Second Language Acquisit
Task-Based Language Teaching

Second Language Acquisition and Task-Based Language Teaching

Mike Long

WILEY Blackwell

This edition first published 2015
© 2015 John Wiley and Sons, Inc.

Registered Office
John Wiley & Sons Ltd, The Atrium, Southern Gate, Chichester, West Sussex, PO19 8SQ, UK

Editorial Offices
350 Main Street, Malden, MA 02148-5020, USA
9600 Garsington Road, Oxford, OX4 2DQ, UK
The Atrium, Southern Gate, Chichester, West Sussex, PO19 8SQ, UK

For details of our global editorial offices, for customer services, and for information about how to apply for permission to reuse the copyright material in this book please see our website at www.wiley.com/wiley-blackwell.

The right of Mike Long to be identified as the author of this work has been asserted in accordance with the UK Copyright, Designs and Patents Act 1988.

Library of Congress Cataloging-in-Publication Data

Long, Michael H.
    Second language acquisition and task-based language teaching / Mike Long. – First Edition.
        pages cm
    Includes index.
        ISBN 978-0-470-65893-2 (hardback) – ISBN 978-0-470-65894-9 (paper)   1. Second language acquisition–Study and teaching.   2. Language and languages–Study and teaching.   3. Task analysis in education.   I. Title.
    P118.2.L668 2015
    418.0071–dc23
                            2014015377

A catalogue record for this book is available from the British Library.

Cover image: Liubov Popova, *Painterly Architectonic* (detail), gouache and watercolor, 1918. Yale University Art Gallery, Gift of the Estate of Katherine S. Dreier, 1953.6.92

Set in 10/12 pt MinionPro by Toppan Best-set Premedia Limited
Printed and bound in Malaysia by Vivar Printing Sdn Bhd

1   2015

Contents

Preface and Acknowledgments

Language teaching (LT) is notorious for methodological pendulum swings, amply documented in published histories of the field. Currently, "task-based" learning and teaching are increasingly fashionable, and many of the very same textbook writers and commercial publishers who made large sums of money out of the structural, notional, functional, topical, and lexical movements of the past 30 years are now repeating the performance with tasks. Most of what they are selling is task-based in name only, however. Miscellaneous "communication tasks" of various kinds, many not very communicative at all, and use of which pre-dates current ideas about task-based learning and teaching, have replaced exercises or activities, but, like their predecessors, are still used to deliver a pre-planned, overt or covert *linguistic* syllabus of one sort or another. Tasks are carriers of target structures and vocabulary items, in other words, not themselves the content of a genuine *task* syllabus. Their role lies in task-*supported*, not task-*based*, LT. Alternatively, such tasks figure as one strand in a so-called hybrid syllabus in textbooks whose authors and publishers claim to combine some or all of grammatical, lexical, notional, functional, topical, situational, and task syllabi under one visually attractive cover, seemingly untroubled by, or in some cases unaware of, their incompatible psycholinguistic underpinnings.

Such materials may or may not have merit, aside from their earning power – certainly, many students around the world have learned languages through (or despite?) their use, some to high levels, for a long time – but they are not what I mean by task-based LT, and I will not be spending much time on them in this book. Instead, I will focus on one of the few genuinely task-based approaches. It is not the only one, not necessarily the best one – an empirical question, after all, to which none of us has the final answer – and may ultimately turn out to have all sorts of weaknesses, but it is the one I have been developing over the past 30 years, with growing, and increasingly valuable, participation by a number of other researchers and classroom practitioners in many parts of the world, and so the one with which I am most familiar. Unlike synthetic linguistic syllabi, it is broadly consistent with what second language acquisition (SLA) research has shown about how learners acquire second and foreign languages and has been implemented in a variety of settings. From the beginning, back in 1980, I have referred to it as (uppercase) Task-Based Language Teaching ('TBLT', not to be confused with 'BLT', the sandwich).

The purpose of this book, however, is not to "convert" readers to TBLT; many will feel they have achieved positive results without it. Some may find it attractive, some may find parts of it worth including in different kinds of programs but reject other parts, and some may consider the whole thing an abomination. Nor is the purpose to provide a survey of the field of LT and applied linguistics, with equal time for all the many proposals out there. LT is a dynamic field, featuring a wide range of views on how best to carry it out, many of which conflict, and not all of which could possibly be correct. This book is intended as a contribution to the debate. My aim is to offer what I believe to be a rational argument for a particular approach, with supporting evidence from theory, research, and classroom experience, followed by a step-by-step description of how to implement TBLT for those interested in doing so. I am especially keen to show the linkage between theory and research findings in SLA, the process LT is designed to facilitate, and TBLT. I will make the case as explicitly as possible and as strongly as I feel warranted. The strength of an argument draws attention to an idea and simultaneously makes it easier for critics to focus on what it is about it that they find objectionable. Explicitness helps remove ambiguities, facilitates testing of ideas, and speeds up identification of flaws. That way lies progress, and faster progress.

I first outlined a primitive rationale for TBLT in courses at the University of Pennsylvania from 1980 to 1982 and sketched the ideas publicly in a plenary address to the Inter-Agency Language Roundtable at Georgetown in 1983, a presentation that appeared in print two years later (Long 1985a). Expanded and modified considerably ever since in response to theoretical developments, the results of empirical studies, and classroom experience, TBLT remains a work in progress. Motivated by research findings in educational psychology, curriculum and instruction, SLA, an embryonic theory of instructed second language acquisition (ISLA; see Chapter 3), and principles from the philosophy of education (see Chapter 4), it has gradually evolved into a comprehensive approach to course design, implementation, and evaluation. First and foremost, it remains an attempt to respond to the growing demand for accountable communicative LT programs designed for learners with real-world needs for functional L2 abilities.

In the first four chapters, which make up Part One of this book, 'Theory and Research,' I review TBLT's rationale, including its psycholinguistic and philosophical underpinnings. In Part Two, 'Design and Implementation,' I devote seven more practically oriented chapters to describing and illustrating procedures, and in some cases problems, in each of the six basic stages in designing, implementing, and evaluating a TBLT program: needs and means analysis, syllabus design, materials development, choice of methodological principles and pedagogic procedures, student assessment, and program evaluation. Finally, in a single chapter that constitutes Part Three, 'The Road Ahead,' I discuss TBLT's prospects and potential shelf-life and identify some issues in need of further research. An appendix lists abbreviations used.

Many people have influenced the ideas in this book, including numerous researchers in SLA and applied linguistics, and many students in my courses and seminars on TBLT at the Universities of Pennsylvania, Hawaii, and Maryland, and summer courses overseas. They are acknowledged and their work referenced in the main text. While I was writing it, several individuals graciously agreed to read and comment on sections, or in some cases, a whole chapter. Others provided additional information on their work when I asked, chased down recalcitrant missing references, gave me permission to include data and examples from their materials development projects, or joined with me in needs analyses and TBLT teacher education sessions and in implementing some of the ideas in the classroom. I am very grateful to the following for their assistance with one or more of these tasks: Nick Ellis, Karen Watson-Gegeo, John Norris, Carmen Munoz, Peter Robinson, Catherine Doughty, David Ellis, Kris Van den Branden, Helen Marriot, Malcolm Johnston, the late, sorely missed, Torsten Schlak, Gloria Bosch Roig, Gisela Granena, Nicky Bartlett, Stephen O'Connell, Susan Benson, Sarah Epling, Hana Jan, Graham Crookes, Howard Nicholas, Megan Masters, Goretti Prieto Botana, Katie Nielson, Marta Gonzalez-Lloret, Assma Al-Thowaini, Buthainah Al-Thowaini, Martha Pennington, Rhonda Oliver, Payman Vafaee, Jiyong Lee, Jaemyung Goo, and Nicole Ziegler. I am also very grateful to the three anonymous reviewers of the final manuscript; their expert comments were very helpful and led me to make a number of changes. Needless to say, none of these people necessarily agrees with everything that follows or is responsible for any errors it may contain. Last, but not least, I owe a huge debt of gratitude to Julia Kirk, Danielle Descoteaux, and Elizabeth Saucier at Wiley-Blackwell. Without their patience and encouragement, the book would never have seen the light of day.

Second Language Acquisition and Task-Based Language Teaching is dedicated to my wonderful son, Jordi Nicholas Long.

Mike Long
University of Maryland
June 2014

Part One

Theory and Research

Chapter 1

Why TBLT?

1.1. The Importance of Second Language Learning and Teaching in the Twenty-First Century

Second language learning and teaching are more important in the twenty-first century than ever before and are more important than even many language teachers appreciate. Most of us are familiar with traditional student populations: captive school children required to "pass" a foreign language (often for no obvious reason), college students satisfying a language requirement or working toward a BA in literature, young adults headed overseas for university courses, as missionaries or to serve as volunteers in the Peace Corps and similar organizations, and adults needing a L2 for vocational training or occupational purposes in the business world, aid organizations, the military, federal and state government, or the diplomatic and intelligence services. Typically, these students are literate, well educated, relatively affluent, learning a major world language, and, the school children aside, doing so voluntarily.

Less visible to many of us, but often with even more urgent linguistic needs, are the steadily increasing numbers of *in*voluntary language learners of all ages. Each year, millions of people are forced to cross linguistic borders to escape wars, despotic regimes, disease, drought, famine, religious persecution, ethnic cleansing, abject poverty, and climate change. Many of these learners are poor, illiterate, uneducated, and faced with acquiring less powerful, often unwritten, rarely taught languages. In some instances, for example, migrant workers in Western Europe, the United States, and parts of the Arab world, the target language is an economically and politically powerful one, such as French, Spanish, German, English, or Arabic. Instruction is available for those with money and time to pursue it, but many such learners lack either. Worse, marginalized and living in a linguistic ghetto, they frequently have little or no access to target language speakers, interaction with whom could serve as the basis for naturalistic second language acquisition (SLA). In some cases, involuntary learners are not created by people moving into new linguistic zones but by powerful languages coming to them. When imperialist nation states use military force to annex territory, they typically oblige the inhabitants to learn the language of the occupier if they hope to have access to education, economic opportunity, or political power, often while relegating local languages to second-class status or even making their use illegal.[1]

The overall picture is unlikely to change anytime soon. Advanced proficiency in a foreign or second language will remain a critical factor in determining the educational and economic life chances of all these groups, from college students and middle-class professionals, through humanitarian aid workers and government and military personnel, to migrant workers, their school-age children, and the victims of occupations and colonization. Moreover, if the obvious utilitarian reasons were not important enough, for millions of learners, especially the non-volunteers, acquiring a new language is inextricably bound up with creating a new identity and acculturating into the receiving community. Occasionally, SLA is a path to resistance for them ("Know thine enemy's language"), but in all too many cases, it is simply necessary for survival. For all these reasons, and given the obvious political implications of a few major world languages being taught to speakers of so many less powerful ones, a responsible course of action, it seems to me, as with education in general, is to make sure that language teaching (LT) and learning are as socially progressive as possible. LT alone will never compensate for the ills that create so many language learners, but at the very least, it should strive not to make matters worse.

It is clear from the above examples – just a few of many possible – that the scope of second and foreign language learning and teaching in the twenty-first century is expanding and likely to continue to do so, and as varied as it is vast. Given the importance of

---

[1] This has happened for thousands of years. Comparatively recent cases include the annexation of much of the African continent by European powers followed by the imposition of English, French, Dutch, Portuguese, and Spanish at the expense of indigenous languages; the British occupation of what are now known as Australia, New Zealand, and North America, followed by imposition of English and the suppression and near eradication of numerous indigenous languages, and often, of the people who spoke them; Spain's and Portugal's colonization of South America, followed by centuries during which the Spanish and Portuguese overwhelmed local languages; the annexation of Hawaii by the United States, followed by decades during which English was imposed and Hawaiian prohibited; the imposition of Russian as the official language of government, administration, education, and the law throughout much of the Soviet Union; and the fascist coup in Spain in 1936, for 30 years after which Franco made it illegal to speak Basque or Catalan, and an imprisonable offense to teach either. These are no more than a few of many such examples in recent world history (see, e.g., Phillipson 2009; Phillipson & Skutnabb-Kangas 2009; Skutnabb-Kangas 2000; Warner 1999).

language learning for so many people and so many different kinds of people, therefore, it would be reassuring to know that LT is being carried out efficiently by trained professionals and that language teachers and learners alike are satisfied with the end product. In fact, there is little evidence for either supposition. While individual programs are professionally staffed and producing good results, they are the exception. Around the world, people continue to learn languages in many ways, sometimes, it appears, with the help of instruction, sometimes without it, sometimes despite it, but there are many more beginners than finishers, and as described in Chapter 2, the field remains divided on fundamental issues to a degree that would cause public consternation and generate costly lawsuits in true professions.[2]

Against this backdrop, it seems reasonable to suggest that new proposals for LT should strive to meet some minimum criteria, with the justification for any serious approach needing to be multi-faceted. Since language learning is the process LT is designed to facilitate, an essential part of the rationale must surely be psycholinguistic plausibility, or consistency with theory and research findings about how people learn and use second and foreign languages. But that is by no means the only motivation required. Given that the subject is language education, a solid basis in the philosophy of education should be expected too. Also of major importance are accountability, relevance, avoidance of known problems with existing approaches, learner-centeredness, and functionality. This book is about Task-Based Language Teaching (TBLT), an approach to course design, implementation, and evaluation intended to meet the communicative needs of diverse groups of learners and which attempts to satisfy all seven criteria. But first, what exactly is meant by "task-based"?

1.2. TBLT and the Meaning of 'Task'

Throughout this book, I distinguish between "Task-Based Language Teaching" (upper case), as in the book's title, and "task-based language teaching" (lower case). The

---

[2] Although often referred to as such, LT unfortunately lacks the characteristics of a true profession, such as law, medicine, engineering, nursing, or architecture. In some parts of the world, language teachers need to have completed recognized degree programs before they are allowed to teach, especially in state schools, but even in those countries, a largely unregulated private sector usually operates, as well. While most teachers strive to be "professional" in the way they go about their work and to perform well for their students, the sad fact is that, in many places, anyone who can find an institution willing to employ him or her can teach a language, even with little or no training, little or no classroom experience, and poor command of the language concerned. Others simply advertise for students and start giving private lessons. The fact that, in many cases, demand for LT far exceeds supply makes that possible. Among institutions offering courses or whole degree programs supposedly preparing students for a career in LT, there is no agreed-upon common body of knowledge of which all practitioners should demonstrate mastery and no common examinations required of would-be practitioners. There is no licensing body, no licenses, and few sanctions on cowboy teachers or language schools. In some countries, even in wealthy first-tier universities with the resources to employ well-qualified staff if they chose to do so, foreign LT is often carried out by tenure-line faculty members, and (more often) temporary lecturers and teaching assistants (TAs), who are literature specialists, with little or no training, expertise or interest in LT, which they often look down upon as a second-class occupation. This would be roughly equivalent to employing biologists to care for the sick, or geologists to design houses – something that does not happen because the expertise required is different and medicine and architecture are professions. Would it were that language learners were as well protected as hospital patients and those with a roof over their heads.

reason is simple. I developed my initial ideas for (upper case) TBLT in courses at the University of Pennsylvania from 1980 to 1982, and first presented them publicly in a plenary talk at the Georgetown Round Table in Washington, D.C., in 1983. The paper subsequently appeared in print as Long (1985a). As so often happens in applied linguistics, however, it was not long before the original proposals were diluted, changed beyond recognition in some cases, and repackaged in a form more acceptable to the powerful political and commercial interests that exert enormous influence over the way LT is conducted worldwide.[3]

As described in detail in subsequent chapters, TBLT starts with a task-based needs analysis to identify the *target tasks* for a particular group of learners – what they need to be able to *do* in the new language. In other words, 'task' in TBLT has its normal, non-technical meaning. Tasks are the real-world activities people think of when planning, conducting, or recalling their day. That can mean things like brushing their teeth, preparing breakfast, reading a newspaper, taking a child to school, responding to e-mail messages, making a sales call, attending a lecture or a business meeting, having lunch with a colleague from work, helping a child with homework, coaching a soccer team, and watching a TV program. Some tasks are mundane, some complex. Some require language use, some do not; for others, it is optional. (For more details on definitions and types of tasks, see Chapter 5, Section 5.5.1.)

After undergoing some modifications, the tasks are used as the content of a *task syllabus*, which consists of a series of progressively more complex *pedagogic tasks*. Pedagogic tasks are the activities and the materials that teachers and/or students work on in the classroom or other instructional environment. 'Task' is the unit of analysis throughout the design, implementation, and evaluation of a TBLT program, including the way student achievement is assessed – by *task-based, criterion-referenced performance tests*. TBLT is an *analytic* approach, with a *focus on form* (see Chapter 2).

In sharp contrast, by the late 1990s, "TBLT" (lower case) as manifested in commercially published pedagogic textbooks and some handbooks for teachers involved "classroom tasks" – often little more than activities and exercises relabeled as tasks (another example of the meaning of a construct being diluted in applied linguistics) – usually unrelated to students' real-world activities beyond the classroom. These counterfeit "tasks" are used to practice structures (see, e.g., Fotos & Ellis 1991), functions or subskills in a traditional grammatical, notional-functional, or skills-based syllabus delivered using linguistically simplified materials, with classroom methodology to match, that is, what I call *focus on forms*. Role-playing a job interview, for example, might be chosen not because job interviews in the L2 were target tasks for a group of learners but because they provided opportunities for practicing question forms. Skehan (an advocate of genuine TBLT) refers to such activities as "structure-trapping" tasks. Ellis (1997) refers to them as "consciousness-raising" tasks or "focused" tasks (Ellis 2003, p. 141).

The syllabus in (lower case) tblt is not task-based at all in the sense understood in (upper case) TBLT; in other words; it is an overt or covert linguistic (usually a gram-

---

[3] The tendency to dilute the meaning of new terms and the constructs behind them is a long-standing affliction in applied linguistics. For example, 30+ years after it originated in England in the work of Brumfit, Johnson, Morrow, and others (e.g., Brumfit & Johnson 1979), what is meant today by 'communicative LT'? The term originally had a fairly precise meaning. Nowadays, it can simply refer to a lesson taught mostly in the L2, even if what is said has nothing to do with genuine communication. "TBLT," "task," "learner-centered," "recast," and "focus on form," as we shall see, are among many other casualties.

matical) syllabus, and the syllabus, methodology, materials, and tests are what Wilkins (1974) called *synthetic*, not analytic. In what Ellis (2003, p. 65) and others refer to as *task-supported*, as distinct from task-based, LT, "focused tasks" are used for the final "produce" stage of a traditional present–practice–produce (sic.) (PPP) approach, with an overt or covert grammatical syllabus. Task-supported LT has its champions and is worthy of consideration – perhaps, as suggested, for example, by Shehadeh (2005), as a bridge between traditional synthetic syllabi and genuine task-based approaches – but is still a synthetic approach. Synthetic approaches may turn out to be useful, at least in part (although, as explained in Chapter 2, the evidence is currently against them), but what is gained by blurring the original meaning of (in this case) 'task-based' until it denotes something quite different, and indeed, opposed to the original meaning of the term?

In fact, it is not hard to see what is gained and by whom. Synthetic approaches, especially grammatical syllabuses, are palatable to commercial publishers and various politically powerful LT institutions because they are what underlie at least 90% of existing, commercially highly successful textbooks sold around the world. Synthetic approaches, including ones that employ structure-trapping tasks, do not entail any fundamental change to the status quo. A true TBLT course, conversely, requires an investment of resources in a needs analysis and production of materials appropriate for a particular population of learners. Textbook series based on a structural syllabus, on the other hand, featured in what publishers refer to euphemistically as their "international list," can continue to be sold around the world to learners of all sorts, however unjustified that may be, on the grounds that they teach "the structures of a language," which are "the same for everyone." This results in enormous profits for authors and publishers alike. With a few exceptions, true task-based materials will rarely have such commercial potential precisely because they are not designed for all learners and do not assume that what all learners need is the same.

Lower case 'task-based,' that is, task-supported, approaches (see, e.g., Ellis 1997, 2003; Nunan 1996, 2004; Willis & Willis 2007) have merits, including their location within the existing comfort zone of most teachers, state education authorities, and publishers, which can make them more acceptable, and so more likely to be adopted, in the short term (and possibly in the long run, as well, as discussed in Chapter 12). They may eventually turn out to be optimal, in fact, but as should be obvious, they are not genuinely task-based, so will not constitute a major focus of this book, which, for better or for worse, is about (upper case) TBLT. How does TBLT measure up against the proposed minimum criteria for a new approach to LT?

1.3. A Rationale for TBLT

1.3.1. Consistency with SLA theory and research findings

An approach to LT should be psycholinguistically plausible. This means that it should rely on learning mechanisms and processes shown to be available to learners of a given age while at the same time recognizing any known constraints on their learning capacity. The tacitly assumed theoretical underpinnings of all synthetic approaches to LT (grammatical, notional-functional and lexical syllabuses, audio-lingual, grammar-translation, and total physical response "methods," etc.) are what are known as skill-building theories of various kinds (see, e.g., DeKeyser 2007a,b; Gatbonton & Segalowitz 1988; Johnson 1996; Segalowitz 2003). Skill-building theories hold that only younger learners, and in some cases, only children younger than seven, can learn a language incidentally, that is, without intending to do so and without awareness of doing so. When it comes to LT for older children and adults (usually envisaged as in the mid-teens and thereafter), therefore, they accord dominant status to explicit learning and explicit instruction. The claim is that language learning is like learning any other complex cognitive skill. Declarative knowledge (knowledge *that* a language works this or that way) is changed through controlled practice into procedural knowledge (knowledge *how*), after which the procedural knowledge is gradually automatized through massive practice, the speed-up process reflecting the power law of learning. Automatization is necessary, as skill builders acknowledge that real-time communicative language use depends on a listener's or speaker's ability to access linguistic knowledge far too rapidly to permit conscious retrieval of declarative knowledge from long-term memory. Rightly or wrongly, such approaches are sometimes referred to as being based upon the *strong-interface* position, which holds that what starts as explicit knowledge "becomes" implicit through practice, or else becomes automatized to such a degree that it becomes accessible sufficiently rapidly to appear to have become implicit, even though that is not the case.

In contrast, TBLT invokes a symbiotic *combination of implicit and explicit learning* that theory and research findings in several fields, including SLA, show are available to students of all ages. The availability of both of these processes, albeit a somewhat reduced capacity for *instance learning* (e.g., the capacity for learning new lexical items and collocations, and for purely incidental learning of form–meaning relationships – see Chapter 3), generally fits well with what is known about adult learning, including adult language learning. The basic tenets of TBLT are motivated by, and broadly consistent with, the past 40 years of SLA research findings, sketched briefly in Chapter 2, and with the embryonic cognitive-interactionist theory of instructed second language acquisition (ISLA) outlined in Chapter 3. Conversely, as explained in Chapters 2 and 3, the strong-interface position is *in*consistent with the evidence of 40 years of SLA research; that is, it is psycholinguistically implausible.

As with any theory, the embryonic cognitive-interactionist theory goes beyond the data in hand, so may eventually turn out to be wrong, wholly or in part, thereby undermining the validity of parts of TBLT. That is the nature of theories, which by definition go beyond the facts in an attempt to fill in the gaps in our knowledge and, more importantly, seek to explain the facts we think have been established. Meanwhile, however, unlike LT approaches and "methods" with no theoretical or research basis, including so-called eclectic methods (an oxymoron), TBLT is a coherent approach and, because it is grounded in a theory and in research findings in SLA, has at least a chance of being correct.

As will become apparent in subsequent chapters, many additional research findings in SLA, educational psychology, language testing, and applied linguistics are drawn upon to justify specific aspects of the design, delivery, and evaluation of TBLT programs. For example, as detailed in Chapter 10, well-documented processability constraints on the effectiveness of instruction (e.g., Pienemann 1984, 1989; Pienemann & Kessler 2011, 2012), including negative feedback (e.g., Mackey 1999), are taken into account in the area of TBLT's (currently, ten) *methodological principles* (MPs), in the form of respect for the internal learner syllabus and developmental processes (MP 8) and respect for individual differences via the individualization of instruction (MP 10). Similarly, as acknowledged in Chapter 11, much of the accumulated wisdom in the literatures on criterion-referenced performance testing and program evaluation is drawn upon in TBLT's approach to the assessment of student learning and the evaluation of TBLT programs.

1.3.2. Basis in philosophy of education

TBLT's philosophical roots lie in *l'education integrale* and the rich educational tradition found in the writings of William Godwin, Sebastien Faure, Paul Robin, Leon Tolstoy, Peter Kropotkin, Elias Puig, Francisco Ferrer y Guardia, and others, and in the practice of the so-called modern schools (*escuelas modernas*) established in many countries in the late nineteenth and twentieth centuries (see, e.g., Suissa 2006). Consciously or not, fundamental principles developed by these theorists and practitioners have been adopted by progressive philosophers of education ever since, often without adequate recognition. They live on in the work of John Dewey, Ivan Illich, John Holt, Colin Ward, and many others, as well as in the growing number of participatory democratic educational projects around the world. The principles are ones to which most language teachers and students subscribe in their everyday lives – principles that need not be forgotten in the classroom. They include educating the whole person, learning by doing, rationalism, free association, learner-centeredness, egalitarian teacher–student relationships, and participatory democracy. Interestingly, the implications of these philosophical principles and those of TBLT's psycholinguistic underpinnings converge in most cases. The details, and their realization in TBLT, will be spelt out in Chapter 4.

1.3.3. Accountability

With the world's population growing as fast as the planet's wealth and natural resources are shrinking, the era of the free ride is over. Accountability is fast becoming a watch-word in publically funded federal, state, and local services, from policing and firefighting to transportation and health care – in most fields, in fact, outside politics and banking. Public education is a favorite target among politicians needing to balance budgets, and foreign and second language programs are among the two or three most vulnerable curricular areas. Demands for accountability in education often come with sanctions attached. Examples include state and federal government funding for schools tied to various dimensions of school performance, moves to evaluate in-service teachers on the basis of student test scores and then to dismiss staff deemed ineffective (often without taking into consideration the fact that they work in schools with high proportions of "at risk" and disadvantaged children), and at the university level, post-tenure review.

If a current educational system cannot deliver, or even if it can simply be *asserted* that a current system cannot deliver, with rebuttals either not provided or provided but not heard due to lack of media access, then one or both of two things happen. First, the "service," for example, second language classes for migrant workers, bilingual education for their children, or foreign LT in schools and universities, is reduced or even eliminated from budgets entirely. Second, consumers financially able to do so vote with their feet, moving their children to the private sector or to so-called charter schools and academies of various kinds. Paradoxically, many of those supposedly superior institutions[4] are publically funded and often tout their foreign language curricula as a selling point. Alternatively, as adults, students may enter the world of for-profit language schools, private teachers, and expensive self-study courses, some of which lure naive customers with claims of dubious validity: "A foreign language, your gateway to the world," "Arabic in ten days!" Customers' hopes and bank balances are hit hard, but wild claims of that kind from segments of the private language sector are increasingly under scrutiny, too. Better late than never, large clients, for example, federal governments, which have long handed over massive sums of taxpayers' money annually to businesses and private vendors of language services and courses of questionable quality, have begun to commission evaluations of what they have been purchasing, leading in some cases to the long overdue cancellation of multimillion dollar contracts.

1.3.4. Relevance

Against this background, and since languages are widely regarded as less critical than mathematics, science or (L1) language arts, it is vital for second and foreign language programs to be well motivated, well designed, and successful. Needs analysis is an essential prerequisite for all three. It is important, however, not only that, objectively, programs be designed rationally but also that their relevance and value be obvious to stakeholders, starting with the students. Learning a new language requires time, effort, and resources (far more than the vendors of most commercial programs claim) on the part not only of the individuals and institutions involved in providing the instruction but also of the learners themselves and their sponsors. The older those learners are, the more likely they are to have a clear goal in mind when they register for a course. A one-size-fits-all approach, using pedagogic materials written with no particular learners or learning purposes in mind, is as unacceptable in LT as it is in other domains.

Before investing in developing new products, manufacturers conduct research to identify gaps in the market – exactly what it is that consumers need or want and will purchase – so they can be sure the investment will be profitable. Since the same household furniture or automobile will rarely appeal to all consumers, whose tastes, preferences, and requirements vary, products are designed for specific groups. Physicians do not prescribe the same medicine to all patients. They would be sued if they did. They first conduct an individual diagnosis (the medical equivalent of a needs analysis), often involving a battery of increasingly specialized tests, and then prescribe a course of treatment designed specifically for that patient, or for all patients with the complaint or condition in question. The same is true of purveyors of most services, be they architects, carpenters, plumbers, painters, travel agents, hairdressers, or restaurateurs. Vast amounts of research underlie most of the products and services offered, as does quality control.

Education is one of the few areas where the one-size-fits-all approach survives, in the form of state education, especially when beholden to centralized, mandated curricula and so-called "standards". But even there, things are changing. The private sector offers

---

[4] The superiority is a myth. See, for example, Ravitch (2010).

a variety of educational alternatives, such as academies and charter schools, for those able and willing to pay for them, and magnet programs and other specialized curricular offerings are increasingly common within regular state systems, each appealing to particular groups. When it comes to language education, adults increasingly do not expect to have to waste time and money learning things they do not need or not learning things they do need. They have a right to expect language courses, like medical treatments, to be relevant and, ideally, to be designed just for them or, at the very least, for learners like them. That is why, to be rational, relevant, and successful, language course development should begin with an identification of learners' goals and an analysis of their present or future communicative needs to achieve those goals.

The growing demand for accountability and the need for relevance are closely related. Mass-marketing of off-the-peg courses suitable for everyone, but for no one in particular, benefit authors' and publishers' bank balances, but they do little for the end user. Language learning requires a huge investment of time, effort, and money on the part of students and, in many cases, their parents or employers. With the need for new languages so crucial for so many, more and more learners, especially college students and young adults, are reluctant to accept courses that were clearly not designed to meet their needs. "General-purpose" (nebulous or no purpose) courses may teach too much, e.g., all four skills, when learners may only need, say, listening, listening and speaking, or reading abilities, and/or too little, e.g., nothing comparable to the content and complexity of the tasks and materials with which learners will have to deal or the discourse domain in which they will have to operate. The same "generic" course is no more likely to be appropriate for everyone, much less efficient and effective, than the same medical treatment, the same dwelling, or the same food will be appropriate. People's language needs, like their other needs, differ, often greatly, and, as repeatedly revealed by the results of needs analyses (see Chapters 5–7), almost always far more extensively from one group to another, and from typical textbook fare, than an outsider would ever anticipate if relying on intuition.

A course that bypasses needs analysis and simply teaches "English," "Spanish," "Chinese," or "Arabic" risks wasting everybody's time by covering varieties of the target language, skills, genres, registers, discourse types, and vocabulary that students do not need, at least not immediately, and by not covering the often specialized target tasks (not necessarily the specialized language itself) that they do need. In attempting to cater to the majority, the course will often be slow-paced and over-inclusive in both the skills and the linguistic domains treated, covering linguistic features "because they are there," as an end in themselves rather than as a communicative tool.

Many learners in FL settings have to be able to read specialized literature in their field, for example, but rarely hear or speak the L2, and never write it. Others require listening and speaking skills, e.g., for tourism, but minimal reading or writing ability. Similarly, *within* a skill area, some learners may wish to be able to comprehend informal colloquial Spanish for a vacation in Madrid, while others may need to be able to understand spoken Spanish in order to follow a lecture series on anthropology at a Mexican university. The variety of Spanish and the genres, registers, and lexis involved in each case will differ considerably, as will the predictability of what is said, the average grammatical complexity of the input, the degree of planning, speed of delivery, the use of idiomatic expressions, visual support, environmental noise, and, last but not least, the background knowledge that the non-native speaker (NNS) brings to the task. (The lecture series may well be easier for the anthropology student than the street Spanish for the tourist.) In a language like Arabic, the spoken variety students require will vary significantly according to the region in which they will be working – Levantine, Egyptian colloquial, North African, or Gulf Arabic, for example. It is literacy that makes Arabic (Chinese, Japanese, and many other languages) so hard and time-consuming for learners whose L1 employs a different writing system. Unless students will need to be able to read and/or write the language, mastering Modern Standard Arabic (MSA, the very different formal variety used for most writing, but for little but the most formal speaking), may be unnecessary, yet most Arabic courses begin with MSA whether learners need it or not, and some begin and end with it.[5] A task-based needs analysis can help avoid such shocking wastes of time and money.

1.3.5. Avoidance of known problems with existing approaches

A new approach to LT needs to avoid its predecessors' known problems. To illustrate, as explained in Chapter 2, the fundamental problem with existing approaches is that the vast majority employ a linguistic unit of analysis and "interventionist" *synthetic* syllabuses and "methods," that is, *focus on forms*, and most of the remainder employ extreme "non-interventionist," *analytic* syllabuses and "methods," such as the Natural Approach (Krashen & Terrell 1983), that rely on a pure *focus on meaning*. One of several problems with purely synthetic approaches is their incompatibility with "natural" language-learning processes. One of several problems with purely analytic approaches is their inefficient, and often ineffective, treatment of learners' persistent grammatical errors and their inadequacy for older learners, whose reduced capacity for purely incidental learning makes supplementary opportunities for intentional learning necessary. It is necessary to address such errors, and to do so in a timely fashion – an issue largely ignored by purely analytic approaches, which eschew "error correction" and any focus on language as object and rely, instead, on provision of additional positive evidence, e.g., more comprehensible input, for the purpose. That is a strategy now proven to be both inefficient and inadequate, as detailed in Chapter 2. TBLT's solution is to employ an analytic (task) syllabus, but with a *focus on form* to deal with problematic linguistic features, and provision of opportunities for intentional learning to speed up the learning process and to supplement the adult's weaker capacity for incidental learning, especially instance learning. MP 6: Focus on form, and MP 7: Provide negative feedback, for example, are two of TBLT's 10 MPs (see Chapter 10), each with numerous realizations in the form of classroom *pedagogic procedures*, which combine to fulfill the purpose while avoiding a return to the equally flawed *focus on forms*.

Avoidance of known problems does not mean that a new approach to LT will entail rejecting everything that has gone before. Thus, of its 10 MPs, only 3 – MP 1: Use task, not text, as the unit of analysis; MP 3: Elaborate input; and MP 6: Focus on form – are original to TBLT. In different combinations, some of the other seven have characterized a number of approaches over the years. It would be counterproductive not to build on

---

[5] For an innovative beginner's course that starts with colloquial spoken (Levantine) Arabic, see Younes (2006).

what has come before, which can mean, with due recognition of sources, judiciously adopting or adapting positive features of alternative approaches.

1.3.6. Learner-centeredness

Learner-centeredness has long been extolled as a virtue in the LT literature. While serious work on individual differences, including affective factors, has been published over the years (see, e.g., Dornyei 2005; Robinson 2002a), their treatment at the level of pedagogy has usually been at a rather superficial level. Teachers are typically encouraged to employ pedagogic procedures likely to create a positive classroom climate. They should praise learners' achievements, for example, respond to errors with sympathy rather than face-threatening negative feedback, and employ games and other activities that make students feel good about themselves and their teacher and vice versa. In other words, the focus has been firmly on the affective domain: "Love your students and they will learn." Few would oppose making the learning experience as pleasant as possible for all concerned, but even such an apparently innocuous statement may deserve qualification. There is some evidence, after all, that a certain degree of tension, or classroom anxiety, can have a positive effect on learning (Scovel 1978), probably because it activates a process known to be critical for language learning: attention.

In TBLT, real learner-centeredness, as distinct from rhetorical hand-waving and everyone just getting along, is addressed first and foremost in the cognitive domain. To begin with, course content is not determined by a multimillionaire textbook writer sipping martinis a thousand miles away on a beach in the Cayman Islands but by a locally conducted analysis of learner needs. Second, attention to language form is reactive, in harmony with the learner's internal syllabus. Third, *teachability* is recognized as being constrained by *learnability*. Fourth, to the extent logistical constraints allow (time, money, student and teacher numbers, access to technology, etc.), individual differences are catered to through the individualization of instruction. The relevance of course content to students' communicative needs and respect for individual differences and underlying psycholinguistic processes is more important for language learning than everyone feeling good about themselves. Students can still be treated with as much delicacy and charm as typically overworked, underpaid teachers can muster, but superficial affective considerations pale in importance for students compared with the self-respect that comes from being treated as rational human beings, associating voluntarily and playing an active role in their own progress in a learner-centered, egalitarian classroom.

1.3.7. Functionality

College students and adults are often attempting to learn a language for the second, third, or fourth time, the results of their earlier efforts having been unsuccessful. They are more likely to recognize the "same, again" when it is served up lightly reheated, and to be more quickly disenchanted this time around. Many college students and most adults, whether voluntary or involuntary learners, require *functional* language abilities, be they for academic, occupational, vocational, or social survival purposes, that they lacked when they were younger, and in general terms, at least, they are more likely to be aware of those needs. They are quicker to spot the irrelevance of generic, structurally based courses in which culturally distant cardboard characters exchange mindless pleasantries about each other's clothing or things they see during a walk in the park. Conversely, in my own experience and that of teachers in other TBLT programs (see Chapter 11), the same students respond immediately and positively to materials and teaching that treat them like adults and have clearly been designed to cater specifically to their communicative needs. TBLT, like any approach that hopes to be successful, must be perceived by students to be enjoyable, intellectually stimulating (even at low proficiency levels), and as LT that works for them.

As will become clear, TBLT meets all the above criteria. This does not mean that it is the best approach to LT, or even a good one. That is a judgment call, based on the plausibility of its theoretical underpinnings and on the research to back it up, including evaluations of its effectiveness. Moreover, other approaches may meet the criteria, too, in which case the judgment will be one of TBLT's and other approaches' *relative effectiveness*. Finally, the criteria themselves may be unsatisfactory or incomplete.

1.4. Summary

Second and foreign language learning affect the educational life chances of millions of learners the world over, and many different types of learners. This book is about an approach to LT that attempts to meet their diverse psycholinguistic and communicative needs. It is about (upper case) TBLT, as distinct from (lower case) "task-based" approaches that, in *task-supported* LT, merely use pedagogic tasks to carry an overt or covert linguistic syllabus of some kind or, in a few cases, to deliver a topical, situational, or content syllabus. Given the importance of language learning to so many, it is essential that an approach to LT meet certain minimum standards. It should be consistent with theory and research findings on how people learn languages, and it should embody progressive social values. Five other criteria considered critical are accountability, relevance, avoidance of known problems with existing approaches, learner-centeredness, and functionality. Subsequent chapters will attempt to show how TBLT measures up against all seven criteria.

1.5. Suggested Readings

Ellis, R. (2003). *Task-based language learning and teaching*. Oxford: Oxford University Press.

Long, M.H., & Norris, J.M. (2000). Task-based teaching and assessment. In Byram, M. (ed.), *Encyclopedia of language teaching* (pp. 597–603). London: Routledge.

Norris, J.M. (2009). Task-based teaching and testing. In Long, M.H., & Doughty, C.J. (eds.), *Handbook of language teaching* (pp. 578–594). Malden, MA: Wiley-Blackwell.

Nunan, D. (2004). *Task-based language teaching*. Cambridge: Cambridge University Press.

Phillipson, R. (2009). *Linguistic imperialism continued*. Hyderabad: Orient Black Swan.

Phillipson, R., & Skutnabb-Kangas, T. (2009). The politics and policies of language and language teaching. In Long, M.H., & Doughty, C.J. (eds.), *Handbook of language teaching* (pp. 26–41). Malden, MA: Wiley-Blackwell.

Robinson, P. (2011). Task-based language learning: A review of issues. *Language Learning* 61, Suppl. 1, 1–36.

Skutnabb-Kangas, T. (2000). *Linguistic genocide in education – or world diversity and human rights?* Mahwah, NJ: Lawrence Erlbaum.

Skutnabb-Kangas, T., & Cummins, J. (eds.) (1988). *Minority education: From shame to struggle.* Clevedon, Avon: Multilingual Matters.

Suissa, J. (2006). *Anarchism and education. A philosophical perspective.* London: Routledge.

Van den Branden, K., Bygate, M., & Norris, J.M. (eds.) (2009). *Task-based language teaching. A reader.* Amsterdam: John Benjamins.

Chapter 2

SLA and the Fundamental LT Divide

2.1. Interventionist and Non-Interventionist Positions

Historical surveys by Fotos (2005), Howatt (1984), Kelly (1969), Musumeci (1997, 2009), Titone (1968) and others have shown that while varying and overlapping at the level of individuals and geographic regions at any one time, the practice of language teaching (LT) over the centuries has swung back and forth between interventionist and non-interventionist positions, between an emphasis on form and on meaning, and between the linguistic code and the learning process. Changes in the twentieth and twenty-first century have often reflected paradigm shifts in philosophy, linguistics, or psychology, but rarely new empirical findings about LT itself. Since the 1960s, the two major orientations have existed side by side. In the past few decades, views held simultaneously by different camps on the effects and effectiveness of instruction have diverged markedly, with proposals running the gamut from *laissez faire* to ball and chain. Teachers and learners have achieved a great deal through the use of all sorts of approaches and "methods." However, while not the only source of relevant data, I believe second language acquisition (SLA) research findings provide important evidence against both

Second Language Acquisition and Task-Based Language Teaching, First Edition. Mike Long.
© 2015 John Wiley & Sons, Inc. Published 2015 by John Wiley & Sons, Inc.

traditional options and in favor of a third, an analytic approach with a focus on form, the one that underlies TBLT.

2.1.1. Interventionist positions

Over the past 60 years, at one end of the spectrum, influenced by structural linguistics and neo-behaviorist psychology, a variety of strongly "interventionist" positions have been advocated by Asher (1981), Brooks (1964), Curran (1976), R. Ellis (1993), Fries (1945), Gattegno (1972), Harmer (1998), Lado (1957, 1964), Lado and Fries (1958), Paulston (1970, 1971), Paulston and Bruder (1976), Politzer (1960, 1961, 1968), Prator (1979), Rivers (1964), Stockwell, Bowen, and Martin (1965), and Swan (2005, 2006), among many others. Despite mostly trivial surface differences in appearance, all these LT approaches and "methods" interfere with what, left alone, might resemble *somewhat* the way young children acquire their native language (successfully). Intervention starts with the language to be taught, and involves such practices as dividing it into bite-size linguistic units of one kind or another (sounds, words, collocations, structures, notions, functions, etc.), presenting them to learners one at a time, and practicing them intensively using pattern drills and exercises, with errors "corrected," before moving on to the next item.[1]

Such views are reflected in almost all mass-produced, commercially published LT materials. This has less to do with their validity than with the fact that "grammar-based" materials are easier to write and simpler to use. Given that in some parts of the world, many language teachers are non-native speakers whose own command of the target language is weak, structurally controlled and sequenced "tramline" materials are understandably popular. It is easier to fall back on the L1 and to stay one rehearsed structure or vocabulary item ahead of the students when working through a mechanical textbook exercise, i.e., to engage in what I refer to as "language-like" behavior, than to conduct a lesson in the target language, using it communicatively and spontaneously, reacting to linguistic problems as they arise, and thereby, to the learner's "internal syllabus." In fact, little but the covers, artwork, and supporting technology for commercial textbooks has changed much in 60 years, and little is likely to change as long as authors and large publishers continue to make vast sums of money from selling millions of copies annually that are based on grammatical syllabi and thinly disguised variants of drill and kill.

Because the grammar of a language does not change much, some pedagogues (often textbook writers, themselves) have periodically tried to justify pervasive use of the same off-the-shelf series to "teach the language" by asserting that "the grammar is the same for everyone." This is to ignore the fact, however, that while grammatical structures may

---

[1] "Correction" appears in scare quotes because, as any experienced teacher knows, what deviant student output often triggers in such classrooms is not correction, but *negative feedback* of more or less overt kinds, provision of which is an illocutionary act. The information the feedback contains may or may not be incorporated by the learner, assuming it is noticed at all, and when it does happen, immediate production of the target version may simply be echoic, and contrary to the way it is often interpreted by novice teachers, not indicate a lasting change to the learner's underlying grammar. Correction, conversely, is a perlocutionary act, implying that just such a modification of the grammar is achieved by the teacher's move.

not change very much, their uses do, a lot (see Chapter 7). The "one-size-fits-all" assertion ignores serious differences in language use corresponding to differences in learner needs and abilities. One wonders if those making such assertions believe the same ready-made clothes are suitable for everyone, or the same drug or medical treatment is good for everyone, no matter their size or what ails them.

Interventionist approaches assume the validity of what in SLA has come to be called the *strong interface* position. On this view, explicit learning and explicit instruction are paramount, and explicit knowledge (knowledge of a language that learners are aware they possess) can, in some versions of the position, supposedly be converted into implicit knowledge. In others (e.g., DeKeyser 2007a), through practice, declarative knowledge (knowledge that) is turned into procedural knowledge (knowledge how), and through further massive practice, automatized, sometimes to such a level that it is sufficient to pass as implicit knowledge (knowledge learners have, but do not know they have), which they deploy automatically. We will return to the questionable validity of the strong interface position, and the more likely roles of explicit and implicit learning, in Chapter 3.

2.1.2. Non-interventionist positions

At the other extreme have been "non-interventionist" positions of the kinds espoused during the last 60 years by Corder (1967), R. Ellis (1985), Felix (1985), Krashen (1985), Krashen and Terrell (1983), Newmark (1966, 1971), Newmark and Reibel (1968), Prabhu (1987), Reibel (1969, 1971), and Wode (1981), among others. While differing somewhat among themselves, members of the second group were often influenced by the growing hegemony of special nativist (Chomskyan) linguistics. Frequently noted were reports from SLA researchers in the 1960s and 1970s of L2 learners' common errors and error types, developmental sequences largely impervious to instruction, and a so-called "natural order" of morpheme accuracy (cf. acquisition), all of which were interpreted as evidence of the continued workings of the language acquisition device (LAD), supposedly used for L1A, and of a relatively minor role for L1 transfer. Also apparently consistent with such views were the findings of large-scale comparative methods studies (see Chapter 11) – notably, in the USA, the Pennsylvania Project (P. Smith 1970) and the Colorado Project (Scherer & Wertheimer 1964), and in Sweden, the Gume project (Levin 1972; Oskarsson 1972, 1973; Von Elek & Oskarsson 1972) – which appeared to show only short-term effects or no effect for instructional method or approach, and by implication, the irrelevance of type of instruction (another interpretation that turned out to be wrong).

Adult SLA was claimed by those in the *laissez faire* group to be much like L1A, with older learners by implication assumed to retain the child's capacity for incidental learning – learning a language, without awareness of doing so or intention to learn, while doing something else, e.g., playing, or studying a content subject through the medium of the L2. Explicit learning and teaching were marginalized or proscribed altogether. On this account, the role of instruction is not to tamper with the language itself, but to focus on the learners, providing students with plentiful access to comprehensible samples of the L2 and opportunities to use it for communication. As Krashen put it, the role of the teacher was to recreate in the classroom the conditions that had made L1A so successful, and to let the innate human capacity for (implicit) language learning, or in his terms, the *acquisition* process, run its natural course. The instructional counterpart of this position became known as the Natural Approach (Krashen & Terrell 1983).

Non-interventionist approaches rest on the *non-interface* position. On this view, pure incidental learning underlies implicit knowledge, explicit and implicit learning are separate processes, and explicit and implicit knowledge are separate systems, stored in different areas of the brain. Explicit L2 knowledge, or in Krashen's terms, *learning*, i.e., (the narrower) conscious knowledge of simple L2 grammar rules, cannot "become" implicit (see, e.g., Krashen & Scarcella 1979). At most, when the learner has sufficient time, knows the rule, and is focused on language as object, it can be used to monitor and edit spoken and written production. These conditions are met in very few cases, e.g., on a discrete-point grammar test, so conscious knowledge of a L2 is not very useful. Most communicative language use depends fundamentally on implicit knowledge, or in Krashen's terms, *acquisition*.

Disagreements resulting from these two conflicting positions remain strong in LT circles to this day. They underlie arguments over such matters as the relative merits of deductive and inductive teaching, the need, or not, for a grammatical syllabus or for linguistically "simplified" teaching materials, the usability of explicit grammar rules, the value of intensive, linguistically focused drills, the relative effectiveness of overt and covert negative feedback, the utility (or, according to some, the uselessness) of "error correction," and so on. They reflect a long-standing division over whether the appropriate starting point in LT is the language or the learner, or, in terms of the important distinction made by Wilkins (1974 and elsewhere), between *synthetic* and *analytic* approaches.

2.2. Synthetic and Analytic Approaches to LT

2.2.1. Synthetic approaches

'Synthetic' and 'analytic' refer to the learner's presumed role in the learning process. A *synthetic approach* begins by focusing on the *language* to be taught, dividing it into linguistic units of one or more kinds – words, collocations, grammar rules, sentence patterns, notions and functions, and so on – sequencing them according to one or more criteria – valency, criticality, frequency, saliency, and (intuitively defined) difficulty – and presenting items to the learner one by one. Timing is determined by where a teacher is "up to" in the pre-set syllabus, not where the learners are "up to" in terms of developmental readiness, i.e., L2 processing capacity. The learner's job is to *synthesize* the items for communicative purposes.

The synthetic approach typically employs a lexical, grammatical, or notional-functional syllabus, or some "hybrid" combination thereof, and in theory, at least, such teaching "methods" as Grammar Translation, the Audio-Lingual Method, the Silent Way, or Total Physical Response.[2] Assuming a central role for explicit instruction

---

[2] 'Method' is a convenient fiction, useful for discussions in "methods" courses. Research in general education by Shavelson and Stern (1981), and in foreign language classrooms by Swaffer, Arens, and Morgan (1982), shows that teachers plan, implement, and recall lessons at the classroom level in terms of activities or tasks, not methods.

and explicit learning, followed by proceduralization of declarative knowledge, and automatization of procedural knowledge, LT is conceptualized as a process of filling the learner's linguistic quiver one shiny new arrow at a time. The syllabus is delivered using linguistically controlled materials and pedagogic procedures suitable for intensive practice of target forms and constructions. The standard Presentation–Production–Practice (sic) (PPP) formula consists of student exposure to "simplified" dialogues and reading passages written using a limited vocabulary and "seeded" with the structure(s) of the day, intensive practice of the structure(s) via drills and written exercises, followed by gradually "freer practice" – in reality, usually pseudo-communicative language use. Lessons are primarily teacher-fronted. Courses typically cover all four skills, whether or not students need all four. Tasks are employed in some cases, but chiefly as an alternative vehicle for practicing the linguistic items on the day's menu, not because they relate to identified student needs to be able to perform such tasks outside the classroom. In synthetic approaches, the L2 is the *object* of instruction.

2.2.2. Analytic approaches

An *analytic approach* does the reverse. It starts with the *learner* and learning processes. Students are exposed to gestalt samples of the L2, as natural and authentic representations of target language communication as possible, and gradually engaged in genuinely communicative (or at least, meaningful) target language production. The learner's job is to *analyze* the input, and thereby to induce rules of grammar and use. There is no overt or covert linguistic syllabus. More attention is paid to message and pedagogy than to language, e.g., to ways of making L2 samples comprehensible, engaging learners with the input, and involving them in communication. The idea is that, much in the way children learn their L1, adults can best learn a L2 incidentally, through using it. Examples of analytic approaches include some immersion education programs, the procedural syllabus, some kinds of content-based LT, including some content and language integrated learning (CLIL), currently popular in parts of Europe and elsewhere, sheltered subject-matter teaching, and Krashen and Terrell's Natural Approach. In analytic approaches, the L2 is the *medium* of instruction.

Wilkins' terms, 'synthetic' and 'analytic,' were originally conceived as ways of classifying types of LT syllabi, but syllabi do not come in isolation. They are implemented using materials and pedagogic procedures suitable for the task at hand. Thus, synthetic syllabi typically rely on linguistically controlled reading passages and dialogues seeded with unnaturally high frequencies of whatever linguistic features and constructions are in focus in a given lesson, and a battery of drills, exercises, and linguistically focused tasks for intensive practice during the proceduralization and automatization phases. Classroom (or computer-mediated) language use is primarily mechanical and meaningful, rarely communicative (for the three-way distinction, see Paulston 1971), and then only during the final "practice" stage of a PPP lesson (see, e.g., Harmer 1998; Thornbury 1999). Pedagogic grammar rules and, especially in foreign language settings, recourse to the native language, including translation, are common options. Early student production is demanded, usually after minimal input (most notoriously in the Silent Way), with non-native-like performance the subject of "error correction." The end-product is assessed via discrete-point tests of various kinds. LT that involves a combination of a synthetic syllabus, synthetic teaching materials, synthetic methodology and pedagogy, and synthetic language testing, where the content and focus of lessons and evaluation of student achievement are the forms themselves, I refer to as *focus on forms.*

Analytic syllabi, conversely, are generally implemented using spoken and written activities and texts, either genuine, i.e., originally designed for native speaker–native speaker (NS–NS) communication, not LT, or modified for L2 learners, chosen for their content, interest value, and comprehensibility. Classroom language use is predominantly meaningful or communicative, and rarely mechanical. Grammar rules, drills, and error correction are seldom, if ever, employed. However, especially when mandated by state school requirements, assessment is often similar to that used in synthetic programs. LT that involves a combination of an analytic syllabus, analytic teaching materials, and analytic pedagogy, where the content and focus of lessons is the message, subject matter, and communication, I refer to as *focus on meaning.*

The fact that such fundamentally contradictory approaches to LT can be defended and implemented simultaneously illustrates the extent to which the field is unaccountable to SLA theory and research findings or to evaluations of practice. Not just the approaches, but the underlying assumptions about how second and foreign languages are learned (let alone best learned), are mutually exclusive. They cannot possibly both be correct, and it is likely that neither is. I have argued for many years (see, e.g., Long 1991, 2000a; Long & Robinson 1998) that a pure focus on forms and a pure focus on meaning are to varying degrees *both* unsupported by research findings – each inadequate, albeit in different ways.

2.3. Problems with Synthetic Approaches and Focus on Forms

The basic problem with the synthetic approach and with *focus on forms* is the assumption that learners can and will learn what they are taught when they are taught it, and the further assumption that if learners are exposed to ready-made target versions of L2 structures, one at a time, then, after enough intensive practice, they will add the new target versions, one at a time, to their growing native-like repertoire (shiny new arrows). In other words, adult SLA is understood chiefly as a process of skill building. On this view, declarative knowledge (conscious knowledge *that*) is implanted first. Subsequently, via intensive use, it is gradually converted into qualitatively different, because analyzed and restructured, procedural knowledge (unconscious knowledge *how*), stored in long-term memory. During the conversion process, the former knowledge system is proceduralized, and then, through massive practice, automatized. Reflecting the power law of practice, performance moves from controlled to automatic processing, with increasingly faster access to, and more fluent control over, new structures achieved through intensive linguistically focused rehearsal (see, e.g., DeKeyser 2007a,b; Gatbonton & Segalowitz 1988; Johnson 1996; Paradis 2009; Segalowitz 2003, 2010). In the most successful (rather rare) cases, automatized procedural knowledge can be accessed so rapidly as to "pass" for implicit knowledge, although it no such thing.

Skill-building models sit uneasily with some rather obvious facts about language, and with 40 years of research findings on interlanguage (IL) development. To start, there are very few grammatical features or constructions that can be taught in isolation, for the simple reason that most are inextricably inter-related. Producing English sentences with target-like negation, for example, requires control of word order, tense, and auxiliaries, in addition to knowing where the negator is placed. Learners cannot produce even simple utterances like "John didn't buy the car" accurately without all of those. It is not surprising, therefore, that IL development of individual structures has very rarely been found to be sudden, categorical, or linear, with learners achieving native-like ability with structures one at a time, while making no progress with others. IL development just does not work like that. Accuracy in a given grammatical domain typically progresses in a zigzag fashion, with backsliding, occasional U-shaped behavior, over-suppliance and under-suppliance of target forms, flooding and bleeding of a grammatical domain (Huebner 1983), and considerable synchronic variation, volatility (Long 2003a), and diachronic variation. Advances in one area sometimes cause temporary declines in accuracy in another, e.g., because the increased processing demands created by control of a new feature result in diminished attentional resources being available elsewhere during production (Meisel, Clahsen, & Pienemann 1981). For example, a learner may produce third person -s accurately in simplex sentences (Melissa works in a bank.), but later fail to supply the -s when it is required in dependent clauses (*Peter said he play every Saturday.), i.e., in a syntactically more complex environment that makes more demands on processing capacity. The assumption implicit in synthetic syllabi and focus on forms is that learners can move from zero knowledge to native-like mastery of nega-tion, the present tense, subject–verb agreement, conditionals, the subjunctive, relative clauses, or whatever, one at a time, produce utterances containing them accurately, and move on to the next item on a list. It is a fantasy.

This is not to deny that explicit instruction in a particular structure, even a complex one, can produce measurable learning. However, studies that have shown this, e.g., Day and Shapson (1994), Harley (1989), Lyster (1994), and Muranoi (2000), have usually devoted far more extensive periods of time to intensive practice of the targeted feature than is available in a typical course. Also, the few studies that have followed students who receive such instruction over time (e.g., Lightbown 1983) have found that once the pedagogic focus shifts to new linguistic targets, learners revert to an earlier stage on the normal path to acquisition of the structure they had supposedly mastered in isolation and "ahead of schedule."

Far from being pliant organisms ready to be inculcated with new sets of language habits, L2 learners, both children and adults, are active, creative participants in the acquisition process. There is plenty of evidence of this. For example, ILs exhibit common patterns and common developmental stages, with only minor, predictable differences due to learner age, L1, acquisition context, or instructional approach. If structures could really be learned on demand, accuracy and acquisition sequences would reflect instructional sequences, but they do not. On the contrary, as demon-strated, for example, by Pica (1983) for English morphology by Spanish-speaking adults, by Lightbown (1983) for the present continuous -ing form by French-speaking children in Quebec being taught English as a second language (ESL) using the Lado English series, by Pavesi (1986) for relative clauses by children learning English as a foreign language (EFL) in Italy and Italian adults learning English naturalistically in Scotland, and by R. Ellis (1989) for English college students learning word order in

German as a foreign language, they are remarkably robust, regardless of different text-book presentation sequences, different classroom pedagogic foci, or whether learners receive instruction at all. As observed in communicative speech samples, rather than "language-like" performance on discrete-point tests, accuracy orders and developmental sequences found in instructed settings match those obtained for the same features in studies of naturalistic acquisition, although instruction can help speed up passage through those sequences.

While ILs are characterized by systematic and free variation, and no two ILs are exactly alike, the striking commonalities observed suggest powerful universal learning processes are at work, as in L1A. In SLA, they are reflected in many ways, including widely attested findings of common errors and error types (Pica 1983) and common interlingual forms and developmental stages (Ortega 2009; Zobl 1980, 1982), some of which appear to be universal. For instance, an initial pre-verbal (*Neg V*) negation stage appears in the ILs not just of speakers of L1s, like Spanish, with pre-verbal negation, in which case one could simply be looking at a case of L1 transfer, but in the ILs of L1 speakers of languages, such as Japanese or Turkish, that have post-verbal negation, even when the target language, e.g., Swedish, also has post-verbal negation (Hyltenstam 1977). The same non-target-like structures appear, regardless of the fact that they are never taught, and despite occasional temporary disturbances caused by teachers and textbooks providing intensive exposure to, and practice with, full native versions from the get-go (Lightbown 1983). The interlingual structures occur in fixed developmental sequences (Johnston 1985, 1997), the same sequences observed in naturalistic SLA, which studies have shown are impervious to instruction (R. Ellis 1989; Pienemann 1984, 1989, 2011). Outside the artificial confines of language-like behavior, such as a pattern drill, instruction cannot make learners skip a stage or stages and move straight to the full native version of a construction, even if it is exclusively the full native version that is modeled and practiced. Yet that is what should happen all the time if adult SLA were a process of explicit learning of declarative knowledge of full native models, their comprehension and production first proceduralized and then made fluent, i.e., automatized, through intensive practice. One might predict utterances with occasional missing grammatical features during such a process, but not the same sequences of what are often completely new, never-modeled interlingual constructions, and from all learners.

The learner's powerful cognitive contribution is visible, too, in so-called "autonomous syntax." As exemplified by the cases of pre-verbal negation described above, most transitional structures are not attested in the L1 or the L2 input, and certainly not practiced by teachers, but, again, created by the learners themselves. For instance, as first shown by Hyltenstam (1984), resumptive pronouns are often observed in the relative clauses of such learner utterances as *That is the man who he stole the car*, or *She is the woman who he loves her*. They are even produced, e.g., by Italian learners of English, when resumptive pronouns are found in neither the L1 nor the L2 (Pavesi 1986). The common error types, developmental sequences, and autonomous syntax documented by Hyltenstam, Pica, Pavesi, and many others are hard to account for, either in SLA theory or in classroom practice, if, as is the case in most classrooms the world over, students are drilled in exclusively standard target language forms, and learning is a process of proceduralizing native-like declarative knowledge. While practice has a role in automatizing what has been learned, i.e., in improving *control* of an acquired form or structure, the data show that L2 *acquisition* is not simply a process of forming new habits to override the effects of L1 transfer; powerful creative processes are at work. In fact, despite the presentation and practice of full native norms in *focus-on-forms* instruction, ILs often stabilize far short of the target variety, with learners persistently communicating with non-target-like forms and structures they were never taught, and target-like forms and structures with non-target-like functions (Sato 1990). The stabilization is sometimes for such long periods that the non-target-like state is claimed to be permanent, i.e., indicating not just stabilization, but permanent linguistic rigor mortis, or fossilization (see Lardiere 2006; Han & Odlin 2005; Sorace 2003; White 2003a; and for an alternative view, Long 2003a).

From robust findings of these and other kinds over four decades, it is clear that *learners, not teachers, have most control over their language development*, and they do not move from ignorance to native-like command of new items in one step, however intensive and protracted the pedagogic focus on code features. Even a simple grammatical rule, like that for English plural, is not acquired suddenly and categorically, but appears to be the end result of a process that Pica (1983) showed starts as item-based learning, plural allomorphs initially occurring only with high frequency, invariant and partially frozen plurals (*scissors, shoes, stairs*, etc.), then moving on to measure words (*dollars, days, years*, etc.), before gradually spreading across noun phrases (NPs) in general. A study by Pishwa (1994) of the acquisition of German subject–verb agreement by 15 Swedish children, aged 7–12, covering 10 observations over 18 months, showed no abrupt restructuring of their IL system, but instead, the same gradual extension of the agreement rule from one structure to another, the sequence governed by the structures' complexity, as judged by their markedness.

IL development is regulated by common cognitive processes and what Corder (1967) referred to as the internal "learner syllabus," not the external linguistic syllabus embodied in synthetic teaching materials. At least with regard to constructions shown to be part of a developmental sequence (see Long & Sato 1984; Ortega 2009), students do not – in fact, cannot – learn (as opposed to learn about) target forms and structures on demand, when and how a teacher or a textbook decree that they should, but only when they are developmentally ready to do so. In Pienemann's terms, and as his classroom studies (Pienemann 1984, 1989; Pienemann & Kessler 2011) and those of others have demonstrated, *learnability*, i.e., what learners can process at any one time, determines *teachability*, i.e., what can be taught at any one time. The effectiveness of negative feedback on learner error has been shown to be constrained in the same way (Mackey 1999). Instruction can facilitate development, but needs to be provided with respect for the learner's powerful cognitive contribution to the acquisition process, and appropriately timed, in harmony with the internal learner syllabus.

Synthetic syllabi will almost always be embodied in pedagogic materials that were written without reference to students' present or future communicative needs, as identified via a thorough needs analysis, and so are inefficient. They risk teaching more skills, vocabulary, genres, and so on, than students can use, but also less, through not teaching language abilities they do or will need. They will also almost always have been prepared in ignorance of any particular group of students' current developmental stages, especially so if in the form of commercially published textbook materials, which are mass-produced for everyone, but for no one in particular. Moreover, as experienced teachers know, and as shown, e.g., by the Pienemann (1984) study, learners within a class will often be at different developmental stages, even when labeled as having attained X or Y level of proficiency or having scored within a specified range on a placement test. Learners can achieve roughly similar overall proficiency and test scores despite strengths and weaknesses in different areas of their IL repertoires.

2.4. Problems with Analytic Approaches and Focus on Meaning

The analytic approach and *focus on meaning* have several advantages over their multiply flawed synthetic counterparts, but suffer from different problems. On the plus side, learners and teachers are no longer faced with trying to meet a psycholinguistically unrealistic timetable in the form of an externally imposed linguistic syllabus, and thereby with virtually guaranteed repeated failure. Liberated from the tight linguistic controls in most synthetic teaching materials and the unnatural classroom language use that accompanies their delivery, students are exposed to richer input and more realistic language models. In other words, the learning task for adults is not made more difficult than it already is by having to be accomplished using the impoverished input that classroom studies have shown characterize lessons with a focus on forms (see, e.g., Dinsmore 1985; Long & Sato 1983; Nunan 1987). Analytic lessons can be more interesting, motivation maintained, and attention held, as teachers and students are free to use the L2 to communicate about topics of interest – potentially, topics of relevance to meeting communicative needs beyond the classroom – instead of yet another memorable dialogue in which Dick and Jane ask and answer questions about the clothes they are wearing or the location of objects on a table visible to both. As evidenced most clearly by the results of French immersion programs in Canada, given enough time, very high levels of achievement are possible via some programs with a focus on meaning.

There are at least four problems, however. First, and most crucially, a pure analytic approach and focus on meaning assume that the capacity for implicit learning remains strong in adults. Yet even though implicit language learning is an option throughout the life span, for reasons detailed in Chapter 3, it is no longer as powerful a language-learning capacity as it was during early childhood. Were it fully intact, there would be plentiful cases of adults achieving abilities comparable to those of native speakers simply as a result of prolonged immersion in a L2 environment. Many have looked, but not a single such case has ever been documented. As demonstrated by Abrahamsson and Hyltenstam (2009), even the ILs of highly proficient speakers, judged to be natives on the basis of short speech samples, turn out to exhibit non-native-like features when scrutinized.

Second, implicit learning takes time, and LT needs to be efficient, not just minimally necessary and sufficient. Most classroom courses meet for just a few hours a week, and nothing approaching the virtually full-time L2 experience of the successful French immersion programs in Canada. In particular, L2 features that are of low saliency for one or more reasons, e.g., because infrequent, non-syllabic, string-internal, or communicatively redundant, may not even be either *noticed* or *detected* (see Chapter 3) in the input for a long time, if ever, unless learners' attention is drawn to them by a teacher, by artfully crafted pedagogic materials, or by a helpful native speaker. A clear illustration of the role of attention direction in this process was Schmidt's failure to notice the imperfect suffix *-ia* [*used to* go] in his daily naturalistic exposure to Portuguese in Brazil until his teacher focused on it in a classroom lesson one day, whereupon he immediately began to notice *-ia* in the input outside the classroom, which he realized must have been there all along (Schmidt & Frota 1986, p. 279). Some theorists hold that *noticing* in Schmidt's sense (Schmidt 1990, and elsewhere), i.e., consciously attending to and detecting a form or form-meaning connection in the input, is the necessary first stage in the process of acquiring some features and form–meaning connections, especially if new and of low salience, and likely to speed up the acquisition of others.

Third, as a result of possessing a L1, learning from positive evidence alone will no longer suffice. As White (1987, 1991) has argued convincingly, this is important when retreat from an over-generalization is required in cases where the L1 and L2 are in a superset–subset relationship. English and French adverbs of frequency, for example, can appear in some of the same places in a sentence (I drink coffee *every day*/Je bois du café *tous les jours*), but not all. French also allows interruption of verb and direct object (Je bois *toujours* du café), whereas English does not (*I drink *every day* coffee.). English and French children can learn what their L1 allows in each case by exposure to the language in use, positive evidence. English-speaking adults can do the same when learning French as L2, encountering examples of the new option in the input. French-(Spanish-, Japanese-, etc.) speaking adult learners of English as L2, conversely, need to "unlearn" the SVAdvO option, grammatical in the L1, but illegal in the L2. That may never happen if the difference goes unnoticed. At the very least, it will take a long time, eventually occurring either as a case of attrition because of absence of support for the L1 pattern in the L2 input, or as a result of negative evidence, e.g., a teacher drawing students' attention to the problem. This is particularly important, White notes, in cases where retention of the ungrammatical L1 option causes no breakdown in communication, for that is precisely when negative feedback is less likely (A: *In France, when I was ten years old, I drank *every day* wine mix with water with my dinner. B: Really? So young!). Communication clearly having been achieved and the conversation moved on, A is unlikely to have noticed anything was wrong.

Fourth, a purely analytic approach ignores the substantial evidence that L2 instruction that also includes one or more types of attention to language works. It does not change the route of acquisition, e.g., developmental sequences, or acquisition processes, e.g., simplification, generalization, and regularization, but it does speed up acquisition and can improve the level of ultimate L2 attainment in some areas (Long 1983a, 1988). The jury is still out on optimal uses and timing of various kinds and combinations of instruction (explicit, implicit, focus on form, focus on forms, etc.), as well as how best to match type of instruction to students' language aptitude profiles (Vatz *et al.* 2013) and the classes of L2 features on which to expend most effort (Spada & Tomita 2010). However, there is overwhelming evidence that all these varieties of intervention can facilitate learning better than simple exposure to meaningful samples of the L2. For comparative reviews, see, e.g., De Graaff and Housen (2009), R. Ellis (2012), N. Ellis and Laporte (1997), Goo *et al.* (2009), Housen and Perriard (2005), Norris and Ortega (2000), and Spada (1997).

2.5. A Third Option: Analytic Approaches with a Focus on Form

Given the flaws and limitations of both focus on forms and focus on meaning, I have argued since the mid-1980s for a third option, which I call an analytic approach with a *focus on form* (see, e.g., Doughty & Long 2003; Doughty & Williams 1998a; Long 1988, 1991, 2009; Long & Robinson 1998). One of the original methodological principles (MPs) of TBLT (Long 1991, 2000a, 2009), *focus on form* involves *reactive* use of a wide variety of pedagogic procedures (PPs) to draw learners' attention to linguistic problems in context, as they arise during communication (in TBLT, typically as students work on problem-solving tasks), thereby increasing the likelihood that attention to code features will be synchronized with the learner's internal syllabus, developmental stage, and processing ability.[3] Focus on form capitalizes on a symbiotic relationship between explicit and implicit learning, instruction, and knowledge.

As noted above, reliance on implicit learning from simple exposure, i.e., a pure focus on meaning, is inadequate, especially if advanced proficiency is the goal, and inefficient, due to the time required. Learner attention to problem areas of grammar, lexis, collocation, and so on, is needed in the interests of rate of acquisition and level of ultimate attainment. A purely implicit approach might not work with adults, especially with non-salient items, and would anyway take too long. However, to avoid a return to psycholinguistically indefensible lessons full of externally timed grammar rules, overt "error correction," and pattern drills, with all their nasty side effects, the idea is that as many of the problem areas as possible should be handled within otherwise communicative lessons by briefly drawing learners' attention to code features as and when problems arise. In this *reactive* mode (part of the *definition* of focus on form, not an optional feature), the learner's underlying psychological state is more likely to be optimal, and so the treatment, whatever PPs are employed, is more effective.

For example, while comparing car production in Japan and the USA as part of a *pedagogic task* designed to help students develop the ability to Deliver a sales report (the *target task)*, a learner might say something like "Production of SUV in the United States fell by 30% from 2000 to 2004." If the very next utterance from a teacher or another student is a partial recast, in the form of a confirmation check, e.g., "Production of SUVs fell by 30%?," as proposed in Long (1996b), the likelihood of the learner noticing the plural -*s* is increased by the fact that he or she is *vested* in the exchange, so is *motivated* to learn what is needed and *attending* to the response, already knows the meaning he or she was trying to express, so has freed up *attentional resources* to devote to the form of the response, and hears the correct form in close juxtaposition to his or her own, facilitating *cognitive comparison*. These are all reasons why implicit corrective recasts are believed to work as well as they do, without disturbing the fundamental communicative focus of a lesson, and why negative feedback is believed to work better than provision of the same numbers of models of a target form and/or tokens in ambient input (positive evidence). In contrast, with *focus on forms*, the teacher or the textbook, not the student, has selected a form for treatment. The learner is less likely to feel a need to

---

[3] See Chapter 10 for a full discussion of the distinction between methodological principles (MPs) and pedagogic procedures (PPs).

acquire the new item, and so will likely be less motivated, and less attentive. If the form is new, moreover, so, typically, will be its meaning and use, requiring the learner to process all three simultaneously. (We will return to these issues in more detail in Chapters 3 and 10.)

If a problematic form is considered tricky, perhaps because of L1 influence or low saliency, a more explicit brief switch of pedagogic focus by the teacher to the language itself, sometimes for just a matter of seconds, may be beneficial, e.g., "Car or cars?" In either case, and however overt the pedagogic procedure may be that the teacher employs to induce student focus on form, this reactive approach to treating (in the case of plural -*s*) a simple grammar point is operating in tandem with the learner's internal syllabus, in that the focus on form was triggered by a problem that occurred in the student's performance, not by a pre-set syllabus having prescribed it for that day's lesson. A student's attempt to produce a form is not always, but often, an indication of his or her developmental readiness to acquire it.

Learners' attention often needs to be directed to linguistic issues – not only in response to error or communicative trouble, but by extending a learner's repertoire as opportunities arise, e.g., by a teacher reformulating and extending already acceptable learner speech or writing. For example, in a discussion of great soccer players, an elementary-level student might say or write, "I think Xavi is a better player than Pirlo." The teacher might respond with "You think Xavi is better than Pirlo, but do you think he's the best midfielder ever?" The learner (and his or her classmates) is likely to be focused on the teacher's response, given that it concerns something he or she has just said, and – because already partly familiar with the content of the message – has attentional resources available with which to focus on the switch from comparative to superlative forms.

In sum, rather than the limited binary choice offered by analytic and synthetic approaches, and by focus on forms and focus on meaning, it is clear that there are *three* major options in LT, depicted in Table 2.1.

2.6. A Role for Instructed Second Language Acquisition (ISLA) Research

Against this backdrop of fundamental disagreement in LT, one might expect theory and research in SLA to provide some help. After all, although most work in SLA has little

Table 2.1. Three major options in language teaching.

Options in Language Teaching		
Option 2 **Analytic** **Focus on Meaning**	**Option 3** **Analytic** **Focus on Form**	**Option 1** **Synthetic** **Focus on Forms**
Natural Approach Immersion, CLIL	TBLT Content-Based LT (?)	GT, ALM, Silent Way, TPR, etc.
Procedural Syllabus, etc.	Process Syllabus (?), etc.	Structural, Notional-Functional, Lexical Syllabi, etc.

or nothing to do with LT, one of its most applied sub-domains, ISLA, is of obvious potential relevance. Since SLA is the process LT is designed to facilitate, the relationship between the two, and understanding the effects and effectiveness of instruction, and constraints on instruction, is of considerable interest. The problem is, the relationship between SLA and LT has not always been a positive one, such that SLA-based proposals will not necessarily be welcomed with open arms, even when, as will become clear in later chapters, the rationale is much broader than research findings in SLA, as is the case with TBLT. The potential contribution of work on ISLA is addressed in the next chapter, as well as in later parts of the book.

2.7. Summary

LT over the centuries has oscillated between two fundamentally different and mutually exclusive positions: on the one hand, synthetic, focus-on-forms approaches, syllabi, methods, materials, and (although not discussed yet) tests, and on the other, analytic, focus-on-meaning approaches, syllabi, methods, materials, and (less often) tests. The difference during the past 60 years, up to and including the present day, is that, while synthetic, focus-on-forms approaches remain dominant, mostly due to the influence of commercial publishers; there has been simultaneous verbal support for each approach from different wings of the LT field. SLA research findings show that both have serious problems, however, and fortunately, are not the only choices available. As explained briefly, and as will be discussed in more detail in later chapters, a third option, *an analytic syllabus with a focus on form*, captures the advantages of analytic, focus-on-meaning approaches, while avoiding their shortcomings.

2.8. Suggested Readings

DeKeyser, R. (2007). Skill acquisition theory. In VanPatten, B., & Williams, J. (eds.), *Theories in second language acquisition* (pp. 97–113). Mahwah, NJ: Lawrence Erlbaum.

Gatbonton, E., & Segalowitz, N. (1988). Creative automatization: Principles for promoting fluency within a communicative framework. *TESOL Quarterly* 22, 3, 472–293.

Krashen, S.D. (1985). *The input hypothesis: Issues and implications*. New York: Longman.

Long, M.H. (2009). Methodological principles for language teaching. In Long, M.H., & Doughty, C.J. (eds.), *Handbook of language teaching* (pp. 373–394). Oxford: Wiley-Blackwell.

Musumeci, D. (1997). *An exploration of the historical relationship between theory and practice in second language teaching*. New York: McGraw-Hill.

Ortega, L. (2009). Development of learner language. In Ortega, L. (ed.), *Understanding second language acquisition* (pp. 110–144). London: Hodder.

Spada, N. (1997). Form-focussed instruction and second language acquisition: A review of classroom and laboratory research. *Language Teaching* 30, 2, 73–87.

Wilkins, D. (1976). *Notional syllabuses*. Oxford: Oxford University Press.

Chapter 3

Psycholinguistic Underpinnings: A Cognitive-Interactionist Theory of Instructed Second Language Acquisition (ISLA)

3.1. Theoretical Disunity in Second Language Acquisition (SLA)

As evidenced by the steadily increasing numbers of encyclopedias, handbooks and scholarly journals in the field, it is clear that over 40 years of modern SLA research has

Second Language Acquisition and Task-Based Language Teaching, First Edition. Mike Long.
© 2015 John Wiley & Sons, Inc. Published 2015 by John Wiley & Sons, Inc.

produced a large body of fairly robust empirical findings about how people learn languages beyond their L1 and dialects beyond their D1. In particular, a lot of work has been reported on the role of cognitive variables, cross-linguistic influence, individual differences (IDs), and the linguistic environment, as well as about biological and processing constraints on learning. Equally apparent, however, is the relative lack of progress in theory construction and assessment, especially comparative theory evaluation.

Depending on what one considers qualifies as a theory, either of, or in, SLA, as many as 40–60 theories, models, and (sometimes of broader scope than either) "hypotheses" are on offer, many with considerable followings (Long 2007a). Theory proliferation, as opposed to theoretical pluralism, is unhealthy in any scientific field and, on this scale, could be interpreted as showing that SLA is prescientific. Imagine the level of public confidence in physicians were medical science in such a state. However, as I have argued elsewhere (Long 2007b), the situation is not quite as chaotic as it might first appear if one looks at entities above the level of theory.

As part of his extensive work on theory change in science, the American philosopher of science Larry Laudan has drawn attention to the existence of what he calls *research traditions* (Laudan 1977, 1996, and elsewhere). Researchers in any scientific field, Laudan argues, tend to have enduring commitments to clusters of fundamental beliefs – beliefs broader than those of any particular theory that reflects them – and to a corresponding set of epistemic and methodological norms about how a domain of inquiry should be studied. 'Research tradition', then, is a technical term in Laudan's theory of theory change in science for a group of theories with a shared ontology and agreed-upon methodological ground rules. Unlike some theories or parts thereof, research traditions are not directly testable. They can survive the demise of one of their particular subordinate theories.[1]

Viewed this way, most of the 40–60 theories of SLA can be grouped into a smaller number of *research traditions*. For example, Schuman's Acculturation Model (Schumann 1978, 1986) and Gardner's Socio-educational Model (Gardner 1985, 1988) are two of several examples of theories proposed by researchers operating (at the time of those publications, at least) within the same social-psychological research tradition. Gardner seeks to predict French L2 proficiency in formal and/or informal, monolingual, and bilingual contexts in Canada as a function of attitude (partly determined by a community's cultural beliefs and characteristics, e.g., ethnolinguistic vitality), of motivation, and anxiety, and a cognitive variable, language aptitude. Schumann attempts to achieve roughly the same goal via a combination of two constructs, social and psychological distance (each an amalgam of several variables) between native and target-language groups. While different in terms of supposedly causal variables, the two models share similar underlying assumptions and scope. Schumann and Gardner both invoke a combination of social, psychological, and social-psychological variables, albeit in very different combinations, to explain success and failure in SLA at the level of the group, mostly as a function of group membership and intra- and intergroup relations. Each attributes greater importance to affective and situational factors than to linguistic or cognitive variables. Where methodology is concerned, empirical tests of both theories have tended to utilize questionnaires, Likert scales, and other paper-and-pencil

---

[1] For discussion of Laudan's notion of "research tradition," see Gholson and Barker (1985) and Riggs (1992, pp. 109–119).

measures of the putative causal variables – attitude, motivation (and the "integrative motive" construct), social and psychological distance, contact with target-language speakers, and so on – and (with some exceptions in research on the Acculturation Model) employ global L2 proficiency tests as the primary outcome measure. The same is largely true of at least two other models in the social-psychological research tradition, those of Clement (e.g., Clement 1980; Clement & Kruidenier 1985), and Giles' Accommodation Theory (e.g., Giles & Byrne 1982).

While the higher level of abstraction offered by research traditions presents a less fragmented, more coherent view of the field, theoretical disunity is still apparent. At least eight such research traditions appear to be alive and well in SLA, each with two or more, sometimes many more, theories within it. Special nativist, general nativist, emergentist, cognitive-interactionist, functionalist, skill-building, social-psychological, and sociocultural traditions all attract research interest, rarely from the same people. And while grouping SLA theories in this way brings greater coherence to the picture, in other ways, it accentuates fault lines. Like many of the theories within them (Beretta 1991), the research traditions themselves are clearly oppositional, not complementary. The human capacity for language either does or does not involve genetically inherited knowledge of language universals. The language-learning process is primarily an individual, internal mental process or a "co-constructed" social phenomenon. SLA either is subject to biologically scheduled maturational constraints (underlying the well-attested age differences), including one or more sensitive periods, or it is not. The language acquisition capacity employed so successfully in child L1A remains available to the adult, available only in diminished form, or is unavailable. Social context either does influence interlanguage (IL) development in more than trivial ways or it does not. The main drivers in SLA are cognitive variables, affective variables, or input but not, or only rarely, all three. And so on.

Evidently, there is no dominant research tradition, much less a dominant theory, i.e., one that is superior to its rivals by all the varying assessment criteria used by scientists in a field and is recognized as such by all in that field (Laudan & Laudan 1989). Moreover, with few exceptions, researchers from different traditions increasingly attend separate conferences, publish in different journals, and, judging by the references they cite, at least, generally ignore work conducted in other traditions. At first sight, therefore, to suggest that SLA research findings can resolve long-standing disputes in language teaching (LT) would seem premature or simply foolhardy. Nevertheless, the major divisions notwithstanding, there are still grounds for believing the field has much to offer LT.

Compared with the theoretical disunity plain to see in the field as a whole, less disagreement exists in the sub-field of instructed second language acquisition (ISLA). Why should this be so? Well, for one thing, many scholars in the research traditions mentioned above have little or no interest in the effects of instruction and seldom intend their work to have more than an indirect relevance for LT, if that. For another, the sub-field's narrower scope helps focus ISLA researchers' attention on the same issues and, as shown by the references they cite, means they are more likely to read each others' publications and hold themselves and one another accountable to the same body of published literature. Whereas work within the special nativist tradition, for example, would never be criticized for ignoring research on social and psychological distance, attitude, motivation, or language aptitude, a suggestion in the ISLA literature, say, that incidental and implicit learning play major roles in adult SLA (a claim I will be making) will quickly be alleged to have given insufficient weight to published findings on intentional learning, explicit instruction and skill building, and vice versa. For these reasons, among others, coupled with fairly consistent findings since the mid-1980s, SLA research in naturalistic, formal, and mixed environments has produced a developing consensus – not unanimity, by any means, with important minority views to both left and right, but a developing consensus – on how instruction can facilitate adult language learning, to the main parameters of which I return below.

3.2. When Knowledge Is Incomplete: The Role of Theory

While, as we shall see, some ISLA research findings are robust and widely accepted, others may be unreliable and conflicting, or their interpretation a matter of dispute. The biggest problem, however, is that they are undeniably incomplete. We by no means fully understand how adults learn second languages and dialects, with or without the aid of instruction, or why so many fail, just some of the factors and some parts of the process. As in any scientific field, so in ISLA, absent comprehensive understanding of the variables and mechanisms involved and of how they interact, what is required is a theory. A theory is as strong and as explicit a statement as possible – both qualities viewed as positive in that they reduce ambiguity and facilitate testing, thereby speeding up scientific progress – always open to modification. It provides an interim understanding of the phenomena (e.g., developmental sequences) deducible from the data, i.e., the sub-set of widely attested empirical observations, or facts (e.g., recurring interlingual structures at different levels of L2 proficiency that go to make up the developmental sequences), in the domain of interest that are considered both salient and important enough to require explanation.[2] Explanations in SLA typically take the form of claims about the interaction of underlying variables and mechanisms, on the one hand, and properties of the L1 and L2, on the other.

Two aspects of the definition are worth highlighting. First, a theory abstracts away from the data and the phenomena they indicate and seeks to explain them, going beyond what is known in the process for the simple reason that if everything were known, a theory would be unnecessary. As a result, it will quite possibly be wrong, at least in part, and quite possibly incomplete (because we do not know all we do not know), but this is a reasonable price to pay, given the benefits. By selecting, relating, and integrating disparate empirical findings, the theory provides a provisional *coherent* explanation of the domain of interest. It motivates *rational* choices for practice where knowledge is incomplete. And because predictions derived from it identify and prioritize research questions, it motivates a research program to test its claims and extend its scope, making the research effort more *economical* in terms of both time and money.

The second point to note is that, however robust, not all research findings may be considered important enough to be referenced by the theory or to require explanation. For example, performance phenomena in second language use, i.e., much of what is subsumed under the rubric of synchronic IL variation, are widely accepted facts about both naturalistic SLA and ISLA. They are considered crucial for understanding L2

---

[2] "The data are evidence for the phenomena; the phenomena are the subject of the explanation, ultimately the theory" (Gregg 1993, p. 285).

development by some (e.g., Adamson 2009; Ellis 1999; Preston 1989; Tarone 1983) but irrelevant by others (e.g., Gregg 1990; Schwartz 1993; White 2003b, 2007) for whom the proper domain of a theory is linguistic competence, not performance.

While deciding which findings to take into account is a judgment call, this does not mean that anything goes or goes away. As evidenced by the coverage in SLA textbooks and the citations in refereed journal articles over the past four decades, there is broad agreement among ISLA researchers as to what constitutes the salient facts to date, about what the phenomena are that an SLA theory needs to explain (Long 1990a), a shared focus facilitated since 2000 by the appearance of increasing numbers of statistical meta-analyses of the findings (see below). A theory that ignored many of those findings or swept them under the carpet would have little credibility and attract little research interest, unless its predictions quickly began to match subsequent observations, which would be unlikely.

As in any scientific field, it is not the case, however, that the entirety of a (casual-process) theory has to be testable. It is sufficient that parts of it should be, those parts ideally linked to the currently untested or untestable ones, thereby making at least indirect assessment feasible. And it is certainly not the case, of course, that a theory should be known to be true, for if that were so, it would no longer be a theory but itself a fact or a set of facts.

A particularly useful approach to understanding the process of theory construction, assessment, and change is provided by Laudan (1977, 1996, and elsewhere). Laudan views science as fundamentally a problem-solving activity:

> the aim of science is to secure theories with a high problem-solving effectiveness. From this perspective, *science progresses just in case successive theories solve more problems than their predecessors.* (Laudan 1996, p. 78, italics in the original)

It follows that what constitutes a "problem," and how problems compare with one another in size and importance, is both crucial for the evaluation process and for measuring progress in SLA or any other field.

Laudan (1996, pp. 79–81) distinguishes two general classes of problems: empirical and conceptual. *Empirical problems* are of three kinds: potential, solved, and anomalous (Laudan 1996, p. 79). *Potential problems* are phenomena accepted as facts about the world for which there is as yet no explanation. *Solved, or actual, problems* are claimed facts about the world that have been explained by one or more theories. *Anomalous problems* ('anomalous' is a technical term for Laudan with a different meaning from 'problematic' or 'contrary to prediction,' its traditional meaning in the philosophy of science) are those problems solved by rival theories but not (yet) by the theory in question. Note that potential or unsolved problems need not be anomalies by this analysis. In Laudan's theory, what makes a problem an anomaly for a particular theory is not whether it currently constitutes a problem for that theory, or looks like doing so for being apparently unsolvable by it, but the fact that a viable rival theory has solved it, while the theory being evaluated has not. Hence, a problem that appears likely to constitute a falsifying instance for a theory may not be an anomalous problem if no other theory can handle it, either, and a fact or a result that does not falsify a theory may yet be an anomalous problem for that theory if it does not account for it, while another theory does.

The second general class of problems in Laudan's scheme, *conceptual problems*, comprises four kinds, one theory-internal and three external. *Internal conceptual problems* arise when (i) a theory is internally inconsistent or postulates ambiguous theoretical mechanisms. *External conceptual problems* exist when (ii) assumptions a theory makes about the world are inconsistent with those of other theories, with prevailing metaphysical assumptions, or with widely accepted epistemology and methodology; (iii) a theory violates the research tradition of which it is a part; or (iv) a theory fails to utilize concepts from more general theories to which it should be logically subordinate (Laudan 1996, p. 78). Gholson and Barker (1985, pp. 764–765) provide examples of the influence of conceptual problems on theory change in the history of physics and behaviorist psychology. They also suggest that a lack of precision in the definition of such central concepts in Piaget's theory of cognitive development as equilibration, construction, assimilation, and organization made them inadequate both theoretically and experimentally, and may account for Piaget's theory seemingly having entered a period of stagnation. In SLA, this bodes ill for sociocultural theory, founded as it is on even more nebulous core constructs, such as "inner speech," "appropriation," "mediation," "self-regulation," and the "zone of proximal development."

Good theories, Laudan argues, and I accept, solve 'problems,' i.e., account for widely accepted phenomena in the field in need of explanation. When two theories are on offer in the same domain, the better theory is the one that solves more problems. For example, it is widely accepted, even by those who reject the existence of so-called critical or sensitive periods for language acquisition, that late starters ultimately do less well than those who begin SLA as young children. Those are undisputed facts; age differences are the phenomena in need of explanation. Some claim that the differences are simply a function of poorer quality and/or quantity of access to the L2, lesser time on task, weaker motivation, and so on, and that some adult starters can even achieve abilities in the L2 indistinguishable from those of a monolingual native speaker (NS). Others, those in the maturational constraints camp, argue that the differences result from a loss of cerebral plasticity (on some accounts, perhaps due to myelinization) and that, whereas those beginning SLA before the close of one or more critical or sensitive periods *may* achieve native-like abilities, no one beginning SLA after the close of a critical or sensitive period *can* do so. A *capacity* has been lost.

Theories embracing the former position cannot explain several repeatedly observed phenomena, including the poorer achievement of late starters with equivalent, lengthier opportunities to learn, stronger motivation, and higher IQ than some young starters. Nor can they explain the *qualitative* changes observed in levels of achievement as a function of the age at which learners are first meaningfully exposed to the target language, or age of onset (AO), as opposed to the gradual decrease in achievement across the life span that would be expected if the no-maturational-constraints position were correct. Conversely, theories acknowledging the existence of biological constraints on language learning, including one or more critical or sensitive periods, can account for the non-linear shapes of the AO-related distributions observed, as well as the equally well-known separation (modularization) of language learning and general cognitive abilities in children, and, arguably, the statistical independence of language aptitude and general intelligence. In Laudan's terms, SLA theories that posit maturational constraints, therefore, solve the problem of child–adult differences in ultimate attainment, a problem that is now an anomaly in Laudan's sense for theories that do not.

The goals of a theory of SLA and a theory of ISLA are different (Long 2000b). Using traditional criteria for the assessment of scientific theories, a theory of SLA may be judged in part by its parsimony, i.e., whether it succeeds in explaining widely accepted facts with recourse to the lowest possible number of factors. For a theory of ISLA, necessity and sufficiency are less important than efficiency. If a factor facilitates language learning, it is fair game for a theory of ISLA, even if it is not necessary, and even though its incorporation adds to the power of the theory, a development that would normally be considered undesirable. Provision of negative feedback, for example, might eventually turn out not to be a relevant factor in a theory of SLA, as argued persuasively by Schwartz (1993), but its empirical track record, to date, as a facilitator of rate and, arguably, level of ultimate attainment makes it a legitimate component – in fact, a key component – of a theory of ISLA.

The following are some widely accepted findings in the field, i.e., salient phenomena or, in Laudan's terms, empirical problems (P), concerning (i) success and failure in adult SLA, (ii) processes in IL development, and (iii) effects and non-effects of instruction. Together, they, and others not addressed here, constitute key components of the *explanandum*, what the theory needs to explain. A minimally adequate theory of ISLA will need to offer an explanation (E), the *explanans*, for at least some of them if it is to be taken seriously. They are problems the theory needs to solve. What follows is my attempt at this, an embryonic cognitive-interactionist theory of ISLA.

3.3. A Cognitive-Interactionist Theory of ISLA: Problems and Explanations

P1. Purely incidental and implicit child L1A is overwhelmingly successful

Given ample exposure to their L1, all but the severely mentally challenged become NSs of that language. Whether with or without the aid of innate knowledge of linguistic universals and of constraints on the way languages can vary, it is widely agreed that most L1 and/or L2 learning from birth to age 6 takes place *incidentally*, i.e., *without intention* – while the learner's attention is focused on something else (a different stimulus, such as toys in the young child's case) – and *implicitly*, i.e., *without awareness* either of the process or the end product, *implicit knowledge*.[3] L1A is overwhelmingly successful, and successful with minimum conscious effort. Humans are biologically "programmed" to do language learning efficiently early in life.

That L1A is also biologically "scheduled" is visible in the common timing and common orders of development across languages within a domain of form–function mapping, such as locative expressions (Slobin 1985). Children traverse the developmental stages, e.g., when they begin to combine two elements, at roughly the same ages, based on conceptual development, regardless of how the mappings are encoded in the languages concerned and regardless of what are often the same languages' markedly different levels of difficulty for speakers of the same L1 who try to learn them as adults.

---

[3] For definitions and discussion of implicit and explicit learning and related concepts, see, e.g., N.C. Ellis (1994, 2009), Stadler and Frensch (1998), and Williams (2009).

The biological scheduling is also reflected in "catch-up" phenomena. Young children initially denied access to L1 input, wholly or partly, e.g., because they are the victims of abusive parents, institutionalized, or hearing children of deaf adults, catch up with age peers once provided with normal access, and then continue along on schedule (Curtiss 1980, 1988; Long 1990b). Late L1 exposure for teenagers or adults, conversely, does not result in "catch-up" or eventual achievement of native levels of proficiency, as shown by such cases as "Genie" (Curtiss 1977), "E.M." (Grimshaw *et al.* 1998),[4] and those of deaf individuals first exposed to a sign language as adults (Mayberry & Eichen 1991; Newport 1990).

The implicit nature of the process is also indicated by the fact that child L1A is uniformly successful in all but a handful of cases (children with certain mental abnormalities). While parents' socioeconomic background and interactional style can affect the level of proficiency, e.g., vocabulary size, children achieve by ages 5–6, factors such as IQ (great disparities among children in which would affect intentional learning) and the environment that strongly influence general cognitive functioning and abilities have lesser, temporary effects on linguistic development, mostly related to rate of learning, e.g., language delay in institutionalized children (Culp *et al.* 1991), not ultimate attainment. Children's resulting knowledge of the L1, as revealed by their ability to pluralize nonsense words (e.g., *wugs*), is implicit, too, although simple parts can subsequently be raised to the level of conscious awareness, e.g., by asking older children and adults when they say *books* instead of *book*.

P2. Purely incidental and implicit adult L2A is highly variable and largely unsuccessful

Seemingly governed not by a single critical period but by a series of sensitive periods for language acquisition, some young children who experience sustained naturalistic L2 exposure early enough can (not necessarily will) attain native-like abilities. The latest starting age (the end of the offset period) at which that is possible increases progressively for (i) phonology, (ii) lexis and collocation, and (iii) (closing in the midteens) morphology and syntax (Abrahamsson & Hyltenstam 2008; Granena & Long 2013a). Both child and adult classroom foreign language learners can also acquire new vocabulary incidentally through exposure while working on pedagogic tasks (Newton 2013; Shintani 2011, 2013) or via extensive reading (e.g., Horst, Cobb, & Meara 1998; Webb, Newton, & Chang 2013), but the yield is often limited (for details, see Section 10.2.5). *Purely* incidental

---

[4] E.M. was born profoundly deaf. Raised in a rural area of Mexico with no contact with sign language, he used a homesign system of gestures for conveying basic meanings until age 15, when he was fitted with hearing aids in Canada and exposed to spoken Spanish in the home for the first time. After four years, his comprehension and production of spoken and written Spanish was still minimal and suggested permanent severe linguistic deficits, mostly comparable with those of Genie. The fact that E.M.'s cognitive and emotional development were normal (although his IQ was low, usually measured in the 80s) and his linguistic isolation, unlike Genie's, had not been the result of child abuse, suggests that the traumas suffered by Genie were not (alone, at least) the causes of her limited language abilities years later as an adult but, rather, the result of closure of a critical period for language development. Genie was 13, 7 when discovered. E.M. was 15 when he first experienced spoken Spanish. Both cases suggest that one or more sensitive periods for first language development are real, with offsets before puberty.

learning of lexis and collocations by adults, while feasible, is usually less successful and, for practical purposes, too slow-paced, although it will normally have to be relied upon to some degree since there is simply not enough time to cover everything explicitly (for a review of research findings, see Boers & Lindstromberg 2012 and Section 10.2.5). Laboratory studies show that, although learning L2 grammar through simple exposure is feasible for adults (Hulstijn 1989; Izumi *et al.* 1999; Izumi & Bigelow 2000; Robinson 1996), outcomes are variable, sometimes likely to be poor (Loewen, Erlam, & Ellis 2009; Robinson 1995a), and again, achieved too slowly for most practical purposes.

Even prolonged (10+ years of) immersion in a L2 environment for older children and adults with little or no form-focused instruction results in limited to minimally functional communicative abilities in most instances, e.g., the "basic variety" described in the European Science Foundation (ESF) project (Klein & Dimroth 2009; Klein & Purdue 1997), and such cases as "Wes" (Schmidt 1983), "Ayako" (Long 2003a), "SD" (White 2003a), and "Patty" (Lardicre 1988a,b, 2007). The prognosis for lengthy exposure is considerably better for school-age children in French immersion programs in Canada, but achievement is still far from native-like in many cases (Swain 1991). With adults, lengthy periods of optimal exposure can result in *near-native* (not native-like) communicative abilities, and then in only a tiny minority of cases (e.g., Abrahamsson & Hyltenstam 2009; Ioup *et al.* 1994; Marinova-Todd 2003), and as documented in the extensive literature on maturational constraints (for review, see, e.g., DeKeyser & Larson-Hall 2005; Hyltenstam & Abrahamsson 2003), never, as far as we know, in *native-like abilities*, the few apparent counterexamples being methodological artifacts (DeKeyser 2006; Long 2005a, 2013a).

The poor results may sometimes be partly due to a variety of adverse factors, ranging from negative attitudinal and motivational profiles, through low language aptitude and lesser time on task, to restricted input and qualitatively and quantitatively poorer opportunities for language use. But the best results for adults are poorer than the routine achievements of young children with early sustained exposure, even when conditions are seemingly optimal, i.e., when learner profiles (attitudes, motivation, etc.) are positive, time to learn is unlimited, and usable input is plentiful. This is shown, e.g., by a study of two exceptional American women's highly successful, but still non-native-like, command of Arabic after 20 years in Egypt (Ioup *et al.* 1994), by two decades of evaluations of Anglophone children's relatively high French proficiency after ten or more years in Canadian French immersion programs (Swain 1991) and again, after four more years at a French-medium university (Vignola & Wesche 1991), and by an examination of the abilities of 30 very advanced learners of English, mostly Harvard students, after an average of ten years of what often amounted to complete immersion in the L2 (Marinova-Todd 2003). Adult L2A can be done incidentally and implicitly up to a point, in other words, from exposure to, and communicative use of, the L2, but the results always fall short, usually far short, of native-like abilities, and – of considerable importance for LT – take much more time than teachers and learners typically have at their disposal.

E1. Adult SLA is maturationally constrained

The existence, scope, and timing of putative maturational constraints on SLA, including one or more sensitive periods, remain contested issues today. However, as with any theory, some simplifying assumptions are necessary. My view of the literature has long been (Long 1990b), and remains (Long 2007c, 2013a), that researchers have provided considerable evidence of such constraints, as well as of their sequential effects, on (i) phonology, (ii) lexis and collocations, and (iii) morphology and syntax, in that order (see, e.g., Granena & Long 2013a). Conversely, while many have looked, not a single case has been found of across-the-board native-like attainment by a late starter that would stand up in court; apparent counterexamples are just that, apparent (DeKeyser 2006; DeKeyser & Larson-Hall 2005; Long 2005a, 2013a). If there really are no matura- tional constraints, adult starters who achieve native-like abilities should be two a penny and pass all the tests to which researchers subject them. Those who deny the existence of constraints need to explain the absence of such individuals in studies that have sought to demonstrate their existence, and the pervasive at least partial failure of adult SLA, and they have not been able to do so. Suggestions that adults retain the same capacity to acquire as young children and simply do poorly because of less time on task, lower motivation, or poorer quality input simply do not bear scrutiny. So, while the precise scope and timing of sensitive periods is less clear,[5] I intend to treat the basic issue, non- native-like attainment by late starters, as a "solved problem" in Laudan's sense of the term, and as both an anomaly in the traditional meaning of that term in the philosophy of science for theories, e.g., so-called full access positions, which hold that children and adults have the same language-learning capacity, and an *anomalous problem* for the same theories in Laudan's technical sense. The meaning of 'adult' for the purposes of what follows, therefore, is also different from everyday use of that term and varies somewhat by linguistic domain. Research findings suggest closure of sensitive periods for the acquisition of native-like phonology as early as ages 4–6 for most people, and before the end of the offset period, at age 12, for everyone else, of the lexicon (lexis and colloca- tions) somewhere between ages 6 and 10, and morphology and syntax by the mid-teens (DeKeyser 2000; DeKeyser & Larson-Hall 2005; Granena & Long 2013a; Hyltenstam 1992; Hyltenstam & Abrahamsson 2003; Long 1990b; Meisel 2011; Munnich & Landau 2010; Newport 2002; Seliger 1978; Spadaro 1996, 2013).

Elsewhere (Long 2007c), I have offered the *Neurophysiological Enrichment Hypothesis* (NEH) as a potential explanation for the behavioral data. The NEH says that exposure to two or more languages, as opposed to only one, before the close of one or more sensi- tive periods conveys a *lasting* advantage on early L2 acquirers – an advantage that persists in adulthood, however adulthood is defined. The precise neurophysiological enhancements that underpin the advantage are unclear at this juncture but may consist of the formation of more, and more complex, neural networks (more nodes and con- nections among nodes), the result of stimulation by richer, more varied input, *before* synaptic sheaths harden as part of the mylenization process, making new ones for new languages more difficult to create in older starters. One indication of this may be the more complex dendritic bundles observed in bilinguals and multilinguals than mono- linguals (Jacobs 1988), although it is not clear that this difference is age-dependent.

---

[5] Where scope is concerned, for example, it is not the case that all morphology and syntactic constructions or all kinds of collocations are affected equally (DeKeyser 2011; DeKeyser, Alfy-Shabtay, & Ravid 2010; Granena 2012; Granena & Long 2013a). And while the timing of sensitive periods for these linguistic domains is gradually becoming clearer, there is some variation from one study to another due to the interaction of the L1's of participants and the nature (production or reception, online or off-line) and difficulty of the target- language measures employed.

The crucial behavioral observation is that younger children catch up with, and given adequate opportunity, ultimately overtake, older child and adult starters (who set off faster) *after* closure of the supposed sensitive periods. Further, the advantage is not lost when the learner undergoes any or all of the *universal* general cognitive changes hypothesized by some to underlie critical or sensitive periods (in such formulations, usually just one critical period), e.g., "less-is-more" changes in processing abilities, the deterioration in the capacity for implicit learning,[6] or attainment of Piagetian formal operations and accompanying metalinguistic awareness. Young starters undergo the same general cognitive changes as everyone else, but those changes do not affect them, suggesting that they are not what underlie sensitive period offsets in the rest of the population. The benefits of an early start are robust and enduring, implying a permanent increase in language-learning potential as a function of early bilingual or multilingual exposure.

As suggested elsewhere (Long 2007c), the enduring benefit of early L2 acquisition experience for later language learning may be visible in the results of a study by Mayberry and Lock (2003). The L2 syntactic abilities (especially for complex grammatical constructions) of deaf adults who had learned either a spoken or a signed language as children were near-native, whereas the abilities of deaf adults who had learned neither fell far short. Mayberry and Lock note that their findings are consistent with those on the beneficial, often critical, effects of early experience on other biological systems, such as visual perception. (Early visual deprivation alters lifelong visual abilities negatively in animals and humans.) In just the same way, they suggest:

> Language may be a genetically specified ability but our previous and present results suggest that the development of language capacity may be an epigenetic process whereby environmental experience during early life drives and organizes the growth of this complex behavioral and neurocortical system. (Mayberry & Lock 2003, p. 382)

More recently, additional results consistent with these and with the NEH were obtained by Petitto *et al.* (2012). They compared the duration of the ability of two groups of babies, aged 4–6 and 10–12 months, who had been exposed from birth either to one language (English, $n = 27$) or two languages (English and another language unrelated to Hindi, $n = 34$), to perceive phonetic contrasts in English and a third language (Hindi), as well as non-linguistic pure tones. While neuroimaging showed that the same brain areas were involved for both groups as for adults, the extent and variability of the language neural tissue were greater in the bilingual babies, the older (10–12 months) group of whom remained sensitive to new sound contrasts when the monolingual babies no longer were, and sound contrasts not in their L2 but in the third language. It seemed that the enriched early bilingual exposure had created superior language-learning potential

---

[6] Many experts (e.g., Reber & Allen 2000, pp. 234–235) deny that the capacity for implicit learning is lost in adults. The results in DeKeyser (2000) may be due to variance in the achievement measure among the early starters being smaller, and it being harder to obtain a significant correlation between language aptitude and AO within that group, therefore. Conversely, a statistically significant positive correlation is obtained in the older group, as they vary both in aptitude and obtained proficiency. Also, both aptitude tests (even oral ones) and grammaticality judgment (GJ) tests (which are what DeKeyser's and other studies employ) allow the use of metalinguistic abilities to some extent, so in part probably measure the same abilities, meaning some positive association between the two sets of scores is to be expected. See Granena (2012) and Granena and Long (2013a) for a more detailed discussion.

in general, at least where new sounds are concerned, but potentially in other linguistic domains, too. Petitto *et al.* (2012) propose the Perceptual Wedge Hypothesis:

> We therefore hypothesize that the number of input languages to which a young baby is exposed can serve as a kind of "perceptual wedge." Like a physical wedge that holds open a pair of powerfully closing doors, exposure to more than one language holds open the closing "doors" of the human baby's typical developmental perceptual attenuation processes, keeping language sensitivity open for longer. (Petitto *et al.* 2012, p. 140)

E2. Adults, so defined, are partially "disabled" language learners

Whereas young starters are positively enabled by early bilingual exposure, monolingual adults, so defined, are, to use Cutler's term (Cutler 2001), partially "disabled" language learners in at least two closely related ways: (i) (counterintuitively) by having learned their L1 so well, and (ii) by a somewhat weaker capacity for implicit learning, due particularly to age-related declines in the efficiency of *instance learning*. Developmental sharpening (see below) during childhood of the way L1 input is processed makes L1A efficient and effective but simultaneously renders the adult L2 acquirer disadvantaged, as a result of the refined implicit processing mechanisms now having been "set" for the L1, and no longer "tuned" appropriately for the new language.

Having successfully learned a native language successfully, normal transfer of training would predict greater adult facility with a L2, but the reverse is true. Adults bring entrenched L1 processing habits to the SLA task and initially attempt L2 processing using mechanisms optimized for the L1 through the process known as "developmental sharpening" (Cutler 2001). *Developmental sharpening* refers to very early tuning of language-learning mechanisms that infants exploit, from the settings applicable to any language when they are born, to narrower settings that make segmentation and mapping more efficient for learning the particular L1 to which they are exposed. Examples include limiting speech perception to just those phonetic contrasts, rhythm and prosodic patterns relevant in the L1, and narrowing the hypothesis space for form–meaning mapping via the whole object, taxonomic, and mutual exclusivity constraints (for review, see Doughty 2003). Having made L1A more efficient, the L1-tuned processing systems work against the adult, who proceeds to apply them to a new language whose parameters differ (see, e.g., Lukyanchenko, Idsardi, & Jiang 2011). This leads to adults adversely "filtering" L2 input to L1-established attractors – what is referred to in the literature as "learnt attention."

A classic example in L1A is the initial ability of infants between the ages of one and four months to perceive the phonemic contrasts in any possible language, but their diminished capacity for the same task just a few months later, when, by around 12 months, they only distinguish contrasts in their mother tongue (Werker & Lalonde 1988; Werker & Tees 1984). According to Werker's Functional Reorganization Hypothesis (Werker 1995), as the infant learns to attend to the relevant sound contrasts and phonetic categories of their L1, their sensitivity to other phonetic distinctions, such as those in a second language, decreases in the period from 6 to 12 months. In the same way, while adults retain the ability to perceive phonemes not present in their L1, provided they are sufficiently different from those that are, the strongly established attractors in the L1 phonetic grid distort the adult's perception of L2 sounds that are different from, but similar to, those in the L1, rendering them undistinguished (Iverson *et al.* 2003; Kuhl 2007; Kuhl & Iverson 1995), resulting in parts of a "foreign accent." While research shows that adults retain some perceptual acuity, "Once native phonemic categorization has taken place, it cannot be altered" (Doughty 2003, p. 286). Another example concerns adults' strong tendency to transfer their L1 segmentation strategy – stress-based for English speakers, syllable-based for French speakers, and mora-based for Japanese speakers – when listening to a L2, regardless of whether it shares the same segmentation template (see, e.g., Cutler 2001; Cutler & Otake 1994; and for a review of findings, Doughty 2003, pp. 276–287).

Potentially problematic L1-tuned associative learning processes in adult SLA include contingency, cue competition, salience, interference, overshadowing, and blocking (Bates & MacWhinney 1989; Ellis 2006a,b). Help will be needed if adult learners are to overcome such L1-induced problems. To illustrate, exaggerated stimuli (an example of what I call "input elaboration," described in Section 9.2), making differences between 'lice' and 'rice,' and so on, discernible to Japanese learners, followed by adaptive training in which the degree of exaggeration is gradually reduced, draws their attention to the problem and can improve perception and production (McClelland, Fiez, & McCandliss 2002). Another example is processing instruction (VanPatten 1996), where artificially high frequencies of target L2 word order cues in the input draw learners' attention to differences in L1 and L2 cue strength at the utterance level, with the aim of blocking use of the default L1 processing strategies. Absent such intervention, given the canonical SVO word order of English, where the first noun is almost always the subject (He saw Mary), most native English speakers initially attempt to parse Spanish using the same first-noun strategy, thereby misinterpreting frequent Spanish OVS utterances (like *La quiere Pepe*/Pepe loves her) as SVO (Her/she loves Pepe).

In addition to the problems caused by having learned a first language successfully, adults' "disabled" status as L2 acquirers results from a diminished capacity (diminished, but by no means extinct) for *implicit learning* around age 12 (Janacsek, Fiser, & Nemeth 2012), due especially to an age-related decline in the efficiency of *instance learning* (Hoyer & Lincourt 1998) and, crucially, from *the interaction of the implicit learning disability with the L1 disability.* Unless "reset" by some form of intervention (see below), such as explicit learning or teaching, implicit processing tuned by and for the native language will filter the L2 through the L1 grid, tending to diminish the size and importance of some differences that are perceived and missing others altogether.

Skill acquisition has traditionally been understood as the gradual transition from declarative to procedural knowledge, followed by automatization (e.g., Anderson 1993; Anderson & Lebiere 1998). Based on generalizations from examples, abstract declarative rules morph into general knowledge in the form of procedural rules, access to and deployment of which increase in speed (fluency) as a result of massive practice. Discontinuous improvements in cognitive performance constitute one form of evidence for switches to rule-based behavior (Blessing & Anderson 1996). Instance theory (Logan 1988, 1990), conversely, holds that skill acquisition consists of the accumulation of concrete examples of the adaptation of general-purpose procedures and of solutions used for earlier problems, the examples stored as separate instances in long-term memory, and their subsequent application to new tasks. The fact that people are often unable to verbalize abstract knowledge about problems they have shown they can solve provides one form of evidence for instance-based learning. Another is when repetition of a specific example of a problem increases performance on that example but not on others. Taatgen and Wallach (2002) argue that both kinds of learning occur, depending on the nature of the task. For an early application of Logan's instance theory to SLA, see Robinson and Ha (1993).

P3. Some classes of linguistic features in adult SLA are fragile

What even relatively successful adult starters typically fail to acquire does not vary randomly. Rather, it is precisely the kinds of non-salient features, e.g., inflectional morphology used to mark gender, case, agreement, tense and aspect, that could be expected to prove difficult for learners whose capacity to notice them implicitly had deteriorated. "Fragile" features, i.e., in this context, those that are late learned or never learned, tend to be of low perceptual saliency, due to their being one or more of infrequent, irregular, non-syllabic, string-internal, semantically empty, and communicatively redundant, and/ or because they involve complex forms, meanings, or form–meaning mappings (see, e.g., DeKeyser 2005; Goldschneider & DeKeyser 2001). Most fragile features turn out to be the same ones that are vulnerable in a range of situations in which language is developed, lost, or impaired late in life or under abnormal circumstances, often resulting in restricted repertoires, such as those associated with pidginization, aphasia, and L1A and L2A by older children and adults (Long 1992), as well as in historical language change (see, e.g., Givon 1979; Lass 1997; McMahon 1994). Morphology is more vulnerable than syntax, inflections are more at risk than free morphemes, and exceptional cases within a language-specific paradigm are especially problematic. There are exceptions to each of these generalizations, however, suggesting that predictions based not only upon linguistic but also on psycholinguistic qualities – frequency, regularity, semantic transparency, communicative redundancy, and perceptual saliency – would likely be more accurate. In other words, a processing dimension is needed. It is not the case that all inflectional morphology and pragmatic rules are vulnerable, for example, but perhaps such categories as non-salient, irregular inflections, and ambiguous, optional pragmatic rules.

E3. Implicit learning is still the default learning mechanism

As noted earlier, *incidental learning* is learning *without intention* to learn at least part of what is learned, i.e., while the learner's *attention* is focused on something else. *Implicit learning* (for overviews, see papers in Stadler & Frensch 1998) is learning *without awareness* of what is learned. For example, when someone is exposed to examples of a pattern, but neither told there is one, nor to look for one, and is asked, instead, to judge the truth/falsity or the semantic plausibility of sentences exemplifying the pattern, yet can later operate on new examples automatically (e.g., in a speeded GJ test) in accordance with the pattern without knowing that he or she knows it, then it can reasonably be inferred that implicit learning of something more than the original examples has taken place. Without intending to do so and without being aware of having done so, the person has obtained generalizable abstract knowledge of the underlying rule or, if not that, of all or part of the underlying patterns to which the original examples conform, as evidenced by better than chance ability to judge whether new, previously unseen examples do or do not conform. The end product, *implicit knowledge*, is knowledge learners have but do not know they have, which they deploy automatically.

Care must be taken to verify that the new knowledge has remained implicit. As demonstrated, for example, by Leow (Hama & Leow 2010; Leow 2000; Leow & Hama 2013), it is possible for sub-sets of learners in a study to show awareness of what they have learned, even though the learning took place incidentally, while they were focused on something else; hence, the need for careful tests of the kind described by Rebuschat (2013) to remove ambiguities that can surround diagnoses of implicit learning. In such cases (e.g., the first experiment in Rebuschat & Williams 2012), there is incidental learning, but not implicit learning, as shown by the learners' awareness. Implicit and explicit learning, memory, and knowledge are separate processes and systems, their end products stored in different areas of the brain,[7] as evidenced by amnesiac patients who can lose the ability to retain new explicit knowledge while maintaining their implicit knowledge intact. It is clear that much of what NSs know about such matters as permissible phonological and spelling sequences (e.g., that English words can end in *-ft* but not *-tf*) in their L1 was acquired, and remains, at an unconscious level, i.e., implicit. The same is true of collocations. Adult NSs of English recognize what is wrong when a non-native says that "Napoleon did a big mistake when he invaded Russia," and know that it should be "Napoleon made a mistake," but when asked, cannot say *why* "do a mistake" is wrong ("I don't know. We just don't say it that way") and "make a mistake" is correct, and have probably never thought about it until now. Like thousands of other collocations, it had always been a tiny part of their vast store of implicit L1 knowledge, now suddenly raised to the level of conscious awareness.

The classes of fragile features with which late starters tend to have difficulty in a L2 are just those that could be expected to be problematic if acquisition were still primarily an implicit process, suggesting, again, that implicit learning remains the default mechanism in adult SLA. Additional evidence for this claim comes from studies of adults' performance on non-linguistic learning tasks by Berry and Broadbent (1984) and Stanley *et al.* (1989). As Doughty (2003) has pointed out, improvement in performance in those studies always *precedes* subjects' ability to verbalize what they know, suggesting that implicit, not explicit, learning is the default mode. Doughty claims the same is true of SLA. After reviewing the extensive experimental L1 literature on adults learning to perform complex tasks, she concluded:

> Taken together, the findings on modes of processing during control of complex systems show five things: (i) without extensive or targeted practice, subjects learn to control the variables in the systems successfully, but they cannot articulate the bases for their decisions; (ii) with time and practice, they gain the ability to describe their mental models; (iii) improvement in performance always *precedes* the ability to explain how

---

[7] According to Ellis (2008a, p. 3), "Implicit learning and memory are located in areas of the perceptual and motor cortex. Explicit learning is handled by areas in the prefrontal cortex involving attention, the conscious apperception of stimuli, and working memory. Explicit memory is located in the hippocampus and related limbic structures."

to control the complex system; (iv) explicit, declarative information is only helpful in improving performance in cases where complex tasks involve few and obvious variables; and (v) implicit practice at the relationships underlying the algorithms is beneficial. In sum, the findings of a pervasive implicit mode of learning, and the limited role of explicit learning in improving performance in complex control tasks, point to a default mode for SLA that is fundamentally implicit, and to the need to avoid declarative knowledge when designing L2 pedagogical procedures. (Doughty 2003, p. 298)

The kinds of tasks studied by Berry and Broadbent differ from language learning in some ways, of course. In a replication of work by Reber, Walkenfeld, and Hernstadt (1991), this time with adult L2 learners, Robinson (2005) observed the same effects for the implicit learning of an artificial grammar as in the original study, but he found no relationship (in a repeated measures design) between the implicit artificial grammar learning and the same learners' incidental learning – some of it implicit, as assessed using the same measures of the extent of awareness of what was learned in the artificial grammar – of an unknown third language, Samoan. Nevertheless, it is clear that, although weaker than in young children, and now tuned incorrectly for the L2 as a result of successful use for L1A, the capacity for incidental and implicit language learning is far from extinct by age seven or the mid-teens, with adult learners having to rely on explicit learning, as some theorists have claimed (DeKeyser 2000; Paradis 2004, 2009).[8]

Despite the faulty tuning, and despite the marked decrease in power noted in the capacity for implicit learning in early adolescence, followed by a further gradual decrease across the life span (Janacsek, Fiser, & Nemeth 2012), incidental and implicit learning remain options for adults, and there is evidence of their continued working in L1A, the learning of rules in artificial language grammars, and L2A (see, e.g., Aslin & Newport 2012; N.C. Ellis 2002a, 2006b, 2009; Hamrick 2013; Leung & Williams 2006, 2011a,b; Rebuschat in press; Rebuschat & Williams 2009, 2012; Saffran, Newport, & Aslin 1996; Williams 2004, 2005, 2009), as well as other complex non-linguistic tasks (Mathews *et al.* 2000). There is evidence that adults are sensitive both to regularities and inconsistencies in instances of potential patterns they encounter in the grammars of artificial languages, and that they will generalize to novel strings, i.e., engage in rule-like language behavior, when the contexts within which patterns occurred were consistent, and exceptions infrequent, but stick with separate learned instances and not generalize when exceptions are frequent, suggesting that statistical learning and rule learning are products of the same learning mechanism (Reeder, Newport, & Aslin 2009, 2010).

The literature on maturational constraints and sensitive periods in SLA typically compares the ability of young starters and adults to learn hard linguistic constructions or tricky semantic contrasts, such as that between the Spanish preterit and imperfect. Despite occasional claims to the contrary, while no adult starters have yet been found who have attained native-like abilities across the board (see Abrahamsson & Hyltenstam 2008; Long 2013a), cases have been documented of adults having learned at least some such constructions and distinctions (e.g., Donaldson 2011; Ioup *et al.* 1994; Montrul & Slabakova 2003). Of those, some, at least, are almost certain to have been learned implicitly, e.g., nine sub-types of dummy subject constructions in Dutch (Van Boxtel 2005;

---

[8] More recently, DeKeyser (2007a) has suggested that explicit learning will only work in the early stages, for easy grammar learned in classrooms by adults with high language aptitude.

Van Boxtel, Bongaerts, & Coppen 2005) by adult immigrants to Holland, as the rules at work are extremely subtle and the items rarely, if ever, taught in the classroom. Nick Ellis writes of adult SLA (see also Ellis 1999; N.C. Ellis 2002a,b):

> the bulk of language acquisition is implicit learning from usage. Most knowledge is tacit knowledge; most learning is implicit; the vast majority of our cognitive processing is unconscious. (N.C. Ellis 2005, p. 306)

   That said, there is also some evidence that the ability of adults, as opposed to young children, to learn a language implicitly, may be limited to adjacent items. Observational and experimental studies show, for example, that adults remain capable of absorbing statistical regularities in possible sequences of sounds and symbols in phonology and orthography, with unconscious tallying of transition probabilities or contingencies, e.g., between syllables in an unknown language. As Williams (2009, p. 329) puts it, the dominant approach is to regard statistical learning as contingency learning ... associative learning of the predictability of outcomes given cues (Shanks 2005). It is less clear whether more complex linguistic structures can be learned implicitly, and unambiguous evidence of *purely* implicit adult SLA, e.g., from laboratory experiments, is hard to come by. This is partly due to the difficulty of creating unambiguous opportunities for, and accurate, sensitive measures of, implicit learning (see DeKeyser 2003, pp. 319–320, for a review of the measurement problems),[9] but also because pure implicit learning, with no involvement of explicit learning at any stage, may be rarer than was once thought (Williams 2009). Many would accept that the literature on L2 vocabulary learning from extensive reading, where the reader's focus is on the meaning of a text, constitutes evidence of incidental learning (for review, see Hulstijn 2003), but the possibility exists that readers do sometimes pause and bring unknown words into focal attention if they impede comprehension. It also might seem that the many studies showing that implicit *instruction* results in measurable learning (Goo *et al.* 2009; Norris & Ortega 2000) are evidence of implicit learning, but it is impossible to be sure that, despite the instruction being implicit, the learners in those studies were not learning intentionally and explicitly, e.g., when presented with recasts. Again, it is very hard to demonstrate implicit learning unambiguously.

   The difficulties notwithstanding, recent studies of the learning of grammatical form–meaning connections (Leung & Williams 2006) and of word order in Japanese (Williams & Kuribara 2008) and German (Rebuschat & Williams 2009) suggest that implicit learning of *linguistically relevant regularities*, at least, is possible. In one study by Rebuschat and Williams (2009), for example, 15 English-speaking subjects heard 120 training sentences reflecting three German word order patterns but containing English lexical items (thereby making the sentences interpretable for meaning by beginners), 40 V2 (*In the evening ate Rose excellent dessert at a restaurant*), 40 V1 (*Since his teacher criticism voiced, put Chris more effort into his homework*), and 40 VF (*George repeated today that the movers his furniture scratched*). Sixty sentences were semantically plausible, e.g., for

---

[9] Modified (belief judgment) elicited imitation tasks have been proposed as a new possibility for implicit learning treatments (Erlam 2006, 2009). Learners repeat stimuli of appropriate length in words or syllables and semantic complexity, and say if they agree or disagree with the statement. They are subsequently tested on grammatical structure embedded in the imitated sentences.

VF (finite verb placed in final position in all subordinate clauses) 'George repeated today that his students about their classes cared' (plausible), and 60 implausible, e.g., 'Kate confessed today that her horse the corridor murdered.' To maintain subjects' focus on meaning, the task they were presented with, which took about 40 minutes to complete, was to repeat each sentence and to judge whether or not it was plausible. They were then confronted with a surprise aural grammaticality judgment test (GJT) lasting about 15 minutes and consisting of 60 new sentences, only half of which followed any of the three grammatical rules modeled in the training sentences. Without receiving any feedback on their correctness, they had to decide on the grammaticality of each sentence, report their level of confidence for the judgment (guess, somewhat confident, very confident), and indicate the basis for their judgment (guess, intuition, memory, rule knowledge). They were also asked to verbalize their understanding of any rules they thought they had learned. Fifteen subjects in a control group merely heard the 60 test sentences and were asked to judge their grammaticality. Results showed that the trained subjects judged the grammaticality of 62% of the test sentences correctly and statistically significantly above chance. Their performance on ungrammatical sentences, conversely, was at chance, suggesting incidental learning of abstract word order patterns. The trained subjects performed statistically significantly more accurately than the controls, whose 43% accuracy rate was statistically significantly below chance. The experimental group was statistically significantly better than the controls at recognizing grammatical sentences as such, but not significantly different on ungrammatical ones.

A statistically significant difference in the level of confidence reported by experimental subjects when accepting grammatical strings as opposed to ungrammatical ones showed that they were, in fact, partly aware of having acquired some knowledge during the training phase. Similarly, their statistically superior performance (65% accuracy) when basing their judgments on rule knowledge, compared with their lowest accuracy rate (56%) when basing them on guesses, suggested they had indeed acquired some unconscious structural knowledge. Unlike the source attributions and confidence level data, verbal reports were largely unrevealing of subjects' awareness of having learned something – more evidence that verbal reports can often result in underestimates of learning.

Rebuschat and Williams are careful to point out that, while their study showed adults capable of acquiring new syntactic knowledge implicitly, of doing so quite quickly and without potentially helpful feedback, and of applying what they learned to stimuli with the same underlying structure but new surface features, the GJ results simultaneously showed that what was learned was somewhat limited. The fact that the trained subjects only accepted 71% of grammatical sentences, and also 47% of ungrammatical ones, suggested that their judgments were based in part on memory of patterns encountered during the training when assessing sentences as correct and on guessing when test sentences did not reflect a training pattern. Moreover, the self-report data suggested they had focused on word order within clauses rather than the crucial issues of clause type and clause sequence. Judgments were probabilistic, not categorical, as would have been the case had subjects acquired linguistic rules. The results in a comparable study by Williams and Kuribara (2008) were similarly limited.

Rebuschat and Williams' analysis of precisely what their subjects had really relied upon when making their GJs is reminiscent of those by critics of the early research on implicit learning by Reber and associates (e.g., Reber 1979; Reber *et al.* 1980), analyses which showed that subjects in some of those studies of implicit learning were using recognition of bigrams and trigrams, rather than implicitly acquired rules, to recognize grammatical strings of letters or numbers. Despite claiming to have demonstrated an adult capacity for implicit L2A, Rebuschat and Williams are admirably cautious about just what kinds of linguistic entities can be handled implicitly. A consensus seems to be emerging that implicit learning operates well for acquiring closely associated sequences, or chunks, such as collocations, but that explicit learning is important for recognizing and producing items that are ambiguously related or not as closely associated spatially or temporally, e.g., long-distance discontinuous dependencies and the morphophonological marking of arbitrary grammatical categories, such as gender (N.C. Ellis 2005, p. 334, 2009; Frigo & McDonald 1998). It may be the case that implicit learning of structure above the level of immediately adjacent items is limited to recognition of similarity in patterns and that acquisition and categorical application of abstract grammatical rules require explicit learning and knowledge, and in most cases, focal attention (Pacton & Perruchet 2008), although there is evidence from vision research of so-called task-irrelevant learning, i.e., learning of associations between attended and not focally attended ambient stimuli (Williams 2009, pp. 341–342).

On the other hand, carefully designed and executed though the laboratory studies to date have been, it could be that they *under*estimate the adult's capacity to learn grammatical rules implicitly in the real world. Both naturalistically and in classrooms, but not in the experimental work, learners are typically allowed (i) more exposure than is possible in most lab studies, (ii) production opportunities, and (iii) opportunities to learn from the negative feedback that deviant learner output often elicits. Nevertheless, an expert and pioneer in studies of implicit second language learning, Williams (2009) concludes as follows:

> Humans possess a powerful learning mechanism that can absorb the statistical structure of the environment, defined as contingencies between events. This type of learning is successful in the areas of lexical segmentation, phonological and orthographic structure, phrase structure and grammatical form-meaning connections, represented at a sufficient level of abstraction to be independent of lexical content. But there appear to be limits to what can be learned in this way. There is evidence that implicit learning is temporally constrained, so that associations between events are only learned if they are adjacent or brought into adjacency through some other means (by attention or by the use of meaningful context in which they occur). Whether this causes problems in the learning of long-distance dependencies in language is debatable. But there also seem to be problems in going beyond the statistical properties of the input to deeper regularities that depend on abstract notions, as exemplified by the (above, implicit learning) studies on word classes, scrambling, and possibly soft mutation. In the cases of word classes and scrambling, there is evidence for similar difficulties in naturalistic SLA. (Williams 2009, p. 339)

A plausible usage-based account of (L1 and L2) language acquisition (see, e.g., N.C. Ellis 2007a,b, 2008c, 2012; Goldberg & Casenhiser 2008; Robinson & Ellis 2008; Tomasello 2003), with implicit learning playing a major role, begins with initially chunk-learned constructions being acquired during receptive or productive communication, the greater processability of the more frequent ones suggesting a strong role for associative learning from usage. Based on their frequency in the constructions, exemplar-based regularities and prototypical morphological, syntactic, and other patterns – [Noun stem-PL], [Base verb form-Past], [Adj Noun], [Aux Adv Verb], and so on – are then induced and abstracted away from the original chunk-learned cases, forming the basis for attraction, i.e., recognition of the same rule-like patterns in new cases (*feed-fed, lead-led, sink-sank-sunk, drink-drank-drunk*, etc.), and for creative language use.

In sum, as explained in E4, while incidental and implicit learning remain the dominant, default processes, their reduced power in adults indicates an advantage, and possibly a necessity (still an open question), for facilitating *intentional initial perception* of new forms and form–meaning connections, with instruction (focus on form) important, among other reasons, for bringing new items to learners' focal attention. Research may eventually show such "priming" of subsequent implicit processing of those forms in the input to be unnecessary. Even if that turns out to be the case, however, opportunities for intentional and explicit learning are likely to speed up acquisition and so becomes a legitimate component of a theory of ISLA, where *efficiency*, not necessity and sufficiency, is the criterion for inclusion.

E4. Explicit learning (including focal attention) is required to improve implicit processing in adult SLA, but is constrained

Because the capacity for implicit learning, especially instance learning, is weaker in adults, and tuned for L1 processing, optimally efficient adult language learning requires help from *explicit learning* (not necessarily via explicit teaching). *Explicit learning* is a conscious operation, in which the learner *attends* to aspects of a stimulus array in the search for underlying patterns or structure. It is *intentional* learning, usually (but see below for possible exceptions) with *awareness* of the learning that is taking place. In language and other domains, it generally works best for simple material, with few variables and salient markers of relevant distinctions (N.C. Ellis 1994, 2005; Rosenshine 1986). Explicit learning results in *explicit knowledge*: people know something and know they know. The capacity for explicit probabilistic sequence learning appears to increase at the same age, around 12, that the capacity for implicit probabilistic sequence learning shows a notable decrease in power (Nemeth, Janacsek, & Fiser 2013).

The primary purpose of explicit learning in this embryonic theory is not, as in skill-building theories, to create a separate store of declarative knowledge, to be proceduralized over time, and, through automatization, to serve as the basis for increasingly skilled performance. Considerable fluency clearly can be achieved by some individuals that way (DeKeyser 2007a,b; Johnson 1996; Segalowitz 2003, 2010), with highly automatized procedural knowledge sometimes even resulting in performance that can pass as implicitly based.[10] Few would deny, however, that, as Krashen argued back in the late 1970s, it is implicit knowledge (Krashen's *acquisition*) that underlies the vast majority of spontaneous communicative language use, with the kinds of off-line "language-like" tasks

---

[10]   N. Ellis questions whether this achievement is, in reality, automatization of explicit knowledge: "Executing different conscious procedures a little faster as a result of practice is not an automization of explicit knowledge – it is only speeded up processing" (N.C. Ellis 2005, p. 333).

for which explicit knowledge is best suited of limited value to learners requiring functional L2 proficiency.

Intentional learning and explicit L2 knowledge can facilitate implicit learning in other ways than skill building (Long 1991). First, they can encourage selective attention to, and either detection or noticing (see below) of, linguistic features that might otherwise go undetected or unnoticed for a long time, perhaps even permanently, especially non-salient, non-meaning-bearing, communicatively redundant, complex, fragile features, such as pronominal copies in Spanish topic-fronting (*La guitarra* **la** *toca Pepe/The guitar* **it**-*fem. sing. plays Pepe*) or inversion in English sentences expressing negative polarity (*Very rarely* **had the creature** *been captured on film*). Second, they can facilitate "noticing the gap," i.e., perceiving mismatches between native input and deviant learner output. Third, they can provide the basis for utterances (stretched output) whose processing aids development of implicit knowledge of the same rules or items. (This is *not* the same as saying explicit knowledge *becomes implicit* through proceduralization and automatization.)

The fourth, and most important, role of intentional learning and explicit knowledge, as indicated in E3, above, is to modify entrenched automatic L1 processing routines, so as to alter the way subsequent L2 input is processed *implicitly*, the default learning process. Learner awareness of a problem triggers a temporary switch to selective attention to form (and helps explain why recasts are as effective as they are). With Nick Ellis and others, what I claim is that *explicit learning (not necessarily as a result of explicit instruction) involves a new form or form–meaning connection being held in short-term memory long enough for it to be processed, rehearsed, and an initial representation stored in long-term memory, thereafter altering the operation of the way additional exemplars of the item in the input are handled by the default implicit learning process*. It is analogous to setting a radio dial to a new frequency. The listener has to pay close attention to the initial crackling reception. Once the radio is tuned to the new frequency, he or she can sit back, relax, and listen to the broadcast with minimal effort. Ellis identifies what he calls

> the general principle of explicit learning in SLA: Changing the cues that learners focus on in their language processing changes what their implicit learning processes tune.
> (Ellis 2005, p. 327)

The prognosis improves for both simple and complex grammatical features, including fragile features, and for acquisition in general, if adult learners' attention is drawn to problems, so that they are *noticed* (Schmidt 1990 and elsewhere). This is the first of four or five main stages in the acquisition process (Chaudron 1985; Gass 1997), in which what is noticed is held and processed in short-term, or working, memory long enough for it to be compared with what is in storage in long-term memory, and, as a result, a sub-set of input becomes intake. *Instruction is successful which recruits temporary episodes of explicit learning as an aid to subsequent implicit processing.* Initially induced by explicit instruction in this way or from negative feedback, noticing enhances implicit processing of subsequent exemplars of the same sounds, features, constructions, lexical items and collocations. As Nick Ellis puts it,

> Form-focused instruction pulls learners out of their implicit habits, their automatized routines, by recruiting consciousness. Habits are implicitly controlled attractor states.
> (Ellis 2008b, p. 25)

An issue of obvious interest in LT for adults is how explicit and implicit learning interact with rule complexity. While L2 studies are few and far between, findings tentatively suggest that explicit learning works best when rules are simple and categorical, whereas implicit learning is more useful for chunk learning of concrete elements in close proximity to one another, e.g., collocations, but also for fuzzy rules or when material is complex, with non-salient underlying patterns (DeKeyser 1995; Robinson 1996; Williams 1999). In such cases, learning is instance-based, with implicit understanding of the underlying structure developing, often over a long period, as a result of the learner encountering numerous examples of the target forms and constructions and generalizing from those. This would account for the finding by Granena and Long (2013a) that measured aptitude for implicit learning correlated statistically significantly with adult (AO 16–29) starters' acquisition of lexis and collocations through long-term residence in the L2 environment.

Meanwhile, it is important to remember, once again, that a theory of ISLA, and a related approach to LT, such as TBLT, will seek to be as *efficient* as possible, regardless of whether particular components are necessary and/or sufficient, and despite the undesirable side effect their presence has on the theory's power. Therefore, the fact that studies (e.g., De Graaff 1997; DeKeyser 1994, 1995; N.C. Ellis 1993; Robinson 1996) and reviews (e.g., Goo *et al.* 2009; Norris & Ortega 2000) have frequently shown explicit learning to be faster than implicit learning, at least when simple linguistic targets are involved, means that a role for explicit learning must be recognized.

The effectiveness of explicit learning is constrained, however. As noted in Chapter 2, teachers usually cannot teach, or learners learn, what they want, when they want. Studies by Ellis (1989), Lightbown (1983), Mackey (1999), and Pienemann (1984, 1989), among others, show that what is encountered that way must be within learners' current processing range for explicit learning or teaching to be successful. The existence of backsliding, U-shaped behavior and zigzag IL development, along with robust developmental sequences, complete with interlingual structures not encountered in the input, and often not in the learners' L1, either, are further evidence of the limits of explicit learning and teaching, as are examples of so-called autonomous syntax, as discussed in Chapter 2 (see Long 2009 and Section 10.2 for more examples, discussion, and implications for teaching methodology).

E5. Attention is critical, at two levels

Attention is critical for learning at each of two levels on a continuum (Doughty 2001; Robinson 1995a; Schmidt 1995, 2001). First, it is an essential prerequisite for *noticing*, i.e., the moment when a learner's use of controlled, focal attention *at the level of conscious awareness* results in perception – but not metalinguistic awareness, and not necessarily understanding – of new forms and form–meaning connections in the input, and of differences between the input and the learner's own output, or "noticing the gap" (Robinson *et al.* 2012; Schmidt 1995, p. 26, 2010). Second, attention improves the efficiency of implicit input processing at the lower level of *apperception* (Gass 1988, 1997, pp. 8–16) or *detection* (Tomlin & Villa 1994). This lower level of automatic attention occurs outside focal or selective attention and *without awareness* either of the act of registering something in the input or of the result. Lower-level registering of the presence of items in the input can occur when one or more features of an item match those of an existing representation first noticed at the higher level and stored in long-term memory. The lower level detection activates the existing representation and strengthens it (N.C. Ellis 2005; Gass 1997; Robinson 1995a). As indicated earlier, whether detection *without* prior noticing is sufficient for adult learning of *new* L2 items is still unclear – perhaps one of the single most critically important issues, for both SLA theory and LT, awaiting resolution in the field. For an important early study of the matter, see Hamrick (2013). Even if it turned out *not* to be sufficient (as both Robinson 2003a and Schmidt 1990 argue), this would still leave intact the claim that implicit learning from subsequent input plays a central role in acquisition *after* initial representations are first established in long-term memory through the application of focal attention and noticing, i.e., with awareness.

Several studies, e.g., Eckman, Bell, and Nelson (1988) and Gass (1982), have shown that learners who are taught object of preposition (OPREP) relative clauses (*The man that I warned her about …*), the fourth most marked on Keenan and Comrie's (1977) noun phrase accessibility hierarchy, but who are not exposed to the less marked subject, direct object, and indirect object relatives, can improve on all four ("Buy one, get three free"). Gass argues that these findings simultaneously demonstrate that implicit learning by adults is a reality and that, while useful, attention is not always essential. Nevertheless, using eye-tracking methodology, a direct relationship has been found between the amount of attention paid to new words while reading and the learning of those words (Godfroid, Boers, & Housen 2013). *Noticing* in Schmidt's sense, where the targets are the subject of focal attention, facilitates the acquisition of new items, especially non-salient ones, and as Schmidt maintains, and as demonstrated by 20 years of studies, from Schmidt and Frota (1986) to Mackey (2006), "more noticing leads to more learning" (Schmidt 1994, p. 18). Crucially, however, as claimed by Gass (1997), and as embodied in the tallying hypothesis (N.C. Ellis 2002a,b), once a new form or structure has been noticed and a first representation of it established in long-term memory, Gass' lower-level automatic apperception, and Tomlin and Villa's detection, can take over, with incidental and implicit learning as the default process. The initial representation in long-term memory functions as a selective cue and primes the learner to pay attention to, and perceive, subsequent instances in the input. If the initial representation in long-term memory is attended to while processing subsequent input for meaning, "its strength will be incremented and its associations will be tallied and implicitly catalogued" (N.C. Ellis 2002a, p. 174). Later, Ellis writes:

> Although noticing is not necessary for priming and tallying, attention is … with everything in our stimulus environment being tallied. Nor are we restricted to being conscious learners, with only that which is focally attended and of which we are aware being the totality of what is learned. It is something between these two extremes. There is implicit associative learning that results from stimuli that are attended and automatically processed following pre-established task-relevant routines, even though this level of attention might not be sufficient for awareness, for seeing the stimulus. (N.C. Ellis 2005, p. 311)

E6. The Interaction Hypothesis

Inching closer to the classroom, ideas are needed as to how explicit and implicit learning can best be harnessed and brought to bear on the acquisition task in a fashion that allows efficient progress and does not entail attempts to combine explicit and implicit teaching as separate endeavors with conflicting theoretical underpinnings, as has sometimes been proposed (see, e.g., R. Ellis 1993; Fotos & Ellis 1991; Willis 1993). My position is known as the Interaction Hypothesis (Long 1981, 1982, 1983b, 1996b), which accords special status to the role of brief episodes of selective learner attention to critical segments of the input (focus on form), especially, but not only, to implicit negative feedback, at moments when attention and other factors are likely to be optimal (see below). The Interaction Hypothesis holds that important brief opportunities for attention to linguistic code features, and for *explicit learning* (cf. explicit teaching) to improve implicit input processing, occur during *negotiation for meaning*. During that activity, the positive and negative feedback that target-like and deviant learner output and some kinds of communication problems (but *not only* communication problems) elicit from interlocutors is of particular importance for acquisition:

> environmental contributions to acquisition are mediated by selective attention and the learner's developing L2 processing capacity, and ... these resources are brought together most usefully, although not exclusively, during *negotiation for meaning*. Negative feedback obtained during negotiation work or elsewhere may be facilitative of L2 development, at least for vocabulary, morphology, and language-specific syntax, and essential for learning certain specifiable L1-L2 contrasts. (Long 1996b, p. 414)[11]

When learners run into communicative trouble, they are likely to switch their attention from meaning to form long enough to solve the problem and notice the necessary new information (Faerch & Kasper 1986; White 1987), especially forms presented in contingent NS responses:

> *negotiation for meaning*, and especially negotiation work that triggers *interactional* adjustments by the NS or more competent interlocutor, facilitates acquisition because it connects input, internal learner capacities, particularly selective attention, and output in productive ways. (Long 1996b, pp. 451–452)

Interaction facilitates output, too, and pushed output also facilitates noticing (Izumi *et al.* 1999).

Considerable evidence for the Interaction Hypothesis has accumulated over the past three decades. For extensive discussion and reviews of supporting literature, see, e.g., Ellis (2008b), Gass (1997, 2003), Gass and Mackey (2007), Gass, Mackey, and Pica (1998), Gor and Long (2009), Mackey (2007, 2012), Mackey, Abbuhl, and Gass (2012), and Pica (1994). Statistical meta-analyses have reported significant positive effects of task-based interaction on the acquisition of targeted linguistic structures (Keck *et al.* 2006), for interaction in general (Mackey & Goo 2007), and for corrective feedback, in particular (Li 2010; Russell & Spada 2006). Mackey and Goo (2007), for example, concluded their review as follows:

> Interaction plays a strong facilitative role in the learning of lexical and grammatical target items. The 28 interaction studies qualified for the present meta-analysis showed

---

[11] The "specifiable L1–L2 contrasts" for which negative feedback is predicted to be essential, at least for maximally efficient learning, include, e.g., L2 items involved in transitions from L1 superset to L2 sub-set relationships of the sort identified by White (1987 and elsewhere), discussed earlier in Section 2.4.

large mean effect sizes across immediate and delayed post-tests, providing evidence of short-term as well as longer-term effects on language acquisition. (Mackey & Goo 2007, p. 405)

E7. The role of negative feedback, including recasts

The Interaction Hypothesis accords a significant role in SLA to negative feedback. Due to sociolinguistic constraints, whereby overt negative feedback would constitute face-threatening behavior, almost all negative feedback outside classrooms is implicit and incidental, much of it in the form of recasts, which have been found to be omnipresent in every type of NS–non-native speaker (NNS) and NNS–NNS conversation studied to date. A pioneering investigation of their role, and of the role of conversation in SLA in general, was conducted by Sato (1986, 1988) as part of her larger, longitudinal study of naturalistic L2 acquisition (Sato 1990) motivated by Givon's claims concerning the shift from presyntactic to grammaticized speech in language change (e.g., Givon 1979). In addition to a series of laboratory-type elicitation tasks focusing on pronunciation and syllable-structure issues (Sato 1984, 1985), Sato's data consisted of taped spontaneous conversations between NSs and two Vietnamese brothers, Than and Tai, whose very early naturalistic English development she observed each week for a year. When it came to inflectional morphology, Sato showed how the two children initially used conversational scaffolding, specifically their interlocutors' prior establishment of reference to a past event, to compensate for their lack of overt inflectional past time marking. The following excerpt from a conversation between a NS and one of the Vietnamese children beginning English as a second language (ESL) reported by Sato (1986, p. 36) contains two examples of recasts, one syntactic, one lexical, both in the form of confirmation checks. As seen here, however, recasts (italicized) are no magic wand and, even when triggered by severe communication breakdowns, can fail to elicit immediate improvements in learner output (even if they are beneficial in the longer term), as in (4):

---

(4)

	NS: Oh, Mary said that you went to um-went to a game by the Fever?
Tai: nou tan hi go yEt	
no-Thanh-he-go-yet	
	You didn't go yet? To the Fever?
wat?	
What?	
	Did you go to see the Fever play soccer?
yEs	
Yes	
	When was that?
nat nat nau	
not-not-now	
	Oh. uh-*later?* Oh. I see. Who else is going?
tan hi go in da pro	
Than-he-go-in-the [pro]	
	(Sato 1986, p. 36)

Later, like adult learners of German (Meisel 1987), the brothers moved to alternative surrogate systems of their own, such as the use of temporal adverbials (*Yesterday I go*) and order of mention, but neither boy progressed very far with past time inflectional morphology during the first year of the study.

In an explicit discussion of the issue, Sato (1986) proposed that conversation is *selectively facilitative* of grammatical development, depending on the structures involved. The beneficial effects of conversational scaffolding and situational knowledge on communication makes overt past time marking on verbs expendable in most contexts, which may hinder acquisition by lessening the need to encode the function in speech morphologically. There is some evidence that conversation nourishes emergent L2 syntax, on the other hand (Sato 1988), and most of the few attempts at complex syntactic constructions (what Sato called "syntactic precursors") produced during the children's first year of English occurred in a conversational context. (Studies of collaborative syntax across utterances and speakers in talks between NSs and adult beginners or more proficient learners remain serious lacunae in the L2 database.)

Since Sato's work, recasts have established a fairly strong track record as facilitators of SLA. They constitute the most frequent form of negative feedback inside classrooms (see, e.g., Ellis, Basturkmen, & Loewen 2001; Lyster & Ranta 1997). Some go unnoticed by learners or are misinterpreted by them as confirmations (Lyster 1998), but research findings have shown that the grammatical, phonological, and especially, lexical, information they provide is noticed in a sufficient number of cases – typically from one- to two-thirds in conversations involving adult learners (Goo & Mackey 2013; Mackey 2012; Richardson 1995; Yamaguchi 1994) – to induce faster IL development than comparable amounts of mere exposure (Long 1996b, 2007d; Long, Inagaki, & Ortega 1998; Mackey & Goo 2007; Ortega & Long 1997). What is learned from recasts, it is important to note, is more than the particular forms or form–meaning connections modeled in them; learners are able to induce underlying rules and apply them to new instances, e.g., rules of English irregular past tense morphology to novel verbs (Choi 2000).

Recasts are crucial points at which implicit and explicit learning converge in optimal ways. Information about the target language supplied (implicitly) reactively in response to learner output has several potential advantages from a psycholinguistic perspective over the same information in non-contingent utterances, i.e., as positive evidence, or models. Recasts convey needed information about the target language *in context*, when interlocutors share a *joint attentional focus*, and when the learner already has *prior comprehension* of at least part of the message, thereby facilitating form–function mapping. The learner is *vested* in the exchange, as it is his or her message that is at stake, and so will probably be *motivated* and *attending*, conditions likely to induce *intentional* learning and facilitate *noticing* of any new linguistic information in the input. The fact that the learner will already understand all or part of the interlocutor's response (because it is a reformulation of the learner's own) also means that he or she has additional freed-up *attentional resources* that can be allocated to the form of the response and, again, to form–function mapping. Finally, the immediate *contingency* of recasts on deviant learner output means that the incorrect and correct utterances are juxtaposed and, quickly so, lessening the amount of working memory required for the comparison. This allows the learner to consider the two forms side by side, so to speak, and to observe the contrast, an opportunity not presented by non-contingent utterances, i.e., models. As Saxton (1997) stresses, writing of the role of recasts in child L1A, positive evidence, i.e., the occurrence of the correct form (e.g., *didn't go* and *later*, as previously mentioned) in ambient, *non*-contingent speech, simply provides instances of what is acceptable in the target language, whereas the same form occurring in a corrective recast simultaneously provides information about both what is and what is not acceptable. Saxton's "Direct Contrast Hypothesis" says, in a nutshell, that corrective recasts (negative evidence) work, and work better than models (positive evidence), because they can inform the learner not only that the form modeled in the recast is grammatical but also, crucially, that their own form is ungrammatical. Models (positive evidence) can serve only the first function. I believe Saxton's claim to be correct, although, as indicated above, that it is only one of several reasons why recasts are often successful.

Evidence of the value of implicit corrective feedback, including recasts, has grown steadily in recent years, with a variety of data-gathering procedures employed to supplement the rather crude measure offered by immediate uptake in output logs. In a study involving 28 college-age ESL students, for example, Mackey (2006) used online learning journals, questionnaires, written responses to a question about their perceptions of lesson goals, and oral stimulated recall protocols (introspections while they viewed video clips from lessons during which they had received recasts of problematic utterances containing questions, plurals, and past tense forms) to show links between feedback, noticing and the development of question formation.

In another promising development, O'Rourke (2008) conducted eye-tracker research on computer-mediated conversation in L2 German that provided behavioral evidence of learner focus on form and noticing leading to uptake. Gaze and keystroke data showed a student briefly interrupting her focus on communication to attend to the information contained in recasts, often involving her in reading and rereading her native interlocutor's responses, comparing the input with her own output, and then incorporating the information in her subsequent output. O'Rourke writes:

> The gaze data show that just prior to this correction she re-reads Steffi's 'Mihr geht es gut', the start of the most recent line in the output pane, then fixates on the word 'Ich' in her own draft ('Ich geht mer gut'), and then implements the change. [More examples are described.] We can thus confirm with near certainty what we could only conjecture from the output logs: that Ciara does indeed take up Steffi's implicit recast.... these gaze data also point to focus on form on occasions when none of the other data sources give us any strong reason to suspect it. (O'Rourke 2008, p. 246)

In a second eye-tracker study, Smith (2010) evaluated 12 ESL learners' eye movements for the duration of eye fixation on recasts immediately following their delivery by a NS during task-based synchronous computer-mediated communication (SCMC). Smith's results showed learners noticing 60% of intensive recasts they received, with lexical recasts much easier than grammatical recasts for students to notice, retain, produce more accurately on a written posttest, and use more productively in subsequent chat interactions. Successful uptake following recasts was relatively rare. Like O'Rourke, Smith notes that, coupled with the fact that the eye-tracker data had shown learners attending to a substantial proportion of the recasts, his results suggest that overt uptake, as measured by immediate improved production, may tend to underestimate the positive effect of recasts on acquisition, as suggested by previous researchers (see, e.g.,

Mackey 1999) who have produced evidence of recasts on delayed, but not immediate, posttests.

Several reviews of the literature, e.g., Long (2007d) and Mackey (2012), and three statistical meta-analyses since 2006, have found strong evidence of the efficacy of recasts. For example, echoing similar conclusions to those of Russell and Spada (2006), Mackey and Goo (2007, p. 409) found that "(R)ecasts seem to be developmentally helpful, with large effect sizes across all post-tests," and in a third meta-analysis, of 33 studies, Li (2010) found a medium overall effect for oral corrective feedback, that the effect was maintained over time, and that whereas the immediate and short-term effects of explicit feedback were greater, the longer-term effect size for recasts was slightly larger than the short-term effect, more effective than explicit feedback on long-delayed posttests, and more enduring, even increasing over time (Li 2010, p. 343).

This is not to say recasts are a panacea or without controversy. There are suggestive findings, for example, of an inverse relationship between the salience of linguistic targets and the optimal degree of explicitness required in negative feedback (Long 2007d, pp. 107–110; Ono & Witzel 2002; Ortega & Long 1997), and some, e.g., Lyster (1998), have advocated the use of more explicit forms of negative feedback in general. It could be that less salient targets will require focal attention, whereas more salient ones can be handled via detection. It has been suggested that the success of recasts has been a laboratory phenomenon not necessarily to be found in real classroom lessons (Foster 1998; Foster & Ohta 2005), but this and other charges have been refuted empirically (Gass, Mackey, & Ross-Feldman 2005; Goo & Mackey 2013). Overall, as the meta-analyses show, recasts have a solid track record in both L1A and SLA, and to the extent that implicit negative feedback does the job, teachers and learners are freed up to devote their primary attention to tasks and subject-matter learning.

P4. Success and failure in adult SLA vary among and within individuals

Thus far, I have attempted to explain the adult SLA process as if, given the same alignment of learner, environmental, and linguistic variables, success and failure were common across all learners and, at the level of the individual learner, within and across all linguistic domains. But such is not the case. It is well established that, in addition to their poor overall prognosis compared with children, adults with the same L1 and roughly the same AO, length of residence (LOR), access to the L2, and so on, often vary considerably (i) among themselves and (ii) at the individual level, in how they fare with different L2 features and constructions. The well-documented considerable disparities in ultimate attainment among and within seemingly comparable learners with seemingly comparable learning opportunities are two more problems in need of explanation. For example, why do the ILs of some speakers of Spanish (or Japanese – see, e.g., Stauble 1984) still exhibit preverbal negation (*No have job*) after many years of residence in the target-language community, whereas other Spanish and Japanese speakers go on to master the full English negation system? Or why do some speakers achieve near-native abilities in English, including with complex syntax and pragmatics, yet continue to make errors with uses of articles?

E8. Individual differences, especially input sensitivity, and linguistic differences, especially perceptual saliency, are responsible for variability in, and within, ultimate L2 attainment

AO, the single most robust predictor in the SLA literature, typically responsible for about 30% of the variance in achievement scores, can go some way toward accounting for differences in ultimate attainment among groups of adult starters. However, since whatever age-related maturational constraints exist are by definition universal in their scope and timing, they cannot constitute an explanation for why, say, one learner with an AO of 25 and a LOR of ten years does far better than a second learner with the same AO and an equally plentiful opportunity to acquire. Nor can maturational constraints, alone, even potentially explain why a learner reaches near-native control of, say, English negation or the simple past tense, but stabilizes (or if such a thing exists, fossilizes) with obviously non-native-like control of articles or the passive, or continues to invert subjects and verbs in subordinate clauses (*I asked why did he quit his job*).

The same is true of other ID variables. Language aptitude, for example, the second most powerful predictor after AO, can explain part of the variance among learners (for review, see Dornyei & Skehan 2003; Granena 2012; Skehan 2012) but has insufficient explanatory potential at the level of differential achievement within learners. Where ISLA is concerned, scores on aptitude tests often correlate with language test scores in the 0.40–0.50 range, and so seemingly account for as much as 20% of the variance in group scores. However, that may be to overestimate the importance of aptitude since most tests, such as the Modern Language Aptitude Test (MLAT), focus predominantly on aptitude for explicit learning, which happens to be the way most foreign LT is conducted, meaning that positive correlations would be expected. Correlations between aptitude for either explicit or implicit learning with L2 achievement via naturalistic acquisition in L2 settings, on the other hand, are lower. Nevertheless, AO and language aptitude remain the two strongest predictor variables in SLA, which explains the interest in interactions between the two variables in the recent SLA literature (see, e.g., Abrahamsson & Hyltenstam 2008; DeKeyser 2000; Granena & Long 2013a,b). Also, newer, more sophisticated aptitude measures, such as LLAMA (Meara 2005) and Hi-Lab (Doughty 2013; Linck *et al.* 2013), may actually reveal even stronger relationships, especially where aptitude for implicit learning is concerned.

In addition to explaining how adults achieve whatever they do in a second language, a minimally adequate theory, as noted, must also account both for differences among learners, and within individuals, differences at the level of linguistic features and constructions. An explanation loses credibility if it can be shown that it only applies to some learners and/or only to some linguistic domains and/or only to some linguistic features within domains. A claim, say, that L1 transfer accounts for some well-attested aspects of developmental sequences, e.g., that speakers of a L1, like Spanish, with preverbal negation, stick with the first two stages of the seemingly universal sequence for ESL negation (No V, and Don't V) longer than speakers of a L1, like Japanese, with postverbal negation (see Zobl 1982), stands up well. It fails as an explanation (and Zobl did not advance it as an explanation) for stabilization (let alone fossilization, if such a thing exists) within those stages, however, for the simple reason that many L1 speakers of Spanish traverse the entire four-stage sequence for English negation without difficulty.

The claim fails the universality test, in other words, as does the multiple effects principle (MEP; Selinker & Lakshmanan 1992), which privileges L1 transfer in combination with a second variable to be determined. It simply does not work for all learners or all structures, as failure occurs differentially at the level both of individuals with the same L1 and individual structures.

The same is true of a seemingly endless list of affect variables (attitude, motivation, extroversion, self-esteem, ego permeability, anxiety, willingness to communicate, etc.). Some may be important as "starting-line" variables, in that they can be relevant in determining whether learners will be diligent in seeking out opportunities to use the L2 or whether they will pay attention to input and participate in class, but none has been shown to have more than marginal long-term influence on learning outcomes. Simple zero-order correlations between one or more of them and L2 proficiency evaporate when AO and cognitive variables (aptitude, IQ, short-term memory, etc.) enter the analysis (see, e.g., Long 1990b; Oyama 1978; Purcell & Suter 1980). Affect variables can sometimes be important in getting learners to the starting line, in other words, but cognitive variables take over when learners confront the learning task itself.

In fact, most of the many putative explanations that have been advanced for adult SLA failure over the years lack predictive potential. They concern either universal human characteristics or pervasive qualities of the linguistic environment, so could only work for all learners and (in the case of trait variables, such as aptitude or IQ) all structures if they worked at all, or state variables (attitude, motivation, anxiety, self-concept, etc.) that have an uneven empirical track record and seem as much a product as a cause of learning success or failure. Explanations that have been advanced for success or failure in the SLA literature but which *cannot* account for ultimate attainment differences across learners (for an extensive list and critical discussion, see Long 2003a) involve (i) unchanging facts about L1–L2 relationships (e.g., the MEP); (ii) cognitive abilities and processes that are presumably universal, or at least vary only in degree, not kind (e.g., processing constraints, automatization of incorrect forms or rules, the ease of using simpler IL systems); (iii) changes in language-learning ability (e.g., loss of sensitivity to language data, complete or partial loss of access to UG, and other effects of maturational constraints), which are supposedly part of the human biological inheritance, so universal; or (iv) pervasive characteristics of language use (e.g., absence of negative feedback and/or presence of positive feedback on error in non-instructional talk, the ungrammaticality of much natural speech, communication breakdown, and unwillingness to risk restructuring), which are, again, presumably the same for everyone.

Proposed explanations in terms of factors that do vary at the level of the individual might appear to have potential for explaining IDs in ultimate attainment (but not universal non-native-like attainment, precisely because it is universal). They include satisfaction of communicative needs, social-psychological variables, (in)sensitivity to feedback, and inability to notice mismatches between input and output. The first two fail empirically at the level both of individuals, e.g., the case of "Wes" (Schmidt 1983), and groups (Schumann 1986), and lack potential for explaining learner success with some linguistic domains or structures but not others, in some individuals but not others.

Insensitivity to negative feedback (Lin & Hedgcock 1996) might work if it were only deviant structures that stabilized (or fossilized), but native-like structures do, too, and correct and incorrect rules and structures must be subject to the same mental processes.

Also, it is highly unlikely that an individual would be differentially sensitive to positive and negative input, as opposed to input in general. Accordingly, I have claimed elsewhere (Long 2003a) that (given otherwise comparable abilities and learning opportunities) one factor, *sensitivity to input* (not to negative input only), is the most likely predictor of success and failure at the level of the individual. Input sensitivity appears to be a factor that can be quite variable among learners, as suggested by the case of "Wes," and more pervasively, by the literature on language aptitude (Dornyei & Skehan 2003; Granena 2012; Granena & Long 2013b). Sensitivity to input is arguably a key component of language aptitude, tapped, for instance, in both the spelling clues and words-in-sentences sub-tests of the MLAT (Carroll & Sapon 1959), as well as several Hi-Lab sub-tests, and involved in three of the four components that Carroll proposed made up language aptitude: phonetic coding ability, grammatical sensitivity, and inductive language-learning ability.

Input sensitivity, alone, however, cannot explain differential success at the level of linguistic domain or structure within learners. An adequate theory will have to recognize facilitative and inhibitory characteristics of domains and target structures, especially perceptual saliency, which, as we have seen, is in turn often a function of frequency, communicative value, semantic weight, and so on. The salience factor, of course, is one to which DeKeyser (2005) has consistently drawn attention, with insightful analysis of its components and development of a saliency measure (DeKeyser 2001; Goldschneider & DeKeyser 2001) that has already proved valuable in a number of studies. Perceptual salience, alone, however, can no more explain differential success with the same features and constructions across learners than ID variables can explain differential achievement of the features within learners. The combination is what is required. In sum, the claim here is that it is *the interaction* of *input sensitivity* (a constant within the individual, but varying across individuals) *and perceptual saliency* (which varies across structures) that has the potential to account for success and failure at the level both of individual learners and individual structures. What is required now is an operational definition and a valid measure of input sensitivity to make it possible to test the hypothesis.

3.4. Summary

While not the only motivation required for an approach to LT, a theory of ISLA should be part of its rationale and will be all the more necessary as long as a sufficient body of research findings and a complete understanding of parts of the adult language-learning process are unavailable. The theory should aim to solve what Laudan refers to as "problems" in the field, i.e., in this case, to explain at least some of the more salient among widely attested and accepted ISLA phenomena. The embryonic *cognitive-interactionist theory of ISLA* sketched in this chapter accords significance to AO, language aptitude, a symbiotic relationship between implicit and explicit learning, the effectiveness of the latter subject to processing constraints, to construction learning, and, more generally, to trait over state, and cognitive over affect, variables. Of special importance is the interaction between input sensitivity and the perceptual salience of linguistic features, the hypothesized combination of learner-internal and input differences minimally required to account for the facts about variation in between-learner and within-learner achievement. Like all theories, however, this one goes beyond what is known, meaning that serious empirical research is required to test some of its claims. Meanwhile, it is this theory and related empirical findings that provide the main psycholinguistic underpinnings for TBLT.

3.5. Suggested Readings

DeKeyser, R.M. (2005). What makes learning second language grammar difficult? A review of issues. *Language Learning* 55, Suppl. 1, 1–25.

Doughty, C.J. (2003). Instructed SLA: Constraints, compensation, and enhancement. In Doughty, C.J., & Long, M.H. (eds.), *Handbook of second language acquisition* (pp. 256–310). New York: Basil Blackwell.

Ellis, N.C. (2005). At the interface: Dynamic interactions of explicit and implicit language knowledge. *Studies in Second Language Acquisition* 27, 305–352.

Ellis, N.C. (2006). Language acquisition as rational contingency learning. *Applied Linguistics* 27, 1, 1–24.

Gass, S.M. (1997). *Input, interaction, and the development of second languages.* Mahwah, NJ: Erlbaum.

Goo, J., & Mackey, A. (2013). The case against the case against recasts. *Studies in Second Language Acquisition* 35, 1, 127–165.

Granena, G., & Long, M.H. (2013a). Age of onset, length of residence, language aptitude, and ultimate L2 attainment in three linguistic domains. *Second Language Research* 29, 3, 311–343.

Granena, G., & Long, M.H. (2013b). *Sensitive periods, language aptitudes, and ultimate L2 attainment.* Amsterdam: John Benjamins.

Hyltenstam, K., & Abrahamsson, N. (2003). Maturational constraints in second language acquisition. In Doughty, C.J., & Long, M.H. (eds.), *Handbook of second language acquisition* (pp. 539–588). Oxford: Blackwell.

Laudan, L. (1996). A problem-solving approach to scientific progress. In Laudan, L. (ed.), *Beyond positivism and relativism. Theory, method, and evidence* (pp. 77–87). Boulder, CO: Westview, 1996.

Long, M.H. (1990). The least a second language acquisition theory needs to explain. *TESOL Quarterly* 24, 4, 649–666. Also in Brown, H.D., & Gonzo, S. (eds.) (1994). *Readings on second language acquisition* (pp. 470–490). Englewood-Cliffs, NJ: Prentice Hall Regents1994.

Long, M.H. (1996). The role of the linguistic environment in second language acquisition. In Ritchie, W.C., & Bhatia, T.J. (eds.), *Handbook of second language acquisition* (pp. 413–468). New York: Academic Press.

Long, M.H. (2003). Stabilization and fossilization in interlanguage development. In Doughty, C.J., & Long, M.H. (eds.), *Handbook of second language acquisition* (pp. 487–535). Oxford: Blackwell.

Long, M.H. (2007a). Second language theories. In Long, M.H. (ed.), *Problems in SLA* (pp. 3–20). Mahwah, NJ: Erlbaum.

Long, M.H. (2007b). Problem-solving and theory change in SLA. In Long, M.H. (ed.), *Problems in SLA* (pp. 21–40). Mahwah, NJ: Erlbaum.

Mackey, A. (2012). *Input, interaction, and corrective feedback in L2 learning.* Oxford: Oxford University Press.

Mackey, A., & Goo, J. (2007). Interaction research in SLA: A meta-analysis and research synthesis. In Mackey, A. (ed.), *Conversational interaction in second language acquisition* (pp. 407–452). Oxford: Oxford University Press.

Robinson, P., & Ellis, N.C. (2008). Conclusion: Cognitive linguistics, second language acquisition and L2 instruction – Issues for research. In Robinson, P., & Ellis, N.C. (eds.), *Handbook of cognitive linguistics and second language acquisition* (pp. 489–545). New York: Routledge.

Robinson, P., Mackey, A., Gass, S.M., & Schmidt, R.W. (2012). Attention and awareness in second language acquisition. In Gass, S.M., & Mackey, A. (eds.), *The Routledge handbook of second language acquisition* (pp. 247–267). Abingdon, Oxford: Routledge.

Sato, C.J. (1986). Conversation and interlanguage development: Rethinking the connection. In Day, R.R. (ed.), *Talking to learn: Conversation and second language acquisition* (pp. 23–45). Rowley, MA: Newbury House.

Schmidt, R.W. (2001). Attention. In Robinson, P. (ed.), *Cognition and second language instruction* (pp. 3–32). Cambridge: Cambridge University Press.

Williams, J.N. (2005). Learning without awareness. *Studies in Second Language Acquisition* 27, 2, 269–304.

Williams, J.N. (2009). Implicit learning. In Ritchie, W.C., & Bhatia, T.K. (eds.), *The new handbook of second language acquisition* (pp. 319–353). Bingley: Emerald Group Publishing.

Chapter 4

Philosophical Underpinnings:
L'education Integrale

4.1. TBLT's Philosophical Principles: Origins and Overview

Education of *all* kinds, not just TBLT as described in this book, serves either to preserve or challenge the status quo, and so is a political act, whether teachers and learners realize it or not. To take a simple example, a language-teaching (LT) textbook storyline and accompanying visuals that feature members of only one gender and/or ethnic group in important roles because that is the way things are organized in the surrounding society will tend, whether intentionally or not, to validate and perpetuate that form of social organization. Conversely, a textbook that features a diverse set of characters in leading roles can help open people's eyes to alternatives and the potential in all people. In Chapter 1, I sketched a few of the powerful forces and sometimes tragic situations that lead many millions of children and adults to become language learners each year. For all those reasons, and given the obvious political implications of a few major world languages – generally those of nations whose strong economies and powerful militaries provide them with global political influence – being taught to speakers of so many less powerful ones, a responsible course of action, it seems to me, is to make sure that LT

Second Language Acquisition and Task-Based Language Teaching, First Edition. Mike Long.
© 2015 John Wiley & Sons, Inc. Published 2015 by John Wiley & Sons, Inc.

and learning are as socially progressive as possible. LT alone will never compensate for the all the ills in the world, it goes without saying, or the pressing needs that motivate so many language learners, but at the very least, it should strive not to perpetuate matters or to make them worse.

In this chapter, I will describe and explain the nine core principles that constitute TBLT's progressive philosophical underpinnings and also point out some of the ways in which most fit well with TBLT's psycholinguistic rationale, described in Chapters 2 and 3. Together, they motivate and are reflected in the theory and practice of TBLT. The connections are sometimes direct and transparent, sometimes indirect and less obvious at first. As will become clear, the full realization of some of them depends on the expertise and classroom behavior of teachers and students and on how well task-based pedagogical materials are crafted. Several of the principles are consistent with other LT approaches, of course, or, in other cases, could be made so.

It is perfectly possible for institutions and teachers to disagree with, or even oppose, any or all of the nine principles for cultural, religious, political, or other reasons, yet still implement TBLT, based on its psycholinguistic rationale (Chapters 2 and 3), its functionality and relevance to learner needs (Chapters 5–7), and its growing empirical track record (Chapter 11). I would suggest, however, that history has attested to the soundness of the principles and that they at least deserve to be considered by anyone interested in making a small, but positive, contribution to a more tolerant, more peaceful, more humane world. So if readers choose to reject one or more of the principles, the following account should at least serve to raise their awareness of the principles to which they *do* subscribe.

The origins of the nine philosophical principles that help to shape TBLT date back centuries, but some are rooted in the work of the English clergyman, journalist, novelist, and philosopher William Godwin (1756–1836), especially his *An Enquiry Concerning Political Justice and Its Influence upon Modern Morals and Manners* (1793). Godwin was the father of Mary Godwin, of Frankenstein fame, and later, father-in-law of her husband, the English Romantic poet Percy Bysse Shelley, whose political beliefs (see Scrivener 1982) Godwin greatly influenced. Godwin's ideas were subsequently developed by Leo Tolstoy (1862, 1863/1967), author of such works as *Ana Karenina* and *War and Peace*, by the Russian prince, biologist, and geographer Peter Kropotkin (1890/1913, 1899/1985, 1903), of whom more later, by the French journalist and newspaper editor Jean Grave (1900), and many others. Godwin's views on education and the language of schooling, in particular, were to influence decades of famous experimental free schools, a tradition currently being revived in many countries. Take this quote, which many educators and not a few whole education systems might do well to consider today, over 200 years later:

> Modern education not only corrupts the heart of our youth by the rigid slavery to which it condemns them, it also undermines their reason by the unintelligible jargon with which they are overwhelmed in the first instance, and the little attention that is given to accommodating their pursuits to their capacities in the second.
>
> William Godwin, *An account of the seminary* (1783), p. 31

The early free school experiments worked well even under what were often adverse conditions. They included those of Elias Puig in Catalonia, Jose Sanchez Rosa in Andalusia, Leo Tolstoy at his Yasnaya Polyana estate in Russia, Sebastien Faure's *La Ruche*

(The Beehive), and Madeleine Vernet's *L'Avenir Social* (The Social Future), both just outside Paris, Paul Robin's Prevost Orphenage at Cempuis, and Franciso Ferrer y Guardia's *Escuela Moderna* in Barcelona. The experimental schools, especially Ferrer's Escuela Moderna, have themselves gone on to inspire numerous "modern schools," alternative schools, and alternatives to schools, in many countries ever since.[1]

Implicitly or explicitly, Suissa (2006) points out, these and other educators in the same tradition ever since have a clear moral vision. They seek to build free, egalitarian societies in which coercion and oppression of all kinds are banished, and in which every individual, not just a fortunate elite, can realize his or her potential. The schools tend to have a socially conscious curriculum designed to offer students opportunities to learn rational thinking, mathematics, science, arts and humanities, and simultaneously, the value of individual freedom (as opposed to mere license), equality, free association, mutual aid, cooperation, and social justice. The free school in Ferrer's time, as now, was seen as the ideal society in embryonic form – building the new society within the shell of the old.

The early experiments were motivated by a number of core principles, notably, *l'educacion integrale* – roughly, educating the whole person – and *learning by doing*. Those ideas have been adopted by many educational theorists and philosophers of education ever since, often without awareness and/or due recognition of their roots. The principles have become widely accepted in progressive societies and in progressive education even in societies that are not very progressive. They live on in the work of, among others, John Dewey (1933, 1938, 1939/1966), especially his advocacy of "experiential learning" (see also Kolb 1984; Lave & Wenger 1991; Manicas 1982), Paulo Freire (1970), John Holt (1964/1995, 1967/1995, 1972), Ivan Illich (1971), Paul Goodman (1952, 1966), and Colin Ward (1996). They underpin growing numbers of free schools and life-long education projects for adults around the world.

The closely related principles of *l'éducation integrale* and *learning by doing* play a central role in several areas of general educational practice today, such as Montessori schools. Maria Montessori's (1870–1952) child-centered, teacher-decentered philosophy and advocacy of *exercices de la vie pratique*, or "exercises in daily living" (see Kramer 1978), reflect much of the same tradition. The use of the "exercises" in so-called Montessori schools, whose practices around the world (rather like immersion education and TBLT) increasingly tend to vary, despite bearing the same name, has stood the test of time. Another example is so-called problem-based learning (PBL). The December 2002 issue of the US National Education Association's *Advocate Online* discusses PBL, which

> is based on the premise that students will 'want to know' and solve problems when the problem is presented in a context that simulates real-world, and thus personally relevant, situations [and furthermore that] acquiring knowledge in the context in which it is meant to be used facilitates recall and application of concepts and skills learned. (Gijselaers 1996)

---

[1] For descriptions of the early, and some more recent, experimental schools, see, e.g., Amster *et al.* (2009, pp. 123–180), Avrich (1980), Duane (1995), Fremeaux and Jordan (2012), Goldman (1917), Haworth (2012), Motta (2012), Perez *et al.* (n.d.), Shantz (2012), Shotton (1992, 1993), Smith (1983), Spring (1975, 1994a), Suissa (2006), Ward (1996), and Wright (1989a,b).

PBL and task-based learning have been used in the education of medical students for some time (see, e.g., Virjo, Holmberg-Mattila, & Mattila 2001) and has recently become widespread in undergraduate courses in other disciplines. Additional examples of learning by doing include the use of simulations and gaming in many fields, case studies in business schools, and case studies, mock trials, and moot courts in law schools.

The philosophical ideas underlying TBLT are ones to which many language teachers and learners already subscribe in their everyday lives – sometimes consciously, sometimes less so – principles that need not be abandoned on entering a classroom. In addition to *l'education integrale* and *learning by doing*, they include a belief in *individual freedom, rationality, emancipation, learner-centeredness, egalitarian teacher–student relationships, participatory democracy, mutual aid*, and *cooperation*. These are the core philosophical principles that motivate TBLT, and as we shall see, their implications for language learning for the most part sit well with those of TBLT's psycholinguistic underpinnings.

4.2. *L'education Integrale* and Learning by Doing

Usually referred to by its French name, *l'education integrale* means integrated, whole person, mind-and-body education.[2] First articulated by the French utopian socialist Fourier, the concept of *l'educacion integrale* was taken up and developed by Proudhon, and then by Bakunin, Paul Robin, and others. It is closely related to a second core principle, *learning by doing*. Both owe much to the belief, argued explicitly by Kropotkin (1890/1913, 1899/1985), that the separation of manual work and mental, or intellectual, work is one of the major causes of the inhumane social stratification still found in many countries. If knowledge is power, then providing socioeconomic elites with crucial information and skills while simultaneously denying them to others serves to perpetuate a two-tier system of haves and have-nots:

> To the division of society into brain workers and manual workers we oppose the combination of both kinds of activities; and instead of 'technical education,' which means the maintenance of the present division between brain work and manual work, we advocate *l'education integrale*, or complete education, which means the disappearance of that pernicious distinction. (Kropotkin 1890/1913, 1899/1985, p. 172)

For anyone who believes in the potential of all people, regardless of race, class, and gender, and in equal access to both the basic necessities and the good things of life, integrating the intellectual and the manual is an obvious step toward equality of opportunity. Equality of opportunity is what most language teachers and learners – indeed, most people – will say they agree with if asked, but it is not much in evidence today. Too many societies effectively condemn large segments of their populations to lives of

---

[2] For histories, analyses, and references to sources on integral education, see Avrich (1980, pp. 3–68), Fidler (1989), Shotton (1993, pp. 1–32), Suissa (2006), and, especially, Smith (1983, pp. 18–61).

drudgery, repetitive physical work, and wage slavery by streaming them at an early age into school systems designed to teach what they will need for such work, and little else.[3]

It was not just opposition to generation after generation of social elites exploiting workers, ethnic minorities, and the poor that inspired the early free schools, however; those who taught in them saw the positive value for children and adults of *l'education integrale*, in which intellectual reasoning abilities and practical experience were combined, and of *learning by doing*. People learn best through personal experience, through practical hands-on work with real-world tasks. Theories and abstract concepts come alive when made visible in everyday life. What is learned is better understood, better remembered, and more easily retrieved if tied to real-world activities or tasks:

> Through the eyes *and* the hand to the brain – this is the true principle of economy of time in teaching. (Kropotkin 1890/1913, 1899/1985, p. 175)

A famous early example of *l'educacion integrale* was Sebastien Faure's school, *La Ruche* (The Beehive), founded in 1904. In a rational, liberating, non-coercive, coeducational environment, "problem" children rejected by the traditional French education system learned mathematics, science, and other academic subjects effectively through operating an on-site agricultural school cooperative, producing eggs, milk, cheese, vegetables, and honey and selling them in nearby Paris to help support the school financially. In Ferrer's Escuela Moderna, established in Barcelona in 1901, children participated in practical training, museum and factory visits, and field trips to study physical geography, geology, and botany (Suissa 2006, p. 80), part of a great emphasis Ferrer placed

---

[3] In the United Kingdom from 1944 until 1976, children's results at age 10 or 11 on the notorious "11+" exam (effectively an intelligence test acting as a surrogate aptitude test) decided whether they would spend the next five years at a "secondary modern" or a "technical" school, or the next seven or eight years at a more academically oriented "grammar" school. Given that until the late 1960s fewer than 10% of children in the United Kingdom attended university, given that 99% of those 10% came from grammar schools and the even more elitist and perversely named "public" schools, and given that a university degree was a requirement for the professions and most better-paying jobs, an exam of dubious validity taken at age 10 or 11 effectively determined a person's career opportunities and life chances. Most children at "secondary mods" and "techs," as they became known, abandoned secondary education as soon as they turned 16 (then the minimum age for the end of compulsory schooling), and most went to work in monotonous, low-paid, blue-collar jobs in factories, on building sites, in public transport, and so on, or joined the police force or the military. At the tender age of 10 or 11, in other words, most children had been designated the next generation of the long-suffering British working class. Meanwhile, the mostly middle-class children who had passed the 11+ and had been assigned to grammar schools were told that they were destined to become the country's future leaders. In reality, that usually meant white-collar office jobs as middle managers in the corporate sector, and perhaps a career in the professions, working for the country's true leaders who were, and largely remain today, the products of the fourth tier of British education, the "public" schools. (In the United Kingdom, 'public school' means a school that is supported by independent, 'public' money, i.e., the money of private citizens, not the state. Such schools are closed to the general public, even those who live in their geographical catchment areas. They would be called "private" schools everywhere else.) The Labour Party attempted to change the system in the late 1960s by introducing "comprehensive" schools – state schools for all children who would traditionally have gone to secondary modern, technical, and grammar schools. In recent years, however, paralleling similar moves in the United States, progressively more right-wing governments from both Tory, Liberal-Democrat and Labour parties have reversed the trend, inventing creative ways of reintroducing a stratified secondary and tertiary education system, complete with "school choice," "vouchers," "specialist schools," "academies," "free schools" (sic), and "league tables."

on learning by doing (Ferrer y Guardia 1909, 1913). Why make children learn about nature from books, Ferrer asked, if the real thing lay just outside the classroom door?[4] In what could almost have doubled as an argument against traditional synthetic approaches and for TBLT, Kropotkin wrote:

> By compelling our children to study real things from mere graphical representations, instead of making these things themselves, we compel them to waste the most precious time; we uselessly worry their minds; we accustom them to the worst methods of learning; we kill independent thought in the bud; and very seldom we succeed in conveying a real knowledge of what we are teaching. Superficiality, parrot-like repetition, slavishness and inertia of mind are the results of our method of education. We do not teach our children how to learn. (Kropotkin 1890/1913, 1899/1985, p. 176)

TBLT is an example of *l'education integrale* and of learning by doing at several levels. It aims to equip learners to meet their present or future real-world communicative needs, as identified through a task-based learner needs analysis, the first step in course design (see Chapters 5–7). Then, inside the classroom (see Chapters 8–10), instead of studying the new language as object, in the form of static texts, separately, in order to use it to communicate at some later date, *students learn language through doing pedagogic tasks.* The intellectual work of language learning, that is to say, is integrated with the practical experience of doing (initially less complex versions of) the communicative tasks for which the language is being learned. *Learning is task-based, not text-based.* As illustrated in later chapters (see, especially, Section 8.4.4), experiential learning is guided by a sequence of *pedagogic tasks* of gradually increasing complexity, culminating in one or more *target tasks* for those learners, as identified by the needs analysis. Task selection is designed for transfer of knowledge and abilities to serve learners' real-world academic, vocational training, occupational, or social survival needs.

Pedagogic tasks, like the *target task-types* that motivated their inclusion in a syllabus (see Section 8.3.1), combine language learning and action at various levels. Most obviously, doing pedagogic tasks through the medium of the target language means that implicit and incidental learning are allowed to fulfill their important symbiotic roles in the acquisition process – for adults, as well as children – as described in Chapter 3. Almost all pedagogic tasks have a hands-on, problem-solving quality designed to arouse learners' interest and hold their attention. Following live or recorded street directions from a native speaker by tracing out a route on a road map, navigating a video simulation, or walking the streets of a real town, for example, are more likely to prepare learners to follow street directions to find their way in an unfamiliar location (the target task for some of them) than studying a reading passage describing the route that someone else took from A to B, or reading/hearing a dialogue showing someone asking for and receiving directions. Actually *doing* a task, or, initially, a simple version thereof, is more relevant, comprehensible, and memorable than reading about someone else doing it. The basic, time-tested idea reflected in such contemporary slogans as "learning by doing," "child-centered," and "educating the whole person" is that practical hands-on

---

[4] Ferrer had worked as a Spanish language teacher in France for several years, and it was a legacy of a million French francs bequeathed him by one of his French pupils, Mlle. Meunie, that enabled him to return to Spain and open the Escuela Moderna (Avrich 1980, p. 6).

experience with real-world tasks brings abstract concepts and theories to life and, because fully contextualized, makes the language involved more understandable and memorable. New knowledge is better integrated into long-term memory and more easily retrieved for use if tied to real-world events and activities. The first two of TBLT's 10 methodological principles (MPs; see Section 10.2.2) are MP1: Use task, not text, as the unit of analysis, and MP2: Promote learning by doing.

4.3. Individual Freedom

While few people spend much time thinking about such matters, or if they do, feel a need to articulate their views explicitly, most believe in individual freedom, meaning that individuals should be free to pursue their goals and live their lives as they see fit, as long as the exercise of their freedom does not infringe upon the freedom of others. If they think further, they may also recognize a distinction between freedom and license; the former is absolute and taken, the latter conditional and granted. Thus, in many societies, licenses are required for a variety of familiar activities, from fishing and driving to practicing a profession and marriage. They are applied for and, if conditions are met, granted, but they can also be denied or revoked, and often are.

Less obvious until it happens to you or to the group or whole society of which you are a member, things that are considered rights in many societies and that most people may not even think about, or as the saying goes, "take for granted," may also be denied or taken away, showing that the presumed rights were in reality just (temporary, conditional) licenses. In some societies, "freedom of speech," for example, is OK until it threatens the interests of those in power, at which point public advocacy of certain views may be proscribed, access to certain internet sites blocked, gatherings of three or more people prohibited, and so on. "Free speech" was really just *licensed* all along, in other words, not a right. As shown every day on the nightly news, some groups may never have, or have, but lose, all sorts of "rights" that others take for granted – the right to provide water, food, and shelter for themselves and their families, to practice a particular religion, to attend school, to get a job, to form a union, to vote, to hold public office, to eat in the same restaurant as members of a different group, to travel, work, or live outside the zone or country in which they were born, to write or say what they believe, and to access education or public services through their native language or even speak that language at all. Things can become so extreme in some periods and in some countries that whole groups defined by race, ethnicity, religion, sexual orientation, or political beliefs can lose the right to exist at all. Persecution amounting to a holocaust, genocide, or ethnic cleansing becomes the order of the day.

The critical importance of genuine individual freedom becomes clear when considered against the backdrop of such (in some parts of the world, continuing) tragedies. Paradoxically, however, there may be a downside to individual freedom in education, where it is sometimes equated with freedom to attend school or not or, once in school, to enjoy freedom from a predetermined curriculum imposed from above. Learners are considered capable of determining their own interests and are entitled to do so. Students who seek out knowledge when they are ready are likely to be motivated and happy, the reasoning goes, and to do better than those who have unwanted knowledge thrust upon them. This may be true in most cases, but is purely student-initiated learning sufficient?

To the best of my knowledge, not forcing knowledge on children (or adults) is a sound educational principle, especially not according to the dictates of an externally imposed timetable in the form of a standardized curriculum for all pupils of a certain age, as is attempted in most state schools and most private ones. Rather, the general idea should be to provide input on demand, i.e., to respond to child- or adult-initiated learning. But is this shortchanging them? Like everyone else, after all, and even more than most adults, *children do not know what they don't know* and may never stumble upon whole bodies of knowledge and skills they might love if they knew of their existence.

A limitation of learning by observing other people and one's environment is that one only experiences "positive evidence," i.e., examples of a sub-set of what is possible, of what exists – that which happens to occur and that one notices. This works well enough for young children, as evidenced by the success of child L1A, supplemented as it is by implicit negative evidence, and is no different for infants and young children in any environment. However, it can surely become an increasingly significant issue as they grow older. How will children learn, or even know that it is possible to learn, or learn about, X or Y subject matter – say, a new language, sport, or science – if left to their own devices, with no one bringing the items to their attention? This is not the easily discredited claim that there exists a fixed body of essential knowledge all children must learn when adults say so, analogous to the externally imposed synthetic syllabus. Rather, it is to ask whether a purely child-centered, child-initiated model, learning from positive evidence alone, analogous to a *purely analytic* LT syllabus, is efficient and does not run the risk that children will achieve less, perhaps far less, and do so more slowly than they would be capable of with moderate, sensitive intervention.

For example, it might be years, if ever, before most children "discovered" not only that there are many languages in the world but also that learning one or more of them is both possible and richly rewarding. By then, it could be too late or, at least, far more difficult to do anything about, given fairly convincing evidence that the human brain is especially tuned for language learning in the early years, i.e., during one or more sensitive periods, but decreasingly so with increasing age, with results for late starters almost always being inferior and never native-like. Similarly, "stumbling upon" mathematics, physics, computer science, or whatever as a teenager, if it happens at all, and finding one loves it, does not necessarily rule out subsequent high levels of achievement but certainly makes them a big ask, and surely an unnecessarily big ask. It may simply be too late to catch up and realize one's potential.

TBLT embodies an intermediate position that I think is defensible. Instead of a preset linguistic syllabus imposed on all learners regardless of their individual needs or psycholinguistic readiness to learn (long demonstrated by SLA research to fail, as discussed in Chapters 2 and 3), course content is determined by learner needs, identified by a pre-course needs analysis, with overt and covert attention to language as object triggered by the design of pedagogic tasks and by problems with learner comprehension or output. In other words, the emphasis shifts from the traditional interventionist, proactive, modeling behavior of synthetic approaches to a more reactive mode for teachers – students lead, the teacher follows – with a correspondingly important role assigned to explicit and implicit negative feedback on learner-initiated production (MP7). Instead of teaching the structure of the day, teachers respond to the learners' internal syllabus – *focus on form, not focus on forms* (MP6) – and to the extent logistical constraints allow, to individual differences (IDs). It is in the provision of focus on form that the intermediate position is realized. Sensitive to learners' current developmental stage, teachers draw their attention to problematic items and options that the L2 offers for dealing with them that might never be noticed, or only noticed after an unnecessarily long time, if learners were left purely to their own devices. In other words, TBLT recognizes individual freedom and freedom to learn, but also the need to provide guidance when the timing is right.

4.4. Rationality

The philosophy of education underlying TBLT emphasizes the power of reason, rational thinking, and science to bring about positive social change. In early twentieth-century Spain (among other places), such views presented a significant challenge to those promulgated by the unholy alliance of the state and the powerful Catholic Church, whose priests supervised all Spanish schools and equated education in the few available, not with rationality but with the development of blind patriotism and acceptance of church dogma. In this light, the critical importance attached to reason, observation, and science is easily understood, as is what would otherwise be the surprising number of leading scientists who have figured among the ranks of those who have advocated philosophical principles like those presented here. Two of the better known examples are the major geographer, zoologist, and evolutionary biologist of his day, Peter Kropotkin, and in modern times, the leading linguist and cognitive scientist of his generation, Noam Chomsky.[5]

Reasoning skills and practical scientific inquiry were central components in the curricula of the early free schools, and it is no accident that the international organization established by Ferrer to support them was called The Society for Rational Education. In his prospectus for the Escuela Moderna, which opened in Barcelona in 1901, Ferrer wrote:

> I will teach them only the simple truth. I will not ram a dogma into their heads. I will not conceal from them one iota of fact. I will teach them not what to think but how to think. (Avrich 1980, p. 20)

Rationality pervades all aspects of TBLT. The approach itself is motivated and shaped by current understanding of theory and research findings in SLA and related fields, with explicit recognition that the understanding may sometimes turn out to be wrong and in need of revision. Courses are designed with conscious awareness of the need for

---

[5] It is not only scientists who have embraced these ideas, of course. There have always been numerous active sympathizers in literature and the arts. They include such writers as Leo Tolstoy, Percy Bysse Shelley, Emile Zola, Paul Adam, Laurent Tailhade, Felix Feneon, Octave Mirbeau, Stephane Mallarme, Franz Kafka, Oscar Wilde, Albert Camus, Stuart Merrill, Andre Breton, Dylan Thomas, Herbert Read, Aldous Huxley, Andre Breton, Dario Fo, Henry Miller, Jaroslav Hasek, Lawrence Ferlinghetti, Kenneth Rexroth, John Cowper Powys, Alex Comfort, Kenneth Patchen, Adrian Mitchell, Allen Ginsberg, Frank Herbert, Upton Sinclair, J.R.R. Tolkein, Paul Goodman, J.M. Coetzee, and Ursula Le Guin, and the painters Gustave Courbet, Paul Signac, Georges Seurat, Henri Toulouse-Lautrec, Camille Pissaro, George Bellows, Francis Picabia, Pablo Picasso, Maurice de Vlaminck, Man Ray, Augustus John, Kees van Dongen, Mark Rothko, and Jackson Pollock, among many others.

relevance to learner needs, the needs having been identified systematically by a needs analysis that follows best practice. Materials are designed, and instruction is delivered in keeping with the results of the needs analysis and consistent with what research findings suggest are putatively universal MPs and effective pedagogical procedures (PPs). The criterion-referenced performance measures employed to assess student achievement are task-based, as it is tasks that students need to be able to perform beyond the classroom, and to compare student abilities against objective external performance criteria (see Chapter 11), not against those of their classmates. Finally, the rationale for the ways courses have been designed and will be delivered, and their results assessed, is explained to students at the outset so that they understand *why* they are learning the way they are and what is expected of them and of their teacher.

4.5. Emancipation

The potentially emancipatory role of education had been stressed by Godwin, who saw the existing state system as a powerful means for social control – the way children were socialized into their roles serving the interests of those in power. And it was not just state education systems that were to be feared, the by then ex-clergyman warned:

> Even in the petty institutions of Sunday schools, the chief lessons that are taught are a superstitious veneration for the Church of England and to bow to every man in a handsome coat. (Godwin, quoted in Smith 1983, p. 12)

In the late nineteenth and early twentieth centuries, the period during which several of the first free schools were opened, it was understandable if their founders saw education as a path to emancipation for the poor and downtrodden and for women. The Catholic Church held a suffocating grip on most aspects of society in southern Europe, nowhere more so than in Spain. What little public education existed was dominated by the Church, of miserable quality, and available only to boys. Just one town in three had a school. Two-thirds of the population was illiterate (Smith 1983, p. 5).[6]

In sharp contrast, inspired chiefly by Pierre Robin's school at Cempuis, which had opened in 1880, Ferrer's Escuela Moderna welcomed both boys and girls. Its values were openly antistatist, anticapitalist, and antimilitarist, and it had a clear commitment to social justice. It was a free school where, in Emma Goldman's words, 'free' meant "to free the child from superstition and bigotry, from the darkness of dogma and authority" (Goldman 1931, p. 458). Parents and other adults flocked to lectures and classes provided for them in the evenings and at weekends. The ideas caught on. Fourteen new Ferrer-inspired schools opened in Barcelona and 34 others elsewhere in Catalonia, Valencia, and Andalusia. Textbooks produced especially for the original school and published by its in-house press were adopted in 120 secular schools started by the League of Freethinkers – schools that, like the Escuela Moderna, also provided literacy classes and other courses for adults. Unsurprisingly, all this was viewed with alarm by both the Spanish state and the Catholic Church, with the latter especially troubled by

---

[6] Surely, it is a tragic waste of talent, and massively unjust, that several world religions seek to deny girls and women access to education to this day.

the fact that the Escuela Moderna was coeducational. There were 30 students, 18 boys and 12 girls, from all social classes, when the school opened, and more than 120 when, after five years of continuous harassment, it was finally shut down by the state.

Some would argue that emancipation is not the goal of the language teacher or the applied linguist. Our job is to teach the language, not to meddle in efforts for social change, especially not when teaching overseas. But how far are those who hold that view willing to push it? By inaction and self-censorship, should teachers, applied linguists, textbook writers, and publishers help perpetuate "received values" in many societies concerning, for example, the (oppressed) status of women or that of other groups defined by, and persecuted for, even executed for, their sexual orientation or religious or political beliefs? Is everything about local "cultures" to be accepted and respected just because it is "part of the local culture"? Or are not local cultures the sum of social practices taught and learned – not genetically inherited or in any way essentially human (or such differences would not occur) – and the values they embody the ones imposed and protected for centuries by those in power – men, heterosexuals, or members of a particular race or religious group – because maintenance of the status quo suits their interests? If, say, young girls and women, albinos, homosexuals, or holders of left-wing political views are systematically mistreated, e.g., by being denied access to education, employment, a life outside the home, or most other rights and privileges enjoyed by boys and men, or worse, is the language teacher to acquiesce? Is everything relative? Are there no universal values? Is rape, murder, or ethnic cleansing ever OK? Would it not be appropriate for pedagogic materials to depict such things as girls in school and women attending university, voting (for those who believe in such rituals), seeking medical assistance unaccompanied by males, demanding second opinions, working in mixed company while practicing medicine, law, dentistry, and so on, driving a car or playing sports? Or should all such models and references be expunged because they offend "local culture"? Whose culture? Whose values? Whose interests?

Unlike extreme relativism, TBLT, based as it is on rationality, assumes that there are some values that can, and should, be defended as universals because they reflect the essence of what it means to be human. TBLT, like some other non-task-based approaches to LT (see, e.g., Auerbach 1992; Auerbach & Wallerstein 2005), has a socially conscious curriculum. This does not mean that the teacher will intentionally provoke conflict, and certainly not abuse his or her position as teacher, which, rightly or wrongly, traditionally confers considerable status and power over students in most societies, to seek to inculcate values that clearly are in no way universal, e.g., by mixing LT with religious proselytizing. Rather, instead of tacitly condoning sexism, racism, classism, and so on, that may be institutionalized locally and are present to some degree in all societies, such issues may well be treated, directly or indirectly, in task-based materials, with students encouraged to reach their own conclusions. Target tasks for a particular group of learners may be those required for successful completion of a university degree or to practice a particular profession, regardless of whether the race, gender, or political or religious affiliation of the students in country X traditionally curtails such plans. There is admittedly a fine line between encouraging awareness and a critical view of traditionally unquestioned practices, on the one hand, and seeking to impose one's own set of beliefs, on the other, but those who oppose LT (of any kind, not just TBLT) having an emancipatory function need to recognize that a hands-off attitude is itself just as "political" and just as interventionist, for it helps perpetuate the status quo.

Such a stance is not to politicize LT. As more and more language teachers and applied linguists have recognized, like all education, LT is inherently political. All education systems embody the values of the societies or individuals who design and implement them (see, e.g., Apple 1996; Lankshear & Lawler 1987). For more than two centuries, critics, such as Godwin, and for considerably less time, "critical theorists," have drawn attention to the fact that one of the principal functions of schooling, and often its major achievement, especially in the case of state education systems, is to socialize students into uncritical acceptance of the existing social order. For many, this only becomes apparent when proposed changes suddenly threaten the previously unchallenged hegemony of their own beliefs, e.g., when proponents of one set of religious or political beliefs try to alter the curriculum to impose their views about such issues as sex education, scientific evolution, economics, or school prayer on everyone else. When apologists for fascism or anti-Semites try to rewrite holocaust history, for example, they are fighting an existing view of the holocaust reflected in the history curriculum. When health-care workers attempt to introduce sex education into the school curriculum and encounter vociferous opposition from religious fundamentalists, they expose the fact that the existing curriculum reflects the fundamentalists' belief that sex education is better left to parents or should not occur at all. When the same religious fundamentalists seek to introduce compulsory school prayer and encounter opposition from liberals, they are challenging the existing acceptance of the doctrine of separation of church and state. In other words, if teachers do not notice propagation of the current social order in school curricula or LT materials, it is not because the propagation is not there but probably because the teachers' views coincide. Hence, not preparing students as social change agents is just as much a political stance, since it is implicitly to accept and perpetuate the existing social order by socializing new members into it.

Even when conducted with the noblest intentions, LT can help perpetuate oppressive social systems that protect the interests of powerful elites at the expense of those of the great majority of ordinary working people (see, e.g., Auerbach & Burgess 1985; Luke, McHoul, & Mey 1990; Tollefson 1989, 1991, 1995; Wallerstein 1983). Most obviously, LT can, and often has, served the interests of imperialism and linguicism (Phillipson 1988, 1992). Many teachers are initially oblivious to this hidden potential of their work, but most wish to make amends once they become aware of it. However, as Auerbach and Burgess (1985) pointed out, a common response is what Freire (1981) called assist-encialism – educators seeing their role as interceding on behalf of their students with solutions to their problems. Freire claimed that showing students how to solve problems does not help them in the long run as much as showing them how to pose problems. Problem-solving can lead to outsiders imposing solutions in the name of learner-centeredness. Worse, students may unintentionally be socialized not just into acceptance of the particular set of problems "solved" in a course but also into acceptance of the idea that problems are givens. Problem-posing, Freire argued, can lead learners to problematize knowledge and their surroundings. Wallerstein (1983) provides an early explicit application of these ideas to English as a second language (ESL). As indicated earlier, in TBLT, an attempt is made to lead students to an understanding of the difference between license and freedom, and to the possibilities of emancipation, for themselves and for others.

4.6. Learner-Centeredness

Educators in the philosophical tradition underlying TBLT were among the first to focus attention on the latent potential inside every child, often likening it to a flower that will develop from within if allowed to do so. Anticipating Piaget and Erikson, as Avrich (1980, p. 15) notes, they also recognized that there are universal, biologically determined, natural stages of development, including cognitive stages, from simple to complex, largely beyond external control, through which all children pass, and must be allowed to pass. Echoes of these ideas are to be found nearly 200 years later, where the child's innate learning capacity is a foundational explanatory concept in work in linguistics, first language acquisition, and cognitive science:

> Acquisition of language is something that happens to you; it's not something that you do. Language learning is something like undergoing puberty; you don't do it because you see other people doing it; you are designed to do it at a certain time. (Chomsky 1988, pp. 173–174)

Reading should not be forced on children too early. Timing was crucial. Schools and teachers should respond to children's needs and interests when they emerged, not try to impose their own:

> According to the received modes of education, the master goes first, and the pupil follows. According to the method here recommended, it is probable that the pupil should go first, and the master follow. (Godwin 1793, 1986)

Direct instruction was to be de-emphasized, and more attention paid to providing feedback on intrinsically motivated, student-initiated learning (Goodman 1966; Smith 1983).

Learner-centeredness in LT has a rather disappointing track record, often having meant little more than a focus on the affective dimension, as reflected in the title of a popular book on the subject 30 years ago, *Caring and Sharing in the Foreign Language Classroom* (Moskowitz 1978, 1991). Teachers should be nice to students, empathize with them, and maintain a relaxed, friendly atmosphere, and students should be nice to one another: "through sharing which leads to caring, students communicate on a personally meaningful level, breaking through shyness and cliques as they truly get to know each other while learning another language."

Unfortunately, "love your students and they will learn" won't stand up in court. Delivering the same irrelevant, preset, psycholinguistically insensitive, synthetic syllabus to all students, in however "caring and sharing" an atmosphere, is learner-centered in only the most superficial sense. Moreover, too relaxed a classroom climate may not even be beneficial. A review of research findings by Scovel (1978) found that neither too much, nor too little, anxiety was conducive to language learning. In fact, a moment's thought would lead one to expect that a certain tension in lessons would help maintain student attention better than the dull predictability (and often, outright monotony) of much traditional LT – and attention, as we saw in Chapter 3, is a critical requirement (necessary, but not sufficient) for language learning (for an overview of the role of ID variables in SLA, see Dornyei 2005).

TBLT is learner-centered in two fundamental, meaningful senses. First, course content is determined by learners' present and/or future communicative needs. The tasks in a TBLT syllabus are there for a reason; they have been identified by a needs analysis as relevant for particular groups of students. Rather than off-the-peg textbooks, TBLT then employs task-based materials (see Chapter 9) written to meet the identified needs. Instead of simplified language of the kind found in commercially published materials, the task-based materials provide *elaborated* input (see Chapters 9 and 10) – language that is modified to enhance comprehensibility, e.g., by the deliberate use of linguistic redundancy, without removing unknown linguistic items or constructions, for it is precisely those items to which learners must be exposed if they are ever to be learned. Input elaboration is also what happens during teacher–student and student–student negotiation for meaning as task-work proceeds. As befits a learner-centered approach, the degree of elaboration is determined not by a textbook writer's guess at what will be understood by hypothetical students at an opaque and psycholinguistically meaningless global proficiency level ("high intermediate," "1+," "B2," etc.) but by what real students, in fact, turn out to require to accomplish a task, which will not be the same for everyone. One of TBLT's (currently) ten MPs is MP3: Elaborate, do not simplify, input.

Second, attention to linguistic problems is determined not by a preset linguistic syllabus in the form of a mass-marketed commercial textbook but by students' psycholinguistically determined readiness to learn. As first demonstrated by Pienemann (1984, 1989; discussed in Chapters 2 and 3), *teachability* is constrained by *learnability*. The teacher and other students respond to students' linguistic problems as they arise, i.e., in a *reactive* mode. It is students who trigger the *focus on form* they require, in other words, not the day's date, and not a textbook writer who has never set eyes on those students (and in some notorious cases, has little classroom teaching experience at all). TBLT caters to what Corder (1967) called the internal "learner syllabus," not one that is externally imposed. Rather than the approach to LT explicit or implicit in generic commercial materials or as stipulated by a brand-name "method," TBLT strives to cater to IDs, and the MPs employed are there because their use is broadly supported by theory and research findings on how people learn languages, while the PPs used to deliver them are chosen systematically to suit particular learner characteristics (see Chapter 10). Such practices, explained to, and understood and appreciated by, teacher and students alike, needless to say, serve to produce a *psycholinguistically*, not just affectively, positive classroom climate.

4.7. Egalitarian Teacher–Student Relationships

Educators opposed to hierarchy, coercion, and oppression of all kinds, whether social or individual, have always recognized children as equals and advocated egalitarian teacher–student relationships in the classroom. Teachers in the experimental free schools did not set out to replace church and state tyranny with authoritarian behavior of their own. Their role was to respond to student interests and student-initiated searches for understanding, which were a far better motivation for learning than the dictates of an externally imposed curriculum whose content and timing were largely arbitrary and certainly meant nothing to the child. The approach placed egalitarianism, individuality, and diversity above standardization, conformity, and homogenization. Catering to IDs was the new norm and is reflected in TBLT's MP10: Individualize instruction.

The fostering of egalitarian teacher–student relationships is an example of a philosophical principle that can be encouraged but whose implementation ultimately lies in the hands of teachers and students. There is little that can be done to prevent teachers who wish to do so from maintaining an authoritarian stance in the TBLT classroom. And there is little that can be done to prevent students from allowing, or even facilitating, such behavior, especially in societies with long traditions of venerating teachers, good or bad, and accepting dictation, drills, and rote memorization as the way education (really, training) is best accomplished. What can be done, however, is to point out the consequences of such behavior for language learning, and the positives to be derived from egalitarianism.

Authoritarian teachers will tend to favor teacher-fronted "lockstep" lessons, with themselves dominating classroom talk and maintaining firm control over turn-taking, including turn-allocation. This will almost inevitably result in perpetuation of the classic initiation–response–feedback (IRF) sequence at the level of exchange structure in classroom discourse (see, e.g., Sinclair & Coulthard 1975), with teachers owning the vast majority of initiation and feedback moves and students largely limited to responding. There will be little opportunity for negotiation for meaning, even if the task-based materials were designed in part to facilitate that. Although not impossible, it is very difficult to "proof" materials against intentional or unintentional subversion by teachers or students. Individualization of instruction will also be unlikely if teachers maintain a lockstep organization.

In contrast, an egalitarian approach to teacher–student relationships will not only improve classroom climate but also create advantageous psycholinguistic conditions for language learning. Students treated as equals are likely to talk more and to have their own communicative and psycholinguistic needs met, since the syllabus will be one designed to meet their needs, as identified by the needs analysis, with teacher interventions to deal with problematic code issues triggered by students' problems (*focus on form*), not by whatever is on the page the class is (supposedly) "up to" in a grammar-based textbook never written with them in mind. As illustrated in Chapters 10 and 12, the egalitarian nature of classroom discourse will mean students are encouraged to initiate topics, not merely to return teachers' serve in the response slot of the IRF structure. They will be free to negotiate for meaning with the teacher and with their fellow students. They will seek assistance with the language as object when they need it, and in tune with their psycholinguistic readiness to learn, not when a distant textbook writer decreed that they should (miraculously, all) need it. The teacher will be a guide, not a dictator.

4.8. Participatory Democracy

Two very different systems are referred to as 'democratic.' Under the first, *representative* democracy, popular participation consists chiefly of citizens being asked, or in some countries, required by law, to vote once every four or five years for who will "represent" them in some sort of parliament. In some societies, elections are an obvious farce, due to massive fraud, or else a rubber-stamping operation in which candidates are selected by a one-party state, sometimes with only one "candidate" offered for each post. Even in supposedly free elections, however, all too many of the lucky winners – in an age of mass marketing and ubiquitous mass media, mostly those with the money to buy enough advertizing, or sometimes, simply to buy enough votes outright – proceed to represent themselves and the interests that paid for their election, not the voters, let alone the ever larger disillusioned segments of the population in many societies who no longer bother to vote at all. (As Emma Goldman famously wrote, "If voting changed anything, they'd abolish it.")

The second system, *participatory* democracy (sometimes referred to as direct, or grassroots, democracy), is very different. People elect *delegates*, not representatives, to councils or assemblies of various sorts – those responsible for day-to-day operations in industry, agriculture, or a municipality. Delegates are mandated to follow the policies agreed upon by those who elect them and are instantly recallable (and replaced) if they fail to do so. The idea is that people affected by a decision should be the ones making the decision.

In a system of representative democracy, people abdicate responsibility and, against all the evidence, hope that politicians will represent their interests. A few do; most do not. People vote; politicians govern. In a participatory democracy, conversely, people stay directly involved through the system of strictly mandated, instantly recallable delegates. The delegates are not a ruling class allowed to decide on policies and laws that will regulate the general population, often very much against its interests; they are delegates – people selected to do the general population's bidding, and directly answerable to it if they do not. Decisions agreed to by delegates only become binding if subsequently ratified by the base.

While the prospects for representative democracy, let alone participatory democracy, at the societal level around the world seem rather dim at present, there is little reason for teachers and students not to operate that way, and many already do. Typically, school or classroom rules and policies are those agreed to by joint meetings of teachers and students, functioning as equals, as well as, in some cases (e.g., many Basque Ikastolas), members of the surrounding community. Again, organizing a school or an adult learning center of some kind along these lines is an example of using the present to model the way a more just future society could operate – building the new society in the shell of the old – and *the importance of the means by which goals are attained being consistent with those goals.*

Participatory democracy in a TBLT course may take many forms. Some important ones include an initial presentation by the teacher of the results of the needs analysis conducted on the current group of learners, or perhaps ones just like them the previous year, with discussion and a request for students to speak up if they think anything has been missed or if any other changes are needed. With course goals established and agreed upon by teacher and students, the next step (in any LT course, not just a TBLT program) should be for the teacher to explain the approach to be taken to achieve, and eventually, assess achievement of, those goals with these particular students, given any constraints they are aware of, together with an explicit *rationale* for that approach – the approach and the rationale again being discussed and modified if warranted. This is especially important with adults, as TBLT will often differ considerably from their experiences in previous language courses. For example, they may be unfamiliar with the use of tasks, and of focus on form, not forms, to deal with grammatical problems or with the use of small group work in societies whose education systems have trained students to assume that rote learning, memorization, and lockstep work with an exclusive focus on the teacher is the only legitimate way of learning anything, including languages. Similarly, a TBLT program may be students' first experience of criterion-referenced assessment (see Chapter 11), meaning that they will now be working to reach an externally determined standard, no longer to outperform their classmates. The idea that everyone can succeed – in systems using grades, potentially all get an "A," and not as a result of grade inflation – will be new to many. The technical level at which these presentations and discussions are conducted will need to be appropriate for the students concerned. Also, with beginning students, this is one of the rare occasions when use of the native language may be justified.

In my experience, learners of just about any kind and any age appreciate being brought into the process from the start, recognizing that they are equal partners in the enterprise, not simply objects to be pushed around, that they have rights, as well as obligations, and that their opinions matter and can influence how a course turns out. It is surprising how often they have useful, sometimes completely unexpected, information to contribute that then helps the whole course run more smoothly than would have been the case if they or the teacher had remained ignorant of each others' concerns and the constraints under which they might be operating. It is worth holding such sessions at regular intervals during a course (also an excellent opportunity for genuinely communicative use of the target language), feedback to the teacher being as important as feedback to the students. The result can be a radical shift from the "us and them" relationship common in many classrooms to one of participatory democracy, mutual aid, and cooperation.

4.9. Mutual Aid and Cooperation

Based mostly on his studies of ants, bees, birds, and mammals in Siberia and Manchuria, Peter Kropotkin (1902/1987) argued in *Mutual Aid: A Factor of Evolution* that forming groups for social purposes, or mutual aid, was a major factor in evolution, *in addition to* competition and struggle within and among species for limited resources and natural selection, the central mechanisms in Darwin's theory. Cooperation among members of a species for the purpose of hunting for food, defense against enemies, protecting the young during the breeding season, and struggle against a harsh environment, e.g., clinging to one another to keep warm during winter or herding closely together for mutual defense when confronting predators, was often the key to survival. Animals, including humans, have always lived in social groups for these purposes, with tribes predating families, which accounts for human survival, while many species physically better equipped for battle have become extinct. The idea that life is inevitably a permanent struggle of each against all, and of survival of the fittest, is a convenient rationalization for the competition inherent in hierarchically organized societies but one that is at odds with the facts.

The validity of Kropotkin's thesis has been increasingly recognized in recent years, e.g., by Dugatkin (1997), Hewetson (1987), McKay (2008), Miller (1976), Purchase

(1996), and the late noted evolutionary biologist, Stephen J. Gould (1997). After discussing Darwin's and Kropotkin's theories, Gould concluded:

> I would hold that Kropotkin's basic argument is correct. Struggle does occur in many modes, and some lead to cooperation among members of a species as the best pathway to advantage for individuals. If Kropotkin overemphasized mutual aid, most Darwinians in Western Europe had exaggerated competition just as strongly. (Gould 1997, p. 20)

Gould urged skepticism when judging any and all claims about human society based on arguments from nature, but continued:

> If Kropotkin drew inappropriate hope for social reform from his concept of nature, other Darwinians had erred just as firmly (and for motives most of us would now decry) in justifying imperial conquest, racism, and oppression of industrial workers as the harsh outcome of natural selection in the competitive mode. (Gould 1997, p. 20)

More recently, some have argued that cooperation and mutual aid are basic, instinctive human values, evidenced, for example, by altruism and spontaneous acts of gallantry, as when, at great personal risk, a passer-by rushes into a burning house or jumps into a fast-moving river to rescue individuals unknown to him or her (see, e.g., chapters in Mansbridge 1990). And it is true that when oppressed peoples have risen up and overthrown coercive state tyrannies of right or left, they have often set about organizing themselves on the basis of free association and cooperation. The complete reorganization of Spanish society by those fighting the combined forces of Franco, Hitler, and Mussolini, and later those of Stalin, during the revolution of 1936–1939, is an example on a large scale (see De Santillan 1937/1996; Leval 1975; Mintz 2013; Orwell 1938/2000), but there have been numerous others down the ages. Certainly, there is nothing natural or inevitable about raw competition in human affairs:

> If authority and restraint are necessary, how are we to explain that in the [so-called] primitive societies which exist today without recourse to authority or government, "freedom but not license is the principle of the group and the characteristic of the individual"?...The history of governmental and class society is at most only 7,000 years old, whereas the primitive communist society has existed since modern man himself appeared on the earth – at the very lowest estimate, for 70,000 years. The social principle in animal societies has existed for a far longer period still. (Hewetson 1987, p. 8)

Converging evidence for the instinctive nature of altruism and cooperative tendencies in humans and other animals, and for Kropotkin's mutual aid thesis, is to be found in the results of experimental studies (e.g., Warneken 2013; Warneken & Tomasello, 2009a,b; Warneken *et al.* 2007) demonstrating spontaneous altruistic behavior in chimps and in human infants as young as 18 months. The altruistic behaviors occur without reward, suggesting that both species are naturally altruistic and that the roots of human altruism run deep. Moreover, the fact that children as young as 18 months evidence instrumental helping without rewards argues against the claim, proposed by some, that altruism is the result of learned behavior, of socially imposed norms. Extrinsic rewards, Warneken and Tomasello (2008) showed, can even *undermine* altruistic tendencies in 20-month-old children. The fact that both species exhibit altruism simultaneously makes it unlikely that human altruism could account for their different evolutionary trajectories. Of special importance in that regard, cleverly designed experiments by Hamman, Warneken, Tomasello, and others have demonstrated that what distinguishes humans from other primates is not altruism per se but that, by age three, children *collaborate* to help one another; they are not limited to instrumental helping (e.g., Hamann *et al.* 2011). Children show a commitment to social goals; chimps do not.

Mutual aid and cooperation are readily apparent in several areas of TBLT, e.g., in its considerable use of collaborative pair work and small group work, and once again independently motivated by findings in language acquisition and general education. The use of supportive peer–peer interaction during the integration of language learning and task completion is consistent with research findings in general education by Barnes (1976/1992) and Barnes and Todd (1977, 1995) on "talking to learn" in first language development and children's subject matter learning at school, and with SLA findings on the role of negotiation for meaning in acquisition (see, especially, Sato 1986, 1988, 1990), captured three decades ago in Hatch's previously quoted famous statement:

> language learning evolves out of learning how to carry on conversations....One learns how to do conversation, one learns how to interact verbally, and out of this interaction syntactic structures are developed. (Hatch 1978, p. 404)

Such collaborative talking to learn is further supported by the considerable body of empirical evidence in favor of the Interaction Hypothesis (briefly described in Chapter 3), now amounting to well over 50 studies, including those reviewed in statistical meta-analyses by Li (2010), Mackey and Goo (2007), and Russell and Spada (2006).

As described in Chapter 10, the relative privacy afforded by the cooperative small group setting is conducive to collaborative conversation for language learning, especially for shy students, and especially for the early stages of work on new tasks, before the confidence is in place for language production in front of the teacher and the whole class. Note that this contrasts with the traditional use of group work – *after* lockstep teaching of declarative knowledge, and *after* whole-class practice – as a way of automatizing proceduralized knowledge more quickly by increasing student talking-time. Task-work in general, and collaborative work on closed, two-way tasks in particular (see Chapter 8), provides the opportunities for interaction and negative feedback, and for both the implicit and explicit learning that successful SLA requires. "Two-way," or "jigsaw," pedagogical tasks are egalitarian in that information is distributed at the outset such that parts are held uniquely by each member of a small group; they fit well with the natural inclination to offer mutual aid in that their successful completion requires students to work together cooperatively, exchanging and integrating that information at the level of the group, in order to accomplish a common purpose.

Students from some cultural backgrounds can initially be skeptical about the value of learning from classmates, having been brought up to believe that the teacher is the only legitimate source of knowledge. A rational explanation of *how* and *why* group practices are beneficial for language learning – especially, but not only, in large classes – plus experiencing the benefits themselves, will, in my experience, rapidly change their attitude. Like so many other things, there is nothing "cultural" about using or not using group work in the classroom. There may be a *tradition* of not using it in some societies, but traditions can quickly change once people realize there are better ways of doing things.

Similarly, students in some societies are raised to believe that life is a rat race and that competition, not cooperation, is the only way ahead. Once again, a rational explanation as to how language learning in TBLT is achieved, and how it is measured, i.e., through task-based, criterion-referenced performance tests (see Chapters 11 and 12), followed by enjoyable experiences of the system in practice, can change attitudes. Students come to understand that to help classmates is to help themselves and that how well a classmate does on a test in no way affects their own chances positively or negatively. On a criterion-referenced test, after all, they are all "competing" against an external criterion or criteria, not with one another, so helping classmates achieve common goals is good for everyone, including their teacher. The purpose of a TBLT course is not for some to do better than others but for all students to succeed.

4.10. Summary

TBLT's philosophical underpinnings consist of a set of nine core principles: *l'education integrale*, learning by doing, individual freedom, rationality, emancipation, learner-centeredness, egalitarianism, participatory democracy, and mutual aid and cooperation. A synergistic relationship exists between the philosophical principles and TBLT's psycholinguistic underpinnings. With very few exceptions, the implications of both converge on a coherent framework for TBLT and a defensible set of criteria for evaluating practice.

It is perfectly possible for individual teachers and whole education systems to implement TBLT even if they disagree with any or all of the philosophical principles because, as explained in Chapter 1, the rationale for TBLT is broad and includes its psycholinguistic underpinnings, relevance to student needs, and functionality. For many educators and students, however, increasingly disillusioned as they are with coercive systems of education in general, and authoritarian classrooms in particular, TBLT's philosophical underpinnings may offer some cause for relief and for optimism that alternatives *are* available.

4.11. Suggested Readings

Auerbach, E.R., & Burgess, D. (1985). The hidden curriculum of survival ESL. *TESOL Quarterly* 19, 3, 475–495.

Avrich, P. (1980). *The Modern School movement*. Princeton, NJ: Princeton University Press.

Crookes, G. (2009). Radical language teaching. In Long, M.H., & Doughty, C.J. (eds.), *Handbook of language teaching* (pp. 595–609). Malden, MA: Wiley-Blackwell.

Gribble, D. (1998). *Real education. Varieties of freedom*. Bristol: Libertarian Education.

Smith, M.P. (1983). *The libertarians and education*. London: George Allen & Unwin.

Smith, M.P. (1989). Kropotkin and technical education: An anarchist voice. In Goodway, D. (ed.), *For anarchism: History, theory, and practice* (pp. 217–234). London: Routledge. Also in The Raven 10, Vol. 3, 2, 1990, 122–138.

Spring, J. (1994). *Wheels in the head: Educational philosophies of authority, freedom, and culture from Socrates to Paulo Freire*. New York: McGraw-Hill.

Suissa, J. (2006). *Anarchism and education. A philosophical perspective*. London: Routledge.

Warneken, F., & Tomasello, M. (2009). The roots of human altruism. *British Journal of Psychology* 100, 3, 455–471.

Wright, N. (1989). *Assessing radical education*. Milton Keynes: Open University Press.

Part Two

Design and Implementation

Chapter 5

Task-Based Needs and Means Analysis

5.1. Why Needs Analysis?

As noted in Chapter 1, among the original motivations for TBLT were the worrisome inconsistency of second language acquisition (SLA) research findings with both traditional approaches to language teaching (LT), and the growing need for relevance and accountability. First, SLA research findings in the 1970s and 1980s were casting serious doubt on the validity of *synthetic* approaches to syllabus design, but equally so, of purely meaning-based *analytic* alternatives (the terms are Wilkins') espoused at the time by Corder, Felix, Prahbu, and most notably, Krashen. Second, it was imperative that

Second Language Acquisition and Task-Based Language Teaching, First Edition. Mike Long.
© 2015 John Wiley & Sons, Inc. Published 2015 by John Wiley & Sons, Inc.

language programs be visibly relevant to learner needs and, thereby, potentially account-able. The role of SLA theory and research findings in motivating TBLT was discussed in Chapters 2 and 3. It is now time to consider a major part of the solution to the rel-evance problem. TBLT provides this by making a carefully conducted task-based learner needs analysis (NA), the first step in course design. NAs are time-consuming and should not be an additional burden placed on teachers' shoulders. Serious LT programs will recognize their importance and assign the work to well-qualified applied linguists, either on permanent staff or contracted especially for the purpose, and/or to teachers with the required expertise temporarily released from other duties.

Those who had been heavily involved in teaching English for specific purposes (ESP) in the United Kingdom, Latin America, Asia, Africa, the Middle East, and elsewhere in the 1970s and 1980s took course *relevance* very seriously. Millions of adult learners around the world pay with their own time and money to acquire the very different *func-tional* language abilities they need, often urgently, to achieve their equally different edu-cational or career goals or to meet immediate social survival needs in a new country, whether as tourists or newly arrived immigrants. Given demonstrably different commu-nicative needs, reliance on the same "general-purpose" textbook series year after year (while for obvious reasons, a practice favored by textbook authors and publishers), and teaching "the language" (sic), not the students (a practice supported by some prominent applied linguists on the grounds that "English is English is English"), do not bear scrutiny.

The first step in LT course design is (or should be) to conduct a NA. In an era of greatly increased student diversity, if "learner-centered" is to mean more than mere rhetorical arm-waving, (a) recognizing individual and group differences and (b) account-ability to learners' needs will both be accorded the importance they deserve. (As described in Chapters 2–4, learner-centeredness in TBLT also has psycholinguistic and philosophical dimensions.) The alternative to needs-based LT is to hope to satisfy the needs of majorities, or, at least, pluralities, of learners through "general-purpose" courses. This approach, however, rides roughshod over minorities in the process and ultimately over the needs and potentialities of the individuals who make up both majorities and minorities. Using the results of a systematic NA as the input to syllabus design is one of the features that distinguishes TBLT as described in this book from all other task-based approaches I am aware of, not to mention task-supported and task-oriented LT, and is a desirable feature of task-based education, in general.

Learner goals and needs can differ widely, both within and across groups. Some students may require advanced proficiency in the language spoken in a country to which they have immigrated, or to which they plan to emigrate, whether voluntarily or because they are forced to do so. How successful they are will have a major impact on their educational and employment opportunities and on those of their families. The new language will likely become the dominant one for their children, and the native language of their grandchildren, who may well lose the family's ancestral language altogether. In contrast, another group may only need to be able to read the professional or scientific literature in their field, which may only be published in English. Other learners may require proficiency in three or all four skills in a second or foreign language, in order to gain access to different kinds of higher education programs overseas, for widely varying occupational purposes, or for vocational training. Still others may be part of a linguistically mixed marriage or domestic partner arrangement. Another group may want Arabic, Hebrew, Tibetan, and so on, for religious reasons, or any number of languages for missionary purposes. And there will be those who would simply like to be able to communicate at an elementary level while on vacation overseas or to establish friendly relations with immigrants moving into their neighborhood.

These and many other language-learning goals will require very different levels of proficiency; different strengths in receptive and productive skills; knowledge of different language varieties, genres, registers, vocabulary, and collocations; and different pragmatic abilities. A NA will identify which goals and communicative language needs are present in particular groups of students and thereby make the appropriate program design and delivery possible. Before getting into the nitty-gritty of NA, further consideration of the daunting variety of reasons why languages are learned today should make the importance of NA clearer.

5.2. Needs Analysis and Learner Diversity

NA is of ever greater importance today due to the increased number and diversity of foreign, and especially second, language learners. Part of the increase is due simply to rapid population growth, but other forces are at work, few of them positive. Two world wars and countless regional conflicts have produced millions of involuntary language learners obliged to seek refuge in countries in which their L1 is not spoken. Millions more involuntary learners have been created by famine, disease, poverty, "ethnic cleansing," deforestation, religious persecution, and government oppression. Climate change will add millions more. Language teachers will be ever busier as long as governments make exploitation and poverty the norm and social upheaval the consequence.

People of all ages, social classes, and educational backgrounds are caught up in such events, with the result that groups once considered nontraditional learners are now viewed as normal in language and literacy classes in the receiving countries. Teachers are growing accustomed to dealing with classes made up of illiterate peasant farmers and their families, doctors, lawyers, and scientists abruptly obliged to seek retraining or reaccreditation in a new land, children faced with learning from school teachers speaking what to them is an incomprehensible language, and traumatized older people suddenly unable even to make simple purchases in shops, much less to explain medical problems to doctors and nurses who may themselves be recent immigrants. Many teachers of English, Dutch, French, German, Spanish, Japanese, Swedish, and other languages now specialize in working with immigrants and refugees. The quality of the work they do is of crucial importance for their students' education, employment, and general well-being. Their own job satisfaction (if seldom the financial rewards) can be equally high.

The number of voluntary language students has also grown rapidly and again reflects an increasingly wide range of student types and needs. These more traditional classroom learners include infants and young children enrolled in bilingual and immersion programs, students undergoing foreign language study in schools and universities (not exactly voluntarily in some cases), adults studying foreign languages to broaden their cultural horizons, for tourism, or because they would like to be able to communicate with the linguistic minorities moving into their neighborhood, international students working toward degrees at overseas universities, missionaries and religiously motivated lay workers on charitable aid projects overseas, participants in numerous international volunteer programs, diplomats and employees of international organizations, such as the United Nations (UN), and non-governmental organizations (NGOs), business people seeking a functional command of a language for a vocational training program or for their current occupational needs, perhaps related to an overseas posting or because they work in the tourist industry, people needing a reading ability in a language to cope with the international academic or professional literature in their field, and finally, the hundreds of millions of unsuspecting citizens the world over who are routinely subjected to a barrage of English-language radio and cable television programming, films, music, newspapers and magazines, as well as government-sponsored radio and television broadcasts of more overt political propaganda.

New categories have emerged, however, even among this second group of mostly voluntary learners. The maintenance or recovery of ancestral, heritage, and community languages is increasingly popular among second-, third-, and fourth-generation immigrants, and more and more programs designed to achieve those goals are becoming available for both children and adults. The vast potential size of this category of learner in some countries in the decades to come is obvious when it is considered that, for example, out of a total population of roughly 313 million people in the United States in 2012, some 60 million spoke a language other than English at home (with an estimated 32 million Spanish speakers easily the largest group).

In addition, although most struggles are far from over and the few successes are in constant danger of reversal, decades and sometimes centuries of resistance by workers and indigenous peoples to racism, religious persecution, foreign occupation, and state oppression have won some ethnolinguistic minorities the freedom, and others a license, at least, to attempt to revive and use their own languages and dialects as a crucial step in what most hope will eventually be their complete liberation from tyranny. (For some detailed case studies, see Fishman 1991; Skutnabb-Kangas 2000; Skutnabb-Kangas & Cummins 1988; Skutnabb-Kangas & Phillipson 1994.) Basque, Catalan, Hebrew, Hawaiian, Irish Gaelic, Navajo, Nahuatl, Tzotzil, Sami, Quechua, Inuktitut, Welsh, Mayan, Navaho, Maori, Pitjantjatjara, and Warlpiri are well-known examples. These and numerous other "minority" languages are now being learned by children and adults on five continents in everything from remote Koori schools in the vast Australian outback, through small evening community classes in church basements and immersion education in autonomous worker-controlled Basque school cooperatives (Garagorri & Eguilior 1983; *Ikastola Irekia* n.d.; Sanchez Carrion "Txepetx," 1991), to large state-supported programs reflecting national language policies, such as that of Australia (Lo Bianco 1989; and see papers in Grabe 1994 for national and regional reviews).

In some cases, the prospects for language revival or reversing language shift (Fishman 1991) are bleak. In others, generally situations of stable bilingualism involving at least some domains where the use of the threatened language is required, there are grounds for optimism. The existence of enough adult speakers, especially women, who wish their children to learn the language concerned, is the critical factor, according to Fishman, who finds it to be

> the heart of the intergenerational transmission mechanism: the normal, daily, repetitive and intensively socializing and identity-forming functioning of home, family and neighborhood. (Fishman 1991, p. 162)

There are numerous other cases, however, especially those of oppressed indigenous peoples, where even the most favorable parental attitudes and the most skilled intervention by applied linguists will fail unless accompanied by a viable program for economic and political, not just linguistic, autonomy for the community concerned. The resurgence of Catalan and Basque after the end of the Franco dictatorship in 1975 constitutes a model for ethnolinguistic minorities in many parts of the world.

The above developments have resulted not only in a vast increase in the numbers of people seeking instruction in an indigenous language or in a foreign or second one but also in greater numbers of adult learners, and for many groups a greater seriousness of purpose. The importance of literacy, advanced functional language proficiency, and high-quality language instruction has not gone unnoticed by the world's governments, military-industrial complexes, and intelligence agencies (see, e.g., Clifford & Fischer 1990), multinational corporations, education systems, labor unions, health-care providers and purveyors of other social services, and by the learners themselves. Thus, while both major parties have continued to make Draconian funding cuts to public education and social programs since the 1980s, Republican and Democrat administrations in the United States have established National Foreign Language Resource Centers and National Flagship language programs at several universities, and a university-affiliated language center, the Center for Advanced Study of Language (CASL) at the University of Maryland, devoted to basic and applied research, all designed to upgrade the quality of foreign language instruction in the United States, and devoted increased funding for consortia of US military and diplomatic programs for their own personnel during the same period.

Many schools and universities are hastening to introduce new foreign languages as one way of adapting to shifting centers of world economic power and the creation of new trading blocks and patterns of international commerce. Thus, in a not uncommon pattern, partly as a response to Spanish entry into the European Economic Community (but also because of its avowed internationalist perspective), all 1500 students at Almen Ikastola, a worker-controlled Basque-immersion school in the famous Mondragon Cooperative Federation, receive 20 minutes a day of English instruction from age six (rising to three hours a week at age ten), 90 minutes of Spanish a week from age eight (rising to two hours a week at age ten), two hours a week in either French or German from age 14, and two hours a week in whichever language, French or German, was not chosen at 14, starting at age 16 (Zubizarreta, p.c., 1994). Similarly, many Australian primary and secondary schools have reduced their traditional emphasis on European languages and upgraded and extended offerings in Japanese, Indonesian, and Chinese. The rapidity of the changes has sometimes created problems, as shown by a survey by Nicholas (1993) in which some two-thirds of Australian school teachers of Japanese reported that their own as yet limited command of the language meant they were unable to conduct whole lessons in the L2.

At the adult level, several Australian universities now provide undergraduate majors in such subjects as law, economics, and commerce, combined with an Asian language, and at least two, the University of Central Queensland at Rockhampton and Griffiths University in Brisbane, offer Japanese immersion B.Ed. degree programs for primary and secondary school teachers, respectively. The signing by the Canadian, US, and Mexican governments of the euphemistically named North Atlantic Free Trade Agreement (NAFTA) in 1993 is likely to result in many new English, French, and Spanish for vocational and occupational purposes programs (Tucker 1994). The spread of content-and-language integrated learning (CLIL) through the public education systems of several European countries (see, e.g., Muñoz 2007; Naves 2009) and other parts of the world, with knock-on programs in increasing numbers of universities, has produced yet another group of adult learners – secondary- and tertiary-level teachers of mathematics, history, social studies, law, medicine, and so on – who need to improve their command of (usually) English, French, or German, in order to deliver their regular content courses though that language to students with whom they share an L1 but who are also non-native speakers (NNSs) of the medium of instruction.

Most of the above-mentioned "new" categories of learners (by no means an exhaustive list) have really populated language courses for a long time, but in less noticeable numbers and different proportions. Their increased presence today makes for more heterogeneous populations of classroom students overall. They differ in many ways capable of affecting language acquisition in or out of classrooms, including age, race, class, gender, first language, interests, language-learning purpose, cultural background, social status, attitudes, motivation, self-concept, language aptitude, memory, intelligence, educational achievement, literacy, previous foreign or second language-learning experience, cognitive style, and prior exposure and current access to the target language(s). The status of, and relationships among, the learners' native language, the target language(s), and other languages in the environment also differ. Some of the languages involved have primarily religious or cultural significance for small groups of speakers, while others serve as a lingua franca in the surrounding community. Some are both spoken and written and used in government, education, law, and commerce, while (for some speakers, at least) others have a reduced set of functions, for example, for religious ceremonies or dance chants, and little or no literature.

In sum, the same forces that increased the number of language learners in the world have also increased their diversity. Thus, while it was always unrealistic to propose a single monolithic approach, brand-name method, set of materials, or test battery for all students, such a proposal would be even less defensible today. What is needed instead is a flexible approach embodying a set of psycholinguistically and philosophically motivated principles whose realization will vary systematically at the level of *pedagogic procedures* to take account of individual differences among teachers, learners, languages, and settings. Student diversity means that wherever time and resources permit, it will be incumbent upon program designers to conduct a careful learner NA before implementing a new course, as well as to monitor possibly changing needs while the course is underway. When so much time and money is invested in LT, and when the outcome is so crucial for so many people, it should come as no surprise that those who invest time and money in the effort – governments, funding agencies, employers, and the learners themselves – expect courses to be relevant to their needs. In an era of shrinking resources, there is an increasing demand for accountability in public life, and language education is no exception. Off-the-peg, general-purpose language courses, sometimes known less flatteringly as languages for no, or nebulous, purposes (LNP) courses, are less and less likely to suffice, if they ever did. For many of today's students, language learning is simply too important.

5.3. Doubts about Needs Analysis

Before proceeding to a consideration of the nuts and bolts of NA methodology in Chapters 6 and 7, some caveats are in order, for by no means everyone is as positive about NA or specific-purpose course design as the discussion so far might suggest. A few reputable applied linguists have claimed that NA is unnecessary or even counterproductive.

5.3.1. General English for all

To begin with, it has been argued (see, e.g., Quirk *et al.* 1972, pp. 13–14) that while specialized varieties of a language clearly differ in measurable ways, they equally clearly all contain a common core of sentence patterns, verb tenses, and so on. On those grounds, some have suggested that teaching one variety of a language, say, "general" English, therefore, is as good as another, and that modeling specialized varieties is either unnecessary or can or should at least wait until after the common core has been dealt with. As Bloor and Bloor (1986) pointed out, however, using the same logic, if the common core is present in any variety, it can be acquired by presenting the relevant one for a particular group of learners, which has the added advantage of simultaneously exposing them to any peculiar properties it has. Moreover, Bloor and Bloor argued, to the extent that language is either learned or retrieved in context, presentation of appropriately contextualized language samples for specific groups of students should make acquisition easier and more relevant (as discussed in Chapter 3, a view reflected in TBLT's methodological principle (MP) 2: Promote learning by doing). This position finds some support in research findings by Selinker and Douglas (1985, 1989) and others suggesting that some IL processes, such as transfer, avoidance, and (putative) fossilization, operate differentially in (rather vaguely defined) "discourse domains," of which a general "life story domain" and a work-related "technical domain" supposedly constitute two.

5.3.2. The *ex post facto* process syllabus

In a second potential argument against NA, advocates of process syllabuses (see Section 8.2.7) maintain that a syllabus is the product of negotiation by teachers and learners, and in a very real sense can only be described and its content analyzed after a course is over (Candlin 1984). It is easy to see how attempts to determine course content based on a pre-course NA would be considered very optimistic from the process syllabus perspective. For now, suffice it to say that redefining the definition of syllabus, as process syllabus advocates do – from what was planned to an evaluation of what was actually done after a course is over – makes sense in an obvious way, but (a) leaves open the very real possibility that what was done may not have been relevant, or optimal, unless one believes that teachers and students are more reliable sources of information than domain experts on how to meet their needs, as opposed to helping identify what those needs are, and (b) is better thought of as an additional source of information, not a substitute for a traditional syllabus. We return to a fuller articulation and critique of the process syllabus in Chapter 8.

5.3.3. Felt needs or objective needs?

Third, some critics dispute the technical ability and/or the right of course designers to assess learners' needs objectively, in some cases further suggesting that learners' wants, or "felt needs," are more important than their needs as assessed by others, or "perceived needs," in cases where the two conflict (see, e.g., Benesch 1996; and for useful discussion, Berwick 1989). By way of response, while the technical quality (reliability and validity) of a NA will undoubtedly vary with the expertise of those conducting it and the options available to them, as will the quality of any aspect of LT, the solution to poor NA is improvement, not abandoning the effort. As for the relative importance of real and felt needs, course designers and teachers are as ethically and professionally responsible for providing what a careful NA tells them is appropriate for their students as providers of any professional service are for prescribing what careful diagnoses tell them is appropriate for their patients or clients.

It has become fashionable to decry expertise in general in some quarters, due to the power those who have it can exercise over those who do not, medical expertise being a favorite target. The real problem is surely not expertise itself, however, but the abuse of power by a minority of callous professionals, and in the medical example, in societies where health care is privatized, exploitation of patients by profit-gouging hospital corporations and insurance companies. As a final safeguard, in most cases (although not in all, to be sure), it is open for patients or language learners to seek a second opinion and/or to vote with their feet if they dislike what is proposed. Needless to say, as proposed in Chapter 6, course designers or teachers who detect a mismatch between "felt" and "objectively perceived" needs should check to ensure that the NA has not missed something, discuss the discrepancy with the students, and reconcile the two as sensitively as possible, just as they would when methodological or pedagogic preferences were at odds with practice.

5.3.4. Learner heterogeneity

Fourth, it is claimed that needs in some classes are too heterogeneous to make NA worthwhile, and also that some populations simply have no L2 needs at all, or at least, not ones analyzable or predictable at any useful level (see, e.g., Willis 1993). Responses to heterogeneity of needs within a class will be dealt with in Chapters 8–10 (see also Long 1985a). With respect to the latter problem, young children and some school-age foreign language learners are frequently cited examples of learners with no needs, or no easily predictable needs, and there certainly are cases, such as children in a bilingual Japanese or Korean kindergarten, of populations with no current needs for the L2 and/ or whose future needs for English or some other language are unclear at best, and could ultimately range from great to none at all. It may be possible to give some minimal shape to such programs, based on the experiences of similar groups, on trends in demographics, education, and employment opportunities, or on information from parents about their plans for themselves or their children. Education in Japan (and South Korea), for example, is sufficiently structured – with systems of "feeder" schools, clear pecking orders among universities, and long established university English entrance examination formats, beginning to change as a result of the Japanese Ministry of Education's English curriculum reform – that many children's educational career paths are broadly predictable quite early on. Several English-language NAs for Japanese secondary school pupils have appeared (e.g., Ogata 1992; Orikasa 1989). In cases where no clear predictions are possible, and there certainly are some, especially where the students are young children, other aspects of TBLT, including materials and MPs, are still relevant and have been shown to be effective (see, e.g., Shintani 2011, 2013; Shintani & Ellis 2010). Preparing for such courses is a TBLT course designer's dream, in fact, as they are free to choose high-interest, age-appropriate pedagogic tasks without some of the usual constraints a NA typically brings, and to deliver them using TBLT methodology and pedagogy.

In any case, the difficulty or impossibility of conducting a useful NA in some situations does not constitute an argument against NA for the vast majority of learners, who generally do have definable needs, nor one for a return to courses based on a linguistic analysis of "the" target language and the inevitable corollary, a synthetic syllabus. The psycholinguistic considerations outlined in Chapters 2 and 3, alone, would preclude that. It can reasonably be argued that almost every learner has needs, that every course should therefore be viewed as LT for specific purposes, especially courses for adults, and that what varies is simply the degree of specificity with which those needs can be identified or met, ranging from minimal to very high.

5.3.5. Surface linguistic features or underlying technical competence?

What might appear to be a fifth, indirect challenge to conventional NA is the argument by Hutchinson and Waters (1987), and elsewhere, discussed approvingly by Swales (1985b, pp. 175–176 and 188–189) that specialized subject-specific LT materials are unnecessary because what specific-purpose LT should focus on is the underlying competence students will need to cope with their new academic program or occupation, not the surface performance features of the new linguistic repertoire itself. Hutchinson and Waters pointed out that even native speakers (NSs) entering a program of study in a field that is new to them, e.g., electrical engineering, typically have no experience of the new subject itself or of the specialized language associated with it yet are eventually able to cope with classes in electrical engineering. What is good for the NS should be good for the NNS, so the languages for specific purposes (LSP) teacher's job is to bring the NNS' non-area-specific underlying competence up to scratch – not to NS levels but to levels adequate for them to cope with new information in the area of eventual specialization. Subject-specific materials will be unnecessary for this, Hutchinson and Waters claim. Rather, with extensive use of pair and group work, students need to do simple technical problems on general topics in their chosen field, which they have to solve using English. The problems and accompanying spoken or written texts can be drawn from popular sources (specialist to non-specialist or non-specialist to non-specialist communication) in the general area of work or study, for the aim is to practice students in the interpretative strategies they will need to handle new information and problem-solving in their field, not to rehearse them in the specialized technical language of that field, in which few materials writers or teachers are likely to be competent in any case. While originally proposed for overseas students entering technical education in the United Kingdom, Hutchinson and Waters claimed their argument held for LSP in general, an extension about which Swales (1985b, p. 176) was more skeptical.

Neither Hutchinson and Waters nor Swales denied the usefulness of analyses of learners' communicative needs, but given what they thought should be the focus of classroom instruction, they questioned the utility of detailed analyses of subject-specific target discourse for the purpose of materials design. The emphasis in NA, they suggested, should be on the kinds of communication learners would have to handle in their field of work or study, on how to solve problems involving new information using knowledge they already possessed. The informational content of pedagogic materials should still be relevant to the students' area of specialization, but in an effort to respond to students' interests, not because of any technical language or information they might contain.

5.3.6. The dark side?

Finally, there is an alleged dark side to NA, one that has led some to oppose it and/or courses based upon it. This is the claim, expressed, for example, by Widdowson (1983, 1987), that special-purpose courses ostensibly designed to meet learners' needs result in narrow language training, restricted competence, and few or no productive, creative, or transferable linguistic abilities. Students are outfitted with a linguistic straitjacket, so to speak. General-purpose courses are preferable, Widdowson claimed, because they offer education, not training, and broader language competence. Similarly, due princi-pally to TBLT's focus on task-based NA as the starting point in course design, another well-known British applied linguist who read an early draft of an article on task-based approaches (Long & Crookes 1992) pronounced our ideas as "social engineering of the worst sort," akin to Margaret Thatcher's policies toward the British working class. If it ever became popular, he said, TBLT would condemn poor people to dead-end jobs by limiting their access to the L2 to just enough of the language to toss hamburgers, sweep the streets, or clean hotel rooms. A variant of the criticism is that TBLT focuses exclu-sively on referential tasks (an allegation that is simply untrue), whereas, we are reminded, language also serves interpersonal functions, for play and for phatic communication.

While there is, to my knowledge, no evidence against the idea that task-related lan-guage abilities are transferable, and some (very preliminary) evidence that they are (Benson 2013; Najar 1992; and see Chapter 8 and Section 11.4), this is clearly a poten-tially serious problem. It is certainly easy to imagine how "relevance" could provide thin cover for "social engineering of the worst sort." For example, unscrupulous state agencies or employers might commission foreign language courses designed to teach recently arrived immigrants or unemployed local residents a rudimentary command of a lan-guage minimally sufficient for them to perform menial work on terms others are no longer willing to accept, and little else. A large resort hotel, the major employer in an area heavily dependent on tourism, such as Hawaii, for example, might make a (tax-deductible) "charitable" donation to a nearby public school that was desperate for funding from any source after years of defunding of public education, the money to be used to provide young school leavers with a course in, say, "Japanese for hotel workers." The course might focus exclusively on a very narrow set of job-related linguis-tic objectives sufficient for porters, restaurant workers, cleaning staff, or golf caddies to understand simple requests and commands in the language of the hotel's most fre-quent overseas guests, but nothing else. It is easy to imagine young men and women becoming trapped in such jobs, prevented from obtaining further education or better work by the long hours, low wages, and lack of benefits endemic in the tourist industry and/or due to their limited command of the language in question. In my view, however, while such exploitation is a very real possibility, it would be better seen as the result of

Machiavellian government policy, pernicious business practices, and gross dereliction of duty by educational administrators, not as the result of NA or of specific-purpose course design per se. It would involve an abuse of NA but is neither its inevitable corollary nor reason to forego its positive effects.[1]

In response to the criticism, I would take migrant workers as an example and ask the following question. Is designing an initial course to meet such learners' communicative needs – basic referential communicative needs if their needs are basic and referential – social engineering, or would social engineering be delivering a general-purpose course *not* designed to satisfy those or anyone else's particular needs, because it would leave them unable to do what they need to be able to do? Is designing courses that meet learners' needs not far more "empowering," to use a rather hackneyed term, than serving up weeks of "generic" LT, complete with bland reading passages about what happened when John and Mary went for a walk in the park (followed by intellectually demanding questions about where they went for a walk, whether they went for a walk in the park, what they were wearing, whether they saw any birds, and so on)? How useful is it to have students read trouble-free generic dialogues supposedly showing someone ordering food in a restaurant, speaking to a bank teller, or making a reservation on the phone, when research has shown time and time again (see, e.g., Bartlett 2005; Cathcart 1984; Granena 2008; Chapters 7 and 9) that such models typically bear little resemblance to how people really do either, followed by metalinguistic work and/or drills on the lexis and grammar points contained in the texts? Is reading what tend to be stilted "simplified" versions of third parties (often cardboard stereotypes) talking *about* life not far more likely to doom learners to dead-end jobs, if they can get them at all with the poor command of the L2 they typically take away from such courses, than helping students actually learn to *do* things like describe their work history at a job interview, order food in a restaurant, open a bank account, or make or take a telephoned dinner reservation?

I would argue that by often graduating students with as few functional abilities as those with which they began a course, it is advocates of supposedly generic, synthetic, linguistically based syllabuses who risk leaving students vulnerable to social engineering. Conversely, if a NA is task-based and well executed, what is taught in task-based social survival courses for such students can be much needed, immediately usable, and far more relevant to poor people's lives. An example is in order.

Tens of thousands of newly arrived Latino migrant workers wait shivering in supermarket parking lots in cities all over the United States on freezing winter mornings hoping someone will hire them for a day's work. These so-called "day laborers" need to be able to recognize the skill-sets sought by the owners of small construction and landscaping firms who shout from the windows of their pick-up trucks as they pull in, looking to exploit the cheap labor available from the desperate workers who swarm around their vehicles in the hope that this is their lucky day, when they will be chosen. The workers need to be able to bargain when they are offered less than the already derisory US minimum wage for what is usually hard physical labor, and to reach a verbal agreement about lunch breaks and transportation to and from the job site. Then, if, as sometimes happens, the contractor refuses to pay them at all at the end of the day,

---

[1] For a procedure for task-based NA in the tourism industry, see Long (2013c). See also O'Neill and Hatoss (2003).

confident that few non-English-speaking migrant workers will dare seek redress through the court system, or have the means to do so, they need to have the language required to demand what is owed them.

Migrant day laborers in the United States are just one example of learners who need to satisfy very basic referential communicative needs as quickly as possible; language for play and for phatic communication can come later. Moreover, task-based instruction need not cease once basic needs are satisfied; it is important to remember – "first" does not mean "only." I believe the same considerations justify an initially utilitarian focus in task-based courses designed to prepare graduate students to handle lectures, domain-specific journal articles, and lab sessions at an overseas university, consular officers to conduct visa interviews at an embassy overseas, or physicians volunteering for an emergency international relief program to elicit a patient's medical history in what may be a very different cultural, as well as linguistic, not to mention stressful, environment. The principle probably applies to task-based instruction in most educational domains beyond LT.

While some oppose the very idea of NA, most applied linguists and practicing language teachers require no convincing of its importance and are simply interested in improving the way it is done. Experienced teachers (and many students) know that general-purpose courses are inadequate for people with specialized needs, which is to say, most people. Even within a supposedly specialized area like English for academic purposes (EAP), some skills and tasks are generalizable, but others are not specialized enough:

> At one point we thought we had the answers…After completing our needs assessments, we offered instruction in note taking, summary writing, general reading skills (such as "comprehension"), and the research paper. But as we begin to reexamine each of those areas, we find that though some generalizations can be made about the conventions and skills in academia, the differences among them may be greater than the similarities; for discipline, audience and context significantly influence the language required. Students must therefore read somewhat different material in each academic discipline they encounter. (Johns 1988, p. 55)

Illustrating with summary writing, the research paper, note-taking and problem-solving, Johns noted that research had shown that EAP task-types can vary considerably according to such factors as academic discipline, student level, professor, lecture format, course text, and expert–novice status. The same is true with task-types in English for science and technology (EST), English for occupational purposes (EOP), vocational English as a second language (VESL), and survival English programs. It is time to move on from arguments about whether NA is justified. It clearly is, and once this is recognized, and given that language teachers may initially know little or nothing about their students' specialist communicative domain(s), the question arises of how to find out, and which unit(s) of analysis to employ for the purpose.

5.4. The Growth of Needs Analysis

Although it is not always called that, NA has long been a given in the professions and in the provision of many other social services. A physician asks questions, takes X-rays, and runs tests to determine what is wrong with a patient, i.e., conducts a medical diagnosis, before prescribing a treatment. Engineers and architects study clients' space and functional requirements before drawing up plans for a new building. These are examples of NA. What the physician recommends may also be constrained by such factors as medical ethics or other health problems from which the patient may be suffering. The architect's proposal will take into account such factors as rock and soil conditions, zoning regulations, and the time, funding, space, technical expertise, and equipment available. In L2 course design, the study of these limiting conditions and of the modifications required to implement a project appropriately for local circumstances is known as *means analysis* (see Section 5.6).

5.4.1. The Council of Europe's unit credit system

NA and means analysis are more recent in LT (for overviews, see Berwick 1989; Brindley 1984, 1989; Brown 2009; Chambers 1980; Hawkey 1980, 1983; Long 2005b, 2013b; Mackay 1978; Swales 1985a,b; Van Hest & Oud-de-Glas 1990; West 1994). An early realization of their importance was triggered by the arrival of increasing numbers of international students at British universities in the 1960s and 1970s. An initially small circle of applied linguists charged with helping them develop sufficient English to cope with their studies in what were often specialized scientific fields quickly realized the need to gather information on the language, and uses of language, required for them to be successful in those fields. They made NA a priority, followed by the development of appropriate, usually locally written, materials. The history of the Special English Language Materials for Overseas University Students (SELMOUS) group, subsequently renamed British Association of Lecturers in English for Academic Purposes (BALEAP), is documented in Jordan (2002).

Another major impetus was provided in the 1970s and 1980s by the suddenly greater flexibility which formation of the European Economic Community, or "Common Market," provided corporations and individual citizens of member countries to cross national and linguistic frontiers for trade or employment. The workers concerned often intended to return home after a fixed period of a few months or years, and so were not necessarily inclined to learn English, French, German, and so on. Rather, they were often interested in just enough, and the right kind of, English, French, or German for their work and to satisfy basic communicative needs. Some, such as bankers, sales representatives, middle managers, and office staff for corporations and international organizations, also knew they might be posted to third and fourth countries during their careers, making learning whole languages an even more unrewarding prospect.

Accordingly, the Council of Europe sought to establish a non-language-specific "unit credit system" that could apply across languages and countries, which segmented adult learners' communicative needs into a number of well-defined units of language work that could also apply across languages and countries (see, e.g., Trim *et al.* 1973). The need for cross-linguistically valid analyses encouraged the use of potentially universal semantic or functional categories, since workers in different countries presumably needed to express the same meanings, even if particular languages encoded them in different forms. As described in Chapter 7, this stimulated important work on notional syllabuses (e.g., Wilkins 1976) and related work for school-age learners (e.g., Van Ek 1976).

The relationship between learners' communicative needs and notional-functionalism was not unidirectional but symbiotic. An orientation toward meaning and communication in the linguistic description fed energy back into the growth of NA. If language ability was to be defined in terms of meanings that people could communicate, it made sense to measure and define learners' target proficiency, or communicative needs, in such terms, as well. Whereas it was usually not at all clear whether a learner required a particular structure, it was thought to be relatively straightforward to establish whether they needed to express time, space, sequence or duration, or to request, offer, decline, hypothesize or define, with whom, in which modalities, with roughly what level of formality and politeness, and so on.

General language courses and units defined in structural terms were obviously not the answer. The problem was that while German automobile mechanics might not require anything like a complete command of French for a two-year assignment in Lyons, a typical general-purpose French course would not provide them with the specialized French that they certainly would require. Most obviously, they would not learn the technical lexicon involved, but also not the appropriate register and speech acts (direct, explain, instruct, etc.) required to talk to co-workers (French mechanics) in a noisy repair bay, or the register and speech acts (apologize, deny, offer, etc.) for dealing with impatient French owners of German luxury cars experiencing engine trouble. A German manager or sales representative for the same car manufacturer would need to be able to perform some of the same functions in French, but also many different ones. In terms of tasks, he or she might have to deliver sales pitches for new models, purchase advertizing and exhibition space, and negotiate contracts with importers and dealers. An Italian chef in Edinburgh might initially need little English at all if he or she shared accommodation with Italian co-workers from the same restaurant, spoke mostly Italian in the kitchen, and played for an expatriate Italian soccer team at the weekend. He or she would need to converse in the local variety of English fluently enough, however, when doing his or her first tasks of the day: buying fresh food for the restaurant at the market, discussing quality and price, and inquiring about expected delivery times. Later, his or her language needs might greatly expand if he or she began to make Scottish friends.

As his contribution to the work of the Council of Europe applied linguistics team for the unit credit system project, Richterich (1972) initially devised a product-oriented procedure for analyzing learners' predictable objective needs, as opposed to their subjective needs, felt needs, or wants (for discussion, see Berwick 1989, p. 55; Brindley 1989, p. 70). Following Chambers (1980), the approach is often referred to as target situation analysis (TSA), contrasted with present situation analysis (PSA), which assesses learners' current abilities. (For a discussion of the relationship between current abilities and future needs, see McDonough 1994.) TSA, as defined by Chambers (1980, p. 29), focused primarily on identifying learners' long-term communicative needs by entering the target situation and collecting data on the functions, forms, and frequencies of the kinds of communication that occur there, from which a selection was later made for teaching "on some pragmatic pedagogic basis." Analysts need to keep their eyes on the ball, Chambers argued, and, although they must be taken into account, not be unduly sidetracked by constraints on program design. Constraints, which must be monitored as a course progresses, include such matters as (often changing) short- and medium-term needs, e.g., fluctuating learner interests in L2 use in various social domains. The analyst must also be wary of competing, sometimes inaccurate, views of needs emanating from sources with some useful knowledge of a situation, but often incomplete knowledge, e.g., employers who know something about what their employees have to do, but (usually) little about the language they need to do it, or who may even be out of touch with what really happens on the factory floor altogether (or hotel floor; Jasso-Aguilar 1999/2005; and see Chapters 6 and 7 for further discussion). Chambers (1980, p. 30) was clear about priorities:

> Needs determined by TSA are the real needs, which all efforts should be made to fulfill; constraints limit the attainment of those aims and should as far as is possible be minimized.

Richterich's system was for use by experts before a course began and took as its starting point the language situations in which a particular type of worker would be involved, subsequently broken down into the participants, or agents, communicative functions, objects and means, as well as many subcategories of each. Later versions of Richterich's work (Richterich 1979; Richterich & Chancerel 1978) were more process-oriented, to be conducted as a course progressed, and involved both experts and learners. Working with learners and employers, programs would ideally build up student profiles over time, along with a bank of curricular options to satisfy typical needs, and then allow learners to negotiate the content and procedures for a particular course.

5.4.2. Munby's Communication Needs Processor (CNP) and its critics

A more formal version of this general approach to TSA was Munby's Communication Needs Processor (CNP; Munby 1978, 1984), a model influenced by Halliday's writings on language and meaning potential (e.g., Halliday 1975) and by North American work on communicative competence (Hymes 1971, 1974). In Munby's system, the first step was to develop a profile of students' communicative language needs by gathering information about the (vocational, educational, occupational, etc.) field for which the L2 was required, or purposive domain, and the institutional and psychosocial settings in which learners would be operating. Next came information about their communicative purposes, social relationships and roles, and instrumentality (medium, mode, and channel), and about language use in that field. Then followed the learners' current and target proficiency level in different skills, the (standard/non-standard) variety or dialect required, as well as target communicative events, for example, writing term papers, conducting religious services, or making a sales presentation (in TBLT, roughly equivalent to, although sometimes larger than, target task-*types*), and needed interactional styles, or communicative key. From this detailed description, applied linguists (not an algorithm) then derived a list of language functions and skills, and finally, again on the basis of their intuitions, their linguistic realizations. This output specified the syllabus content, although the designer would still have sequencing and other work to do in order to transform the whole into a pedagogic syllabus.

Productive use of the CNP was reported by several practitioners (e.g., Hawkey 1983, 1984; Roberts 1981). The approach was harshly criticized by others, however. Davies denounced it as simplistic and part of a

> sterile reductionist trend in applied linguistics which promotes a belief in blueprints, in simple all-embracing answers to the real and difficult and probably intractable problems of language learning and teaching. (Davies 1981, p. 332)

He pointed to CNP users' dependence on their own intuitions when it came to specifying linguistic syllabus content and also to the lack of empirical support for the model. Coffey (1984) found it overcomplicated and static. Brumfit (1979) objected to Munby's ignoring the way that, in his view, learners' personal needs determined language use, and for assuming NAs could be conducted a priori by experts and in isolation from other educational issues. Widdowson (1981) castigated the model, and subsequently, NAs done that way in general (Widdowson 1983, 1987), maintaining that they produced lists of skills and functions that could only be of value if their role in discourse, or what the learner did with them, was also specified, that Munby's model's atomization of language precluded that, and that the whole approach said nothing about how the end product was acquired. Brindley (1984) questioned Munby's (deliberate) exclusion of affective and cognitive learner characteristics, such as motivation and learning style, from the analysis, as well as teaching resources and pedagogic options (see also Mead 1982), and also Munby's assumption that an adequate analysis could be conducted without the learner's direct involvement. Coleman (1988, p. 156) objected to Munby's "idealization of the individual and unwarranted generalization from the individual to the group." It was impractical to study individuals' needs in large organizations, Coleman argued, and even the needs of different groups were not necessarily homogeneous and static, but changed, and were influenced by those of other groups with whom they interacted. For example, university lecturers with insufficient English reading ability to use English source materials were unlikely to assign such materials to their own students.

Some of these criticisms were arguably less refutations of Munby's views than reflections of different assumptions about the relevant dimensions of NA. It is true that needs are in the eyes of the beholder, perceived differently according to who is looking (see Berwick 1989). However, if both learners and outside experts agree that A, B, and C are among the "language situations" (physics lectures, job interviews, etc.) in which the learners have to be able to participate, and if the experts have not imposed what they perceive as needs on learners, but consulted with them, then what is required in those "language situations" – what Hutchinson and Waters (1987, p. 55) call "necessities" – is arguably not going to change much, if at all, as a function of "personal needs," learner attitudes, motivation, learning style, or what Hutchinson and Waters (1987, p. 57) call "wants." Those factors will be relevant at other stages of program design, of course, especially where methodology and pedagogy are concerned, but Munby was purporting to deal with the selection of syllabus content – and an idealized description – not with methodology and pedagogy.

With respect to criticisms of the sources of information utilized, as Richterich (1979) noted, many learners have little or no idea of their future language needs and little linguistic awareness in general, which would seem to justify, if not require, generalizations and predictions based on surveys of language use by groups of similar learners. Moreover, if it were really necessary to wait to involve each new group of learners in every NA, input from them could only feed into any materials written for their course with difficulty. Writing materials overnight for classroom use the next day is not unknown, but is unsatisfactory. It would also mean that generalizations about learners or "language situations" were either impossible or limited. Yet that is clearly not the case. It would be a foolish designer who, on learning that next year's intake were to be (say) Arabic speakers starting English-medium university courses in subjects X, Y, and Z, did not consult the previous year's experiences with such learners and/or the extensive documentation of prior NAs and descriptions of target discourse for subjects X, Y, and Z that have been published by applied linguists at King Faizel, Khartoum, Abdul Azziz, Yarmouk, and Sultan Al Quaboos universities, among others (e.g., Arden-Close 1993; Flowerdew 1993; Zughoul and Hussein 1985; and for review, Swales 1984; Swales & Mustafa 1984), and who instead set out to reinvent the wheel. Groups of students will obviously each be unique in some respects, as will individuals within the groups, but they will certainly also share a great many needs in common, and the tasks posed such students by, say, lecture courses in biology or chemistry are unlikely to change greatly from one year to the next, except with respect to the kinds of technology employed in their delivery and in student note-taking.

The issues with respect to the frequent heterogeneity of needs within large organizations raised by Coleman are legitimate practical concerns in the real world of NA, in my experience found even in much smaller organizations than the case about which he writes, Indonesia's Hasanuddin University, with its 140 administrative units, 1000 staff, and 11,500 students. Coleman conducted what was effectively a language audit (see Section 6.2.6) of Hasanuddin, although not called that, which showed minimal use of English reading materials, even in science and technology fields, where, objectively, they were obviously needed, and despite the fact that roughly 80% of the books in the University's library were in English. A study of the needs of individual faculty members or students at Hasannudin would have appeared to show little or no need for English. Even "required" readings in English that appeared on some syllabuses turned out not really to be required, Coleman discovered, as most staff could not handle English materials themselves, most students simply refused to read English (or very much at all – library use was virtually nonexistent), relying almost exclusively on lectures and lecture notes delivered in Indonesian instead, and most staff did not wish to alienate students by forcing the issue.

Coleman suggested that in large organizations, at least, there should be two stages to a NA. First, patterns of current and projected language use by different target groups in the institution should be established, i.e., a language audit conducted, which would allow identification of which groups (e.g., the lecturers) influence others' (e.g., the students') L2 use currently and are likely to do so in the future. Only when such groups have been identified, Coleman maintained, can it be known on whose subjective and objective needs the NA should focus in stage two. At Hasannudin, it was decided to devote the finite EAP teaching resources first to working on developing basic study and library skills, and then reading skills, among first-year undergraduates. The hope was that when some of those students were later employed as lecturers at Hasannudin (a university which hired most of its staff from among its own graduates), they would have a different attitude toward library use and L2 reading and would pass that attitude on to their students through what they required in their courses.

Coleman's insights are valuable and will be returned to later, but some of his criticisms of Munby's approach are less convincing. Based on his experiences at Hasannudin, Coleman claimed that Munby's CNP was impractical because it was too labor-intensive and time-consuming for use with large institutions, yet those appear to be practical limitations on use of Munby's system, not flaws in the system itself. Coleman (1988, p. 156) further criticized Munby for assuming that the identity of those whose needs are to be analyzed is known at the outset (arguing for two-stage NAs), the unwarranted generalization from the individual to the group, and for assuming "there is a one-to-one relationship between the identification of needs and ways of satisfying them" (p. 155). These three issues reflect valuable practical insights from Coleman about identifying appropriate sources of information for NAs and selecting the most useful recipients of LT, insights with which most course designers, including Munby, I suspect, would agree. I have encountered the forces to which Coleman draws attention operating in relatively small organizations, for example, individuals in senior positions in companies whose antiquated views about the need for foreign languages – essentially "Let the rest of the world learn English" – had influenced employees below them. In my view, however, the issues raised are, again, not legitimate criticisms of Munby's procedure itself but of some of its potential misuses.

None of this is to deny the CNP's complexity, or to suggest it was without flaws. The complexity tended to sideline teachers and learners, as did the time needed to gather data and then feed them through the processor. Both factors conspired to create (often lucrative) employment for NA specialists, who could easily be perceived as, and sometimes were, detached from the daily realities of the classroom and whose work, once completed, was difficult, as well as expensive, to modify, if need be, once teachers, materials, and learners met. Devisers of subsequent procedures and instruments (e.g., Holliday & Cooke 1982) sought to make them simpler and less time-consuming for these reasons and, where possible, to involve teachers and learners rather than outside experts (see, e.g., Allwright & Allwright 1977; Nunan 1988).

A common procedure is to present incoming students with a written checklist of previously identified common activities or tasks for learners of their type, for example, white-collar office workers. They are then asked to check off the ones that apply to them and perhaps to rank them or to use a simple ordinal scale to rate the frequency or importance of those activities and/or the difficulty they think they (will) have with them in the L2. A variety of item formats are possible, a few of which are illustrated in Figure 5.1. Depending on the level of literacy, L2 proficiency, and general sophistication of the students concerned, a simple questionnaire like this can be administered orally or in writing, in the students' native language(s), if necessary, or in the L2, individually or in groups, with the teacher providing explanations of items, as needed. It should be remembered, however, that while short, simple, speedy, user-friendly systems are attractive in obvious ways, the amount and quality of information they produce tend to be more limited, and teachers and learners will sometimes be unable to provide needed information at all, for example, if they have yet to begin the job concerned or have little experience doing it. There is nothing intrinsically heretical or elitist in supposing that when circumstances permit, specialized work in applied linguistics will be better done by specialists.

Name _____Native language_____

Occupation _____Time in occupation_____

1. I *speak* English at work   YES   NO

Who to? _____

What about? _____

How much on average? _____

Do you use the telephone in English?_____

2. I *read* English at work   YES   NO

What kinds of things do you read? (Check those that apply.)

letters__   faxes__   the internet __

technical manuals__   e-mail messages__

reports__   books___   advertisements __

other (specify)_____

3. How important are listening, speaking, reading and writing English for you? Check ( ) the
   boxes below.

	not important	not very important	fairly important	very important
listening				
speaking				
reading				
writing				

4. On a scale of 0 to 4, how problematic are these at work?
   (0 = no problem, 4 = most problem)

   listening ___   speaking ___   reading ___   writing ___

5. The most useful thing for me in this course would be grammar classes. (Circle one.)

   strongly disagree   disagree   neutral   agree   strongly agree

Figure 5.1. Sample item *formats* for a simple, in-class NA checklist for white-collar office workers.

6. On a scale of 1-5 (1 = least useful; 5 = most useful), how useful would work on each of the following be for you?

Grammar	____	Speaking	____
Vocabulary	____	Reading	____
Pronunciation	____	Writing	____
Listening	____	Note-taking	____

7. Rank the following *speaking* tasks in terms of their importance for you.
(1 = the most important, 2 = the second most important, and so on. 0 = irrelevant for   my work.) Then, using the same system, rank the difficulty of those items for you. (1 = most difficult, and so on.)

	Importance ranking	Difficulty ranking
Greeting customers and other visitors		
Taking telephone purchase orders		
Responding to complaints by phone		
Making telephone sales calls to clients		
Attending group meetings		
Presenting sales reports		
Interviewing job applicants		

Other (specify):

1. _____

2. _____

3. _____

Figure 5.1. *Continued*

In my experience as part of teams writing notional-functional EAP reading materials for university students in Mexico and Montreal in the 1970s (see, e.g., Long *et al.* 1980), Munby's work was valuable. At the very least, it provided a useful checklist of relevant variables to be taken into account when writing materials and a logical sequence to the activities involved in doing so. I believe, however, that three more serious issues were largely ignored by critics.

First, as explained in Section 5.5, it is not at all clear that language use can be predicted from situation or communicative event or, more to the point, that it needs to be, since task is a more relevant and viable unit of analysis in syllabus design and one about which more reliable information is available from task-based occupation analyses, domain experts, and other sources. Second, even if target linguistic forms could be specified reliably and validly using the CNP, their use as syllabus content is of doubtful validity from an acquisition standpoint for reasons discussed in Chapters 2 and 3, since the result is a synthetic linguistic syllabus. Third, the final step in Munby's procedure, i.e., specification of the appropriate linguistic realizations of communicative micro-functions, is left to the syllabus designer's or materials writer's intuitions (as Munby 1978, p. 152, explicitly recognized, it should be noted) or, preferably, to collection and analysis of samples of target discourse (see Chapter 7). This is a major limitation, as Davies (1981, pp. 334–5) pointed out. What is worse, however, is that practitioners tend to know a field by the work, or tasks, they do in it, and (with few exceptions) little about the linguistic forms they use in the process, while applied linguists, conversely, know about language but are usually unfamiliar with either the tasks or the language of that field. It is not just that they will be forced to rely on intuition that is a problem, therefore, but also the fact that their intuitions about unfamiliar target situations are almost guaranteed to be unreliable, while insiders' knowledge of their field is ignored.

Although much of the work of the Council of Europe was geared toward languages, especially English, for occupational purposes (EOP), NAs were also being conducted in university settings during the 1970s, prompted by the surge in numbers of students crossing linguistic borders for higher education, by an increase in the number of English-medium courses and even of whole English-medium universities in some countries, and by the fact that published materials, including textbooks, in many scientific and technical fields were available only in English. Coleman (1988), for example, reported that 80% of Hasannudin University's Central Library holdings were in English, 15% in other languages (e.g., Dutch), and only 5% in Indonesian, most students' native language. In the University's medical library, 80% of books were in English and 18% in Dutch. The textbook problem continues today, and will assuredly continue to do so, especially at the graduate level, since the pace of theory development and research in the sciences, medicine, engineering, and so on, means that knowledge in those fields develops rapidly, requiring the continued updating or rewriting of textbooks.

Teaching operations mounted especially for those students became known as EAP. Much of the pioneering work was done by the SELMOUS group of applied linguists working at universities in the British north and midlands (see, e.g., Jordan 1978; Jordan & Mackay 1973; Mackay 1978; Mackay & Mountford 1978; Morrison 1978), and as part of several British projects overseas, notably at the University of Khartoum (see, e.g., Swales 1985a,b, 1986, 1991; Swales & Mustafa 1984), at the Universidad Nacional Autonoma de Mexico (Mackay 1978), and at the Universidad Autonoma de Mexico, Xochimilco (see issues from the period of our department's bilingual journal, *Lenguas Para Objectivos Especificos/Languages for Specific Purposes*). Related research was conducted in the United States during the same period (see, e.g., Dubois 1980; Gopnik 1972; Lackstrom, Selinker, & Trimble 1973; Selinker, Tarone, & Hanzelli 1981; Trimble 1985). Exceptions exist, but in general, whereas British and Canadian efforts, as well as the excellent work by both expatriates and native scholars in Latin America and the Arab world, often constituted the first stage in materials development projects in or for English as a foreign language (EFL) settings, the US work tended to be more linguistically oriented and focused primarily on ESL or genuine NS texts. Valuable analyses were produced of the characteristics of university lectures (e.g., Benson 1989; DeCarrico & Nattinger 1988; Flowerdew 1995a; Lebauer 1984; Young 1995), of written discourse in specific subject areas (e.g., Castaños 1976, 1977; Tarone *et al.* 1981; Wood 2001), as well as of particular academic genres (Swales 1981, 1986a,b, 1989). Such descriptions have appeared as masters and doctoral theses, in journals, including the *ESPMENA Bulletin*, *English for Specific Purposes*, and *English for Academic Purposes*, in edited volumes, and increasingly, in journals in such fields as business, medicine, and tourism. (For useful overviews, see Flowerdew 1995b; Flowerdew & Peacock 2001; Hyland 2009; Swales 1990a, 2001.)

5.5. Task as the Unit of (Needs) Analysis

While language abilities needed by heterogeneous populations vary widely in terms of skills and linguistic systems, they do so more concretely with respect to the tasks that learners will have to perform. At the one extreme, many refugees and migrant workers, sometimes illiterate or barely literate in their native language, as well as the L2, must learn to do such things as use a cell phone or computer (perhaps for the first time), find, interview for, and then keep an entry-level job, obtain school admission for their children, rent lodgings, follow street directions, negotiate the public transport system, secure emergency health care, and open a bank account. Some of these tasks are common to university students and blue-collar workers, white-collar professionals, and government officials arriving in another country, too. However, some members of the latter groups may not be planning trips to SL environments at all and, even if they are, may have little problem with any of them, but great difficulty with other tasks, such as understanding lectures on economics or chemical engineering, changing an airline reservation, completing the hospital internship of a vocational training course taught in the L2, buying a car, negotiating a business deal, or making an after-dinner speech, only a few of which are of much concern to most refugees or migrant workers. The various groups' communicative language needs – the lexis, collocations, pragmatics, skills, genres, and registers required for the tasks they must perform – are clearly not the same, for the simple reason that what they have to *do* in and through the target language – their *target tasks* – are so different.

5.5.1. Tasks defined

From the above and other examples so far, it should be obvious that a key feature distinguishing TBLT from most other "task-based" (and "task-supported") approaches, is that by 'task' is meant the non-technical, everyday, real-world use of the term:

> a piece of work undertaken for oneself or for others, freely or for some reward. Thus, examples of tasks include painting a fence, dressing a child, filling out a form, buying a pair of shoes, making an airline reservation, borrowing a library book, taking a driving test, typing a letter, weighing a patient, sorting letters, making a hotel reservation, writing a cheque, finding a street destination and helping someone across a road. In other words, by "task" is meant the hundred and one things people do in everyday life, at work, at play, and in between. Tasks are the things they will tell you they do if you ask them and they are not applied linguists. (Long 1985a, p. 89)

More precisely, these are *target tasks*, i.e., the things the NA will identify as what our students need, or will need, to be able to *do* in the L2. A similar notion is conveyed by Crookes (1986a, p. 1), who defines task as "a piece of work or an activity, usually with a specified objective, undertaken as part of an educational course or at work," and by Skehan (1998), who states that a task is an activity in which "Meaning is primary; there is a goal which needs to be worked on; the activity is outcome-evaluated; there is a real-world relationship."

Several alternative definitions of 'task' have appeared in the applied linguistics literature. The following are representative examples. Some, in my opinion, have been too abstract and opaque to be of much practical use. Candlin, for example, defines task this way:

> one of a set of differentiated, sequencable, problem-posing activities involving learners and teachers in some joint selection from a range of varied cognitive and communicative procedures applied to existing and new knowledge in the collective exploration and pursuance of foreseen or emergent goals within a social milieu. (Candlin 1987, p. 10)

Like Candlin's, most definitions, moreover, have been characterizations of classroom tasks – coming, as they do, from task-*supported* approaches developed without reference to analyses of learner needs beyond the classroom – so they tend to refer to language and language learning. They, too, are sometimes rather vague. A task is

> a workplan that requires learners to process language pragmatically in order to achieve an outcome that can be evaluated in terms of whether the correct or appropriate propositional content has been conveyed. To this end, it requires them to give primary attention to meaning and to make use of their own linguistic resources, although the design of the task may predispose them to choose particular forms. A task is intended to result in language use that bears a resemblance, direct or indirect, to the way language is used in the real world. Like other language activities, a task can engage productive or receptive, and oral or written skills, and also various cognitive processes. (R. Ellis 2003, p. 16)

> [an activity in which] the target language is used by the learner for a communicative purpose (goal) in order to achieve an outcome. (Willis & Willis 2001, p. 173)

> a piece of classroom work which involves learners in comprehending, manipulating, producing, or interacting in the target language while their attention is focused on mobilizing their grammatical knowledge in order to express meaning, and in which the intention is to convey meaning rather than to manipulate form. The task should also have a sense of completeness, being able to stand alone as a communicative act in its own right. (Nunan 2004, p. 4)

> any structured language learning endeavor which has a particular objective, appropriate content, a specified working procedure, and a range of outcomes for those who undertake the task. "Task" is therefore assumed to refer to a range of workplans which have the overall purpose of facilitating language learning – from the simple and brief exercise type, to more complex and lengthy activities such as group problem-solving or simulations and decision-making. (Breen 1987b, p. 23)

In fact, 'exercise type' and 'group problem-solving or simulations and decision-making' are types of *pedagogic tasks*, of which much more later. Sometimes, the definitions make it clear that the author is talking about the use of tasks to deliver a grammatical syllabus, i.e., task-*supported* LT. Thus, R. Ellis makes a distinction between "focused" and "unfocused" tasks:

> Focused tasks, then, have two aims; one is to stimulate communicative language use as with unfocused tasks, the other is to target the use of a particular, predetermined target feature in meaning-centred communication...a task-based syllabus...can be entirely unfocused (as in Prabhu's [1987] Communicational Teaching Project) or it can be focused (i.e. informed by a list of structural items). (R. Ellis 2003, p. 65)

The real-world nature of tasks in TBLT and the eschewal of a grammatical syllabus, overt or covert (as is also the case in the work of Crookes, Robinson, Skehan, Norris, Gilabert and others), distinguish it from (lower case) "task-based" approaches and reflect the fact that, unlike those approaches, TBLT begins with a NA. However, as will become clear in later chapters, even pedagogic tasks in TBLT are more tangible, simpler versions of target tasks and are defined that way, not in language-learning terms.

Task has at least five advantages as the unit of analysis in course design. (1) Organizing materials and lessons around tasks is compatible with the SLA theory and research findings about how people learn languages summarized in Chapters 2 and 3. (2) Task as the unit of NA is consistent with, and supported by, the philosophy of education principles described in Chapter 4. (3) Task-based analyses of language use surrounding accomplishment of target tasks reveal more about the dynamic qualities of target discourse than do text-based analyses, an issue to which we turn in Chapter 7. (4) Conceptualizing needs in terms of tasks helps circumvent the domain expert's usual lack of linguistic knowledge and the applied linguist's usual lack of content knowledge. (5) Existing descriptions created by knowledgeable insiders in both the public and private sectors of the work involved in education, vocational training, occupations, jobs, and more are almost always task-based, so can save the applied linguist valuable time and effort. At this juncture, let us briefly consider points (4) and (5).

5.5.2. Avoiding the traditional bottleneck in needs analysis

The use of task as the unit of analysis helps avoid some notorious NA bottlenecks in traditional approaches to LSP, to which, as will become plain, TBLT nevertheless owes a considerable debt. A pervasive problem in traditional LSP course design is that of finding informants who are competent in the academic, occupational, or vocational area of interest and also knowledgeable about language use in that area. Such people are few and far between. In their absence, there is a danger that materials will be based on materials writers' intuitions about the target domain, intuitions that tend to be unreliable even on the rare occasions the writer is familiar with work in the area of interest. It is here that one of several advantages of task as the unit of NA becomes clear. The domain expert's (usual) lack of linguistic knowledge, mirroring the needs analyst's (usual) lack of content knowledge, is only a problem if the kind of LT envisaged is text-based, not task-based, and especially if a synthetic linguistic syllabus is to be employed for working on the texts.

NAs for language-centered courses, understandably, will themselves be language-centered and will be difficult to accomplish satisfactorily with domain experts, who are almost always linguistically naive. Non-linguistically focused analytic syllabuses, conversely, will require accurate information about subject matter for content-based or immersion programs, and about target tasks for TBLT – information that domain experts will often be able to supply easily and reliably. This will be supplemented in TBLT by holistic samples of language use surrounding those tasks whose collection and analysis (see Chapter 7) is the responsibility of the applied linguist, who will be linguistically sophisticated. Domain experts may be called upon to provide guidance as to the appropriate domains in which to sample target discourse, and often with such matters as obtaining relevant documents and tape recordings, but analyses of those data will be performed later by applied linguists, materials writers, teachers, and learners, and even then (see Chapter 7) not via conventional linguistic procedures, such as register analysis. Thus, selecting task as the unit of analysis in syllabus design and, therefore, in NA, avoids a bottleneck in traditional linguistically focused approaches to LSP.

5.5.3. The availability of ready-made task-based analyses

Ready-made occupational descriptions exist in many sectors, such as federal, state and local government, business, unions, education, and the military. The fact that the descriptions are almost always at least in part in the form of lists of tasks to be performed is another argument in favor of adopting task as the unit of analysis. They are often accompanied by specifications of minimum acceptable levels of performance, for example, "take dictation at 80 words per minute," "type at a rate of 45 net words per minute," "read above the eighth grade level," "determine the distance between two locations using a map with no more than 10% error," or "put on four levels of chemical protective clothing within eight minutes." These can be useful in determining proficiency level when setting course goals.

When ready-made descriptions are unavailable, linguistically naive but work-experienced informants are usually able to provide reliable task-based descriptions of what their work involves, for, as noted above, activities and tasks are the normal units in which people tend to think about what they do each day. The task is a natural, meaningful unit for people, in other words, a second argument in its favor. Classroom teachers, for example, have been found to plan, deliver, and recall lessons as a series of activities or tasks (Shavelson & Stern 1981). The lack of informants' linguistic awareness does not matter in a NA for a teaching program that, following Hutchinson and Waters (1987), does not try to teach the specialized language of a target domain at all or, as in TBLT, rarely does so explicitly.

One of the first applied linguists to appreciate part of the potential of task in NA was Bell (1981, pp. 159–70), who illustrated with the case of a canteen assistant working in a self-service operation. Bell was able to adopt a ready-made job analysis for a counter hand from Boydell (1970). Basic duties and responsibilities included "complying with instructions received from counter charge hand or supervisor," "complying with food hygiene regulations," and "determining a customer's requirements and obtaining them from the display unit." Tasks involved in the third of these included the (rather awkwardly worded) sub-task, "dealing with a customer's complaint about food which is supposed to be hot, when served, being cold." To complete that sub-task satisfactorily, the assistant needed to know several things, including the customer's and the company's rights, how to recognize a complaint, and what to do next. Skills required included judging whether the food really was cold or not, informing the customer of the judgment, placating the customer, and offering fresh food or a refund. Using this information, Bell produced an algorithm for dealing with a complaint in the form of a chart, as well as a table to facilitate identification of faults (e.g., dirty plates, or cups in a vending machine failing to drop), and analysis of possible causes, locus of responsibility, effects on customers and employees, action to be taken, and preventive measures. This was innovative work, ahead of its time. Unfortunately for present purposes, since Bell (1981, p. 165) was explicitly "committed to a functional approach in the design of our syllabus," at this juncture he set out to try to "list the speech acts which are needed by the learner, and, possibly, select a limited number of formal manifestations of each, which we will teach" (p. 165), that is, to produce a linguistically based, not a task-based, syllabus.

5.6. Means Analysis

At one or more stages in developing a new course, designers need to consider a wide variety of situational factors in addition to those discussed so far, factors identified through a means analysis. The traditional domain of a NA is *what* is taught. That "content" influences *how* a program is implemented. Consideration must also be given, however, to a range of factors falling outside the domain of needs. Munby (1978, p. 217) recognized the importance of political and social matters, such as the relative status of the Ll and L2, of logistical matters, such as the money, time, and human resources available, and of methodological matters, such as learners' previous language-learning history and local pedagogic preferences. Munby viewed such variables primarily as constraints to be dealt with after a NA had been completed. Holliday (1994, 1995), Holliday and Cooke (1982), Nunan (1988), and others, conversely, have advocated taking them into account from the outset. As noted earlier, Widdowson (1981 and elsewhere) warned against attributing undue importance to learner needs in a NA and the static, goal-oriented approach to course design which he claimed resulted from this, and argued in favor of a focus in NA on learning needs and the process-oriented approach that supposedly resulted from the second orientation. Hutchinson and Waters (1987, p. 62) proposed a similar distinction between target needs, relating to course content, and learning needs, which concern such matters as students' learning background, concept of teaching and learning, and methodological preferences.

Several writers (e.g., Canagarajah 1999; Dudley-Evans & Swales 1980; Holliday 1994, 1994; Robinson 1981; Tarone & Yule 1989; Taylor 1993) have discussed ways in which training factors and/or cultural differences can give rise to tensions between teachers' and learners' expectations about classroom processes (for further discussion, see Section 12.1). For example, mismatches have sometimes been found between teacher preferences for communicative teaching methodology and learner preferences for more traditional approaches (Butler 2011; McDonough & Chaitmongkol 2007; Nunan 1988, p. 95; Savage & Whisenand 1993). Tensions can also arise between program designers and what they believe research findings show to be beneficial to learners, on the one hand, and on the other, local teachers and/or learners who hold different beliefs equally firmly. As described in an insightful discussion of the issue by Holliday (1994), the likelihood of conflict is increased when designers are cultural outsiders, for example, foreign-trained expatriate applied linguists, and teachers and students predominantly insiders who received their education locally.

To illustrate, applied linguists and SLA researchers have for years put forward pedagogic arguments and a psycholinguistic rationale for small group work (see Long & Porter 1985, for review), and in particular (as described in Chapter 9 and 10), for certain kinds of negotiation for meaning that can be facilitated when group work is combined with appropriate pedagogic tasks (see Pica 1994; Pica *et al.* 1996). However, a long-standing successful reliance on adult- and teacher-centered instruction, sometimes accompanied by silent observation, sometimes by rote memorization, is well documented in informal learning and classroom practices in many parts of the world. It is noteworthy, for example, that in an otherwise remarkably innovative LT project, Prabhu's (1987) implementation of the procedural syllabus in Bangalore (see Section 8.2.6) eschewed group work partly because of local teacher and student expectations about classroom roles and instruction. More recently, some comfort may be derived from research findings showing local acceptance and productive use of task-based small group work and negotiation for meaning by students in such cultural contexts as Japan (Fujii & Mackey 2009; Mackey, Abbuhl, & Gass 2012; Mackey *et al.* 2012), Thailand (McDonough 2004), and Singapore (Mackey & Silver 2005).

The potentially problematic tension between course designers' beliefs and local cultural values was treated explicitly by Taylor (1993) with reference to an EST writing program in Micronesia. He pointed out that language teachers have long recognized the importance of culture in NA, but generally, the culture of the target language or of the discourse community to which students desire entry rather than that of the learners themselves. The result, according to Taylor, is the hegemony of Western scientific beliefs and inappropriate educational models in the Pacific and elsewhere. Topping (1992, quoted in Taylor 1993, p. 16) pointed out how formal literate education often ignores the crucial role of oracy, of direct experience and dialogue:

> Coming from a world where even preschool children understand the holistic relationships of moon and tides, of seasons and fish, of weather and insects, and so on, to one of piecemeal, segmental, linear reasoning, the children of the Pacific have been subjected to the conflict of contradictory cognitive patterns. (Topping 1992, p. 27)

With a few notable exceptions, for example, Flowerdew (1986), Kennedy (1988), Swales (1985a, p. 212), and the "ecological" approach to NA of Holliday and Cooke (1982), there has been a parallel tendency to ignore the learner's culture in ESP course design.

Successful pedagogic adaptations to culturally based learning styles have been made in other educational contexts. One example is provided by modification of reading lessons, teacher questioning patterns, and other dimensions of teacher–student classroom interaction to suit the peer-orientation and collaborative discourse construction of the "talk-story" routine of native Hawaiian and Hawaiian Creole English-speaking children (Au & Jordan 1981; Boggs & Watson-Gegeo 1985; Sato 1989), based on the original work on talk-story of Watson-Gegeo (1975). Practical examples of accommodations that might be made in LT programs are few and far between. One is Barron's (1991) traditional engineering course in Papua New Guinea, which began by having students build traditional artifacts as an introduction to modern technological concepts and as a way of seeing the links between them. However, for ESP programs to be successful in a place like the Northern Marianas, Taylor suggested, traditional local patterns of participation and learning must be studied, catered to in a NA, and reflected not only in program content but also in culturally congruent classroom methodology. This can help overcome what may otherwise become notoriously disruptive discontinuities in patterns of language use expected at home and at school. Examples of such mismatches include those between Warm Springs Native American children's preference for group over individual performance and cooperation over competition (Phillips 1972), and between Inuit children's expectation that learning is achieved by looking and listening, and the greater importance some non-Inuit teachers assign to verbal participation (Crago 1992).

An important target task for students in the Northern Marianas course was writing summaries of technical readings for their content courses. Taylor reported that the learning of complex navigation charts, canoe- and house-building, weaving, agriculture and fishing techniques, and so on, in Micronesia generally occurs through

> prolonged observation [imitation] and eventual [cooperative] participation, without specific, direct instruction. This observation and instruction takes place in group settings; except in a few specific separate male/female activities and highly skilled apprenticeship situations, it does not occur on a one to one basis. (Taylor, 1993, p. 18)

Instead of a conventional "silent seat-work" approach to summary writing, therefore, he suggested greater attention be paid to prewriting activities. First, in-class group discussion, teacher-led if necessary, should clarify the writing task's relationship to students' work in their technical courses. Given the importance of oral history in Micronesian cultures, group-developed oral summaries should come next, with the teacher shaping and reworking them orally with the students and writing them on the board in real time, thereby engaging students in a less threatening, shared, group approach to writing. This is not the conventional approach of providing a written model for emulation, but modeling, or demonstrating, the writing process while learners observe, before later engaging in it. It is a key aspect of culturally congruent instruction in Micronesia. The teacher's role would gradually be assumed by students, still working with the others as a group. Later, students would perform the task independently.

Taylor's example is valuable and probably applicable in many other settings. Fortuitously, it is a case where local cultural patterns coincide with much thinking in SLA and on the teaching of writing. Matching instruction with students' cultural background will sometimes involve tougher calls, however. For example, difficult decisions must sometimes be made in situations where students are accustomed to, and so now expect, a highly teacher-centered, "transmission" model of education (Barnes 1976/1992), with plenty of explicit grammar instruction and a heavy dependence on rote memorization, or in cultures where speaking out in class may be frowned upon and where, as in Japan, students have been socialized into accepting some version of the saying that "the nail that sticks up will be hammered down." Solutions are not easy, but a possible one is to organize lessons so that multiple learning options are available simultaneously, for example, through a variety of individual and group tasks at different work stations. Students select those with which they feel most comfortable, while nearby, models of what are perhaps new ones to them are visible, audible, and, it is hoped, increasingly attractive.

The range of factors considered in a means analysis by Holliday and Cooke and others (e.g., Allwright 1982; Brindley 1984; Nunan 1988; Swales 1990a) is very broad. It includes political, economic, support personnel and administrative matters, classroom facilities and equipment, the level and L2 ability of teachers, cultural factors, the cultural setting, the linguistic environment (e.g., whether or not there is access to the L2 outside the classroom), the cultural background of teachers and learners, preferred teaching and learning styles, and class size. While presenting a potentially daunting new dimension to the designer's task, a sensitivity to these factors can ultimately have a major positive impact on the way a program is implemented, for example, in materials design and pedagogy (not methodology), and on the eventual likelihood of success (Kennedy 1988; Mountford 1988). Thus, if a NA is worthwhile, a means analysis must also be. It can influence the chances of a new program being accepted by rank-and-file education workers (Markee 1986, 1993; Van den Branden 2009; and see Section 12.1), with grass-roots change initiated and fully understood by teachers and learners being academically and politically desirable, and more likely to succeed.

TBLT obviously presents more than the usual potential of any new approach for mismatches with traditional LT practice and locally received views about how languages should be taught (for further discussion, see Section 12.1). In some parts of the world, the enhanced role of the student it involves, its emphasis on creative, communicative language use and learning by doing, and the importance assigned to implicit, as well as explicit, language learning, among other qualities, will not play well. If rote memorization and drill and kill are the norm, and the teacher has unquestioned authority and is regarded as the source of all knowledge, change may come slowly. Initial reactions to its emancipatory potential may also deter arbiters of education policy in some countries for political or religious reasons. Such factors must obviously be taken into account during a means analysis and, in extreme cases, might first require a new approach to language teacher education if there is to be any chance of success. Put another way, the likelihood of TBLT being welcomed with open arms is remote in some societies, and its initial adoption there will likely depend on the existence of well-trained teachers and program administrators in just a few institutions, after which its success there may encourage others. These issues will be a major focus of Chapter 12, where TBLT's potential will be assessed from the perspective of the literature on the diffusion of innovation.

5.7. Summary

While the utility of NA has occasionally been questioned, the great and growing diversity of students, the importance and urgency of satisfying their equally diverse, often highly specialized, communicative language needs, and the increasing value placed on course relevance, both real and perceived, are the ultimate justifications for NA as a prerequisite (necessary, but not sufficient) for successful course design.

NA has a long history of steady growth in applied linguistics. Quite complex models have been employed in the identification of the frequency and centrality of linguistic features and constructions, and/or functions and speech acts associated with occupations, academic disciplines, and the like. While valuable from a methodological point of view, demonstrable differences in the *target tasks* for widely different learner groups, and (as we shall see in Chapter 7) in the language associated with them, make *task*, in its everyday real-world sense, a logical unit of analysis when identifying and satisfying needs.

Tasks are also suitable units around which to develop materials and lessons compatible with theory and research findings about SLA and the philosophical principles described in Chapters 3 and 4, respectively. They avoid the problem with traditional linguistically based analyses, in which insiders know about tasks, but not about language, and applied linguists know about language, but are usually ignorant about the content area. A task-based approach also means that ready-made NAs, which are almost always couched in terms of background knowledge, tasks, and performance requirements, can be used in course design. Finally, field experiences suggest strongly that constraints of several kinds, identified by a means analysis, should be taken into account, preferably simultaneous with, and as part of, the NA. The question that now arises is how best to identify and analyze target tasks and the language required to perform them. These practical methodological issues will be the focus of Chapters 6 and 7, respectively.

5.8. Suggested Readings

Brown, J.D. (2009). Foreign and second language needs analysis. In Long, M.H., & Doughty, C.J. (eds.), *Handbook of language teaching* (pp. 269–293). Oxford: Wiley-Blackwell.

Hyland, K. (2009). Specific purpose programs. In Long, M.H., & Doughty, C.J. (eds.), *Handbook of language teaching* (pp. 201–217). Oxford: Wiley-Blackwell.

Hyland, K., & Hamp-Lyons, E. (2002). EAP: Issues and directions. *Journal of English for Academic Purposes* 1, 1–12.

Long, M.H. (2005). A rationale for needs analysis and needs analysis research. In Long, M.H. (ed.), *Second language needs analysis* (pp. 1–16). Cambridge: Cambridge University Press.

Long, M.H. (2013). Needs analysis. In Chapelle, C. (ed.), *Encyclopedia of applied linguistics*. Oxford: Wiley-Blackwell.

Swales, J.M. (1990). *Genre analysis*. Cambridge: Cambridge University Press.

Swales, J.M. (2001). EAP-related linguistic research: An intellectual history. In Flowerdew, J., & Peacock, P. (eds.), *Research perspectives on English for academic purposes* (pp. 42–54). Cambridge: Cambridge University Press.

Chapter 6

Identifying Target Tasks

6.1. Sources of Information

There are many potential sources of information available to those responsible for a needs analysis (NA) (see Table 6.1), and some debate continues in the field as to the relative value of each. The issue is an important one if, as Chambers (1980, p. 27) asserts, "whoever determines needs determines which needs are determined." The position taken here is that, as with periodic discussions of the merits of qualitative and quantitative research methods in other contexts, no single potential information source (or

Second Language Acquisition and Task-Based Language Teaching, First Edition. Mike Long.
© 2015 John Wiley & Sons, Inc. Published 2015 by John Wiley & Sons, Inc.

Table 6.1. Sources of information for NA

Source	Source/evaluation	Sample use
Published and unpublished literature	Crookes (1986a)	Numerous LSP programs
Learners	Brindley (1984) Brindley and Hood (1990) Nunan (1988)	Beatty and Chan (1984) Ramani *et al.* (1988) Savage and Storer (1992)
Teachers and applied linguists	Lamotte (1981) Selinker (1979) Zuck and Zuck (1984)	Numerous LSP programs
Domain experts	Huckin and Olson (1984) Selinker (1979) Zuck and Zuck (1984)	Coleman (1988) Ramani *et al.* (1988) Tarone *et al.* (1981) Bosher and Smalkoski (2002)
Triangulated sources	Lincoln and Guba (1985) Long (2005b, 2013c) Lynch (1995)	Cowling (2007) Cumaranatunge (1988) Jasso-Aguilar (1999/2005) Gilabert (2005) Long (2005b) Oliver *et al.* (2012) Sullivan and Girginer (2002) Spence and Liu (2013) Svendsen and Krebs (1984) Zughoul & Hussein (1985)

Source: Updated from Long (2005c, p. 25).

method of obtaining information) for NA merits privileged status. Instead, as with different classes of research methods, different sources of information can profitably be used in a NA, depending on the type of course being designed, the time available, and the kind of information sought. Use of *multiple sources* typically provides more detailed information and has the additional advantage of allowing cross-checking for informal validation, and ideally, triangulation, of findings; coupled with use of *multiple measures*, it can help allay the serious threat to validity that Chambers' aphorism implies. The only limit on sources and measures should be information overload. Before embarking on a vast data-gathering project, analysts should look ahead and be clear that the kind and amount of information they plan to collect can be analyzed and used, given any limitations of time, money, and personnel.

6.1.1. Published and unpublished literature

A great deal of information about the communicative needs of particular groups of learners and how to assess them has been available in the professional literature for some time (for useful surveys, see Brown 2009; Robinson 1981, pp. 7–17, and her 200-item accompanying bibliography, pp. 110–119; West 1994). Several specialized journals, notably, the *ESP Journal, English for Academic Purposes*, and the *ESPMENA Bulletin*, have often included reports of NA findings, as do *English Language Teaching Journal*, *TESOL Quarterly, Modern Language Journal*, and several regional and national language-teaching (LT) publications. Other studies have been featured in edited collections, for example, Hagen (1988), Lambert and Moore (1990), Long (2005d), Mackay and Mountford (1978), Richterich (1983), Selinker, Tarone, and Hanzelli (1981), and Van den Branden (2006a). Competent course designers should be familiar with this literature, or at least know of its existence, and can avoid reinventing the wheel if they are. Regrettably, some of the best research is unpublished, as it is done on contract for internal use by private companies, publishers, and other large organizations, and its procurement, when possible at all, requires more effort than a trip to the nearest university library.

Other sources of information for NAs are job descriptions in both the public and private sectors. Most large corporations, and not a few small ones, maintain written statements of the duties of their employees from middle managers on down. (Owners, directors, and senior managers rarely seem to have such job descriptions, for reasons we will not dwell on here.) These can be invaluable for the course designer, for apart from saving time, they are more likely to provide accurate descriptions due to their (a) having been the work of insiders, that is, those intimately familiar with the work, not applied linguists, and (b) compiled and revised over time. Companies commissioning language courses for their employees are usually more than willing to provide such internal documents, as they readily perceive the likelihood of increased relevance of the courses to follow, but they may insist that the information contained in them go no further. Almost all such job descriptions take the form of lists of tasks workers must be able to perform, sometimes taxonomized and sometimes accompanied by references to relevant background knowledge and the minimum standards at which the tasks are to be carried out, usually expressed in terms of speed and accuracy.

Ready-made information is also widely available in the world's militaries and government sectors, where task-based training manuals and job descriptions are the norm. The US Army, for example, publishes a periodically updated *Soldier's Manual of Common Tasks* (e.g., U.S. Department of the Army 1994), Skill Level 1 of which deals (in 556 pages) with 86 tasks, such as the following: load an M203 grenade launcher; identify terrain features on a map; engage targets with an M60 machine gun; employ hand grenades; react to a nuclear hazard; give first aid for frostbite; and perform mortuary affairs operations. Each task lists conditions under which performance is to be assessed, the performance standards expected, training exercises, examples, any specific language to be used while doing the task, and an evaluation procedure and checklist.

Task 113-571-1016 in the 1987 version of the *Manual*, for example, is "Send a radio message." The *Conditions* (p. 37) are

1. two operational radio sets, both warmed up and set to the same frequency
2. frequency (obtained from local command)
3. message to be transmitted
4. call signs for sender and receiver
5. situation: net is in the clear and there is no need to encrypt.

The *Standards* for the task (p. 37) are to send a voice radio message using correct radio procedures, correct pro-words, and correct phonetic alphabet and numbers. Five steps (or sub-tasks) are listed in the *Training Information* outline (pp. 37–39), with examples (of which, for reasons of space, only the first is included here), to be completed in sequence:

1. Listen to make sure the net is clear. Do not interrupt any ongoing message.
2. Call distant station using the call sign and tell the operator you have a message for his/her station.
    Example:
    "D81D, this is Z94D. (priority) Over."
    Your call should sound like this:
    DELL TAR AIT WUN DELL TAR – THIS IS ZOO LOO NIN ER FOW ER DELL TAR – (PRIORITY) OVER.
3. Receive response from the distant station's operator that he/she is ready to receive.
4. Send the message using correct pro-words and correct pronunciation of letters and numbers.
5. Get receipt of the message.

Three tables follow (pp. 40–43). The first lists 21 common pro-words and their explanations, for example,

> All after – I refer to all of the message that follows…
> Over – This is the end of my transmission to you and a response is necessary. Go ahead; transmit.
> Roger – I have received your last transmission satisfactorily, loud and clear.

The second is a chart of what is referred to as the 'phonetic alphabet' (an illustration of how technical, as well as sub-technical, terms can have different meanings in different fields), for example,

A	*B*	*C*	*D*	*E*	*F*
Alfa	Bravo	CHARLIE	DELTA	ECHO	FOXTROT
(AL FAR)	(BRAH VOH)	(CHAR LEE)	(DELL TAR)	(ECK OH)	(FOKS TROT)

The third lists (American English) alphanumeric pronunciation:

> 44 FOW-ER FOW-ER, 90 -NIN-ER ZE-RO, etc.

There then follows a detailed *Evaluation Preparation Procedure* (p. 43), essentially a vignette suitable for a task-based, criterion-referenced performance test (see Chapter 11). The text is included in full here as it illustrates some basic properties of task-based performance assessment, as well as some of its problems (matters considered in Chapter 11):

> Set-up: Position two operational radio sets in different rooms or tents or at least 70 feet apart outside. Secure two call signs and a radio frequency through the normal command chain. Select a message 15–25 words in length containing some number groups such as

map coordinates and times. Print the call signs for the sender and the receiver, along with the message to be sent, on a 5 × 8 card. Perform a communications check to ensure operation of the radios. Have an assistant who is proficient in radio operation man (sic) the receiving station. Provide the assistant with the call sign. If the soldier has not demonstrated sufficient progress to completing the task within 5 minutes, give him (sic) a NO-GO. This time limit is an administrative requirement, not a doctrinal one, so if the soldier has almost finished the task correctly, you may decide to allow him (sic) to finish.

Simulations such as this are common in the *Soldier's Manual*, as they are in TBLT. Some approximate the target task quite closely; others fall short of the full "communicative event," which is probably just as well; a brief note (p. 426) appended to the "setup" for "React to nuclear hazard" informs the reader that

> To evaluate the soldier's reaction to a nuclear attack without warning, you may simulate the task by saying "Brilliant flash," or by using the flash attachment of a camera.

Last comes the *Evaluation Guide* (p. 44) for 'Send a radio message', which follows the *Manual*'s standard format of 'pass' or 'fail' for each step (or sub-task) in task completion:

Send a radio message	
Performance measures	*Results*
1. Listens to determine if net is clear	P F
2. Contacts distant station	P F
3. Receives response from station that it is ready for message	P F
4. Sends a message using correct radio procedures, correct pro-words, and correct phonetic alphabet and numbers	P F
5. Gets receipt for message	P F
6. Completes all steps in sequence	P F

The soldier is finally to be scored "GO" if all steps are passed, and "NO-GO" if any steps are failed. If "NO-GO," he or she is to be shown what was done wrong and how to do it correctly.

There are many positive features to the task-based procedure used in the *Soldier's Manual* and elsewhere in the military. The tasks themselves are meaningful to trainers and trainees, as (usually) are the conditions under which they are performed. Tasks are broken down into sequenced, manageable steps or sub-tasks. Needed ancillary knowledge is provided in context. Performance is evaluated objectively, in a reasonably authentic manner, again using sub-tasks in a way that allows identification and remediation of any stage at which a procedure is breaking down.

The government sector, too, offers useful information for task-based NAs. Since 1939, for example, the US federal government has published several editions of the *Dictionary of Occupational Titles (DOT)*, available in most reference libraries. The two-volume revised (fourth) edition (U.S. Department of Labor 1991) lists task-based descriptions of some 12,000 occupations. They are grouped into nine broad categories (professional, technical, and managerial; clerical and sales; service; machine trades; etc.), 83 divisions (e.g., within machine trades: metalworking, printing, and textiles), and 564 groups (e.g., within printing: typesetters and composers, printing press occupations, and typecasters). The occupational definitions are the result of "comprehensive studies [75,000 on-site job analysis studies from 1965 to the mid-1970s alone] of how similar jobs are performed in establishments across the nation and are composites of data collected from diverse sources" (U.S. Department of Labor 1991, p. xvii).

The *DOT*'s definitions of occupations are composites, descriptions of how similar jobs are performed, with minor variations, in many establishments. By way of illustration, a museum attendant's job varies slightly from place to place, depending on such factors as a particular museum's size, location, and contents, and the kinds of additional staff available. The occupation of museum attendant, however, has been found to have common characteristics. After an opening lead statement, those are listed (U.S. Department of Labor 1991, p. 84) as task element statements.

109.367-010 MUSEUM ATTENDANT (museums)
   Conducts operation of museum and provides information about regulations, facilities, and exhibits to visitors. Opens museum at designated hours, greets visitors, and invites visitors to sign guest register. Monitors visitors viewing exhibits, cautions persons not complying with museum regulations, distributes promotional materials, and answers questions concerning exhibits, regulations, and facilities. Arranges tours of facilities for schools or other groups, and schedules volunteers or other staff members to conduct tours. Examines exhibit facilities and collection objects periodically and notifies museum professional personnel or governing body when need for repair or replacement is observed. GOE: 07.04.04 STRENGTH: L GED: R4 M3 L4 SVP: 3 DLU: 86

DOT listings are easily accessed alphabetically or by area. They are multiply cross-referenced to each other and to outside sources, e.g., the US Employment Service's *Guide for Occupational Exploration* (*GOE*), intended primarily for career guidance counselors and potential career entrants, which lists the kinds of interests, aptitudes, entry-level preparation, and other traits appropriate for different occupations. They are accompanied by codes referring to the type and duration of specific vocational preparation (SVP) required for the occupation, as well as one of five operationally defined levels of physical strength (S = sedentary, L = light, M = medium, H = heavy, V = very heavy), and one of six broadly defined levels of general educational development (GED) broken down into reasoning development (R), mathematical development (M), and (rather uninformatively) language development (L), based on US school curriculum grade levels and college standards. Finally, date of last update ("DLU") indicates the year in which the most recent information on the occupation was gathered.

The body of each definition includes a lead statement, task element statements, and (sometimes) "may" items. The opening sentence is the lead statement, which provides a brief overview or summary of the occupation, followed by a colon. Task element statements then list the specific tasks a worker performs. "May" items describe duties required of workers in this occupation in some establishment but not others. To illustrate, here is the entry for hotel clerk (U.S. Department of Labor 1991, p. 209):

238.367-038 HOTEL CLERK (hotel and rest.) alternate titles: motel clerk; motor lodge clerk

Performs any combination of following duties for guests of hotel or motel: Greets, registers, and assigns rooms to guests. Issues room key and escort instructions to BELLHOP (hotel and rest.) 324.677-010. Date-stamps, sorts and racks incoming mail and messages. Transmits and receives messages, using telephone or telephone switchboard. Answers inquiries pertaining to hotel services; registration of guests; and shopping, dining, entertainment, and travel directions. Keeps records of room availability and guests' accounts, manually or using computer. Computes bill, collects payment, and makes change for guests [CASHIER (clerical) I 211.362-010]. Makes and confirms reservations. May post charges, such as room, food, liquor, or telephone, to ledger, manually or using computer [BOOKKEEPER (clerical) 210.382-014]. May make restaurant, transportation, or entertainment reservation, and arrange for tours. May deposit guests' valuables in hotel safe or safe-deposit box. May order complementary flowers or champagne for guests. May rent dock space at marina-hotel. May work on one floor and be designated Floor Clerk (hotel and rest.). May be known as Key Clerk (hotel and rest.); Reservation Clerk (hotel and rest.); Room Clerk (hotel and rest.) or according to specific area in which employed as Front Desk Clerk (hotel and rest.). GOE: 07.04.03 STRENGTH: L GED: R3 M3 L3 SVP: 4 DLU: 81

The *DOT* and similar attempts to develop taxonomies of human performance have been reviewed and criticized on a variety of grounds (see Crookes 1986a; Fleishman & Quaintance 1984; McCormick 1976; McCormick, Jeanneret, & Meecham 1972; Miller *et al.* 1980; Peterson & Bownas 1982). Some criticisms concern reliability and validity. Sampling of establishments and jobs for the *DOT*, for example, has been non-random, and data-collection procedures have sometimes varied in different parts of the country. Data-gathering has mostly been through interviews with, and/or observation of, better, rather than typical, workers. While standardized and relatively objective, some aspects of the methodology used for job analysis, for example, completion of pre-specified sets of observational categories on task sheets, have been satisfactory for blue-collar occupations but not necessarily suitable for all jobs. Of particular concern in the present context is that

[the methodology] can be applied most practically to manufacturing jobs or, more generally, to any type of a structured job that can be broken down into discrete tasks performed over a limited amount of time. It is less suited to unstructured jobs, such as certain service jobs that entail widely varying tasks. (Miller *et al.* 1980, p. 146)

This last point reflects a parallel concern about TBLT, discussed only tangentially in Chapter 5, namely, whether attempting to portray everyday life in terms of tasks is reductionist in ways that affect the validity of TBLT and/or is avoidable. My own experience suggests that there is a tendency for validity to decline somewhat as the communicative needs (occupational or otherwise) being studied increase in abstractness and generality, that is, as they become more removed from, and less consistently tied to, particular individuals, times, and places. This is an impressionistic observation only, but it is consistent with the findings of a reliability study of the ratings of *DOT* worker functions and traits (Cain & Green 1983), which found ratings for manufacturing job descriptions more reliable than those for jobs in the service sector. (The study concerned functions and traits – SVP, strength requirements, three GED components, etc. – not tasks, it should be stressed, and was based on written job descriptions, not site visits.) In defense of task-based NA, however, it should be recognized that every unit of analysis (structure, notion, function, topic, etc.) and methodology proposed for NA in LT is reductionist to some degree, and that task and task-based NA atomize needs less than other approaches. Further, some limitations of task-based, or any other, NA can be at least partially remedied by the use of multiple data-collection and analysis procedures (described below) and by conducting an analysis of target discourse (see Chapter 7) – a feature of TBLT but of few other approaches.

Despite, but bearing in mind, these limitations, the *DOT*'s task-based occupational descriptions are valuable for TBLT course designers, materials writers, and teachers. (Copies of *DOT* entries can also make for interesting class discussion with students from, or about to enter, the fields concerned and can sometimes stimulate combined student NA and language-learning projects.) However, the descriptions may need supplementing in two ways: by (1) verification in the particular settings for which students are being prepared, in order to identify any local job or position variation in target tasks, and (2) collection of language samples. The former involves recourse to one or more additional information sources on the occupations of interest, and one or more methods of collecting data from those sources; the latter requires an analysis of target discourse.

Verification in the particular target setting in which students work or for which they are preparing is a process that will usually also serve to flesh out *DOT* definitions and provide useful detail. This tends to be more important in service and "white-collar" areas, since the *DOT* has tended to make finer distinctions among manufacturing than other occupations, e.g., including 70 entries for different kinds of sewing machine operator, compared to only six for Secretary. Position descriptions sometimes also include additional useful information not in the *DOT*'s occupational listing. For example, a well-known international hotel chain's position description for guest services agent, roughly equivalent to the *DOT*'s hotel clerk, or front desk clerk, described earlier, lists the typical 'work schedule,' 'training and experience required,' 'tools and equipment used,' and 'cognitive demands,' in addition to the tasks, or 'functions and duties,' involved.

The detail of job or position descriptions generally far surpasses that of occupational descriptions. Employers, after all, usually know what they want their own employees to do more precisely than can be specified by a list of common tasks required of employees in that type working in different kinds of establishment. The occupation of secretary (sometimes upgraded to 'office coordinator' or 'office manager') may serve as an illustration. There is no entry in the *DOT* for what is a very common occupation the world over, university department secretary. The nearest listings the *DOT* offers are those for school secretary (education) and secretary (clerical). The latter (U.S. Department of Labor 1991, p. 171) is broader:

201.362-030 SECRETARY (clerical) alternate titles: secretarial stenographer
    Schedules appointments, gives information to callers, takes dictation, and otherwise relieves officials of clerical work and minor administrative and business detail. Reads and routes incoming mail. Locates and attaches appropriate file to correspondence to be answered by employer. Takes dictation in shorthand or by machine [STENOTYPE OPERATOR (clerical) 202.362¬022] and transcribes notes on typewriter, or transcribes from voice recordings [TRANSCRIBING-MACHINE OPERATOR (clerical) 203.582-058]. Composes

and types routine correspondence. Files correspondence and other records. Answers telephone and gives information to callers or routes call to appropriate official and places outgoing calls. Schedules appointments for employer. Greets visitors, ascertains nature of business, and conducts visitors to employer or appropriate person. May not take dictation. May arrange travel schedule and reservations. May compile and type statistical reports. May oversee clerical workers. May keep personnel records [PERSONNEL CLERK (clerical) 209.362-026]. May record minutes of staff meetings. May make copies of correspondence or other printed matter, using copying or duplicating machine. May prepare outgoing mail, using postage-metering machine. May prepare notes, correspondence, and reports, using word processor or computer terminal. GOE: 07.01.03 Strength: S GED: R4 M3 L4 SVP: 6 DLU: 89

Readers familiar with the workings of university departments will recognize omissions from this description, and university department secretaries themselves (insiders) would assuredly spot even more. The job description for a department secretary at a large state university with which I am familiar provides breadth and depth to the *DOT* entry with a realism that might well discourage applicants who saw it from ever seeking the position. Its size precludes quotation of the full document, which runs to 11 single-spaced pages (compared with the half-page *DOT* entry), but some brief excerpts will serve to illustrate the degree of useful detail and specificity that authentic job and position descriptions, as opposed to occupation descriptions, can provide the course designer, along with use of task as the unit of analysis at this level, as well.

Following a brief introduction and overview, the description lists 'major duties and responsibilities,' divided into four areas: 'office management,' 'curriculum and instruction,' 'fiscal and inventory,' and 'personnel.' These, in turn, are broken down into sub-areas, each consisting of a set of tasks requiring anything from a single sentence to a half-page paragraph to describe. Thus, 'office management,' designated as involving 10% of the secretary's time, is divided into 19 sub-areas, of which the following are four of the simpler ones for an outsider to understand:

(1) Maintains a log of incoming federal and campus mail addressed to the chair and department, noting date received, sender, subject matter, assigned to and response dates if any. Reads all incoming mail addressed to the department and chair and answers routine correspondence, such as program inquiries, admission procedures, independently whenever personal replies by the chairman (sic) are not necessary. Completes questionnaires independently, researching when necessary for statistical data, submits to the department chairman (sic) for approval.

(2) Greets and ascertains the purpose of callers, answers inquiries and/or refers them to the proper department or person, schedules appointments for interviews for important foreign visitors and observers for the chairman (sic), director and staff.

(11) Attends various meetings regarding purchasing, registration, graduate manual, personnel, management, office training and immigration. This may involve new materials or updating instructions pertaining to rules, regulations and procedures.

(12) Processes all travel requests (departmental and research), and travel completion reports, submits them to the Department Chair, Dean, and Office of Research Administration for approval. Types requisition for airfare and travel advance, travel completion report forms and narrative report.

Such detail would tell a course designer a lot more about this secretary's target tasks than the *DOT*'s "reads and routes incoming mail," "answers inquiries," "files correspondence and other records," "schedules appointments for employer," and so on, although the *DOT* entry is essentially correct as far as it goes. A job description will usually also suggest documents, specimens of which it would be useful for the designer to collect as a partial basis for a subsequent analysis of target discourse, as well as for possible use in materials design. Indicated in this case are copies of pages from the departmental mail log, samples of incoming and outgoing correspondences of various types, purchase orders, travel-funding requests, and visa application forms, to name but a few. Audio-recordings of entire days of spoken (including telephone) language use in the office, or failing that, of a stratified random sample thereof, would also be important.

Despite the advantages of the level of detail found in job or position descriptions, even they can sometimes conceal, or at least fail to make explicit, much of what a job or position really entails. In the case of the university department secretary, for example, completing university administration questionnaires about student enrollments and completion rates, staff travel and vacations, department budget projections and the like, referring visitors or telephone callers to the appropriate staff members, as well as the duties listed in (11), all assume a wealth of accumulated knowledge on the individual concerned's part about where the needed information is stored, how this particular university, department, and faculty do things, and much more. The needs analyst would have to obtain such information about these dimensions of the job via other means, such as non-participant observation and interviews with department secretaries. In extreme cases, some entries can conceal as much as they reveal. Thus, from some familiarity with the department front office in question, I can attest to the knowledge and personal skill needed by the secretary just to accomplish (14) in the 'curriculum and instruction' area:

(14) Deals with students on a personal basis daily, both native and non-native speakers of English, by answering questions regarding policies and procedures, or referring them to the chairman (sic). Maintains an up-to-date student directory and card file.

And what horrors lurk behind the innocent-sounding final item under 'office management':

(19) Reminds faculty members of all deadlines.

In sum, the initial bases for many task-based NAs exist in published and unpublished forms in both the public and private sectors, with militaries, governments, educational institutions, private corporations and employee unions constituting just some of the sources available in the vocational and occupational domains. There is also a considerable literature describing academic genres and tasks for school and university students (see, e.g., Marx & Walsh 1988; Ostler 1980; Swales 1990a), examples of which are dealt with in Chapter 7. The descriptions are almost always task-based and offer "ready-made" NAs for those familiar with the professional literature or, at least, with where to look. However, as noted earlier, it is important to verify generic descriptions of occupational, vocational, academic, or survival needs in particular target settings, as this will often reveal local variation from the abstract ideal. There may be tasks that are common in an occupation, for example, but which are not required of the holder of a particular job or position, or (more often) tasks that are not typically required in an occupation but are required in a particular job. Finally, as illustrated below, alternative sources, and procedures for gathering information, as well as analyses of target discourse, sometimes reveal demands on individual position holders that would be difficult or impossible to predict from neatly printed descriptions of either occupations or jobs.

6.1.2. The learners

The learner(s) for whom a course is to be prepared will ideally be a major source of information on every aspect of the design and subsequent implementation of a program, starting with their needs. Learners obviously have a right to input on the matter; it is their time, often their money, and their life chances, that are at stake. Some learners are articulate and/or knowledgeable (not necessarily the same thing) about their current or projected L2 needs and, if asked, are able and willing to supply detailed, usable information, even through the L2 (see, e.g., Ramani *et al.* 1988; Tarantino 1988). Others, such as recent immigrants and beginners in Australia's Adult Migrant Education Program (AMEP), have been reported by teachers as less able in this regard, and/or as feeling teachers should decide what form a program should take (Brindley 1984; Brindley & Hood 1990). Patience and some ingenuity can be required, particularly with learners with zero or low L2 proficiency, illiterates (in the L1 and/or L2), and people from cultural backgrounds in which interviews may not be recognized speech events (see Wolfson 1976) and written tests unknown. In some cultures, moreover, where interviews or questionnaires are concerned, direct questions, especially from strangers, may be inappropriate and/or not to be answered "directly" (see, e.g., Eades 1992; Phillips 1972), and expressing criticisms or strong opinions in public frowned upon.

A moment's thought will show that reification of the learner as the principal or, as some would have it, the sole authority on needs is almost never justified, and often impossible, even in the case of highly educated, articulate adults. Those who, in the name of learner-centered instruction or political correctness, would privilege learners' subjective, or felt, needs over all others should ask themselves the following questions: Can the students in question articulate their (perceived) needs? How good are their perceptions? How good are their perceptions compared with other sources? Even if they are good, can process information be used responsibly in a course that is already under way? Are the benefits of (this interpretation of) a "negotiated" syllabus more valuable than those accruing from a carefully pre-planned one?

Many learners are pre-service, that is, preparing for education, for an occupation, or for life in a new country, none of which they have yet experienced or know much about at all. Thus, even at the gross level of undifferentiated language skills, some English for academic purposes (EAP) learners' anticipated greatest difficulty with L2 writing before they began an educational program has been found to be supplanted by problems with speaking skills once the program started (Beatty & Chan 1984; Christison & Krahnke 1986; Jordan 1993; Zughoul & Hussein 1985). Beatty and Chan (1984), for example, using a questionnaire to compare the perceived academic needs of 24 students entering the Graduate School English Language Center in Beijing in preparation for graduate study or for periods as visiting scholars (in practice, usually quite similar experiences) in the United States with those of 22 Chinese scholars who had already been residents at US universities (Berkeley and UCLA) for a minimum of six and an average of 13 months. Respondents in both groups were specialists in the physical and life sciences and engineering. The results showed that the group with first-hand experience of the target academic setting rated almost all questionnaire items as of increased importance. Both groups felt understanding lectures was the single most important activity, followed by such research skills as reading and writing research proposals, papers, journal articles, and abstracts. Tasks rated more important by the experienced than the inexperienced group included reading charts and graphs, taking lecture notes, and functioning in graduate seminars, presumably reflecting their growing awareness of the relative importance of such activities in US graduate programs. Other tasks rated higher by the experienced group included writing resumes, filling out application forms, and seeking information and help from the university, perhaps reflecting a realization of the greater importance of individuals initiating bids for assistance of various kinds in the United States compared with the tendency for such matters to be taken care of more uniformly and by the host institution in the PRC. The researchers ended their article by stressing the value of pre-course NAs by post-experience informants:

> first it is essential to do a needs assessment before teaching, and second, the people who have adapted to the target situation are the ones who should be asked. Instead of relying on their own perceptions and those of people who have not yet gone through the experience…, curriculum developers are advised to poll the people who…know what is important for them to learn. Sensitivity to the immediate needs and perceptions of incoming [pre-experience] students must be displayed while gently initiating and guiding them in the direction in which they will need to go. (Beatty & Chan 1984, p. 59)

Such conclusions are probably well founded, although they would be strengthened by data validating the experienced group's perceptions, for example, by comparing them with those of other stakeholders, notably their content area teachers, or better still, with the students' performance in the graduate programs.

The importance of comparing results from more than one source is shown in a study by Zughoul and Hussein (1985) of the English-language needs of students at Yarmouk University in Jordan. The researchers administered two questionnaires, one to 1147 students, and the other to 90 faculty members at Yarmouk. They found that students' English listening, speaking, reading, and writing skills were rated considerably higher by the students themselves than by the faculty. Where needs were concerned, both faculty and students rated listening the most important skill for students but diverged in their rankings thereafter, with students rating speaking ability the second most important, for example, whereas faculty considered it least important, and instead thought reading ability almost as crucial as listening. Again, although Zughoul and Hussein report that the faculty's perceptions were consistent with their own impressionistic observations and with the apparent degree of use of the four skills at Yarmouk, the differences of opinion alone do not invalidate the students' perceptions; independent objective measures of their English abilities and of language use at the university would be needed in order to address the validity issue adequately.

While pre-experience learners will often make for unreliable informants, experienced in-service workers can usually report quite accurately on the tasks their jobs involve.

Several limitations upon what even they can provide the analyst should be borne in mind, however. First, many courses have to be prepared before the students arrive at the teaching institution concerned. Second, as shown by a NA of Thai aquaculturalists (Savage & Storer 1992; see below), even well-educated informants (understandably) can often provide only general, insufficiently detailed information about language needs for those tasks unless prompted by some form of role-play or guided participant observation activities, or else, as in Selinker (1979), by a series of carefully planned initial and follow-up lessons. Third, language learners are rarely themselves applied linguists, so there is no reason for them to have more than naive intuitions about their language needs, even if they have experience with other aspects of the educational, occupational, or other settings giving rise to those needs. Even when they do know both about language and the field concerned, Lamotte (1981), an applied linguist graduate student with five years' experience as a physical therapist, showed how unreliable retrospection can be when compared with objective analysis of language use. Finally, when learners do have good insights and intuitions about their needs, even their language needs, better sources of information are often available. Depending on local circumstances, such as the longevity and stability of a program and its staff, these may include language teachers with prior experience of such learners, people now undergoing or who have completed the education program (Allen & Spada 1983) or are already employed in the occupation (Tarantino 1988) for which the prospective learners are preparing, current or future subject-area teachers (Horowitz 1986; Mackay & Bosquet 1981) or employers (Watts 1994), documents, such as job descriptions and course reading lists, and last but not least, the extensive published NA literature.

None of this is to suggest that learners should be excluded from the NA process. Far from it. Rather, where circumstances permit, objective and felt needs should be cross-validated and triangulated among teachers, learners, and external sources, preferably (a) before a course begins, (b) at its inception, and (c) as it proceeds. Such practice respects learners' rights and raises teachers' and students' understanding of why they are doing what they are doing. It can lead them to reflect usefully on means and ends (Nunan 1988, p. 5) and can serve as one component in learner training (Ellis & Sinclair 1989) or as a basis for parts of the program itself. It is the valuing of learner-identified subjective needs above all others that should be avoided.

A reportedly successful use of learners as informants for both NA and course design was described by Savage and Storer (1992). The context was an Asian Institute of Technology (AIT) English language program for the staff of an aquaculture demonstration project in Udornthani in northeast Thailand. NA for the program began with an AIT teacher making a one-day site visit to discuss their work-related needs with the learners. The latter listed them, among other things, as being able to use English to describe and explain the aquaculture project's research and recommendations to visitors (many of whom were English speakers), often using figures and graphs, to write monthly reports and summaries thereof, and to read and write memos, scientific reports, and farmer report forms. The researchers were not satisfied, however:

> This information was inadequate in that it merely prescribed a set of content to be taught. (Should we now offer a course called 'Writing Office Memos'?) It did not tell us what the learners could already do in English and what language learning concerns they thought needed to be addressed. This led us to a two-day planning workshop (Savage & Storer 1992, p. 190).

The workshop was held at AIT in Bangkok. Sessions were videotaped and teachers took detailed notes. Seven art staff and seven student counterparts carried out work-related tasks together to generate information for the eventual two-week period of intensive language instruction, whose general aim was to get students to a stage where they could continue to develop their English ability by themselves. The tasks included such exercises as giving oral reports on fieldwork and writing monthly reports, with the collaboration between teachers and staff members serving to identify language needs more precisely in the minds of both teachers and future students. It transpired, for example, that quantitative data on report forms did not have to be translated into English and that qualitative data could be in note form, not complete sentences. Teachers were able to observe students using English and "were thus better able to comment on their needs; the participants themselves were better able to discuss their learning needs" (Savage & Storer 1992, p. 190).

The final course, which took place on-site in Udornthani, reflected the needs identified by learners and teachers during the previous two sessions, as well as methodological options found successful then, e.g., group work on occupation-based tasks, followed by report-back sessions, which had proved useful for diagnostic purposes at the second NA meeting. The seven aquaculturalists who had participated in that session helped orient the 17 colleagues who were now joining them as students, suggesting learning strategies they had found useful and explaining unfamiliar aspects of the teaching methodology, such as the group work and report-back format, and the negotiable choice of the tasks themselves. Teachers kept detailed daily logs during the intensive course, later using them to see whether and how learner- and teacher-identified needs had been met during the course and also whether and how they had been reinterpreted and allowed to change as the two weeks unfolded. Following Hutchinson and Waters (1987), Savage and Storer (1992, pp. 196–197) stressed the importance of continuing participatory evaluation throughout the course, principally through explicit discussion of tasks and task-work during the report-back sessions. Very much in the spirit of Breen and Candlin's process syllabus (see Section 8.2.7), they advocated continual adjustments to content and methodology as required in the light of students' evolving perceptions of their language needs as a course proceeds. In this way, students can participate not only in NA but also in defining content and methodology for an emergent language program.

6.1.3. Applied linguists

It is tempting for applied linguists to act as their own informants when conducting a NA. After all, most will know quite a lot about language and may have had extensive LT experience, sometimes with students of the kind involved in the analysis, and perhaps even in the very program for which the NA is being conducted. While their observations and introspections may well be valuable in such cases, the use of alternative sources, especially experts in the domain for which students are preparing, cannot be overemphasized. The plain fact of the matter is that applied linguists' intuitions about language use in walks of life with which they are only passingly familiar are likely to be almost as unreliable and invalid as those of any other outsider. A professionally responsible designer will go to experts in the domain, not to ask about language use, in which the domain expert will usually be inexpert, but about content and tasks.

Examples of mismatches between applied linguists' intuitions about discourse and communication in unfamiliar areas have occasionally been reported explicitly. In a pioneering case study of this issue in EAP reading, for example, Selinker (1979) described four consultations with a genetics professor, a native speaker (NS) of English, over a period of a few months, much in the tradition of linguistics fieldwork. The expert informant provided his own interpretations of the target article and also responded to carefully planned questions from Selinker and a class (mostly) of English as a second language (ESL) teachers, all untrained in genetics, who met frequently between consultations. Together they endeavored to explicate a single five-page article surveying research on the repair of genetic material in living cells.

Many categories of difficulty emerged, of which the following were just nine of the most common. Selinker (1979, p. 211) recognized that the categories were heterogeneous, reflect mixed levels of analysis, and sometimes overlapped. First, there was the problem of understanding such technical terms in the field as pyrimidine, dimer, and enzymatic photoreactivation, the only solution for which appeared to be for the teacher to become familiar with the subject matter, at least at the level of a basic introductory genetics text. The second problem involved common words used technically in a particular field, in this case, for example, 'insult' to mean a cause of damage in DNA. The difficulty here was not only to learn the field-specific meaning of a term, and often the new collocations it entered into when used that way, but also, crucially, to recognize when a word was indeed being used in something other than its familiar non-technical sense. Third, the strength with which the writer was making a claim, as reflected, in expressions of levels of certainty and generality, was sometimes ambiguous, especially for those unfamiliar with the amount and gradations of "hedging" common in scientific discourse, due to scientists being aware that many observations have multiple interpretations and that today's inference may be disconfirmed tomorrow. Hedges are often encoded with modals, but also in other ways less obvious to outsiders, as in the following sentence from the article in question (Hanawalt 1972, p. 83):

> It has been estimated, for example, that a bacterial gene may be duplicated over 100 million times before there is even a 50% chance that it will have been altered.

This sentence, the genetics professor was able to show, contained two hedges: the agentless passive, 'It has been estimated,' and perhaps most alarmingly for the non-specialist, the phrase '100 million times.' The latter, on the face of it, looked like a large number expressing author confidence and/or designed to impress the reader. In fact, however, 100 million had a specific meaning in this context, namely, ten to the nth power, which is the 'mutation frequency,' that is, the rate at which genetic material undergoes hereditary changes.

A fourth problem was for the non-specialist to determine when an apparent 'contextual paraphrase,' for example, 'replicate with extraordinary fidelity' for 'duplicate,' really was an alternative way of referring to the same scientific concept employed for stylistic effect, as opposed to something different. A fifth difficulty concerned the recognition of semantic differences occasionally marked only by variation in low-level grammatical choices, for example, in tenses and articles or in singular/plural changes, for example, scheme/s and efficiency/-ies. Sixth, modals often appeared to be used with meanings not captured by sentence-level linguistic descriptions. How something could "demonstrate...in principle," for example (as opposed to either demonstrate or not demonstrate), was only understandable by appreciating (later in the article) that Hanawalt had been hinting at an alternative explanation he would suggest for a previously unquestioned interpretation of a body of research findings. Other difficulties lay in recognizing and then interpreting mismatches between explicit and implicit rhetorical structures, including definitions and classifications, subtle shades of meaning indicated by punctuation choices, for example, use of a semicolon versus a comma, and the multiple readings sometimes possible of uses of sentence connectors, such as however, then, and yet, as in

> One is impressed by the remarkable stability of the DNA molecule, an essential factor if species of organisms are to remain unchanged over many generations of growth. Yet the DNA must exist in a milieu of deleterious factors such as ultraviolet light (UV) that can destroy its genetic message. (Hanawalt 1972, p. 83)

Having illustrated the complexity confronting even the NS, untrained in a specialized field, who attempts to read insider communication, Selinker concluded with some useful pointers regarding the detail required of an adequate linguistic and rhetorical description of such discourse, compared with the need for a pedagogically feasible sub-set of "safe rules" and general principles sufficient to get the non-native speaker (NNS) by in some contexts, but not others. Such safe rules (see Lackstrom, Selinker, & Trimble 1973) would probably suffice for EAP/English for science and technology (EST) students' own writing and for reading textbooks, where rhetorical functions are often made explicit, but less so for reading specialist-to-specialist communication, such as academic journal articles, where implicit information and unmonitored use of all of a language's linguistic and rhetorical resources abound.

In an interesting replication, Huckin and Olson (1984) set out to see if Selinker's procedure could be streamlined to make it usable in real-world NA, when teachers frequently have little idea of their students' needs until a course is about to begin and then have little time to conduct the analysis. Serving as the naive readers of the same genetics article by Hanawalt themselves, Huckin and Olson first read the text independently, formed their own interpretations of its meaning, compared them, found them to be similar, compared them with those of Selinker's ESL teacher group, and found them to differ, and to do so in similar ways. They then conducted an interview of over an hour with each of two specialist informants, Hanawalt, a Stanford University biologist and author of the target text (who had read Selinker's article), and Hohn, a genetics expert at the University of Wurzburg, a NS of German with a non-native, but excellent, command of English (who had not read Selinker's article).

The two geneticists' interpretations of the article agreed with one another and with Huckin and Olson's (1984, p. 122) interpretations totally "on every point." The two experts both felt that the differences in the way Selinker's group had interpreted lexical and grammatical details in the article, for example, two putatively different uses of 'must,' were sometimes inaccurate and would in any case make little or no difference to its overall interpretation, and that questions from Huckin and Olson about such details generally had little relevance for understanding the basic meaning structure of the text. Conversely, questions pertaining to rhetorical structure and purpose often did affect overall interpretation. The use of '100 million times,' for example, was confirmed as having the technical meaning Selinker's informant (but not the naive readers) had identified, but also the rhetorical purpose of impressing readers with the magnitude of genetic stability, which had been Selinker's naive group's initial interpretation, disconfirmed by their expert consultant. In general, whereas Huckin and Olson found most of the nine classes of questions suggested by Selinker 'unfruitful' (p. 127), they agreed with Selinker that a 'top-down' use of questions of overall rhetorical structure and purpose allowed them to establish "a mutually understood frame of reference with each informant which then allowed us to discuss lower-level details in proper perspective" (p. 127). A misunderstood rhetorical perspective could also lead an analyst astray, however. For example, Selinker's group had interpreted 'in principle' and 'might' in "Several types of repair mechanisms ... demonstrate, in principle, three ways in which an organism might respond to damage of its DNA" as a hint of things (i.e., an alternative explanation) to come. However, that turned out not to have been what Hanawalt had had in mind. Rather, he said he used 'could' and 'might' almost interchangeably and had simply meant that the mechanisms referred to were three possible ways the organism might respond, that is, again, what an initial, lay reading might suggest.

Huckin and Olson inferred that the use of a top-down approach to text analysis is the key to reducing the time that the use of expert informants can otherwise take, thereby making the procedure a more viable option for practitioners. They concluded that needs analysts should also have some familiarity with important conventions and ways of arguing in the field, for example, a grasp of scientific methodology; that the chance of informants providing pedagogically useful interpretations of a text is likely to increase if needs analysts can adopt the content area specialist's, rather than the (applied) linguist's, perspective; and that the most useful specialist informant for a language for specific purposes (LSP) text is its author.

Regrettably, there appear to have been very few other studies of this kind. However, Tarone *et al.* (1981) used insider knowledge to help explicate the overall rhetorical structure of two professional journal articles in astrophysics. In that field, the structure typically takes the form of a logical argument wherein authors select the combination of accepted procedures and equations that best solves a problem. The academic informant also helped clarify the rhetorical functions played by passives and, contrary to popular belief about scientific writing in general, in this genre in astrophysics, at least, the more frequent active verb constructions. The informant was Icke, the fourth author, a Dutch astrophysicist. While not a NS, Icke had native-like English and "very strong intuitions regarding the rhetorical and grammatical structure typically used in good writing in this field" (Tarone *et al.* 1981, p. 125, fn. 2). It may be that in specialized areas in which practitioners are highly educated, applied linguists can hope to find domain experts with useful knowledge about language use in their field as well. Like Selinker, meanwhile, Tarone *et al.* were clear about the critical importance for NA of insider expert knowledge:

> We cannot stress enough the importance of Icke's contribution to our analysis. His knowledge of the subject matter was absolutely essential to our analysis of the rhetorical structure of these papers. (Tarone *et al.* 1981, p. 125, fn. 2)

The insider's subject matter knowledge was also found important by Zuck and Zuck (1984), who compared specialist and non-specialist evaluations of anticipated text difficulty for students, and their approaches to assessing student comprehension of a text. Zuck and Zuck used a short (two-page) article from *BioScience* about whether islands really provide unique opportunities for modeling more complex continental biological systems. The specialist judges were six biologists (three NSs and three NNSs); the non-specialist judges were ten ESL teachers (five NSs and five NNSs). They were all asked to perform three tasks: to rate the anticipated difficulty of the article for beginning biology students, to list a maximum of ten words or phrases they considered essential to understanding the passage, and to write from three to five short questions that could be used to evaluate student comprehension of the passage's main idea. (The ambiguity of the way in which the second task was formulated, allowing subjects to list ten or fewer items if they chose, and allowing differences in the number of questions posed on the third task, unfortunately introduced three unnecessary sources of uncontrolled variance into the study's results, making a replication desirable.)

Overall difficulty ratings for the article were similar across groups. NNS ESL teachers rated it as very difficult, at 5.8 on a scale of 1–6, NS ESL teachers at 4.6, and NS biologists at 5.7. (The NNS biologists' rating was inconclusive.) Written comments revealed, however, that the NS biologists were responding to the perceived difficulty of the biological concepts (e.g., patchiness) for beginning biology students, whereas both NS and NNS ESL teachers were reacting to the perceived difficulty of the language in which the text was written. Subjects interpreted the second task differently; key words and phrases listed were inconsistent both within and across groups. However, NS ESL teachers generally identified words that indicated the main idea, and NNS ESL teachers the words they had to look up themselves. NS biologists, on the other hand, mostly listed words or word uses that a naive reader would not easily find in a dictionary, i.e., common words used technically, and NNS biologists mostly listed words they had trouble with themselves. Finally, specialists and non-specialists, whether NSs or NNSs, showed three within-group similarities and between-group differences in the kinds of comprehension questions they wrote. First, questions asking the definition of terms were almost exclusively the province of the ESL teachers. Second, similar to a finding by Selinker (1979), whereas biologists' questions reflected recognition of the tentative nature of the original author's argument, expressed, for example, through plentiful use of 'may,' ESL teachers' questions were mostly posed as if all information in the text was factual and certain. Third, answers to the ESL teachers' questions were more local, often based on information contained in a single sentence or paragraph, whereas answers to the subject specialists' questions were more global, tending to involve interpretations of larger units of text or even of the whole article, and to require inferences more often.

Considerably more work is needed extending the line of inquiry represented by these four studies both within and beyond EAP and EST. For reasons explained earlier, what such research reveals about particular linguistic and rhetorical properties of texts in a target area will be less useful for TBLT than for synthetic approaches to syllabus design. However, the work is still important for task-based NAs for what it shows about the relative value of different sources of information, particularly applied linguists and domain experts.

6.1.4. Domain experts

While the professional literature, the learners themselves, and applied linguists will often have much to offer as sources of information for NAs, the limitations of what they can reasonably be expected to provide help to clarify the crucial importance attributed to domain experts in TBLT. By definition, they are likely to have most knowledge about an academic field, a vocational training program, an occupation, survival skills needed in another country, and so on. Therefore, when at all possible, and assuming the work has not already been done and reported in the professional literature, needs analysts should seek out the engineering professor rather than the future engineering student or EAP teacher, the post office manager and postal clerk rather than the would-be postal worker, and personnel officers who actually conduct job interviews in the field of interest rather than the retrospections of applied linguists about (probably field- and culture-specific, possibly idiosyncratic) job interviews they once underwent.

Having identified domain experts as usually the single most useful source of information (not the only source, it should be stressed, and not invariably a reliable source, as Coleman's study at Hasanuddin University showed), the important point to grasp is the kind of information that should be sought from them. Domain experts are experts first and foremost in content, or tasks, seldom in language. They should be asked about what people in their domain have to know and have to do, only very rarely about what they have to say.[1] Notice, for example, that the genetics professor who served as an informant in Selinker's case study was rarely asked to act as an authority on language per se, although he was asked about such things as the meanings of lexical items and technical terms in his field. Instead, his role was chiefly to explain how genetics and genetics discourse work, e.g., the constant testing and revision of predictions made by models, the clear differentiation of 'observed facts' and 'interpretations,' and the use of 'hedges,' as well as to provide brief explanations of basic concepts treated in the target article.

Needless to say, there are exceptions. The case of the Dutch astrophysicist (Tarone *et al.* 1981) has already been noted. In addition, Ramani *et al.* (1988, p. 86) reported that some of the Indian scientists they interviewed were very clear about their perceived language needs, sometimes at quite a detailed level. For example, one felt his students had to learn the strategies employed by established scientists to stake claims of priority in noticing phenomena related to the topic of a paper but not elaborated on in it. In general, however, domain experts who have reliable introspections about language are exceptions, not the rule. As might be expected, most are relatively unreliable sources on language use in their domain, and beyond the obvious macro level ("I need to learn English"), even about their own language needs and difficulties. This has been found not just at the detailed linguistic level but also where higher-level discourse events are concerned. For example, Marriot (1991) described how a monolingual English-speaking Australian shop assistant in a duty-free store failed to make sales of watches to Japanese tourists who were interested in buying, due to her lack of Japanese, compounded by her

---

[1] There may be exceptions to this. The military trainer instructing soldiers in army radio communication could provide important information about the particular code used in army radio transmissions. However, even that could be handled, albeit less efficiently, by a study of a representative sample of transmissions.

additional failure to recognize discourse cues when the tourists attempted to complete the transaction in English (see Section 7.4.2). Interviewed subsequently, the woman (who had worked in the store for four years) claimed that she was able to "get through" transactions with Japanese customers despite their poor English (sic) and that their politeness made them easy to serve. Marriot (1991, p. 205) concluded:

> In other words, this server did not diagnose the existence of any serious language problems. Such a finding is consistent with previous research. For example, using the technique of the follow-up interview, Neustupny confirmed that summarizing assessments of participants in an encounter do not reflect the range of actual problems which occur in the discourse. (Neustupny 1988)

On the basis of his experience, Selinker (1979, pp. 213–214) suggested several criteria for the 'good specialist informant.' Originally proposed for EAP informants, they are reworked and generalized here as among those desirable (although assuredly rare in the same individual) in an expert selected as an informant for a NA in any domain. A good informant, in Selinker's view, should be a NS, well trained and competent in the field of interest, used to dealing with NNSs attempting to function in that domain, caring about their success in doing so, able to explain what experts in the domain do, and willing to revise initial answers after follow-up questions if wrong the first time. Selinker further suggested that informants should have a feel for the technical language in the domain, and an openness to LT and LSP as important activities, and a willingness to familiarize themselves with basic issues in LT/LSP in order to understand the kind of information the analyst wants. These last three qualities are of less concern for TBLT, however, since the basic subject matter for a task-based NA will be non-linguistic. While samples of target discourse will be gathered for later analysis and potential use in task-based materials, they will rarely require commentary by informants, few of whom will have the necessary linguistic expertise, in any case.

6.1.5. Triangulated sources

Reference has already been made to the value of triangulating perceived and/or objective needs among learners and other informants, but the triangulation process itself can take different forms and deserves some elaboration (see Cicourel 1974; Denzin 1970; Lincoln & Guba 1985; Lynch 1995). Triangulation is a procedure long used by researchers working within a qualitative, or naturalistic, tradition to help validate their data and thereby, eventually, to increase the credibility of their interpretations of those data. The process involves the ethnographer comparing different sets and sources of data with one another, e.g., by presenting workers', management's, and the researcher's own perspectives on the causes of a labor dispute and on changes needed to the parties concerned, and asking them to reflect on those interpretations (see, e.g., Greenwood & Gonzales Santos 1992). Triangulation can involve comparisons among two or more different sources, methods, investigators or (according to some experts) theories, and sometimes combinations thereof (Lincoln & Guba 1985, pp. 305–307).

A NA might sample the opinions of Chilean medical faculty and students as to the nature and extent of the students' reading needs in English, and compare one with the other, and/or either or both with the reading requirements for state or national medical examinations. If the faculty and student views were both assessed via a questionnaire, that is, if the method were held constant, that would be a case of *triangulation by sources*. If the faculty and/or student views (sources held constant) were studied via a question-naire and interviews, that would constitute *triangulation by methods*, as would the comparison of faculty and student opinions with the findings of the document analysis (study of the examination requirements). A comparison of results from faculty inter-views, student questionnaires, and the document analysis would be *triangulation by sources and methods*. Not to be confused with any of those mentioned above, checking findings from two (or 200) more individuals of the same type using the same procedure, e.g., the findings from one faculty interview against those from another faculty inter-view, simply constitutes what Lincoln and Guba (1985, p. 305) call multiple copies of one type of source, not triangulation of different sources. Similarly, comparing findings from faculty interviews with reading requirements listed on course syllabi written by the same faculty members would be a case of comparing different methods of accessing the same information from the same source, not triangulation of sources.

Triangulation by methods can involve use of different data-collection procedures, such as logs, non-participant observation, interviews, questionnaires, and testing, or, for those working within a quantitative paradigm, different research designs, e.g., a multiple case study of EAP students' progress through a medical course, and a quasi-experimental, criterion group design comparing examination scores of students able and unable to read medical texts in English. Researchers in the qualitative, naturalistic mode, Lincoln and Guba (1985, p. 306) point out, could not avail themselves of this option since the design in naturalistic inquiry is emergent, not pre-specified.

Triangulation by investigators involves comparing the findings of different researchers who are studying or have studied the same phenomenon, either separately or as members of a research group. For example, analysts might compare their emerging findings on EAP lecture comprehension needs with those of previous studies in the area (e.g., Arden-Close 1993; Flowerdew 1992, 1995b; Murphy & Candlin 1979; Olsen & Huckin 1990), or simply compare two or more sets of the earlier findings. Needless to say, care must be taken to ascertain the importance of any similarities and differences among the contexts, populations, subject areas, and methodologies involved in the previous studies and in the situation for which the new program is to be designed. In an honest, but surely (for researchers employing qualitative methods) rather troubling comment on this option, Lincoln and Guba note:

> The use of different investigators, a concept perfectly feasible for the conventionalist [i.e., one working in the quantitative paradigm), runs into some problems in the naturalistic context. If the design is emergent, and its form depends ultimately on the particular inter-action that the investigator has with the phenomena (Axiom 2), then one could not expect corroboration of one investigator by another. The problem is identical to that of expecting replicability for the sake of establishing reliability. (Lincoln and Guba 1985, p. 307)

Lincoln and Guba (1985) also consider *triangulation by theories* an unacceptable concept in naturalistic inquiry, in fact "epistemologically unsound and empirically empty" (p. 307). This is because facts are theory-determined, something with which few philosophers of science or researchers of any methodological persuasion would argue (see Chalmers 1999, pp. 42–60), and "do not have an existence independent of the theory within whose framework they achieve coherence" (p. 307), a controversial claim for members of many different camps. Is it not frequently the case that at least a sub-set of the facts and phenomena recognized by complementary, and even by rival, theories – "problems" in need of explanation, in Laudan's terms (see Section 3.2) – are the same (they are rivals in the same empirically defined domain, after all), and that conflicts among their supporters concern arguments over which theory can best explain them?

In any case, triangulation by sources and/or by methods is an important procedure whose use has, until recently (see Bosher & Smalkoski 2002; Jasso-Aguilar 1999/2005; Oliver *et al.* 2012; Svendsen & Krebs 1984), been observed in only token fashion in most of the NA literature, although it has been used effectively in SLA and classroom research (see, e.g., Hawkins 1985; Johnson Nystrom 1983; Lynch 1995). Many NAs for English for specific purposes (ESP) programs involve data from different sources and/or gather them via different methods. Every published study I am aware of that has done so has found differences, often large differences, in the views of different classes of informants (see, e.g., Iwai *et al.* 1999; Markee 1986; Ogata 1992; Oliver *et al.* 2012; Orikasa 1989). Orikasa (1989), for example, used four different questionnaires to survey Japanese high school students, their English as a foreign language (EFL) teachers, a small group of the high school's administrators (including the principal and three vice principals), and the EFL faculty members in all departments (Commerce, Economics, Law, Letters, Medicine, and Science and Technology) of the university to which the high school concerned was affiliated. Questions covered the five areas suggested by Brown (1995, pp. 43–45) for such cases: priorities, abilities, problems, attitudes, and solutions. Students differed from the other three groups in the relative importance they attributed to speaking over reading and writing skills. High school EFL teachers rated students' abilities much higher than the students themselves (in sharp contrast with the earlier reported reverse finding by Zughoul & Hussein 1985, for Yarmouk University faculty). The high school EFL teachers ranked listening as the most problematic skill, whereas the university EFL teachers rated reading as the one causing most difficulty. Finally, the high school teachers revealed a considerable lack of consensus among themselves over goals and procedures, for example, the use of spoken English in the classroom. Similarly, in her study of Japanese high school students' language needs, Ogata (1992) used questionnaires to survey three groups, Japanese teachers of English, NS assistant teachers, and students. While she found that all three groups strongly supported preparation for the notorious Japanese university entrance English examinations, she identified a discrepancy between the relative importance of (especially oral) communicative abilities perceived by the students compared with the other two groups. Unfortunately, Orikasa and Ogata, like most analysts, both stopped there, content to report the differences and leave it at that.

A case where triangulation by sources and methods was used productively is the study of the language and tasks performed by maids in a Waikiki hotel by Jasso-Aguilar (1999/2005). Jasso-Aguilar utilized multiple sources (hotel maids, supervisors, the executive housekeeper, and a human resources staff member) and multiple methods (participant observation, unstructured interviews, and questionnaires), followed by triangulation of sources and methods, to help determine the dependability of the findings obtained. She reports that triangulation enabled her not only to identify discrepancies but also to *explain* several of them. They were due to such factors as racial differences among sources, differences in typical guest requirements across shift times, difficulty with English, and with the written mode, in particular, making questionnaires and unstructured interviews differentially effective data-gathering procedures for informants of varying L2 proficiency, and differing interests and perspectives of employers and employees concerning such matters as the importance of the maids being able to "chit-chat" with guests.

In cases where findings from different sources and/or methods conflict, it is important to find out which are right, or more likely to be, and are to be followed when designing a program. Are none of them right? Or are all of them (at least those involving different sources)? Are conflicting findings simply evidence for Mohan and Marshall Smith's thesis that different views of tasks (paraphrasing somewhat) reflect the "fact" that all views of them are socially constructed? Assuming one rejects the postmodernist and epistemological relativist view that different views of reality, including tasks, simply reflect the fact (sic) that all of them are socially constructed (in which case there would be no such thing as facts, and one would not be bothered by conflicting findings, or indeed by "findings" at all), this is exactly where triangulation, as opposed to informal cross-checking, can help the needs analyst. So, too, can one or more independent measures of the variable concerned, such as the L2 proficiency of students or the knowledge and competence of a flight attendant (FA). For example, an objective measure of students' L2 proficiency could, in principle, have helped decide between the conflicting views of students' proficiency uncovered in such studies as Orikasa's (1989) and Zughoul and Hussein's (1985), as well as gradually build up a body of experience as to the likely reliability of different sources on such matters in future NAs. Predictive validity studies comparing different perceived and objective needs with subsequent student performance are another option for evaluating alternative information sources.

6.2. Methods

In addition to substantive findings about the discourse of physics lectures, chemistry textbooks, and the like, applied linguists have developed a considerable body of expertise in the various procedures available for NA, building on NA methodology in education (e.g., Stufflebeam *et al.* 1985) and (insufficiently, in my view) on social science research methods in general (e.g., Bailey 1982; Bernard 1994; Lincoln & Guba 1985; Reinharz 1992; Strauss & Corbin 1990). Several alternatives exist (see Table 6.2), some requiring more expertise or time than others, and some being more appropriate than others for different situations or for use with different kinds of informants. They include both inductive and deductive procedures (Berwick 1989). The former involves use of expert intuitions, participant and non-participant observation, and unstructured interviews, from which categories of needs are derived; the latter involves procedures and instruments with pre-set categories, such as structured interviews, questionnaires, and criterion-referenced performance tests.

6.2.1. The use of multiple measures and their sequencing

It is difficult to overemphasize the likelihood that use of multiple measures, as well as multiple sources, will increase the quality of information gathered, whether or not the

Table 6.2. Methods of data collection for NA

Procedure	Source/evaluation	Sample use
Non-expert intuitions	Auerbach and Burgess (1985)	Most LSP textbooks
Expert practitioner intuitions	Huckin and Olson (1984) Selinker (1979)	Lamotte (1981) Tarante et al. (1981) Lett (2005)
Unstructured interviews	Bailey (1982) Spradley (1979) Hoadley-Maidment (1983)	Ramani et al. (1988) Fixman (1990)
Structured interviews	Bailey (1982) Bernard (1994)	Mackay (1978) Brindley (1984)
Interview schedules	Bernard (1994)	Mackay (1978) Tarantino (1988)
Surveys and questionnaires	Bailey (1982) Bernard (1994) Johnson (1992) Oppenheim (1966)	Horowitz (1986) Ferris and Tagg (1996) Iwai et al. (1999) Mackay (1978)
Language audits	Coleman (1988) Watts (1994) Long (2013c)	Mawer (1991) Watts (1994)
Ethnographic methods	Bernard (1994) Watson-Gegeo (1988)	Boswood and Marriot (1994) Mohan and Marshall Smith (1992) Roberts, Davis, and Jupp (1992)
Participant observation	Bailey (1982) Bernard (1994) Lincoln and Guba (1985)	Hodlin (1970) Jasso-Aguilar (1999/2005)
Non-participant observation	Bernard (1994) Lincoln and Guba (1985)	Bosher and Smalkoski (2002) Cumaranatunge (1988) Jacobson (1986) Jupp and Hodlin (1975) Svendsen and Krebs (1984) Oliver et al. (2012)
Classroom observation	Chaudron (1988) Van Lier (1988)	Schmidt (1981) Allen, Frolich, and Spada (1984)
Diaries, journals, and logs	Bailey and Oschner (1983)	McDonough (1994) Reves (1994)
Role-plays and simulations	Berwick (1989)	Berwick (1989) Roberts (1982)
Content analysis	Braine (1988) Flowerdew (1994)	Benson (1989)
Discourse analysis	Sinclair and Coulthard (1975) Hatch (1992)	Crookes (1986a) Ventola (1983)
Analysis of discourse	Jacoby (1999) Jacoby and McNamara (1999)	Marriot and Yamada (1991) Medway and Andrews (1992) Sullivan and Girginer (2002)

Table 6.2. (*Continued*)

Procedure	Source/evaluation	Sample use
Register/rhetorical analysis	Biber (1988) Selinker (1988)	Conrad (1996) DeCarrico and Nattinger (1988) Trimble (1985)
Computer-aided corpus analysis	Flowerdew (1994) Conrad (1996)	Kennedy (1990) Willis (1990)
Genre analysis	Swales (1990b)	Swales (1986) Thompson (1994)
Task-based, criterion-referenced performance tests	Brown and Hudson (2002) Hudson and Lynch (1994) Norris *et al.* (1998) Norris *et al.* (2002)	Brown *et al.* (2002) McNamara (1996) Norris *et al.* (1999) Robinson and Ross (1996) Teasdale (1994)
Triangulated methods	Long (2005b, 2013c)	Bosher and Smalkoski (2002) Cowling (2007) Gilabert (2005) Jasso-Aguilar (1999/2005) Lambert (2010) Long (2005b) Cowling (2007) Oliver *et al.* (2012) Spence and Liu (2013) Wozniak (2010)

Source: Updated from Long (2005c, pp. 31–32).

findings are used for triangulation by methods and/or sources. In particular, carefully sequenced use of two or more procedures will produce better quality information. In the case of a NA for a large public or private institution, for example, after meeting with senior personnel (often those commissioning the study) to gain an overview of the institution and of its functioning, it is almost always better to begin with more open-ended procedures, such as interviews or non-participant observations. Those procedures are time-consuming and labor-intensive, and qualitative data are harder to summarize, but they are also more likely to reveal what the outsider does not know, and does not know he or she does not know, about the domain in question. Starting – or even worse, starting and finishing – with a questionnaire runs the risk of precluding discovery of relevant information, as survey items are effectively tests of the survey designer's preconceptions about the needs in question, so those of an ignorant outsider. A questionnaire, with its right/wrong statements, rankings, and other closed-item formats (used for ease of scoring with large samples), is better thought of as a method of obtaining broad coverage of a large pool of informants quickly *after* relevant information has been gathered. That is to say the questionnaire should be informed by the findings from the open-ended procedures. Quite often, following analysis of the survey results, additional targeted follow-up procedures are found to be called for.

To illustrate, at the request of the Office of Intramural Training and Education of the US National Institutes of Health (NIH), several Maryland and Georgetown graduate students from my annual TBLT seminar conducted a study with me of the language needs of approximately 4500 international visiting fellows, research fellows, clinical fellows, post-docs, and graduate students at NIH (Long 2010; Serafini, Lake, & Long 2013). Located in Maryland, just outside Washington, D.C., the NIH is a major national center in the United States for highly specialized basic and applied research in the biological and medical sciences, including such fields as biochemistry; genetics; developmental, cell, and molecular biology; neuroscience; ocular pathology; biophysics; immunology and infectious diseases; physiology; and pharmacology. The aim was to identify those tasks that the NNSs of English are required to accomplish in English, both at work at NIH and in their daily lives off campus, along with as much information as possible about the tasks' frequency, difficulty, and criticality.

The study began with individual semi-structured interviews, lasting roughly 30 minutes each, of 25 research fellows and post-docs and six principal investigators (PIs). Questions were intentionally open-ended, including "Can you describe a typical day at NIH?" and "What are the five most important things you do at the NIH?" Similar questions probed participants' "social-survival" tasks off campus (purchasing cell phone contracts and Internet service, obtaining a driver's license, completing tax returns, etc.). Questions to PIs generally focused on their perceptions of the tasks and difficulties faced by their lab personnel, the idea being to uncover any discrepancies between their views and those of the people who worked under their supervision. They included such items as "What problems, if any, do you think graduate students or post-docs have at NIH?" and "Do you find they have problems with their English or other communication skills?"

Initial findings from the semi-structured interviews were used as the basis for three versions of a questionnaire, one designed for each of the three groups: PIs (23 items), NS post-docs and fellows (12 items), each taking five to seven minutes to complete, and NNS post-docs and fellows (37 items), requiring eight to ten minutes. Before distribution, the surveys were reviewed by three groups, reflecting both insider and outsider perspectives, in order to identify and correct any problematic items: applied linguists (the author and the seminar students), NIH staff at the Office of Intramural Training and Education, and two linguistics doctoral graduate students unfamiliar with the project. The NIH staff, in turn, enlisted the help of colleagues to make sure that terms employed in the items were those used by, and thus meaningful to, NIH insiders. Only then were the surveys administered to the target NIH populations online, using Survey Monkey™ (www.surveymonkey.com). NSs of English were included to enable tasks that are difficult for all fellows and postdocs to be distinguished from those made difficult for NNSs by linguistic and/or cultural differences. The surveys were sent to 3800 trainees and 1200 PIs. Completed surveys were obtained from 790 NS and NNS trainees and 230 PIs, overall response rates of 21% and 19%, respectively. Thirty-one and a half percent (274) of the trainee respondents were NSs, and 68.5% (597) NNSs.

The surveys produced a wealth of information about several dimensions of trainees' communication needs at work and off campus. There was broad agreement about the relative frequency and importance of the tasks and task-types that they undertake as part of their work, and as to which ones are more vulnerable to insufficient English language proficiency. Discrepancies between PI, NS, and NNS trainee perceptions were identified in some cases, however. For example, 90% of PIs and 83% of English NS trainees thought cultural differences caused communication problems at work, whereas only 59% of NNS trainees thought so, suggesting that some NNS trainees underestimate the difficulties they face.

After results of the surveys had been quantified and compared, and a few discrepancies disambiguated, four students returned to NIH to conduct non-participant observations and to make audio-recordings, later transcribed and analyzed, of the highly specialized target discourse of what both the interview and survey data, from all sources, had shown to be one of the most critical, and problematic, target task-types, participation in the weekly lab meeting. The lab meeting usually takes place on Fridays and is when the PI and the typically half a dozen fellows and post-docs in his or her lab spend about three hours reporting and discussing their research findings that week. One of the graduate students also shadowed a NNS post-doc for an entire day in her lab, making recordings and taking notes on all her language use.

To take another example (for details, see Long 2013c), given adequate time and resources, a study of the language needs of tourist industry workers might usefully begin with a literature survey to preempt wheel reinvention. If information of the type required does not already exist, the next step might be to conduct in-depth, unstructured interviews with members of different categories of stakeholders, such as one or more operators of different sized hotels, souvenir shops, restaurants, tour companies, and rental car services, as well as with tourists themselves. The purpose of this set of interviews would not be to produce a final inventory of target needs, but merely to obtain a better idea, based on insider knowledge, of the scope and dimensions of the sampling elements and sampling frame to be covered in a survey (see Section 6.2.5).

Summarizing findings from Massey University's audit of language use in New Zealand's tourist industry, Watts (1994) noted that tourism involves many service categories, including formalities (consulates, customs, immigration), transport (airlines, railways, taxis), accommodation (hotels, condominiums), sightseeing (travel agencies, guided tours), entertainment (casinos, concerts, theaters), food and drink (kiosks, restaurants, bars), shopping (duty-free stores, chemists, department stores), and other services (hospitals, banks, post offices, information centers). He pointed out that such sectors would change with increased choice of so-called ecotourism and other more specialized types of foreign travel.

Based on the Massey audit, a questionnaire might then be designed for broad coverage of representative members and numbers of each category, that is, a stratified random sample of the total population. The questionnaire would be mailed out or, if possible, used as the basis of face-to-face interviews. This would be combined with in-depth structured interviews, utilizing the results of the earlier open-ended round, with small representative subgroups of the same stratified random sample. Since all the information gathered thus far would involve introspection and retrospection, interim conclusions would preferably be cross-checked against results of participant observations and/or non-participant observations of actual native and foreign language (FL) use, for example, through daily logs kept by members of the target groups. Proficiency measures, ranging from language self-assessment procedures to task-based, criterion-referenced performance tests (see Section 6.2.9), would help elucidate the gap between needs and present abilities. Finally, analyses of representative target discourse samples, for example, audio- or videotaped recordings of service encounters between foreign tourists and travel industry personnel would be collected, as in studies of communication between

Japanese tourists and shop assistants in Melbourne (Marriot 1991; Marriot & Yamada 1991). The analysis of target discourse would provide useful additional information for training some categories of staff and help in the preparation of teaching materials.

Few published NAs have utilized as many or as varied procedures as these, much less in the order suggested, but a study by Cumaranatunge (1988) comes close. The population of interest was the 10,000 or more Sri Lankan women who left for jobs annually as domestic "aides," i.e., servants, in the Middle East (until 1991, at least), about 34% of them in Kuwait. These women were known to face serious communication problems on arrival, since few knew any Arabic or English. A preliminary survey showed the latter to be more in demand for the better jobs. In the order in which they were applied, Cumaranatunge's NA involved the following procedures and sources:

1. A questionnaire in their Ll was administered to 30 women currently working as domestic aides in Kuwait. One purpose was to obtain a detailed job description and target situation analysis (TSA). To that end, some items in the questionnaire (and in the structured interviews that followed) asked respondents which of the 12 activities and settings listed, for example, 'to explain an illness to a doctor' or 'at the post office,' required them to use English. Illustrating the importance of allowing new insider categories to emerge from informants, however, especially in the early stages of a NA, some open-ended questions were included. An invitation to supply other examples of important 'activities' and 'settings,' for example, elicited several useful ones, such as 'to read the menu,' 'to fill in the disembarkation form,' and 'to ask for help if my sponsor does not arrive with a visa.' The three most important, as established by the percentage of respondents mentioning them, proved to be 'to speak to master/mistress,' 'to understand my duties,' and 'to explain an illness to a doctor' (Cumaranatunge 1988, p. 130).

2. Structured interviews followed, covering somewhat different questions and topics, with 46 people, including women who had recently returned to Sri Lanka, 86% of them after working in Kuwait, aides currently working there, employment agents in Sri Lanka and Kuwait, and five employers in Kuwait. (Few employers would agree to be interviewed, considering it an infringement on their privacy.) The purpose of interviewing recruits, agents, and employers, Cumaranatunge (1988, p. 128) wrote, was "to validate the information already given and to gain another perspective."

3. Informal interviews came next. They were conducted in both countries with government officials, airline staff, travel agents, Sri Lankan Embassy staff, airport officials, and bank officers.

4. There followed two weeks of field study and "participant observation" in Kuwait. (Since there is no evidence that Cumaranatunge herself worked as a domestic aide, 'participant observation' must, in fact, refer to non-participant observation.) "From the point of view of situation analysis and developing a real feel for the workplace," Cumaranatunge (1988, p. 129) wrote, "this was perhaps the most useful of the data-gathering procedures used." Three aides were observed at work in their households, and some others while minding children in a park. Visits were made to the airport, bank, post office, bazaar, and other sites where the women would use the target language. Impressionistic estimates of the level of language proficiency required were also made during these visits. The Sri Lankan Embassy allowed access to employee complaint files and to interviews between embassy staff and both employ-

ers and employees. Cumaranatunge (1988, p. 129) reported learning from the embassy visits that the women's problems extended far beyond language difficulties to include "deportation, attempted suicide, imprisonment, absconding, pregnancy, rape, sexual and physical harassment, among other things."[2]

5. Finally, 44 job advertisements were analyzed for age of the worker required, country of destination, job category, and language requirement.

Cumaranatunge reported examples of discrepancies in the information obtained from different sources and, unlike some researchers, attempted to reconcile the findings. One concerned the activities and situations, for example, 'asking directions,' in which aides (88%), agents (36%), and employers (0%) thought English would be necessary. While aides liked to have freedom to move about outside the home, Cumaranatunge reported, "both employers and agents wished to discourage this for socio-cultural reasons" (p. 130). A similar difference was found in the three groups' view of the need for English to obtain travel documents. The analysis of job advertisements also required correction. Whereas 'housemaid' was the most frequent position listed, interviews with domestic aides and field observations both revealed that there was little job specialization in practice, and that most women aides were expected to do any kind of work, including helping in the kitchen and looking after children. Again, the job descriptions did not mention some of the most unpleasant and difficult duties; those were only reported by the domestic aides interviewed in Kuwait. Perhaps the clearest example of conflict concerned the 'problems' reported by different sources:

> Domestic aides complained of sexual and physical harassment and verbal abuse, and of not being permitted to go out or to talk to anyone. Agents mentioned culture shock, loneliness and resistance to discipline, whereas employers spoke of theft, disobedience and lack of training'. (Cumaranatunge 1988, p. 131)

Finally, Cumaranatunge elicited rankings from the aides of the relative importance of receptive and productive, spoken and written skills they perceived themselves to need. The rankings were coupled with the information on activities and settings, and also with the impressionistic estimates of required proficiency levels made during Cumaranatunge's field observations and site visits. She found there was a low tolerance for error in certain written tasks, such as addressing letters and completing forms, but high error tolerance in most spoken production, partly because of the generally low level of English proficiency in the Middle East. Together, this information offered useful information for course design.

---

[2] The 1991 Gulf War was ostensibly conducted to achieve the "liberation" of Kuwait and "restoration of democracy." According to reports by reputable foreign journalists and international human rights organizations since then, however, what has, in fact, been restored is outrageous wealth, privilege, and absolute power to the country's traditional ruling families, a few trappings of representative democracy, such as the right to vote, and a stable supply of oil. The rights of migrant workers, male and female, on the other hand, seem somehow to have been overlooked. Many are reported to have been subjected to even more grotesque treatment than before, not excluding cases of torture and summary execution. See, for example, *Walls at every turn. Abuse of migrant domestic workers through Kuwait's sponsorship system.* New York: Human Rights Watch, October 6, 2010. Unfortunately, such flagrant abuses of domestic workers are by no means unique to Kuwait.

Cumaranatunge closed the rather brief report of her study by noting that her sources had not included prospective learners, that most of the data had been limited to sources and information on Kuwait, just one of roughly eight countries in which Sri Lankan women worked, and that the sample size in some categories had been small. She also alluded to the difficulty she had experienced as a woman in trying to gather information in Kuwait and to the reluctance of many returned "aides" to talk about their experiences abroad, due to the social stigma attached to domestic labor in West Asia. Both factors, she considered, had made her field visits and (non-)participant observation all the more important. Despite those limitations, Cumaranatunge's study appears to have been one of the finest NAs conducted to date, and one of the very few to begin to engage seriously with the problematic issue of the validity of alternative sources and procedures available to the analyst.

Other illustrations of the carefully sequenced use of multiple methods (and multiple sources) in a NA include work on the language needs of immigrant health professionals when communicating with patients and colleagues in a clinical setting (Bosher & Smalkoski 2002), the goals in learning and teaching Dutch as a FL of a random sample of 700 FL learners of Dutch, and 800 teachers of Dutch as a FL around the world (Gysen & Van Avermaet 2005), and the Dutch as a second language needs of 453 adult migrants to Flanders by Van Avermaet and Gysen (2006). Both Belgian studies involved large-scale interviewing and questionnaire surveys, among other procedures. Also worthy of note is work in rural Western Australia by Oliver *et al.* (2012). In a study of the language and literacy needs of indigenous aboriginal Australians at a vocational education training (VET) center, Oliver *et al.'s* sources were 12 students, 15 center staff, including the center's senior administrators and teachers, five lecturers at the technical and further education (TAFE) community college to which some students moved after completing their VET courses, ten local employers, and 57 community members, including family members and elders. The methods employed were adjusted with an eye to cultural appropriateness and community acceptability. They included semi-structured individual and focus group interviews, digitally recorded where appropriate and permitted, field notes, non-participant workplace observations, samples of training materials used at the center, and information about the occupations to which the students aspired found in the *Job Guide* (similar to the US *DOT*). This is an important study.

6.2.2. Sampling

Whichever procedures and types of instruments are selected for a NA, they must be used with an appropriate sample of the population of interest (see Bailey 1982, pp. 83–108; Bernard 1994, pp. 71–101). The issue is whether or not the people whose views or behaviors are sampled are representative of the population of interest and, hence, whether findings from a study of the sample can be generalized to the population afterwards. Too often, NAs (and much other second language research) utilizes a *convenience sample*, that is, whoever happens to be around and willing to participate. Some convenience samples are really "captive samples," such as the researcher's own students, where "willingness" is sometimes asserted rather than demonstrated. Tightening up of the Institutional Review Board (IRB) process in some countries, notably the United States, over the past 20 years has gone a long way to improving the situation. A *purposive sample*, that is, a group selected by the analyst as representative of the target population of interest (e.g., Dr. Smith and Professor Molina because they are reputedly "typical" chemistry department teachers), may seem like an improvement, but it is only as good as the researcher's criteria for typicality, and application of them, which are unknown.

A *random sample*, in which each member of the population has an equal chance of being selected, is much preferable, but costly in time and money when a population is large. In such situations, a *systematic random sample* is often used, that is, a selection of every nth person from the sampling frame, for example, every nth name on an alphabetized list of all the entering first-year Japanese graduate students at a Canadian university. A random sample may still distort the true picture in the population, since the group of respondents selected could inadvertently include roughly equal numbers of graduates and undergraduates, or students from the humanities, and social, natural, and applied sciences (whose reading and other needs have been found to differ in several studies), when the largest group of Japanese might, in fact, be graduate engineers. A way of avoiding this possibility is to draw a *stratified random sample*, that is, to sample randomly, but proportionately, within each subgroup or strata, of the population of interest (see, e.g., Chaudron *et al.* 2005). If engineers make up 60% of the population, let 60% of the sample be engineers, and so on. Finally, in cases where identifying the sampling frame is problematic, for example, because data on some departments are simply unavailable, a *cluster sample* may be used, that is, a random sample drawn just from one or more sub-groups for which the sampling frame can be identified.

6.2.3. Expert and non-expert intuitions

Their own non-expert intuitions about target language use are the stock in trade for many commercial textbook writers, yet they are notoriously unreliable. Several researchers have found considerable differences between the language used in target situations and that used elsewhere, as well as between the former and the language modeled for those situations in LT materials (Scotton & Bernstein 1988; Wong 2002). Examples include business meetings (Williams 1988), service encounters (Bartlett 2005; Granena 2008; Mason 1989; see, also, Ventola 1983, 1984), and academic seminars (Lynch & Anderson 1991). Auerbach and Burgess (1985, pp. 478–490) strongly criticized authors of "survival English" textbooks for presenting learners with materials that modeled oversimplified language, inauthentic communicative structure, and unrealistic situational content.

An example of the problem was reported by Cathcart (1989), who, after a 'contextualized distributional analysis' of four doctor–patient encounters audiotaped by the participants, warned against reliance upon writers' intuitions as a basis for ESL materials. Many such service encounters are simply too important. L1 studies (e.g., Frankel 1984; Todd 1984) and L2 research (e.g., Candlin, Bruton, & Leather 1976) have shown doctor–patient consultations to be a clear example of unequal power discourse, with doctors typically dominating conversations, as reflected in their control of topic, use of directives, and asking the majority of questions, while patients' predominant role is that of question-answerer. Cathcart (1989, pp. 109–111) found that common conversational topics in her data included discussion of symptoms, physical examination, diagnosis and discussion of the nature of an illness, prescription, prognosis, future appointments, and (in a shift in the level of analysis also found in Candlin, Bruton, & Leather 1976) pre-closing. There was sometimes also talk about prior visits and non-medical personal matters. Frequently occurring utterance functions (p. 116) for doctors, she found, included prognosis (speculate about an illness), action/information (tell the patient what he or she is doing during an examination), treat/direct (tell the patient what to do), diagnosis/information, acceptance (acknowledge the patient's comment), interrogation, and making sure (request clarification). Functions for patients included giving information (requested by the doctor), accepting, and giving unsolicited information. There were relationships between topics and functions, Cathcart showed, and some variation in the traditional pattern of doctors doing all the question-asking of passive patients. The presence of a third party (e.g., a child patient accompanied by its mother), age, class, gender, education, and medical sophistication of the patient might make for variability in language use, but the tiny *n*-size precluded any determination of underlying causes in this instance.

Cathcart provided lists of relative frequencies of grammatical structures in the data but warned that frequency data alone provided a misleading picture without information about use. Present simple verb forms, for example, tended to occur not to describe habitual action sequences but in conditionals and other complex structures ("If she gets another one, we'll put her on..."). Modals occurred mostly as hedges ("It should fade away," "She may not be able to eat") and to express possibility ("We may not need to..."), not, for example, for advice-giving ("You should drink a lot of water"), as modeled in some ESL materials. There were a lot of complex structures in the data, again unlike the typical textbook dialogue materials for this service encounter, some of which are both overly simple and designed more to illustrate a grammatical pattern than as realistic models of target language use, for example,

> DOCTOR: Here's a prescription. I'd like you to take one of these pills three times a day.
> PATIENT: Is there anything else I should do?
> DOCTOR: Yes. You should drink a lot of liquids and get a lot of rest.
>   (Rost & Stratton 1978, p. 133, cited in Cathcart 1989, p. 105)

In one of the conversations she studied, Cathcart found (1989, pp. 118–120) that the lexis was broken down into three main noun categories: general terms (day, afternoon, thing), sub-technical terms (tonsilitis), and three main verb categories, idiomatic phrasal and prepositional sub-technical relating to illness or medicine (put someone on a medication, pick up an illness), common verbs used sub-technically (get and have an illness), and verbs for prediction, speculation, or planning (see how, think). Again, Cathcart noted the discrepancies between the lexis observed and that typically modeled in (even supposedly specialized) ESL materials.

Based on her findings, Cathcart went on to make some rather debatable recommendations for materials and pedagogy, to which we will return. The main point at present, however, is the valuable additional evidence her study provided of the unreliability of non-expert intuitions about domain-specific language use, even when the intuitions are those of applied linguists, and to stress the urgent need for a lot more research of this kind. For TBLT, future work would be strengthened by additional task-based analyses of the target discourse samples and linkage between those and the other analyses. Just such an important recent contribution, a comparison by Epling (2011) of the language printed on the labels affixed by pharmacists to the containers of prescription and non-prescription drugs in the United States and that modeled in pedagogic materials, is described in Chapter 9.3.3.2.

Finally, there is some evidence that even in the rare cases of an applied linguist who is also an expert practitioner in another field, his or her intuitions about the language used in that field may still be unreliable. Lamotte (1981) found that, despite holding a master's degree in physical therapy and having previously practiced as a physical thera-pist for five years, there were considerable differences between her (presumably expert) intuitions about the language used by physical therapists with their patients, retrospec-tions about which she first wrote down at great length, and the language they actually used, samples of which she then recorded at a local hospital. Lamotte was a language teacher and halfway through a two-year master's degree in applied linguistics at the time of her study, so had some expertise in language use. She found that her linguistic intui-tions about therapist–patient communication were unreliable, despite her unusual com-bination of insider occupational knowledge and linguistic knowledge. In contrast, she *was* able to use introspections to provide a fairly accurate list of the tasks performed by a physical therapist.

6.2.4. Interviews

One of the more direct ways of finding out what people think or do (in some cultures, at least) is to ask them, a function served by various kinds of interviews and question-naires. The interview is a key data-gathering tool in many branches of the social sciences, most notably in anthropology and linguistics fieldwork, and with suitable modification for informants from cultures in which formal structured interviews, at least, are not a recognized speech event (see Wolfson 1976), it can serve the applied linguist well, too. Needless to say, allowances must be made for cross-cultural differences that may exist between interviewer and interviewee in value systems, in beliefs about such matters as teacher and student roles and relationships, in the appropriateness of discussing certain topics (e.g., age, religion, and politics) at all, and of great importance for a NA, in notions of relevance, views about the appropriateness of criticism, and truthfulness.

Interviews are more open to bias and inconsistency of various sorts than question-naires, for example, through interviewers communicating their attitudes about the matter at hand (such as the importance of the language they teach to the interviewee's work) to interviewees, thereby influencing their responses, interviewees telling inter-viewers what they think they want to hear (the so-called "halo effect"), interviewers leading respondents, asking different questions or the same questions in different ways, and unintentionally distorting data by filtering the way they report of interpret responses through their own perceptions. Much of this can be dealt with by the needs analyst being aware of the problems and, if need be and numbers warrant, by inter-viewer training. Having interviewers of the same race, ethnicity, sex, social class, and cultural background as interviewees also increases the likelihood of obtaining good data, especially where attitudes and opinions on sensitive issues are involved. (See

Bailey 1982 and Briggs 1986 for helpful reviews of research findings on these and related issues.)

Although time-consuming, open-ended or *unstructured interviews* allow in-depth coverage of issues and have the advantage of not preempting unanticipated findings by the use of predetermined questions, categories, and response options, a potential limitation of structured interviews and questionnaires. Moreover, while some may decline an interview, the acceptance rate is much higher than the response rate for mailed questionnaires, based on my experience with two NAs in Montreal, one for a large francophone insurance company, the other for a canning factory. In each case, a small team of teachers and I started by conducting semi-structured interviews (in English and French) with a stratified random sample of the workforce in the two institutions that had requested that ESL programs be mounted for their employees. By a *semi-structured interview* is meant that while some general topics were predetermined, the order in which they were dealt with was not, and nor were the particular questions initiating their treatment. Further, plenty of opportunity and encouragement were given for interviewees to raise topics we had not thought of. Based on the data from the interviews, questionnaires were designed for all workers within the categories of potential students. In the case of the insurance company, the questionnaires were distributed by section or department heads, filled out, and collected during office hours, resulting in a nearly 100% return rate, which meant that inferences from samples to populations were largely unnecessary. This combination of in-depth coverage via interviews of a sample of the targeted population, followed by narrower, more focused, but global, coverage of virtually the entire workforce likely to be involved in language training, would seem to offer close to an optimum procedure in projects where potential students are already doing the occupation or academic program concerned, and when time and access are available before the program begins.

Interviews with stakeholders are undoubtedly one of the more widely used data-gathering devices for NA in applied linguistics, although fluency in the informants' L1 is usually a requirement (see Hoadley-Maidment 1983). They require a good deal of time on the part of the applied linguist, not just in informing the prospective interviewee of the interview's purpose, obtaining consent, arranging and conducting the interviews but also in analyzing and summarizing the results, from audiotapes and/or notes taken during or immediately after each meeting. Clearly explaining the purpose and benefits of a NA to respondents before interviewing begins is very important. Having formal approval and cooperation from the institution involved, e.g., by management formally notifying workers in advance that the "study" is approved, can be critical. As illustrated by the participatory action research conducted on behalf of some of the Mondragon cooperatives (Greenwood 1991; Greenwood & Gonzales Santos 1992), this is not a problem in worker-owned and controlled entities, since the study will then have been decided upon democratically by the workers themselves, not imposed from above.

Unstructured interviews are exploratory, use no fixed format, and allow the interviewee's notion of relevance to prevail instead of being constrained by a set of pre-planned questions. In Lincoln and Guba's (1985, p. 269) words, unstructured interviews are appropriate when the interviewer "does not know what he or she doesn't know and must therefore rely on the respondent to tell him or her." The quality of information produced can be greatly enhanced by awareness of basic interviewing micro-skills, such as initial use of a few general "warm-up"/relaxation questions ("How do you like living/

teaching here?" "How does working here compare with country/institution X?"), making sure the interviewee does the talking, and use of follow-up probes when further detail or explanation is sought, including explicit requests for more information, "pumps," like 'uh huh,' and other encouraging verbal and non-verbal back-channel signals, and silences that the interviewee fills. Many valuable insights on these and related procedural matters are available and well worth reading (see, e.g., Bailey 1982, pp. 181–217; Bernard 1994, pp. 208–255; Reinharz 1992, pp. 18–45; Spradley 1979).

Once unstructured interviews have been completed and the data from them analyzed, *semi-structured* or *structured interviews* may follow. As the names imply, these differ from unstructured interviews and from each other in the degree to which questions have been pre-formulated (and hence, the issues pre-determined) by the interviewer. In extreme cases, structured interviews are oral administrations of a questionnaire, then often referred to as an *interview schedule*, as exemplified by some telephone interviews or by census takers who visit sample respondents' homes with a lengthy list of printed questions on a form that the interviewers fill out. Structured interviews and interview schedules have the advantage of being quicker to conduct, and of producing data that, because organized, will not require hours to categorize, and because standardized, will allow easy comparison across respondents.

Use of interviews is widely reported in NAs in ESP. As noted earlier, Ramani *et al.* (1988) conducted unstructured interviews with Indian scientists. Fixman (1990) summarized findings of 32 semi-structured interviews, mostly with middle and senior managers, in nine companies of different types and sizes, designed to identify FL needs of US corporations. Brindley (1984) described the development, piloting, and use of structured interviews in NA and objective setting for Australia's AMEP. Cumaranatunge (1988) employed structured and unstructured interviews with, among others, Sri Lankan domestic aides and with various kinds of civil servants, respectively. Mackay (1978) discussed the use of an interview schedule with Veterinary Medicine faculty at the National Autonomous University of Mexico (UNAM), noting three important advantages of structured interviews over questionnaires: they allow interviewers to make sure all questions are answered, clarify any misunderstood or ambiguous items, and follow up avenues of interest disclosed by answers that were unforeseen when the questionnaire was designed.

The use of an interview schedule was also reported by Tarantino (1988), this time with Italian physicists, chemists, and computer scientists at the University of Bari. The aim (Tarantino 1988, p. 35) was to identify the perceived relative difficulty of the four basic language skills at macro- and micro-levels, which semantico-grammatical areas caused most problems with each skill and level, whether having studied English at school influenced language abilities in the physicists' specialized professional domains, and whether "the translation method" produced satisfactory results for EST communication. After piloting the questionnaire with ten informants and revising some items (always critically important steps), the final version was administered as a structured interview, yielding much useful and detailed information for other EST practitioners on the perceived abilities and needs of such learners.

It is sometimes difficult to tell how many of Tarantino's detailed findings, especially those concerning specific linguistic and rhetorical problems (verb sequence, use of modals, adjuncts and connectives, paragraphing, etc.) were gleaned from the interviews, from her previous work as a teacher of some of the informants, or as appears to have been the case, both. Previous error analyses of informants' written work had motivated some of the questionnaire items, she stated (p. 35). If informants of this kind really do have reliable intuitions about detailed language problems, it would considerably increase the value of the structured interview in NA. Unfortunately, as has been the case in virtually the entire NA literature, Tarantino provided no independent evidence on informants' language abilities with which to assess the issue. In a potentially revealing aside, however, she mentioned one mismatch of which she was aware:

> To my surprise, in papers written in the TL by the three respondents (5.66%) who had claimed to have no problems whatsoever in writing, I found errors in the same areas indicated as problem sources by the rest of the interviewed. It can thus be inferred that the difficulties in this skill are more widespread than the data show. (Tarantino 1988, p. 43)

A more troubling possible inference, of course, is that this discrepancy was the tip of an iceberg. Criterion or predictive validity studies are clearly needed. How do perceived problems reported in structured interviews (or on questionnaires) compare with those revealed by language samples from the same informants, especially where (different kinds of) domain experts' ability to provide useful information about domain-specific language needs (or use) is concerned? The issue should be of more concern to those conducting NAs for synthetic linguistic syllabi than analytic task-based ones, of course.

Ramani *et al.* (1988) reported successful use of unstructured interviews with faculty and students in management and electronic design technology (EDT) as part of a NA at the Indian Institute of Science in Bangalore. The format allowed informants to explain how work and genres in their fields were organized using their own "insider" categories, not the researchers' pre-formulated ones emanating from applied linguistics. One example of the benefit of this was that the analysts learned that whereas they had taught the "project report" as the single written genre required of EDT students, the staff actually required several different documents:

> a Pre-Study report comprising a product brief, wish specifications, product survey, a Study report dealing with methods of investigation, theoretical principles, and conversion of the wish specifications to target specifications, and an Engineering report. (Ramani *et al.* 1988, p. 86)

It was not sufficient to learn of the existence of different kinds of reports in the field, however. The interviews also revealed specific expectations about what each document should contain and how its writing should correspond to a particular stage in the research and development process. Ramani *et al.* (1988, p. 86) concluded:

> Needless to say, an ESP course designed without reference to these expectations and to the interrelation between the process of research and that of writing (i.e., without ethnographic data) would only be marginally relevant to these students.

6.2.5. Questionnaire surveys

The advantages and disadvantages of questionnaire surveys are in large part the mirror image of those of unstructured interviews. Questionnaires, especially if mailed or, as in the NIH study, distributed via e-mail and conducted online, group-administered or administered by third parties, can procure sizeable amounts of focused, standardized, organized data from a large sample of respondents relatively quickly and cheaply. They can do so, moreover, with the option of anonymity (should that be important to respondents) and with less chance of interview bias, since the questions asked, the order in which they are asked, and the precise way they are asked can be carefully planned and fixed. On the other hand, response rates can be low, and the type of information and range of responses obtained are limited by the use of pre-determined questions and response options and formats. In a sense, that is, unstructured interviews serve to identify relevant questions, whereas questionnaires assume knowledge of the right questions and test hypotheses about those answers.

Considerable expertise exists in questionnaire design and item-writing in the social sciences in general (see, e.g., Babbie 1973; Bailey 1982, pp. 109–180; Bernard 1994, pp. 256–288; Henderson, Morris, & Fitz-Gibbon 1987; Oppenheim 1966). Some pitfalls to avoid include double-barreled questions ("Do you read and write letters to customers in English?" "Are your students able to understand your lectures in English and ask clarification questions clearly when necessary?"), overly complex or technical wording ("Do you ever have difficulty with business call pre-closings?"), leading questions ("Should sales staff be able to speak Spanish fluently"), ambiguity ("Do you have difficulty understanding everyday French?"), abstractness ("Do you find reading English difficult?"), sensitive or threatening questions ("Do you skip reading assignments if they are in English?"), and, especially, irrelevant questions. Items suffering from one or more of these flaws will usually surface quickly if writers try to answer them themselves or when the instrument is pilot-tested.

Items may be open, with no pre-specified response categories or choices, or closed, where the respondent must choose from one or more specified options. As might be imagined, the strengths and weakness of each type roughly parallel those of unstructured interviews and questionnaires themselves. Open questions, for example, can elicit a wider range of information and more detail, and may be more suitable for complex issues, but involve loss of standardization, and are more difficult and time-consuming to code and interpret. Closed items provide standardized, easily coded and quantified data but may limit possible responses and may result in overly simple treatments of complex issues.

Return rates for questionnaire surveys are notoriously low, with figures below 50% common in some fields. This is especially true of mailed questionnaires, for example, 25% in an audit of language use and needs in Australia's international trade (Stanley, Ingram, & Chittick 1990, reported in Watts 1994, p. 77) and of e-mailed questionnaires, for example, 21% and 19% in the NIH study (Serafini, Lake, & Long 2013), reported earlier in Section 6.2.1. The problem, of course, is that external validity will probably be affected negatively, since those who do respond may well not represent the original sampling unit. Preemptive measures are called for. One is to procure "official" sponsorship, if possible even including distribution and collection of the questionnaire by the institution itself rather than have the applied linguist, usually an outsider and often with low status, handle that end of things. Another is to organize "proctored" group administrations of the questionnaire, with responses collected as respondents leave the room. A third is to make an extra effort (usually through a cover letter) to inform potential respondents of the identity of those doing a study, its purpose, the importance of the information being sought, the importance of the information they have to offer, the confidentiality with which it will be treated, the uses to which it will be put, and the benefits to them in responding, for example, improved job performance, new promotion prospects, or better prepared students, as the case may be.

A fourth strategy to improve response rate is to make the questionnaire as short, as attractive to look at, as easy to read and respond to, and as obviously well designed as possible, the last indicating seriousness of purpose on the analyst's part to people whose valuable time is being encroached upon. In this regard, questionnaires, like any data-collection procedure or instrument, should always be adequately pilot-tested with individuals like those with whom they will eventually be used, and revised and piloted again if need be. A fifth is to offer an inducement of some kind, such as a summary of the results for everyone who responds and indicates they would like to receive one. A sixth is to try to personalize the survey so that respondents do not feel like a number on a sheet of paper. Some options utilized in a survey of the use of classroom research findings in language teacher education programs (Long 1983e) were to hand-address envelopes, address them to named individuals ("Dr. Mary Smith," as opposed to "The Chair"), include a serious but friendly cover letter explaining the study, and include a hand-stamped, self-addressed return envelope. (Even with these measures taken, the return rate for my survey was still only 55%.) A seventh is to time the study so that the questionnaire does not arrive at an inopportune moment (the last week of classes, exam week, closing days of the financial year, etc.) for the respondents. An eighth is to mail second copies of the questionnaire and/or make follow-up phone calls to non-respondents at a reasonable interval after the first mail-out. Return rates of 50% are still considered high for mailed questionnaire surveys, however, so some variant of the "in-house, insider-handled" administration is the preferred option if available to the analyst.

The option of online surveys distributed via e-mail makes conducting survey research today easier, cheaper, and potentially quicker than the use of paper, and responding far easier, too. Response rates could therefore be expected to rise substantially. However, as part of the NA at the NIH mentioned earlier for the roughly 4500 international research fellows and postdocs (Long 2010), the questionnaire component conducted online using Survey Monkey still produced a response rate of only 23%, suggesting that several of the strategies listed for hard-copy surveys are likely to remain relevant in the electronic age, even though technology has greatly simplified some logistical aspects of such research.

Administration of a questionnaire is among the most widely used procedures in NA (see, e.g., Brown 1995; Inman 1979; Johns 1981; Jordan & Mackay 1973; Ostler 1980; Richterich & Chancerel 1977/1980, pp. 59–77; Utley 1992; Zughoul & Hussein 1985). Mackay (1978) describes three uses of questionnaires (and provides the instruments themselves), one as the basis of an interview schedule for veterinary faculty at the UNAM, a second with students from the same university department, and the third for a survey of ESP needs and program resources in Southeast Asian Ministers of Education Organization (SEAMEO) countries. Mackay (1978, p. 23) makes the important point, potentially true of all NA methodologies, that because of the way language teachers make their living, there is a danger they will exaggerate the importance of, and need for, their particular language for groups of learners, and he illustrates some steps that can be taken to help avoid the problem. A questionnaire on EAP reading needs, for example, should not "lead" respondents by asking how much reading they assign or do in English (or other target language) for their courses or research right away. Instead, they can be asked about the availability of relevant literature in the faculty member's or students' Ll, and then about such matters as required course readings in "other languages," before any mention is made of English. Mackay also noted how a faculty member, having done graduate work overseas, could easily influence his or her personal use of professional literature in a FL and choice of any L2 readings assigned to students – another example to support Coleman's claim about how one sector in a large institution, such as a university, can influence language use in another.

Several writers have pointed out that the rapid and extensive coverage achievable through questionnaires can lead analysts to overlook potentially serious issues of validity. A notable example is Horowitz (1986), who began a study of tertiary academic writing needs by noting the variable nature of the lists of skills and tasks that had figured in previous questionnaire surveys of EAP writing, and by recalling the concern expressed by Johns (l981) and Zemelman (1978, cited in Johns, 1981, p. 52), among others, as to whether the results of such studies reflect what the respondents do, think they do, think the researcher thinks they ought to do, or want the researcher to think they do. Horowitz also noted the danger that questionnaire items may reflect analysts' invalid, preconceived notions as to the relevant categories of tasks in a domain. A logically prior activity to asking respondents about those tasks, he suggested, should be to discover and classify (in that case, EAP writing) tasks from the perspective of those assigning and doing them.

To that end, Horowitz collected and examined a corpus of actual writing assignments and essay examinations at a US university. Of approximately 750 faculty members contacted, 36 responded with usable data (a 4.8% return rate). The data represented assignments from 29 courses (28 undergraduate and one graduate) in 17 departments. Aside from essay questions, seven major categories (target task-types) emerged from the data: summary of/reaction to a reading, annotated bibliography, report on a specified participatory experience (e.g., a field observation), connection of theory and data, case study, synthesis of multiple sources, and research project. Many assignments specified the expected content through sets of questions to be answered or detailed headings and sub-headings, that is, were very controlled. Recognition and reorganization of data were emphasized, rather than invention and personal discovery. Other findings useful to EAP writing teachers, including examples of the task-types and information about which categories of assignments were typical of which departments, need not concern us here. (Interested EAP writing teachers should consult Horowitz 1986.) We will return later, however, to Horowitz's suggestions for how such findings might influence syllabus design and pedagogic tasks. Replications of Horowitz's study are clearly needed with undergraduate and graduate courses from a systematically sampled range of disciplines and universities. Meanwhile, the differences between the task-types he identified and those typical in lists presented to respondents in traditional surveys are a salutary reminder of the need to work on quality before turning to quantity in a NA.

A final use of questionnaires is as a checklist during a first class meeting. Even in a well-designed course, where content has been determined on the basis of a thorough NA, it is still helpful for teachers to use a simple in-class questionnaire when meeting their students for the first time. It is possible, after all, that a particular group of students may differ from the normal intake for that course or program in ways that can be easy to discover, and which are better identified at the start of a course than once it or over.

A brief discussion of needs the first day, followed by administration of a short questionnaire (five minutes), analyzed outside class, can alert the teacher to any such deviations, and simultaneously serve to make clear to students *why* course content is the way it will be, that is, begin to demonstrate the course's relevance. Figure 5.1 (in Chapter 5) showed examples of the variety of *formats* available for items in such simple in-class questionnaires with an imaginary class of white-collar office workers. (It would likely confuse students to mix so many different formats in a single questionnaire, of course.) The sample items could easily be modified (and expanded upon) for other English for occupational purposes (EOP), English for vocational purposes (EVP), EAP, and survival skills groups.

6.2.6. Language audits

A related use of questionnaires is to conduct a *language audit*. Language audits are difficult to define because in practice they often include some activities and produce some of the same information typical of a NA. However, whereas a NA provides detailed information about the needs of individuals, a language audit works at the level of institutions or organizations, is intended primarily to identify their existing linguistic resources, rather than their needs, and is usually conducted through a quantified general survey. As noted earlier, Coleman (1988) effectively recommends that a language audit precede a NA in large institutions, partly in order to identify the individuals whose needs should be targeted for analysis. An audit produces (a) a TSA in the form of the language skills required by an organization, as determined, for example, by job descriptions and records of current language use, (b) a profile of existing language abilities, assessed by language test scores or proficiency self-ratings, and (c) a recommendation concerning the amount and form of language training (or external provision of language assistance), if any, required to raise the profile to the standards identified by the TSA. In the business sector, Utley (1992, pp. 34–35) characterizes an audit as an exercise in defining any FL skills existing in a company, present and future needs for FL skills, the staff likely to require them, to what extent and for what purpose, and the options available to the company (e.g., instituting a FL training program, or buying outside translation and interpreting services) to deal with any gap identified between present abilities and current and future needs. An audit is useful for providing a quick overview of a situation and for identifying mismatches between perceptions and reality, between what is going on and what should be.

Watts (1994) reports on a pilot language audit of the New Zealand tourist industry that employed a questionnaire to survey 96 major tourist organizations and companies, including airlines, information centers, duty-free shops, and hotels in five main tourist destinations. The questionnaire was designed to assess the importance respondents attached to FL proficiency, which languages were most important, the proficiency levels felt desirable and those actually held by industry staff, the kinds of FL materials produced for visitors, the arrangements made for business-related communication in FLs, and the degree to which staff recruitment and training policies recognized FL skills in applicants. Fifty-nine questionnaires were returned for a high 61% response rate. FLs were shown to be important for tourism (notably, Japanese, German, French, Chinese, and Spanish, paralleling findings in Australia), especially for tour operators, airlines, and hotels. The audit revealed discrepancies between, first, the relatively high importance tourism organizations said they attached to FLs and the rather minor role FL ability actually played (relative to commercial experience and technical skills) in recruitment and training, and second, between the FL proficiency levels perceived as desirable for staff and the abilities they actually possessed. Only certain specialist, "frontline" staff positions, e.g., tour guides, front-desk staff in hotels, and duty-free shop assistants, were perceived as requiring higher proficiency, and few staff overall reported themselves as having such proficiency. Watts noted that such findings required detailed follow-up studies of language needs in the tourist industry, similar to those in Australia by Marriot (1991) and Marriot and Yamada (1991), described in Chapter 7. (For more on language audits and NAs for TBLT in the tourist industry, see Long 2013c.)

6.2.7. Participant and non-participant observation

Interviews and questionnaires involve informants in introspecting about tasks and reporting on them, and researchers in interpreting those data, three processes that can filter or distort even "perceived reality." They tap respondents' perceptions, attitudes, and opinions. Document study, as illustrated by Horowitz's examination of university writing assignments contained in syllabi, course handouts, and so on, can provide a more direct glimpse of what happens in a target domain (see also Benson 1989; Flowerdew 1994). Participant and non-participant observation have the advantage of allowing direct, in-depth, contextualized study of what participants actually do, of the activities of interest in their natural environment (natural, that is, except for the presence of the outside observer in the case of non-participant observation). As two pioneers in this area put it,

> It is essential for the teacher to investigate and experience the social reality of a place of work... The investigator's role is not one of detached observer. He (sic) must develop a real 'feel' for the work place so that he can understand the experiences, tensions, and frustrations which affect communication there. (Jupp & Hodlin 1975, p. 38)

Ethnographic procedures, of which some kinds of participant and non-participant observation are two, are designed to lessen the cultural distance between outsider (observer) and insider (observed). They are used to seek out insider views of the culture. Crucially, this involves eschewal of pre-conceived (outsider), *etic* analytic categories of events, formulated before observation begins, in favor of insider *emic* categories, meaningful to the insiders, which emerge from the data and the observer's developing interpretation of them – interpretations that are validated reflexively against insider views, for example, through triangulation. Note that many forms of non-participant observation, such as the use of pre-determined, etic categories in coding systems like the Communicative Orientation to Language Teaching (COLT) (Allen, Frolich, & Spada 1984), to record, and simultaneously analyze, classroom talk, are very valuable for some kinds of research and teacher education but have nothing to do with ethnography. There is a vast literature on both participant and non-participant observation. The interested reader is again referred to texts on qualitative research methods, in general (e.g., Bailey 1982, pp. 247–282; Bernard 1994, pp. 136–164; Kirk & Miller 1986; Lincoln & Guba

1985; Reinharz 1992, pp. 46–75; Strauss & Corbin 1990), as well as to work on ethnography and ethnographic methods, in particular (e.g., Agar 1986; Goetz & Le Compte 1984; Hammersley & Atkinson 1983; Hymes 1962; Nobblit & Hare 1988; Shieffelin & Ochs 1986; Spradley 1980; Spradley & McCurdy 1972; Watson-Gegeo 1988, 1992). While the study by Jasso-Aguilar (1999/2005) of the needs of Waikiki hotel maids is one of the very few to have employed participant observation as one of its data-collection methods, to my knowledge, there have been no NAs to date that meet the criteria for true ethnographies. For most writers on the subject (see, e.g., Hammersley & Atkinson 1983; Watson-Gegeo 1988), those usually include microanalysis of social patterns within a cultural group, and of the values and beliefs underlying them, in context. That typically requires lengthy immersion in the target setting, sometimes for periods of years; use of multiple data-collection procedures, especially, but not only, participant and non-participant observation, recordings and note-taking; entering the field "unbiased," for example, without fixed hypotheses to test, and instead allowing meaningful units of analysis, and often the research questions themselves, to emerge from the data; adoption of an insider's perspective on events, including use of emic categories in the description and analysis, i.e., units with meaning for the participants within their, not (necessarily) the analyst's, culture; validation of interim analyses by trialing them on participants, often through a process of triangulation; and in general, focusing on the particular, not the universal, seeking understandings of events rather than generalizations valid beyond the original setting, and in some cases believing such generalizations to be impossible in principle where human behavior is concerned.[3]

A study by Hodlin (1970, reported in Roberts *et al.* 1992, pp. 185–188) constitutes one of the earliest uses of participant observation for the purposes of a NA. Hodlin spent a week working in the packing department of a British factory that made cake mixes and breakfast cereals. She was presented to, and accepted by, the other workers as a temporary student employee, although her supervisor knew that she was really also conducting a field observation in preparation for an anti-racist training course to be run by the Pathway Industrial Unit. Hodlin employed a combination of participant observation, (presumably surreptitious) tape-recordings, and field notes to produce job descriptions, vignettes of some of her co-workers, and data on the kind of work-related and "social" language required for the job, as well as the range of attitudes toward racial issues among line workers and supervisors, comparing the atmosphere in three sections where she worked.

Several researchers have explicitly referenced ethnographic methods as part of their approach to NA, not least the earlier described work of Boswood and Marriot (1994) on socialization of business English teachers in Hong Kong. Non-participant observations have been reported for some time (e.g., Allwright & Allwright 1977; Courtney 1988; Cumaranatunge 1988; Franco 1986; Jacobson 1986; Jupp 1980; Jupp & Hodlin

---

[3] Most IRBs recognize that the requirement that researchers obtain institutional approval, and then informants' consent, before conducting research can be problematic if applied too strictly where true ethnographic studies in some settings are concerned. Karen Watson-Gegeo (p.c. 6/18/2011) reports that IRBs generally accept that written consent is impossible to obtain when fieldwork is conducted in a non-literate society, for example, and further, that asking for written consent in some societies is culturally inappropriate because of the values and assumptions around writing. The key issues are that human subjects understand what they are agreeing to in allowing themselves to participate in research or in allowing a researcher into the community or their homes, or access to their children.

1975; Mohan & Marshall Smith 1992; Nore 1990; Ramani *et al.* 1988; Savage & Storer 1992; Svendsen & Krebs 1984). Ethnographic methods have also been insightfully employed in other crucial areas of applied linguistics, such as the investigation of language and discrimination in the workplace (Roberts, Davis, & Jupp 1992, especially chapters 4 and 5).

In an EOP (factory) setting, Jupp and Hodlin (1975, pp. 38–39) advocated first seeking an overview of the general work situation through interviews with managers and a swift site tour, followed by interviews with NNS employees and close observations of the departments from which students would be drawn, including collection of job descriptions and recordings of work-related language use:

> [The observation] is best done by the teacher spending a day or so working at the factory, although obviously not incognito. It is important to move around a lot and understand all the main categories of work. (Jupp & Hodlin 1975, p. 40)

A straightforward (but time-consuming) procedure in academic settings consists of longitudinal case studies in which NNS learners are observed in content classrooms (Mohan & Marshall Smith 1992; Yalden 1987, p. 132) to see the kinds of tasks they have to deal with. Out-of-class interviews are conducted with their teachers and with the learners themselves, and conclusions are drawn about students' level of success in dealing with them. Study of student assignments (laboratory reports, essays, exams, etc.) and feedback from the content instructors after a course is over obviously both improve the likely validity of such findings. Schmidt (1981) reported an EAP study of this kind focusing on a business administration student.

Another EAP study utilizing some ethnographic procedures was Jacobson's (1986) non-participant observation of students' strategic competence needs in an undergraduate physics laboratory. Jacobson observed and audiotaped four lab sections taught by different instructors, but covering the same materials (finding the ratio of specific heats from sound resonances for three different gases). He taped four introductory lectures and two pairs of students working together, and interviewed the coordinator and four instructors. Jacobson concluded that most student difficulties were not with general English skills but were task-related (although he did not use such terminology). For example, students had difficulty not with reading in general but with knowing how to use information they had read in a manual to assemble the apparatus required for an experiment, and not with understanding lectures but with selecting the information they needed from lectures. Similarly, interviews with the instructors confirmed that, partly due to their heavy marking load and lack of time to do otherwise, they paid little attention to grammatical errors in NNSs' written work. The main problem they found was not the NNS students' writing per se, but such matters as their not knowing which supporting information to include, and detail to exclude, from a written explanation.

Jacobson felt that the NNS students' problems were matters of strategic competence, of how to obtain information and use it to achieve their purposes. He isolated four strategies for handling information in the physics lab:

> (a) evaluating and selecting information needed for a specific purpose, (b) synthesizing information from more than one source, (c) applying information to new or different situations, and (d) establishing working relationships with others in the lab (Jacobson 1986, p. 182).

To illustrate, carrying out an experiment was complex because it involved identifying appropriate (sometimes conflicting) information from several sources, such as the manual and an instructor's introductory lecture; writing a lab report was problematic because it involved producing a coherent written synthesis of information from the first two sources plus the findings from the students' own experiment. Solving problems that arose during such tasks as setting up the equipment for an experiment and getting it to work was made more difficult by the NNSs apparently finding it hard to establish and benefit from the more social, more verbal working relationships their American NS classmates routinely employed. NNSs tended to work in silence with one another or with a NS, whereas NS pairs tended to talk through their problems with one another or with the instructor as they worked. In other words, NNS students might have no apparent difficulty with listening, speaking, reading, or writing in general, as measured by so-called "proficiency" tests, but nevertheless encounter problems with tasks requiring their use. To address those problems, Jacobson (1986, pp. 184–186) went on to suggest pedagogic activities of kinds common in TBLT, although not exclusive to it. NNSs could be encouraged to develop strategies for establishing social working relationships with other students, for example, Jacobson suggested, by dividing information needed to complete a task among members of a group (a "two-way" task) and accepting only a group project.

A more overtly ethnographic approach was advocated for EAP NA by Swales (1985a, p. 219), who noted that

> it is not only texts that we need to understand, but the roles texts have in their environments; the values, congruent and conflictive, placed on them by occupational, professional and disciplinary memberships [i.e., insiders]; and the expectations those memberships have of the patternings of the genres they participate in, be they monographs, textbooks, lectures, examination papers, memos, minutes, testimonials. (Swales 1985a, p. 219)

Johns, too, suggested that EAP researchers should focus on elucidating how NNS students might accomplish a major task they faced, which she suggested was to

> distance themselves from the academic milieu, the texts they study and their own cultural expectations in order to analyze the nature of the culture which they intend to enter. (Johns 1988, p. 57)

(For an exemplary use of this approach, see the work of Boswood & Marriot 1994, discussed in Chapter 7.2.1.)

In another study referred to previously, Ramani *et al.* (1988) reported the use of a four-step quasi-ethnographic procedure in a NA for two units, the Centre for Electronic Design Technology (CEDT) and the Department of Management Studies, at the Indian Institute of Science in Bangalore. Over a one-month period, the analysts (1) observed the students in their natural academic environment, (2) used unstructured interviews to ask students and (3) subject specialists, about their communication practices, needs, and problems, and (4) in light of their findings, introspected as language specialists as to the justification for items (such as "mechanics of writing") in their existing syllabus. Ramani *et al.* noted that the above sequence could be modified and suggested that introspection, in particular, could also usefully occur before observation began, so as to identify potentially unjustified syllabus items with a view to assessing the need for them.

The observation stage, of interest here, was aimed at understanding what a student's normal day was like and at identifying "critical" communicative events in the life of the department (Ramani *et al.* 1988, p. 84). The potential mismatch between insider and outsider perspectives that ethnographic methods can help overcome became apparent in differences in the researchers' and EDT staff members' perceptions of the purpose of one such critical communicative event, the student seminar. The CEDT staff attached considerable importance, it turned out, to maintaining a clear separation between (the intended) use of the seminar for students' public defense of technical decisions made during the design process, on the one hand, and (what often resulted instead) presentations of progress reports on students' work, on the other. Ramani *et al.* reported that the applied linguists (a) had not noticed the distinction, (b) would not have thought it important if they had, (c) might have recast it in terms of the traditional rhetorician's distinction between "argumentation" and "narration," that is, outsider categories, and if so, (d) would have failed to "indicate its communicative value in the repertoire of the CEDT community" (p. 85).

From a very different environment, Svendsen and Krebs (1984) described the use of non-participant observation in NAs for vocational English as a second language (VESL) in a study of two health-care occupations: central supply technician and hospital transporter. They suggested observers begin by interviewing people in the department in which the NNSs are to work. The idea is to secure different perspectives on the jobs and how they fit into the overall operation in the relevant hospital departments: those of upper management, supervisors, and line workers, including holders of the target positions. There follow a number of site visits. The aim is for teachers/analysts to learn as much about the target occupations as possible, as well as to collect data, for example, through audio-recordings, and if possible, to identify difficulties NNS trainees are experiencing. How many visits and recordings depends on the complexity of the jobs and setting involved, as well as the extent of students' language difficulties, but for jobs of moderate complexity, such as the two health-care occupations, Svendsen and Krebs reported an average of six to nine hours a week of observation and taping during the first three or four weeks of a course. Workers are shadowed at different times of day as they do their jobs, recordings of spontaneous talk are made, supplemented by written notes on context, and collection of relevant written materials, e.g., forms, procedures, and training manuals. Ideally, a NA will also include on-site observation of the particular NNSs who intend, or who have already begun, to do the jobs concerned. In some VESL programs, at least part of the language instruction, too, is conducted on site (see also Nore 1990), exploiting the realism and (potential) authenticity this provides. Finally, the accuracy of data and teachers' interim interpretations of them are verified with experienced industry personnel. We will return to Svendsen and Krebs' pioneering study when considering how to go about analyzing and using target discourse samples.

Reminiscent of the revised understanding of student seminars and project reports reported by Ramani *et al.* as a result of their study, Svendsen and Krebs stressed the discrepancies that can exist between analysts' assumptions about occupational language needs and what an on-site analysis sometimes reveals. A trainee central supply technician, for example, might hear supervisors explain and instruct them in their routine tasks, such as washing, wrapping, and sterilizing medical supplies, using imperatives, for example, "First you fill the sink with warm water. Then you put in two squirts of the disinfectant, and so on." Imperatives with those functions might look like worthy candidates for instruction for someone working with a structural syllabus. However, NNS trainees actually understood the activity mostly by watching the accompanying demonstration, Svendsen and Krebs reported (p. 157). Imperatives signaling assignments or changes of duties ("Now report to X-ray"), on the other hand, often did need to be understood from decontextualized language alone, especially in central supply, where technicians handled a variety of tasks throughout the day. Instructions often occurred in more elaborate forms ("You want to go ahead and try to wash this one?") than are customarily taught in general purpose courses ("Wash the tray"), Svendsen and Krebs, noted (p. 157), as well as with greater use of pronouns and deictics ("Put this one over there with those others"), again due to the context-embedded nature of much task-related conversations.

Hospital transporters had what looked like more advanced language needs, since much of their work involved communicating appropriately with nurses and patients, reporting their location, and receiving instructions on where to pick up and deliver patients, sometimes over the telephone. Also important was a relaxing "wheelchair or trolley-side manner." That involved approaching patients with use of their name and some reassuring words, informing them of what was going to happen to them next ("Now I'm gonna help you sit up/take you downstairs to X-ray"), encouraging them, and ideally, engaging in relaxing phatic communication with both nurses and patients. Contrary to expectations, however, central supply technicians also engaged in social chit-chat. Many of their tasks, such as taking inventory and filling orders, required them to read lists of words, numbers, and quantities on labels and forms, and to match orders with items on a cart or shelf, but little or no spoken language. The same was true of the hours spent wrapping supplies prior to sterilization. Precisely due to this lack of spoken interaction, supply technicians liked to chat to each other as they worked, just as transporters liked to sit around and talk when traffic was slow.

Svensen and Krebs pointed out that VESL students often needed help in understanding the job itself and proposed that the language program should provide this, even if it meant using the students' native language to do so. For example, they suggested that if central supply trainees understood how disease was spread, they would be less likely to make mistakes, such as reusing possibly contaminated water. If transporters were taught to recognize the psychological and physical manifestations of illness, they would be more likely to understand the importance of maintaining friendly contact with a patient ("Are you doing OK, Kelvin?") throughout an entire transport. The last suggestion fits perfectly with TBLT's focus on preparing students to handle target tasks, the language to do so being taught and learned along the way. Unless under extreme time constraints, however, such task-based instruction would, of course, be carried out in the L2. To do otherwise would be to discard one of the many important benefits of TBLT, namely, that the availability of real-world tasks (or of pedagogic approximations to them) shown by a NA to be important to students obviates the need for materials writers or teachers to contrive artificial lesson content.

6.2.8. Journals and logs

The use of different kinds of diaries, journals, and logs for pedagogic purposes, in teacher education, and for research, has been reported and discussed in applied linguistics and LT since the early 1980s (see, e.g., Bailey 1990; Bailey & Oschner 1983; Brown

1985; Howell-Richardson & Parkinson 1988; Jarvis 1992; McDonough 1994). Dialogue journals, in which students submit entries about their experiences inside and/or outside the classroom, and teachers write regular responses, usually to content rather than form, have been found to play a useful role in writing courses (Peyton & Reed 1990; Spack & Sadow 1983), and more generally to serve as a valuable source of information for developing learner-centered curricula (Auerbach 1992). The use of logs and journals described here is narrower, in that the main purpose is to gather information for a NA, which influences the content of at least part of what learners write (and sometimes are asked to write), as well as the focus of teachers' written responses. Dialogue journals sometimes contain logs, but logs can also be used separately in NAs. Logs are records, usually audiotaped or in the form of written notes, which learners make of their language use, perhaps over a week at the office, factory, or university, perhaps longer. They are like language audits of individuals.

Successful use of diaries and logs in NAs and/or as sources of informal feedback for teachers and students about the degree to which needs are being met have been reported by Lundstrom (1994), McDonough (1994), Parkinson and Howell-Richardson (1990), Reves (1994), and Savage and Whisenand (1993), among others. As part of the five-day workshop in the EOP program for Thai aquaculturalists described earlier, for example, Savage and Whisenand had learners keep logbooks, student–teacher journals used to record language-learning and teaching experiences. Student entries were reviewed daily by teachers in order impressionistically to assess (a) problems students felt they had with English and (b) the degree to which they saw that day's classroom activities as helping to resolve those problems. In other words, the logbooks served for work-related writing practice, as a partial basis for an informal analysis of perceived student needs, and as a continuing formative evaluation of attainment of program objectives as the five-day workshop progressed.

The study by Reves (1994) is particularly interesting because it also involved a comparison of her findings with those of a task-based NA for the same program carried out by different researchers four years earlier (Alexandrou & Revard 1990), which had used logs, interviews, and a questionnaire. Reves' study involved a semester-long, non-credit EAP reading course in the University of Hawai'i's English Language Institute (ELI) for students with TOEFL scores ranging from 500 to 600. Students were required to submit journals every two weeks. The first assignment had them answer four specific questions about their reading requirements for the semester, their perceived views of their reading strengths and weaknesses, their goals for the ELI course, and how they would like to achieve them. For the second assignment, they discussed how they read a textbook and how they prepared for an exam. Thereafter, students were free to write about topics covered in the ELI course, summarize things read in or out of class, discuss their reading skills, and so on. In the earlier study, Alexandrou and Revard (1990) had five learners in the same course keep logs, recording what they read, the time spent reading and the purpose. Based on findings from the logs, three interviews were then conducted with each of the five students. Based on findings from the interviews, questionnaires were written and administered to 101 students then enrolled in the ELI's EAP reading courses and to eight faculty members in the students' major departments. From lists provided, students indicated the frequency with which they encountered each of 27 text-types (textbooks, personal lecture notes, academic journal articles, lab manuals, etc.), and rated their difficulty, the importance of 12 reading task-types (reading to prepare for exams, research a term paper, perform lab procedures, build a model or project, etc.) and their difficulty; and the importance and difficulty of 30 reading micro-tasks (outlining important information in a text, reviewing lecture notes, reading graphs, charts, tables and diagrams, using context to guess word meanings, looking up words in a dictionary, locating sources through a library computer database, etc.). The content teachers listed course reading materials and tasks and indicated any different problems they felt NSs and NNSs had with them and how they thought ESL classes might help.

Examining her students' diaries, Reves found that students could easily list some of the major reading tasks they faced and their purposes, but she also found, like Brindley (1984), that perceptions changed somewhat as the semester progressed. Several students later reported having to read quite a number of novels for some courses, for example, a genre initially mentioned only for pleasure reading. Students were generally rather vague about their course goals, their reading strengths and weaknesses, and the kind of teaching they wanted. They became more specific about instructional processes as the course proceeded, however (a finding also reported by Brindley), presumably in part because of their increasing familiarity with relevant terminology and the options available.

Comparison of findings from Alexandrou and Revard's earlier study with those from the logs revealed a much wider range of text- and task-types in the former. For example, five of the 11 most frequently used text-types identified by Alexandrou and Revard's questionnaire findings were not even mentioned in any of the journals. Reves attributes this not so much to the difference in measures the two studies employed as to the extra depth and detail of Alexandrou and Revard's study, and to the fact that learners' opinions about tasks were sampled later in the semester, when students were more aware and sophisticated about those needs. Within-sample variability could have accounted for the differences in findings, of course. Alexandrou and Revard had noted considerable variation in their informants. They differed as to the kinds of exam questions they encountered, for example, and whereas graduate students had to write term papers and used journals and reference books frequently, undergraduates did not. Differences in sampling frame, sample size, and/or changes in the ELI's intake over the four-year period between the two studies could also have played a role. These were different measures applied to two different samples from the same program at two different times, it should be recalled. Studies employing multiple measures with the same learners are clearly called for.

Elsewhere, the journals produced at least some common findings regarding the perceived difficulty and importance of text- and task-types. There were differences across studies in how learners viewed learning processes, however. Reves' students identified two of their goals as increasing reading speed and comprehension, and learning more vocabulary and grammar as ways of achieving them. Alexandrou and Revard's questionnaire offered 'using context to guess meaning of word' as an option, but not learning vocabulary or grammar per se. Reves noted the way learner and researcher categories differed here and elsewhere, with logs, like unstructured interviews, potentially valuable in revealing learner perspectives on language learning. While endorsing the "top-down" approach to processing reflected in Alexandrou and Revard's study, she pointed to the possibility that the use of outsider (etic) categories might result in learners failing to see that their felt needs were being recognized in the NA or, later, addressed in lesson content. (See Nunan 1989 for a discussion of these issues and the desirability of developing mutual understandings of teachers' and learners' process agendas.) Finally, Reves reported that the journals allowed students to express their personal feelings about events in and out of the ELI classroom – something that pre-structured, objective measures tend to preclude – and provided her with not just a one-time snapshot of students' perspectives but also continuing valuable insights into their attitudes and concerns throughout the course. Some students reported greater awareness of their own needs as a result of the journal-writing process, and even a few who found the procedure a chore recognized part of its value:

> I do not like to write journal very much, but I think it should be helpful to teacher because it can make you know what students think about your classes. (Reves 1994, p. 20)

These studies, and that of Lundstrom (1994) of the English and Japanese language needs of a Waikiki travel agent, show diaries and logs to be potentially rich sources of insights into learner (and teacher) needs. They have the important advantage of preserving insider notions of what is relevant. They have the obvious disadvantage, on the other hand, of being time-consuming both to write and to analyze. What is recorded may be idiosyncratic and impressionistic and may require confirmation via other sources and methods. In this regard, McDonough's (1994) study is the only one (to my knowledge) to have involved multiple teacher diaries in the same classroom (for one month of a nine-month co-taught EAP course at the University of Essex). McDonough reported considerable variation among the four teacher diarists about such matters as which learners (in a relatively small class of nine students) prompted diary entries at all, as well as in the teachers' attitudes and experiences toward those learners and to the course in general.

6.2.9. Proficiency measures

Students in any kind of LT program should be tested for diagnostic and placement purposes before a program begins, or where that is impossible, soon after it starts. The reliability and validity of measures and procedures used should be established for the population tested. In the case of TBLT, traditional language tests will be superseded by task-based, criterion-referenced, direct or indirect performance tests (see Section 11.1). A university EAP student, for example, may be required to watch a graded series of simulated or authentic video-taped lecturettes and to answer a set of multiple-choice questions on the information contained in them, the key information bits and test items having been identified by subject-area specialists, i.e., domain experts, as those which good NS students in the area of specialization would be expected to handle. In an elementary Japanese course, a future tourist might be required to role-play purchasing specified items from a Japanese shopkeeper, the shopkeeper's role being presented on audio- or videotape and the student's performance measured by his or her ability to identify from what the seller said such things as which items were and were not available, the cheapest product among a set of options for a needed item, and the total cost.

Task-based measures of this kind are in great demand and are gradually becoming available. For present purposes, suffice it to say that task-based tests form an integral part of the present situation analysis (PSA) and are used to assess entrants' current ability to perform either full versions, or where that is logistically unfeasible, simulations, of target tasks and/or less complex approximations to them (complexity defined according to criteria described in Chapter 8.4.4). Since such measures will eventually also serve for exit, or achievement, testing in TBLT programs, full discussion and illustration of the available options will be reserved for Chapter 11.

6.2.10. Triangulation by methods and sources: the flight attendants study

As noted earlier, gathering information from multiple sources, using multiple methods, is highly desirable but should not stop there. Results from each should be compared and, where discrepancies are identified, triangulation employed to understand the causes and disambiguate the findings. Little work of this kind has been completed to date. However, a study of the tasks and language use involved in the work of airline FAs (Long 2005c) deliberately employed multiple sources and multiple methods (sequenced from most to least open-ended), along with triangulation of methods and sources, in an initial exploration of the issues and potential yield of such an approach. One aim of the study was to see whether outsiders, in this case, applied linguists, could make reliable sources of information on the work – tasks and language use – of a FA, given that it appears to be fairly repetitive, carried out in a relatively constrained discourse space, and "public," in the sense observed many times by today's frequent fliers, or whether insiders, in this case, FAs, would still be required. If the latter, as proved to be the case, the credibility of LT materials written on the basis of authors' intuitions about such "public" fields, let alone more obscure ones, would be placed in doubt. A second, more important aim of the study was to compare the effectiveness of various methods for NA, as well as their relative suitability for tapping different sources.

Written sources consulted were the *DOT*, pre-service FA training manuals, a book-length FA union contract, various in-service FA competency and recertification tests, a cabin crew organizational chart, a flight-operations manual, and standard forms and routine flight paperwork. While more accurate than the introspections of the four applied linguists who served as informants (all frequent air travelers), most of the 15 tasks listed in the *DOT* entry for FA were limited to in-flight FA–passenger interaction and services, lacked position-specific duties (e.g., reference to cabin class or exit door) and any indication of frequency or importance. While a useful starting point, the eventual inadequacy of the *DOT* and outsider information was easily established by triangulation with that obtained from insiders – four experienced, working FAs from two airlines. Also crucial were the written sources, which represented insider-to-insider communication and proved to be by far the richest mine of information on domain-specific, technical, and sub-technical language tasks and background knowledge, not least on such matters as computerized bidding, scheduling, pay calculation, service flow patterns for different types of aircraft, equipment location and checking, safety proce-dures, in-flight emergencies, and basic medical procedures, which are among the most important parts of a FA's work and ability set.

Methods utilized were written introspections about language use and tasks (although the word 'task' was intentionally excluded from instructions, so as not to lead inform-ants), unstructured interviews of about an hour with each of the eight FAs and applied linguists, and samples of target discourse from surreptitious recordings of a pre-flight briefing, segments of in-flight FA–passenger service, FA–FA talk during in-flight breaks, and FA–FA conversation on an airport shuttle. The applied linguists' (outsiders') understanding of a FA's work, as evidenced by their written introspections and transcripts of the interviews, focused almost exclusively on a narrow range of visible in-flight service duties (greet passengers as they enter the plane, help passengers find seats, serve meals, serve drinks, put movie screens down, pass out customs forms, etc.), even when prompted by interviewers to go further. One applied linguist described them as "like waiters, or waitresses in the air…basically they give things to you, and tell you what you need to do.…They're kind of…hands that come round and give you things…servodroids." The FAs themselves provided a far richer, more complex and more detailed account, of much broader scope, including events before they board a plane, and then, before the passengers board, mentioning more tasks, with safety responsibilities the most important aspect of their duties – something reflected in the written document sources, too.

Where source × method interactions were concerned, written materials were found to be the best source on both tasks and language use. This would most likely not be the case in domains where talk is less standardized than is the case with FAs, where, for safety reasons, international norms must be followed both about what is done and, to a large extent, what is said to passengers. Insiders were richer sources of information on both tasks and language. Unstructured interviews allowed insiders to show their vastly superior knowledge better than did written introspections. Audio-recordings were more useful for regular language use on the job than for technical or sub-technical language or for information on tasks. However, they were valuable for obtaining data on some important components of a FA's work, including pre-flight briefings, phatic communication among FAs, and for subtler intertextual, open-ended, and implicit qualities of FA talk. For a more detailed report of the study and quantified results, see Long (2005c, pp. 48–66). For some more recent uses of triangulation by methods and sources, see the NA for a business English course designed for Mitsubishi Heavy Industries by Cowling (2007) and the study of the language needs of French mountain guides by Wozniak (2010).

6.3. Summary

Several *sources* of information are available to the needs analyst. Unsurprisingly, domain experts, that is, insiders, along with authentic documents of various kinds, are by far the most valuable. They will almost always constitute a more reliable source of information than outsiders, such as language teachers or pre-experience language students, on the tasks involved in performing well in a particular occupation, academic field or vocational training program, and on the standards required. Multiple *methods* exist for gathering the information, the use of two or more of which is highly desirable. They should be carefully sequenced from more open-ended methods, such as unstructured interviews and non-participant observation, for depth of insight, to more closed methods, such as questionnaires and criterion-referenced tests, for breadth of coverage. *Triangulation* of sources and methods is desirable, especially when initial results reveal discrepancies among the findings.

6.4. Suggested Readings

Arden-Close, C. (1993). Language problems in science lectures to non-native speakers. *English for Specific Purposes* 12, 3, 252–261.

Boswood, T., & Marriot, A. (1994). Ethnography for specific purposes: Teaching and training in parallel. *English for Specific Purposes* 13, 1, 3–21.

Coleman, H. (1988). Analysing language needs in large organizations. *English for Specific Purposes* 7, 2, 155–169.

Gilabert, R. (2005). Evaluating the use of multiple sources and multiple methods in needs analysis: A case study of journalists in the Autonomous Community of Catalonia (Spain). In Long, M.H. (ed.), *Second language needs analysis* (pp. 182–199). Cambridge: Cambridge University Press.

Jasso-Aguilar, R. (1999/2005). Sources, methods and triangulation in needs analysis: A critical perspective in a case study of Waikiki hotel maids. *English for Specific Purposes* 18, 1, 1999, 27–46. Revised and expanded version in Long, M.H. (ed.), *Second language needs analysis* (pp. 127–158). Cambridge: Cambridge University Press. 2005.

Lett, J.A. (2005). Foreign language needs assessment in the US military. In Long, M.H. (ed.), *Second language needs analysis* (pp. 105–124). Cambridge: Cambridge University Press.

Long, M.H. (2005d). Methodological issues in learner needs analysis. In Long, M.H. (ed.), *Second language needs analysis* (pp. 19–76). Cambridge: Cambridge University Press.

Long, M.H. (2013). Identifying and satisfying language needs in the tourist industry. In Bosch Roig, G.I. (ed.), *Teaching foreign languages for tourism: Research and practice* (pp. 21–44). Bern: Peter Lang.

Oliver, R., Grote, E., Rochecouste, J., & Exell, M. (2012). Addressing the language and literacy needs of aboriginal high school VET students who speak SAE as an additional language. *Australian Journal of Indigenous Education* 41, 2, 229–239.

Van Avermaet, P., & Gysen, S. (2006). From needs to tasks: Language learning needs in a task-based approach. In Van den Branden, K. (ed.), *Task-based language education: From theory to practice* (pp. 17–46). Cambridge: Cambridge University Press.

Vandermeeren, S. (2005). Foreign language needs of business firms. In Long, M.H. (ed.), *Second language needs analysis* (pp. 160–181). Cambridge: Cambridge University Press.

Van Els, T., & Oud-de-Glas, M. (eds.) (1983). *Research into foreign language needs*. Augsberg: University of Augsberg.

Chapter 7

Analyzing Target Discourse

7.1. Conventional Approaches to Language Analysis for Language Teaching (LT)

Two conventional approaches to language in needs analysis (NA) were described succinctly by Pauline Robinson (1981, p. 18) in her survey of theory and practice in English for specific purposes (ESP):

> either texts (spoken or written) are identified, the language of which constitutes the language syllabus for the students, or some sort of language syllabus is identified and then texts are sought or created to embody that language.

Second Language Acquisition and Task-Based Language Teaching, First Edition. Mike Long.
© 2015 John Wiley & Sons, Inc. Published 2015 by John Wiley & Sons, Inc.

The first approach, that is, involves gathering samples of language use in the domain of interest, producing some sort of linguistic description, perhaps involving a register or rhetorical analysis, and basing syllabus content on the results. The second approach is utilized in most general-purpose LT, not just languages for specific purposes (LSPs), and means adoption of a pre-set linguistic syllabus of some kind, e.g., structural or notional-functional, and either adopting or contriving texts to illustrate the workings of those structures, notions, or functions. Both result in classroom lessons in which the focus is on language as object.

Robinson continued:

> At the learning stage, some then advocate that students be exposed to the texts selected and, through appropriate activities or tasks, acquire the target linguistic features. Others adopt some form of explicit description and teaching of the linguistic features, perhaps not always embodied in texts. (Robinson, 1981, p. 18)

There is a methodological choice, in other words, between acquisition through exposure to authentic texts while working on something else (activities and tasks), i.e., incidental learning, on the one hand, and on the other, a focus on forms, i.e., explicit teaching of the items in a pre-set linguistic syllabus. For reasons explained earlier (Chapter 2), TBLT eschews a pure diet of either of these options, regarding both as theoretically and empirically discredited. Language development occurs under each but is inefficient, incomplete, or both. In TBLT, *tasks, not texts*, constitute syllabus and primary lesson content. Conventional linguistic analyses are replaced by *analysis of target discourse*, sample authentic **texts** by *target discourse samples* (TDSs) (with authenticity not necessarily judged according to native speaker (NS) norms), and either pure incidental learning or pure focus on forms by *focus on form*, that is, by *use of intentional learning to facilitate and improve upon purely incidental learning*, in harmony with the learner's internal syllabus.

In fact, there is considerable evidence for the idea that it is not "special language" that causes comprehension problems in LSP so much as a lack of background knowledge about content and how a field works. In a study of Hungarian students' ability to read and translate two English economics passages with the aid of a dictionary, for example, it was found that the students had little difficulty with a text which dealt with problems that were familiar to them from their professional training, but did have difficulty with a second one which analyzed consumer behavior from a psychological perspective, a topic not part of their general economics curriculum. Errors the students made showed that while grammatical difficulties could impede understanding, absence of grammatical difficulties did not guarantee full comprehension. Where vocabulary was concerned, similarly, more errors were caused by conceptual gaps than by unknown words.

As Robinson noted (1981, pp. 19–32), linguistic analyses of technical varieties used in specialist–specialist communication have always had limitations, even for use in synthetic linguistic syllabi. Describing vocabulary frequencies in a field, for example, does not mean that LSP teachers know the technical meanings of the lexical items identified or that they will recognize when familiar items are being used as technical terms. As shown by comparisons of applied linguists' and expert informants' comprehension of specialized texts (Huckin & Olson 1984; Selinker 1979; Tarone *et al.* 1981; Zuck & Zuck 1984), understanding technical work meanings requires content, rather than linguistic, knowledge. Nor is it necessarily the case that technical vocabulary will be unknown to non-native speakers (NNSs) or the most difficult for them, at least for those already working in the domain concerned. Lecturers switching between formal and informal registers and use of informal, colloquial expressions have been reported to cause most trouble for NNSs (see, e.g., Hutchinson & Waters 1987; Jackson & Bilton 1994). Many English for academic purposes (EAP) and English for science and technology (EST) courses concentrate on so-called sub-technical, "inter-level" vocabulary items, that is, non-discipline-specific words and lexical phrases, such as those expressing logical relationships (Coxhead 2000; Coxhead & Nation, 2001; DeCarrico & Nattinger 1988; Simpson-Vlach & Ellis 2010) and describing common scientific processes, that fall between the most frequent and the subject-specific.

Morpho-syntactic frequency data from register analyses are equally limited without extensive supporting information since, as was shown by Cathcart (1989; see Chapter 6.2.3), knowing, for example, which verb tenses and forms are used most frequently is not the same as knowing the functions they serve and could easily mislead a materials writer who lacked the functional information. In an effort to address this problem, some researchers have sought to link grammatical and lexical frequency data to function (Biber 1988) and text-types (Grabe 1987). Adopting a rhetorical approach, others (e.g., Trimble 1985) have shown how writers' rhetorical purpose influences their choices among grammatical options, such as active and passive voice (Tarone *et al.* 1981) or past and present tense (Malcolm 1987) in scientific journal articles. None of this is to imply that vocabulary frequency studies and other kinds of register analyses are not useful. Far from it. They have repeatedly demonstrated their worth, and have become richer and ever more widely available with the advent of rapid computer-assisted analyses of larger corpora, including programs that yield information on different collocations for the same word in different fields or genres (see, e.g., Biber, Conrad, & Cortes 2004; Kennedy 1990; Simpson *et al.* 2002; Simpson-Vlach & Ellis 2010; Sinclair 1987), and the use of more systematically derived samples.

Improvements in the quality and quantity of purely linguistic information should not be seen, however, as a substitute for a satisfactory analysis of learners' communicative needs or of target tasks. Courtney (1988) warns, moreover, against an additional potential side-effect of an exclusively transactional focus, in his case, with respect to a NA for a communication skills course for trainee computer operators at the Oman Technical Industrial College:

> Despite our efforts to avoid such things, improved descriptions can still leave us with essentially linguistic caricatures. We are looking for task-specific language, so it is easy to ignore other aspects and obtain a language specification that assumes that computer operatives only require instructional abilities more relevant to robots than human beings. (Courtney 1988, p. 200)

7.2. The Dynamic Qualities of Target Discourse

A major problem for which a task-based NA offers a solution, although only a partial one, is that of how to move beyond traditional static linguistic approaches to analyzing texts in target discourse domains and, instead, to do justice to the *dynamic structures of language use surrounding the completion of target tasks.* To take the target task Present an automobile sales report as an example, a purely linguistic analysis of a corpus of automobile sales reports might produce a list of 50 verbs, X%, Y%, and Z% of which were marked for simple past, past continuous, and past perfect, ten cohesive devices, the 30 most frequent collocations, and more linguistic detail of that kind. Unfortunately, such information would be of limited value for a materials writer (or a student). The way the forms were used would remain unknown unless a separate functional analysis was conducted. Even if the two sets of information were then combined, as can happen in a good notional-functional syllabus, the communicative value of the language would remain disconnected from the task that gave rise to them. How the forms and functions were used to do the task would remain a matter of guesswork.

In a text-based course, students are left to study one or more frozen (usually, contrived) records of task completion by others, typically featuring an unnatural frequency of target forms that illustrate the structure(s) du jour. The exemplar texts consist of full native language use, or in linguistically simplified versions, often very stilted use, with students encouraged to regurgitate the models from the get-go, as if they already knew the language. They will not experience, or themselves recreate and thereby understand, the dynamic relationships among the forms and functions and doing the task that gave rise to the model of their use by others now presented to them as a finished product. In a task-based approach, students work on pedagogic tasks, i.e., initially simpler versions of the full target task, gradually developing the language they will need for the full version as they proceed.

Exactly how to identify and analyze communicative needs in a target discourse domain in such a way as to reveal the dynamic properties of language use in that domain remains problematic, however, and has occupied scholars in a number of areas of applied linguistics and sociolinguistics outside TBLT. Several insightful non-task-based solutions have been proposed, including the following three, summarized briefly below. While the units of analysis differ, each has something to offer in the way task-based target language use is understood.

7.2.1. Boswood and Marriot's "ethnographic approach" to NA

In a series of valuable papers, Boswood and Marriot (Boswood 1992, 1994; Boswood & Marriot 1994) have proposed and illustrated an approach to analyzing the *communicative events* in which learners participate (Boswood 1994). Influenced, as was Munby (1978), by Hymes' notion of communicative competence, but of the opinion that the true force and value of Hymes' ideas had yet to penetrate LSP, Boswood (1992, 1994) drew attention to the salience and common social recognition of communicative events, such as church services, phone calls, trials, classes, debates, broadcasts, shareholders' meetings, and reading and writing letters and reports. Boswood's first argument for the validity of *event* as a unit of analysis, in other words, was the same as the one noted earlier for task, namely, what might be termed its "social-psychological reality;" participants and (often) non-participants alike, for example, understand (roughly, to be sure) what is meant by a trial (an event) or giving evidence (a task).

The system of analysis that Boswood (1994, p. 41) offered segments target communicative events for learners into 13 major components: participants, purposes, channel and related technology, mode, topics and subject matter, spatial setting, temporal setting, psychosocial setting, act sequence, rules for interaction, norms of interpretation, non-verbal media, and language variation. For the purpose of syllabus design, the information derived in this way must be supplemented by information on students and other stakeholders, and also by information about three other components: the target event's critical importance (in terms of training needs), the gap between intake and target ability, and text analysis, which Boswood said may be based on grammatical, discourse, lexical or skills features, or a combination thereof.

The 13 components listed above are treated as putatively universal variables, realized in terms of values in specific real instances of events, and as ranges of values in idealized events, or event genres. The key difference in analyzing target needs as events is that the focus will be less on the spoken or written linguistic texts involved in each, and more on participants' roles and the dynamic structures of the socio-cultural events in which the texts are embedded. There is a difference, in other words, between *text genres* – narrative, argumentation, description, and so on – and *event genres* – wedding ceremonies, job interviews, university lectures, and so on (Boswood 1994, 42–43). There is also a difference between *speech activity* (Gumperz 1982, 166), such as 'lecturing on linguistics,' which Boswood pointed out highlights the activity of particular participants, and an *event genre*, 'lectures on linguistics,' which is inclusive of both lecturer and audience. There are differences, similarly, between a claim letter, which is a text, a claim for damaged goods, which is the event type in which the text is embedded, and reading or writing a claim letter, which are activities within the event or event type. NA in traditional LSP has erred in focusing over much on authentic texts, such as a particular claim letter (or when generalized, claim letters, the text genre), and in tending to ignore the variety of communicative events in which the text may be involved, e.g., a trial arising out of the complaint or a class devoted to teaching students how to respond to such letters.

Traditional LSP NA, Boswood noted, has concentrated on more formal, conventionalized events, because they are easier described, and has avoided the messier informal ones, such as daily office interaction or small group discussions, even though the latter constitute an important part of students' lives. Traditional NA has also

> focused on linguistic features of conventionally organized texts rather than on the contextual components which explain and give meaning to these preferred organizations. In effect, this involves analyzing the effect of the rules rather than the rules themselves or their operation. This focus on etic rather than emic analysis results in a lack of explanatory power in ESP analysis which limits its pedagogic value. (Boswood 1994, p. 44)

The analysis of communicative events, and courses based on them, Boswood stressed, must also focus on rules for interaction and norms of interpretation. Depending on the students and the type of course involved, the relevant rules and norms might be those used in a broad cultural system (French), particular professional communities (tertiary level students in Paris), particular occupational communities (attorneys), particular communicative events (trials), or particular stages or acts within an event (cross-examinations). Analysis is most usefully conducted diachronically (temporal sequencing) and synchronically (choices among alternatives) in terms of an event's communicative act structure, as exemplified by Ventola's (1987) account of a service encounter. What episodes, and acts within episodes, go to make up an event, and what markers are used to mark the boundaries between episodes and to transition from one to the next? Understanding the communicative value of rules and norms will require their presentation to learners not in decontextualized texts, but with enough non-trivial cultural information for learners to deal with mismatches between their "world structures" and notions of literacy and ideology and those of the target (national, ethnic, professional, corporate, academic, etc.) cultures, i.e., with "sociolinguistic interference" (Hymes 1971, p. 287). The level of delicacy of such an analysis will depend in part on informant intuitions and pedagogic needs, Boswood (1994, p. 50) explained, so that a true ethnographic study of a target communicative event would be far more detailed than the procedure he was advocating, "ethnographic NA."

In an interesting extension of these ideas to business ESP and business ESP teacher education in Hong Kong, Boswood and Marriot (1994), then at the City University of Hong Kong, argued for a reconceptualization of the goal of business ESP teachers as that of acculturation into the business discourse community, and for a parallel recasting of ESP teacher education as ESP practitioner training, the goal of which, again, is acculturation, or socialization, of "novices" (in this sense, post-experience general-purpose English as a second language (ESL) teachers) into the ESP practitioners' discourse community (for discussion, see Freeman & Cazden 1991; Johns 1988; McKenna 1987; Swales 1990a), using principles of ethnographic inquiry to achieve both. Whereas speech communities develop and sustain themselves principally through procreation and marriage, it has been pointed out, discourse communities recruit their members "by persuasion, training or relevant qualification" (Swales 1990a, p. 24). That being the case, Boswood and Marriot noted that the learner's objective (achieved through site visits, panel discussions with community members, analysis of video segments of communicative events, e.g., a business presentation and a transaction at an airport transit desk) is not just to master the linguistic registers of communication among business ESP teachers or in the business world itself, however useful that may be. Rather, it is to understand the expertise, events, genres, systems of in-group organization and communication, and shared belief systems and goals that define the target discourse communities and, within them, the overlapping communicative networks of community members. Eventually, their effectiveness will be improved by a parallel overlap between their own community networks arising from their likely joint roles as entrepreneurs themselves (marketing business ESP training) and mediators of business discourse for their language students in the business world.

Boswood's basic units of analysis, events and event genres – phone calls, news broadcasts, wedding ceremonies, university lectures, job interviews, reading and writing letters and reports – sometimes resemble TBLT's target tasks and target task-types, respectively. Making phone calls, listening to radio news broadcasts, and conducting or going for job interviews, for example, are all target task-types. Attending an undergraduate economics lecture and attending a graduate electrical engineering lecture are target tasks; attending university lectures is a target task- type. Events and target task-types differ in at least two ways, however. First, communicative events, such as wedding ceremonies, university lectures, and trials, in Boswood's schema tend to be larger in scope than most target task-types in TBLT, such as filling out forms, taking lecture notes, or entering a plea. Second, in the interest of inclusiveness, events are neutral with respect to participants and roles, whereas task-types imply agency and action.

Events are superior to tasks for some purposes in the greater degree of contextualiza-tion they preserve, but as units of NA, their holism will often mean a loss of useful specificity for the course designer. To illustrate, 'trials' are a communicative event. They involve many kinds of participants, purposes, act sequences, and so on, all amenable to useful analysis with Boswood's system. However, language teachers are typically dealing with only one class of participants in trials at a time, e.g., attorneys, and target tasks and target task-types for attorneys differ significantly from those of many other participants in trials. Target task-types for criminal lawyers might include reading police reports, locating relevant precedents using a computer database for lawyers, interviewing clients, questioning potential jurors, entering a plea, introducing exhibits into evidence, recon-structing alleged criminal acts from visual information displays, raising an objection, examining and cross-examining witnesses, making opening and closing statements, and addressing juries. Target task-types for judges, jurors, plaintiffs, defendants, witnesses, expert witnesses, sergeants-at-arms, clerks, stenographers, guards, and other partici-pants in the same trials would all be very different. While pedagogic tasks can usefully be embedded in communicative events as analyzed by Boswood when pedagogic mate-rials are written, a NA for course design must identify which actors in those events our students are and the nature of their target tasks.

7.2.2. Mohan and Marshall Smith's "language socialization" approach to NA

A similar proposal to Boswood and Marriot's (1994) for reconceptualizing language learning as socialization into a new culture was made in the EAP context by Mohan and Marshall Smith (1992). Mohan and Marshall Smith were highly critical of the dominant psychological "language acquisition" orientation to language learning (as they saw it), and argued for an anthropologically oriented "language socialization" approach. The former, they stated (Mohan and Marshall Smith 1992, pp. 81–87), defines the learning task as mastery of an underlying system of grammatical knowledge, linguistic compe-tence; the latter sees the learning task as that of becoming a competent member of a cultural group, with language acquisition as one (important) part of that process (see, e.g., Schieffelin & Ochs 1986; Watson-Gegeo 1988, Watson-Gegeo & Nielsen 2003). The "acquisition" view of tasks, Mohan and Marshall Smith claimed, assumes that all subjects have the same, and a constant, "definition of the task." In contrast, they stressed the importance of distinguishing the adult or expert's task and the novice's version of it, which is progressively expanded into it. The theoretical basis for most studies of task-based language learning, they asserted, had been Krashen's Input Hypothesis, and most studies in that tradition have (allegedly) treated context as a given, ignoring its role in making new linguistic items comprehensible, and further ignoring how contextual information itself becomes known and is socially constructed – how it makes not just sentences (sic) but also tasks themselves comprehensible. As previous chapters have made clear, and as subsequent sections will show, some of these allegations (e.g., those concerning the role of Krashen's theory, the static notion of task, the failure to distin-guish expert and novice notions of task, and the widespread ignoring of context in making input comprehensible) are simply unfounded. Fortunately, however, the "lan-guage socialization" position Mohan and Marshall Smith wished to advance does not depend on the validity of their straw man criticisms of the "language acquisition" approach.

To illustrate the "socialization approach," Mohan and Marshall Smith reported on a five-month, quasi-ethnographic study of Chinese students at a Canadian university, in which the researchers focused on task because it provides a common unit of analysis in the language and content learning areas and thereby facilitates an understanding of how the two can be integrated. They warned, however, that use of task or any other common unit of analysis does not guarantee that the findings of the different (acquisition and socialization) approaches to research on tasks will be compatible. Moreover, they rejected the idea that tasks are "out there waiting to be discovered" by the individual learner, so to speak (a possible interpretation of TBLT, and of much of the ESP literature, but an erroneous one), viewing them instead as sub-components of a "larger cultural activity," learned cooperatively. Drawing on the ideas of Vygotsky and Bruner, they defined the relevant research issues (in a way entirely compatible with TBLT theory and practice) as

> the processes by which novices come to adopt the role of experts in culturally organized activities; the interactional nature of their progress, which can often be described as an increase in control or responsibility; and the ways experts structure interactions so that novices can participate in activities that they are not otherwise capable of. (Mohan & Marshall Smith 1992, p. 87)

Mohan and Marshall Smith described how eight Chinese students were (impressionistically, at least) increasingly able to complete the assignments in a task-based graduate course in adult education despite their lack of background in the field and despite the fact that their English language proficiency (roughly 500–550 on the TOEFL) was below the standard usually required. The researchers stated that the full study utilized field notes based on non-participant observation, interviews and informal discussions with the students and their professor, study of assignments and materials distributed for the course, and a field diary. Perhaps because of space limitations (a frequent problem in reporting qualitative, especially ethnographic, research), they presented little evidence to support their conclusions but claimed that the Chinese students were able to participate successfully, e.g., by completing some of the five required assignments, because

> the course supplied and developed the context for the learner's tasks, a context that was constructed by the cooperative interaction of the instructor and the students. (Mohan & Marshall Smith 1992, p. 97)

Aside from the "richly interpretative" nature of such comments and conclusions, it is notable that most examples of 'cooperation' the authors report in fact involved worthy, but rather unremarkable, efforts by one party, the instructor, to make the course manageable (for any students, not just NNSs): clear and explicit organization, a statement of objectives and of procedures for achieving them, deliberate keying of lectures (exploiting repetition and redundancy) to a sequence of five clearly formatted assignments, use of discussion groups and tutorials for students to ask clarification questions about course content, systematic provision of background knowledge and feedback for and on the assignments, breaking down wholes into achievable parts, and an explicit developmental coherence to the assignments, leading cumulatively toward achievement of course objectives. The course appears to have been well planned and taught, in other words, but hardly to have provided a basis for Mohan and Marshall Smith's attempted demolition of "acquisition-oriented" approaches to task-based learning, nor (alone) for constructing their "socialization-oriented" theoretical edifice among the ruins. That said, it is clearly valuable to know what can be done by experts to facilitate novices' entry into a new culture, such as an overseas education system. Mohan and Marshall Smith are clearly right in claiming that context more broadly conceived than has been the case in many "acquisition-oriented" studies is an often neglected resource in this regard, and an important one for course designers to consider in their efforts to make tasks accessible to NNSs. Data of the sort their study provides can help illuminate how learners move toward task accomplishment, including development of such things as coping strategies, rather than simply language development.

A constructive position on the "acquisition–socialization debate" is that of Cole (1985, p. 158), cited approvingly by Mohan and Marshall Smith (1992, p. 88), namely, that

> task or "activity" can be a link between psychology and anthropology. Seen in Vygotskian terms as both a unit of cognitive organization within the individual and a unit of social organization within the culture…It may be that a division of labour can be made between the experimental study of micro-processes of discourse below the level of task and the naturalistic study of macro-processes surrounding the task.

In my view, both kinds of work are necessary and complementary. While a division of labor may be possible, however, "acquisition" and "socialization" inquiries must also be systematically related to one another, not simply left to proceed in isolation.

7.2.3. Watson-Gegeo's true ethnography and "thick explanation"

In an important, beautifully written paper that should be required reading for graduate students in many areas of SLA, applied linguistics, and sociolinguistics, Watson-Gegeo (1992) advanced the notion of "thick explanation":

> the integration of micro- and macro levels of contextual data collected and analyzed in a qualitative, ethnographic framework, to achieve a more holistic understanding of children's socialization. (Watson-Gegeo 1992, p. 52)

Building on the work of Clifford Geertz, Watson-Gegeo (1992) argued that there is a need to integrate two levels of contextual analysis, the horizontal and the vertical. The horizontal dimension refers to "behaviors, interactions and events as they unfold in time, together with the immediate circumstances affecting them" (p. 53). The vertical dimension treats "institutional arenas of activity within the larger culture and society that, although appearing to lie outside the immediate (horizontal) context, shape the context and behavior within it in profound ways" (p. 53). To be adequate, Geertz (1973) had argued, a description must transcend a "thin" behaviorist account to include background cultural information and participants' interpretations of behavior and events, thus making the description rich, or "thick." Crucially, Watson-Gegeo argued:

> thick description, however, can still result in a thin explanation if the researcher pursues an exclusively micro- or macro-analysis. A thick explanation takes into account all relevant and theoretically salient micro- and macro-contextual influences that stand in a systematic relationship to the behavior or events one is attempting to explain. (Watson-Gegeo 1992, p. 54)

The test to determine the boundaries of a study is that "to be included, a level must be shown to be part of the same system as the phenomenon under study" (p. 54), that is, must make a substantial contribution to the explanation.

Watson-Gegeo illustrated with a brief summary of a (by then) 18-year longitudinal study (see, e.g., Watson-Gegeo & Gegeo 1995; Watson-Gegeo & Nielsen 2003), part of which had investigated educational problems for Kwara'ae children in rural areas of the western Solomons Islands (Malaita). Extensive micro-level ethnographic work in the children's homes and classrooms identified serious problems, among them, home–school differences in values and language use, the school system's disregard for the home language and submersion (cf. immersion) of the children in a restricted class-room version of English, poorly trained teachers, and inappropriate materials. However, this "thin" explanation, Watson-Gegeo pointed out, could not explain why some of the children with the strongest home preparation for schooling fared among the worst after kindergarten, and also failed to address the underlying causes of why rural education was the way it was. To that end, Watson-Gegeo and Gegeo set about thickening the thin explanation through an examination of macro-level sociopolitical factors. They based this on a literature review of the history of education in the Solomons, an analysis of government documents, interviews with parents, teachers, and Ministry of Education officials, and a reanalysis of the home and school interactional data in terms of their sociopolitical significance.

Numerous institutional-interactional linkages were revealed, to which, for space limitations, the following brief summary does not do justice. Among many problematic underlying factors, the researchers noted that rapid school expansion as part of a drive for universal primary education in the Solomons had taken place during a 25-year period of a weak economy and as poorly trained, poorly paid, local teachers were rapidly replacing expatriates (the country became independent in 1978). Funding for education had shrunk everywhere, but especially in the countryside, because the emerging middle-class elite in the capital, Honiara, favored projects in urban areas, especially in Honiara, where they lived. All this encouraged high turnover and urban drift among teachers and school principals. Meanwhile, outdated, culturally incongruent materials written in English and originally intended for younger pupils engaged the children at a lower cognitive level than they had already reached in their native language (Kwara'ae) at home (possibly having an even more demotivating effect on the more "advanced" children). Their own bad experience of school, their children's repeated "failure," and the evident loss of morale among school staff themselves, led parents to lose respect for teachers and what hope they held that their own children could use education to break the cycle of failure and poverty. Inevitably, they communicated those attitudes to their children, who then tended to perform as they perceived themselves destined to do.

7.2.4. TBLT

TBLT attempts to make the connection between the internal, cognitive, and external, social (horizontal and vertical) dimensions of tasks in several ways. The first is by maintaining a clear distinction between target tasks and pedagogic tasks. The former represent the end-state, product-oriented, expert view of what the learner needs to be able to do, the view sought from domain experts in a task-based NA, for example. The latter adopt the learner's, or in the case of "pre-experience" students, the novice's, perspective. Pedagogic tasks are worked on, usually in a series of increasing complexity (see Chapter 8.4.4), as gradual approximations to the full target task. While the target tasks are those that the NA has identified as required by the learners, the language or other means used to accomplish pedagogic tasks are negotiable (see Chapters 9 and 10). Given the nature and extent of learner control over interlanguage (IL) development (described in Chapters 2 and 3), that would be the case whether the curriculum "allowed" negotiation or not.

Another way that cognitive and social dimensions are linked in TBLT is, as indicated earlier, by at least some pedagogic tasks being embedded in what Boswood calls 'communicative events.' It is true that, in Cole's and in Mohan and Marshall Smith's terms, some pedagogic tasks in TBLT do have a primarily internal, cognitive, "language acquisition" function, in that they are deliberately designed to increase the frequency of such phenomena as negative feedback and other negotiation work, more complex output, or the probability of learners detecting new linguistic features in the input. Moreover, many experimental studies of relationships among task-types and IL use have also employed the narrower, "cognitive-only" definition, in order to achieve the control an experiment requires. However, such cases are by no means the only forms pedagogic tasks can, and often do, take in materials design. Pedagogic tasks in TBLT are contextualized socially in a variety of ways, not least by invoking learners' knowledge of the world for their resolution and/or, as indicated below, their reconceptualization.

The third and final way in which the cognitive and social dimensions of tasks are linked concerns TBLT's role in preparing students as agents of social change (emancipation being one of its underlying philosophical principles, as described in Chapter 4.5.), for themselves, and potentially, for others. Steps are taken, both in pedagogic task design and in the area of methodology, to make learners aware of their potential as social actors, not merely passive observers, in determining task outcomes and, where necessary, in redefining tasks. For example, instead of simply teaching the minimum language required to describe a health problem to a doctor, pedagogic tasks in a "survival" course for newly arrived Asian or Middle Eastern women immigrants (from some cultural backgrounds) to an industrialized Western society may raise awareness about their rights in the new country, both as patients and as women, as well as strategies for changing power imbalances in service encounters – encounters they may never have experienced before in their country of origin, let alone as potential equals and without a male chaperone. Similarly, in addition to improving lecture comprehension strategies, pedagogic tasks in an EAP listening comprehension course may include work on such matters as culturally acceptable ways of interrupting speakers to elicit reruns of difficult sequences and to improve learners' efficient use of office-hour appointments, tutorials, teaching assistant (TA) sections, and study groups.

7.3. Discourse Analysis (DA) and Analysis of Discourse (AD)

I make a distinction (possibly idiosyncratic) in TBLT between discourse analysis (DA) and analysis of discourse (AD). Both treat discourse, i.e., language in use for communication, and each may employ structural categories (utterance, sentence, turn, T-unit, c-unit, etc.), functional categories (model, repetition, confirmation check, recast, etc.), or both, as part of the analysis. They usually differ in other ways, however, including purpose, focus, and scope. Broadly, whereas a DA sets out to provide an exhaustive account of the "grammar" of language use in a given speech event or other domain, and to meet similar requirements to those observed in syntactic or semantic analyses of sentences, an AD has less lofty aspirations. The aim of an AD in TBLT is to data-mine representative samples of language use associated with successful accomplishment of target tasks and target task-types for input in task-based materials. The AD will often focus on multiple dimensions of language use (functions, grammatical forms, lexis, collocations, etc.) without the usual obligation on the true discourse analyst to relate different dimensions of the analysis to one another (although such relationships may be identified in an AD), let alone to identify hierarchical relationships, and to account for all the data, as stipulated by Sinclair and Coulthard (1975; see below). It is tempting to label DA and AD as "theoretical," or "basic," and "applied," respectively, but (a) those are not mutually exclusive categories, and (b) as Kropotkin pointed out,

> The name of "applied science" is quite misleading, because, in the great majority of cases, invention, far from being an application of science, on the contrary creates a new branch of science.... only after the invention has been made, science comes to interpret it. (Kropotkin 1899/1985, p. 184)

7.3.1. Discourse analysis

The product of a DA is a description of language use as a hierarchical system of levels in which elements at one level are made up of elements at lower levels. A 'cycle' in Bellack *et al.*'s (1966) analysis of classroom lessons, for example, is made up of various sequences of two or more of four possible moves at the level below it: 'structure,' 'solicit,' 'respond,' and 'react.' A cycle consists of a structuring and/or a soliciting move, plus one or more responding or reacting moves. One cycle ends and a new one begins when another structuring or soliciting move occurs, as in the following constructed example from a social studies lesson:

T: CYCLE 1 (STRUCTURE) Today we're gonna talk about the different kinds of labor unions you read about for homework. (SOLICIT) Who can explain the difference between trade, or craft, unions, like the Teamsters or the UAW, and industrial unions, like the Spanish CNT, the French CGT, the Swedish SAC or the (international) Industrial Workers of the World, the IWW?

S: (RESPOND) Industrial unions are organizations of all workers in an industry in one union across trade lines. Pilots, flight attendants, machinists, baggage handlers, ticket agents, and so on in one airline workers union, for example, or at a higher level, in one transport workers union.

T: (REACT) Right // <u>CYCLE 2</u> (SOLICIT) What kind are most unions today?
S: (RESPOND) Trade unions.//
T: <u>CYCLE 3</u> (SOLICIT) And which sort has historically been most effective?

Approaches to DA vary with respect to the dimension(s) of communication dealt with and the categories employed. DA may be performed without any immediate application in mind, in the same way that some linguistic analyses are initially conducted to produce a grammatical analysis for theoretical purposes only. To be observationally adequate, it is argued, however, a DA must satisfy four criteria (Sinclair & Coulthard 1975, pp. 15–17):

1.   It must use a finite descriptive apparatus. In other words, it must specify the categories it will use to classify language use in the domain of interest and not introduce new ones on an *ad hoc* basis whenever data are encountered which do not fit into the existing ones. If this is not done, the system may only be giving the illusion of classification, that is, not really showing how discourse in the domain is constituted.

2.   Categories must be precisely relatable to exponents; that is, they must be clearly and explicitly defined. Failing that, the use of the system will not be replicable and it will be open to the analyst to fudge when problematic data turn up. In practice, meeting this criterion means developing operational definitions of categories, compiling a written list of coding conventions, training coders in the system, and conducting inter-rater reliability checks. While exceptions exist (e.g., Crookes 1986b), very few published DAs (including Sinclair & Coulthard 1975) have in fact provided data on reliability.

3.   The system must be comprehensive. It must be capable of handling all the data. Recourse to a 'miscellaneous' category, e.g., 'other' (for more than a very small proportion of the data, at least) will make it possible technically to meet the requirement, but will again only be giving the illusion of an exhaustive analysis.

4.   There must be one or more impossible combinations of categories. If a system allows any category at one level of analysis to consist of any category or series of categories at the next (lower) level of analysis, that is akin to saying that the largest unit of analysis of interest, e.g., a business letter, an economics lecture, or a classroom lesson, may have any structure at all, which is to say, no structure. A DA will have no predictive power, offer no insight into how, say, language lessons are constructed, unless it can specify constraints on what is possible, i.e., one or more structures that lessons will never exhibit. Just as a comprehensive linguistic analysis of the sentence must specify what constitutes ungrammaticality, so a DA of a lesson must specify what makes (say) a teaching exchange "ungrammatical," e.g., the sequence: *response, feedback, initiation.

7.3.2. Analysis of discourse

AD, on the other hand, tends to be motivated by applied concerns, such as issues in education (Allen, Frolich, & Spada 1984; Barnes 1976/1992), language acquisition (Hatch 1978; Hatch & Long 1980; Sato 1990), or the law and criminal justice (Coulthard

& Johnson 2007; Eades 1992, 1995, 2013). The applied purpose is reflected in the analytic focus and (usually) in the lack of interest in dealing with a complete corpus. Fanselow's system for analyzing L2 classroom discourse, Foci for Observing Communications Used in Settings (FOCUS) (Fanselow 1977), for example, treats several dimensions of classroom talk and relationships among them, and was developed in part to provide language teachers with feedback on the extent to which they are exploiting more than one medium to communicate lesson content. Categories employed for that purpose in one dimension of the analysis include 'linguistic,' 'aural,' 'visual,' 'paralinguistic,' and 'symbolic.' FOCUS does not include categories, on the other hand, for analyzing some other interactional dimensions of classroom conversation, such as whether teacher or student utterances function as models, repetitions, extensions, recasts, and the like, which a more psycholinguistically motivated system might do.

Another example of the applied purpose and focus of AD is Diana Eades' critically important forensic linguistic work on behalf of aboriginal defendants in some high-profile Australian criminal trials, e.g., the Condren and Kina cases (see Eades 1993, 1994, 1995, 1996). Eades' work has often taken the form of expert court testimony drawing upon her extensive knowledge of Aboriginal English in Queensland and elsewhere. That testimony has, in turn, allowed defendants' counsel to dispute the authenticity of alleged confessions obtained by white police officers from aboriginal suspects in custody in prison cells.

As part of Kevin Condren's 1987 appeal of his 1984 murder conviction, for which he was serving "life," for example, Eades showed that (a) the syntactic structure of Condren's supposed answers to police yes–no questions, and (b) pragmatic aspects of his supposed answers to WH questions, as transcribed (supposedly verbatim) by police officers during his "confession," differed radically from Condren's speech in court and to Eades' herself, and from Aboriginal English speech norms, respectively. Thirty-one percent of Condren's alleged answers to yes–no questions in the confession transcript took the form "(yes) + pronoun + auxiliary":

> Q: When you hit her with the steel picket, did you aim for her head?
> A: Yes, I did.
> Q: Was Patricia bleeding when you walked away?
> A: Yes, she was.
>
> (Eades 1994, p. 123)

Yet use of 'unsupported verbal auxiliaries' in such answers is rare in Aboriginal English, Eades' previous research had demonstrated. Moreover, only 1% of Condren's answers to yes–no questions in an interview with Eades took that form, and none of his answers to such questions in his trial had done so. Similarly, Eades showed that the supposedly verbatim transcriptions of the police interrogation violated pragmatic rules of aboriginal conversation concerning the specificity of information appropriate in responses to direct questions. For example, the police transcript showed Condren answering police questions with detailed specificity, e.g., as to precise times, numbers of weeks, and the length of a weapon in feet, whereas such unhesitating, unqualified, and quantified responses to questions are very rare in aboriginal talk. Aboriginal specificity rarely involves use of numbers, Eades (1994, p. 122) reported, and is, instead, frequently relational, employing social, geographic, or climatic comparisons ("When did that happen?" "Not long before the sun went down"). Condren's alleged confession, in sharp contrast, exhibited an alarming number of precise answers with quantifiable specification, e.g.,

Q: When did you do this?
A: Quarter past four.
Q: How long has she been your woman?
A: Three weeks.

(Eades 1994, p. 122)

These observations led Eades (1994, p. 121) to conclude that "the 'confession' was not in Condren's variety of Aboriginal English," and that "I [did] not believe that it was a verbatim record."

Eades' work – surely, an outstanding illustration of the value of applied linguistics in modern society – was accomplished without a DA in the sense of Sinclair and Coulthard (1975). There was no claim, for example, concerning hierarchical relationships among the units and sub-units that go to make up a 'confession,' nor were Eades' analyses exhaustive in the sense of including all the language used by the defendants and police officers concerned. The fact that Eades' evidence in the initial 1987 appeal was heard, but ruled legally inadmissible by the Appeals Court, should not be taken as a reflection on its quality. After all, Condren had been convicted in 1984 despite the fact that another man had confessed to the murder, and despite evidence that he (Condren) had been in a police lockup 50 miles from the crime scene on a charge of drunkenness at the time. The Australian High Court reversed the Appeal Court's decision in 1989, finding both the linguistic and other evidence 'cogent' and admissible, and ordering a new appeal be allowed. That appeal was successful in 1990, the original conviction quashed, and Condren released having served seven years for a crime he did not commit.

ADs conform to Sinclair and Coulthard's second criterion, that of clear category–datum relationships. To do otherwise would render an analysis impossible to replicate and immune from third-party scrutiny. The other three criteria are often ignored, however. For example, where scope is concerned, there is usually no interest in providing an exhaustive description of everything in confession statements, classroom lessons, or NS/NNS conversations. Instead, researchers may focus on one or more aspects of classroom talk, such as feedback on learner error (Chaudron 1977) or teacher questions (Long & Sato 1983), on supposedly key catalytic events in language acquisition, some of which may be quite rare (Nelson 1987), or on a phenomenon, such as 'gratuitous occurrence' (Eades 1993, 2013), which can have a crucial bearing on how testimony is interpreted. ('Gratuitous occurrence' is the term Eades uses to describe the tendency of aboriginal people in Australia to agree with any question, regardless of whether or not the respondent really agrees, or even understands, as a defense strategy in formal interviews, especially in situations involving hostile questioners and a serious imbalance of power.)

For the same reason, ADs tend to be flatter, more serial, and either less, or not at all, hierarchical. For example, using 'utterance' or 'turn' as the unit of analysis, several ADs by researchers interested in the role of implicit negative feedback in language acquisition (e.g., Farrar 1992; Oliver 1995) have focused on sequences, roughly at the level of move, consisting of (1) a grammatical or ungrammatical learner initiation, followed by (2) one of four main categories of caretaker or NS response, including corrective recasts of the learner's utterance, and (3) a learner's reaction, either ignoring or incorporating (all or part of) the grammatical information supplied by the interlocutor. With one possible set of functional labels added, here are the examples of recasts, one syntactic, one lexical, both in the form of confirmation checks, from Sato's work we considered in Chapter 3, section E7:

> NS: Oh, Mary said that you went to
>   um- you went to a game by the Fever?
>
>   TAI: nou tan hi go yEt (INITIATION)
>
> NS: *You didn't go yet?* (RECAST) To the Fever?
>
>   TAI: wat? (IGNORE)
>
> NS: Did you go to see the Fever play soccer?
>
>   TAI: YEs
>
> NS: When was that?
>
>   TAI: nat nat nau (INITIATION)
>
> NS: Oh uh- *later?* (RECAST) Oh I see.
>   (MOVE ON) Who else is going?
>
>   (Sato 1986, p. 36)

The next example, from Long (1980a), shows incorporation, or learner uptake of the auxiliary modeled in the recast:

> NS: Uh yes . a woman drinking (and bottle) wine uh bottle and man drinking (a) beer
>   (INITIATION)
> NNS: Yes and *she's drinking* a glass or a bottle of wine? (RECAST)
> NS: No uh she? *She's drinking* in (no) glass (INCORPORATION)[1]

While DA and AD are usually readily distinguished, they are not mutually exclusive or in competition. It is possible to find work that serves an applied function while meeting most or all four criteria for an adequate DA. Sinclair and Coulthard's own analysis of classroom talk is a case in point; the system for classroom DA proposed by Wells (1993) is another; Ventola's (1987) model of service encounters, sketched in Section 7.4.2, is a third. Some ADs, likewise, can usefully be improved by refining them to meet one or more of the other requirements for DA. It would be interesting to know, for example, if the likelihood of implicit negative feedback being provided in NS/NNS conversation is conditioned by higher-order discourse events of some kind. Finding out would entail relating the above-mentioned three-step sequences at the level of move to what is going on higher up the conversational tree structure. In TBLT, however, as in most ESP work in the 1970s and 1980s, analyses of language use surrounding perform-ance of target tasks are almost always ADs.

---

[1] Studies have shown that even when feedback is "ignored," or when interlocutors move on, thereby denying them an immediate opportunity to demonstrate uptake, learners have often noticed it, with beneficial results on their subsequent performance (see, e.g., Li 2010; Mackey 1999; O'Rourke 2008; Smith 2010). On the other hand, if simply "echoic," immediate incorporation can mean less for long-term IL development than first appears. And in the present example, production of "she's" cannot be taken to imply that the auxiliary will be supplied following a full NP, as opposed to a pronoun.

7.3.3. Sampling and data collection

Exactly how many target discourse samples (TDSs) are collected, how they are obtained, and how extensive they need to be will vary from one setting and set of target tasks to another. The occupation of tour guide, for example, which usually involves many different target tasks and variants thereof, is likely to require more samples, and more careful sampling, than that of tour-bus driver. There is no simple relationship between the complexity of an occupation and the quantity or variety of TDSs involved, however, and such factors as size and the number of other participants, e.g., co-workers or students, can greatly affect what would otherwise be involved in two tasks in the same occupation, academic or vocational education program, or survival setting. Other things being equal, the range of tasks involved in a job is generally broader for the same occupation in smaller organizations, for the simple reason that workers in small organizations tend to have to be "generalists." The co-pilot in a short-hop, 12-seat commercial aircraft, for example, may deal directly with passengers and may even be responsible for checking seat assignments and explaining safety procedures – tasks that are handled by flight attendants on larger aircraft.

In most cases, a task-based NA will indicate domains of language use fairly clearly, especially if the NA was performed in part through participant or non-participant observation. Conferring with domain experts to check on proposed sampling is nevertheless strongly recommended. To illustrate, a hotel front-desk clerk might alert an analyst to the need to sample by time, e.g., overnight telephone conversations with guests calling the front desk from their room, not just daytime calls. Among other differences, tasks handled over the phone at night can differ (in some hotels) in that they include fewer requests for missing or additional items in rooms than tend to occur in the afternoon and evening, when guests check in and see their rooms for the first time, but more outgoing international calls (due to time-zone differences) and more requests from guests for (relatively less predictable) idiosyncratic "emergency" services, and often a correspondingly greater need on the clerk's part to stall or improvise. Talk by secretaries and receptionists in many university department offices, similarly, varies somewhat predictably according to time of day with respect to such matters as the number of people present, pace and noise level, proportion and frequency of telephone and face-to-face conversations, and the likelihood of interactions occurring with faculty, students, administrative staff and members of the public, and of being predominantly "social" or narrowly job-related. Language use can also vary spatially at surprisingly local levels, rather than according to the usual social-class, ethnic, racial, or regional factors, as shown by a study of the "workplace isoglosses" marked by differing lexical choices among 1,253 workers in sections of the same pottery factory within a single building (Tway 1975).

The number and extensiveness of TDSs will also vary from one course to another. In just the same way that time and resources will lead wise analysts to collect only as much information as they will be able to use in course design, so the intensity and duration of a course will affect the quantity and diversity of samples it is useful to gather. A short course may dictate that teachers and students work on the most critical sub-set of tasks identified by the NA, for example, the decision as to which ones determining the TDSs required. The sequence of events is not always NA, followed by collection of TDSs, it should be noted. In practice, analysts often start collecting copies of written documents (e.g., organizational charts, job descriptions, training and safety manuals, sample forms and letters, syllabi, handouts, and textbooks) from the outset and often begin recording, or asking participants to do so for them, soon thereafter.

A detailed description of the process of collecting discourse samples for a task-based study of the US naturalization interview was provided by Winn (2005). She adopted the interactional sociolinguistic approach to analyzing cases of misunderstandings in gate-keeping interviews pioneered by Gumperz (e.g., 1982), who held that an interviewee's grammatical accuracy was less important for success than their mastery of bureaucratic ways of communicating. Winn described several stages in the data-collection process. First, as in any anthropological study, it was necessary to gain entry to the field, which Winn managed through an Immigration and Naturalization Service (INS) officer acquaintance, followed by a formal written approval from the district director. After interviewees' written consents were obtained, 63 interviews with a range of INS officers were audio-taped, accompanied by note-taking by Winn, acting as a non-participant observer. Soon realizing that the data being collected were voluminous and potentially usable for addressing any number of questions, Winn settled on four issues that could directly inform curriculum development and classroom practice: the nature of naturalization interview discourse, what differentiated successful and unsuccessful interviews, the factors that affected applicants' chances of naturalizing, and the implications for ESL/US citizenship preparation courses. She devised a simple protocol to help focus her note-taking on those issues and subsequently added notes she had taken to the transcripts she made of about half the recordings. In typical AD fashion, Winn coded a variety of different dimensions of the data, including "tasks, functions of questions, types of interviewer accommodation [repetition, rephrasing of questions, etc.], causes of misunderstandings, reasons for communication breakdowns, and instances of negotiation for meaning" (Winn 2005, p. 276), relating them to passing and failing interviews. Winn also conducted a number of follow-up interviews, initially unstructured, later structured, with the INS officers she had observed.

Although not of immediate concern here, Winn's general finding, on the basis of her observations and follow-up interviews with the INS officers, was that, of the 63 observed, the ten applicants who failed did so because of their inability to communicate in English, not (alone) for lack of knowledge of US history and government, but that it was not grammatical accuracy that concerned the interviewers but applicants' inability to understand and convey meaning, even with the help of accommodation on the interviewers' part. In a related study, Seig and Winn (2003) found that immigrants, too, perceived their greatest problems being their English abilities, both in the interviews and the reading and writing tests, not the factual knowledge. Accordingly, rather than the typical broad curriculum taught using a content-based approach and focusing on US history and government, Winn recommended a task-based preparation course, with prospective naturalization applicants focusing on the interview process and protocol and experiencing practical, hands-on role-plays and similar activities. She identified nine sub-tasks – swearing to tell the truth during the interview, verifying the accuracy of personal information, accepting or declining the option of a legal name change on naturalizing, establishing "good moral character," professing allegiance to the US Constitution and the American form of government, passing a dictation test of English writing ability, passing a test of English reading ability, passing a test of US history and government, and consenting to take the US Oath of Allegiance at the eventual swearing-in ceremony – pointing out that, directly or indirectly, each one constituted a test of applicants' English ability.

Reflecting on her experience, Winn (2005, pp. 293–294) identified several factors that had facilitated her collection of TDSs and might reasonably be expected to apply in other settings, too. They were possession of an inside connection to facilitate entry to the field, patiently following official channels when requesting formal permission to make recordings, building rapport with interviewers over time, which resulted in greater information sharing, positioning herself as a learner, wishing to learn from the experts (insiders), observing and recording a goodly number of instances, thereby increasing the likely validity of generalizations made, using follow-up interviews with participants, collecting data from related events (in this case, citizenship classes, etc.), and methodological flexibility and creativity when confronting unexpected logistical challenges.

7.4. Analysis of Target Discourse: Five Cases

There is an emerging consensus among those who have conducted field research on language use in a variety of settings that the principal communicative problem facing new practitioners is not so much the specialized language appropriate for those settings itself, if indeed there is much specialized language at all, but rather, knowing how, when, and with whom to use it, i.e., the purpose it serves. After studying spoken and written language use in a British architect's office, Medway (1994) observed:

> helping people learn the technical vocabulary and conventional forms specific to an occupation will not produce effective language users... Workers could probably use most help, not over the language itself, but in achieving a more conscious awareness of the situational factors of which they need to be taking account. (Medway 1994, p. 11)

By way of illustration, a written "site instruction" was sent by "Joe," a junior architect in the firm, to the contractor, specifically to the building site supervisor, "Luc," ostensibly telling Luc to lower part of the ceiling in a new building already under construction: "Lower ceiling @ corridor 327 as per attached sketch SK 26-01 and revise to acoustical lay-in tile as shown." The formal conventions for such communications, e.g., article omission, use of simple imperatives, and accompanying graphics to convey detail, Medway suggested, while important for message clarity and for maintaining the architect's credibility, were relatively easy to learn on the job, where he claimed most specialized language use has to be acquired. What was much more important, he argued, was knowledge of the judgments and appraisals relevant to the decision, many of which lay "outside the words themselves" (Medway 1994, p. 4).

Exactly which approach to AD a designer or teacher takes, which dimensions of TDSs he or she analyzes, will depend on a number of factors. The kinds of students involved, and the extent, if any, to which value is attached to overt classroom treatment of features of linguistic or discourse structure, will be influential. So, too, will whether or not the analysis is to be of the conventional kind, done by the teacher or materials writer before a course begins, or performed collaboratively by teachers and students as part of the course itself, or both. Some general methodological considerations, as well as examples of the kinds of information that can emerge from ADs and then be taken into account when designing materials, are briefly illustrated below.

7.4.1. The railway ticket purchase

The following four short conversations (see the dialogue below) are representative of a larger series of 21 that I audio-taped one morning some years ago at the ticket window of a small country railway station in eastern Pennsylvania.

At the ticket window
   Ticket clerk (**TC**), customer (**C**)

Dialogue A

TC: How you doin'?

C: Alright and yourself?

TC: Tripper?

C: Right

TC: (2) That's Bethayres to Logan?

C: Right Mmhm

TC: (8) (XXX)

TC: [stamps ticket] (5) OK Eleven
   she be and Thank you

C: Right

Dialogue B

TC: Morning Yes (mam)

C: Morning Senior citizen one-way Terminal
   (By the way)

TC: OK That'll be one-twenty

C: [gives money]

TC: [giving change] That'll be two

C: (Thank you) OK (5) [returning to counter]
   Is there a train expected before the nine
   o one?

TC: Yes There's an eight fifty-two due
   next Then comes the nine o one

C: Thank you

Dialogue C

C: I need a couple of bargains Did you get rid
   of the doggie?

TC: Yeah I had to finally send him away
   (He) was here until eleven o'clock (and)
   no body claimed him so (2) Ok

C: Really?

C: [holding up cigarettes and candy] Three
   seventy and twenty-five right?

TC: Right

TC: Mmhm

C: Ok

Dialogue D

C: Nine o one train's passed yet?

TC: No not yet   Not yet? Ah (xx)

TC: Ok what would you like?

C: (6) Five bargain ticket [sic], please

TC: [stamps ticket] That'll be nine twenty-(seven)

C: [gives money]

TC: That'll be ten Thank you

C: (Is it) OK that my blue car is parked (in front of here)? (2) In front (1) in the uh (xx) Here is the Volkswagen?

TC: Yeah well that's-

C: Red Volkswagen?

TC: Well I don't know That's for handicapped people (there xx)

C: Oh OK I'm gonna put (it) park over there

They involved the same ticket clerk, who had worked there for several years and who was the sole employee at the station. His was a one-man operation situated inside the waiting-room, mercifully heated during the long winters, serving passengers mostly bound for Philadelphia, the final station for all inbound trains, or else further out into the countryside. It was the kind of quiet station where people simply walked across the tracks for outward-bound trains. About half the passengers were regular commuters with season tickets whom the clerk knew by sight. As the only employee, he also operated a small kiosk selling newspapers, cigarettes and candies, which were laid out to the side and just in front of the ticket counter, over which he took the money for tickets and sundries alike. As a regular commuter from the station for several months prior to and after the recording, I judged the conversations that day as typical of many I heard.

Tasks reflected in the dialogues included buying and selling train tickets in all four, sundries in C, and a sub-task, making change, in A, B, and D. Other tasks included greeting an acquaintance in A and B, informing passengers/inquiring about a train arrival in B and D and about parking in D. The only other relatively major item was an exchange about a lost dog in C. All but the last were predictable tasks to find a ticket clerk and railway passengers engaged in at that station, but there were degrees of predictability even within this tiny sample. Buying and selling tickets would be safe bets to figure in the daily routine of the vast majority of railway ticket clerks the world over. Buying and selling sundries, however, would be unknown at many ticket windows, including those at large stations in most major cities. Dealing with parking issues would be less unusual when, as at the station in question, the only parking available belonged to the railway and was visible from the waiting room. The "lost dog" episode is an example of the kind of unpredictable social talk that can alarm NNSs, teachers, and needs analysts alike.

Albeit crude, and (for reasons of space) based here on a tiny corpus, these preliminary observations are typical of more detailed findings from a range of task-based analyses of talk in a variety of workplace settings. First, where size is concerned, the smaller the institution, the more the fewer workers there tend to function as generalists, and the broader the range of tasks they perform, including some that would be handled by other more specialized employees in larger institutions doing the same work. The railway clerk sold sundries and (although not illustrated here) also performed platform flagging duties and made station announcements over a loudspeaker, among other things, tasks that would normally be handled by other personnel, not ticket clerks, at a larger station. While small size generally means more diverse tasks for participants, it also often means increased familiarity, personalization, and shared background knowledge among interlocutors, with resulting possibilities for inexplicitness and ellipsis, as shown here in the clerk's ability to *initiate* some ticket purchases, his ability to do so using a single word ('Tripper?'), the usual lack of need for him to specify a destination, and in the passengers' use of anaphoric reference ('the doggie') with first mention of an item. These options would rarely prevail at a busy city railway terminus serving numerous destinations and thousands of passengers each day. Second, the context-embedded nature of talk allows use of deixis, e.g., 'here' and 'that' in D, and of further cases of ellipsis, e.g., no mention of the sundries whose prices are called out in B. Third, even in the case of a relatively narrowly circumscribed occupation like that of railway ticket clerk, considerable variation arises due to local circumstances, much of which would be unpredictable, and in fact difficult to understand, without contextual information. Here, that would include information about physical plant and layout, the fact that the station only served passengers on one line, to and from a major city terminus (known as the 'Terminal'), and that the operation was small enough and the clerk experienced enough with it that he recognized many passengers and, in some cases, could remember their usual destinations and the kind of ticket they customarily purchased. Only with that information, for example, is it possible to explain how it could be the clerk, not the passenger, in A who initiated the sale by suggesting the kind of ticket ("Tripper?") and the itinerary ("Bethayres to Logan?") in which the passenger was interested (in contrast with the situation at a busy city terminus ticket window) with no preceding talk other than an exchange of greetings, or how so much ellipsis could be acceptable in A, B, and C.

Several other features common to a variety of specialized and semi-specialized domains of language use are reflected in the four short pieces. There is the colloquial, perhaps idiosyncratic, language the clerk uses, e.g., to accompany the sub-task of giving change ("Eleven she be," "That'll be two"), and the proportion of talk (apparently) not intrinsically related to the key participant's central role, in this case the occupation of ticket clerk. As with the lost dog and parking restrictions, this "social talk" (see 7.4.5., below), moreover, is less predictable and requires less formulaic, more complex, language of participants. Finally, in the area of the technical lexicon, 'ticket,' the vocabulary item most people, including many applied linguists (confirmed with several groups of graduate students in TESOL and applied linguistics), would predict, based on intuition, to occur frequently in conversations with railway ticket clerks, in fact, only occurs in D. Elsewhere, the imprecise generic term is replaced by more informative specific ones indicating particular types of ticket: tripper, senior citizen, one-way, and bargain. This is a common phenomenon in specialist-to-specialist communication. Thus, carpenters rarely refer to 'wood,' 'hammer,' or 'nail' when talking to one another, but, e.g., to 'two-by-four,' '12 ounce,' 'two-inch,' and so on. Also, as is often the case with a specialized lexicon, regional variation abounds (cf. British 'cheap-day-return,' West Australian "multi-rider," etc.). Preparing students for exactly which of the plethora of possibilities occur in a particular location will require local knowledge, acquired through analysis of TDSs. Interestingly, the purchaser in D, who was the only person to use 'ticket,' was also the only NNS among the four passengers. One wonders if she had been the innocent victim of LT based on materials writers' intuitions, as opposed to an analysis of TDSs, about what transpires at railway ticket windows, such as the following embarrassing example, for which I must accept responsibility:

The helpful ticket clerk
PASSENGER: How far is it to Oxford?
TICKET CLERK: About sixty miles.

PASSENGER:	How long does it take?
TICKET CLERK:	An hour.
PASSENGER:	How much does it cost?
TICKET CLERK:	Two pounds.
PASSENGER:	Uh two tickets, please.
TICKET CLERK:	There are no trains on Sundays.

(Long 1977a, p. 7)

Several of the above-mentioned observations parallel those reported in published and unpublished ADs of language use in a variety of settings, including the study by Svendsen and Krebs (1984) of two health-care occupations, central supply technician and hotel porter. Svendsen and Krebs found that speech in the hospital, like that at the railway ticket office, was often more colloquial and idiomatic than that which would typically be modeled in a conventional ESL classroom, and that, as noted earlier, there was greater use of pronouns and deictics ("Put this one over there with those others"), due to the context-embedded nature of much of the task-related talk. Perhaps the first to report the phenomenon were Hutchinson and Waters (1987), who drew attention to the colloquial, idiomatic, and context-embedded nature of communication in a technical classroom ("You just shove this little chappie in here like that").

Svendsen and Krebs (1984, pp. 158–159) noted the greater importance of spoken language ability when things went wrong and when the unexpected occurred (cf. the ticket clerk's handling of passenger B's inquiry about the lost dog and passenger D's parking problem). Central supply technicians needed to be able to communicate a problem appropriately ("We're out of 2×2 gauze." "The sterilizer's not working"). They also noted that while language requirements for the two occupations differed, workers in those and most other entry-level jobs need to be able to report problems, seek clarification or confirmation that tasks are being done correctly ("Like this?" "That one?"), understand imperatives and numbers, and give co-workers feedback on their level of understanding, as well as socialize. The extent to which such "social" talk is really phatic communication or part of the job is a matter to which we will return.

7.4.2. Japanese tourist shopping

Tourism has been a mainstay of many economies for some years now, Hawai'i being a prime example. While often taking a devastating toll on indigenous cultures, on land, water, and other natural resources, there is little sign that governments or the giant corporations involved are concerned enough to change matters, e.g., by economic diversification. After all, it is local workers, not politicians or corporate executives, who are evicted from their homes to make way for unwanted developments or who see their farms dry up so that golf courses may be properly watered.

Travel from Asia to English-speaking countries, in particular, has increased rapidly, and where a foreign language for occupational purposes (FLOP) is concerned, receiving countries have been playing a losing game of catch-up ever since. For example, Japanese visitors to Australia, just 49,000 in 1980, more than doubled to 108,000 in 1985, and had increased to a staggering 452,000 by 1990 (Marriot & Yamada 1991, p. 155). Surveys show that of four major tourism components, sightseeing tours in Australia for these visitors are always conducted in Japanese, shopping in either English, Japanese, or both, and accommodation and transportation mostly in English.

Marriot and Yamada (1991) set out to determine how best to evaluate the Japanese conversational abilities of Australian English speakers serving Japanese tourists in shopping encounters. They compared two naturally occurring service encounters in Japanese in a Melbourne duty-free store selling opals. One was between a female Australian server, herself a NS of Japanese, and a male Japanese tourist, both in their 40s, and the other between an Australian male server, a NNS of Japanese, and two female Japanese tourists, all in their 20s. Data were obtained from tape-recordings of the two conversations between both servers and the two female Japanese customers, and from follow-up interviews.

In related work on Japanese shopping encounters in Japan, Sugito and Sawaki (1979, pp. 285–288, reported in Marriot & Yamada, 1991, pp. 156–157; see also Tsuda, 1984) had drawn attention to the power vested in sellers, in part through their richer technical lexicon, power reflected in the tendency for them, not the potential buyers, to initiate new topics and stages in shopping discourse. Marriot and Yamada confirmed this finding for both opal sellers. The female Japanese NS initiated 78 of 89 (88%) new lexical items, and the Australian male NNS 92 of 136 (68%), many concerning opals: e.g., *honmono* (genuine article), *jinkooteki* (artificial), *borudaa opaaru* (boulder opal), *mekki* (plating), *masshiroi* (pure white), and *mezurashii* (rare), or the particular sales context: e.g., *o-miyage* (gift), *o-kadioku* (bargain), *hoshoosho* (guarantee), and *takkusu* (tax).

While roughly comparable where specialized vocabulary was concerned, the two differed in other ways. Most obviously, the Australian NNS made a variety of Japanese grammatical errors and, in a subsequent interview, freely admitted to a strategy of leaving a number of utterances unfinished in an effort to avoid looming grammatical choices he knew he could not make accurately. (This phenomenon was misinterpreted positively by the customers as an appropriate display of politeness and humility, their follow-up interview revealed.) This was 'presentational deviance' in Neustupny's (1995a,b) terms, that is, an inability to communicate more than the basic propositional content of a message. Speakers display presentational deviance when they lack the linguistic or pragmatic knowledge to communicate such things as appropriate marking of attitude, e.g., deference or politeness, in a message or to an interlocutor. Presentational deviance was also exhibited by the NS server. For example, she used the appropriate *desu/masu* honorific style and other honorific forms (which are obligatory from the always subordinate server to the always superior status customer in Japanese sales encounters) more consistently, frequently, and appropriately than the Australian NNS, but also deviated from Japanese norms, mostly in the direction of excessive informality, overuse of colloquial forms, and insufficient overt politeness, perhaps through having started this work after leaving Japan.

The most significant differences between the NS and NNS sellers' performance, however, lay in their management of the major structural elements and topical content of the conversations. This involved what Neustupny (1995a,b) calls 'propositional deviance' on the Australian NNS's part, that is, an inability to produce or comprehend as needed, at both the utterance and discourse levels. The discourse structure in each transaction was analyzed following Ventola (1987), whose pioneering work in this area had identified the main elements in such service encounters as

Greeting, Attendance-Allocation, Service Bid, Service (sub-stages, in terms of Need Specification and Need Compliance), Resolution, Pay (potentially consisting of two sub-stages,

Requesting and Giving Payment, and an optional Giving and Receiving Change), Goods Handover, Closing, and Goodbye.

The two conversations were found to require some modifications to Ventola's scheme, including a new sub-element, Need Stimulation, within her Service category, in part because of the complexity of the interaction involved in purchasing opals. (Ventola's encounters had involved comparatively straightforward purchases: stamps at the post office, a plane ticket at a travel agency, and souvenirs at a gift shop.) Cultural background (Australian English in Ventola's work, Japanese in Marriot and Yamada's) motivated some of the differences, as explained below.

Still within the domain of propositional deviance, Marriot and Yamada found that the male Australian server engaged in a considerable amount of monologic discourse, providing a lot of valid technical information about the product and service options available during the service element of the transaction. He was able, that is, to perform Need Stimulation through providing enough information about the product and prices, and Need Compliance by giving out more such information in response to customer inquiries. He failed to ask about such matters as the purpose of the purchase and the customers' price range, however. Also, whereas the Japanese NS server initiated every sub-stage of the service element, the NNS server sometimes left the customers to do so. In the process, he failed to pick up on at least two cues from them that they were ready to purchase a particular opal, and also a later signal from one of the women that she was interested in a second purchase. Following satisfactory completion of Resolution and Pay, the NS server, in contrast, was careful to return to a new inquiry about possible additional Needs. Unlike the Japanese NS server, the Australian NNS also failed to engage the customers at a more personal level, e.g., by talking about the weather or asking about their stay in Australia, which is considered important to many Japanese in this sort of transaction.

Interestingly, Marriot and Yamada report that whereas the Australian had great difficulty with the highly complex honorifics systems, and was aware that he did, he had apparently not noticed his problems with some of the appropriate interactional and topic-related behavior, despite having lived in Japan for a year, studied Japanese at university for two years, and then worked part-time in the duty-free store for a year. In other words, focus on form appeared necessary with respect to certain aspects of discourse structure and pragmatic appropriateness:

> Norms pertaining to interaction management for specific contexts are extremely varied and are also difficult to acquire unconsciously; unless specific training is provided, we cannot expect Australians to improve their interactive competence in such situations. (Marriot & Yamada 1991, p. 164)

Of the little occupational language training the man had received from the company, most had been help with the technical lexicon for talking about opals (which had obviously been useful), along with a few tips about such matters as 'helping Japanese customers overcome shyness,' e.g., by taking out a tray of opals as soon as they began to look. An American or Australian customer might react negatively to such a move, potentially akin to 'hustling,' or perhaps respond with a routine like 'just looking' (as might some Japanese tourists, Marriot 1991, p. 206 reports, on the basis of interviews with a number of them). This "pushing" strategy led to the two servers omitting Service Bid, which Ventola had found customary in Australian English service encounters, and moving straight to 'merchandise.' Marriot (1991) and Marriot and Yamada (1991) introduced a new category, Need Stimulation, into Ventola's scheme to take account of this culturally motivated difference.

Marriot and Yamada (1991, p. 166) concluded that their case study showed how "interactive competence for specific situations requires a wide range of skills, some of which will be industry-specific or position-specific." By no means all the relevant skills were linguistic, either, they emphasized. Socio-cultural and socio-economic competence were probably more crucial (see also Neustupny 1995a,b). This was confirmed by further case studies of shopping encounters between monolingual Australian English speakers and Japanese tourists, reported by Marriot (1991). There were clear instances of performance deviance by both Australians and Japanese, i.e., an inability to communicate according to internal native norms for a situation. Japanese tourists employed language mixing and switching during conversations with the monolingual English speakers, for example, while on the Australian side, servers who were experiencing difficulty in communicating with the tourists at all (as when trying to inform a monolingual Japanese customer of the unacceptability of US currency in the Australian store) resorted to message avoidance, sometimes being unintentionally rude and ineffective (initially losing a sale), as a result:

SERVER: No, no that's U.S. I think, excuse me (looks at the card) Yes, that's U.S. No, only Australian.
CUSTOMER: *A dame na no?* (Isn't it any good?]
SERVER: I'm so sorry, very sorry
CUSTOMER: *Kore dame?* (Is this no good?]
SERVER: (Looking at the tourist next to the customer) I'm very sorry
CUSTOMER: *Dame?* [Is it any good?]
SERVER: Thank you very much
CUSTOMER: Doomo sumimasen
SERVER: Ah yes just leave it   I'll put it back. Thank you very much, no don't worry
                                                            (Marriot 1991, p. 207)

Buying/selling a train ticket and an opal are two instances of the task-type, buying/selling something. Given the frequent need in heterogeneous classes, and/or due to time constraints, to work on pedagogic tasks derived from task-types, rather than from the target tasks themselves, it is instructive to compare them for similarities and differences. Perhaps most important, with relatively minor modifications (see below), the discourse structure of both types of purchases conformed broadly to Ventola's model for this sort of service encounter. A second obvious similarity concerned the role of peculiar local logistical factors in both situations, factors that would have been difficult to predict without an on-site NA. For example, at the railway station, the close proximity of the sundries kiosk to the ticket counter made it possible for some Need Specification to be signaled non-verbally, and the visibility of the parking-lot from the ticket office window made the exchange about parking restrictions with passenger 4 (a) reasonable, and (b) able to take the form it did. Similarly, the fact that opals in Australia were kept in closed glass display cases normally motivated more spoken interaction with customers than might otherwise be necessary, although in the instances described, at least, not necessarily with Japanese tourists, because of a particular sales strategy, Need Stimulation, employed with them.

There are also several salient differences, however. The routine nature of a ticket purchase compared with the purchase of a relatively rare and unfamiliar luxury item affected such matters as the shared knowledge of technical terms ('tripper', 'senior', 'Terminal') in the former, and the unequal distribution of technical terms, and a resulting power imbalance, in the latter. Second, the certainty and clarity of the railway ticket buyers about their requirements contrasted with the typical situation in the duty-free store. As Marriot and Yamada pointed out, people buying an expensive gemstone usually do so only rarely, often know little about the product or the specialized language used in the trade, and may be unsure of whether they intend to buy at all or, if so, exactly what, when they enter the store. Prior knowledge on the commuters' part made the need for negotiation, and the complexity and explicitness of the resulting discourse, all far lower than in the opal purchases, as did, third, the familiarity of the server and some of the buyers in the former case. The core component, Service, in particular, was cryptic at the railway station, with no need for Need Stimulation. Need Specification was sometimes performed by the seller, not the buyer. The fact that the commuters were usually short of time, compared with the leisurely pace of the tourist holiday shopping, may have been another factor bearing on discourse structure and complexity.

For reasons of space, many other similarities and differences between these two variants of the same task-type are left unstated here. Suffice it to say, tourist gift shopping, at least, obviously constitutes a partly different kind of buying and selling from the more numerous, functional, routine transactions witnessed at railway stations, post offices, supermarkets, and the like. While some features of the discourse will be common to most examples of buying and selling, therefore, both NAs and ADs will often be required before a course is designed to ascertain where any differences lie. Target task-type will be too general a unit of analysis for course design; inventories of target tasks are what are needed, along with analyses of TDS that go with them.

7.4.3. Doing architecture

A third example of an AD, this time of the often more abstract, open-ended, context-reduced talk common in "white-collar" professional occupations, is Medway and Andrews' (1992) insightful interim report on a study of language use in a British architect's office (see also Medway 1994). Medway and Andrews began by pointing out that some professional discourse, e.g., most of a lawyer's work, serves principally to instigate more language production, while some, e.g., talk by aircraft pilots, produces non-linguistic outcomes, like landing a plane. Some language-related tasks, such as dictating letters, consist primarily of language activity, while others, such as producing drawings, are primarily non-verbal. Most talk among architects might be expected to create a non-verbal product in the form of new or converted buildings. In fact, however, while some of the conversations observed did indeed result in non-verbal tangibles, such as drawings, it turned out that much of an architect's work, too, involved linguistic outcomes rather than physical structures (which are erected by construction workers, after all, the authors pointed out, not white-collar professionals). Many tasks that an architect performs concern contracts, environmental impact statements, or planning permission, for which speech, reading, and writing are critical throughout.

Medway and Andrews spent two days in the office as non-participant observers. They made audio-recordings, collected documents, asked questions, and obtained explanations from the participants about their work. Their 1992 report concerned findings on talk among the firm's three partners, focusing on one episode in particular, a 'briefing update' (a term used by the participants). The briefing lasted some 37 minutes, including interruptions. In it, RC, one of the partners, updated a second, who had just returned from a vacation, in the presence of the third (and the researchers), on the progress of their joint proposal to build new housing and offices for a local housing association. The briefing was found to reflect considerable discursive skill on RC's part. While consisting primarily of a spoken narrative by RC, texts of various other kinds were cleverly integrated. These included graphical representations, such as architectural drawings, "bracketed" conversations embedded in the larger narrative, such as recalled excerpts from a conversation with another party or a telephone call to a client, made by agreement in the presence of the listeners, and 'consultations' of source documents, such as committee minutes or a planning application, often interwoven with physical manipulation of papers and meta-discursive comments:

> Now on the housing front, among these papers is their development programme. Very interesting. And the Shaston Station Housing is mentioned in it, /2/ as being part of it. /3/ [Flicks through document] Turn that up. /8/ And among the things that they've got there. (Medway & Andrews 1992, p. 19)

The whole briefing, the researchers showed, was rich in implicit and explicit reference to past, current, future and hypothetical spoken, written, and graphic texts. Deliberate acts of 'consultation', conscious interruption and 'bracketing' made some references obvious, but in addition, they pointed out, "texts from elsewhere are simply present in the current spoken text, in substance or as ghosts" (Medway & Andrews 1992, p. 19).

The intertextuality of the briefing was sometimes intense. At one point, RC said:

> Not yet. Er/3/. . just thinking of the order in which things happened. Er/4//what did Jim say to me? [Can't find. Thinks, hand on head, eyes closed] Jim said something to me. I wrote it down somewhere. /3/Lost it. /6/ But he said /6/ send a copy of the plan to Luke Jones. (Medway & Andrews 1992, p. 21)

Medway and Andrews (1992, p. 21) commented:

> Jim's request led to RC's written note which should have informed the current oral report. Similarly, part of this current text, which was itself occasioned by the problematic nature of a prior text (the initial drawing RC had prepared) gives rise to a third text, RC's phone call, a later successful version of which will presumably inform a subsequent oral text (another discussion amongst the partners) and then another graphical text (the revised drawing), which will form the basis of a further oral text (the board's discussion) which will lead to a written text (the board's minutes) which will provide a grounding for any number of further textual productions.

As well as substantive information about such matters as potential modifications to the initial plans, the briefing included reference to political matters concerning the deliberations of committees and boards responsible for granting approvals and contracts, e.g., rumors and inferences about the preferences and allegiances of members of a crucial committee, and inferences as to what might motivate those individuals' past and future attitudes to the partners' submission. Instead of dismissing such comments as irrelevant small talk, the researchers pointed to their potential importance in the life of the project, given the influence of public officials and others in determining the chances of the firm's proposal eventually becoming the successful bid:

> Such gossip and speculation...are probably highly functional in the long run...anything which contributes to that understanding in general, whether or not immediately relevant to the job in hand, is considered "business". (1992, pp. 6–7)

In sum, a central finding was the crucial and pervasive role of talk in doing architecture. Medway and Andrews reported seeing this in a wide variety of activities during their two-day site visit. Linguistic sophistication was required by juniors negotiating with seniors, by an architectural technician dealing with a site foreman, and by a staff member framing a detailed written presentation to a planning officer. The architects also used language collaboratively, not always to communicate information, but to think through a problem together out loud. Such dialogue was often fragmentary, with incomplete utterances and many pauses, sometimes while both speakers worked separately on rough sketches of the problem. When a solution was found, there was joint verbal confirmation of the fact. Workplace language use, in other words, Medway (1994, p. 12) pointed out, often includes using language to learn, to create new knowledge on the job. Or as Medway and Andrews (1992) put it, given that architects do not pour concrete and physically make buildings, considerable importance is attached to building with words.

The insights provided by Medway and Andrews offer potential additional depth to ADs in other settings. Perhaps the talk between ticket clerk and passengers described earlier that was not intrinsically related to ticket sales, e.g., the "social chit-chat" about a lost dog, should also be seen as functional in the long run, although not immediately relevant to the job at hand. It was presumably in part through texts of that nature that ticket clerk and passengers learned about each other and built the social relationships upon which subsequent familiarity was grounded, both personal, as reflected in greetings, and functional, as reflected in the clerk's ability to predict ticket requirements. The "social talk" among the hospital porters and central supply technicians reported by Svendsen and Krebs may well have served the same purpose. The Australian duty-free shop assistant's failure to engage the two Japanese women customers at the personal level, described earlier as an example of propositional deviance, is an even less ambiguous example. Marriot (1991, p. 161) reported that, at one point, perhaps aware of her male Australian NNS co-worker's difficulty in handling small talk in Japanese, the female Japanese NS server entered the conversation he was having with the two Japanese women to ask pleasantly about their travel in Australia. The "small talk" appeared to be appreciated by the customers, she reported, for the two women proceeded to volunteer several pieces of additional personal information in their replies. Both in that instance and when the female NS server adopted the same strategy with the male Japanese customer, Marriot (1991, p. 161) pointed out, the "small talk" involved a reduction of distance between the server and customer, which could be seen in a brief change, from formal to informal style, in the Japanese male customer's speech.

In light of Medway and Andrews' analysis, the seemingly sparse verbal encounters surrounding the railway ticket purchases, like the briefing update, can now also be seen as involving the skillful interweaving of texts of different kinds. Some greetings ("How you doin'?" "Alright and yourself?") reflected familiarity from previous meetings. The inquiry and response about the fate of the lost dog clearly showed mutual recognition of a shared past text. The clerk's responses to queries about arrival times linked (memorized) reference to written schedules, current responses to passengers' queries, and impending physical events (train arrivals). Verbal and visual texts were combined when, while listing their prices orally, a passenger held up sundries to indicate intention to buy, eliciting verbal confirmation by the clerk, and when the clerk's ticket-stamping or change-counting were accompanied by verbal commentary ("Eleven she be," "That'll be two").

There are lessons here for a much neglected dimension of the authenticity of any LT materials (see Chapter 9), not just task-based materials. ADs of this kind make salient the intertextuality and open-endedness of most TDSs. Even the ostensibly simple, "stand-alone" ticket purchases contained embedded texts and referred to previous, co-occurring, and future ones. They neither began nor ended with the words spoken, and they involved far more than what the transcripts would appear to indicate. By contrast, most materials writers present learners with self-contained, stand-alone dialogues and reading passages in which all needed information, and no more, is introduced and utilized within a single text. Typical spoken or written discourse models for LT have a beginning, a middle, and an end, little or nothing is left unstated, and allusions are rare. Whether this facilitates comprehension or acquisition is an empirical question, but authentic it is not.

7.4.4. Buying and selling a cup of coffee

Bartlett (2005) recorded 248 interactions at three locations selling coffee: a coffee cart on the University of Hawai'i campus, and two nearby shops, each part of well-known chains. 168 were transcribed and analyzed. A general pattern emerged, usually involving the following sub-tasks: either greeting the server or responding to a service bid (Can I help you?), specifying the order, possibly confirming the order and options, sometimes adding information about a menu item, responding to the server's additional offer of service (Anything else?), paying and closing (the last sometimes performed non-verbally). Bartlett (2005, pp. 314–315) offers several examples, of which the following was representative, although shorter than some (S = server; C = customer):

s: Can I help you ma'am?
c: Can I try an iced macadamia latte?
s: Did you want that blended or on the rocks?
c: Blended
s: OK. Did you want whipped cream on that?
c: Yes
s: Anything else for you?
c: (non-verbal response)
s: OK. That'll be three forty-eight
c: (customer hands over money)
s: Thank you. Fifty cents is your change. Would you like your receipt?
c: (non-verbal response)
s: OK. It'll be ready for you in just one minute

Transactions involving frequent customers tended to be shorter and more concise:

s: Hi. What can I get for you?
c: A tall coffee and the *Honolulu Advertiser*

```
s:   1.91
c:   (customer hands over money)
s:   Out of two. Nine cents is your change. Here's your coffee sir
```

Like 'ticket' at the railway station, the word 'coffee' occurred rarely, and when it did, was a specific term denoting a brewed or drip coffee of the day at all three locations. More precise terms were required for the size of the drink, e.g., *short, tall* (=small), *grande, venti*, and its type, e.g., *frappuchino* (referred to as a *frio* at one store), *latte, chai, macchiato, espresso,* and *Americano*. And as at the railway ticket office, given the close proximity of the interlocutors and the intensely context-embedded nature of the talk, with menus on the wall and display cases between them, pronouns and deictics were plentiful. Again like the railway ticket office talk, there was a high degree of implicitness and ellipsis in both server and customer turns, due to shared background knowledge, with servers often initiating a purchase, predicting a regular customer's order (Bartlett 2005, p. 321):

```
s:   Hi. Americano?
c:   Yeah
s:   Anything else today?
c:   No thanks (hands over money)
s:   Three four five ten out of twenty. Thank you
```

And finally, just as was the case with the railway ticket purchases, conversations with regular customers sometimes featured intertextuality and the unexpected (Bartlett 2005, p. 318):

```
s:   Hot or iced?
c:   Hot. I was wondering if anyone found my bag
s:   Oh. You were the one that called yesterday?
```

as well as phatic talk (Bartlett 2005, p. 319):

```
c:   Hi
s:   Hi. How are you today?
c:   Small coffee. I need a new card
s:   Small coffee. Are you busy this morning?
c:   I don't know. I haven't started yet. I keep on forgetting to get my card
s:   Do you have a card or do you need a new card?
c:   I need a new card. Actually two stamps. With this one it's three stamps
s:   You keep forgetting do you?
c:   She can vouch for me
s:   (hands over coffee) There you go
c:   Thank you
s:   You're welcome
c:   Thank you
s:   (hands over change) There you go. Have a great day
```

Bartlett compared her findings to models for roughly comparable restaurant service encounters in ESL textbooks, which often proved to be little more than drills in disguise

(What do you want to drink? I'd like __ tea, please. Do you want __ milk with that? No thanks. But I'd like __ sugar; or Would you like a __? Yes, I'd like a __; or May I have a __? And would you like a __?). She then made the critical move between analysis of target discourse and materials design, synthesizing her findings to produce a data-based, *prototypical dialogue* for buying coffee:

s: Hi. Can I help you?
c: Can I get a grande latté with vanilla?
s: Did you want that blended or on the rocks?
c: Blended, I guess
s: 2% or skimmed?
c: Uhm 2%
s: 2%. OK. Any whipped cream?
c: Sorry?
s: Did you want whipped cream on that?
c: Yes
s: Anything else?
c: No, that's it. Oh no. Can I get- are those scones?
s: Yeah, we have cranberry and blueberry
c: I think I'll have one of those (pointing)
s: A blueberry scone?
c: Yeah. The one in the back
s: This one
c: Yeah that's it
s: Ok. For here or to go?
c: To go
s: Ok. That'll be three forty-eight
c: (hands over money)
s: How about a frequent user card?
c: Oh sure
s: Thank you. 52 cents is your change (hands over change).
     And your card. Ok. It'll be ready for you in just one minute
c: Thank you
s: There you go (hands over drink). Have a nice day
c: You too

(Bartlett 2005, p. 338)

The result is noteworthy for several features. Idiosyncratic behaviors and terms, e.g., *a skinny* and *a frio* used at only one coffee site, are removed. Conversely, widely attested idiomatic uses, e.g., *There you go, That'll be 3.4* and *Can I get*, and other genuine language, e.g., *blended, skimmed, 2%* and *For here or to go?*, are retained. This is true, even if the language is domain-specific, e.g., specific names for drinks, and avoidance of the unused generic term *coffee*. Such language would not normally appear in commercially published pedagogic materials, but is what students need to know to perform the task successfully. Also included are deictics and pronouns, e.g., *that, those, one of those, the one in the back*, several cases of ellipsis, e.g., *Anything else? Any whipped cream? For here or to go?*, and of intertextuality, e.g., gestures, *And your card*, and non-verbal turns, all of which constitute realistic reflections of the context-embedded nature of the encounter. Also important are examples of functions of grammatical forms used for purposes other than those typically modeled in pedagogic materials, such as *did* used as a mitigation device, e.g., *Did you want that blended?*, instead of as a tense marker. Many of the modifications Bartlett made to produce the prototype dialogue would be applicable to the production of task-based prototypes in any discourse domain.

7.4.5. When small talk is a big deal

'When small talk is a big deal' comes from the title of a chapter by Holmes (2005) in which she reported on a study of the importance of social talk in a range of New Zealand workplaces for members of two groups: recent immigrant workers for whom English is a second language and workers with an intellectual disability. The Wellington Language in the Workplace (WLW) project, on which her findings were based, documented the pervasiveness of small talk, or social talk, and the crucial importance of effective sociopragmatic skills for acceptance by one's fellow workers.

Ability to do a job, and even to do it very well, can be insufficient for a new worker to be completely accepted and integrated. Small talk is needed to express friendliness, establish rapport, and maintain solidarity. A typical example is this early morning exchange between Diana, a manager, and Sally, her administrative assistant, when Diana enters Sally's office to collect the mail:

DIANA: good morning Sally, lovely day
SALLY: yes don't know what we're doing here we should be out in the sun
DIANA: mm pity about the work really
SALLY: how are your kids?
DIANA: much better thank goodness + any mail?

(Holmes 2005, p. 353)

Such exchanges are so normal for cultural insiders that they are hardly noticed, but not necessarily for new arrivals. Failure to understand that at least some minimal social talk was expected when co-workers met at the start of the day, rather than launching directly into work-related matters, could lead to new workers being regarded as unfriendly or rude. A tricky area for many of them was recognizing when such questions as "How are you?" or "How's it going?" were purely social, not intended as serious inquiries designed to elicit, for example, detailed descriptions of the addressee's health. Conversely, difficulty could also arise from failure to recognize when small talk was inappropriate, or that signals were now coming from a higher status interlocutor that it was time to get back to work or to shift to work-related talk.

When NSs join a new workplace, they have to learn its prevailing interactional norms, including such subtleties as the levels of formality and politeness (or impoliteness), and the kinds of humor considered appropriate. Such matters can be especially difficult for NNSs and for NSs with intellectual disabilities, as neither group will have been socialized in the same ways as their new NS colleagues. They may bring with them different, culturally specific understandings of appropriate ways of complimenting, responding to compliments, complaining, apologizing, refusing, teasing, and so on, and about what constitutes culturally acceptable topics for social talk within the workplace and the wider society (Clyne 1994).

The WLW data included recordings of talk among white-collar and blue-collar workers in offices and on the factory floor. Analyses revealed what are considered appropriate, non-controversial topics for small talk in New Zealand workplaces, including the weather, ritualized inquiries about health, work, social activities outside the workplace, sport, generalized complaints about the economy, and positive comments on someone's appearance. Yet shared knowledge, and lack of it, about such things as *which* sports are popular could still cause problems. Compare:

ANN: great match on Saturday eh
BEA: yeah awesome

and:

CARL: great match on Saturday eh
BEN: what match?

(Holmes 2005, p. 354)

Ben was a newly arrived immigrant.

Different cultural values could also cause misunderstandings, as when what was intended as a compliment by someone from a cultural background where large families are regarded positively was interpreted as a criticism by someone from a different cultural background:

RECENT CHINESE IMMIGRANT: Such a big family!
PAKEHA NEW ZEALANDER: Yes, but it has advantages too

(Holmes 2005, p. 355)

The WLW project findings, along with those of Clyne and others, show the unquestionable importance of small talk in the workplace in cases where NNSs are employees. The earlier "crosstalk" study (Gumperz 1982) had been triggered in part by British hospital patients' complaints about "rude" foreign doctors and nurses, whose "shortcoming," it turned out, was often a lack of what in the United Kingdom was considered an appropriate "bedside manner," not a lack of English or medical expertise. In their study of two entry-level occupations, those of hospital porters and central supply technicians, Svendsen and Krebs (1984) had also noted the importance of friendly, stress-reducing language for patients, as well as the need for NNSs to know sufficient socially acceptable formulae to be able to get themselves out of trouble when problems or the inevitable communication breakdowns occurred, e.g., to request help in the form of repetitions of an instruction they had not understood the first time around. It was important, they reported, for new NNS workers to be able to *socialize*. Difficulties with small talk with clients and colleagues was one of the findings of a study of the communication problems of immigrant students in a training program for nurses in the United States, too (Bosher & Smalkoski 2002).

In fact, it seems likely that the importance of social talk is not limited to situations of prolonged daily contact among fellow workers, but extends even to brief service encounters, and perhaps to most occasions when NSs and NNSs meet. As noted earlier, the inability of Marriot and Yamada's Melbourne duty-free shop employee to engage in appropriate small talk resulted in a lost sale to Japanese customers. Even the potentially routine railway ticket sales were helped along by the willingness of both the ticket clerk and the NS passengers to engage in small talk. Encounter A began not with a request for a certain kind of ticket, but with

| TICKET CLERK: | How you doin'? |
| PASSENGER: | Alright and yourself? |

and encounter B with a cheery greeting:

| TICKET CLERK: | Morning Yes (mam) |
| PASSENGER: | Morning |

A task-based NA or task-based materials that focus exclusively on the referential dimension of tasks and ignore the social dimension of the talk through which they are accomplished, even in the most mundane cases, will clearly be selling learners and teachers short. How to move from the findings in both the referential and social dimensions of analyses of discourse like those exemplified to the design of task-based materials is taken up in Chapter 9.

7.5. Summary

The primary focus of language analysis in TBLT is the dynamic qualities of target discourse – how language is used to accomplish *tasks* – not simply the linguistic features of static *texts*. Once target tasks have been identified, samples of language use surrounding their accomplishment are mined for anything likely to facilitate task performance. However, the focus of an AD is not on achieving an exhaustive, generative model of the kind sought in a true DA, but, again, on dimensions considered important for successful task completion. Analyses of samples of genuine language use quickly reveal properties they share that are rarely modeled in commercially produced pedagogic materials. Language use, even in relatively formal situations, is often more colloquial than that found in textbooks, usually because, unlike textbook models, it is context-embedded. Conversations are also typically less self-contained and more open-ended than contrived textbook "dialogs." Those characteristics, in turn, allow use of other devices rarely found in pedagogic models, notably, extensive ellipsis and intertextuality. Finally, even fairly simple, constrained tasks, such as service encounters, whose focus is usually thought of first and foremost in terms of referential communication, are facilitated by the use of "small talk."

7.6. Suggested Readings

Bartlett, N.D. (2005). A double shot 2% mocha latte, please, with whip: Service encounters in two coffee shops and at a coffee cart. In Long, M.H. (ed.), *Second language needs analysis* (pp. 305–343). Cambridge: Cambridge University Press.

Biber, D., Conrad, S., & Cortes, V. (2004). *If you look at* …: Lexical bundles in university teaching and textbooks. *Applied Linguistics* 25, 371–405.

Boswood, T., & Marriot, A. (1994). Ethnography for specific purposes: Teaching and training in parallel. *English for Specific Purposes* 13, 1, 3–21.

Holmes, J. (2005). When small talk is a big deal: Sociolinguistic challenges in the workplace. In Long, M.H. (ed.), *Second language needs analysis* (pp. 344–372). Cambridge: Cambridge University Press.

Marriot, H.E. (1990). Intercultural business negotiations: The problem of norm discrepancy. *Australian Review of Applied Linguistics* 7, 33–65.

Mohan, B., & Marshall Smith, S.M. (1992). Context and cooperation in academic tasks. In Nunan, D. (ed.), *Collaborative language learning and teaching* (pp. 81–89). Cambridge: Cambridge University Press.

Swales, J.M. (1990). *Genre analysis*. Cambridge: Cambridge University Press.

Watson-Gegeo, K.A. (1992). Thick explanation in the ethnographic study of child socialization: A longitudinal study of the problem of schooling for Kwawa'ae (Solomons Islands) children. In Corsaro, W.A., & Miller, P.J. (eds.), *Interpretive approaches to children's socialization. Special issue of New Directions for Child Development 58* (pp. 51–66).

Chapter 8

Task-Based Syllabus Design

8.1. Some Minimum Requirements

To be minimally adequate, proposals for a language teaching (LT) syllabus type (or for a particular LT syllabus illustrative of that type) should provide a rationale for the *unit of analysis* employed, and for the systems used for *selection* and *grading* (*gradation, sequencing*) of syllabus content in terms of that unit. That is to say, proposals should specify three things: (i) the type(s) of linguistic entities, e.g., lexical items, structures,

Second Language Acquisition and Task-Based Language Teaching, First Edition. Mike Long.
© 2015 John Wiley & Sons, Inc. Published 2015 by John Wiley & Sons, Inc.

notions and functions, or non-linguistic entities, e.g., topics, situations, or tasks, chosen as course currency, (ii) course content, i.e., what is to be taught in a course (and by implication, what need not be), and (iii) the order in which it is to be taught, i.e., how that content is to be sequenced. This is true of any type of syllabus, not just a task syllabus.

Choices in the three areas should reflect the designer's psycholinguistic assumptions. For example, choice of a linguistic unit of analysis of some kind commits the designer, materials writers, and teachers to some form of synthetic approach when it comes to methodology and pedagogy. It would make no sense to specify course content as a series of grammar points if an analytic approach is to be employed in the classroom, or as a series of tasks if a synthetic approach is what is intended. Syllabus, methodology, and assessment need to be compatible and coherently interrelated.

The unit of analysis selected for a syllabus is in many ways the most important decision course designers make, for the unit chosen will inevitably affect decisions in other areas, whereas the converse is not necessarily true. For example, choice of a linguistic unit, say, grammatical structure, or non-linguistic unit, say, task, for the organizational unit in the syllabus will require grammatical structures or tasks, respectively, to be the currency in any needs analysis (NA) that is conducted, in course materials, methodology, pedagogy, and assessment.[1] Similarly, it would make no sense to adopt a linguistic unit of analysis if teachers intended to use a "method" like the Natural Approach that eschewed a classroom focus on language forms, just as it would be impossible to deliver an analytic syllabus using pedagogic procedures associated with "methods" designed to practice isolated grammatical structures, such as the Audio-Lingual Method, Total Physical Response, and the Silent Way. Conversely, while unusual, a designer could in theory decide in favor of either norm-referenced or criterion-referenced tests without ruling out any options with regard to the unit of analysis operating in the course syllabus, materials, methodology, or pedagogy. It might be that the synthetic syllabus designer is confident students will be able to handle a communicatively based criterion-referenced evaluation, or that the designer of an analytic syllabus feels equally confident that students will be able to do well on a discrete-point measure.

8.2. The Unit of Analysis

Linguistic constructions and features of one kind or another are by far the most commonly employed units, resulting in so-called structural, or grammatical, syllabi. Other syllabi employ lexical items and collocations, notions, functions, topics, or situations as their organizing unit. For examples and detailed discussion of the strengths and weaknesses of several linguistic and non-linguistic syllabus types, see Long and Crookes (1992, 1993), Robinson (1998, 2009), R. White (1988), and Chapter 2.

---

[1] Summative evaluations comparing the relative effectiveness of courses or whole programs that use either linguistic or non-linguistic units of analysis, and either synthetic or analytic approaches, are the only cases where forms of assessments may legitimately not always cohere with what has gone before. For example, it is sometimes of interest to know whether students who undergo a task-based course can handle the kinds of grammar-based, discrete-point tests mandated by education authorities in many countries as well as, or better than, students who take a traditional grammar-based course, and vice versa. As noted in Section 11.5.4.2, the answer is generally "yes."

Since language teaching is designed to facilitate language learning, the unit of analysis for syllabus design should be compatible with second language acquisition (SLA) research findings about how languages are learned. For reasons explained in Chapters 2 and 3, synthetic linguistic syllabi lack support from SLA research findings; indeed, they fly in the face of what is known (or, at least, thought to be known) about (a) the (L1 or L2) language-learning process, and (b) how languages can be taught (as opposed to how they can appear to be learned and taught).

8.2.1. The structural, or grammatical, syllabus

The chief, usually implicit, justification for the continued popularity of the structural, or grammatical, syllabus is that the L2 can fairly easily be divided into bite-sized pieces whose mastery will serve all learners because of the (unwarranted) assumption that "the language is the same" for all learners. More positively, in the hands of materials writers of the caliber of a Geoffrey Broughton, Robert O'Neill or Michael Swan, with engaging story lines, rapid changes of activities, and spiral recycling and re-combinations of grammar points, they can hold learners' attention long enough for language learning of the skill-building kind to take place, while making lessons orderly and relatively painless for teachers to deliver. As Skehan (1998) has noted, such materials offer clear learning goals for classroom lessons and lend themselves to easily constructed systems of (discrete-point) assessment. In other words, materials focusing on linguistically based units are easiest to write, easiest to teach from (even by untrained teachers with poor command of the L2), and easiest to sell to the widest possible audience. Many publishers have large amounts of money invested in textbook series based on such syllabi, and along with their authors, receive vast amounts from their sales, so maintaining the status quo has obvious advantages from their perspective.

Unfortunately, the structural syllabus' logistical advantages do not compensate for the psycholinguistic implausibility of all synthetic approaches discussed in Chapters 2 and 3. Moreover, in addition to its incompatibility with SLA research findings, the grammatical syllabus has several other problems. Especially for students at elementary levels of proficiency, structurally graded materials tend to provide unnatural samples of target language use, often resulting in what Widdowson (1972, and elsewhere) refers to as *usage*, i.e., models whose need to conform to the "structure of the day" results in misrepresentations of how native speakers really *use* a given construction, verb tense, and so on. Native speakers very rarely hold whole conversations using the same verb tense or aspect throughout, yet characters in structurally graded textbooks often do. There is a difference between the misleading textbook or teacher model, "John is reading a book," uttered when John is in full view of both speaker and listener (*usage*), and "The police are arresting demonstrators," spoken into a microphone by a radio news reporter for the benefit of listeners far away who cannot see what is going on, or "The economy is contracting," a written metaphor used by a political commentator to describe an abstract process that is not directly observable – both realistic examples of *use* of the present progressive.

Structurally based materials, Widdowson (1971, pp. 38–39) further notes, can be functionally restricted. The imperative mood may be modeled in grammatically based materials for its use in commands (*Give me the gun*), but not as an instruction in a recipe

(*Stir in the butter, and season to taste*), an invitation (*Have another sandwich*), advice (*Buy the cheaper one*), or a prayer (*Forgive us our trespasses*). Conversely, just as a single form rarely serves a single function, the same function can usually be realized by a variety of forms (an argument used for the notional-functional syllabus). The same piece of advice, *Buy the cheaper one*, for example, might be expressed in several other ways – *Why not buy the cheaper one? You should/I would buy the cheaper one, Buying the cheaper one would be smarter*, and so on.

The same problems arise with the lexical grading found in grammatically based materials. If a textbook writer is limited to the most frequent X00 words in stage 1 of the main textbook, or in an accompanying graded, or so-called "simplified," reader, it is inevitable that dialogues and reading passages written to conform to those specifications will often model lexical usage, not use. Specific nouns will give way to generics (*columnist* to *journalist, French Brittany* to *dog, titanium* to *metal*), and lower frequency words and expressions will be replaced by higher frequency ones (*village* to *town, stream* to *river, earn money* to *make money, fall asleep* to *go to sleep*, etc.), even if information is lost in the first case and meaning is altered in the second. (A solution to this problem – input elaboration, instead of simplification – will be offered in Section 9.2).

A more sophisticated argument in favor of the structural syllabus begins with the idea that teaching linguistic structures builds explicit declarative knowledge (*conscious knowledge that*) of grammar, e.g., awareness that in English, adjectives precede the nouns they modify. In the standard skill-building model, through controlled exercises and drills of various kinds, declarative knowledge is then proceduralized, and subsequently, through massive practice, automatized. (This position was discussed in Chapter 2.) Going a step further, while recognizing the timing problem, i.e., the difficulty of matching such instruction to learners' inner developmental stage, R. Ellis (1993, 1997, 2003), endorses what is sometimes referred to as the "weak interface" model. Provided the timing is right, *explicit knowledge* of new structures can help learners develop *implicit knowledge* of the same items through increasing the likelihood that learners will perceive those items in the input, monitor their own output, and notice the gap between what they produce and the grammatical target version. On this view, in other words, the role of tasks in (lower case) task-based, i.e., task-supported, language learning is twofold: "consciousness-raising," i.e., increasing learners' awareness of grammar, which can in turn promote implicit knowledge of the same forms, and providing a vehicle for practicing those forms. Tasks, that is to say, serve as vehicles through which to deliver a *grammatical* syllabus. The psycholinguistic problems with this approach were pointed out by Robinson (1994) and discussed extensively in Chapters 2 and 3, so they will not be repeated here.

We will conclude by noting that in addition to all the above logistical and psycholinguistic limitations, the structural syllabus does not lend itself easily to communicative language teaching, and in no way caters to the large-scale variation in students' communicative needs. Indeed, needs analyses and structural syllabi are strangers.

8.2.2. The notional-functional syllabus

Notional-functional syllabi emerged from the work of the Council of Europe in the 1970s, notably that of Wilkins (1974, 1976, 1981). The aim was to provide a language-independent unit-credit system applicable in principle to any language by avoiding specification of proficiency in terms of learners' control of linguistic features (which would inevitably be language-specific). This was achievable by considering language abilities in terms of learners' mastery of three types of semantic categories: (i) semantico-grammatical, such as time (past, present, and future), place, distance, duration, and sequence; (ii) modality, such as necessity, possibility, probability, and certainty; and (iii) communicative function, such as accusing, denying, requesting, offering, compliment-ing, apologizing, defining, and hypothesizing. With a notion or function as the organ-izing unit for a lesson, forms and lexical items that would typically be treated separately in a structural syllabus would be brought together. A lesson on 'sequence' might include work on the simple past and past perfect tenses, together with items like *before, after, first, second, third, then, next,* and *finally.* A unit on 'suggesting' might treat '*How about changing?*,' '*Why don't you change?*,' '*Have you thought about changing?*,' and '*You could change*,' along with such items as *perhaps, possibly, maybe,* and so on. They could make the 'communicative value' of linguistic forms more salient to learners (Widdowson 1978, p. 11). (To the best of my knowledge, like so much in LT, these were data-free claims, with no research ever conducted to determine whether notional-functional syllabi were in fact superior in this or any other respect.)

By focusing on how meanings are expressed, notional-functional syllabi lend them-selves more readily to communicative teaching approaches and so have greater potential for reflecting students' communicative needs. As noted in Section 5.4, they were the units of analysis in some early efforts at needs identification, such as that of Munby (1978). Any increased relevance they offer, however, along with the improved student motivation that perceived relevance brings, are the result of the NA itself, not an intrinsic advantage of the notional-functional or any other (including task) syllabus type.

The notional-functional syllabus was not without problems. Most fundamentally, as several critics pointed out (see, e.g., Brumfit 1981; Cook 1985; Paulston 1981), there was no connection either with general learning theory or with research findings on how second and foreign languages are learned. There is no more evidence that notions and functions constitute more viable acquisition units than grammatical structures, or that they, unlike grammatical structure, can be taught and learned one at a time. In practice, moreover, what learners encounter in the input is still tokens of linguistic constructions that realize notions or functions, not the notions or functions themselves. In addition, the assumption that after the target language has been fragmented into notions and functions, or any other linguistic unit, and presented one at a time, learners will eventu-ally be able to synthesize the pieces for communication, is unfounded. The fragmenta-tion process, moreover, extracts the resulting pieces from the discourse context that gives them communicative value (Crombie 1985a,b; Widdowson 1978) – a problem with synthetic linguistic syllabi of whatever kind. And how many pieces are there? Relevant target tasks for particular learner groups can be identified and quantified; there is no claim to be teaching *all* target tasks. But such is not the case with structural or notional-functional syllabi, which both purport to teach the same "grammar" for everyone.

The notional-functional syllabus has other problems. The same utterance or sentence can simultaneously realize two or more notions or functions, which can often seem to be endlessly divisible, with one nested in another, and two or more going to make up a third. For example, depending on discourse context, *When food supply decreases, chick-ens reduce their numbers* is an observation and/or a generalization. Standing alone,

Chickens have an innate mechanism for population homeostasis is an observation or a generalization, but in the sequence *When food supply decreases, chickens reduce their numbers. Chickens have an innate mechanism for population homeostasis*, it is still a generalization, but at a higher level, simultaneously a conclusion, or a deduction, and so on. On what rational basis are notions and functions to be sequenced? Are apologies harder or more frequent than requests? Is sequence more useful than duration? What are the linguistic realizations of notions or functions, how are they to be determined, other than by native speaker intuitions, and how should the realizations themselves be selected or sequenced? The sequence may well be different from that common in structural syllabi, due to structures being grouped in terms of the notions or functions they realize, but that does not make them any more learnable on demand.

Wilkins (1981) subsequently modified his views, moving closer to the structural syllabus his ideas had originally been designed to replace, and reaffirming (again, without any evidence) that "an extensive mastery of the grammatical system" was essential to anything more than "a rudimentary communicative ability" (1981, p. 85). The field's gradual loss of confidence in the notional-functional syllabus, White (1988, pp. 78–81) suggests, lay behind proposals for hybrid structural/notional-functional syllabi (e.g., Brumfit 1984; McKay 1980; Stern 1983; Ullman 1982; Yalden 1987). But as noted by Long and Crookes (1993, p. 18), "the prospects of two unmotivated units combining to produce one motivated hybrid would seem rather dim."

8.2.3. The lexical syllabus

Advocates of the lexical syllabus (e.g., D. Willis 1990; Kennedy 1990; Sinclair 1987; Sinclair & Renouf 1988) recognize that structural syllabi sit uneasily with communicative approaches and with well-established facts about language acquisition, such as accuracy orders, developmental sequences, and processing constraints, i.e., with Corder's internal "learner syllabus." Consequently, they tend not to assume that newly presented forms will immediately be incorporated into a student's developing interlanguage system, and focus, instead, on raising students' awareness of new words and their meanings, to be integrated over time. Selection, i.e., in this case, which words and collocations are included in materials, is not based on an analysis of learners' communicative needs (although I see nothing in principle to preclude that where lexically based materials are concerned). Rather, it tends to reflect materials writers' intuitions as to potentially interesting *topics* for a given group of students, leading in turn to the creation of *pedagogic tasks* (chosen for language-learning purposes, not because they are related to real-world communicative needs), and the writing of *texts* to accompany the tasks, with the lexical targets highlighted in the texts.

When developing a lexical syllabus and lexically based teaching materials, e.g., the Collins Birmingham University International Language Database (COBUILD) corpus and related textbook series (Willis & Willis 1988), corpora are mined (i) to determine word frequency, which becomes the major criterion for both selection and (at a macro-frequency level) grading, and (ii) as a source of genuine examples of native speaker usage of the words and their collocates. Collocations containing the most frequent words in utterances or sentences are itemized as illustrations of authentic use and incorporated into the texts written for LT. Most frequent items are covered first. The first stage in the COBUILD series uses a vocabulary of 700 words, the second stage 1500 words, and the third stage 2500. There is no expectation that the words or collocations will be learned in the order in which they are presented, which in any case is not sequenced or controlled within the three frequency bands.

In sum, the lexical syllabus entails a synthetic approach, with lexical items and collocations replacing grammatical structures as the unit of analysis. Its greatest weakness and greatest strength, respectively, are visible in D. Willis' own (internally contradictory?) characterization of what is involved:

> The syllabus specification must, directly or indirectly, consist of an inventory of language forms. I have suggested, however, that a successful methodology must rest on language use. (Willis 1990)

The deployment of real examples of language use is a positive development that some other syllabus types would do well to imitate. (As explained in Section 9.2.1, this cannot be achieved simply by adopting ready-made, "authentic" texts.) The synthetic approach, on the other hand, coupled with the fact that course content is not determined by a NA, but by materials writers' or teachers' choices of topics and texts, based on intuitions about students' interests, are both problematic. The same materials are supposedly satisfactory for all learners, regardless of their varying needs.

It is perhaps significant that, the COBUILD textbooks, supposedly a model for lexically based materials, in fact employ a seven-strand *hybrid* syllabus: listing tasks and topics; texts and features; writing; social language; verbs/tenses and clause patterns; noun phrases, pronouns, adjectives, prepositions, and adverbial phrases; and spoken and written discourse. Lexical selection and grading are not, it appears, a sufficient basis for syllabus design. 'Tasks' are not what one might think, either, but a potpourri of what are often more akin to rather opaque macro-functions, e.g., (in Book 1) talking about families, describing things, expressing likes and dislikes, discussing and comparing buildings, and explaining answers. Moreover, 'describing things' is at once broader and more abstract than 'discussing and comparing buildings,' and could include both that and 'expressing likes and dislikes.' (The fact that genuine tasks often "contain" other tasks, or sub-tasks, is an issue for genuine task-based syllabi, too, however, and one to which we return.)

The tensions obvious among selection criteria for the course syllabus, as reflected in its seven strands, are also on display in the five basic principles listed in the introduction to the *Teacher's Book* (Willis & Willis 1988, ii–vi) as guiding its methodology:

1. People learn a language most effectively by using language to do things – to find out information, to solve problems, to talk about personal experiences, and so on.
2. A focus on accuracy is vital.
3. As far as possible learners should be exposed to real language.
4. Grammar is learned rather than taught. Coursebooks and teachers provide useful guidelines on the language, but learners should additionally be encouraged to think and deduce for themselves.
5. Learners need strategies for organizing what they have learned – they need rules, patterns, and categories.

The *Collins COBUILD English Course*, the authors state (Willis & Willis 1988, p. 11) – even though it in fact relies on a multi-strand hybrid – "realizes these well-established principles through a new language syllabus – a lexical syllabus." Yet it is surely obvious by now that principles 2 and 5, at least, are anything but well established, and also that principle 1, students learning a language through using it to do things, is at least partially incompatible with principle 2, a vital focus on accuracy. (The pedagogy Willis and Willis advocate (p. iii) also stresses the need for accuracy and "controlled repetition of various kinds.") Principle 3, the need for exposure to real language, might appear well motivated (but see, again, Chapter 9.2), but it is unlikely that 'real language' will be lexically graded, e.g., so as to use the 700 commonest words in English, as is the case with texts in Book 1. And why do students need rules, patterns, and categories for *what they have learned* (principle 5)? Native speakers do not. The usual argument for meta-linguistic knowledge invoked by advocates of synthetic approaches is that rules help students learn the language. But principle 5 assumes the reverse: once learned, students need rules. Pointing out problems with a particular course does not, of course, necessarily invalidate a syllabus type. However, the COBUILD course was held up by creators of the lexical syllabus as an exemplary implementation of their ideas.

Sinclair and Renouf (1988) stress the emphasis on utility as the main benefit of the lexical syllabus – what is most frequent is most valuable to students. They also claim, without offering any evidence, that lexical selection is a shortcut to selection of other linguistic material:

> if the analysis of the words and phrases has been done correctly then all the relevant grammar, etc. [i.e., structures, notions and functions] should appear in a proper proportion. (Sinclair & Renouf 1988, p. 155)

Sinclair and Renouf (1988) criticize modern second language syllabi for ignoring content, and notional-functional syllabi as "incomplete." Finally, they assert that the lexical syllabus is "neutral" with respect to "the use of tasks to practice effective communication," since it is "an independent syllabus, unrelated by any principles to any methodology" (p. 155). Indeed, they maintain (p. 145) that all syllabi should be independent of methodology. Their stance contrasts sharply with the minimal requirement argued for in Section 8.1., the need for choices as to unit of analysis, syllabus type, and methodology to be coherent and psycholinguistically compatible.

8.2.4. Topical and situational syllabi

There is often an overlap between these two syllabus types, so they are treated together here. Situational syllabi, the name suggests, could reasonably be expected to refer to organization around *where* language is used – at the restaurant, at the airport, at the supermarket, and so on – and topical syllabi around *what* language is used to talk about – food, transportation, work, sport, politics, family life, and so on. In practice, however, many so-called situational syllabi are really structural-situational, with situations mere backgrounds for the broad contextualization of grammatical constructions, sequenced "within situations" in the usual manner for structural syllabi. Courses of this kind include *Voix et Images de France* (CREDIF 1961), the Australian government's *Situa-*

tional English (Commonwealth Office of Education 1967), and Louis Alexander's once widely used *First Things First* (Alexander 1967). Thus, a structurally graded, lexically controlled dialogue might supposedly take place in the garden, but in fact be designed to provide examples of the present continuous:

JEAN: Where's Sally, Jack?
JACK: She's in the garden, Jean.
JEAN: What is she doing?
JACK: She's sitting under a tree.
JEAN: Is Tim in the garden, too?
JACK: Yes, he is. He's climbing the tree.
JEAN: I beg your pardon? Who is climbing the tree?
JACK: Tim is.
JEAN: What about the dog?
JACK: The dog's in the garden, too. It's running across the grass. It's running after the cat.

First Things First (Alexander 1967, p. 31).

Structural-situational courses are obviously open to the same criticisms as overtly structural syllabi.

A more legitimate use of 'situational' concerns courses organized "around situations and [that] deal with structures as they arise" (Mohan 1977, p. 251). After analyzing a representative sample of situational course books, Mohan concluded that even those did not really deal with situations, but rather, "topics, which are illustrated by situations which show how an interaction in that topic area might develop" (Mohan 1977, p. 251), e.g., the topic 'shopping' covered in such 'situations' as "shopping for food, shopping for clothes" (Mohan 1977, p. 251). Examples of topic-based course materials include *English Topics* (Cook 1975), and the rather misleadingly named *Notions in English* (Jones 1979) and *Notion by Notion* (Ferreira 1981). Topics included in Jones' book are the weather, shops, drinks, entertainment, money, and geography. The subtitles to many topics suggest that, once again, supposedly topic-based materials are synthetic in nature, as illustrated by the inclusion of such overtly linguistic items as 'questions,' 'articles,' 'the past,' 'isn't it?,' and 'preposition + noun' in the lists of 'topics' or 'notions.'

In theory (but as far as I am aware, unknown in practice), situational and topical syllabi could be both realistic and motivational if based on needs analyses carried out in terms of the frequency of target situations or topics of importance for specific groups of learners. Even then, however, they would be faced with at least two major problems. First, such "situations" as 'at the airport' can involve an infinite number of other situations, or sub-situations: at the ticket counter, in security, on the shuttle, at the bookstore, in a shop, at a restaurant, in the waiting room, in customs, at passport control, and so on. And that assumes we are talking about passengers, not those engaged in the numerous occupations found at an airport. Second, as was argued in a little known but important article 50 years ago (McIntosh 1965), it is almost impossible to predict language from situation unless such additional factors as the interlocutors (passenger, customs inspector, shop assistant, cashier, waiter, flight attendant, etc.), and/or "immediate situation" (ticket counter, restaurant table, currency exchange, passport control, etc.) are also specified. The same is true of topics. A conversation about 'soccer' can go in many directions, with consequences for genre, register, pragmatics, grammar, notions, functions, lexis, collocations, and phonology. Different speakers with vastly different knowledge of, or interest in, soccer might focus on rules of the game, an upcoming game, a game they watched last weekend or in which they participated or would simply like to hear about, the relative merits of various players, teams, leagues, referees, or "national styles" of soccer, club owners, player salaries, soccer finances, betting and bribery, FIFA, the World Cup, predictions about tournament outcomes, rising stars, famous soccer cheats, famous soccer cleats, soccer hooligans, soccer and politics, and more. The list of "soccer topics" is endless, and so is the language they would require. Whether 'at a soccer game' (situation) or talking, reading, or writing about 'soccer' (topic), in other words, the language needed is, as McIntosh claimed, mostly impossible to predict. Tasks have an advantage in this respect. Use of specific language items in broad-ranging, "open" pedagogic tasks (discussing an issue, expressing opinions, etc.) is hard to predict, too, as demonstrated, e.g., by Cox (2004). However, as seen in the case studies considered in Chapter 7.4, the language used to perform specific target tasks, such as checking in at the airport or changing currency or buying a meal there, can vary, but not to nearly the same extent.

8.2.5. The content syllabus

Many varieties of content-based language teaching have become popular in recent years. They include early-exit and late-exit, transitional and maintenance, bilingual programs (e.g., Cummins 2009), so-called "dual language" programs, in most of which L1 and L2 children in the same class may spend half the day learning through one language, half through the other (e.g., Cloud, Genesee, & Hamayan 2000), "sheltered subject-matter" teaching (Krashen 1991), what is now regarded as traditional content-based language teaching (e.g., Brinton, Wesche, & Snow 2003; Crandall 1993; Crandall & Tucker 1990; Met 1991; Mohan, Leung, & Davison 2001), and content-and-language integrated learning (CLIL; e.g., Dalton-Puffer 2011; Lasagabaster & Ruiz de Zarobe 2010), the last being especially popular in parts of Europe and now spreading to East Asia and the Middle East. Genesee *et al.* (2006) provided a useful overview of research findings on the efficacy of some variants. Research on CLIL is in its infancy, with most studies only descriptive and often poorly designed (see Bruton 2011a,b, 2013).

Traditional content-based programs are especially common in state secondary schools with large numbers of immigrant children who have insufficient command of the major medium of instruction to be placed in regular classrooms with target language-speaking age peers, e.g., English for Spanish-speaking Latino children in the USA. Providing minority language students with courses that could in theory meet their second-language-learning needs and simultaneously deal with their education in mathematics, science, social studies, and so on, is understandably a very attractive idea for school districts confronted with a major social problem, for dealing with which they are drastically underfunded. While also spreading to tertiary institutions and to countries further afield, CLIL has so far been implemented chiefly at the secondary level in Europe, although more and more tertiary-level programs are appearing in many countries. Instead of an attempt to handle education through a *second* language for large populations of immigrant children, CLIL is intended as a way of achieving higher levels of proficiency in a *foreign* language (often English) by children who are native speakers of the dominant language in the country concerned. Unfortunately, there are serious difficulties with all these approaches. A detailed critique is well beyond the scope of this book, so just a few issues are highlighted here.

In practice, the syllabus for content-based courses typically consists of the materials for teaching the subject concerned, e.g., social studies. That can mean the regular text-book, a modified version thereof, or some combination, made comprehensible through additional schema-building, paraphrasing, occasional switches to the students' L1, and other pedagogic procedures available to trained, experienced teachers. Theirs is not an easy task. Textbooks originally designed for native speaker age-peers present all sorts of problems, in that the language, content, and cultural knowledge assumed is often absent among recently arrived immigrant children. Understanding frozen texts – especially ones not intended for language learners – becomes the focus of many lessons, and is wholly inadequate for language-learning purposes. Due to the fact that children in these classes may have what Cummins terms basic interactional skill (BICS), but typically lack cognitive-academic language proficiency (CALP), teachers are soon bogged down with explaining the meaning of unknown vocabulary items and collocations, and with "mining" videos and reading passages for grammatical items that will often be beyond students' current processing capacity. As a result, content-based lessons typically feature a focus-on-forms approach, the principal difference being that the content of the frozen texts is different from, and certainly more useful to students than, the typical "content" (or absence of much content) of the texts and dialogues in traditional focus-on-forms language teaching materials. Students do learn some L2 and some content this way. The real question, however, is whether there are better alternatives. In my view, there clearly are, with TBLT one of them (see, e.g., Long & Adamson 2012), and more generally, improvements in the way foreign languages are taught (by qualified foreign language teachers).

Especially in southern Europe, CLIL has largely been the result of political pressure on politicians from parents dissatisfied with the level of English or other foreign languages achieved by their children via three hours a week of traditional foreign language instruction. It is quite astonishing that an educational change with such massive potential for harm to content mastery – even *if* the language-learning benefits turn out to be real – could have been introduced on such a wide scale with no research to back it up. Put simply, there is every reason to believe that learning science, social studies, and so on, through a language which neither the regular content teacher nor the children typically speak very well, will result in poor quality language development, due, among other reasons, to what is likely to be deviant input from the teacher, whose own command of the foreign language is often weak, and certainly poorer quality input than that provided by trained foreign language teachers. Worse, the content curriculum is likely to be diluted as a result of the teacher's and students' inadequate command of the medium of instruction; linguistic simplification has been known to have that effect (Long & Ross 1993; Lynch 1987; Mackay 1993). There has been vanishingly little research on either of these fundamental issues, yet CLIL continues to spread, largely fueled, it seems, by a dangerous cocktail of hope and hype. For an important critique, see Bruton (2011b, 2013). For a laboratory study showing some potentially nasty side effects of CLIL, see Long *et al.* (2013).

8.2.6. The procedural syllabus

The five years from 1979 to 1984 were witness to one of the most innovative language teaching programs in many decades. Located at the Regional Institute of English in Bangalore, India, and led by N.S. Prabhu and Esther Ramani, the Bangalore/Madras Communicational Teaching Project is best known for its development of the procedural syllabus. Reacting against the traditional "Structural-Oral-Situational Method" long used in India, Prabhu sought a new, culturally appropriate approach to teaching that would focus on communicative, rather than linguistic, competence, and harmonize means and ends:

> Communicative teaching in most Western thinking has been training *for* communication, which I claim involves one in some way or other in preselection; it is a kind of matching of notion and form. Whereas the Bangalore Project is teaching through communication; and therefore the very notion of communication is different. (Prabhu 1980, p. 164)

In the years immediately following closure of the Project, Prahbu wrote up the rationale for the procedural syllabus and described its use in Bangalore in his book, *Second Language Pedagogy* (Prabhu 1987).

Very much in line with the priority Krashen accorded *acquisition* over *learning*, Prabhu considered grammatical rules too abstract and too complex for students to master explicitly; instead, he claimed, a focus on meaning would result in their unconscious assimilation (1987, p. 70). Consequently, a procedural syllabus is analytic:

> …any attempt to guide that [learning] process more directly (and whether or not explicitly) is rejected as being unprofitable and probably harmful. There is therefore no syllabus in terms of vocabulary or structure, no preselection of language items for any given lesson or activity and no stage in the lesson when language items are practiced or sentence production as such is demanded. The basis of each lesson is a problem or task.…(Prabhu 1984, pp. 275–276)

The focus on meaning would best be achieved through engaging students in cognitively challenging "reasoning-gap" activities that required them to infer new from given information. In the Bangalore Project (BP):

> [A]n activity which required learners to arrive at an outcome from given information through some process of thought, and which allowed teachers to control and regulate that process, was regarded as a "task". (Prabhu 1987, p. 24)

By way of illustration, Prabhu (1987, pp. 138–143) reports that students in the eight primary and secondary school classes involved in the project might be asked to interpret information presented in tables, e.g., provided with information in an imaginary train time-table, asked to calculate the time from one town in India to another. Given distances between other locations on a map, they might be asked to calculate distances between towns. They might listen to "whodunit" stories and complete them with appropriate solutions, or identify factual inconsistencies between information heard in dialogues and that in given narrative or descriptive accounts. Tasks in the procedural syllabus, that is to say, were not the *target tasks* of TBLT, identified by a learner NA. They can best be thought of as pre-set *pedagogic tasks*, unrelated to any *target tasks*, i.e., to students' use of English outside the classroom. There was no task syllabus in the BP in the sense used in TBLT, in other words; rather, BP *pedagogy* was task-based (in principle, at least).

Pedagogic tasks in the Bangalore curriculum were of three broad types. Information-gap tasks required transfer of information from one form to another, e.g., visual to verbal. Reasoning-gap tasks required students to make deductions or inferences in order to derive new from given information. Opinion-gap tasks required students to decide on and communicate their own attitudes, values, preferences, and responses to given information. The purpose of the communicative activities was to engage students in critical reasoning, which, if sustained long enough, Prabhu claimed, was "a condition favorable to the development of grammatical competence" (1987, p. 53). Student interest was to be maintained by making the tasks intellectually demanding enough for students to perceive them as difficult, but feasible, as presenting a "reasonable challenge," a rough measure of which was that "at least half the class should be successful with at least half the task" (Prabhu 1984, p. 277).

Clearly, task performance in the procedural syllabus was a means to an end – grammatical competence – not an end in itself, i.e., the critical goal it constitutes in TBLT, and as a subsequent process evaluation by Beretta (1989, 1990) showed, the program was really an example of task-supported, not TBLT. The *criterion for success* was also different. In TBLT, if a NA has identified a set of target tasks as those which students need to be able to handle, half of them completed by half the students is an unacceptable outcome.

Since he considered a pedagogic focus on language as object unproductive, Prabhu reasoned that a fixed syllabus was redundant and to be avoided. The purpose of a lesson was the stimulation of learning, after all, not to have students master a particular text:

> lessons in the classroom are not acts of texts, or language presentation, but rather contexts for discourse creation. (Prabhu 1987, p. 95)

Therefore, teachers should be provided with general guidelines and sourcebooks of loosely constructed teaching materials, not tightly constructed commercial textbooks. That idea, needless to say, was not at all popular with publishers, especially in a country with a potential market the size of India's, or with the British Council, which eventually withdrew its support for the project.

There was no evaluation component built into the BP's design. In an effort to provide some relevant data on its effectiveness, Beretta (1986) and Beretta and Davies (1985) conducted a *post hoc* intact-groups comparison of four project classes and four roughly comparable classes in the same schools that had been taught using a traditional structural approach. The traditional classes outperformed the project classes statistically significantly on a discrete-point grammar test, whereas three of the four project classes did statistically significantly better than the comparison classes on tests of listening and reading comprehension, and all four did better on a "task-based" test modeled on the kind of reasoning-gap tasks used during the project. Causal claims were impossible, the evaluators recognized, due to the lack of random assignment of students or intact groups to each condition, and because three of the four BP classes had "better qualified, more highly motivated teachers, who were accustomed to being observed and treated as guinea-pigs" (Beretta & Davies 1985, p. 123). The results, nonetheless, are consistent with the BP leaders' view that a communicatively oriented syllabus will prepare students better for communicative use of a L2 than a traditional structural syllabus.

The BP was remarkable in several ways. It was locally produced, short-lived, relatively small-scale – eight classrooms, 18 teachers, and 390 children aged 8–15, for periods of one to three years – and conducted in the difficult conditions (large classes, meager classroom resources, etc.) then pervasive in Indian public secondary schools. It was subject to criticism by some academics and evaluators at the time and subsequently (see, e.g., Beretta & Davies 1985; Brumfit 1984; Greenwood 1985; Tickoo 1987), yet it had a considerable impact – in the applied linguistics literature, at least, if not on English language teaching in India. What made it a radical departure from standard British communicative language teaching (CLT) was not the tasks themselves, but in theory, at least, the classroom focus on task completion instead of the language used in the process. Similarly, again, to Krashen's proposals and the methodological prescriptions and pro-scriptions of the Natural Approach (Krashen & Terrell 1983), input was not to be lin-guistically graded, or as Prabhu puts it, "preselected," but roughly tuned as a natural by-product of the spontaneous adjustments teachers (and other native speakers) make when communicating with less proficient non-native speakers. Again, as in the Natural Approach, the solution to learner errors was not traditional overt error correction, but the incidental correction that occurs when teachers respond to the content of what learners say, e.g., with what are now referred to in the literature as recasts.

In some other respects, classroom instruction in the BP was quite traditional, due chiefly to a felt need to meet student expectations and adhere to prevailing local cultural and educational norms and practices. Thus, by design, most instruction was teacher-centered, with an emphasis on "receptive language." Tasks were first conducted as teacher-fronted, whole-class activities (the "pre-task"), and then by students working on sometimes more complex versions of them (the "task"), usually individually. Group work was discouraged because of the fear that learner–learner interaction would promote fossilization (Prabhu 1987, p. 82). Even if there really is such a thing as fossilization (which, although widely accepted in the field, is, in my opinion, far from clear – see Long 2003a), this was a needless fear within the short duration of a basic-level language program, research findings have shown (for reviews and data, see Long & Porter 1985; Pica 1987; Pica *et al.* 1996). Also, despite the pedagogic procedures stipulated by Prabhu, teaching was in practice often linguistically quite tightly controlled, with traditional error correction evident in videoed demonstration classes and other lessons (for an exchange on this issue, see Beretta 1989, 1990; Prabhu 1990a,b). Beretta found that while 47% of the teachers involved were well informed about the methodology expected, and implemented it fairly consistently, and 13% had mastered it sufficiently to be ready to modify it, 40% were not well informed and did not know how to use it.

While innovative, the procedural syllabus – as illustrated by the BP, at least – suffers from at least four shortcomings, in my view. First, there is no NA, meaning that syllabus content – the pedagogic tasks chosen for classroom use – are a hit-or-miss affair, dependent on a teacher's or course designer's intuitions, and unlikely to satisfy any particular group of learners' communicative needs. Needs are hard to define in most school-age learners, making the methodology employed with the secondary school pupils relatively more important than selection issues in the case of the BP itself, but they become crucial with college-age students and adults. Second, the procedural syllabus offers no criteria for classifying or sequencing tasks, which are handled impressionistically. This is by no means a problem unique to the procedural syllabus, it must be said. Third, the criterion for success of '50% of the task by half of the class' is unsatisfactory because it concerns task difficulty, makes success a norm-referenced issue, and reveals nothing about intrinsic task complexity, thereby precluding generalizations to new materials. If tasks appear in a syllabus because they reflect student needs, as is the case in TBLT, criterion-referenced assessment is called for (see Chapter 11.1). Fourth, as argued in Chapters 2 and 3, there are several reasons having to do both with rate of learning and level of ultimate attainment why a *focus on form* is a necessary component of optimally efficient classroom input and interaction. Prabhu's tacit recourse to implicit negative feedback will only partially suffice in that regard.

These criticisms should be seen in context, however. The procedural syllabus was not a task syllabus – at least, not in the sense employed in this book – and was not claimed to be. The BP's positive features lay mostly in the (stipulated) pedagogy, which was especially innovative, given received wisdom about language teaching at the time. The focus on pedagogic task completion, rather than immediate linguistic accuracy, is very much in line with TBLT, and some of the Bangalore reasoning-gap tasks are similar to "building block" tasks for elementary-level students in TBLT (see Chapter 9.3.2). In my view, the work of Prabhu and Ramani, conducted with regular teachers and students in difficult circumstances, often in the face of institutional hostility, deserves to be recognized as one of the most important developments in language teaching in decades. The BP asked serious questions about traditional language teaching and offered some creative answers. If there were flaws and limitations, that is surely to be expected of radical new ideas. In the long term, the test is whether the new thinking serves to advance the field, and in the case of the procedural syllabus, of that there is no doubt.

8.2.7. The process syllabus

Another example of an analytic syllabus, the process syllabus (Breen 1984, 1987a,b, 2001; Breen & Candlin 1980; Breen & Littlejohn 2000; Candlin 1984, 1987; Candlin & Murphy 1987) constitutes a second approach to course design in which what at first look like the pedagogic tasks in TBLT play an important role. Rather than theory and research findings in SLA, the rationale for this syllabus type is based on proposals for curriculum design in general education (e.g., Freire 1970; Stenhouse 1975). The focus is on the learner and learning processes, not language or language-learning processes, and on process, not product:

> …conventional syllabus design has oriented toward language as primary subject matter.…
> An alternative orientation would be towards the subject matter of *learning* a language. This alternative provides a change of focus from content for learning towards the process of learning in the classroom situation. (Breen 1984, p. 52)

A pre-set syllabus, Breen and Candlin argued, is a mirage; syllabi are constantly subject to negotiation and reinterpretation by teachers and learners, and in a very real sense, can only be specified once a course has finished. That is, they constitute records of what was done, not plans for what will be. The negotiation process, they maintain, furthermore, is what drives (language) learning.

The process syllabus, as described by Breen (1984, p. 56), addresses the overall question: "Who does what with whom, on what subject matter, with what resources, when, how, and for what learning purpose(s)?" It specifies sets of options at four levels, final selections among which are left to teachers and students. Course design consists of providing the resources and materials needed for (i) making general decisions about classroom language learning (who needs to learn what, how they prefer to learn it, when, with whom, etc.); (ii) alternative procedures for making those decisions (the basis for an eventual "working contract" between teachers and their students); (iii) alternative activities, e.g., teacher-led instruction, group work, and laboratory use (see Breen, Candlin, & Waters 1979); and (iv) alternative tasks in the form of a bank from which students may select to realize the 'activities':

> [I]t is at the level of tasks that the actual working process of the classroom group is realized in terms of what is overtly done from moment to moment within the classroom. (Examples at task level would include such things as agreeing on a definition of a problem, organizing data, deducing a particular rule or pattern, discussing reactions, etc.). (Breen 1984, p. 56)

From the examples provided by Breen, it is immediately apparent that pedagogic tasks in the process syllabus and TBLT are very different animals. A task in the process syllabus is defined as:

> any structured language learning endeavor which has a particular objective, appropriate content, a specified working procedure, and a range of outcomes for those who undertake the task. "Task" is therefore assumed to refer to a range of workplans which have the overall purpose of facilitating language learning – from the simple and brief exercise type, to more complex and lengthy activities such as group problem-solving or simulations and decision-making. (Breen 1987b, p. 23)

The definition and examples make the pedagogic focus plainer. It is clear that the meaning of 'task' in the process syllabus is even further removed from its meaning in TBLT than 'task' in the procedural syllabus. Such items as agreeing on the definition of a problem, discussing reactions, exercise type, group problem-solving, and simulations show that we are now dealing with activities and processes that might normally fall within the domains of lesson planning ('workplans') and classroom management, not with anything related to real-world tasks learners need to be able to perform outside the classroom. As with the process syllabus, in fact, no needs analyses are conducted for implementation of the process syllabus. To do so, after all, would imply that a syllabus could or should be planned in advance, and would in a superficial sense deny learners the opportunity to negotiate lesson content.

In one sense, the process syllabus is even more radical than the procedural syllabus. It intentionally involves a redistribution of power and authority in the classroom that critics claim would be culturally unacceptable in some societies, and requires more competence on the part of teachers and students, who, rightly or wrongly, are accustomed to relying on a single textbook (see, e.g., Kouraogo 1987; R. White 1988; and for an alternative view, papers in Breen & Littlejohn 2000). Needless to say, these could well be viewed as positive features, not problems. As described in Chapter 4, the desire, and ability, to take control over, and responsibility for, their own learning has been demonstrated time and again by people from all sorts of cultural backgrounds, often under the most adverse circumstances (see, e.g., Freire 1970, 1972; Hirshon 1983; MacDonald 1985; Vilas 1986), as well as by 150 years of successful libertarian education (see, e.g., Avrich 1980; Haworth 2012; Hern 2008; Holt 1972; Illich 1971; Shotton 1993; M. P. Smith 1983; Spring 1975, 1994a,b; Suissa 2006; Ward 1996).

That said, in my view, the process syllabus suffers from several of the same problems as the procedural syllabus. First, the absence of a NA renders selection a hit-or-miss affair, with the activities and materials available in the bank of tasks unlikely to be relevant to students' real-world needs. The desire to allow students and teachers to negotiate syllabus content leads to Breen and Candlin's intentional avoidance of its pre-specification. I would argue, however, that the fact that the content of the genuine task syllabus in TBLT is determined by the results of a learner NA allows learners to "negotiate content" in a very meaningful and more fundamental way, while simultaneously allowing syllabus planning and optimal use of class time. As will become clear in Chapters 9 and 10, additional negotiation opportunities occur in TBLT in the way students perform pedagogic tasks, and in the numerous options open to teachers in the area of pedagogic procedures. A well-conducted analysis of learner needs (not wants) makes limitations on negotiation of syllabus content within the classroom unproblematic in the same way that a doctor's medical diagnosis makes the range of treatments available to patients narrower, but more relevant for a cure.

If selection is a problem in the process syllabus, so is grading. The criteria for grading tasks proposed by Candlin (1987) are rather abstract, often opaque, and either difficult or in some cases seemingly impossible to operationalize and measure objectively: cognitive load, communicative stress, particularity and generalizability, code complexity and interpretative density, content continuity, and process continuity. That may not be a problem if learners are supposed to be free to negotiate the tasks they work on, rendering prior grading obsolete, but it must still be a problem from the point of view of their changing appropriateness in terms of students' psycholinguistic readiness to learn.

Finally, there is vanishingly little reference to the SLA literature in publications about the process syllabus. To the extent that language learning differs, at least in part, and some would say massively, from learning subjects like history, geography, mathematics, and science, this is problematic. Is reliance on negotiation of the choice and organization of classroom work really sufficient to drive the language-learning process? Is the kind of L2 input that results "naturally" from negotiating sufficient? Will a focus on code features, whether explicit or implicit, ever occur or be considered necessary? Does what is learned via a process syllabus transfer to real-world language use outside the classroom? The literature on the process syllabus is silent on these issues and other matters of a psycholinguistic nature.

8.2.8. The task syllabus

For reasons explained in Chapters 2–4, it goes without saying that *task* is the unit of analysis in TBLT. Unlike linguistic syllabi of all kinds, assuming selection is based upon the results of a learner NA, as in TBLT, a genuine task syllabus does not attempt to impose the same program on all learners. In particular, it does not try to impose the same set of lexical items and collocations and/or the same pre-set, psycholinguistically unmotivated sequence of linguistic features and constructions on whole groups of learners simultaneously, regardless of whether any or all of those learners need them, or if they do, are developmentally ready to incorporate them into their L2 repertoire, and hence, regardless of whether the items are *learnable* and *teachable* in Pienemann's sense at the time they are presented. Instead, as explained in Chapters 2 and 3, students are helped to develop their language abilities gradually to meet the demands of increasingly complex tasks, linguistic problems being treated reactively, as they arise. This approach is consistent with SLA research findings and compatible with the idea that learning grammar evolves out of language use, not the other way around. Instead of putting the cart before the horse by teaching "the grammar" first, so that students can (it is assumed) subsequently use it to communicate, as attempted by focus-on-forms approaches, it is worth recalling Evelyn Hatch's justifiably much-cited observation once again:

> …language learning evolves out of learning how to carry on conversations….One learns how to do conversation, one learns how to interact verbally, and out of this interaction syntactic structures are developed. (Hatch 1978, p. 404)

Given that its content will have been determined by an analysis of learners' current and/or future communicative needs – the tasks they need to be able to accomplish through the L2 – neither does a genuine task syllabus ignore *differences* in the vocabulary, collocations, registers, skills, and uses of linguistic features and constructions in the varied discourse domains in which learners must operate. That is to say, it is *not* assumed that the same language, or the same syllabus, will suffice for all learners. Having learners work on the tasks they need to be able to handle prepares them to do exactly that, while learning the language they need in the process. Learning by doing tasks, moreover, is consistent with the fundamental philosophical principles of education discussed in Chapter 4. Finally, negotiating initially less complex versions of full target tasks involves learners in a dynamic process of language use to accomplish those tasks, not passive study of language as object in the form of static *texts* – texts that, even when they constitute realistic samples of language use (which is rare), are, at best, *frozen records of other people's language use*. Watching Barcelona or Arsenal play soccer is unforgettable and inspiring, but is no substitute for young players getting out on the practice field and trying to do it themselves – putting in the long hours required to master the necessary technical skills. And when out on the field, for beginners to try to play like Xavi, Iniesta, Messi, Neymar, Koke, Wilshire, Cazorla, or Ozil right away is equivalent to low proficiency language learners trying to (re-)produce full native speaker texts from the get-go. Both are mirages and doomed to failure. (Selection and grading in task syllabi will be dealt with in Sections 8.3 and 8.4.)

8.2.9. The hybrid syllabus

So-called "hybrid" syllabi purport to employ two or more units simultaneously, e.g., structures and tasks (R. Ellis 1993) or lexis and collocations and tasks (Willis 1993). They are increasingly popular with authors and publishers of commercial textbooks (see, e.g., Richards, Gordon, & Harper 1995; Willis & Willis 1988), which sometimes contain as many as five or six units in parallel strands, ignoring the psycholinguistic incompatibility of linguistic units and synthetic approaches, on the one hand, and non-linguistic units that, potentially, at least, entail analytic approaches, on the other. For a critique of the structures + tasks proposal, see Robinson (1994).

Examination of hybrid courses usually shows the grammatical strand to be central, with items from other dimensions of language use mere appendages to it. A "structure-trapping" task is used to practice the structure of the day, and so on. It could be argued that because the pedagogic tasks in such syllabi are not tasks in the sense of TBLT, but simply another form of exercise for practicing structures, they are not incompatible with the synthetic approach implicit in the syllabus' linguistic dimensions. If so, however, we are no longer dealing with a task syllabus, and the textbooks ought not to be marketed as 'task-based.'

8.3. Selection

Selection and grading are all too often the product of arbitrary decisions, based, respectively, on a materials writer's intuitions about student "interest" and linguistic "difficulty." Instead, as Chapters 5–7 have made clear, selection of syllabus content in TBLT is determined rationally and empirically, according to the results of a learner NA. However, the target tasks identified by the NA for a group of learners constitute only the *raw* input data for a TBLT syllabus.

For two reasons, target tasks are not usually themselves the components that go to make up a task syllabus. First, the list of target tasks produced by a NA may be too long to include in a course of limited duration, so target tasks with features in common are grouped together, as members of *target task-types*. Second, the communicative needs within a group of students may vary, such that teaching all the target tasks would be an uneconomical use of class time, and irrelevant for some students at least part of the time. Therefore, as when insufficient time is available, if there are two sub-groups of students in a class with some target tasks in common, but some unique to each group, target tasks that share common features are again grouped together as members of *target task-types*. Given their abstract nature, target task-types are also unsuitable as units for a task syllabus, however, so *pedagogic tasks* are derived from the target task-types, sequenced according to their intrinsic *complexity*, and entered into the syllabus (see Figure 8.1). In TBLT, with one exception (see below), the syllabus is made up of *sequences of pedagogic tasks*. Examples of the two processes – the moves from target tasks to target task-types, and from target task-types to pedagogic tasks – now follow.

8.3.1. Target tasks and target task-types

In the best-case scenario, (i) a NA will have shown that the same target tasks are important for all students in a class, and (ii) there is time available to teach all of them. In that situation, pedagogic tasks are derived directly from each of the target tasks, and sequenced according to criteria discussed in Section 8.4. It is those pedagogic tasks, sequenced rationally, that go to make up a task syllabus. In cases where one or both of

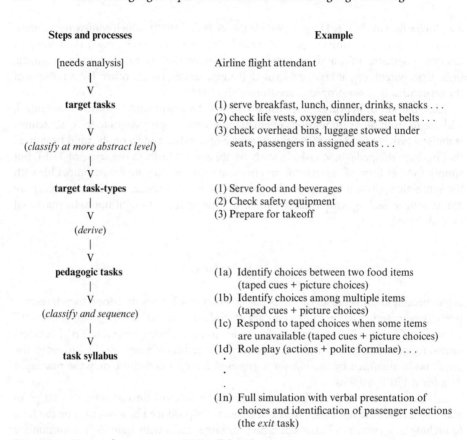

Steps and processes	Example
[needs analysis]	Airline flight attendant
↓	
target tasks	(1) serve breakfast, lunch, dinner, drinks, snacks . . .
	(2) check life vests, oxygen cylinders, seat belts . . .
↓	(3) check overhead bins, luggage stowed under
(*classify at more abstract level*)	seats, passengers in assigned seats . . .
↓	
target task-types	(1) Serve food and beverages
	(2) Check safety equipment
↓	(3) Prepare for takeoff
(*derive*)	
↓	
pedagogic tasks	(1a) Identify choices between two food items
	(taped cues + picture choices)
↓	(1b) Identify choices among multiple items
(*classify and sequence*)	(taped cues + picture choices)
	(1c) Respond to taped choices when some items
↓	are unavailable (taped cues + picture choices)
task syllabus	(1d) Role play (actions + polite formulae) . . .
	.
	.
	.
	(1n) Full simulation with verbal presentation of
	choices and identification of passenger selections
	(the *exit* task)

Figure 8.1. Steps and processes in TBLT syllabus design.

these conditions is not met, however, target tasks undergo two transformations before becoming part of a task syllabus. First, they are grouped into *target task-types*, and then, *pedagogic tasks* are derived from the target task-types. Let us consider two examples of the process by which target tasks are grouped together into target task-types. (For a third example, in the context of the English program at a Japanese university, see Lambert 2010.)

The first example is illustrated in Figure 8.1. A study of methodological options in NA (described briefly in Section 6.2.10) identified over 100 target tasks for airline flight attendants (for details, see Long 2005c, pp. 48–62).[2] Several target tasks involved passenger service, including those related to the task-type 'Serve food and beverages.' Some critically important target tasks, many of them performed before passengers board an aircraft, were related to safety, including a group that could be brought together as members of the target task-type 'Check safety equipment.' A third group concerned target tasks that flight attendants perform about the cabin shortly before takeoff, which

---

[2] The focus of the study was the relative value of sources of information, methods of obtaining that information, and source × method interactions. For various reasons, the occupation of flight attendant was the example chosen. The roughly 100 target tasks identified were by no means intended as an exhaustive description.

could be classified into a target task-type, 'Prepare for take-off.' (These were just three of many other target task-types.) Figure 8.1. lists a few of the target tasks in each set, the three target task-types they go to make up, and a few of the pedagogic tasks that might be developed for the first target task-type, 'Serve food and beverages.' Why the pedagogic tasks are sequenced the way they are will become clear in the next section.

The second example concerns filling out application forms – often a daunting "social survival" target task-type for recent arrivals in a second language environment. Despite their differences, common elements in such target tasks as filling out application forms for opening a bank account, renting an apartment, obtaining a driver's license, registering a child in school, and so on, may justify their being subsumed under the target task-type, 'Filling out an application form.' Teaching each of the original target tasks could require more time than is available, and/or the NA may have revealed that subgroups of students within the class are likely to need to be able to do some, but not others. The idea is that grouping the various target tasks concerned with filling out application forms of various kinds into a single target task-type can go some way to solving both problems. If students learn to fill out a generic application form, the abilities they master in doing so will serve them when confronted with a real-world task of filling out, say, an application form for opening a bank account, as well as for new cases, such as filling out an application for a library ticket or a credit card.[3]

Learners will never actually have to 'fill out an application form' (the target task-type), but rather, specific application forms for the above or other purposes (the target tasks). That is to say, target task-types are superordinate categories – convenient abstractions to help deal with logistical problems that can arise with short courses and/or heterogeneous groups. Because they are abstractions, they cannot themselves figure as items in a task syllabus. Instead, in the second stage in the process (see Section 8.3.2), pedagogic tasks are derived from the target task-types, and it is the pedagogic tasks that are then sequenced to form the task syllabus, embodied in tangible form in task-based pedagogic materials. It is pedagogic tasks that teachers and students work on in the classroom.

8.3.2. Pedagogic tasks

To begin with, pedagogic tasks are simpler, sometimes much simpler, versions of the target task-type or of one or more of its components. They gradually increase in complexity – the *complexity of the pedagogic tasks, not linguistic complexity* (see Section 8.4.4) – until they reach the full complexity level of the target task(s) that motivated their inclusion.

Tasks may be simplified in several ways, the most obvious of which involves breaking a target task down into its component pieces or sub-tasks. For example, depending on the starting proficiency of the students concerned, the first pedagogic task (PT) for the

---

[3] Precisely which application forms share sufficient similarities to justify being treated as exponents of a single task-type, and whether the abilities learned through mastery of examples of a task-type will generalize to other examples, are empirical matters, important not only for syllabus design but for the transferability and assessment of task-based abilities, to which we return in Section 11.4. Determining which forms have sufficient in common will involve collecting samples of each and conducting an analysis of (in this case, written) discourse, as described in Chapter 7.

task-type 'Filling out an application form' might only deal with the first section, common to almost all application forms (although the level of required detail varies), in which applicants must provide personal information – name, address, telephone numbers, email address, and so on, and in some cases, similar information about immediate family members, if any. Depending on the kinds of applications identified by the NA as relevant for the students in question, the second PT in the series might focus on sections pertaining to educational qualifications and/or prior work experience. Alternatively, the second PT might serve for practice in providing information about the applicant's financial situation – assets, debts, and obligations, including property owned, existing or previous checking and savings bank accounts, car loans, mortgages, and the like. A third PT might deal with how to list the applicant's training, skills, abilities, and experience relevant for a particular job. A fourth PT might involve provision of information about sources for personal, academic, or work references. These PTs all involve simplification of the full target task-type by breaking it down into sub-tasks, in this case in the form of sub-sections of typical application forms. If the NA showed some of the potential PTs to be irrelevant for some students and/or for some types of application forms, they would not be included.

Another example of simplifying a target task by breaking it down into sub-tasks is described by Gilabert (2005) in the report of a task-based NA he conducted of work often performed in English by Catalan journalists. One of the target tasks identified was 'Interviewing a source.' Gilabert ascertained that this task involved six steps or sub-tasks: deciding on the decision-making process, contacting the source, documenting the interview, making arrangements for the interview, interviewing, and translating the transcript or interview for publication. Some sub-tasks themselves consisted of two or more parts. The target sub-task, 'Documenting the interview,' for example, comprised gathering different information sources (previous interviews, documents, Internet items, etc.), selecting materials for questions, and producing a set of questions. The target sub-task 'Making arrangements for the interview' also consisted of three parts: calling or emailing the source to request an interview; calling or emailing the source to arrange time, place, and topics for the interview; and sending an email or fax message to the source to confirm arrangements.

Additional ways of simplifying target tasks include use of pre-tasks that build schema, or background information, to assist with the PTs that follow, allowing more time and opportunities for attempts at task performance, and *elaborating the input* (see Chapters 9.2. and 10.2.3) used in full native–native performance of the corresponding target tasks. In the case of filling out an application form, this can often mean elaborating (not simplifying) the quite complex, sometimes elliptical, language used in many forms, some of which can even cause headaches for native speakers. Once again, which PTs and which approaches to simplifying a task are employed will depend on which target tasks have been identified for particular groups, and on students' starting proficiency level.

The one exception to the statement that target tasks do not themselves go to form a task syllabus is the *last* task in a module of TBLT materials, when either a genuine or a virtual version of the full target task serves as the *exit task* for that unit. The exit task is used to assess students' ability to perform the target task, for it consists either of a genuine example of that target task or a virtual proxy. To continue with the current example, the exit task might assess students' ability to fill out an application form for one of the original target tasks, and/or, with an eye on transfer of task-based abilities, an application for a post office box or for membership of a club or to enter a high school or college. If students can complete the exit task successfully, it shows that after traversing the series of progressively more complex PTs, they can now deal successfully with the target task whose identification by the NA warranted their presence. Further examples of the two syllabus design processes and of PT sequences in the form of task-based classroom materials are provided in Chapter 9.

8.4. Grading

Having dealt with choice of the unit of analysis, and with selection, we now turn to the third and final stage in designing a task syllabus, grading, or sequencing. In TBLT, *grading* means the *rational sequencing of pedagogic tasks*. The general LT literature offers a variety of potential criteria by which to sequence items in a syllabus. They include valency and criticality, frequency, learnability, and complexity, or difficulty. The last two, in particular, have been the subject of considerable debate and many data-based studies within the TBLT literature. While some progress has been made, grading remains the most problematic dimension of task syllabus design, and in my view, one of the two issues (the other being the above-mentioned generalizability, or transferability, of task-based abilities) most in need of convincing data-based solutions (see Chapter 11).[4]

Before discussing grading in TBLT, however, it is worth noting that the need for grading in LT is not a given. In three important but, regrettably, now seldom cited, papers published over 40 years ago, Newmark and Reibel (1968), Reibel (1969, 1971), and Newmark (1966, 1971) made a strong case for the irrelevance of, at least, traditional grammatical approaches to sequencing. If done correctly, they argued, the end-product could only be a series of texts, the eventual sum of whose linguistic properties might collectively reflect genuine language use, but any one of which, due to linguistic grading, would inevitably constitute a distorted sample, and thereby impede learning. (See, also, Allwright 1976; Dakin 1973.) While a serious concern for the structural and lexical syllabus and for authors of structural and lexically based materials, this criticism does not apply to task sequencing, fortunately, for two reasons. First, selection of tasks in a TBLT syllabus has been based on an analysis of learner needs, which vary greatly, meaning that no one course, and certainly no one pedagogic task, attempts or presumes to reflect all possible tasks. Second, because tasks vary greatly, it is neither assumed, nor necessary, that any one of them will reflect the potential components of all tasks.

8.4.1. Valency and criticality

The valency, or communicative value, reach, or coverage (*disponibilité*), of grammatical constructions has often been proposed as a way of ordering items in a structural syllabus. Items with higher valency are more useful, so more important, so should occur earlier in a syllabus. While seemingly logical enough, the problem with this criterion is

---

[4] As is often the case with "problems" in TBLT, more research has been carried out on the issues in the past 30 years than has ever been conducted on the very same problems (e.g., identifying objective criteria for selection and grading) in grammatical, lexical, or notional-functional syllabi, where intuition still seems to be considered satisfactory.

that as long as valency is judged impressionistically, agreement beyond a few simple examples turns out to be problematic. Thus, while some might accept, at least impressionistically, that subject relative clauses are in some sense more useful than genitives (*The man who stole the car*...vs. *The man whose car was stolen*...), or that the simple present tense in English (*John goes*...) is more useful than the past perfect (*John had gone*...), would they also claim that subject relatives are more useful than object relatives (*The man who stole the car*...vs. *The man stole the car that*...), that the simple present is more useful than the simple past, or that relative clauses are more useful than conditionals? The obvious way out is to examine linguistic corpora to see how various structures are used, and how often. But at that point, valency becomes another word for frequency. Also, even if a given structure occurs more frequently or appears to have a wider range of meanings and/or functions, it may be that its linguistic complexity makes it less suitable for early treatment than a less widely used, but linguistically simpler, structure that can be employed for the same purpose. However widely used, and useful, a structure may be, after all, it is almost always optional; the same meaning can be expressed using alternative forms. Moreover, frequency data in the language as a whole may not be representative of frequency within a particular group of learners' domain(s) of interest.

Although still not without problems, valency arguably has greater potential as a grading criterion for tasks, for whereas many linguistic constructions (relative clauses, the subjunctive, passives, etc.) can usually be avoided, tasks and task-types cannot. An airline flight attendant cannot simply skip tasks involved in ensuring passenger safety. A college student cannot simply decide not to attend lectures or lab sessions (at least, not without drastic consequences). And whereas the *criticality* of structures, too (an extreme form of valency) is also difficult to identify, the criticality of tasks can usually be measured fairly easily. Job descriptions and advertisements often state explicitly that some qualifications and/or the ability to do X or Y are 'required,' whereas others are merely 'desirable' or 'preferred.' Acceptance into university graduate programs typically requires applicants to hold degrees in subject F or G, to have taken courses in H or I, and to have completed J or K kinds of scholarly work at the undergraduate level. Applicants for faculty positions teaching those students almost always require college degrees in F or G, or a related discipline, proven ability to teach courses in C or D, and a track-record in E or F (obtaining external research funding, publishing in major refereed journals, etc.), as distinct from such 'desirable' qualifications as teaching credentials, administrative experience, proficiency in language(s) X or Y, the ability to teach courses in J or K, and so on. Almost all the standard methods of identifying target tasks described in Chapter 6 can be designed to yield a fairly accurate idea of *both* valency and criticality. Interviews and questionnaires often ask respondents explicitly about both, for example, without necessarily using the terms themselves. Logs and participant and non-participant observation, too, will yield the requisite information.

8.4.2. Frequency

Teaching the most frequent items in a language first seems an eminently reasonable idea, for even though frequency counts are based on texts produced by and for native speakers, learners are more likely to encounter frequent items, and so need to be able to deal with them. Moreover, assessing frequency has become more feasible now that several large corpora of spoken (not just written) texts are available, along with computer software packages for analyzing them. Lexical frequency information, often broken down by, and very different in, speech and writing, has become a useful dimension of several dictionaries, e.g., the *Collins Cobuild Dictionary*, *Oxford Advanced Learner's Dictionary*, and *Longman Dictionary of Contemporiary English*, and can also be found in Leech, Rayson, and Wilson (2001). Biber *et al.* (1999) provide corpus-based frequency data on English grammatical items.

There are problems, however. First, to the extent that a well-designed course is tailored to the communicative needs of particular groups of learners, as is the case in TBLT, frequency information based on "general" English, Mandarin, and so on, as opposed to data on language use in specific discourse domains, will be of limited value. Generic or "core" verbs and noun phrases are more frequent, but they fail to convey the full meaning of the words native speakers would use as collocates in specific contexts (laugh, instead of chuckle, snigger, sneer, or giggle; chair, instead of armchair, stool, rocker, or recliner). It is one thing to say that a wounded soldier walked across the road, quite another to say he staggered across the road. A snake does not simply move through tall grass; it slithers. There is nothing to prevent frequency information being based on data from specialized domains, but determining how representative a text is of a discourse domain is no easy matter (Biber 1993). The situation is gradually improving, however. Progressively more work has begun to appear on such matters as the frequency and dispersion of lexical items, collocations, and lexical phrases in university lectures within and across academic disciplines (e.g., Coxhead 2000; Coxhead & Nation 2001; DeCarrico & Nattinger 1988; Hyland & Tse 2007; Simpson-Vlach & Ellis 2010), and on the frequency and dispersion of grammatical structures within and across four registers of English: conversation, fiction writing, newspaper writing, and academic prose (Leech, Rayson, & Wilson 2001).

Second, frequency information about structures does not tell a syllabus designer, materials writer, language tester, or a student how those structures are used. Related information is needed about function, which can vary from one discourse domain to another, as Cathcart (1989) showed with respect to the use of imperatives in doctor–patient communication (findings discussed in Chapter 6.2.3). Some progress has been made on this issue (see, e.g., Biber 1988; Grabe 1987). Third, frequency has been shown to be only one of several influences on acquisition (or better, accuracy) orders and sequences, e.g., the famous morpheme orders of the 1970s (see, e.g., Larsen-Freeman 1976). Such factors as learnability (Pienemann 1984, 1989), perceptual saliency (Goldschneider & DeKeyser 2001), and (closely related) difficulty (DeKeyser 2005) may be more important. To take an obvious example, the fact that a grammatical pattern, such as the English passive, is frequent in a particular discourse domain does not warrant its appearance early in a structural syllabus if it is unlearnable early.

Frequency data on linguistic forms of various kinds is of only secondary importance, at most, in a task-based syllabus. The relative frequency and criticality of *tasks*, on the other hand, are both fairly easy to ascertain as part of a NA, and provide useful information for sequencing. Frequency is important in designing a genuine task-based syllabus, but *frequency of tasks*, not words or grammatical patterns.

8.4.3. Learnability

With roots in the Zweitspracherwerb italienischer (portugiesischer) und spanischer Arbeiter (ZISA; Second language acquisition by Italian (Portuguese) and Spanish workers)) Project (Clahsen, Meisel, & Pienemann 1983; Meisel 2012; Meisel, Clahsen, & Pienemann 1981), Pienemann's work in the 1980s (see, e.g., Pienemann 1984, 1989) gave new life to learnability in SLA and language teaching. Pienemann defined learnability as what students are capable of processing. He showed that in principle, because developmental stages reflected universal cognitive processing constraints (Clahsen 1987), a student's current developmental stage in *any* language could be identified, along with which grammatical structures could be taught – those at the same stage and the next one, but not beyond that – and which not yet. *Learnability determined teachability.* (See, also, Mackey 1999.) An obvious potential application was to sequence structures in grammatical syllabi according to developmental sequences, either empirically attested or as predicted by Processability Theory (PT; Johnston 2000; Pienemann 1998, 2011; Pienemann & Kessler 2011). Pienemann (1985) and Pienemann and Johnston (1987) demonstrated the possibilities by mapping out parts of a structural syllabus based on PT for English. Johnston (1995) did the same for Spanish.

The idea that instructional sequences should be harmonized with developmental sequences makes sense, of course, as discussed in Chapter 2. It is supported by a number of research findings (e.g., Bardovi-Harlig 1995; Bonilla 2012; Ellis 1989; Lightbown 1983; Pienemann 1984, 1989) showing that, except within the confines of tightly controlled language practice of some kind, the order in which learners master increasingly more complex grammatical constructions in a sequence cannot be changed by instruction that introduces the items in a different order. For users of structural syllabi, the PT work remains a valuable resource with which to motivate the design of pedagogic materials. There are limitations, however. Most obviously, few structures have been studied sufficiently (and those mostly in English) to have established developmental sequences empirically. Fairly robust findings exist for German word order and English negation, questions, and relative clauses, but for few other structures. (For a review of what is known, see Ortega 2009.) Absent robust empirical findings, relying on PT is the logical solution, but the movement constraints that define production stages in PT end at what could informally be termed "intermediate" proficiency levels, and concern grammar only (a valuable contribution in itself) and production only.[5] Since TBLT does not use a grammatical syllabus, this is not a problem. Meanwhile, the PT-based predictions for stages and structures in developmental sequences can help teachers decide what is learnable, and therefore, teachable, at any stage, and so which linguistic constructions constitute viable targets for focus on form.

8.4.4. Complexity and difficulty

For decades, 'complexity' and 'difficulty' were routinely advocated as the main criteria for sequencing items in a *grammatical* syllabus. The terms were used interchangeably,

---

[5] Work has recently begun on the capacity of PT to predict receptive command of grammatical structures. Early results, using an auditory GJT, are not encouraging (Spinner 2013).

with little attention paid to defining or measuring either one, i.e., for explaining how complexity or difficulty was to be judged. Would the same structure be equally easy or difficult for speakers of typologically different L1s, for example? When the issue was addressed at all, it was usually simply by saying that syllabus designers and materials writers (often the same people) should use their intuitions – which is exactly what they did, often with very different results. The situation has improved in recent years.

The first way in which the notion of complexity or difficulty (in this instance, used synonymously) has been made meaningful is through valuable work on the development of a metric by which to quantify the qualities that make linguistic features more or less *perceptually salient* (Goldschneider & DeKeyser 2001), incidentally providing an explanation for the average accuracy order observed in the famous "morpheme studies" of the 1970s and 1980s. As noted in Chapter 3, features are non-salient when one or more of infrequent, irregular, non-syllabic, string-internal, semantically empty, and communicatively redundant, and/or because they involve complex forms, meanings, or form-meaning mappings. Lack of perceptual saliency, in turn, has been identified as crucial in determining what makes learning grammar difficult (DeKeyser 2005).

Such information is applicable by those designing a synthetic syllabus who wish to decide how much attention to devote to various grammatical items, and how to sequence linguistic features rationally, perhaps guided by the developmental stages defined by Processability Theory.[6] Also, even though TBLT eschews a linguistic syllabus, it is information that is useful for teachers to be aware of when deciding whether to withhold or provide *focus on form* of varying degrees of explicitness. For example, results from three studies comparing the relative efficacy of models and recasts (Doughty *et al.* 1999; Long, Inagaki, & Ortega 1998; Ono & Witzel 2002) can be interpreted as suggesting that implicit negative feedback in the shape of recasts might be better employed with salient linguistic targets, such as word order or English past tense morphology. More overt negative feedback, such as focused recasts, prompts, and meta-linguistic statements, may be required – or at least, more effective sooner – for less salient targets, such as English prefixes *in-* and *un-*, where even native speakers are sometimes unaware of misuse of the unmarked form (*unattentive, *unadmissable, etc.). This could encourage selective attention to linguistic features that might otherwise go unnoticed for a long time, even permanently, especially fragile features. Examples include pronominal copies in Spanish topic-fronting (*La guitarra **la** toca Pepe*), inversion in English sentences expressing negative polarity (*Only very rarely **had the creature** been captured on film*), or Korean sentences involving conjunction, in which different conjuncts are used, depending on the type of sentence, e.g., not -*ese* in imperatives (pi-ka o-**nikka/*-ase**, wusan-ul kace ka-<u>la</u>, 'Take an umbrella with you <u>since</u> it is raining').

A key issue for TBLT is how to determine the *relative complexity*, not of grammatical features and constructions, but of *tasks* (as distinct from the easier problem of texts). This is important because if increasing the complexity of tasks increases the complexity and/or accuracy of the language students use to accomplish them, then having students work on progressively more complex tasks should lead to interlanguage development. In early discussions of the topic (Brown & Yule 1983; Brown *et al.* 1984; Long 1987), it was suggested that use be made of such factors as the number and distinctiveness of a

---

[6] See Johnston (1995, 2000) for applications of PT theory to syllabus design for Spanish and ESL, respectively, and Kessler, Liebner, and Mansouri (2011) to L2 English within a TBLT course.

task's components, of the elements or steps in a task, the number of solutions to a problem, and a task's location in time and space (here-and-now or there-and-then orientation). Thus, identifying a suspect would be a less complex task if the people in a police lineup varied by age, race, gender, and build, and more complex if, say, all were middle-aged white men of similar height and body shape, and had similar facial features. Making an airline reservation is more complex, the more choices exist as to which company to use, itineraries, departure and arrival times, fare, (window, center, or aisle) seats, and so on. Reporting a single-car collision with a tree is less complex than reporting a traffic accident involving two cars, and less complex, again, than one involving three or more cars, two of which were of the same make and color, and two pedestrians, each with a dog. In a valuable series of studies and papers on how to classify and sequence tasks, Robinson (2001a,b, 2002b, 2003b, 2005, 2007a,b, 2009, 2010, 2011a,b), Robinson and Gilabert (2007), and Robinson, Ting, and Erwin (1995) has drawn a useful distinction between the two terms, task complexity and task difficulty, that has subsequently become widely adopted – within the literature on TBLT, at least – and added a third parameter, task 'condition.' See Table 8.1.

Complexity in TBLT refers to inherent, unchanging qualities of a task that make it more or less challenging than another task at a given moment in time. Factors affecting task complexity include the existence, or not, of a shared context and perspective (a task's displacement, or not, in time and space, i.e., here and now vs. there and then), the number of elements involved in a task, and the degree of difference among those elements (see Table 8.1). Thus (these are my own examples, and also my own rationales, with which Robinson may or may not agree), other things being equal, a task with a here-and-now orientation, such as talking about a traffic accident with a bystander while both are observing the scene (or, in a classroom lesson, a picture or video of it), i.e., one that requires what Cummins (1979, 1980a,b, and elsewhere) refers to as "context-embedded" language use, is a less complex task than one that involves a there-and-then orientation, such as describing the same accident later to friends who did not witness the scene or testifying about it weeks later in court, i.e., what Cummins describes as "context-reduced" language use. Displacement in time and place requires more of the speaker or writer because nothing can be assumed of the hearer or reader. The greater complexity of the task can also result in more speech and more complex speech, e.g., because background information will be needed to set the scene and explain how the accident came about, as well as use of more sequence markers (*before, after, then, next, later*, etc.), past tenses, and full noun phrases, instead of pronouns and deictics, to identify and disambiguate events and actors. Similarly, the more elements involved, and the more similar those elements, e.g., two black mid-size cars, a motorcycle, and three pedestrians, rather than just one car and a truck, the more complex the task. More, and more similar, elements can lead to more, and more complex, language, e.g., due to additional modifiers being required to distinguish *which* car did what, when, and to whom.[7] Table 8.1 includes a list of other dimensions of tasks that Robinson claims affect task complexity.

---

[7] Whether or not studies show that more complex tasks do, in fact, result in more language, and more complex language, will be discussed in Chapter 9.

Table 8.1. Characteristics for pedagogic task design and sequencing decisions

Task complexity (cognitive factors)	*Task condition (interactive factors)*
(Classification criteria: cognitive demands)	(Classification criteria: interactional demands)
(Classification procedure: information-theoretic analyses)	(Classification procedure: behavior descriptive analyses)
Subcategories:	Subcategories:
(a) Cognitive variables making cognitive/ conceptual demands	(a) Participation variables making interactional demands
+/− Here and now	+/− Open solution
+/− Few elements	+/− One way flow
−/+ Spatial reasoning	+/− Convergent solution
−/+ Causal reasoning	+/− Few participants
−/+ Intentional reasoning	+/− Few contributions needed
−/+ Perspective-taking	+/− Negotiation not needed
(b) Cognitive variables making performative/ procedural demands	(b) Participant variables making making interactant demands
+/− Planning time	+/− Same proficiency
+/− Prior knowledge	+/− Same gender
+/− Single task	+/− Familiar
+/− Task structure	+/− Shared content knowledge
+/− Few steps	+/− Equal status and role
+/− Independency of steps	+/− Shared cultural knowledge

Source: Robinson, P. (2009). Syllabus design. In Long, M.H., & Doughty, C.J. (eds.), *Handbook of language teaching* (pp. 294–310). Oxford: Wiley-Blackwell.

In TBLT, the order in which target tasks are addressed via a sequence of pedagogic tasks of gradually increasing complexity may depend on the relative frequency and/or criticality of the target tasks, as determined by the NA. Once that has been decided, however, *pedagogic tasks in a TBLT syllabus are sequenced according to complexity – task complexity, not linguistic complexity*. Very much in keeping with the rationale for TBLT described in this book, the Cognition Hypothesis (Robinson 2001a,b, 2003b, 2009, and elsewhere) holds that increasing demands on the *cognitive/conceptual dimension* of pedagogic tasks promotes interlanguage development by causing learners to focus on, and notice, L2 features required to express the new cognitive/conceptual distinctions, resulting in more uptake. This speeds up grammaticization and encourages use of more complex syntax. Increasing task complexity on the *performative/procedural dimension*, on the other hand, e.g., by reducing planning time or task familiarity, improves learners' *access* to, and *control* over, current L2 abilities, and improves the likelihood that abilities learned will transfer to task performance in the real world.

To repeat, it is on the basis of their *relative complexity* that PTs are sequenced in TBLT. For example, two reading tasks involving articles on renewable energy, one from a newspaper, the other from a scientific journal, may feature different percentages of technical and non-technical lexical items, drawn from varying frequency ranges. Given the average length in words of sentences in the articles, and the average number of syllables per word, application of the Flesch–Kincaid Grade Level Readability Formula may identify them as appropriate for different grade levels or for students of different ages. The two articles' differential *complexity*, as defined by the frequency and domain-specificity of those lexical items, sentence length, and the kind of reasoning they embody and require on the reader's part, do not change, so reading the newspaper article could be expected to be sequenced before reading the journal article, perhaps serving as a schema-building activity.

The second dimension in Robinson's model is task *condition*, under which interactive factors are grouped (see Table 8.1). Within a unit or a lesson, the same pedagogic task may produce different experiences for students according to the conditions under which it is performed. Changes in task condition may come about through a teacher's or materials writer's manipulation of what Robinson labels *participation variables*, such as whether a version of a task is open (has multiple, perhaps an infinite number of, solu-tions) or closed (has only one or a small, finite number of solutions), one-way or two-way (in terms of how information is distributed at the outset of a task, and whether or not information held uniquely by individuals in a pair or group must be exchanged for the task to be completed), or convergent or divergent (whether or not students must agree on a solution), which has consequences for the interactional demands on those working on the task. Task condition also varies as a function of *participant variables*, such as the number, (same or mixed) gender, L2 proficiency and cultural background of students who work on it together, and whether they work alone or with one or more classmates, with or without teacher assistance. Teachers and materials writers can control and manipulate these and other interactive factors, but they are not factors used to sequence two or more pedagogic tasks. Conditions affect the way students experience a single task. Their importance, following Robinson, drawing on work in L1 psychology (e.g., Broad 1997; Schank & Abelson 1977), is that richer and more varied experience of the same task under different conditions increases the likelihood that the language "scripts" learned for doing the task will transfer to real-world settings beyond the classroom.

Whereas complexity is fixed, the third dimension of a task, its *difficulty*, may vary for two students, due to individual differences between them. For example, when the students read the newspaper article on renewable energy, one may have higher or lower L2 proficiency, better or poorer reading skills, or higher or lower language aptitude and working memory than the other. And over time, the same readers' vocabulary sizes should increase, as may the background knowledge they bring to the task, making the same texts less *difficult* for those readers or for the same reader on his or her second encounter with the same task. *Complexity*, in other words, is unchanging, a product of a task's intrinsic properties and the cognitive demands it makes on learners. *Difficulty*, conversely, is variable, a function of the combination of the complexity of a task and the abilities individual learners bring to the table, coupled with modifications teachers may make to task condition. For example, the cognitive demands tasks make on learners may be temporarily decreased by schema-building (here, on renewable energy) that precedes the readings, by planning time, or by the time students are allowed to complete them. Complexity is the metric by which a syllabus designer, materials writer, or teacher in TBLT can classify and compare pedagogic tasks, in order to sequence them. Difficulty is a measure of the challenge the same pedagogic task or target task presents to two or more learners, or to the same learner over time, due to differences in the learners, or in the situations under which they perform the task, not in the task itself.

Pedagogic tasks are graded and sequenced based solely on the *cognitive demands* they make. *Interactive factors*, i.e., the conditions under which those tasks are performed, e.g., in open or closed, one-way or two-way, convergent or divergent, or same or mixed proficiency versions, are adjustments that can be used to make initial performance of a single pedagogic task easier by producing simpler versions of the same task, not for sequencing two or more different pedagogic tasks. Given the names and occupations of eight dinner guests, for example – four men and four women, two each of whom are factory workers, and two each middle-class professionals – and told to arrange their seating around a table with no limitations on who sits with whom, is easier than being given the same information and instruction, but with the constraint that no two men or blue-collar workers must sit side by side. The first version is an *open task*, meaning that any solution is acceptable; the second version is a *closed task*, meaning that there is a single correct solution (or, paralleling the same open/closed distinction in teacher questions, in some cases, a small, finite number of correct solutions). Choosing (any) three favorite books to take to a desert island is an open task, as is having to give one's opinions about a particular painter or tourist destination, on what makes a top-class athlete or why Barcelona play soccer so magnificently; there is a very large, potentially unlimited number of possible opinions, choices, and reasons. Being asked, on the other hand, to explain the causes of earthquakes and tsunami, which of three famous seventeenth-century Dutch and Flemish painters in a list of 10 died before the age of 40, which 8 of 11 Barcelona first team players in 2012 also played for the World Champion Spanish national team, or the sequence in which certain historical events occurred, are all closed tasks; there is one correct answer or only a very small, finite number of correct answers, in each case.

In his model, the Triadic Componential Framework (TCF; Robinson 2007a), task complexity factors, as noted above, are divided into two groups, *resource-directing* and *resource-dispersing* (also referred to as *resource-depleting*). Resource-directing dimensions, again, are those that increase cognitive task demands, e.g., by involving more reasoning in a task, more steps or components, or more elements that are hard to distinguish from one another because they are very similar. Robinson's claim is that such factors force learners to focus more attention on linguistic features, e.g., to use more modifiers or relative clauses to differentiate people, places, or things, thereby stimulating language development. Resource-directing features include +/− here and now, +/− few elements, +/− spatial, causal, and intentional reasoning, and +/− perspective taking. Resource-dispersing dimensions are those that force a learner to allocate attentional resources to more things at once, e.g., through having to talk to a customer on the telephone while simultaneously taking written notes on her order. Resource-dispersing dimensions do not affect the learner's level of attention to linguistic features, but do affect procedural demands and automaticity. They include +/− planning, +/− prior knowledge, +/− single task, +/− task structure, +/− few steps, and +/− independence of steps. Increasing task complexity along resource-directing dimensions, Robinson predicts, can result in an increase in both linguistic complexity and accuracy, which are related and serve the same ends, e.g., when catering to the need for increased linguistic precision created by a more complex task. This is possible because, following work in L1 psychology (Baddeley 1986, 1996; Navon 1989; Neumann 1996), Robinson views attention as consisting of multiple attentional resource pools that can operate simultaneously through a central executive; depleting one will not affect others, so speakers can attend simultaneously to form and meaning, to accuracy and complexity. Increasing complexity along resource-dispersing/depleting dimensions, on the other hand, he predicts, may increase fluency, but affect accuracy and complexity negatively.

Robinson's work on task complexity and task sequencing has been insightful and influential, and the TCF is appealing in many ways, but its sheer complexity creates problems and has been said to make it less useful for practitioners:

> Intuitively it may be assumed that the variables distinguished by Robinson do play a role in determining task complexity, but it is far from clear how these variables have to be operationalised, which of them are predominant, how they interact and how fine-grained they should be ... One may wonder how all [the 36] variables [in the 2007 version of the model] can be operationalised and differentiated and how for instance the supposedly different kinds of reasoning should be tested in an experimental setting. (Kuiken & Vedder 2007, p. 265)

Some task dimensions listed by Robinson as issues of (potentially resource-depleting) task complexity, such as +/− planning time and +/− task familiarity (prior knowledge), seem equally likely to work as task conditions. Objective measures of 'spatial reasoning,' 'causal reasoning,' 'intentional reasoning,' or 'perspective taking' could prove elusive. Moreover, as D. Ellis points out (2011, p. 13), even the seemingly most transparent variables, such as number of elements, are difficult to operationalize non-controversially. A researcher might claim to have included ten, but perhaps only five were salient and noticed by the participant in an experiment. If so, how complex was the task?

Robinson (p.c., May 15, 2013) does not view the TCF as especially complicated. There are three categories in the TCF, it is true, but only one of them, task complexity, is proposed as the operational basis for classifying target task demands, then designing pedagogic tasks based on that classification, and then sequencing tasks. For use in task syllabus design, the Simple/Stabilizing interlanguage, Automatizing access to interlanguage, and Restructuring and Complexifying (SSARC) model (Robinson 2010, 2011b) recommends matching the demands of a target task to the 12 dimensions of task complexity, increasing the complexity of relevant resource-dispersing dimensions first, and second, the complexity of resource-directing dimensions. Not all 12 dimensions will be relevant to all target task performances. For example, progressively increasing the complexity of pedagogic tasks for requesting a bank transfer will not involve causal, spatial, or intentional reasoning. They may involve dual task demands if the task is done over the phone while doing something else, but not if face to face in the bank, and so on. Task difficulty factors will probably turn out to be important, but are under-researched to date, so cannot play a role in sequencing decisions. They figure in the TCF to promote inquiry and research into what makes some dimensions of complexity more or less difficult for individual learners to handle. The third and final category, task conditions, also has no consequences for sequencing, only for task classification. Target task conditions are not used and adjusted during sequencing, but held constant every time increasingly cognitively complex versions are performed. Thus, a bank transfer is always a two-way task, so pedagogic task versions would always be two-way to help elaborate and consolidate schemata for performing that task.

Robinson's claims about the benefits for language learning of increased task complexity contrast with those of an alternative model for task sequencing proposed by Skehan (1998, 2001, 2003) and Skehan and Foster (2001). Skehan's Limited Attention Capacity Model (LACM) of task complexity is conceptually simpler, although sometimes to the extent that more elucidation is required before claims can be tested. The model assumes that humans possess finite attentional resources governed by a single control mechanism. Content and form compete for these finite attentional resources, and since humans process for meaning first, an increase in task complexity will mean more attention is required for conceptualizing the message itself, leaving less for the language they use to express the message. Hence, an increase in task complexity, e.g., through the learner having to deal with new, more complex content, is likely to result in a decrease in accuracy. Typically, there is likely to be an increase in only one of accuracy, complexity, or fluency at a time, and then at the expense of the other two. In the event that a focus on message form leads to an improvement in accuracy, it is likely to come at a cost to fluency, and possibly to complexity, as well. There is a trade-off. A decrease in task complexity, conversely, will free up attentional resources, potentially leading to improvements in the quality of one or more of the three dimensions of speech production.

There is no grammatical syllabus in Skehan's approach to language teaching, which is genuinely task-based (as is Robinson's), although without a prior NA to guide task selection. As with the Procedural Syllabus, therefore, for Skehan, what are referred to in TBLT as pedagogic tasks do not need to be selected with reference to a list of target tasks. Unlike Robinson, who sees more complex tasks triggering more complex and more accurate language, Skehan maintains that the increased use of a learner's finite attentional resources required by cognitively challenging tasks, tasks that require attention to content, or meaning, leaves fewer resources available for focusing on language form, resulting in a decline in the complexity, accuracy, or both, of learner output. Skehan further claims that various task characteristics can be manipulated to induce learners to focus attention relatively more or less on accuracy, complexity, or fluency. Tasks with a clear "macrostructure," for example, encourage accuracy, whereas "a need to impose order on ideas" enhances complexity (Skehan 1998, p. 112). To achieve balanced L2 development, tasks should be sequenced with regard to three dimensions of complexity. First, there is a task's *code complexity*, reflecting the morphosyntactic and lexical density and variety required. Second, there is a task's *cognitive complexity*, the thinking required. A familiar task, topic, or discourse genre reduces cognitive complexity, as do lesser processing requirements, brought about by clearly organized material. Third, a task's *communicative stress*, i.e., the conditions under which it is performed, varies according to such factors as the number of participants involved, the time available for task completion, the length of texts, and the degree to which students can control interaction.

Both Robinson's TCF and Skehan's LACM have been subjected to a considerable number of empirical tests. See, e.g., Bygate, Skehan, and Swain (2001), Cadierno and Robinson (2009), Ellis (2004), Foster and Skehan (1996), Gilabert (2004), Gilabert (2007a,b), Gilabert, Baron, and Llanes (2009), Ishikawa (2006, 2008a,b), Kim (2009),

Kuiken, Mos, and Vedder (2005), Kuiken and Vedder (2007), Michel, Kuiken, and Vedder (2007), Nuevo (2006), Rahimpour (1997, 1999), Rahimpour and Hosseini (2010), Revesz (2009, 2011), Robinson (1995, 2007b, 2010, 2011b), Robinson, Cadierno, and Shirai (2009), Robinson and Gilabert (2007), and Robinson, Ting, and Erwin (1995). Attention has been devoted to relationships among the three dependent variables in most task complexity studies, accuracy, complexity, and fluency, but the way they have been measured has varied enormously, with 84 different measures employed in studies so far (Jackson & Suethanapornkul 2013), and the learnability of targeted structures by students of different proficiency largely ignored (Norris & Ortega 2009. Based on 39 measure contrasts from nine studies that met the requirements for inclusion in their statistical meta-analysis of results concerning Robinson's Cognition Hypothesis (CH; Robinson 2001a, 2005, 2007a, 2011b; Robinson & Gilabert 2007), Jackson and Suethanapornkul found that increases in resource-directing task demands yielded a small positive average effect size (0.28) for accuracy, and a small negative average effect size for fluency, both results as predicted by Robinson's CH. Findings from 28 measures utilized in a total of seven studies showed tiny improvements in lexical complexity, however (an average effect size of 0.03), and contrary to the CH's predictions of positive effects for complexity, a negligible decrease in syntactic complexity (an average size of −0.02).

A detailed, critical review of both models and of some of the studies is provided by D. Ellis (2011). Comparisons of findings in favor or against each one is virtually impossible, Ellis points out, for several reasons. Tasks employed have varied greatly across studies and sometimes been vaguely characterized, often pitched at the level of task-type or genre (e.g., picture description, narrative, personal information exchange, decision-making, writing a letter to a friend), rather than that of the smaller scale, more tangible and more precisely defined pedagogic tasks in TBLT. Studies have not sampled data from comparable *phases* commonly observed in certain task-types, yet the phases have been known to produce different results (Bygate 1988), or from comparable task-types. Some studies have involved speech, some writing. Some have used monologic formats, some dialogic. The dimensions of task complexity and task condition manipulated have run the gamut from +/− complex reasoning, through +/− number of elements, +/− planning time, +/− structured, and +/− here and now, to +/− contextual support, often in varying combinations. Not all three dependent macro-variables, accuracy, complexity, and fluency, have figured in several studies. When they have, they have been measured in a variety of ways (for the many options, see Ellis & Barkhuizen 2005), including S-nodes per T-unit, motion verb and motion clause complexity, self-repair, error-free speech, the percentage of participants producing non-prototypical uses of tense-aspect markings, the raw frequencies of tense-aspect morphology used to mark specific semantic categories, turn-taking, clarification requests, confirmation checks and comprehension checks, recasts, language-related episodes, lexical errors, lexical density, lexical variation, appropriateness, quantity of output, and (operationalized in different ways) spoken fluency. Methodological differences aside, results within and across studies have been mixed (see, e.g., Kim 2009), with most findings failing to reach statistical significance, and trends in the data not always occurring in the predicted directions. Undaunted, several researchers have interpreted their results as showing support for either Robinson's or Skehan's position. Ellis' conclusion (2011, p. 11), conversely, is that not a single published study provides unambiguous support for either model. Unfortunately, I have to agree.[8]

Ellis offers what at first sight might seem a radical proposal: conduct studies using native speakers, not L2 speakers (or writers). The rationale is appealing. Unlike L2 learners, who vary in age, L1, L2 proficiency, IQ, educational background, and more, native speakers by definition (assuming minimal controls on IQ and educational background) have a full, homogeneous, and comparable, command of their L1. Using them as subjects in task complexity research, initially, at least, offers a simple way of controlling for accuracy, processing demands and (to a lesser extent) fluency, thereby allowing any changes in the one remaining dependent variable, linguistic complexity, to be isolated as the effect of changes in task complexity. Why search in the dark for that relationship in non-natives before first ascertaining its existence in natives?

A study that pursued the native speaker option was that by Foster and Tavakoli (2009). In an earlier work, Tavakoli and Foster (2008) had found a positive relationship between task complexity and linguistic complexity among L2 speakers – a result in keeping with the predictions of both Robinson's and Skehan's models. Task complexity was assessed as a function of *storyline complexity*, requiring speakers to provide background information while describing foreground events during the retelling of a picture-guided cartoon story. Previous work had shown that the need to explain background events (the conditions, reasons, and purposes of an event) often involved use of subordinate clauses, thereby increasing syntactic complexity. Task complexity was affected by the *inherent structure* of a narrative. A tight narrative structure, with a clear time sequence, from beginning to middle to end, was less complex than one with a loose structure, in which events were unrelated, allowing them to be narrated in any order, and on which the speaker therefore had to impose a structure (Skehan & Foster 1997, 2005). Retelling a familiar restaurant scenario depicted in a video produced less complex language than retelling a more unpredictable video narrative (Skehan & Foster 1999). The clear time sequence of a tightly structured narrative was claimed to make processing easier, freeing up attentional resources to devote to improving accuracy and fluency. The Tavakoli and Foster (2008) study replicated the earlier findings. More complex narratives (those with greater storyline complexity) resulted in use of more complex language, whereas less complex (tightly structured) narratives resulted in more accurate language, and a trend in the data toward greater fluency.

Foster and Tavakoli (2009) conducted a modified replication of their 2008 study, this time with 40 university undergraduate literature or psychology majors, all English native speakers. Accuracy is a non-issue for native speakers, and so was not assessed. Fluency did not vary as a function of task complexity. Nor did lexical diversity, measured using D (Malvern & Richards 2002), i.e., mean length of utterance (MLU) corrected for text length. There was an effect for task complexity on syntactic complexity, however. The

---

[8] A lot of people have put considerable time and effort into the task complexity issue. Given that the work typically entails individual data-collection sessions, transcription and coding before quantification, statistical analyses, and interpretations of findings can even begin, it tends to be very labor-intensive. Rather than more and more one-off studies using a miscellany of variables, measures, and analyses, what is needed is a unified *research program*, albeit conducted by individual researchers and research groups at different locations. The sum of their efforts would be greater than the parts, replication would be feasible, and unnecessary duplication avoided.

ratio of clauses to AS units (Foster, Tonkyn, & Wigglesworth 2000) was significantly higher for narratives with two story lines (i.e., those requiring interweaving of background and foreground information), and MLU was significantly higher for dual narratives with an inherently tight structure. Conversely, tight inherent structure of narratives (lower complexity) facilitates fluency among non-natives, but does not affect native speaker performance. Natives tend to pause at syntactic boundaries; non-native pauses occur more often in the middle of clauses. Less complex narratives allowed non-natives to plan and deliver clause-length utterances more fluently. Task complexity did not affect lexical diversity in either group. On the basis of these two studies, therefore, the first with non-natives, the replication with native speakers, storyline complexity affects syntactic complexity the same way with L1 and L2 speakers. It seems that syntactic complexity is in part, at least, a genuine task effect, not wholly a L2 processing effect. L2 speakers with inadequate command of subordination devices in English (relative clauses, *if/when* clauses, *unless/although/in case* clauses, etc.) have more difficulty with more complex (dual storyline) narratives, so may be less accurate or less fluent than on a narrative with a single story line. As Foster and Tavakoli put it:

> Dual storylines provoke greater use of subordinate clauses in English; single storylines do not. A native speaker selects subordination to weave two storylines together, not because a secure knowledge of English allows it but because the nature of a narrative ... requires it. (Foster & Tavakoli 2009, p. 885)

Numerous studies assessing the effects of manipulating various parameters of task complexity and task condition have been reported over the past 20 years. For reviews of various sub-sets of them, see, among others, D. Ellis (2011), R. Ellis (2003, pp. 195–235), and Robinson (2007b). Most studies have been theoretically unmotivated. Many have been methodologically flawed, e.g., confounding token and type – using only one task to exemplify each of two task-types supposedly under investigation, and not always even two versions of the same task. With respect to task condition, for example, a researcher might set out to compare the linguistic accuracy and complexity of speech and/or writing when students are asked to state opinions on causes of the so-called "Arab Spring" (an open task) and when required to identify which of a list of 20 individuals and events were instrumental in the upheavals in three of the countries concerned (a closed task). Whatever the results, it would be unwarranted to attribute any differences observed to the +/− open task condition parameter. Each task is but one exemplar of open and closed task-types, so the effects may well be due to something about those particular tasks, not to their being open and closed. Moreover, the two tasks differ in so many other ways. At most, a researcher might conclude that results were consistent with the hypothesis that open or closed tasks (in general, i.e., at the level of task-type) are associated with more or less complex linguistic production. A more reasonable approach would be to compare production, or (arguably, more relevant for assessing the differential potential of various task-types for acquisition) incorporation of linguistic input contained in the task materials (uptake) of two versions of the *same* task, e.g., the table seating-arrangements task mentioned earlier, where in one version, the same eight guests can be seated freely (open), or in another, with tight constraints as to which guests (male and female, blue-collar and white-collar, etc.) can sit next to one another (closed).

Finally, it is worth remembering that there is no reason to expect a one-to-one relationship between values of any single parameter, or any one combination of values of task complexity parameters, on the one hand, and on the other, linguistic complexity, quantity or quality of interaction, uptake, or any other dependent variable, even if individual learner differences (L2 proficiency, IQ, aptitude, etc.) are taken into account. In practice, teachers and students, not just researchers and materials writers, often play a significant role in determining task complexity and/or difficulty. For instance, intentionally or unintentionally, they may short-circuit what a researcher or materials writer planned by ignoring elements of a task designed to make it more complex, e.g., by simply omitting any reference to a second car in their report of the traffic accident, or by changing task condition. Participant "interventions" of this sort have affected the outcome of several classroom and experimental laboratory studies designed to assess relationships between task complexity and linguistic accuracy and complexity (see, e.g., Kong 2002; Kumaravadivelu 1991; Y.-G. Lee 2002). "Proofing" a task, to make it more resistant to unhelpful modifications in the classroom (unhelpful from a language-learning perspective, that is), has become an interesting topic for research. We will return to these matters in Chapter 9, when we will consider ways in which task-based teaching materials, i.e., pedagogic tasks, can be classified and sequenced, including examples using the complexity criterion, as well as other issues in pedagogic task design.

8.4.5. Some research findings on pedagogic task-types

With the above caveats in mind, the following are some research findings to date on relationships between *pedagogic task-types* and the conditions under which they are performed, on the one hand, and on the other, classroom processes (negotiation work, provision of feedback, etc.), performance quality (complexity, accuracy, fluency), and learning outcomes (uptake, acquisition of new forms, etc.). While findings have been reasonably consistent (not necessarily uniform) across laboratory and classroom settings, they have been rather mixed on some dimensions of task-types. The references provided are to sample studies and findings, by no means all that have been obtained, for those interested in reading further and perhaps contributing to the research effort themselves. More comprehensive and detailed reviews are available elsewhere, e.g., R. Ellis (2003, 2012), Gass (1997), Mackey (2012), Long and Porter (1985), Pica (1994, 2009), Pica, Kanagy, and Falodun (1993), and Samuda and Bygate (2008). For a statistical meta-analysis of the effects of resource-directing task-types on complexity, accuracy, and fluency, see Jackson and Suethanapornkul (2013). The following, to repeat, are merely sample studies and findings, with some references to initial sources for those interested in the original research.

8.4.5.1. One-way tasks **One-way tasks** are tasks, such as opinion-gap tasks, where information-exchange is optional, as when learners express their views on an issue, and/ or tasks where one party holds all the information needed for task completion (e.g., has and describes a picture that a classmate, who does not have it, must draw or identify). One-way tasks sometimes produce little negotiation work of the sort known to be important for language development, and no more negotiation work when performed in small student groups than what typically occurs in teacher-fronted lockstep lessons. For laboratory studies, see, e.g., Gass, Mackey, and Ross-Feldman (2005) and Long (1980a, 1983b). For classroom studies, see, e.g., Fujii and Mackey (2009), Pica (2002),

Pica and Doughty (1985a,b), and Shintani (2011). There is some evidence from laboratory studies, however, that one-way tasks allow more modification of output than two-way tasks (Iwashita 2001; Shehadeh 2001).

8.4.5.2. Two-way tasks   **Two-way tasks** (sometimes also referred to as "reciprocal," or "jigsaw," tasks), i.e., those, like "Spot-the-Difference" and map-route tasks, where (a) each participant holds unique information (b) that must be exchanged for the task to be completed successfully, have been shown to be superior to one-way tasks in the amount of negotiation for meaning they engender. For laboratory studies, see, e.g., Gass, Mackey, and Ross-Feldman (2005) and Long (1980a, 1983b). For classroom studies, see, e.g., again, Foster (1998), Gass, Mackey, and Ross-Feldman (2005), Newton (1991), Pica (1987), Pica and Doughty (1985a,b), and Slimani-Rolls (2005). However, some classroom studies (Eckerth 2008; Foster & Ohta 2005) have found no effect for task-type and/or (Foster 1998; Slimani-Rolls 2005) an effect, but little negotiation work and considerable differences at the level of individual students. Negotiation for meaning leads to improved comprehension. For laboratory studies, see, e.g., Van den Branden (2000). For classroom studies, see, e.g., De la Fuente (2002) and Ellis, Tanaka, and Yamazaki (1994). In a small-scale classroom study (Newton 2013), two-way tasks were found better than opinion-gap tasks for learning new vocabulary items.

8.4.5.3. Open tasks   **Open tasks**, in which there is no single correct answer that learners must identify (e.g., debates, deciding which books and music they would take to a desert island, ranking countries), can offer more opportunities for extended turns at talk. Open tasks can result in more complex, and sometimes more accurate, language. For laboratory studies, see Berwick (1990), R. Brown (1991), Duff (1986),[9] and Tong-Fredericks (1984). For classroom studies, see Bygate (1987) and Skehan (1998).

8.4.5.4. Closed tasks   **Closed tasks** require students to find the correct solution, or one of a small, finite number of correct solutions to the problem posed by a task. They can lead to more negotiation for meaning, more feedback, more uptake, and greater fluency than open tasks. For laboratory studies, see, e.g., Berwick (1990), Crookes and Rulon (1986), Manheimer (1993), Newton (1991), Paul (1991), and Rankin (1990). For classroom studies, see, e.g., Julkunen (1990) and Tong-Fredericks (1984).

8.4.5.5. Convergent tasks   **Convergent tasks** require learners to reach agreement on the solution to a problem, such as which of four student applicants is most deserving of financial aid. There is some evidence that convergent tasks produce more interactional modifications and negotiation for meaning than divergent tasks. For laboratory studies, see Duff (1986) and Skehan and Foster (2001).

---

[9] R. Ellis (2003, p. 90) criticized my earlier citation of Duff's work as an example of a study of open and closed tasks, instead of divergent and convergent tasks, missing the point that Duff's tasks – a debate, and reaching agreement on items to be taken to a desert island – were, respectively, examples of *both* divergent and open, and *both* convergent and closed, tasks. He comes close to recognizing his error later (2003, p. 123) and when he refers to "open tasks with divergent goals" (2003, p. 126).

8.4.5.6. Divergent tasks   **Divergent tasks**, such as debates or arguing the merits of different sports teams or candidates for political office, can result in more output, and output of greater syntactic complexity. For laboratory studies, see Duff (1986) and Skehan and Foster (2001).

8.4.5.7. Complex tasks   **Complex tasks** are those involving one or more of more reasoning demands, more components, more steps, more (and/or more similar) items, unfamiliar content, reference to (there-and-then) displaced time and space/less (here-and-now) contextual support, and so on, e.g., describing a crime scene without, instead of with, the benefit of a photograph. According to Robinson's Cognition Hypothesis (CH), these are **resource-directing tasks**, i.e., those that increase attentional demands (through involvement of more similar steps and components, etc.), oblige learners to focus on language features, and thereby increase opportunities for acquiring new language. Because more complex tasks tend to prompt learners to focus more attention on the input in their attempt to cope with the greater complexity, more noticing is likely, and more benefit, therefore, from procedures used to induce focus on form, including recasts (Revesz 2009; Robinson & Gilabert 2007). They can result (as Robinson's model predicts) in increased accuracy, complexity, lexical diversity, and use of more developmentally advanced constructions, in learner output, but sometimes (as Skehan's model predicts) with a trade-off: lower syntactic complexity, and/or fluency. Resource-directing tasks stand in contrast with **resource-depleting tasks**, i.e., those that increase procedural demands by dividing learners' attention (through involvement of fewer, easier distinguished steps or components, by denying planning time, or by requiring simultaneous performance of two tasks, etc.), are less useful for acquisition, but helpful for improving learners' control over what they already know, potentially resulting in greater automaticity. For laboratory studies manipulating the $+/-$ elements, here-and-now/there-and-then, and $+/-$ reasoning demands dimensions, see, e.g., Kuiken and Vedder (2007), Michel, Kuiken, and Vedder (2007), Rahimpour (1997), Revesz (2009), and Robinson (1995b, 2001b, 2007b). For classroom studies, see, e.g., Revesz (2011). More complex tasks impose heavier communicative demands on learners, so can sometimes result in more interactional modifications and self- and/or other repairs (Gilabert, Baron, & Llanes 2009; Poulisse 1990; Shortreed 1993), but not always (Nuevo 2006), and in more attention to form-meaning mappings (Robinson 2003a; Skehan 1998), and more language-learning opportunities (Revesz 2009; Robinson 2001b). As discussed in Section 8.4.4. and in a statistical meta-analysis of task complexity studies (Jackson & Suethanapornkul 2013), however, results on task complexity to date, across and even within studies (e.g., Kim 2009; Nuevo 2006), have been mixed, so must be treated with caution.

8.4.5.8. Planned tasks   **Planned tasks**, i.e., those for which learners are allowed to think about the task and the language they will use for a few minutes (typically five to ten) before beginning their attempt, i.e., to plan strategically, can (not necessarily will) result in more lexically or syntactically complex language than unplanned performance of the same tasks. For laboratory studies, see, e.g., Crookes (1989) and Ortega (1999). For classroom studies, see, e.g., Foster (1996) and Foster and Skehan (1996). Strategic planning often results in more fluent language. For laboratory studies, see, e.g., Ellis

(1987), Mehnert (1998), and Ortega (1999). For classroom studies, see, e.g., Foster and Skehan (1996) and Skehan and Foster (1997). Results for accuracy have been mixed, both within and across studies, possibly because of differences in the types of linguistic features (e.g., easy and hard, salient and non-salient) that have served as dependent variables, and/or because some studies have targeted specific linguistic constructions, e.g., relative clauses, whereas others have looked at global accuracy measures, e.g., supplied in obligatory contexts (SOCs), target-like use (TLU), or clauses per c-unit, and/or because underlying knowledge representations (as opposed to conditions, such as time, governing access, and retrieval) simply do not vary very much within the short duration of most studies. For laboratory studies, see, e.g., Crookes (1989), Mehnert (1998), and Ortega (1999). For classroom studies, see, e.g., Mochizuki and Ortega (2008), Philp, Oliver, and Mackey (2006), and Skehan and Foster (2005, 2007). Other task-type dimensions can play a moderating role, as well. For instance, accuracy can improve when planning is applied to clearly structured (so less complex) tasks, presumably because less attention needs to be applied to content (Skehan & Foster 1997, 1999). For reviews of findings and methodological issues in research on planning, see R. Ellis (2005, 2012) and Ortega (1999).

8.4.5.9. Familiar tasks   **Familiar tasks**, i.e., tasks known to students as a result of task repetition and/or content familiarity, can lead to more negotiation (but cf. Gass & Varonis 1984), improved comprehension and (possibly because familiarity with a topic or task content frees up attention for learners to focus on form) increased fluency, use of more lexically complex language, and in some cases, greater accuracy. For laboratory studies, see, e.g., Bygate (2001) and Gass *et al.* (1999). For classroom studies, see, e.g., Lynch and Maclean (2001), Pinter (2007), Shintani (2012), and Van den Branden (1997). There is some indirect evidence that familiarity needs to be with the same task, not just with tasks of the same type (Bygate 2001; Plough & Gass 1993), potentially indicating a serious problem for the generalizability of task-based abilities. The amount of negotiation work during the first attempt at a storytelling task can influence the extent of linguistic improvement in subsequent retellings (Ko, Schallert, & Walters 2003). Contrary to other findings, however, familiar tasks can sometimes lead to less negotiation for meaning, including less feedback on partners' errors, and less modified output, than unfamiliar tasks (Mackey, Kanganas, & Oliver 2007).

8.4.5.10. Mixed proficiency tasks   **Mixed proficiency tasks** here refers to those performed by mixed proficiency dyads, i.e., student pairs, one of higher (HI), and one of lower (LO), proficiency. Mixed proficiency dyads tend to negotiate more and successfully resolve more language problems. For laboratory studies, see Yule and MacDonald (1990). For classroom studies, see Kim and McDonough (2008) and Watanabe and Swain (2007).

   Despite the existence of numerous data-based studies, of which those referenced above are but a fraction, clear and consistent findings are few and far between. I believe there are several reasons for this state of affairs. First and foremost, many of the varied findings seem due to methodological differences in how studies ostensibly of the same issues are carried out. The long list of measures of dependent variables employed is an obvious example. Second, some studies have purported to compare two task-types, but, confounding type and token, have employed only one of each type, with the result that any differences observed may have been due to the particular tasks employed, rather than the class to which they supposedly belonged. Moreover, planning and other task conditions might help with some of the particular tasks, but be unneeded for others, and/or be differentially useful, depending on learner proficiency and, hence, task difficulty. Third, it is also possible that some particular tasks differ sufficiently from others of the same type such that within-task-type effects are, alone, capable of producing variation in dependent variables. Fourth, this kind of research is labor-intensive, typically involving transcription and coding of recordings of student task performance, with classroom conditions being especially problematic for the recordings themselves. The result is use of small n-sizes, with all the usual dangers that poses to findings. Fifth, many tasks simultaneously constitute examples of two (or even more) task-types, so that two or more influences may be at work, together or in competition, in producing the observed outcomes. For example, if two students are asked to agree on the correct sequence of six pictures to represent a story, each holding three at the outset, their task can be classified as closed, two-way, and convergent. Sixth, the way task designers, researchers, and teachers intend a task to be carried out may not be how students actually do so. For example, intentionally or not, they may not notice, or notice but simply ignore, some of the items added by the designer to subsequent versions of pictures with the intention of making the later versions of a task more complex. Seventh, learner proficiency differences and other individual differences (L1, aptitude, IQ, gender, cultural background, motivation, etc.) across studies could mask what may really be underlying similarities in results. Eighth, the ways that constructs like accuracy, complexity, and fluency have been operationalized have differed greatly from one study to the next, again potentially masking genuine commonalities in effects for task-types. For instance, in one study, 'accuracy' may refer to a global measure, such as errors per c-unit, but in others, TLU of specific linguistic features, such as articles, plurals, or relative clauses, the difference compounded by the fact that the choice of target features has rarely taken learnability for the students concerned into account.

There are other possible reasons for the current lack of clarity and consistency in findings, but eight will do for now. What is needed are *research programs*, not series of one-off studies. Research within a research program would be motivated by, and test, the same theory or theories, use the same, or a sub-set of the same, measures, and so on. That way, results would be directly comparable and cumulative. The same (considerable) effort would have a far higher yield, and progress would be faster. Useful discussions of some of these factors have begun to appear. See, e.g., R. Ellis (2012), Jackson and Suethanapornkul (2013), and Norris and Ortega (2009).

8.5. Summary

Proposals for any type of syllabus need to explain and justify the unit of analysis chosen, and the criteria by which items for inclusion will be selected and sequenced. Linguistic units of analysis and synthetic (structural, notional-functional, lexical, most topical and situational, and hybrid) syllabi have long been popular, chiefly due to the ease with which they can be (i) understood by teachers and students, (ii) used as the basis for dialogues, texts, drills, and exercises, and (iii) packaged by publishers as (allegedly) appropriate for students of all kinds. In fact, they suffer from many defects, not least their (a) frequent irrelevance for students' communicative needs, and (b) lack of psycholinguistic validity. As a class, non-linguistic units and analytic (some topic and situational, content, procedural, process, and task) syllabi hold more promise in both respects, but most ignore students' communicative needs and SLA research findings on psycholinguistic requirements, too.

Criteria for selection and grading tend to be considered 'solved' problems within synthetic approaches – simply "teach the L2 grammar" and rely on teachers' or materials writers' intuitions about relevance to student interests and "difficulty." TBLT takes selection seriously, relying on a task-based NA to determine syllabus content. Grading is a problem for all syllabus types, although not always recognized as such. Intuition is unsatisfactory; people's intuitions differ greatly, and they cannot all be right. Valency, criticality, and frequency are seductive, but unsatisfactory for several reasons, unless applied to the results of a task-based NA, and even then are insufficient. Learnability is a relevant criterion for all syllabus types, but ignored by most. Complexity is crucial, but difficult to operationalize in laboratory and classroom, alike, and vulnerable to intentional or unintentional modification by teachers and students. The rational sequencing (grading, or gradation) of items remains the most problematic issue in the design of syllabi of all types and an active area of research in TBLT. Findings on task-type effects to date have varied, in part due to methodological differences across studies. One or more unified research programs would speed up progress in the field.

8.6. Suggested Readings

Ellis, R. (1993). The structural syllabus and second language acquisition. *TESOL Quarterly* 27, 1, 91–113.

Jackson, D.O., & Suethanapornkul, S. (2013). The Cognition Hypothesis: A synthesis and meta-analysis of research on second language task complexity. *Language Learning* 63, 2, 330–367.

Long, M.H., & Crookes, G. (1992). Three approaches to task-based language teaching. *TESOL Quarterly* 26, 1, 27–56. Reprinted in Van den Branden, K., Bygate, M., & Norris, J.M. (eds.), *Task based language teaching: A reader* (pp. 57–81). Amsterdam: John Benjamins. 2009.

Long, M.H., & Crookes, G.V. (1993). Units of analysis in syllabus design: The case for task. In Crookes, G., & Gass, S.M. (eds.), *Tasks in pedagogical context. Integrating theory and practice* (pp. 9–54). Clevedon: Multilingual Matters.

Norris, J.M., & Ortega, L. (2009). Towards an organic approach to investigating CAF in instructed SLA: The case of complexity. *Applied Linguistics* 30, 555–578.

Ortega, L. (2009). Sequences and processes in language learning. In Long, M.H., & Doughty, C.J. (eds.), *Handbook of language teaching* (pp. 81–105). Oxford: Wiley-Blackwell.

Robinson, P. (1994). Implicit knowledge, second language learning and syllabus construction. *TESOL Quarterly* 28, 1, 161–166.

Robinson, P. (2009). Syllabus design. In Long, M.H., & Doughty, C.J. (eds.), *Handbook of language teaching* (pp. 294–310). Oxford: Blackwell.

Robinson, P. (2011). Second language task complexity, the Cognition Hypothesis, language learning, and performance. In Robinson, P. (ed.), *Second language task complexity. Researching the Cognition Hypothesis of language learning and performance* (pp. 3–37). Amsterdam: John Benjamins.

Robinson, P., & Gilabert, R. (2007). Task complexity, the Cognition Hypothesis and second language learning and performance. *International Review of Applied Linguistics* 45, 195–215.

Skehan, P. (1998). *A cognitive approach to language learning.* Oxford: Oxford University Press.

White, R. (1988). *The ELT curriculum: Design, management, innovation.* Oxford: Blackwell.

Chapter 9

Task-Based Materials

9.1. Desirable Qualities of Pedagogic Tasks (PTs)

For reasons explained in Chapter 7, TBLT lessons are built around tasks, not texts. Spoken or written texts are static records of someone else's (previous) task accomplishment, i.e.,

Second Language Acquisition and Task-Based Language Teaching, First Edition. Mike Long.
© 2015 John Wiley & Sons, Inc. Published 2015 by John Wiley & Sons, Inc.

a by-product of tasks. Basing lessons on texts (as in much content-based language teaching) means studying language as object, not learning language as a living entity through using it and experiencing its use during task completion. Learners need to learn how to do a task themselves. There is a world of difference, for instance, on the one hand, between learning to make a particular kind of social, business, or emergency medical telephone call through acting one out, as in a role play, and/or making a real one to given specifications, and on the other, in a text-based program of some kind, listening to, or reading, a "dead" script of someone else's effort. When pre-existing ("found") texts or, preferably, elaborated versions thereof, occur as sources of input in language lessons, learners should encounter them as meaningful steps in accomplishing tasks. The pedagogic tasks (PTs) will initially be simple, then of gradually increasing complexity, and eventually of the full complexity of the target tasks identified by the needs analysis that fed into the design of the course.

The most important quality of any type of LT materials is *relevance* to students' L2 communicative needs. It is one thing to show that students can perform well on a discrete-point grammar test, quite another to demonstrate that they can do whatever it is they need to be able to do in and through the L2. Obvious though this might seem, courses frequently employ so-called "four skills" materials for students who mostly, or in some cases exclusively, need just one or two of those skills. They use "generic" grammar-based materials that cover many things students do not need, and fail to cover many things they do need. In TBLT, the fact that the syllabus is based on the results of a learner needs analysis greatly improves the chances that the materials embodying the resulting syllabus will be relevant.

Beyond (i) *relevance*, desirable qualities of any LT materials, not just task-based materials, include (ii) *motivational qualities* – student *interest* and, thereby, the all-important *attention* often being maintained through ensuring that tasks present sufficient intellectual challenge, and (iii) the greatest possible approximation to *real-world language use*. Relevance is usually immediately perceived by students and can be motivation enough, but there is still plenty of room for gifted materials writers to use their imagination; after all, relevant, but poorly written, materials can still be boring. Ingenuity is required to produce tasks that are obviously relevant to students' needs outside the classroom, whose content is of high intrinsic interest, that are fun to do, and that (with Durkheim's and Merton's theories of social anomie in mind) are just challenging enough to intrigue learners, but not so challenging as to discourage them.

Exposing students to realistic samples of language use is the hardest problem. Instead of stilted, linguistically "simplified" dialogues and reading passages, followed by drills and exercises of various kinds, a currently fashionable attempt at a solution is to bring "authentic" spoken or written materials into the classroom, i.e., genuine *texts*, such as song lyrics, news broadcasts, films, newspaper articles, and textbook chapters, originally created by and for native speakers (NSs), not for LT to non-natives. The use of authentic materials is especially common in content-based LT, particularly in tertiary education. However, for reasons explained below (Section 9.2), such "authentic" texts are often inappropriate for all but advanced learners, given the psycholinguistic constraints imposed by their current L2 developmental stage. Moreover, even when psycholinguistically appropriate, the *uses* to which the texts are put in the classroom are rarely authentic.

9.2. Input Simplification and Elaboration

9.2.1. Genuineness, input simplification, and authenticity

The periodic debates over "authenticity" in LT mostly concern the (usually, simply asserted) relative utility of spoken or written *texts* originally intended for NS consumption, compared with that of texts designed for teaching a language to non-native speakers (NNSs) of that language. The former are commonly referred to in the pedagogy literature as "authentic" texts, the latter typically as "simplified." Simplified, in this context, means texts written (or re-written) using relatively short utterances or sentences, a limited range of relatively high frequency vocabulary, a low ratio of dependent to main clauses, and a narrow range of syntactic constructions and verb tenses. Publishers issue simplification guidelines concerning permitted vocabulary levels, verb tenses, and so on, for authors writing at the various "levels" of their series of "graded readers" and "graded listening materials." Such materials are (usually) more easily comprehended than unsimplified spoken or written input; however, not unlike so-called "basal readers" for L1-acquiring children, they tend to be stilted, repetitive, and dull.[1] Worse, as detailed below, they are of limited value for language development, yet (given that students will never again encounter these particular texts again), this is supposedly their main purpose.

Widdowson (1976, 1996) noted that even when texts originally produced by NSs for real communicative purposes – what he called *genuine* texts – are utilized in LT, i.e., even when the *sources* of texts are authentic, the *uses* to which they are put in classrooms often are not. Teachers and authors of commercially published pedagogic materials may require learners to memorize or translate a speech, write down a passage one sentence at a time while listening to it read aloud (dictation), listen to a telephone conversation (often scripted, not genuine) while filling in words or phrases missing from a transcript, or supply one party's responses while listening to the other side in a taped spoken dialogue. Taking notes about isolated words or phrases while listening to a taped business telephone conversation, even if the conversation is genuine, is not an authentic task, Arnold (1991) points out. In a real office, a sales representative, for instance, would be taking notes about the content of the message or even filling out an order form while participating in the conversation. A classroom simulation of *that* activity would be an authentic PT. Note that the spoken and written *texts* in such a case, i.e., the telephone conversation and the notes or completed order form, *would result from the task*, e.g., taking a customer's telephone order, not the other way around.

In many instances, the inauthenticity of PTs is compounded by that of the language to which students are exposed through them, due to the texts involved having originally been written to be read, not spoken, and so differing in myriad ways from genuine spoken discourse. Scripted talk, read aloud, typically lacks such features of natural conversation as sandhi variation (Hendrichsen 1984), false starts, interruptions, overlaps,

---

[1] In fact, simplification does not even always help comprehension, sometimes because it serves to remove useful redundancy in texts, e.g., by deleting explicit intra- and inter-utterance/sentential markers of logical relationships among clauses and propositions (Blau 1982). Simplification of passives, nominalizations and participles helped neither L1 nor L2 reading comprehension, nor shortened required reading time, in a study of Dutch and American college students' performance with an EST text (Ulijn & Strother 1990).

echoic responses, a reliance on the here and now (context-embeddedness), ellipsis, redundancy, and intertextuality, among others (see Chapter 7.4). It also avoids issues of unfamilar varieties or accents – the written code for any language typically being far more standardized – known to be a potentially serious problem with spoken varieties of a language, especially for second language speakers (see, e.g., Anderson-Hsieh & Koehler 1988). It usually entails removal of the visual support that accompanies and facilitates many real-world listening tasks (a problem sometimes remediable through use of video with listening materials when target tasks make that appropriate). Even when texts are genuine, they may lack authenticity with respect to learner needs, e.g., because they reflect different varieties of the spoken language from those to which students will be exposed outside the classroom, or because they are drawn from discourse domains or genres different from those in which learners will operate. There are considerable differences, for example, between radio or television broadcasts involving specialist to non-specialist communication and talk among insiders, on the one hand, and on the other, academic lectures on the same topics, or between unimpeded face-to-face conversation and noisy, overheard, third-party speech.

The above are significant problems with traditional approaches to materials design, but not the only ones. There are strong grounds for believing that it is not just artificiality, boredom, and a lower probability of positive transfer that should be expected from materials and pedagogy bearing little resemblance to learners' future real-world tasks. More serious is the fact that *psycholinguistic* properties of *both* genuine and linguistically simplified texts reliably make them of lesser value for any but advanced learners.[2] This is because genuine texts almost always utilize language processable in real time by NSs, but not by learners with limited target language knowledge, while simplified texts make processing possible, but do so by removing from the input the very linguistic material to which learners need to be exposed if they are to progress. Simplification, that is, improves *comprehensibility* (of texts learners will never encounter again) at the expense of *language learning*, which is the real goal. An alternative approach to modification is needed, and one exists: *input elaboration*.

9.2.2. Input elaboration

Elaboration is an approach to improving the comprehensibility of spoken or written texts that grew out of research findings on foreigner talk discourse in the 1970s and

---

[2] Here, as is so often the case, research is needed at just that point at which SLA research findings end and applications to language teaching begin. It is clear that some sorts of modifications are needed for "beginners," and few or none for "advanced" students, who can and need to confront tasks and texts of full target complexity. But where is the line to be drawn, where the transition? Impressionistically, based on my own years of classroom teaching experience, plus some admittedly high inferences from the published experimental SLA literature, I believe the transition from elaborated to genuine texts often occurs best in the ILR 2–3 range. In addition to lacking a solid empirical basis, however, any such generalization must obviously be conditioned by the level of "technicality" and target discourse-specificity of the texts concerned and students' background knowledge of the "technical" field. Another serious gap in the applied research concerns the relative effectiveness in computer-aided instructional environments of building elaborative modification devices into texts, on the one hand, and on the other, providing learners with links from potentially difficult items to pop-up paraphrases, and other forms of help, as needed. See Doughty and Long (2003) for critical discussion of some materials that provide progressively more simplified "help" of the second kind.

1980s. Contrary to what was asserted by some second language acquisition (SLA) theorists at the time, it was found that, aside from the use of slower rate of delivery and shorter utterance length, both of which improved comprehensibility, NSs *simplified* their speech rather little. Instead, they succeeded in getting their message across mostly by means of discourse-level alterations, seemingly made with different degrees of awareness, which helped non-native interlocutors cope with quite complex (retained) vocabulary and syntax. Rather than the *input* itself being simplified, the *interactional structure* of NS–NNS conversation was modified during *negotiation for meaning* (more so on some kinds of tasks than others, e.g., closed tasks and two-way tasks) by more frequent use of such devices as simple and brief treatment of conversational topics, a here-and-now orientation, confirmations, (exact or semantic, self- and other-, complete or partial) repetitions, reformulations, confirmation checks, comprehension checks, clarification requests, and various other kinds of scaffolding, such as decomposition, lexical switches, a NS preference for yes/no or or-choice over wh questions, and NS acceptance of unintentional NNS topic-switches. (For data and reviews of the literature, see Long 1981, 1983b,c,d, 1996b; Mackey 2007). Similar findings hold for NNS–NNS conversation (Pica *et al.* 1996).

Elaboration in materials design – and as a methodological principle (see Chapter 10.2.3) – involves adding redundancy and regularity to a text, and often, more explicit signaling of its thematic structure, followed by gradual removal of the "crutches" the modifications provide as learner proficiency increases. *Redundancy* is achieved by such devices as repetition, paraphrase, provision of synonyms of low frequency lexical items in appositional phrases, a preference for full NPs over pronouns, and more overt marking of grammatical and semantic relations already retrievable from context, e.g., use of optional Japanese particles to mark topic, subject, object, directionals, and locatives. As illustrated below (Section 9.3.1), it is important to note that not only materials writers, but teachers, too, can add redundancy, e.g., by segmenting and repeating input. *Regularity* is attained through such devices as parallelism, more frequent use of canonical word order, retention of optional constituents, e.g., subject pronouns in pro-drop languages, full noun phrases (NPs) instead of anaphors, and matching order of mention to order of occurrence (*The plane took off before the family reached the airport*, in preference to either *The family reached the airport after the plane took/had taken off* or *When the family reached the airport, the plane had taken off*). Greater *explicitness* of logical relationships often involves the use of (optional) overt marking of grammatical and semantic relations, mentioned above, and the addition of intra- and inter-sentential linkers, such as *but, so, however, although, therefore, on the other hand, as a result*, and *whereas*. (For additional details and examples, see Long 2007e, pp. 130–138.)

9.2.3. The Paco sentences

Several of the simplification and elaboration processes and features can be seen in the sample texts in Table 9.1, and their quantified effects in Table 9.2. Simplification of the single original (genuine) 18-word sentence in (1) results in three shorter sentences in (2), with an average length of 6.33 words. The syntactic complexity has been reduced from four s-nodes (have, work, provide for, fall asleep) in one sentence to an average of 1.33 per sentence. The cataphora in the genuine sentence has been lost, as has the

Table 9.1. The Paco sentences

1. *Genuine (NS–NS baseline) version*
Because he had to work at night to provide for his family, Paco often fell asleep in class.
2. *Simplified version*
Paco had to make money for his family. Paco worked at night. He often went to sleep in class.
3. *Elaborated version*
Paco had to work at night to earn money to provide for his family, so he often fell asleep in class next day during his teacher's lesson.
4. *Modified elaborated version*
Paco had to work at night to earn money to **provide for** his family. As a result, he often fell asleep in class next day during his teacher's lesson.

	provide for means	a	educate
		b	leave
		c	support

Source: Long (2007e, p. 136). Republished with permission of Taylor and Francis Group LLC Books.

Table 9.2. Descriptive statistics for the Paco sentences

	NS	Simplified	Elaborated	Modified elaborated
Words	18	19	27	29
Sentences	1	3	1	2
s-nodes	4	4	5	5
Words per sentence	18	6.33	27	14.5
s-nodes per sentence	4	1.33	5	2.5

Source: Long (2007e, p. 137). Republished with permission of Taylor and Francis Group LLC Books.

intra-sentential linker *because*, and the pronominalization of Paco. Instead, as a result of the simplification, we are left with three short choppy sentences, with an unnatural repetition of *Paco*, and at least two cases where some of the original meaning has been lost: *to provide for* (his family) is more contextually appropriate, and carries a more precise meaning, than *to make money for* (his family), and whereas someone who is exhausted may *fall asleep* unintentionally wherever he or she may be, everyone *goes to sleep*, in bed if he or she is lucky enough to have one, at the end of a normal day. How will students master cataphoric reference and pronominalization or learn the collocations *provide for* and *fall asleep* – genuine NS language use – if such items disappear from the input as a by-product of simplification? The simplified texts have probably been made more comprehensible, although exactly what is understood is no longer quite the meaning of the original, but they have become less useful for language learning, their ostensible purpose. (As discussed in Chapter 8.2.5., (i) loss of realistic models of native-like use and (ii) bleeding of semantic detail are potentially damaging side effects of CLIL.)

The elaborated version of the genuine sentence in (3) is linguistically more complex that the original. Sentence length has increased from 17 to 27 words, and s-nodes from four to five, this as a result of addition of the redundant (for a NS) *to earn money* as an implicit paraphrase of *to provide for* (*to earn money to provide for his family*). Rather than remove the probably unknown *provide for* from the input, *provide for* is retained and the input elaborated by way of compensation. *Fell asleep* has also been retained. It will be up to a combination of the greater overall comprehensibility of the elaborated version, supplemented if need be by help from the teacher, to be sure that students appreciate the distinction between *go to sleep*, with which they are presumably already familiar, and *fall asleep*. One intra-sentential linker *because* expressing causality has been lost, but has been replaced by another *so*, now positioned immediately before the result (of working at night) to which it refers: *so he often fell asleep*. Further redundancy has been provided by the addition of *during his teacher's lesson*, designed both to elucidate *in class* and to clarify the temporal relationship between the night work and its classroom consequence the following day.

Having improved comprehension without sacrificing meaning or exposure to unknown target forms, and without recourse to unnatural, staccato, basal-reader-type sentences, it now remains to deal with the unwieldy nature of a sentence that elaboration has simultaneously rendered linguistically more complex than the original – 27 instead of 18 words, and five s-nodes instead of four. Recall that the research on foreigner talk discourse found that one of the two simplifications NSs often made to their speech to NNSs was to shorten utterance length. Simply splitting the elaborated version in (4) takes care of the problem, producing two sentences of acceptable complexity: an average length of 14.5 words, and an average syntactic complexity of 2.5 s-nodes, per sentence. *So* could be retained if this were spoken input, but is substituted for by *As a result* in the final *modified elaborated* version, as we are dealing on this occasion with the written mode. Two additional devices are illustrated in (4), each designed to increase the saliency of the important target collocation: **provide for** is bolded, and a correct synonym (in this context) *support*, is presented, along with two distracters, *educate* and *leave*, as a further attention-drawing device to induce focus on form. Both are optional, of course, and by no means the only ones available.[3]

It is important to stress that a materials writer does *not* need to go through all the above steps in creating task-based materials. The typical process involves only one step: either modified elaborated texts are written from the get-go, or found genuine texts are rewritten in modified elaborated form. Since the modifications involved are those that (even untrained) NSs and more proficient NNSs make spontaneously when conversing with NNSs, experience shows that materials writers quickly understand what is required and, after about just 60 minutes, can write new modified elaborated texts almost as fast as they would produce genuine texts for a NS audience. Also, for those wishing to measure results, computer software is now available to produce far more sophisticated quantified analyses of different texts and different versions of the same text than those mentioned above (see Crossley *et al.* 2007).

---

[3] Input enhancement has sometimes been found to improve vocabulary development in modified reading materials (see Chung 1995; Kim 2003, 2006). A similar effect can be achieved in listening materials by added stress and/or a brief "priming" pause before key meaning-bearing lexical items. A study by Hulstijn (1992) demonstrated the greater effectiveness of the multiple-choice format than either simple exposure or provision of L1 translations of target lexical items for improving vocabulary learning through reading – a finding confirmed in a replication study by Watanabe (1999).

9.2.4. Effects of simplification and elaboration on L2 comprehension and acquisition

With the exception of slower rate of delivery, including use of pauses (Blau 1990, 1991; Griffiths 1992; Kelch 1985) and macro-markers, i.e., signals or meta-statements about major propositions or transition-points in a lecture, such as *What I am going to discuss next is X*, or *That was the reason why X* (Chaudron & Richards 1986; but see, also, Dunkel & Davis 1994), single adjustments are alone usually insufficient to improve the overall comprehensibility of whole spoken texts, such as lecturettes (Blau 1982; Parker & Chaudron 1987). In concert, however, elaborative devices have usually been shown to improve the comprehensibility of both spoken and written input statistically significantly, or, at least, not statistically significantly less than linguistic simplification. Both simplification and elaboration facilitate comprehension most for students at lower levels of proficiency (Blau 1982; Long 1985b; Tsang 1987), but there is evidence that elaborated input can aid reading comprehension (Oh 2001) and listening comprehension and incidental vocabulary acquisition (Urano 2000) among relatively more advanced learners, as well, with some studies even finding that elaboration assists higher proficiency students more (see, e.g., Chiang & Dunkel 1992). Students' own perceived comprehension of simplified and elaborated spoken discourse is also higher (Long 1985b). Elaboration achieves its positive effects despite producing what are often, in experimental laboratory studies, very considerable increases in utterance/sentence length, syntactic complexity, and overall text length. To illustrate, consider the short excerpts from *Computer literacy for everyone?* in Table 9.3, and the descriptive statistics for the texts in Table 9.4. As assessed by standard readability measures, the difficulty of elaborated texts

Table 9.3. *Computer literacy for everyone?*

Genuine (NS–NS) version
The advent of the personal computer is often claimed to be of great social significance. The widespread availability of word-processing, for example, has supposedly had a major impact on the productivity of those who have traditionally made their living at least in part from the pen, or in recent years, from the typewriter …

Simplified version
This is the age of the personal computer. People usually say the computer is very important for society. Word-processing, for example, is easy for everyone. Many people have to write with a pen or a typewriter as part of their work. Word-processing, people think, increases the amount of writing …

Elaborated version
The advent, or arrival, of the personal computer is often claimed to be of great significance for society. For example, word-processing is easily and widely available to everyone. This widespread availability of word-processing has caused a major increase, people think, in the amount of work, or productivity, of a certain group of people. The group whose productivity has supposedly been helped in this way is those people who have always traditionally made their living, that is, earned money, at least in part from writing, either with a pen, or in recent years, with a typewriter …

Source: Long (2007e, p. 132). Republished with permission of Taylor and Francis Group LLC Books.

Table 9.4. Descriptive statistics for the computer literacy texts

	NS	*Simplified*	*Elaborated*
Words	55	52	98
Sentences	2	5	4
s-nodes	4	8	10
Words per sentence	27.5	10.4	24.5
s-nodes per sentence	2	1.6	2.5

Source: Long (2007e, p. 133). Republished with permission of Taylor and Francis Group LLC Books.

in some studies is several grade levels higher than that of the simplified equivalents, and often higher even than the original NS baseline versions.

Despite elaboration's usually unpleasant side effects on overall text length and overall readability (easily correctable in modified elaborated versions), subjects exposed to elaborated input in many of some 20 studies of listening and reading comprehension to date (for review, see Chung 1995; Kim 2003, 2006; Oh 2001; Silva 2000; Urano 2000; Yano, Long, & Ross 1994) have demonstrated improved comprehension, and often comparable (statistically non-significantly different) levels of comprehension to groups exposed to simplified versions of the same texts (e.g., Brown 1987; Oh 2001; Pica, Young, & Doughty 1987; Tsang 1987; Yano, Long, & Ross 1994). In a study of English and Spanish reading, however, Brantmeier (2005) found little benefit for the elaborative use of analogy to expand meanings of unknown lexical items, the added length of the modified passages actually hindering comprehension. Yano, Long, and Ross (1994) concluded that elaborative expansion of word meanings through parenthetical and appositive constructions provided useful definitional detail to readers, who could then make inferences about otherwise unreadable lexical items. Explicit forms of elaboration (Kim 2003, 2006), however, tend to improve comprehension better than less noticeable implicit forms. Subjects in simplified and (less often) elaborated conditions have also statistically significantly outperformed students confronted with the genuine (baseline) versions in many cases.

To illustrate, in a reading study, Yano *et al.* had 483 Japanese college students read 13 passages (ranging in length from a short paragraph to two pages) in one of three versions: genuine, simplified, or elaborated. Comprehension, assessed by 30 multiple-choice items, was highest in the simplified group, but not statistically significantly higher than in the elaborated group, and (contrary to Brantmeier's results) despite the fact that the elaborated passages were (a) 16% more complex in words per sentence, 60% longer, and nearly one grade level harder in readability than the genuine texts, and (b) 125% more complex in words per sentence, 50% longer, and six grade levels harder in readability than the simplified texts. Subjects in all three conditions had the same amount of time to complete the reading task and comprehension test. Type of text was found to interact with type of comprehension task: replication, synthesis, or inference. Performance on inference items was best among readers of elaborated texts. Yano *et al.*'s results, including the interaction effect for elaboration and question type, were replicated in a study with Korean secondary school learners of English as a foreign language by Oh (2001). In a follow-up study of the genuine, simplified, and elaborated versions of one of the texts, retention of the original propositional content was also best in elaborated texts (Long & Ross 1993), a finding with especially significant implications for educational systems operating through the medium of a second language, or partially so, as in content-and-language integrated learning (CLIL) courses (see, also, Long *et al.* 2013), as it suggests that, unlike simplification of teacher speech or textbook language, elaboration need not result in serious dilution of curriculum content over time.

In a later reading study, Urano (2000) had three randomly formed groups of ten college-age Japanese learners of English as a second language (ESL) read ten English sentences presented to them on a computer screen in one of three versions: baseline (NS), lexically simplified, and lexically elaborated. A fourth group viewed ten distracter sentences for an equivalent time period. Reading comprehension was measured by mean reading-time and comprehension questions on each sentence. A surprise vocabulary test in two sections, form recognition and meaning recognition, assessed incidental vocabulary acquisition. Urano found that both lexical simplification and lexical elaboration produced significantly improved comprehension, as shown by a (shorter) mean reading time, than was required by those in the baseline condition. Incidental vocabulary acquisition, as assessed by the form-recognition measure, was greater for higher proficiency students in the elaborated than in the baseline condition, while lower proficiency students did better with the simplified sentences than those in the baseline group. Incidental learning was small across all conditions, however, probably due to a single exposure to each target lexical item being insufficient.

In a listening study, Toya (1992) provided brief training in the recognition of six devices, first identified by Chaudron (1982) in a study of elaboration in teacher speech, used to provide implicit and explicit explanations of lexical items, and then compared the effects of implicit (IE) and explicit (EE) explanations (two kinds of elaboration) of unknown vocabulary items on the acquisition of those items. 109 Japanese university students listened to two texts three times each, taking a receptive test of the target items' meanings after each exposure, and a delayed post-test, four weeks later. In each text, one-third of the 12 target lexical items received IE, and one-third EE, while the remainder was left unelaborated, as in the original, items and treatment being rotated and counterbalanced in the three forms of each text. Understanding of the target items was found to improve with each exposure, and pre-test to delayed post-test gains were significantly greater in all three conditions. The EE version, however, produced statistically significantly higher scores than both the IE and baseline versions (although that difference had all but disappeared by the delayed post-test, presumably due simply to lack of exposure to the items during the intervening period). The more explicit explanatory devices (definition, naming, and description) appeared to induce more noticing of the targets than did the implicit devices (apposition, parallelism, and paraphrase),[4] but

---

[4] The following were two of the target lexical items (underlined here) and explanation types [EE] or [IE]. (1) "But since they [the Greeks] could not dive into the waters, they could not <u>lay bare</u> these secrets. Lay bare means to make things known." [EE] Or: "But since they [the Greeks] could not dive into the waters, they could not <u>lay bare</u> these secrets, or make these secrets known." [IE] (2) "And they also learned how not to <u>contaminate</u> the oceans. You know, when the water is contaminated, it is dirty and polluted." [EE] "And they also learned how not to <u>contaminate</u> the oceans, or not to make the ocean dirty." [IE] The possibility that EE might have worked better due to the (natural) tendency for target items to be repeated in EE seems not to have been realized, since an item-by-item comparison of post-test means showed that five items whose EE did *not* involve such repetition produced equivalent improvements over IE to those that did.

perhaps also resulted in something more like intentional learning, compared with the more incidental IE condition.[5] The beneficial effects of elaboration were clear, nonetheless. In a subsequent listening study, Derwing (1996) showed that EE instructions were significantly better comprehended by 12 Korean high school English as a foreign language (EFL) teachers than unelaborated and excessively elaborated versions. Also, the EE, IE, and unelaborated versions were significantly better comprehended than the excessively elaborated versions by 74 "high-intermediate" and "advanced" EFL college students from various L1 backgrounds, and by 19 Japanese students attending high school in Canada.

As measured by EFL students' ability to position utensils on drawings of a kitchen, Ellis, Tanaka, and Yamazaki (1994) found significantly greater comprehension of directions in the form of an interactionally modified text (in the making of which learners had been allowed to request clarifications and confirmations), than of either a baseline (NS) or premodified (NNS) version. Vocabulary acquisition was also greater in the interactionally modified condition than in the other two. In a follow-up analysis of several features of the directions, Ellis (1995) found 'range,' the number of different directions in which a target item occurred, to be positively correlated with vocabulary learning, and length of definition and number of defining characteristics (i.e., something akin to excessive elaboration) negatively correlated.

Elaboration achieves roughly comparable improvement in comprehension to simplification in studies like these, despite subjects in the elaborated conditions having to handle significantly longer texts containing significantly more complex input, and do so in the same amount of time. In laboratory studies, greater complexity and length is not a problem, as they are typical by-products of elaboration that *disfavor* the hypothesis. They need not muddy pedagogic waters, however. As noted above, *modified elaboration* – essentially, elaboration, followed by the one form of simplification found typical of NSs in the original foreigner talk research, reduction of utterance or sentence length – will deal with the unwanted side effects of pure elaboration. It should be noted, however, that studies to date have been conducted with languages that use alphabetic writing systems, and may not extend to those, like Chinese and Japanese, that employ ideographic systems, readers of which face many additional challenges (for discussion, see Long & Ross 2009).

The crucial thing about all the comparative findings on comprehensibility, to reiterate, is that elaboration does its work *without* removing from the input the very items to which students must be exposed if they are to progress. Genuine texts contain those items, too, of course, but are simply too complex for all but "advanced" learners, and so largely unusable as input for acquisition. The undeniable improvement in comprehension that simplification achieves comes at a high cost where language acquisition is concerned – removal of many, usually most, of the learning targets. For example, whereas the first 3000 running words in the original version of Robert Louis Stevenson's classic *Treasure Island* contains 145 words not found in the 2000 most common English word families (West 1953) or those in the Academic Word List (Coxhead 2000), the

---

[5]   Toya (1992, p. 94) notes that knowing they would be tested only on the vocabulary items, and not on overall comprehension of the passages, may well have led subjects to concentrate on the former, and pay little attention to the latter. This strategy would have disfavored IE, whose effectiveness resides largely in the impact it has on improving overall comprehension of target forms in context.

simplified Oxford Progressive Reader version at the 1400-headword level contains only 11 such items (Horst 2005, p. 369). Elaboration, conversely, achieves nearly as great an improvement in overall comprehension as simplification while retaining almost all unknown material, meaning that new language is available for acquisition.

It is now time to illustrate the use of elaboration, along with other desirable qualities of PTs in some sample TBLT materials. But first, a word of caution. The only people who know which materials are appropriate for a particular student or group of students are those responsible for the needs and means analysis, or at least, privy to their results, along with the teachers and the students themselves, and students' needs vary enormously. Thus, any or all the sample materials that follow may very well be unsuitable to a greater or lesser extent for the students of interest to some readers. They are offered solely as *examples* of genuine task-based materials, and with the understanding that even in cases where specific examples may be relevant, modifications would likely be necessary to cater to differences in students' age, current L2 proficiency and language aptitude, as well as such factors as the target L2 and whether it is taught in a foreign or second language environment. The focus will be on the design principles reflected in the examples.

9.3. Sample Task-Based Materials

9.3.1. Preliminaries

Sample materials consume a considerable amount of physical space in a book of this kind, so the number it is possible to include below is very limited. The aim will be to illustrate a few of the types of task-based modules that can be developed – a tiny fraction of what is possible. In my experience, the more of them one produces, the more additional possibilities one recognizes. The limited space that can be devoted to samples also precludes more than the briefest of suggestions about classroom organization or illustration of the language use and classroom discourse that would best accompany their delivery. Then again, experienced teachers will not need such guidance, and the more specific they were, the less relevant to particular teaching situations the examples would quickly become.

Second, the best materials are locally produced (assuming a minimum degree of competence on the part of the writers), as it is local program designers and teachers who know their students and their needs best, as well as whatever constraints may be imposed by limited human or financial resources and other dimensions of the teaching context, i.e., their means. For example, a module designed to handle a given target task may require more or fewer PTs, given different starting L2 proficiency and other attributes of the students in different classrooms. It is unlikely, therefore, that many of the sample materials will be suitable for teaching situations of immediate concern to the reader. They are simply intended to illustrate the principles underlying some (not all) genuine task-based materials design, including the way task complexity influences PT sequencing.

Finally, since few teachers around the world have the latest, or in many cases, any, technological aids at their disposal, nothing more than chalk and a blackboard is assumed. If even those are absent, as is the case in many rural communities in developing countries, stick drawings on the ground will suffice in some cases. With those caveats in mind, let us consider some sample task-based materials.

9.3.2. Sample modules for true and false beginners

Not all PTs in TBLT will be obviously, or visibly, related to a target task. This is especially true in the case of learners at the very earliest stages of proficiency. If students are true beginners or "false beginners," what I refer to as "building-block" tasks may be needed early in a sequence of PTs that *are* gradually more recognizable as simple approximations to one of their target tasks. Contrary to what some have argued about communicative LT, it is *not* necessary – and would imply a belief, against all the evidence, that radically different mechanisms and processes underlie earlier and later stages of acquisition – to wait until students have a basic linguistic repertoire in place before TBLT can begin.

To illustrate, the target task **Obtain and follow street directions** (see Section 9.3.3.1) will be a lot easier once students are familiar with such locative and temporal expressions as *on the right, on the left, before, after, beside, between, next to, above* and *below*. That and other relevant language can be learned through doing one or more of the Geometric Figures tasks described below, with no need for a methodologically incoherent switch to a pre-teaching of such items, i.e., focus on forms. The geometric figures tasks chosen for the purpose, e.g., Matching Shapes (Section 9.3.2.1), do not themselves look like the target task, **Obtain and follow street directions**, but provide valuable precursors to other PTs that do quickly become recognizable as less complex versions of the target task. Similarly, such target tasks as **Buy household appliances** and **Assemble laboratory apparatus** will be easier if students are already familiar with basic geometric figures and qualities, e.g., *large, small, square, straight, flat, side, long, short, round, angle, circle/circular, rectangle/rectangular, triangle/triangular,* and *cylinder/cylindrical*. Knowing how to count in the L2 will be useful, too. Again, this emphatically does *not* mean that lists of such lexical items will be taught in decontextualized isolation (focus on forms) in preparation for the PTs concerned. Rather, the usual TBLT methodology will apply. Starting as early as the very first hour of instruction, some basic PTs will be employed whose solution will draw beginning students' attention to some of the items, in context, as they work on the tasks (focus on form). Most needed target language will eventually be learned through doing the PTs in the module for **Obtain and follow street directions**.

"Building-block" tasks are basic, but they can be challenging and fun, nonetheless. They initially tend to be comprehension-based, developing students' receptive abilities first, before moving on to tasks that require production, although they usually facilitate productive abilities, too. (For a review of research findings on comprehension-based and productive-based grammar teaching, see Shintani, Li, & Ellis 2013.) They are communicative tasks, designed to provide massive, concentrated L2 exposure. Students typically have to listen and/or read *for a purpose*, however simple, and then act in some way – *do* something. The focus is always on meaning, not linguistic forms. There are myriad possibilities for stimulating task-based modules for young children (see, e.g., Shintani 2011, 2013), and for adult beginners, of which the following are but a few of many I have used over the years, each easily modified by materials writers and classroom teachers in light of what they know about their learners' current L2 proficiency, age, language aptitude, intelligence, L1 and L2 literacy, eventual domain of L2 use, skills needed, and so on. Such tasks can also serve to demonstrate to students how future TBLT lessons will run, i.e., for learner training, including practices and processes they will often be expected to follow in pair-work or small group work for students for whom such forms of classroom organization are new.

9.3.2.1. Geometric figures tasks (matching shapes) Some of the most basic "building block" tasks, usable with true beginners as early as the very first hour of a TBLT course, are a group I refer to loosely as "Geometric Figures tasks." In practice, not all of them involve geometric shapes. Some deal with two-dimensional, some three-dimensional objects, many with basic mathematical operations. The following example, **Matching shapes,** typically has three, four, or five PTs, depending on how many skills the needs analysis has shown students to require. Since this is the very first concrete example so far, and since it is intended for beginners, and since novice teachers often express skepticism over the possibility of genuine communicative L2 use so early in a course, I will sketch some pedagogic procedures and classroom management options, and try to indicate the desirable qualities of teacher speech, when using the tasks.

PT1. Which one?

The teacher draws several geometric shapes on the board – a big and a small circle, a big and a small square, a rectangle, a triangle, and so on, the exact number to be determined by students' age, attention span, and current abilities. Each shape is numbered, as in Figure 9.1. If the shapes are new to the students, the teacher begins by providing three to five minutes of extensive exposure, *elaborated input* – plenty of complete and partial repetition, segmentation, and so on – and intensive listening practice. Pointing at the numbers and shapes concerned, he or she might say, "Number 1 is a small circle. A circle. A circle. Number 1. Number 1 is a circle, a small circle. Not a *big* circle (pointing at number 2), a *small* circle. Not a small *square*. Number 3 is a small square. Number 1 is a small *circle*. Number 3 is a small square." And so on. Students simply listen at first, but are gradually brought into the "conversation," encouraged to complete the teacher's utterances: "Number 5 is a large _?" Students: "Triangle." The talk is meaningful at this stage, but not genuine communication. Once students seem to be on the way to learning the names of at least some of the shapes, the teacher asks students to identify which figure he or she is describing – **Which one?** The teacher says "a large triangle," "a small circle," and so on, handing that responsibility over to students as soon

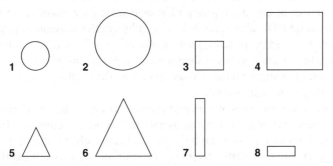

Figure 9.1. Geometric shapes for PT1 (Which one?).

as possible, too, and students identify the shape concerned, with "Number X." Being able to respond simply by using numbers means that even students with the most minimal knowledge of the L2 can participate from the get-go, and their talk, although very limited in scope, is communicative. Next, working in pairs, individual students practice asking their partner to identify shapes they name by number, and then, to name the shapes corresponding to numbers they select. The teacher circulates, praising students when warranted, reminding them of lexical items they have forgotten, and providing "corrective" feedback where needed. The whole activity probably lasts about 15 minutes. It will be reviewed in subsequent lessons, a few new items and numbers being added each time, and with imperatives and locative expressions introduced ("Put/place the blue square between the red circle and the green circle").

PT2. Matching pictures

The teacher next provides each pair of students with two identical sets of paper cutouts (laminated cardboard cutouts last longer) of the geometric shapes that figured in PT1. The sets for each pair are identical, but should differ slightly from one pair to another. The number of shapes in each set can vary according to the students' age, proficiency, and so on, but typically starts with 6–10 shapes per set. Erecting a simple "screen" between them (a book, file or bag, will suffice) to prevent students seeing each other's configuration, members of each pair of students have to describe the layout of their shapes, in whatever arrangement they choose, hidden from their partner's view, and/or use imperatives to instruct him or her as to how to arrange them, so that he or she can produce the same configuration with his or her set. "Through the eyes *and* the hand to the brain...." They are encouraged to ask each other for clarification ("A small circle?" "On the left?"), if and when the need arises. A teacher-supervised demonstration using one pair is recommended before the simultaneous pair-work commences if working in pairs or small groups is new to the students. When the students think they have succeeded in arranging their shapes in the same configuration as their partner ("The small circle is beside the big square." "On the left or on the right?" "On the left. And the big circle is below the big square," etc.), they remove the "screen," receiving immediate visual feedback on their performance. Some sets may include two versions of the same shape, differing in size and/or color, e.g., a small red circle and a small blue circle. Metalinguistic rules about adjective order (*red small circle vs. small red circle) will usually be unnecessary; the correct order will be learned incidentally from the numerous examples in the teacher input. But if students' L1 uses noun–adjective order and errors persist, their attention can briefly be drawn to the problem, in context, as they perform the task (focus on form). When the screen is removed, students can often identify the source of any discrepancies between what they intended and what their partner understood ("Oh, above, not below!"), although the assistance of the teacher or a third student assigned the (rotating) role of observer may be needed for this with some students. Pairs then exchange sets of shapes with a neighboring pair, and more intensive practice ensues, their attention maintained in part by the challenge posed by the differences in the shapes in each new set.

It is important for materials writers and teachers to adjust the *complexity* of PTs to a level that will be sufficiently challenging to hold their students' attention. In the case of the geometric figures game, sets can be sequenced rationally according to the number of figures in a set, and their distinctiveness. For example, a set containing three pairs of shapes (six in total), of different sizes and/or colors, e.g., a big and a small square, a red and a yellow square, and a green and a blue triangle, is less complex, so is sequenced before a second set containing five pairs (a total of ten figures). The second task is less complex, again, than a set of ten geometric figures, all circles and squares of different sizes, but all of the same color. A set that also includes a "surprise" previously unused shape or a non-geometric shape will be more complex, again, and will serve to push students to develop strategic competence. Even near beginners unexpectedly confronted with non-geometric shapes will often come up with imaginative metaphors to get across the idea, e.g., "like mountain" to refer to a shape with a jagged edge. Still more complexity can be created by intentionally including sets that differ in one or more ways, i.e., are *not* identical, leaving students to negotiate the additional information gap when they eventually realize something is amiss, and so on. Use of PTs that present a serious intellectual challenge is a viable way of holding the interest of highly intelligent students while their command of the L2 is still limited. Such students can quickly lose motivation if force-fed commercial materials with trivial content, i.e., that equate limited L2 proficiency with limited intelligence. A set of ten triangles, all the same color, each differing slightly in their size and internal angles, can constitute a brainteaser for the smartest adults, even doing the task in their L1.

PT3. Speed listening

Students listen to recordings of (or when electronic devices are unavailable, to their teacher reading aloud) descriptions of various (in this case, fixed) arrangements, presented on worksheets, of the geometric shapes with which they have been working. For students who will enjoy a slightly greater intellectual challenge, the descriptions may include those shapes, plus one of two previously unseen ones. The simplest items will involve two arrangements of, say, six figures each. The students are given a moment to study the pictures (Figure 9.2). They then listen to a recording of a description of one of the two pictures (or to the teacher reading it aloud), which will deliberately contain some information that rules out one of the pictures. For example, given pictures A and B in Figure 9.2, after several utterances which are true of both arrangements – "The big triangle and the small triangle are above the rectangle. The small triangle is on the right. The circle is beside the square. They are below the rectangle" – they hear "The small triangle is above the circle," which is untrue of picture A, meaning that picture B is the correct answer. In a simple version of this task, students are allowed planning time (in this case, time to study the pictures before the oral descriptions begin), and then listen and choose their answers silently. In a more difficult, speeded version, planning time is

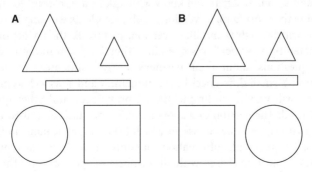

Figure 9.2. Geometric shapes for PT3 (Speed listening).

reduced or eliminated altogether, and in a game-like atmosphere, students call out the answer as soon as they think they know it, representing either themselves, a pair, or a larger group of classmates, and (crucially, to discourage guessing) then have to explain the key part of the description that revealed the correct answer. Again, as in PT2, item complexity also increases as the number and internal complexity of the arrangements increases, with the appropriate level of difficulty determined by the teacher's knowledge of students' L2 proficiency and other abilities, as well as by reduction in the time allowed to complete the task.

PT4. Speed reading

If reading is a skill that students require, PT3 can be repeated in written form, unspeeded or speeded, students this time having to read the descriptions to identify the correct pictures.

PT5. Written descriptions for a classmate

If both reading and writing are needed skills, students write short descriptions for their classmates of drawings of arrangements provided to them by the teacher. Their classmates then have to use the descriptions to arrange geometric shapes in the order indicated, or alternatively, to use the instructions to identify the correct picture among three or four provided. If the end-product does not match the original picture, as it should, the students and/or the teacher working together can follow the statements or instructions one by one until the error is identified.

As is the case with all the sample materials presented in this chapter, PTs can be modified for relevance to students' communicative needs. Thus, PT3 and PT4 are easily adapted for very different subject matter and proficiency levels, e.g., instead of descriptions of arrays of geometric figures, listening to or reading two or more biographies of famous people in a field relevant to the students, or to facts about two or three automobiles, buildings, paintings, commercial products, political parties, philosophies, countries, and so on, with only one description being accurate in each case. The nature of the PTs encourages students to pay close attention to the input. Through use of standard spoken or written input enhancement techniques, salience can be added to target lexical items, collocations, grammatical features and constructions considered important but perhaps unlikely to be noticed quickly enough without it. Finally, the entire module can easily be adapted for presentation via computer if the technology is available.

9.3.2.2. "Spot-the-difference" tasks   Spot-the-difference tasks come in all shapes and sizes, some versions involving listening skills only, some listening and speaking, some reading only, and so on. Teachers will know which skills are relevant for their students. What is probably the most familiar version involves students working in pairs, one with picture A, one with a slightly modified version, picture B, their view of each other's picture obstructed by a "screen" of some kind. They have X minutes to describe their pictures, ask questions about their partner's version and answer questions about their own, to find Y small differences between them. X and Y, as well as picture content and complexity, will vary according to the L2 proficiency and other qualities of the students concerned. The version of a spot-the-difference task described below is what is known as a *two-way task*, i.e., a task in which (a) each participant (in this case, two, but any number) begins with information that only he or she or each group member has, but which (b) must be shared with all members of the group (in this case, a pair) for the task to be completed successfully. The one-way/two-way distinction does not refer to the number of participants involved, but rather, to the direction in which uniquely held information must flow for task completion. There is a substantial store of empirical findings (see, e.g., Pica, Kanagy, & Falodun 1993; Pica *et al.* 1996) on two-way tasks (sometimes referred to as "jigsaw" tasks in the literature on LT pedagogy), dating back to my own dissertation study comparing the speech and conversation of 32 NS–NS and NS–NNS pairs working on a series of six tasks (Long 1980a, 1983b), in which the one-way/two-way distinction was a moderator variable. It was an early example of research on what, since Robinson's important work on pedagogic task-types (e.g., Robinson 2001b, 2009, and elsewhere), is now referred to as a *task condition*. In a nutshell (for more detail, see Chapter 8.4.5), two-way tasks have been shown to produce more negotiation for meaning than one-way tasks because the way information is distributed among participants means that each has uniquely held material the other(s) need(s), and so can participate on a roughly equal footing, even if of lower L2 proficiency than other group members.

The negotiation work two-way tasks motivate typically contains numerous examples of implicit, and sometimes, explicit negative feedback, as well as many other features facilitative of L2 development, as parties sustain the conversation in order to complete the task (Long 1996b). There were 16 NS–NS dyads and 16 NS–NNS dyads in the original study. The NNSs were first-semester ESL students (false beginners, somewhere between + and 1 on the ILR scale), with a (mostly passive) vocabulary of just 100–200 words. Table 9.5 contains a short excerpt from the transcript of one of the 16 NS–NNS pairs at work on a two-way spot-the-difference task. The crudely drawn cartoon-style picture that the female NS and male Brazilian student were discussing (either side of a screen) depicted a rather dysfunctional working-class British family at home in their living-room. The hard-working mother in the background was ironing clothes, while her husband lay sprawled in an arm-chair reading a newspaper, empty beer bottles and a tankard on the floor beside him. Seemingly emulating their father, two grown children lounged on a sofa nearby, wine bottles and glasses on a table (echoes here of Jan Steen's c. 1661–1664 painting, *The Dissolute Household*).[6] The instruction was to find as many differences between the two versions of the picture as possible in five minutes. Unknown to them, there were twelve differences, half involving objects present in one version, but not the other, and vice versa, making it impossible for the NS to take charge and complete the task simply by interrogating the NNS, as he/she would never guess what the new objects in his/her partner's picture might be. Although there was just one picture of the room, this particular pair treated what was happening in different parts of the room as different pictures (hence, the NS's opening "My first picture …"). In what follows, "_" = a half-beat pause, and "." = a one-beat pause, both typically employed by the NS right before and/or after a key information-bearing word, (2) = a two-second pause, T = rising, so-called "try-marking" intonation, "-" = cut-off by self or other speaker, (xxx) = inaudible utterance or part of utterance, and speech by both speakers on the same line = an overlap. Numerous common features of foreigner talk discourse are visible even in this short excerpt. Due to space limitations, I will comment on only a few of them here.

---

[6] Free reproductions of famous paintings are now often available on the Internet. Downloaded copies modified in the ways described could provide a useful source for LT materials of this kind.

Table 9.5. NS–NNS conversation on a two-way task

1	My first picture is a woman _ ironing?	
2		Woman?
3	Ironing. She's got something in her hand	
4	for making clothes flat	
5		Yes she-
6	Yeah and she's ironing	
7		Mmhm
8	blue jeans or uh something like that. And she	
9	has a cup and saucer T (2) on the board?	
10		Mmhm
11	And there's a clock on the wall. that says	
12	three o'clock?	
13		No Five o'clock
14	Oh Is that the only thing?	
15		Is five o'clock only (xxx)
16	OK So that must be the difference. What's	
17	the next picture then?	
18		And. next picture?
19	Yeah	
20		(xx) I must?
21	Yeah	I tell to-
22	You tell me this time	
23		Ok. and next picture. and man and woman .
24		sitting on the sofa maybe. yes?
25	Aha	
26		And drinking (2) uh drinking uh wine
27		maybe
28	On both of them?	
29		Uh yes. a woman drinking (and bottle) wine
30		uh bottle and man drinking (a) beer
31	Yes and she's drinking a glass or a bottle of	
32	wine?	
33		No uh she? She's drinking in (no) glass
34	Oh in the glass?	
35		No glasses
36	Not in a glass? Oh go- like a g- a wine glass.	
37	a goblet?	
38		Oh yes spec- special glass for wine
39	Oh	
40		And man special glass for beer
41	OK	
42		Yes and she have a a (xx) and book and
43		table
44	There's a book?	

Table 9.5. (*Continued*)

45		A a woman sit here
46	Aha OK (2) Whe- there's a lamp? Next to the	
47	woman? At the- at the end of the sofa by the	
48	woman there's a light . a lamp?	
49		Yes
50	Yeah?	
51		A light or lamp . yes
52	And there's a book somewhere?	
53		A book, yeah
54	Where's the book?	
55		Book on on the floor
56	Oh there's no book on *my* floor Uh in front of the	
57	woman there's a footstool (2) Is there a footstall?	
58	Some	(xxx)
59	thing for her to put her feet on?	
60		Yes
61	OK	
62		Mmhm
63	Is the- are there three bottles next to the man's	
64	feet? And one fallen over? The three standing and	
65	one fallen?	
66		Yes
67	It must be the book that's different	(xx) bottle maybe book (is different) And one bottle wine for woman yes?
68	Oh no There- she doesn't have a bottle	
70		Oh oh Bottle is different
71		
72	Yeah	
73		And table (xx) one bottle Yeah?
74	Oh? Not on this one	

Source: Long (1980a).

Already having a rough idea of the NNS' very low proficiency (this was not the first task they had done together in the series of six), the NS correctly anticipates that 'ironing,' will be unfamiliar to the NNS, pausing for half a beat (alerting the interlocutor that something important is coming next) before saying the word, and using rising intonation (a confirmation check). The learner having confirmed his ignorance of the word (line 2), the NS resorts (line 3–4) to exact repetition and use of an informal definition ("She's got something in her hand for making clothes flat") to get the meaning across, with an added confirmation, "Yeah and she's ironing" (line 6). Repetition of 'ironing' right after she has successfully communicated its meaning has the effect of providing the new form again at just the right moment for the learner to connect form and meaning. This is one reason why negotiation for meaning is so useful for lexical (and other language) development; new forms and constructions in the input are delivered, embedded in a context, when the learner is vested in the exchange and attending closely.

NSs use lexical switches both as a strategy and a tactic[7] to avoid or repair communication breakdowns in foreigner talk discourse, often returning to the original word that caused the breakdown immediately after communication has been re-established, seemingly without intention or awareness of doing so, or that they are thereby providing a perfect mini-vocabulary lesson. One example is the switch (line 36–37) from "Oh go- like a g- a wine glass . a goblet." Aware that the learner will not know "goblet," the NS, a skilled foreigner talker, initially avoids the term (a conversational strategy), switching to 'wine glass' – and then, having successfully got her message across, provides the word she had originally intended, 'a goblet,' the learner confirming his understanding with "Oh yes spec- special glass for wine" (line 38). The lamp – light – lamp sequence (lines 48–50) is another example. The pattern is sometimes broken, however, as when the NS does not return to 'footstall' after using another informal definition, "Something for her to put her feet on?" (lines 61–62) to get the meaning of that word across.

Another critical feature of negotiation work is the provision of negative feedback, ideally followed by uptake of the linguistic information contained in one implicit form that negative feedback often takes, corrective recasts. It would be tempting, but unwarranted, to infer that the NS's partial recast (she's drinking) of the learner's "a woman drinking (and bottle) wine uh bottle and man drinking (a) beer" (lines 29–30) in "Yes and she's drinking a glass or a bottle of wine?" (lines 31–32) produced successful uptake when (line 33) the learner clarifies with "She's drinking in (no) glass." However, absent a pre-test, one cannot discount the possibility that the learner already used the auxiliary, albeit variably, before this exchange, or perhaps already did so, but only with pronouns, not full NPs (a woman drinking, a man drinking). This *might* be a classic case of implicit negative feedback (both speakers' focus is on meaning throughout the exchange) successfully triggering an expansion of the learner's repertoire, but it might not. It could also simply be an echoic repetition of *she's* by the learner. However, whatever its status, it probably constituted useful production practice for the NNS.

A final feature (among many others) worth noting here is the extended example of *decomposition* (Long 1980a, 1983b) observed in lines 48–56. In decomposition, a speaker either preempts a potential communication breakdown or repairs one by shifting from a single-utterance, subject-predicate construction to a scaffolded topic-comment construction, realized over three or more utterances in an exchange. The first step is to establish the non-native interlocutor's agreement as to the immediate topic of conversation (the old, or given, information), eliciting confirmation of that before moving on to the new information, often in the form of a question or part of a question that would

---

[7] For a taxonomy of devices used as *strategies* (to avoid conversational trouble), *tactics* (to repair trouble when it occurs), and both *strategies and tactics*, see Long (1983b).

have been asked right away, without the build-up, in NS–NS interaction. To illustrate, in these two examples (from Long 1980a), decomposition is first shown in its role as (A) a strategy to avoid conversational trouble, and then as (B) a tactic to repair trouble that has arisen:

A
NS: Kyoto, right?
NNS: Yeah
NS: Yeah. What does your father do in Kyoto?
B
NS: When do you go to the uh Santa Monica? (4) You say you go fishing in Santa Monica, right?
NNS: Yeah
NS: When?

Returning to our transcript at line 42, and reflecting another positive characteristic of conversation on two-way tasks (when, in contrast to one-way tasks, topic-initiating moves are typically fairly evenly distributed among participants), it is the learner who initiates the exchange concerning the book (which figures in his version of the picture, but not the NS's version). Seeking verification of what sounds like a potential difference between their pictures, at line 46, the NS begins to use a WH question (Where's the book?), but (as she had done earlier with *goblet*) restrains herself (Whe-) in an effort to prevent a communication breakdown, resorting instead to a more elaborate and circuitous, but from the learner's perspective, simpler approach, via a combination of linguistically less complex intonation questions, starting with "There's a lamp?" (line 46). This is expanded and repeated (lines 46–48) "Next to the woman? At the- at the end of the sofa by the woman there's a light . a lamp?" (The repetition itself also contains the helpful lexical switch noted earlier.) Having requested and obtained confirmation that the NNS is following: "Yeah?" (line 50) "A light or lamp . yes," (line 51), the NS brings the topic back to the book, again via a simple intonation question, "And there's a book somewhere?" (line 52), and then following up the learner's confirmation, "A book, yeah" (line 53), with the question she had wanted to ask all along, "Where's the book?" (line 54). It is hard to convey the degree of satisfaction, enthusiasm, and obvious sense of accomplishment expressed by *both* NS and NNS in the final two utterances (lines 55 and 56) in this segment: "Book on on the floor" "Oh there's no book on *my* floor."

9.3.3. Sample modules for elementary learners

Having described a few "building block" PTs usable with students of minimal L2 proficiency, let us now consider examples of modules of PTs clearly and visibly motivated by target tasks identified by a learner needs analysis. While each module was originally written for specific TBLT programs, the templates have all subsequently been used by other programs and in microteaching sessions, with subject matter, and often, the L2, varied.

9.3.3.1. Obtaining and following street directions   The first example (Table 9.6) is a social survival module for the target task **Obtain and follow street directions**. It is suitable for students of limited L2 proficiency, who might be tourists, international students, or immigrants recently arrived in the second language environment, or foreign language learners preparing for such visits. The purpose is to raise student performance to a level at which they can politely request and understand street directions. Previous research conducted as part of a demonstration TBLT program at the University of Hawaii for the teaching of Korean as a FL had shown the need to distinguish directions given for nearby and distant destinations (for details and data, see Chaudron *et al.* 2005). This version of the module consists of eight PTs of gradually increasing complexity. Variants may include more or fewer PTs, depending on students' L2 proficiency. The final task, here PT8, serves as a criterion-referenced test of students' ability to perform the task in a real-world setting, i.e., as the exit task. The city in the example is imaginary, but the module has been used successfully with reference to many real cities relevant for the students concerned, including Langley Park, Maryland, in a first-level ESL course for Latino migrant workers at CASA de Maryland, and in translation, Seoul, in a first-semester Korean as a foreign language course at the University of Hawaii.[8] Some teaching suggestions are included in Table 9.6, along with more meta-language and commentary than space will permit in subsequent cases.

Table 9.6. Target task: obtain and follow street directions

Rationale and overview

The TT for this module is **Obtain and follow street directions**. The module consists of a sequence of seven pedagogic tasks (PTs1–7). The purpose is to raise students' performance to a level at which they can politely request, and understand street directions to both nearby and distant destinations. The first three tasks are to be done in a teacher-fronted, whole class format, although better individual students may be able to take on the teacher's role after hearing some models from you. The aim is to provide intensive exposure to typical NS directions. At this stage, the students are not required to produce, but simply to listen. During PT1, and in PT2 and PT3, they show comprehension by moving their fingers on very simple, two-dimensional street maps. The next task, PT4, still uses the simple two-dimensional maps, and is done in small groups after a demonstration by you. It involves comprehension and some production, but the emphasis here and throughout this module is on *following* directions, since this is what visitors or recent arrivals in a strange city need to be able to do and since, as such, they will rarely be in the role of direction giver. PT5 and PT6 increase the complexity of the directions and involve a real map of a real town (Waikiki). Both PT5 and PT6 provide more intensive practice of something now very close to the full target task. The final task, PT7, provides practice with as close an approximation to the target task as can easily be completed in most classrooms (unless they have special technical equipment). As such, it can serve as the exit test. The seven PTs should take about 60 minutes to complete, but times are approximate and should be adjusted by you according to your students' of progress. Pedagogic adjustments may also be needed in some cases.

---

[8]　A video of a demonstration KFL class using the Korean version of the module (Long *et al.* 2003) is available from the University of Hawaii's Second Language Teaching & Curriculum Center.

Table 9.6. (*Continued*)

PT1 *The real thing*
Materials: Tape-recorder and audio tape (or other digital recording device).
Procedure: Teacher explains that today's lesson is on how to obtain and understand street directions to nearby and distant destinations from a passer-by. Teacher then tells students to listen carefully to the three sample conversations – real examples of NS giving directions – but not to worry if they do not understand everything. He/she then plays the recording through twice (3 × 2 = six brief conversations in all). [5 minutes]

PT2 *Fragments*
Materials: OHP or Powerpoint slides (if unavailable, blackboard) and student worksheets.
Procedure: Teacher displays a series of three simple street maps on the OHP, one at a time. Students look at the same map on their worksheets. One at a time, the teacher then reads out 60 street directions fragments, 20 for each map, twice each at first, and students trace that part of the route on their worksheets with their fingers, stopping where they think the direction takes them. The teacher then repeats that direction twice more, moving his/her finger on the OHP, and students thereby receive confirmation or, if that be the case, see where they went wrong. This is not a test. Students are not asked if they were successful. It is assumed they will need numerous hearings before success becomes routine. These early PTs allow for private practice and improvement first. The 60 fragments, which gradually increase in complexity, are genuine excerpts, or only slightly cleaned up versions, or melds, from the target discourse samples obtained as part of the needs analysis. If this kind of activity is unfamiliar to your students, provide clear explanations and one or two models, as needed, before beginning. In some classes, students may be capable of taking over the teacher's role after sufficient examples. [10 minutes]
See student worksheets 1–3 for the maps, and teacher OHP transparencies (or Powerpoint slides) 1–3 for the same maps, and the accompanying worksheet for the 60 fragments.
Sample items:

1. Go straight up Main Street for two blocks, and turn right.
2. Go to the first corner and turn left.
3. Go to the first corner and take a right.
4. Go down Redfern Avenue. At the second cross street, make a right.
5. Go two blocks up Shipley. Make a right, and then take the first left. The station is on your right.
Etc.

PT3 *Where are you now?*
Materials: OHP or Powerpoint slides (if unavailable, blackboard) and three new simple maps on student worksheets. These maps are more detailed, including some additional street names and very simple three-dimensional drawings or symbols of some frequent types of buildings (school, bank, museum, etc.) and other typical landmarks (shopping mall, university, railway station, etc.).
Procedure: Same as for PT2, except that this time, (i) the directions will tend to be a little more complex because the distances involved will gradually be longer, and (ii) after each one, the teacher will ask the class, gradually shifting to individual students, a question after each one, e.g., What street are you on now? What's the building in front of you? If you are now facing north on Main, is the bank on your left or your right? (Note: Teachers should NOT teach any supposedly unknown vocabulary items first. Students can be expected to learn any such items through doing the task.) Again, allow students to take over the teacher's role if capable of doing so. [10 minutes]

(*Continued*)

Table 9.6. (*Continued*)

See student worksheets 4–6 for the maps, and teacher OHP transparencies (or Powerpoint slides) 4–6 for the same maps, and the accompanying worksheet 2 for the 60 new fragments and questions.
Sample items:

1. Go two blocks on Main, and turn left. What street are you on now?
2. Take the first right on Main. Is the school on your left or your right?
3. Go down Main, past Shipley Road, and take the next right. What street is that?
4. Continue on Redfern Avenue. Make a right, and then an immediate left. What building is in front of you?
5. Go up Main, and make a left on Shipley. Keep going straight on Shipley. How many blocks to the Modern Art Museum, and is it on the left or the right?

Etc.

PT4 *Asking the way*
Materials: Tape recorder and cassette (or other digital recording device). Worksheets with the same maps as were used in PT3. Other sheets each with a mix of 15 of the original 60 directions and questions used in PT3, and 15 new items of the same type.
Procedure: Replay the original three dialogues, once each, and three additional ones. Then divide the students into groups of four. Students work as two pairs inside each group, each pair with a copy of the map and one of the worksheets. One pair reads out the directions while the other follows them for item 1, then reverses the giver and receiver roles for item 2, and so on. Demonstrate the procedure first if this is a new kind of activity for your students. (If more practice is needed, the whole procedure can be repeated with a second pair of worksheets containing another set of 30 items, using the same maps, but with the students this time working in pairs rather than groups of four.)
[10 minutes]

PT5 *Follow the marked route*
Materials: Real three-dimensional tourist maps of the city of interest in the L2 environment for the students concerned, e.g., the map available to passengers arriving at an international airport. The map has five different routes marked on it to and from various sites, ideally in different colors. The audio-recording of ten sets of directions describing the five routes. (The teacher could read these aloud if a recording is unavailable, in which case scripted versions of the directions will be required for the teacher.)
Procedure: Students hear two versions (A to B, and B to A; C to D, and D to C; etc.) of five sets of recorded directions (= 10 in all) while following the routes already marked out by the five colored lines on the map. [5 minutes]

PT6 *Follow the unmarked route*
Materials: The same three-dimensional maps used in PT5, now one per person, and a recording with five new sets of directions from points marked on the map to destinations not marked on it.
Procedure: Students are told they are at point A (B, C, etc.), marked on their maps. They hear recorded directions to new unknown destinations, and trace the routes on the map with their fingers. The directions are in segments, with check questions of the sort used in PT3 (What's the building in front of you? What street are you on now?) as they go. Students complete this task individually, but with answers to the check questions spoken aloud and confirmed or corrected by the teacher or other students as they go. The final question after each set of directions is a variant of "Where are you?" or "What's the building we are now at?" [10 minutes]

Table 9.6. (*Continued*)

PT7 *Finding your way*
Materials: The same three-dimensional maps as in PT5 and 6. Recorded versions of five new
  sets of directions.
Procedure: Students do the same as in PT7, but in one go, i.e., without breaks and check
  questions along the way, labeling the building/space/etc. on their maps at the end of each
  route as evidence that they have successfully reached their destinations. To ensure they really
  have identified the right place, they also answer a check question of the sort used earlier, e.g.,
  "And what's the building next door/across the street?" (Note: This PT can also serve as the
  exit test for this module if a better simulation or, ideally, the real target task, is unavailable.)
  [10 minutes]

PT8 *Exit task: Virtual reality map task (or street performance)*
Using video from the target location and audio of the target discourse, complete a simulation of
  the target task. For a Spanish prototype, see, e.g., *En busca de esmeraldas* (González-Lloret
  2003). (In the case of a second language course, where learners are resident in the target
  community, they can be assigned to obtain and follow street directions to a location
  previously unknown to them, with success or failure assessed by their success in finding their
  destination successfully. Procedures and criteria for such assessments are described in
  Chapter 11.)

The first three tasks are completed in a teacher-fronted, whole-class format, although
better students may gradually be able to take on the teacher's role in PTs 2 and 3 after
hearing a few models. The aim is to provide intensive exposure to typical NS directions.
As in most task-based modules I have written or whose writing I have supervised, this
one begins with receptive skills. As usual, PT1 is designed to give students a glimpse of
the end-product – the target discourse they are aiming at – in the form of NSs performing the task in question. It is followed by one or more (in this case, two more) PTs whose
main function is to provide massive and intensive comprehensible exposure to the relevant language (60 fragments, 20 for each map, twice each at first, more if need be),
without any demands or expectations as yet that students produce the language concerned. The fragments, it is important to note, are not linguistically simplified; they are
examples of real NS language use, elaborated in this instance via partial and complete
repetition, plus the context-embedded nature of the presentation, with the two-
dimensional street maps and the teacher's gestures (e.g., indicating left and right) providing visual support. The idea is to surround students in a linguistic cocoon, rather as
caretakers do for children learning their L1. "Go straight up Main Street for two blocks
(pointing to the map and gesturing), and turn right. Go up Main Street. Go straight up
Main Street . for two blocks. Go straight up Main Street for two blocks. And then turn
right. Turn right. And then turn right. Go straight up Main Street for two blocks and
turn right. Go straight up Main Street for two blocks and turn right." The teacher does
all this while pointing out the route he or she is describing on whatever visual reproduc-
tion of the map is available – from a simple chalk drawing on a blackboard or stick
drawing on the ground to a PowerPoint slide or whiteboard projection, depending on
the program's financial and technological resources.

During PT2 and PT3, students show comprehension by moving their fingers on very simple, two-dimensional street maps with which they are provided. The next task, PT4, still uses the simple two-dimensional maps, and is performed in small groups after a demonstration by the teacher. It involves comprehension and some production, but the emphasis here and throughout this module is on *following* directions, since this is what visitors need to be able to do and since, as recent arrivals in a strange city, they will rarely be in the role of direction giver. PT5 and PT6 increase the complexity of the directions and involve a real map of a real town relevant to students in the course concerned. Both PT5 and PT6 provide more intensive practice, moving closer to the full target task. PT7 provides practice with a very close approximation to the target task.

As in most TBLT modules, initial student work, especially student production, is performed quietly, individually, *soto voce*, or in pairs and small groups, before "public" performance is requested in whole-class format. This is the opposite procedure to that which is common in courses using a synthetic syllabus and teacher-fronted, drill-and-kill language practice. The advantage is that initial performance, whether receptive or productive, which is likely to feature errors of various kinds, can be accomplished "in private," beyond scrutiny by teacher or classmates, and so without the anxiety that some students understandably feel during whole-class work, due to potential loss of face.

PT8 doubles as a further practice task and as the exit task for the module. (Procedures and criteria for use with exit tasks and task-based assessment, in general, will be the subject of Chapter 11.1–11.4.) The eight PTs should take about 60 minutes to complete, probably spread over two or three lessons, but times are approximate and can be adjusted by the teacher according to students' starting L2 proficiency and rate of progress. Other pedagogic adjustments may be needed in some cases.

The PTs in the street directions module are sequenced according to increasing complexity. (i) Tasks involving receptive skills precede those requiring production. (ii) Teachers (or recordings) provide successively fewer repetitions of fragments and (later) of complete directions. Complexity also increases according to (iii) the degree of visual support provided, and (iv) the decrease in the use of segmentation and breaks in directions (stops along the route to identify a building or wrong routes before students go too far astray). Finally, given the findings of a map-directions study by Robinson (2001b), complexity increases according to (v) whether or not the route is marked on the map. Describing a route already marked is a less complex task than working out an (unmarked) route on the same map and simultaneously describing it. Robinson found that lexical variety increased on the more complex (route unmarked) version, but that fluency was greater on the less complex (route already marked) map.

9.3.3.2. Decoding drug labels   Another problem identified by the needs analysis for CASA de Maryland's ESL program was that posed by reading the labels on containers of over-the-counter (OTC) and prescription drugs. The language used on the labels is not of the kind found in elementary level ESL textbooks, but understanding it is very important for working-class immigrant students if they or their children are the patient. It was ranked eighth among the 26 most important tasks by respondents to the CASA NA survey, part of the target task-type **Administer medicine to (self, child, other)** (Nielson 2010). In a valuable study, Epling (2011) set about analyzing the target discourse found on the drug labels and developing PTs to address the problem. Of 12 commercially published ESL textbooks she examined, only three dealt with the problem at all, and then only superficially, offering cartoon drawings of prescription bottles bearing labels with instructions like "2 TABLETS BEFORE MEALS" or "Take 2 capsules in the morning." An on-line source (LaRue 2010) was much more realistic, but still lacked the variety of language and textual structure observed in genuine labels.

Epling next gathered genuine data samples. The US Food and Drug Administration (FDA), she discovered, regulates the kind of information and the way it is displayed on OTC drug containers (see Figure 9.3), mandating a specific graphical organization of the information on package inserts. Unfortunately, while the FDA also regulates the display of information to be included on package inserts for prescription drugs (U.S. Food and Drug Administration 2009), it does not do the same for the label that appears

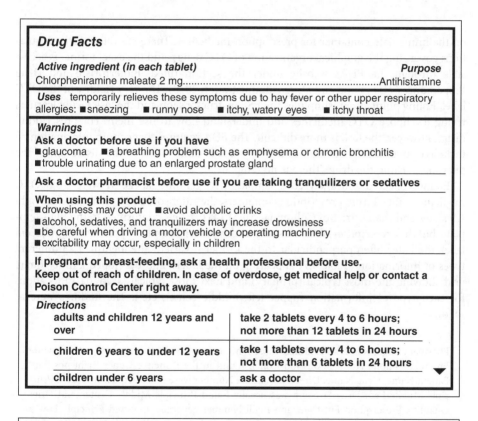

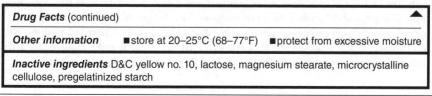

Figure 9.3. US FDA OTC medicine label template (U.S. Food and Drug Administration 2010). Reproduced by kind permission of Sarah Epling.

Table 9.7. Twenty-three types of information on prescription drug labels

Information designations			
Caution note	Prescriber name	Drug strength	Expiration date
Pharmacy logo	Pharmacist name	Drug quantity	Refill number
Pharmacy name	Patient name	Drug physical Description	Refill phone no.
Pharmacy address	Patient address	Directions	Warnings
Pharmacy phone no.	Patient phone no.	Rx number	Insurance information
Pharmacy reference no.	Drug name	Prescription fill date	

Source: Epling (2011).

on the immediate container for prescription medicines. There are rather strict regulations governing the graphical organization of OTC drugs, and the exact format is accessible through the FDA's website under the section titled 'Bioterrorism and Drug Preparedness' (U.S. Food and Drug Administration 2010). The very rigidity of the OTC label, Epling pointed out, simplifies the ESL instructor's job and the task facing learners trying to choose OTC medicines and understand how to use them. For prescription drugs, however, the task is more difficult. The FDA requires that certain information be included on all labels, but how and where this is done is left to the discretion of the pharmacy selling the drug. There is no template.

Epling collected and analyzed a sample of 93 genuine labels. 51 were from OTC medicines, and 42 from prescription containers, the latter sold by 19 pharmacies in eight US states and the District of Columbia. All 51 OTC labels conformed to the FDA template, but the prescription labels – usually both a principle and a supplementary adjacent label, the latter often perpendicular to the former – varied. She identified 23 different types of information (Table 9.7) appearing on the labels, and developed a nine-square grid showing the most typical (primary) and next most typical (secondary) locations for each type of information (upper left, middle center, etc.). The findings were as follows:

> Pharmacy Logo, Name, and Address most commonly appeared Principle Upper Left, while Pharmacy Phone Number was most often found in the Principle Upper Right position. Patient Name, Drug Name, Directions and Rx Number were most frequently located Principle Middle Left. Drug Strength was usually found Principle Middle Center, and Drug Quantity, Prescription Fill Date, and Refill Number generally appeared Principle Lower Left. The location of Prescriber Name greatly varied, being found equally in both Principle Middle Right and Principle Lower Left positions. The designation Warnings was the only information that appeared most often on the adjacent label, in the Upper Left position. All other designations, including the FDA required Pharmacist Name and Caution Note, were usually not present on the label. (Epling 2011, p. 7)

Epling then analyzed the technical and sub-technical vocabulary and collocations appearing on the labels. Of 45 imperatives and directional words and phrases employed, *take* accounted for 71%. The remaining 29% consisted of *shake, inhale, apply, inject, use,*

HS		TAKE WITH FOOD OR MILK.
Health Springs Pharmacy 555-423-5555		
4744 Fictional St.		KEEP OUT OF REACH OF
Hometown, MD 48484		CHILDREN.
DOE, JOHN Dr. Wells, B. (MD)		
KETOP ROFEN CAP 75MG		
Rx 654321		
TAKE ONE CAPSULE BY MOUTH THREE TIMES DAILY.		
QTY 30		
Feb 5, 2011		
Refills left: 1 of 3		
[[Dr. Wells, B. (MD)]]		

Figure 9.4. Prototypical prescription drug label (primary locations) (from Epling 2011, p. 11). *Note*: Items in [[ ]] represent alternative common location. Reproduced by kind permission of Sarah Epling.

instill, as directed, and *may repeat.* Direct objects varied widely. *Tablet(s)* featured 62% of the time, and *capsule(s)* 12%. Other items were *puff, drop, teaspoonful, cap(s)* (the short form of *capsule*), *spray(s), half an inch of ointment,* and zero object, as in *inject intramuscularly* and *apply to infected areas.* A larger sample of labels would undoubtedly reveal more such items.

The final stage of the project involved production of prototypical labels for CASA de Maryland ESL teachers and students based on the findings. To that end, the most common information and locations were synthesized and presented in two prototypical labels (Figure 9.4 and Figure 9.5), the first based on the most frequent primary locations for the information, the second on the most frequent secondary locations. In effect, Epling was distilling the common features of the 42 genuine labels, and editing out idiosyncratic features peculiar perhaps to just one pharmacy, to produce prototypes, just as Bartlett had done with the coffee counter conversations discussed in Chapter 7.4.4. The principal difference, aside from the modality, type of information and language involved, was the importance of the physical location of information in the drug labels.

It is not hard to see how PTs could be developed and sequenced. First (PT1) would come a genuine prescription drug label (Figure 9.6) – this simply to provide students with a glimpse of what the full (written) target discourse looks like. Next (PT2), taking the first prototypical label (Figure 9.4) as the starting-point, much simpler versions would be presented, perhaps beginning (depending on students' proficiency) with just a (real, local) pharmacy name, address and phone number, (fake) patient and physician names, and the name of a (real) drug. The teacher might then (PT3) establish the importance of knowing where to look on a label for which type of information by drawing students' attention to correct and incorrect locations. The next, slightly more

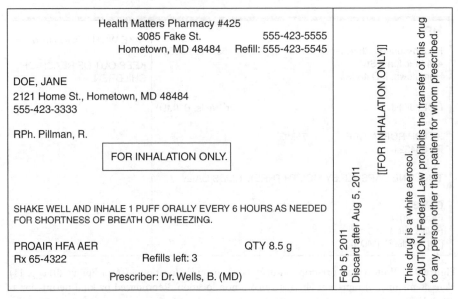

Figure 9.5. Prototypical prescription drug label (secondary locations) (from Epling 2011, p. 11). *Note*: Items in [[ ]] represent alternative common location. Reproduced by kind permission of Sarah Epling.

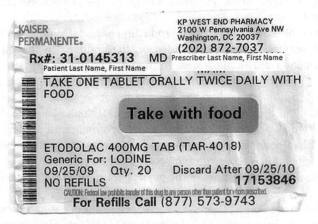

Figure 9.6. A genuine prescription drug label (from Epling 2011, p. 40). Reproduced by kind permission of Sarah Epling.

complex, version of the label (PT4) – more complex for the number of information bits it contained – would include the previous information, plus the dosage instruction, "TAKE ONE CAPSULE BY MOUTH THREE TIMES DAILY," along with the two warnings, students' attention again being drawn to the locations for each type of information. Next (PT5), using genuine lexical items and collocations from Epling's lists (*shake, inhale, inject, puff, drop, teaspoonful,* etc.), several alternative directions and dosages would be substituted, the meanings fairly easy to make clear, given that most items readily lend themselves to simple drawings and/or mime. The same procedure would follow (PT6) with the secondary label (Figure 9.5). Just how far and fast the increase in PT complexity occurred, and hence, the number of PTs required, would depend, as always, on student proficiency, aptitude, and teacher judgment. Such directions as "Shake well and inhale 1 puff orally every 6 hours as needed for shortness of breath or wheezing" might at first look too difficult for students requiring the earlier PTs, but in fact can easily be taught through elaboration – breaking the direction down into manageable segments (*shake well, inhale, 1 vs. 2 or 3 puffs,* etc.), plenty of repetition and visual support, in this case, perhaps including drawings or realia (sample capsules, inhalers, tablets, ointments, etc.) taken into the classroom. Each PT might last 5–10 minutes, a sequence of 6–8 spread out over three or four lessons. The exit task would consist of a test of students' ability to read 10 genuine OTC and prescription drug labels and locate the information required to match each of them to one of ten simple line drawings representing the most critical components of all labels: items (capsules, tablets, etc.), actions (shake, inhale, etc.), and dosage (twice daily, every six hours, etc.).

9.3.4. Sample modules for intermediate learners

9.3.4.1. Negotiating a police traffic stop   One of the target tasks identified by the needs analysis conducted for CASA de Maryland's ESL program in 2009 (repeated in 2010) was **Negotiate a police traffic stop**. Recently arrived Latino and African migrant workers in the USA often work as day laborers in landscaping, construction, and allied trades, or as house cleaners. The more successful among them may eventually acquire their own means of transport, frequently a cheap, much used pick-up truck suitable for ferrying the owner(s) and their equipment from job to job. The vehicles are often in a poor state of repair, and the drivers new to US traffic regulations, or in many cases, to driving at all. These factors, as well as racial profiling in some jurisdictions, result in a higher than proportional number of incidents in which L2 speakers are pulled over by patrolling police cruisers. Most reasons for stops involve vehicle equipment violations (defective brake lights, unlit license plates, unsafe loads, etc.) or traffic violations (erratic lane changes, illegal turns, speeding, failure to stop at red lights, etc.). Police traffic stops are difficult for many NSs to negotiate; for many poor immigrant workers with little or no English, they are very intimidating prospects, indeed, even when they can produce a valid driving license and paperwork showing current registration and insurance.

Knowing how critical the police traffic stop was for numerous students, in what was to prove another very valuable study, O'Connell (2012) examined six commercially published textbooks ostensibly dealing with social survival topics. As is so often the case, such treatment as there was (in just one of the six) was superficial, unrepresentative of genuine target discourse, and clearly designed as thin cover for a grammar drill, in this case, of the past continuous (*Ms. Chi was speeding. Mr. Garcia was driving and talking on his cell phone. He wasn't using a headset*). Some useful lexical items were provided (*speeding, changing lanes, turn signal*, etc.), but so that students could use them in a *report* of a traffic stop they or someone they knew had experienced, not for negotiating a stop themselves – text-based, not task-based.

O'Connell then set about gathering genuine samples of target discourse. This proved more difficult than usual, due to the unpredictability of traffic stops and to US laws on the confidentiality of such encounters, although many are in fact recorded for subsequent use by the police themselves, sometimes by dashboard-mounted video cameras.[9] Nevertheless, through perseverance and the helpful cooperation of four of the five police departments he contacted, plus coincidentally experiencing a police traffic stop of his own (an unplanned case of participant observation in L2 NA), O'Connell was eventually able to obtain the data he needed. The four departments provided sample scripts officers used when making a traffic stop – scripts which provided a rough guide as to what to expect, but from which officers inevitably departed in practice, it turned out – and one made its traffic safety officer available for a 60-minute interview. Two allowed him to participate in their "ride-along" programs, via which civilians can accompany an officer during a shift while out on patrol. He also interviewed one of the officers with whom he was riding.

Some of the crucial information to emerge from the first interview and subsequent comments from the two officers – perhaps obvious to US residents, but not to many others – was the importance of drivers always carrying some form of identification, even if not a driver's license, and of drivers always remaining in their car when pulled over, unless instructed to do otherwise, stepping out being interpreted as a sign of aggression. The situation is the exact opposite in some countries, e.g., Egypt, where remaining seated in the car would be interpreted as a sign of disrespect.[10] One officer noted the difficulty limited English speakers have in understanding the distinction between warnings, which require no further action by them, and citations, especially as the "tickets" look similar, and among the three options one has upon receiving a citation: plead guilty and pay the fine by mail, plead guilty, but go to court to ask for leniency (which does not require the presence of the ticketing officer), and plead not guilty and go to court to contest the charge (which does require the presence of the ticketing officer). Also problematic is the distinction between a regular driver's license and a commercial license, the latter being required to drive any kind of commercial vehicle, as is the ability to speak English. With or without a commercial license, migrant workers driving small pick-up trucks or vans containing landscaping, construction or house-cleaning equipment, and so on, are also frequently unaware that by law in the State concerned, a commercial vehicle can be pulled over at any time for inspection, even if no traffic violation has occurred.

[9] Recordings or transcripts thereof can only be released by court order, even when identifying information is removed.

[10] Once again, cultural information is shown to be critically important – potentially more important than grammatical accuracy. The obligation to remain in one's vehicle when pulled over is well understood by US motorists. Similarly, it is obvious to them, but alas, not to recent arrivals from many societies, that to offer a bribe to the police officer who pulled them over would be treated as a far more serious offense than the traffic violation itself. In some countries, conversely, it is routine for motorists to offer police officers a bribe, and for the bribe to be accepted.

While not allowed to record any stops, O'Connell was permitted to eavesdrop the conversations with motorists who were pulled over during the ride-alongs he made with the two officers, observing five such stops by one, and three by the other. He wrote down as much as he could of the conversation in the moments immediately following each one, eliminating any potential identifying information, with the officer helping him fill in any gaps in what had been said. Table 9.8 contains three examples. It was clear that once officers obtain the documents and information they demand, they typically dominate the rest of the conversation, explaining why the driver was stopped, the outcome

Table 9.8. Police traffic stops

First example:

OFFICER:	Good evening
DRIVER:	( )
OFFICER:	Can I see your license and registration please.
DRIVER:	(Yes.) Why'd you stop me?
OFFICER:	The lights over your license plate don't work.
DRIVER:	Oh (*giving license & registration*)
OFFICER:	You're the owner of the van?
DRIVER:	Huh?
OFFICER:	This isn't your van?
DRIVER:	No, it's my uncle's.
OFFICER:	Okay. And you still live here, in xxx?
DRIVER:	No, I'm living with my uncle, in xxx.
OFFICER:	Okay, what's the full address?
DRIVER:	xxx, xxx.
OFFICER:	xxx xxx. Okay. Okay, please stay in the van and I'll be back with you in a few minutes.

(Roughly 5 minutes pass)

OFFICER:	Okay, so this here is a repair order for that light. The repair order means you have ten days to fix the light – or I mean your uncle does, since it's his van. You-, your uncle then has 30 days to get this page of the repair order back to us. Tell him he can have this signed by any service station that's licensed to do state inspections, or because it's a light and it can clearly be seen that it's fixed or not, you can have a police officer sign it. Okay?
DRIVER:	Yeah, (I need to fix the light and submit this form).
OFFICER:	Exactly. And the directions are printed on there as well.
DRIVER:	But we need someone to sign saying it's been fixed?
OFFICER:	Yes. You can get that signature from any service center that does state inspections, or from any police officer. Not just xxx PD, any police officer. Okay?
DRIVER:	( )
OFFICER:	And if you don't take care of this your tags will be suspended –and you don't want that.
DRIVER:	Okay, so got to a state inspection gas station and get it fixed and have them sign it.
OFFICER:	Within ten days. Or your tags will be suspended.
DRIVER:	( )
OFFICER:	Okay, have a good night.

(Continued)

Table 9.8. (*Continued*)

Second example:

OFFICER: Good evening, I'm Officer xxx with the xxx Police Department.

DRIVER: ( )

OFFICER: Could I see your license and registration, please?

(*Driver talks to passenger, driver gives license and registration*)

OFFICER: (*to passenger*) Oh, this is your car?

Passenger: Yeah

OFFICER: I'll need to see your license too.

(*Passenger gives license*)

OFFICER: So you know what I stopped you for?

DRIVER: Yeah, I was going too fast.

OFFICER: You were going *way* too fast. I clocked you at over 65 as you passed me and then I could hear the car roar as you were accelerating up the hill.

DRIVER: I'm sorry– I just, I hadn't driven stick in a while and wanted to see what his car could do. I know it was stupid, I'm really sorry.

OFFICER: ( )

DRIVER: We're actually both members of the xxx racing team.

OFFICER: Really.

DRIVER: Yeah.

OFFICER: Okay. I'm going to ask you stay in the vehicle and I will be back with you in a few minutes.

(*Roughly 5 minutes pass*)

OFFICER: (*handing back licenses and registration*) Okay, here's the deal. I'm writing you up for speeding, for going 64 in a 45. You know you were going faster than that.

DRIVER: Yeah, I'm sorry.

OFFICER: That's going to knock down the fine, because 20 miles over the speed limit increases the fine considerably. I'm also giving you a break by not giving you a citation for excessive speed, or for negligent driving. I don't care if you're a xxx racer and know how to drive. There are a lot of people out on this road, and driving like that is extremely dangerous.

DRIVER: I know I'm sorry.

OFFICER: So I could write you up for multiple offenses.

DRIVER: ( )

OFFICER: (*giving citation*) You'll see on the citation there that you have three options. You can plead guilty and pay the fine by mail. Or you go to court, still plead guilty but explain to the judge why you were going 64 in a 45. Or number three, you go to court and I go to court and the judge decides if you're guilty or not.

DRIVER: Okay.

OFFICER: And regardless of what you decide, if you don't take care of it in 30 days, they suspend your license. Understand?

DRIVER: Yes, thanks.

OFFICER: Okay. Have a good evening and drive carefully.

Table 9.8. (*Continued*)

Third example:

OFFICER: Good evening, I'm officer xxx with the xxx police department.

DRIVER: ( )

OFFICER: Can I see your license and registration? (*gesturing to passenger in front seat*) And yours too.

(*Driver gives license & registration; passenger gives license. Officer looks at documents*)

OFFICER: So this is your car?

DRIVER: Yes.

OFFICER: Now I don't know what [name of State] law is [the *car has out-of-state license plates*], but in [name of State] you can't turn right on red without stopping.

DRIVER: I didn't stop?

OFFICER: No. I was back there watching the intersection and you slowed down, but you didn't stop. A red light means you're supposed to stop.

DRIVER: Right.

OFFICER: Where are you coming from tonight?

DRIVER: We were at a friend's house, over (xxx)

OFFICER: Over, just over the other side of 193?

DRIVER: Yes.

OFFICER: Okay. And where are you heading?

DRIVER: Home. I live on [street name], just off St. Andrew's.

OFFICER: Right. Okay.

DRIVER: So am I going to get a ticket?

OFFICER: I don't know what I'm gonna do yet. Give me a few minutes and I'll be right back. Make sure you stay in the car.

(*Approximately 20 minutes pass*)

OFFICER: (*handing driver warning print-out*) Okay, so I'm giving you a warning tonight. And though it's just a warning, which means no points and no fine, it is in the system and if we pull you over again, we'll know that you've been given a warning. So be sure to come to a full stop at red lights in the future.

DRIVER: Okay, thank you.

OFFICER: (*returning licenses and registration*) And here're your licenses and the registration.

DRIVER: Thank you.

OFFICER: Okay, have a good evening; drive safely.

Source: O'Connell (2012). Reproduced by kind permission of Stephen O'Connell.

(warning or citation), and the steps the driver must take as a result (no action or action, respectively). Drivers do not need to say much more, but they do need to understand what the officer tells them.

The next task was to distill the commonalities in the eight transcripts available, in order to produce a prototypical example of the police traffic stop. To that end, O'Connell identified the obligatory and optional moves evidenced in the conversations, as shown in Figure 9.7. Things would differ in the event of such eventualities as a driver being unable to produce a driving license or a previous arrest showing up on the officer's computer. The typical pattern, O'Connell observed, was for officers to greet the car occupant(s) and introduce themselves (probably), ask for a driver's license and registration (always), ask for identification cards from passengers (possibly), ask about

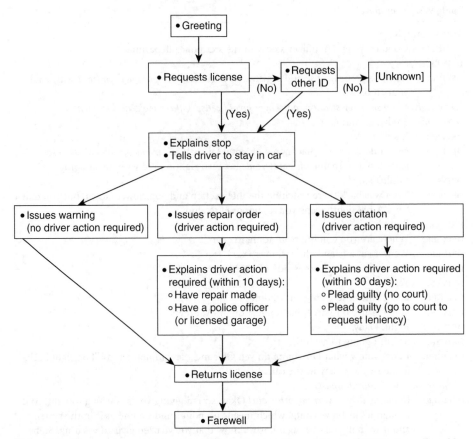

Figure 9.7. Linear schematic structure of the traffic stop (from O'Connell 2012). Reproduced by kind permission of Stephen O'Connell.

ownership of the car (possibly), explain why the driver had been stopped (always), ask where the driver was going (possibly), tell the driver to stay in the car while he checked the information on the computer in his patrol car (always), "lecture" the driver about their violation(s) (probably), issue a warning, repair order or citation (always), explain any action required of the driver or options regarding payment of the fine or court appearance (always), return the license (always), and bid farewell (always). Variations on this basic structure were usually the result of issues introduced by the drivers, not the police officers, e.g., the vehicle belonging to someone other than the driver, mitigating (or exacerbating) circumstances volunteered by the offending motorist (e.g., in the second example, *I hadn't driven stick in a while and wanted to see what his car could do* (sic), and, given the circumstances, the rather astonishing *We're actually both members of the xxx racing team.*

As is so often the case, even in such everyday, "non-specialist" discourse domains, some important sub-technical lexical items and collocations were apparent, items unlikely to be covered in typical commercially published materials. They included *points* (on a license), (license) *plate, in the system* (i.e., an electronic record has been made of the stop), *repair order, tags, clocked, negligent driving, intersection, ticket, warning, citation, issue a warning/citation, lenient,* and *grant leniency.* Such items would not be pre-taught (focus on forms) in TBLT, but learners' attention might well be drawn to them in context (focus on form) when they occurred in elaborated task-based materials, probably using verbal input enhancement by the teacher, and/or visually through italics or bolded print.

Based on the schematic representation of moves in a police traffic stop, stripping away idiosyncratic moves and topics, incorporating language from the genuine originals, and given differences in the two events, O'Connell produced two prototypical dialogues (Table 9.9), one for a traffic stop resulting in issuance of a warning, one for a citation. Building on O'Connell's work, I would suggest a module consisting of the following six PTs, sequenced by task complexity, as sufficient to prepare students to deal with a police traffic stop, should the need arise.

PT1. The police traffic stop: Introduction of the topic (Schema-building)

Tell students the lesson is going to be about police traffic stops. Ask what sorts of things police officers stop drivers for (speeding, running red lights, failing to stop at a stop sign, broken headlight, etc.). Recast student responses, feeding in some of the new target lexical items and collocations and (assuming students are literate in the L2) writing them on the board. Ask students what kinds of questions they think police officers ask drivers after they have stopped them, recasting as needed. Ask students to recount any traffic stops they have experienced – when, where and why they were stopped, and the outcome.

PT2. The real thing

Play a recording (given that the original is unavailable, this will be a reenactment) of one or more of the genuine sample dialogues to give learners an understanding of the overall linguistic demands of the target task. Possibly play the recordings a second time, and then in segments. Play each segment of the police officer's turn one, two or three times, depending on student proficiency and language aptitude, pausing to allow students to summarize, explain and comment on it. After each segment, ask a volunteer to explain the police officer's turn. Then listen to the actual driver's response.

PT3. What happened?

Depending on students' L2 proficiency, use genuine dialogues or elaborated versions. Students listen to the dialogues as many times as needed until they can explain why the driver was stopped, what the outcome was (warning, citation, repair order), and what action, if any, was required. There is plenty of opportunity here for injecting a game-like quality to the PT, and upping or lowering the intellectual challenge, depending on the kinds of students involved. For example, all sorts of drivers' excuses can be inserted in the recordings, with various effects on the police officer. If so, questions can also be asked about what the excuses were, and whether they were successful. More subtly, and especially for students who appreciate a greater intellectual challenge, questions can be asked about matters not directly referenced in the dialogues, but about which reasonable inferences can be made, based on what was or was not stated. Examples include, but are by no means limited to, the age, gender and occupation of the driver, the age, gender, personality and mood of the officer, the kind of vehicle involved, the time of day and location of the stop, and the police officer's receptiveness to any excuses the driver offered.

Table 9.9 Prototypical warning and citation dialogues

(a) The warning

OFFICER:	Good evening ma'am. I'm Officer Smith with the Pleasantville Police Department. Can I see your license and registration please?
DRIVER:	Sure, here they are. (*Gives officer documents*)
OFFICER:	Okay. And is this still your current address?
DRIVER:	Yes, it is.
OFFICER:	Okay. Now, I stopped you because one of your brake lights, your rear left brake light, is out. Were you aware of that?
DRIVER:	No, no I wasn't.
OFFICER:	Okay. Please stay in the car and I'll be back with you in a minute. (5–10 minutes pass)
OFFICER:	Okay, ma'am. I'm giving you a warning on the brake light. (*Gives driver warning*) You need to get that fixed, though, as it's a violation that you could be cited for. Okay?
DRIVER:	Yes, sir, thank you.
OFFICER:	And here's your license and registration. (*Gives driver documents*)
DRIVER:	Thank you.
OFFICER:	Have a safe evening, and be careful pulling out here.

(b) The citation

POLICE OFFICER:	Good evening, sir. I'm Officer Smith with the Pleasantville Department. May I see your license and registration, please?
DRIVER:	Sure. Here they are. (*Gives officer documents*)
OFFICER:	Okay. And is this still your current address?
DRIVER:	Yes.
OFFICER:	Okay. You know why I stopped you, right?
DRIVER:	I was driving over the speed limit?
OFFICER:	Yes, you were driving well over the speed limit. I clocked you on the radar gun at 63. This is a 45-mile-per-hour zone.
DRIVER:	Sorry, I didn't realize I was going that fast.
OFFICER:	Right. Just stay in the car for a few minutes and I'll be right back. (5–10 minutes pass)
OFFICER:	Okay. I'm giving you a citation for speeding. Now, you've got three options for how to proceed. One, you can plead guilty and pay the fine. Two, you can plead guilty but ask for a court appearance, and you'll have a chance to explain whatever reasons you had for driving almost 20 miles per hour over the speed limit. And maybe the judge will reduce your fine or the number of points. Your third option is you plead not guilty and you go to court and I go to court and we both tell our side of the story and the judge makes a decision. You got all that?
DRIVER:	Yes.
OFFICER:	That same information is printed on the citation (pointing) there, as well. (*Gives driver citation*)
DRIVER:	Okay.
OFFICER:	And here's your license. (*Gives driver license and registration*) Now, I could've also given you a citation for reckless driving, which would be an additional $225 fine, but I'm giving you a break.
DRIVER:	Okay, thank you.
OFFICER:	You have a safe evening, and watch your speed.

Source: O'Connell (2012, pp. 18–19.) Reproduced by kind permission of Stephen O'Connell.

PT4. Reading along

Students read the transcripts silently, two or three times, while listening to a recording of them, associating sounds with symbols. Afterwards, they answer the same set of questions, e.g., Why was the driver stopped? What was the outcome? What does the driver have to do?, along with any of the subtler ones.

PT5. Role play 1

PT5 is a two-way task, moving from receptive to productive abilities. Place students in groups of three. Give each of the students playing the officer and driver a cue card. The card for student A, playing the role of the officer, explains why he or she has pulled the driver over. Student B, playing the driver, is given some information about such things as his or her identity, and the ownership of the vehicle. Student C observes. The outcome will be whatever students A and B negotiate. When the exchange is complete, student C will summarize and report the following information, first to students A and B, and then to the class: why the driver was stopped, the outcome, and what the driver needs to do. Roles are rotated, so that all students have an opportunity to play the part of the police officer, the driver and the observer.

PT6. Role play 2: the exit task

The exit task would be in two parts. First, students listen once to recordings of three new traffic stops, answering these questions after each one: Why was the driver stopped? What was the outcome? What action is required? Second, in another role-play, and depending on time and resources available, the instructor, another teacher or an official program assessment specialist plays the part of a police officer. The student plays the part of a driver. The teacher's colleague or the assessment specialist observes. The student must negotiate a hypothetical traffic stop, the key elements of which are fixed and specified on a cue card. The observer/assessor must judge whether the student/driver was able to (i) understand and respond appropriately to the police officer's questions and instructions, and (ii) explain three things to the assessor: Why they were stopped, the outcome of the stop, and what, if anything, they need to do as a follow-up to the stop. (For a rationale and more detailed examples of criterion-referenced, task-based performance tests, see Chapter 11.1–11.4. For another example of the use of role-play as a way of testing task-based communicative abilities, this time those of immigrant healthcare professionals in a clinical setting, see Bosher & Smalkoski 2002).

9.3.4.2. Delivering a sales report   The second example of a module suitable for intermediate learners – perhaps students of a L2 for occupational purposes in a second or third semester foreign language course – concerns the target task **Deliver a sales report**, eventually to be done both orally and, if the NA indicates that is appropriate, in written form. The materials comprise six PTs and take a total of about 90 minutes to complete, typically as part of two or three lessons, although I have often had pre-service and in-service teachers studying TBLT complete all six in about half that time, due to their superior command of the L2.

Computer sales in the USA and Japan

PT1. Desk-top sales in the USA and Japan, 1982–1987

PT1 is a two-way task. Students are divided into groups of four. Pairs or groups of three would be acceptable, although not as useful. Each group member receives two randomly chosen slips of paper (laminated cardboard is more resilient) from a set of eight, each containing information about trends in sales of desk-top computers in the USA and Japan from 1982 to 1987. The eight pieces of information in the group are different. The information can be read aloud, asked about, explained, paraphrased and discussed by the group as often as needed, but must not be shown to other group members. If it becomes helpful, notes can be taken of relevant numbers in other people's clues, but the clues themselves must not be written down verbatim from dictation. The first objective is to complete Table 1 (see Figure 9.8), working together as a group. The eight clues are as follows. They are numbered here for ease of reference, but would not be in the real materials.

1. Japanese sales increased by fifty percent to six million in 1985.
2. US sales rose by one million in 1983 and 1984, and then remained unchanged for two years.

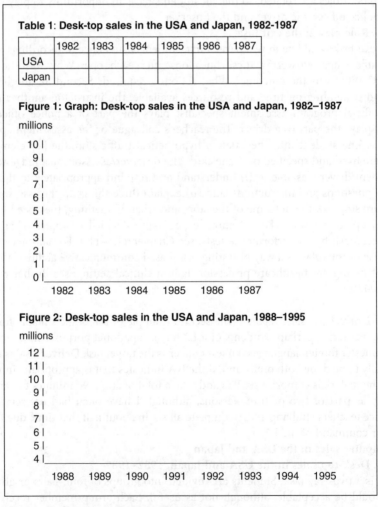

Table 1: Desk-top sales in the USA and Japan, 1982-1987

	1982	1983	1984	1985	1986	1987
USA						
Japan						

Figure 1: Graph: Desk-top sales in the USA and Japan, 1982–1987

Figure 2: Desk-top sales in the USA and Japan, 1988–1995

Figure 9.8. Computer sales in the USA and Japan.

3. Japanese sales were one million in 1982.
4. US sales were double those of Japan in 1982.
5. Japanese sales for 1983 equaled those of the US in the previous year.
6. US sales in 1987 equaled US sales for 1982 and 1983 combined.
7. Japanese sales declined by one million in 1986, and rose again to eight million the following year.
8. US and Japanese sales were the same in 1984.

Students typically start by reading their clues aloud in random order and quickly realize that most are (by design) useless on their own. The information they contain must be pooled for the (two-way) task to be completed. Sooner or later, they discover that clues numbers 1 and 3 provide the only combination of a date and hard sales number, i.e., the necessary "anchor points." Once that is recognized, the other information gradually falls into place. If Japanese sales were one million in 1982, and (clue # 4) US sales were double those of Japan in 1982, US sales were two million that year. If US sales were two million in 1982, and (clue # 2) rose by one million in 1983 and 1984, and then remained unchanged for two years, they must have been three million in 1983, and four million in 1984, 1985, and 1986. And so on. It sounds simple, and is, but depending on students' L2 proficiency, intelligence and (very basic) math skills, about 15 minutes and a considerable amount of negotiation for meaning is usually required before Table 1 is completed satisfactorily. Without realizing it, learners receive a lot of intensive listening and speaking practice, during which the task leads them to attend very carefully to the relevant numbers, dates, and key lexical items and collocations – all useful when reporting and comparing change, and rate of change, (in this instance) in sales over time: *increased by, rose by, remained unchanged, double, equaled, previous, combined, same* and *declined.*

PT2. Graphing the data

Using the data from the now completed Table 1, students draw two lines, one each for the two countries, converting the numbers to visual (graph) form (Figure 9.8).

PT3. True or false?

Students next use the data they have entered in Table 1, and the graph they just completed in Figure 1, to determine whether the following statements are true or false, circling T or F as appropriate. Some items require inferences from the slopes of lines in the graph, often generating discussion among group members.

1. US and Japanese sales both rose in 1985.
2. Six million desk-top computers were sold in the USA from 1982 to 1984.
3. The percentage sales increase in the USA from 1983 to 1984 was higher than that in Japan for that period.
4. Sales in the USA in 1984 were the same as those in Japan in 1987.
5. US and Japanese markets showed similar rates of growth after 1986.
6. Based on the trend from 1982 to 1987, the Japanese market was projected to show greater improvement than the US market in 1988.
7. Japanese sales increased steadily from 1982 to 1984, remained stable until 1986, and then fell sharply.
8. US sales peaked in 1984.
9. US sales were at their lowest in 1983.

10. Based on the 1986–87 data, Japanese sales had probably reached their highest, and were expected to decline after 1988.

Several additional useful lexical items and collocations are included in the true/false statements, some of which will probably already be known by intermediate students, some not: *sold, percentage increase, higher than, the same as, similar, rates of growth, trend, projected, show improvement, market, steadily, remained stable, until, fell sharply, peaked, at their lowest, their highest, expected to,* and *after.* Students pool their knowledge of such items, with help from the teacher or recourse to a dictionary as needed.

PT4. Spot the factual errors

Based on the information in Table 1 and the graph, students (working individually or in pairs) decide which of the following paragraphs is factually correct, circling A, B or C. To make sure they read all three paragraphs carefully (often more than once), they are told that it is possible that more than one paragraph is correct or that none of them are. They must underline any sentences which contain incorrect information. This reading task requires students to *attend* to the input very carefully. Their focus is on meaning, but incidental uptake of new forms in the input is probable – especially of collocations, which students will encounter multiple times within a short period as their eyes flit back and forth between picture and texts. When answers are discussed within the reconstituted groups and/or in a whole-class format, students must justify their answers with reference to the Table they completed and/or the graph they drew. If students are very smart and/or of fairly advanced proficiency, PT4 can be used as a speed-reading task.

A. US computer sales showed a steady increase from 1982 to 1984. They then remained the same for two more years before rising again in 1987. Japanese sales were more erratic. They doubled from 1982 to 1983, and again from 1983 to 1984. They increase another fifty percent the following year, but then declined in 1986. The figures for 1987 were encouraging, but not as good as US sales that year.

B. US and Japanese computer sales both improved over the period 1982–1987. The growth in US sales was fairly steady, with each year's sales either equaling or improving on those of the previous year. Japanese sales rose eight hundred percent during the same period, but the growth was a little more uneven. Japanese sales doubled three times from one year to the next, but they also declined once.

C. US computer sales either remained unchanged or rose by at least twenty-five percent each year from 1982 to 1987, increasing by a total of two hundred and fifty percent during the six-year period. Japanese sales were even stronger, however. While starting lower in 1982, they equaled US sales in 1984 and were higher than US sales each year after that. Japanese sales showed an eight hundred percent increase from 1982 to 1987.

PT5. Complete the model paragraph

Students copy the following paragraph, completing it as they go, using information in Table 1 and the graph. The focus is not on grammatical forms, as is more often the case with what is in effect a modified close passage, but on the recently learned lexical items and collocations, control over which they are in the process of improving.

US computer sales were _____ those of Japan in 1982, but Japanese sales _____ in 1983 and _____ again in 1984, when they _____ US sales for the first time. Whereas US sales then _____ unchanged for the next two years, Japanese sales _____ fifty percent in 1985, _____ by twenty-five percent in 1986, and then _____ sharply to eight million in 1987.

PT6. Describe the graph – the exit task

Students write a new paragraph comparing computer sales in the USA and Japan from 1988 to 1995, based on the data in the second graph, in Figure 2. They complete the second graph as they choose, extrapolating from the shapes of the lines in their first graph. If additional writing practice is desirable, students write one or two paragraphs reporting computer sales in the two countries over the entire 13-year period, 1982 to 1995. If time is available and the needs analysis dictates, students prepare and deliver an oral and/or written sales report related to new products or services in their own field (automobiles, pharmaceuticals, real estate, electronics, healthcare, landscaping, cleaning, etc.) or a field of general interest, using whatever technological aids they would normally employ for the purpose. Sales report modules, like most at the intermediate level, can easily be made more complex and, thereby, suitable for higher proficiency students.

9.3.5. Sample modules for advanced learners

9.3.5.1. A complex political issue   TBLT modules for advanced students offer materials writers a wide range of options, limited only by their imagination, and in some settings, by logistical or resource constraints, such as lack of student access to computers or the Internet. 'Advanced' in this context refers to high school or college students in the fifth semester or higher of a language, or adults at or above ACTFL Advanced, ILR 2 or CEFR B2. My own preference is for modules in the shape of informal research projects, adapted to students' L2 proficiency and cultural background, but also very much to their academic or occupational fields of interest and needs, and pitched at an appropriate level of intellectual challenge. Doing research (in the broadest sense) is what students have to do in the real world and is an activity that holds their attention and lends itself to a hands-on, learning-by-doing approach to language learning. From middle-management on up, it is a common component in the work in many occupational fields, as well, although the issues of interest typically differ, of course. More complex versions of the module for **Deliver a sales presentation** can work well at the advanced level, with genuine or only slightly elaborated texts employed as source materials.

The first example (see Table 9.10) was originally produced in 2002 as an English template for materials production for the TBLT Korean Flagship Program at the University of Hawaii, then housed in the Second Language Studies Department, for which I was Principal Investigator and Director. The short descriptions of steps in the instructional sequence are self-explanatory. The template was subsequently used for further modules in that program and the Persian Flagship program at the University of Maryland, for which I was also PI and Director. Other versions have been produced for regular students of ESL and foreign languages, e.g., on alternative energy sources. Table 9.11 shows the English version of an adaptation for L2 Spanish.

Table 9.10. Structure for a prototype TBLT module for the (ILR 2–3) UH Korean Flagship program

---

Domain: *International relations*
Target task-type: *Conduct and report a political science research project*
Target task: *Research and produce an oral and written report on key elements in, and attitudes toward, the stand-off between North and South Korea over the North's nuclear weapons program*
Duration: 10 classroom hours and approximately 20 additional hours over 2 weeks
Problem/Research Questions:

(1) Who are the major players in the current standoff over North Korean claims to possess nuclear weapons and threats to restart their nuclear weapons program? (2) How do potential solutions proposed by the various parties differ? (3) How do attitudes and opinions of (a) Koreans, and (b) Korean-Americans, vary on this issue with respondents' (i) age, (ii) gender, (iii) educational background, and (iv) in the case of Korean-Americans, length of residence in the US?

Instructional sequence:

1. Teacher introduces the module (everything in Korean throughout) – topic, problem/research questions, materials, and method – making sure students have an initial grasp of the dimensions of the issue (not seeking their answers to the questions), of the resources available to them (Internet, audio- and video-taped news items, current affairs programming, academic publications, newspapers and magazines, interviewees, etc.), and of what is required of them.

2. Students view a selection of video-taped TV news broadcasts, political speeches, current affairs programming, etc., on the topic. Items are discussed and vocabulary and collocations occurring in the input and/or discussions thereof are brought to students' attention (in context). Register differences between different "levels" of Korean in the input are highlighted (in context). Ditto dialectal, gender-related, and other differences. Readings are assigned – probably a medley of sources designed both (i) to provide useful information on the issues, and (ii) to highlight systematic Korean NS language variation.

3. Students are instructed in how to begin to research the issue outside the classroom. This will involve some hours searching the Internet for sources, viewing a growing library of audio- and video-tapes, reading a growing file of newspaper and magazine clippings and academic writing on the topic. They report back on what they are discovering during subsequent class meetings.

4. Teacher helps students (working small groups) design a questionnaire survey of Koreans and Korean-Americans of the issues, responses to which will enable them to provide at least temporary answers to RQ 3, i – iv. Basic instruction is provided in questionnaire and survey design, with opportunities taken for specialized vocabulary and collocation work in this area (sampling procedures, item types, item analysis, generalization to population, etc.). Draft questionnaires are reviewed and critiqued by teacher and students. Drafts are merged to produce one class questionnaire and survey.

5. Lecture on survey research methods by NS Korean faculty member (UH or taped in Korea). Readings on same, with follow-up activities on reading skills.

Table 9.10. (*Continued*)

6. Lecture(s) on current state of North/South Korea relations by NS Korean faculty members, journalists, etc. (UH or taped in Korea). Readings on same, with follow-up activities on reading skills.
7. Arrangements made and attitude/opinion survey conducted (by class acting together) on samples of Koreans and Korean-Americans. Resulting data are analyzed, reported and discussed in class.
8. Live or taped interviews of Koreans and Korean-Americans by NS Koreans observed by students. (Possible written interviews via email, as well.) Students' attention is drawn to language issues in interviews.
9. Students conduct taped practice interviews of one another on the issues. Following critiques of these and focus on linguistic issues arising, students conduct taped interviews of samples of Koreans and Korean-Americans.
10. Tapes are critiqued for language issues. Results of interviews are summarized and reported by students.
11. Students prepare final oral reports of both questionnaire and interview components of the opinion surveys. These are discussed and critiqued in class for both content and language.
12. **Assessment/Exit task(s):** Students make video-taped final reports, and produce written reports, of their study, answering the RQs posed for the module. These will serve as interlanguage samples which Flagship teachers will store as part of each student's portfolio record, and also analyze with the individual students, providing detailed feedback on their language problems and areas for improvement.

Table 9.11. A complex political issue

Domain: *Social studies/international relations/political science*
Target task-type: *Conduct and report a social sciences research project*
Target task: *Research and produce an oral and written report on tensions between the Spanish central government in Madrid and the semi-autonomous regions*
Duration: 10 classroom hours and approximately 20 additional hours over 5 weeks
Problem/Research Questions
(1) Which are the major semi-autonomous regions wanting more independence from Madrid? (2) How do their political and economic situations and demands differ? (3) How do attitudes and opinions of people in favor of more autonomy and those against differ? (b) How do different views on the issues vary with such variables as respondents' (i) age, (ii) gender, (iii) educational background, (iv) occupation, and (v) political affiliation?

Pedagogic tasks
1. Teacher introduces the module (everything in Spanish throughout) – topic, problem/ research questions, materials, and method – making sure students have an initial grasp of the dimensions of the issue (not seeking their answers to the questions), of the resources available to them (Internet, audio- and video-taped news items, current affairs programming, academic publications, newspapers and magazines, interviewees, etc.), and of what is required of them.

(*Continued*)

Table 9.11. (*Continued*)

2. Students view a selection of video-taped TV news broadcasts, political speeches, current affairs programming, etc., on the topic. Items are discussed and vocabulary and collocations occurring in the input are brought to students' attention (in context). Register differences between different "levels" of Spanish in the input are highlighted (in context). Ditto any dialectal, gender-related, or other differences. Readings are assigned, probably a medley of sources designed both (i) to provide useful information on the issues, and (ii) to highlight systematic language variation in Spanish.

3. Students are instructed in how to begin to research the issue outside the classroom. This will involve some hours searching the Internet for sources, viewing a growing library of audio- and video-tapes, reading a growing file of newspaper and magazine clippings and academic writing on the topic. They report back on what they are discovering during subsequent class meetings.

4. Teacher helps students (probably working in two or three small groups) design a questionnaire survey of Spaniards of the issues, responses to which will enable them to provide at least temporary answers to the research questions Basic instruction (in Spanish) is offered in questionnaire and survey design, with opportunities taken for specialized vocabulary and collocation work in this area (sampling procedures, item types, item analysis, generalization to population, etc.). Draft questionnaires are reviewed and critiqued by the teacher and students. Drafts are merged to produce one class questionnaire and survey.

5. Lecture on survey research methods by a native Spanish speaker. Readings in Spanish on the same topics (with follow-up activities on reading skills).

6. Lecture(s) on current state of relations between Madrid and the semi-autonomous regions by one or more Spanish-speaking faculty members, journalists, etc. (taped in Spain if necessary). Readings on same topics (with follow-up activities on reading skills).

7. Arrangements made and attitude/opinion survey conducted (by class acting together) on samples of Spanish-speaking respondents. Data analyzed, reported and discussed in class.

8. Live or taped interviews of Spaniards observed by students. (Possibly, written interviews via email, as well.) Students' attention is drawn to language issues in interviews.

9. Students conduct taped practice interviews of one another on the issues. Following critiques of these and focus on linguistic issues arising, students conduct taped interviews (in Spanish) of samples of Spaniards.

10. Tapes are critiqued for language issues. Results of interviews are summarized and reported by students.

11. Students prepare final oral reports of both questionnaire and interview components of the opinion surveys. These are discussed and critiqued in class for both content and language.

12. **Assessment/Exit task(s):** Students make video-taped final reports, and if appropriate, written reports, of their study and answering the research questions posed for the module. These will be graded. They will also serve as interlanguage samples, stored as part of each student's portfolio record, and analyzed with the individual students, providing detailed feedback on their language problems and areas for improvement.

As should be obvious, once templates are created, they can be used as often as needed, with modifications to fit the research issues of interest for particular groups of students and such local circumstances as their L2 proficiency, the (non-)availability of NSs of the L2 with expertise in the target discourse domain, access to technological aids, and the time at the teacher's and students' disposal. The Korean Flagship was a full-time program, so the module could reasonably be completed in two or three weeks, whereas, used in a foreign language setting, the Spanish module might be spread out over a month or more, given that regular high school and university foreign language classes typically meet for only three to five hours per week. The number and complexity of research questions can be increased or reduced, e.g., by eliminating one or more of the moderator variables (age, gender, etc., of interviewees), thereby increasing or reducing the complexity of the overall project.

9.3.5.2. Attending an academic lecture   Learners studying languages at the proficiency levels (for present purposes) corresponding to "advanced" in this discussion (ILR 2 and above, etc.), especially languages that are "hard" for speakers of their L1 (for English speakers, usually due to typological distance and/or a non-Roman L2 alphabet), are clearly doing so for a serious, often academic or occupational, purpose, not, e.g., for tourism. For many, the goal is to study or take advanced professional training at a university overseas; for others, it is to attend international academic or professional conferences. In either case, a critically important, and frequent, target task will be to **Attend a [subject area] lecture** in the students' field of specialization.

As usual, the first PT in the module will have the learners experience a sample of the real thing. They should listen to a recording, or better, watch a video, of perhaps a five-minute excerpt from a real lecture in their subject area (economics, physics, etc.), delivered by and for NSs of the L2. Such material is ever easier to find on the Internet these days. Alternatively, the program, materials writer or teacher concerned may have a personal NS contact in another department or in the country of interest who can make or secure a recording for them. PT2 will consist of a schema-building session – perhaps 20 minutes of in-class oral work, everything in the L2, based on a short written text on the topic of the lecture, elaborated if need be, and/or on students' existing knowledge of the field concerned. Students in this sort of course can usually be expected to know a lot more about the subject matter than the teacher. Far from presenting a problem, this is a resource that can be exploited, as it is a naturally occurring example of students having information with which to negotiate teacher-student interaction – a condition that teachers and materials writers working with a synthetic syllabus ordinarily strive to create artificially.

There will then follow three or four simpler PTs, the exact number to depend on students' current L2 abilities and knowledge of the field of interest. Next will come short lecturettes, elaborated to the extent students require. For example, they may be broken down into segments, heard twice if need be, with a written L2 outline in note form provided. As these "crutches" are gradually removed, students will be dealing with increasingly complex versions of the full target lecture. The focus throughout will be on their ability to understand information in a lecture that a subject-matter specialist (ideally, the original lecturer), *not* the language teacher, indicates to be what he or she would expect a good NS student to take away. Students' attention will be drawn to lexical items and (especially) collocations in context, as well as any lingering grammatical problems for such advanced students. With PT3 or 4, they will often benefit from reading a written transcript of the lecture while listening to the recording at least once, the written version having important grammatical points and collocations highlighted in one of the usual ways (bolding, italics, underlining, etc.), so as to increase the likelihood of noticing. The module may repeat the sequence with a second or third lecture from the relevant domain. The final PT, which will double as the exit/assessment task, may present students with a new video-taped lecture (a simulation of a target task), followed by a multiple-choice test on the information it contains. Can a student score 80% or better on the *information* (not the language) in the lecture that a domain expert identifies as to be expected of a good NS student in the discipline concerned?

A lot of valuable research has been conducted on the linguistic and discourse structures of university lectures at the undergraduate and graduate levels, within and across disciplines. It is not necessary to reinvent the wheel. Flowerdew (1995b) provides an overview of some of the work. For discourse-level treatments, see, e.g., Clapham (2001), Dudley-Evans (1995), Johns (1988), Thompson (1994), Young (1995), and additional chapters in Flowerdew (1995a), Flowerdew and Peacock (2001), Johns (1997), and Swales (1990a). Chaudron, Loschky, and Cook (1995) is a valuable resource on listening comprehension and lecture note-taking. For work on lexical items and collocations found in reading materials or lectures within and across academic disciplines and more general fields (sciences, social sciences, etc.), see, e.g., Arden-Close (1993), Coxhead (2000), Coxhead and Nation (2001), DeCarrico and Nattinger (1988), Hyland and Tse (2007), Simpson-Vlach and Ellis (2010), and Wood (2001). A materials writer embarking on task-based modules for a specific discipline would also do well to consult the table of contents for complete runs of such journals as *English for Specific Purposes* and *English for Academic Purposes*, potentially saving him- or herself a lot of time. Many MA theses and doctoral dissertations have been completed in these areas, as well.

It is by no means all plain sailing, however. The corpus study by Hyland and Tse (2007), in particular, serves as a valuable cautionary note for teachers and materials writers. Their analysis of a more modern, balanced and representative corpus than those employed in some earlier studies found that fewer lexical items than was once thought really serve students in more than a few fields, as might be inferred from the notion of an "academic vocabulary," and that the common distinction between "academic" and "technical" vocabulary needs to give way to a recognition that while many terms occur across several disciplines, their precise meanings and the ways they are used can vary from one discipline to the next. It might be more accurate, they suggest, "to regard academic vocabulary as a cline of technically loaded or specialized words ranging from terms which are only used in a particular discipline to those which share some features of meaning and use with words in other fields" (2007, p. 249). Even when the same items occur in two or more disciplines, they often have discipline-specific usages. Their research revealed inter-disciplinary variation in the form of "uneven word frequencies, restricted item range, disciplinary preferences for particular items over semantic equivalents, and additional meanings lent to items by disciplinary convention and associations in lexical bundles" (2007, p. 248). They stress the importance of narrowly focused needs analyses. One wonders if many of the same caveats do not apply to "academic collocations," as well.

Regardless, it is clear from Hyland and Tse's work that in addition to the psycholinguistic reasons explained earlier as part of the rationale for the notion of focus on form, it is important to draw students' attention to key linguistic features (lexis, collocations, grammatical constructions, etc.) *in discipline-specific context*. Also, special attention may usefully be applied to particular issues characteristic of lectures, such as contrastive stress. In a lecture on English literature, for example, the lecturer might say something like the following: "Keats, Shelley and Wordsworth were the three most famous of the English Romantic poets. Keats and Shelley died young." If 'Shelley' in the second utterance is slightly stressed and uttered with a falling tone, NSs, but (as can be demonstrated by a simple question about Wordworth's life span) not many non-natives, will understand that, by implication, Wordsworth lived to a ripe old age. Students in other disciplines need to be aware of this or risk missing implicitly provided information to which their native classmates will be alert.

9.4. Summary

Task-based materials should be visibly relevant to learners' communicative needs, motivational, and samples of as close to real-world language use as is possible, given psycholinguistic constraints. By definition, such materials will be task-based and dynamic, not text-based and static. When students encounter texts in TBLT, it is as part of the language use that occurs naturally as a result of task work. Use of *genuine texts* (frozen reports of third-party completion of tasks) to achieve these ends can impede learning by any but very advanced students through confronting them with large amounts of unknown language (new vocabulary, complex syntax, etc.) without compensatory devices to facilitate comprehension. They present too dense a linguistic target, due to the lack of redundancy. *Simplified texts* (the traditional "solution" in commercially published LT materials) improve comprehension through use of shorter sentences and restricted vocabularies and grammars. However, they tend to result in stilted, basal-reader-type material, lacking implicitness, open-endedness, and inter-textuality. It impedes learning by modeling unnatural *usage*, e.g., non-collocations, not *use* (Widdowson 1972) and by removing from the input the very items to which learners must be exposed if they are ever to be learned.

Elaborated texts achieve almost as great an increase in comprehension as simplified ones, but do so without impeding acquisition. Comprehension is improved through adding redundancy (eight types of repetition, paraphrase, etc.) and transparency (clear signaling and marking to increase topic saliency, reversion from subject-predicate to topic-comment constructions, matching order of mention to chronological sequence of events, preference for a here-and-now orientation, etc.), and especially, but not only, in spoken texts, by a slower rate of delivery, and where multi-party, interactional discourse is concerned, by frequent use of clarification requests, comprehension checks and confirmation checks. Retention of unknown linguistic targets (new vocabulary and syntax, collocations, etc.) means learners are exposed to them – with understanding, due to the elaboration – exposure that is essential if the forms are to be learned, and the new forms mapped onto their meanings and functions.

In an era when 'authenticity' is a buzz word in LT materials design, TBLT involves use of *modified* materials in the early (ILR 0–2) stages, at least, and often even after that. In particular, for listening comprehension, the use of *elaborated* (not linguistically simplified), domain-specific spoken discourse samples is optimal. These should be presented to learners not as found objects for study, as in text-based programs, but rather, as a natural component of doing *tasks*. 'Elaborate input,' both in task-based materials and in classroom teacher speech, is theoretically motivated and sufficiently supported empirically to merit its status as one of ten *methodological principles* (MP3) in Task-Based Language Teaching (see, e.g., Doughty & Long 2003; Long 1985b, 2000a; Long & Norris 2000, and Chapter 10). Listening (and reading) comprehension materials, from political speeches, through telephone conversations, to academic lecturettes, should be elaborated, not simplified. Elaborated texts are almost as good for comprehension as simplified versions, and better for language learning, which is a program's primary concern. Traditional belief in the value of so-called "authentic" LT materials needs rethinking.

The best task-based (or any other type of) materials are usually locally written and adapted by the teacher to make them suitable for use with his or her students. For that reason, more materials templates would be especially useful in the field. While most TBLT materials can be delivered face-to-face by a live teacher, in a blended learning course, or via computer in a distance-learning program (Brett & Gonzalez-Lloret 2009; Doughty & Long 2003; Thomas & Reinders 2010), most do not require access to the latest expensive technology. In fact, I maintain that, due to first-hand knowledge of their students and their communicative needs, and the ability to modify instruction as needed in real time, good teachers will generally outperform the most expensive technology-driven programs. Some learners do not have access to live teachers, of course, but those who do should use that option first.

9.5. Suggested Readings

Arnold, E. (1991). Authenticity revisited: How real is real? *English for Specific Purposes* 10, 237–244.

Brantmeier, C. (2005). Effects of reader's knowledge, text type, and test type on L1 and L2 reading comprehension in Spanish. *Modern Language Journal* 89, 1, 37–53.

Brett, D., & Gonzalez-Lloret, M. (2009). Technology enhanced materials. In Long, M.H., & Doughty, C.J. (eds.), *Handbook of language teaching* (pp. 351–369). Oxford: Blackwell.

Derwing, T. (1996). Elaborative detail: Help or hindrance to the NNS listener? *Studies in Second Language Acquisition* 18, 283–297.

Doughty, C.J., & Long, M.H. (2003). Optimal psycholinguistic environments for distance foreign language learning. *Language Learning and Technology* 7, 3, September, 50–80. Retrieved from http://llt.msu.edu

Hyland, K., & Tse, P. (2007). Is there an academic vocabulary? *TESOL Quarterly* 41, 2, 235–254.

Johnson, K. (2003). *Designing language teaching tasks*. New York: Palgrave.

Kelch, K. (1985). Modified input as an aid to comprehension. *Studies in Second Language Acquisition* 7, 1, 81–90.

Kim, Y. (2006). Effects of input elaboration on vocabulary acquisition through reading by Korean learners of English as a foreign language. *TESOL Quarterly* 40, 2, 341–373.

Long, M.H. (1983). Native speaker/nonnative speaker conversation and the negotiation of comprehensible input. *Applied Linguistics* 4, 2, 126–141. Reprinted in Candlin, C., & Macnamara, T. (eds.) (2001). *A reader in applied linguistics*. London: Routledge.

Long, M.H. (1996). Authenticity and learning potential in L2 classroom discourse. *University of Hawai'i Working Papers in ESL* 14, 2, 127–149. Also in Jacobs, G.M. (ed.) (1996). *Language classrooms of tomorrow: Issues and responses* (pp. 148–169). Singapore: SEAMEO Regional Language Centre.

Long, M.H. (2003). Espanol para fines específicos: Textos o tareas? [Spanish for specific purposes: Texts or tasks?]. In Jauregui, K. (ed.), *Espanol para fines especificos. Actas del 11 CIEFE, Amsterdam, 2003* (pp. 15–39). Madrid: Ministerio de Educacion y Ciencia del Reino de Espana.

Long, M.H. (2007). Texts, tasks, and the advanced learner. In Long, M.H. (ed.), *Problems in SLA* (pp. 119–138). Mahwah, NJ: Lawrence Erlbaum Associates.

Long, M.H., & Ross, S. (1993). Modifications that preserve language and content. In Tickoo, M. (ed.), *Simplification: Theory and application* (pp. 29–52). Singapore: SEAMEO Regional Language Centre, 1993.

Oh, S.-Y. (2001). Two types of input modification and EFL reading comprehension: Simplification versus elaboration. *TESOL Quarterly* 35, 1, 69–96.

Parker, K., & Chaudron, C. (1987). The effects of linguistic simplification and elaborative modification on L2 comprehension. *University of Hawai'i Working Papers in ESL* 6, 2, 107–133.

Pica, T., Lincoln-Porter, F., Paninos, D., & Linnell, J. (1996). Language learners' interaction: How does it address the input, output, and feedback needs of language learners? *TESOL Quarterly* 30, 1, 59–84.

Robinson, P. (2005). Cognitive complexity and task sequencing: Studies in a Componential Framework for second language task design. *International Review of Applied Linguistics in Language Teaching* 43, 1, 1–32.

Salaberry, R. (2000). Pedagogical design of computer mediated communication tasks: Learning objectives and technological capabilities. *Modern Language Journal* 84, 1, 28–37.

Widdowson, H.G. (1976). The authenticity of language data. In Fanselow, J.F., & Crymes, R. (eds.), *On TESOL '76* (pp. 261–270). Washington, D. C.: TESOL. Reprinted in Widdowson, H.G. *Explorations in applied linguistics*. Oxford: Oxford University Press.

Yano, Y., Long, M.H., & Ross, S. (1994). The effects of simplified and elaborated texts on foreign language reading comprehension. *Language Learning* 44, 2, 189–219.

Chapter 10

Methodological Principles and Pedagogic Procedures

10.1. Methodological Principles (MPs), Pedagogic Procedures (PPs), and Evaluation Criteria (EC)

The literature has long featured debates over optimal approaches, methods, and techniques for language teaching (LT). The three terms vary in level and scope, not only among themselves, but among writers. For example, 'audio-lingual' and 'grammar-translation' are sometimes referred to as 'approaches' to LT, sometimes as 'methods.' The terms are also problematic in that research has shown that teachers do not stick to a

Second Language Acquisition and Task-Based Language Teaching, First Edition. Mike Long.
© 2015 John Wiley & Sons, Inc. Published 2015 by John Wiley & Sons, Inc.

particular approach or method, except over short periods, and additionally, in that most approaches and methods overlap to such an extent as to become hard to distinguish in practice. Moreover, teachers do not plan, deliver, or recall classroom lessons in terms of methods, even when explicitly trained in them, but rather, in terms of activities, or tasks (Shavelson & Stern 1981; Swaffer, Arens, & Morgan 1982). For these and other reasons, I prefer a distinction, idiosyncratic though it may be, between methodological principles (MPs) and pedagogic procedures (PPs). In addition to avoiding the problems with the previous terms, differences in LT can be defined objectively in terms of shared or distinctive underlying principles, and behavioral realizations of the MPs at the classroom level can be observed and identified reliably. I have provided definitions of the terms, MPs and PPs, on several occasions; the following, with only minor changes to improve clarity, are from Long (2009).

10.1.1. Methodological principles

Methodological principles (MPs) are universally desirable instructional design features, motivated by theory and research findings in second language acquisition (SLA), educational psychology, philosophy of education, general educational curriculum design, and elsewhere, which show them to be either necessary for SLA or facilitative of it. *Facilitative* effects are important because the goal of a *theory of LT* is a maximally *efficient* approach, whereas a *theory of SLA* is primarily concerned with what is *necessary* and *sufficient* for learning to occur (for further discussion, see Long 2000b, pp. 4–5, 2007a, pp. 16–20). Negative feedback, for example, may or may not eventually turn out to be necessary for language development, but numerous studies have shown it to be facilitative, justifying MP7: Provide negative feedback (see Section 10.2.7). There are currently ten MPs in TBLT (see Table 10.1). The theoretical motivation and empirical support MPs enjoy means they are candidates for any approach to language teaching, not just TBLT.

10.1.2. Pedagogic procedures

Whereas MPs are putative language teaching universals, *pedagogic procedures* (PPs) comprise the potentially infinite range of options for instantiating the principles at the classroom level. MPs specify *what* should be done; PPs suggest *how* it can be done. Variation in how is to make instruction appropriate for learners of different ages, aptitudes, cognitive styles, proficiency, or L1 and L2 literacy level, for more salient and less salient target forms, and so on, and is handled at the level of PPs. Given that variations in implementation are designed to respond precisely to particular needs and conditions at the local level, often moment by moment as a lesson unfolds, choices among PPs are usually best left to the classroom teacher, who is typically the expert on local conditions, and will not be dealt with in any detail here. Whereas MPs are founded upon, and can be evaluated against, theory, research findings, and practice in several fields, the paucity of research on their relative effectiveness means that choice among PPs is still mostly a matter of teacher judgment, with different choices potentially justified at different times with the same learners or at the same time with different learners. Consequently, options

Table 10.1. MPs, sources, and EC

	MP	Sources	EC
Activities			
MP1	Use task, not text, as the unit of analysis.	Long (1985a, 2007c); Long and Crookes (1992, 1993); Norris (2009); Robinson (2001a,b); Skehan (1998), Van den Branden (2006a,b)	EC1, EC2; EC3, EC4
MP2	Promote learning by doing.	Avrich (1980); Doughty and Long (2003); Shotton (1993); Smith (1983)	EC1, EC3, EC4
Input			
MP3	Elaborate input. (Do not simplify; do not rely solely on "authentic" texts.)	Long (1996b, 2007c); Long and Ross (1993); Oh (2001); Yano, Long, and Ross (1994)	EC2, EC3
MP4	Provide rich (not impoverished) input.	Gass (1997, 2003); Krashen (1985); Larsen-Freeman and Ellis (2006); Long (1996b); Pica et al. (1996); Shintani, Li, and Ellis (2013)	EC1, EC2, EC3
Learning processes			
MP5	Encourage inductive ("chunk") learning.	Boers and Lindstromberg (2012); N.C. Ellis (2002a, 2002b, 2006b, 2007a,b); Larsen-Freeman & Ellis 2006; Meara (2009); Schmitt (2008); Wray (2000, 2002)	EC1, EC4
MP6	Focus on form.	De la Fuente (2006); Doughty (1991); N.C. Ellis (2005); Goo et al. (2009); Hulstijn (2003); Long (1991, 2000a); Long and Robinson (1998); Norris and Ortega (2000); Schmidt (2001); Shintani (2011, 2013); Williams (2005)	EC1, EC2, EC3, EC4
MP7	Provide negative feedback.	Annett (1969); DeKeyser (1993); Goo and Mackey (2013); Li (2010); Long (2007b); Lyster and Saito (2010); Mackey and Goo (2007); Russell and Spada (2006)	EC1, EC2, EC3, EC4

Table 10.1. (*Continued*)

	MP	Sources	EC
MP8	Respect learner syllabi and developmental processes.	Ellis (1989); Lightbown (1983); Mackey (1999); Ortega (2009); Pienemann (1984, 1989); Pienemann and Kessler (2012)	EC1, EC2
MP9	Promote cooperative/ collaborative learning.	Barnes (1976/1992); Barnes and Todd (1977, 1995); Gass (1997, 2003); Gass and Mackey (2007); Hatch (1978); Jacobs (1998); Liang, Mohan, and Early (1998); Long (1996b); Long and Porter (1985); Mackey and Goo (2007); McCafferty, Jacobs, and DaSilva Iddings (2006); Oxford (1997); Pica *et al.* (1996); Sato (1986, 1988, 1990); Webb (1991)	EC1, EC2, EC3, EC4
Learners			
MP10	Individualize instruction (psycholinguistically and according to communicative needs).	Altman and James (1980); Harlow (1987); Logan (1973); Long (2005a); Robinson (2002a); Sawyer and Ranta (2001); Vatz *et al.* (2013); Wesche (1981)	EC1 EC2 EC4

Source: Updated from Doughty, C.J., & Long, M.H. (2003). Optimal psycholinguistic environments for distance foreign language learning. *Language Learning and Technology* 7, 3, September, 50–80.

among the wide range of PPs for providing negative feedback – for example, from the overt and explicit end of the spectrum, such as use of a rule or explanation, to the covert and implicit end, such as corrective recasts, and many points in between – cannot be judged well- or ill-founded without knowing the context. For instance, explicit corrective feedback might be appropriate for a less salient target feature and/or educated adult learners (e.g., an error with an unstressed, so less salient, prefix, such as *undecisive*, which does not result in miscommunication), implicit negative feedback, such as recasts, might suffice for the same learners with a more salient target (e.g., a stressed, meaning-bearing, free morpheme, such as *did*), and explicit feedback might be wholly inappropriate for either type of target feature with young children.

To say that teachers are best suited to make decisions on PPs does not imply that methodologists abdicate responsibility at the classroom level. Choices should be rational, based on teaching experience and, where available, research findings. Doughty and Williams (1998b), for example, discuss research findings and provide detailed rationales for a continuum of choices, from unobtrusive to obtrusive, among the many PPs available for providing negative feedback. The LT literature would be mightily well served by more such research-based comparative evaluations of the relative appropriateness of behavioral realizations of MPs at the classroom level.

10.1.3. Evaluation criteria

Evaluation criteria (EC) for MPs are the standards by which proposals can be judged, the ways in which their likely validity may be assessed. EC can take several forms, including, most obviously, EC1: Theoretical motivation, EC2: Empirical support, and EC3: Logical argumentation.

To illustrate, in the case of MP7: Provide negative feedback, EC1 is met by the predictions of theories of (S)LA as disparate as Skill Acquisition Theory (DeKeyser 2007a), Emergentism (Ellis 2007b; Larsen-Freeman & Ellis 2006), Cognitive Interactionism (Gass 1997; Long 1996b, Chapter 3; Mackey, Abbuhl, & Gass 2012), Universal Grammar (Lardiere 2012; White 2003b, 2007), and Sociocultural Theory (Lantolf 2012). EC2 is met by the findings of numerous empirical studies, and meta-analyses of studies, of the positive influence of both implicit and explicit corrective feedback on L2 development (e.g., Goo & Mackey 2013; Li 2010; Long 2007b; Mackey 2012; Mackey & Goo 2007; Russell & Spada 2006). EC3 is met by arguments such as that of Lydia White (1987, 1991) concerning the problem of unlearning L1 options on the basis of positive evidence alone when the input gives no indication of their ungrammaticality in the L2, a situation that potentially occurs whenever options in the L2 are a subset of those in the L1 in a given domain, e.g., those for adverb-placement for L1 speakers of French or Spanish learning L2 English.

EC1 and EC3 will often be important, given the paucity of controlled studies in some areas. A lack of research is usually due to the difficulty of conducting studies of some issues in real educational settings, the shortage of people with sufficient training in research methods and sufficient time to invest in the effort, and the lack of adequate funding for the purpose.[1] Since language teaching is not simply something that can be put off for a few years while the research is carried out, alternative criteria are needed. Additional potential EC include those employed in other fields, some of them widely discussed in the philosophy of science literature. An example of a criterion of that type (see below) is EC4: Consistency with accepted theories in other fields. To illustrate, MP7: Provide negative feedback, receives independent support, and meets EC4, because of the well-established importance of negative feedback in almost every other type of human learning and performance (see, e.g., Annett 1969), not just language learning. Conversely, MP5: Encourage inductive ("chunk") learning, would be hard to justify if it were accepted in cognitive psychology that adults are only capable of learning explicitly. (It is not.)

---

[1] Vast amounts of time and money are invested around the world each year in training language teachers, but minimal amounts of either on developing the knowledge base that should form the major component in such training. Compare the established facts and validated procedures to be understood and assimilated by trainee physicians, architects, lawyers, engineers, and future members of other professions with those available to language teachers.

10.2. Ten Methodological Principles

Three of the ten MPs (see Table 10.1) are original to TBLT: MP1: Use task, not text, as the unit of analysis, MP3: Elaborate input, and MP6: Focus on form. The remaining seven can be found in several other "approaches" and "methods," and some, such as MP7: Provide negative feedback, in all of them (Krashen & Seliger 1975).[2] Sources of support for the MPs vary, drawing on theory, research and practice in philosophy of education, SLA, educational psychology, curriculum and instruction, and LT. Support for some is stronger than for others. Several derive convergent validation from work in two or more fields. The 'Sources' column 2 in Table 10.1 provides references to some relevant supporting studies and research reviews for the MPs. Evaluation criteria that are met are noted in column 3. In what follows, little space will be devoted to MPs 1–4 and 6–8 because they have already been discussed at length in this book and elsewhere. More attention will be paid to MPs 5, 9, and 10, which have received less satisfactory treatment in the previous TBLT literature. It is recognized that some readers will assuredly not accept some of the principles, and that, accepted or not, some require additional research support. Once again, however, it is hoped that their nomination for consideration will help focus the debate as to just what do constitute relevant methodological principles in TBLT and for LT in general.

10.2.1. MP1: Use task, not text, as the unit of analysis

Seven independent reasons for use of 'task' as the unit of analysis in all stages of TBLT – from needs analysis to student assessment – were provided in preceding chapters, starting with Chapter 1.3. Unmotivated by a needs analysis, pedagogic tasks (PTs) of various kinds have been deployed in other kinds of communicative LT (see, e.g., Allwright 1977), including courses using a procedural and process syllabus, and in various kinds of task-*supported* delivery of a grammatical syllabus (see, e.g., Bygate & Samuda 2007; R. Ellis 2003; Nunan 2004), but in TBLT, tasks themselves constitute syllabus content, and lessons are built around them. If they appear in the syllabus, it is for a reason, and there is no covert grammatical syllabus.

The disadvantages of building lessons around texts have also been explained, most recently in Chapter 8.2.8 and Chapter 9.2. To recapitulate, in brief, at the level of methodology, MP1 meets the requirements of an analytic approach and enables learners to experience language as a living entity through using it to practice doing the tasks they will face beyond the classroom. In contrast, the focus in text-based courses, including most content-based instruction, with their use of genuine or simplified reading passages and scripted dialogues, is language as object. Texts are frozen records, often unrealistic records, of task accomplishment by others, i.e., a by-product of tasks. Watching someone else do a task or reading about it is not the same as learning how to do it oneself. Students need to learn how to make a restaurant reservation by telephone, understand real

---

[2] Krashen and Seliger claimed negative feedback and rule isolation were the only two features common to all LT methods, but rule isolation is clearly not supposed to occur in several analytic approaches, including the Natural Approach (Krashen & Terrell 1983).

spoken street directions well enough to trace a route on a map or to walk the streets in an unfamiliar neighborhood without getting lost, follow the instructions on a metro ticket vending machine, or follow a police officer's instructions when pulled over, answer his or her questions, and understand whatever follow-up action may be required. They will accomplish this best by doing (initially less complex versions of) the tasks themselves.

10.2.2. MP2: Promote learning by doing

Choice of task as the unit of analysis goes naturally with learning by doing. Again, the rationale for MP2 was provided in earlier chapters, e.g., Chapter 4.2 and Chapter 8.2.8, obviating the need for much discussion here. Interesting tasks of perceived relevance to the communicative needs of students are more likely to hold their attention than repetitive "language-like" drills and exercises. Hands-on, personal experience with *doing* (initially, less complex versions of) real-world tasks – "through the eyes *and* the hand to the brain" – increases the likelihood that abilities learned in the classroom will transfer to the world outside, that what is learned is understandable, because it is context-embedded, better integrated into long-term memory, and more easily recalled. The combination of mental and manual work also creates the conditions required for incidental learning, thus unleashing a powerful language-learning resource (see Chapter 3.3, especially E3) that is stifled by traditional forms-focused instruction.

10.2.3. MP3: Elaborate input

Considerable attention has already been devoted to the rationale, and empirical support, for the use of elaborated, rather than either genuine or simplified, texts (see, especially, Chapter 9.2, and also Chapter 11.5.3). The principal motivation for elaboration is that elaborated input is psycholinguistically more appropriate than either genuine or simplified input. It is better tuned to learners' current processing capacity than genuine input, so it is more likely to be learnable. Elaboration improves comprehensibility without the same level of artificiality that results from simplification, and unlike simplification, does so while retaining unknown linguistic items, meaning that learners are exposed to, and can learn, them. The same arguments apply to teacher speech, in which elaboration will occur naturally as long as genuine task-based communication is the focus, as it will be during task-based learner–learner communication (Pica *et al.* 1996). Examples of elaboration in teacher speech were provided in Chapter 9.2 (see, also, Chaudron 1982). Well-designed PTs induce negotiation for meaning, achieved largely through input elaboration.

10.2.4. MP4: Provide rich input

The simplification that goes hand in hand with synthetic approaches to LT entails fairly strict structural and lexical control exercised by publishers and commercial materials writers over the language modeled in dialogues and reading passages, and results in linguistically impoverished input. The same is true of teacher speech in focus-on-forms instruction. Small L2 samples are presented to students, seeded with the grammar point that is the lesson's real focus, and worked and reworked in drills, exercises, and (in task-supported LT) PTs of various kinds – limited data from which to learn a new language, and as discussed in Chapters 7 and 8, almost always unrealistic data.

Learners need plentiful exposure to rich data. Comprehension-based grammar instruction can help provide this, e.g., through having students work on so-called "listen-and-do" PTs. It tends to be more effective than production-based instruction for developing receptive abilities, as would be expected, especially when the acquisition of new grammatical features is involved, whereas production-based instruction is often better for enhancing productive control of already partially acquired features (for review, see Shintani, Li, & Ellis 2013). Use of elaborated input in such tasks will help greatly in this regard, but alone is insufficient. With potential sales figures in mind, commercially published materials, especially synthetic materials, intended for the widest possible audience, will be the *least* context-, domain-, and task-specific possible – generic L2 samples (supposedly) valid for any purpose, but not for any particular purpose. This is the opposite of what learners require. If they are to be prepared to achieve their context-, domain-, and task-specific communicative needs beyond the classroom, they require materials that expose them to samples of the L2 that are context-, domain-, and task-specific, especially, but not only, if advanced functional proficiency is the goal. As shown by studies that have compared genuine samples of target discourse with what is found in traditional pedagogic materials, the language this entails is often of a kind rarely encountered in commercial textbooks, whereas the analysis of target discourse that underpins genuine TBLT materials (see Chapter 7) means their relevance is assured. Rich input, in sum, is not just a matter of the greater linguistic complexity of elaborated, as compared with simplified, input, but of quality, quantity, variety, genuineness, and relevance.

10.2.5. MP5: Encourage inductive "chunk" learning

Anyone who has taught advanced foreign language learners will know that while grammatical errors may still occur, domain-specific vocabulary and, especially, collocations remain a major problem. This has been documented in many studies (e.g., Bahns & Eldaw 1993). Whereas child L1 and L2 learners appear to store and retrieve target-like collocations from the get-go, even advanced adult L2 learners frequently have to stop and ask themselves whether a particular French noun is masculine or feminine (and therefore requires a masculine or feminine determiner and adjective), whether or not a particular Spanish verb is reflexive, and which items in such English pairs as the following are correct: *arrive at London* or *arrive in London*; *make a mistake* or *do a mistake*; *make a photo* or *take a photo*; *a little minority* or *a small minority*; *hold true* or *hold correct*; *beat around the bush* or *beat around the tree*; *the snake slid across the grass* or *the snake slithered across the grass*; *the child giggled* or *the child guffawed*; *the man grimaced with anger* or *grimaced with pain*; and *the government announced war* or *the government declared war*. Collocation errors persist even among near-native L2 speakers resident in the target-language environment for decades (Granena & Long 2013a; Spadaro 1996, 2013). Since MP5 has received scant attention in the previous TBLT literature, more space will be given to it here.

The author of a number of valuable studies and reviews of research on the learning and teaching of collocations and idioms (see, e.g., Boers & Lindstromberg 2012), Boers has drawn attention to several reasons why L2 collocations constitute such a major learning problem. (i) They may differ from how equivalent words collocate in the learner's L1 (Yamashita & Jiang 2010). (ii) The fact that many of them are made up of familiar words may lead learners to pay less attention to them than to attention-catching new words. Eye-tracking studies have shown learners usually fixate longer on new words (Godfroid, Boers, & Housen 2013). (iii) The semantic vagueness of some collocations, e.g., when the verb in verb–noun collocations, is high frequency and multi-purpose (*have* time, *make* trouble, *do* the shopping) can also make them less salient. (iv) Collocations are numerous, but instances of the same one tend to be spaced far apart. The time lapse can mean that the memory trace from the first encounter has faded before the second encounter occurs (Eyckmans, Boers, & Stengers 2007). (v) Collocates, e.g., 'declare war,' are sometimes interrupted, making recognition that they are, indeed, collocates, less likely (The *war* everyone had feared for so long was finally *declared* on December 1st). (vi) Collocates for some words vary (do/complete/accomplish/perform a task, for example). (vii) Some collocations (e.g., have time/do time/make time, or pay the price/pay the cost) look deceptively similar, the "cue competition" resulting in confusion and error (*He paid the cost of a life of crime).

The size and scope of the collocations problem can be appreciated by considering findings on the presumably lesser task of word learning. Nation (2006) and Nation & Chung (2009) have calculated that learners require knowledge of between 6000 and 7000 word families for adequate comprehension of speech, and 9000 for reading. Intentional vocabulary learning has been shown to be more effective than incidental learning in the short term (e.g., Horst, Cobb, & Nicolae 2005; Laufer 2005; Schmitt 2008), but there is nowhere near enough time to handle so many items in class that way, and teacher speech contains them in insufficient numbers or frequencies to make purely incidental learning feasible, either (Horst 2010). As a result, incidental L2 vocabulary learning through "extensive reading," proven successful in L1A, continues to receive considerable research attention.[3] The predominant focus has been the acquisition of low-frequency words in simplified versions of novels. However, the fact that even the most advanced simplified readers are typically pitched at the 4000-word level makes genuine texts the default resource for items in the mid-frequency (3000–9000) range. The problem is that mid-frequency lexical items typically constitute less than 5% of the words in genuine texts (Cobb 2007).

---

[3] While vocabulary acquisition through extensive reading is often thought of as the product of incidental learning, it is possible that learning becomes intentional if and when the reader fixes his or her attention on an unknown word in an effort to decode its meaning (Godfroid, Boers, & Housen 2013; Paribakht & Wesche 1999). Using eye-fixation time as a measure of attention, Godfroid *et al.* found a "direct, positive relationship between amount of attention and amount of [vocabulary] learning" (2013, p. 509).

Research findings on extensive reading (see, e.g., Horst 2005; Horst, Cobb, & Meara 1998; Pellicer-Sanchez & Schmitt 2010) have shown that incidental vocabulary-learning gains mostly concern receptive, rather than productive, abilities, and while real, are modest, I suspect due to an insufficient *intensity* of exposure. While a single encounter with a new lexical item can trigger recognition abilities, several researchers suggest that around 8–10 exposures (or even higher) appear to constitute a threshold, crossing which leads to a noticeable increase in learning (Horst, Cobb, & Nicolae 2005; Pellicer-Sanchez & Schmitt 2010; Schmitt 2008; Webb, Newton, & Chang 2013), or can sometimes be required, even when those exposures occur in texts as short as two or three sentences (Webb 2007). To supplement learners' typically insufficient encounters with mid- and low-frequency items, and to reduce the forgetting of items learned incidentally that delayed post-tests reveal tends to occur over time (e.g., Waring & Takaki 2003), it seems necessary to build on incidental learning with activities that focus learners' attention on the same target items.

Returning to collocations, it is unclear why child L1 and L2 learners appear better able than adult L2 learners to perceive, store, and retrieve them effectively. It could be, as Wray (2000, 2002) suggests, that although adults can and do process larger chunks of input for meaning, they learn and store individual words separately and try to pair them up later. Or it could it be, as claimed by N.C. Ellis (2001, 2002b, 2003, 2006b), that adults retain the ability to perceive co-occurrences among words without conscious attention, through a slow, input-frequency-driven process of implicit tallying, relevant, according to Ellis, not just for development of the lexicon, but for all linguistic systems. This leads to words frequently encountered in combination becoming associated and stored more efficiently in long-term memory as "chunks" (on analogy with the way information is chunked for more efficient storage), with one word, or sometimes one chunk, then triggering the other(s) in production, resulting in greater fluency. Failure with collocations would then be due to insufficient exposure.

Results consistent with Ellis' position were obtained in an interesting laboratory study by Durrant and Schmitt (2010). Randomly assigned to one of four conditions, 84 college students, non-native speakers (NNSs) of English, were exposed on a computer screen to either 40 or 80 counterbalanced sentences. The target adjective–noun collocations consisted of familiar words forming meaningful but (to avoid prior familiarity with them as collocates) very low frequency pairs, as evidenced by their minimal occurrence in the British National Corpus, e.g., *busy route* in 'Extra buses were introduced on the busy route into the city,' and *excellent drink* in 'Hot chocolate is an excellent drink on a cold evening.' Group 1 saw 40 sentences, each for seven seconds: ten sentences containing the target collocations, ten serving as control sentences (e.g., 'Extra buses were introduced on the route into the city,' and 'Hot chocolate is a wonderful drink on a cold night') that contained the target noun (*route, drink*), but without the paired adjective, and 20 filler sentences. Group 2 saw 80 sentences: the target sentences twice, the first for seven seconds, a second *verbatim repetition* of the first, shown only for three seconds, and the rest for control and filler sentences. Group 3 saw 80 different sentences: 20 containing the target adjective–noun collocations, the second in each pair constituting a *varied repetition*, i.e., the same collocation, but in a different sentence, e.g., 'The busy route between Birmingham and London was closed for a week' and 'Lemon and honey is an excellent drink if you have a cold,' 20 containing the target nouns without their paired adjectives (again, two different sentences for each of the ten targets), and 40 control and filler sentences. Participants in all three groups read the sentences aloud into a microphone. Participants were not told they would be asked to recall anything about the sentences. In the surprise naming test that immediately followed the training, they saw the adjective from each adjective–noun pair for 1.5 seconds, followed, for five seconds, by the first two letters of the noun collocate and dashes for each of the missing letters, e.g., busy + RO_ _ _. Participants had to say the word (*route*) into the microphone if they thought they knew it.

All three groups recalled nouns they had seen with paired adjectives better than those seen only in control sentences, i.e., without their adjective collocate, showing that some memory of an association between the two words had been formed implicitly (without conscious attention) after as little as a single encounter (group 1) or after two encounters (groups 2 and 3). Both repetition groups outperformed the single exposure group, with verbatim slightly more successful than varied repetition. Median recall scores were 3/10 for the single exposure group, 4.5/10 for the varied repetition group, and 5/10 for the verbatim repetition group. If adults can begin to learn collocations so fast and so easily (when assessed very soon after first exposure, at least, and with a test that primes recall), Durrant and Schmitt suggest, their failure to attain native-like levels is more likely due to insufficient L2 exposure than to the word-based approach to learning suggested by Wray. It would be important, they point out, to discover how durable such memory traces are, and thereby, how soon subsequent exposures need to occur for associations to be strengthened, as opposed to having to be formed anew each time. Also, with research findings suggesting 8–10 exposures to be necessary for new words to be learned, would at least that number be required for collocations? Would more meaningful practice than simply reading sentences aloud affect learning? And perhaps most important of all, would explicit teaching and learning be more effective?

No one disputes the fact that adults can and do learn collocations, some to astonishing levels, even if not native levels across the board. Many naturalistic adult acquirers learn them, even when not very advanced overall, often with collocational abilities superior to those of classroom foreign language learners of comparable grammatical abilities. Command of collocations has a lot to do with why some low-level naturalistic acquirers sound more native-like than classroom learners with more advanced grammatical knowledge. Laboratory studies like that of Durrant and Schmitt show they can begin to learn some collocations after only minimal opportunity. Why, then, do so many adults, including those with advanced proficiency, continue to struggle with them? The factors Boers identifies are obviously relevant, all of which concern linguistic and semantic properties of collocates. My hypothesis is that two additional issues are involved, one to do with learning capacity, the other with learning opportunities.

First, as noted in Chapter 3, there is evidence that the dimension of the human capacity for implicit learning most vulnerable to age-related deterioration is (non-rule-based) *instance learning* (Hoyer & Lincourt 1998), and learning collocations is a classic example of instance learning. As predicted, therefore, the area of lexis and collocations, not morpho-syntax, was the domain most affected when first exposure to Spanish in a group of long-term Chinese residents in Spain was late (ages 16–29, compared with groups whose first exposure occurred at ages 3–6 or 7–15), and was the only domain in which language aptitude was relevant in explaining a high level of ultimate attainment (Granena & Long 2013a).[4]

Second, although the total variety (and often, the total amount) of input to which adults are exposed is greater than that which children experience *in the early stages*, the intensity and repetitive nature of exposure to a relatively narrower range of input experienced by children over the short term means that the same smaller number of collocations occur relatively more frequently, and in closer proximity. This is important because, in order to recognize that certain words "go together" with higher than average frequency, learners need to experience their juxtaposition "close together," i.e., during a sufficiently short period of time, for traces of earlier instances still to be retrievable from memory when later instances are encountered. The volume and variety of input to adults over short periods (including vastly greater numbers of collocations) works against their chances of experiencing the same collocations frequently enough, and more importantly, temporally close enough, to perceive them as collocations. If, in a flood of letters, the sequence 'PTR' is encountered, but encountered a second time only hundreds of pairs and triplets of letter combinations later, the fact that it is a combination of higher than usual frequency will be harder to recognize than if it occurs twice within a period of a few seconds. Additional factors are no doubt at play. For instance, some collocations may be more meaningful or emotionally significant for children (e.g., Well done! Clever boy! Put it down. Pick it up. Switch the light off. The battery [of a toy train] ran out), and so have increased saliency and memorability for them.

Whatever the explanation, it is clear that adults, like children, need to learn L2 collocations, and lots of them. The 505 semantically non-transparent multiword items (*take place, at all costs*, etc.) in the PHRASal Expressions List (PHRASE List; Martinez & Schmitt 2012) involve 10% of the 5000 most frequent word families, with 95% of the 505 made up of the 1000 most frequent words in English, and so are clearly relevant even at elementary levels of proficiency. Anything more than basic communicative abilities requires mastery of high numbers; near-native proficiency entails vast numbers. Familiarity with formulaic language of all kinds, collocations included, aids processing speed for both receptive and productive skills; collocation errors, conversely, cause processing difficulties for native speakers (Millar 2010). Statistically significant correlations have been reported between the number of formulaic sequences learners produced during story-retelling tasks and oral proficiency ratings (Boers *et al.* 2006; Stengers *et al.* 2010).

The $64 000 question is how best to facilitate learning. Collocations can be noticed not only because of the saliency that frequency provides, N. Ellis recognizes, but instan-

---

[4] Granena and Long (2013a) reported that, like their lexical and collocational abilities, the late learners' Spanish phonology was also affected by their (post-sensitive period) first exposure and by their language aptitude. They noted, however, that this anomalous finding was probably an artifact of their having employed a monitorable (reading-aloud) task, and predicted that pronunciation would be unaffected by aptitude on either of two free speech tasks they had also employed, but data from which had not been analyzed at the time. In a follow-up study, Granena (2013) presented 20 NS judges with tapes of the same participants performing four tasks; reading a word list aloud, reading a paragraph aloud, story retelling, and online narration. As expected, aptitude scores were statistically significantly related to ratings on the two reading aloud tasks, but not to scores on the free speech tasks.

taneously, as a result of conscious attention (after which, the usual process of implicit tallying applies thereafter to the chunk itself, with frequency again the determining factor). Trying to teach thousands is out of the question, but if explicit treatment of at least some is to be attempted, prioritizing the more frequent ones makes sense, and lists of those are available (Liu 2012; Martinez & Schmitt 2012; Simpson-Vlach & Ellis 2010). Explicit approaches have not been found as successful as some, e.g., Laufer (2005), suggest, however. Boers and Lindstromberg (2012) provide an insightful review of research since 2004. Drawing learners' attention to formulaic strings in spoken or written input does not necessarily lead to memory traces usable in subsequent receptive L2 use, and there are far too many to deal with that way, in any case. Turning learners into amateur corpus analysts by having them identify what they think are multi-word units (so-called "text chunking"), and then comparing their judgments against those of the teacher or other native speakers (NSs), or against results obtained using concordance software, has also generally failed to produce measurable advantages, e.g., for adult students who performed such activities for a year over comparable groups that did not (Boers *et al.* 2006; Stengers *et al.* 2010). Intentional learning, as when students are told in advance that they will be tested on collocations, or when they utilize attention-focusing aids known to facilitate vocabulary learning while reading, e.g., translations and glosses of various kinds (Hulstijn 1992; Watanabe 1999), increases the rate of learning collocations in some studies.[5] But activities designed to encourage students to focus more on collocations on their own, e.g., by having them use collocation dictionaries or concordance data, have had poor results. Grouping collocations thematically or by semantic relatedness (*narrow* escape, *slim* chance) increases, not lightens, the learning load (Webb & Kagimoto 2011), as is the case when semantically related words are presented together (Erten & Tekin 2008; Waring 1997). So does presentation of groups which share synonymous collocates, such as *make* and *do* (Webb & Kagimoto 2011).

Supplementing a regular course with a program of systematic out-of-class written exposure might seem a viable option. However, aside from the time and student self-discipline needed for sufficient extensive reading, success with a purely incidental approach could be expected to be even less assured with collocations than with vocabulary items, due to the typically wide separation of targets in such reading materials. Even what may be thought of as "enhanced incidental learning" through reading, i.e., an input flood, in which exposure to target items is far more frequent and more intensive than in normal reading materials, has had some success, but only limited success. Webb, Newton, and Chang (2013) found that the more exposures intermediate EFL learners experienced – 1, 5, 10, or 15 – to the same 18 verb–noun collocations (*run a risk, raise questions,* etc.) – while reading and simultaneously listening (for a total of 35 minutes) to one of four otherwise exactly comparable versions of a graded reader, the better their scores on unexpected immediate post-tests of receptive and (less good) productive command of the collocations. However, results overall were not encouraging. Students who encountered the collections just once fared no better than a pure control group, and on the most difficult production test, L1-cued translation, students who had encoun-

---

[5] Some "glossing study" results could be due to a covert frequency effect, an artifact of exercises causing students to focus their eyes on the lexical targets several times while flitting back and forth between the collocation in the text and a gloss in the margin, rather than once during normal reading for content. Eye-tracker research could help disambiguate the findings.

tered the target strings 10 times only scored around 30%, and those who had met them 15 times only around 50%. With results like these from 15 exposures, Boers and Lindstromberg (2012) point out, it is optimistic to expect much uptake by students who encounter a collocation just once while doing extensive reading or listening, or do so more often but with the encounters spaced out over time. Such results also put the findings by Durrant and Schmitt into perspective, for as they were careful to point out at the time, the impressive uptake achieved by participants after only one or two exposures was measured just minutes after that exposure (with recall assisted by helpful prompts unavailable in real-time communication), and with those experiencing two exposures doing so not over an extended period, but within a matter of seconds.

Commercially published LT materials feature an array of exercise types designed to teach collocations via focus on forms. Since learning requires repeated encounters with collocations as single units, if such exercises are used at all, it is reasonable to expect greater success from formats that present target collocations as intact wholes. Having learners choose which of a list to use to complete a sentence is more likely to be beneficial than presenting them with separated parts to be matched or reassembled, as when students are asked to correct malformed collocations (*He shot a goal*, *She shot the rifle*, *I made my homework*, *She made her duty*) or when lists of verbs in one column are to be matched with lists of nouns in another. The latter inevitably produce some erroneous groupings that, even when corrective feedback is available, can be expected to leave unhelpful memory traces. And if someone needs to learn new collocations, how will not seeing them help? Four interesting small-scale studies by Boers *et al.* (2013) found disappointingly small effects for any exercise types (all practicing verb–noun pairs), despite learning being assessed via off-line discrete-point tests. Such (non-statistically significant) advantages as were found for one format over another, however, favored those that had students practice with intact collocations.

It is clear that MP5 is well motivated, given the importance of collocations in learning a language, but it is equally unclear how best to realize it into practice, i.e., which pedagogic procedures to call upon. My own two suggestions are as follows, but each comes with the caveat that, to the best of my knowledge, little or no empirical research has been conducted on either. First, whenever possible, add an *extensive reading **and** listening* program (as in Webb, Newton, & Chang 2013) to the main classroom or distance learning course. Rather than simply have students read high interest materials silently (useful though that is), have them read while listening to lively recordings of the texts made especially for language learning by a native speaker with excellent diction and articulation. In addition, the spoken version should be a case of enhanced spoken input. The person making the accompanying sound track would be encouraged to record the texts in such a way as to draw students' attention by adding salience to target lexical items and collocations (a) within the target 3000–6000 range, and/or (b) within or beyond the 3000–6000 range, known to be useful to the particular students concerned, in light of the needs analysis findings concerning their target discourse domain(s).[6] To

---

[6] For instance, students of English for academic purposes needing to attend university lectures might have their attention drawn to occurrences of sub-sets of the lexical phrases identified by Nattinger and DeCarrico (DeCarrico & Nattinger 1988; Nattinger & DeCarrico 1992) and academic formulas by Simpson-Vlach and Ellis (2010).

increase the likelihood of the addition of the simultaneous spoken version paying dividends, salience should be added in ways revealed to be effective by research on foreigner talk discourse (for review, see, e.g., Gass 1997; Long 1983b,d, 1996b), such as use of short (one-beat) pauses (not found when the interlocutor is a NS) before and/or after the target expressions, subtle increases in volume, and within reason, perhaps even a feigned performance need to repeat items involving target collocations in mid-sentence (repetitions occurring at syntactic boundaries being less likely to seem intrusive). Ideally, the same collocations would receive some form of attention-attracting input enhancement in the written texts as well (see Kim 2006), probably via italicization or boldface. PTs used in class would then contain as many of the same items as possible, with students' attention drawn to them in the event that errors occurred (focus on form, not forms).

If adult foreign language learners are to sound like natives, they need to be exposed to realistic (genuine or elaborated) samples of target language use (MP3 and MP4) as input components of PTs, and then helped to incorporate, store, and retrieve collocations within that input as prepackaged chunks. When performing tasks, that is, they must be encouraged to "plagiarize." My second suggestion for a pedagogic procedure through which to realize MP5 is to encourage what might be termed "overt plagiarism." This refers to a variation on a pedagogic procedure (not called that) which I first saw used very successfully, and then used myself, with young adults at the Swan School in Oxford in the late 1960s, and have since employed with adults at the previously mentioned community English as a second language (ESL) program for migrant workers in Maryland.

The procedure is simple. The teacher reads a passage aloud two or three times (or better, to save energy, plays a recording of a native speaker doing so). The passage may be an elaborated version of a genuine text if learners' proficiency level so requires. Passage length is determined by students' proficiency. Starting with the opening sentence, the teacher then reads (or plays a recording of) progressively larger segments as many times as necessary for students to be able to repeat them verbatim, gradually combining progressively larger chunks, until teacher and students can recite most of the entire passage from memory. Once memorization is good, even if not perfect, students are shown the written passage for the first time, and teacher and students read it aloud together two or three times, thereby associating spoken with written form. Provided the teacher's (or recorded) models are lively, the whole process is not nearly as dreary or time-consuming as it may sound, and becomes easier with new passages with practice, just as learning lines in a play or referencing case law becomes progressively easier with practice for actors or lawyers. Students are then encouraged to "plagiarize," i.e., to re-use as large chunks of the passage as they choose when talking or writing about a new topic. While initially skeptical, I found the procedure worked very well. Native-like collocations and larger segments borrowed from the original began to show up in the students' speech and writing on all manner of topics quite unrelated to the contexts in which they had first been encountered. Moreover, the initially large chunks that had been "plagiarized" were broken down over time, and the parts used productively, but with the original collocations intact.

At first sight, the overt plagiarism pedagogic procedure may look like one that could be found in traditional *text*-based LT, where mimicry and rote memorization are staples of focus-on-forms approaches. There are important differences, however. What is being memorized here is not a series of sentences or a stilted dialogue or reading passage seeded with copious examples of the same grammatical patterns or verb tenses, and spoken or written within the confines of a stipulated vocabulary range. Nor is it a linguistically graded text to be mined for grammar points or lexical items, as would happen in such approaches. Rather, it is a gestalt, semantically rich and meaningful, genuine or elaborated sample of the target language. Students are led to notice, and then re-use, meaningful chunks from the input in new contexts, chunks representative of native speaker usage. It is broadly consistent with the model of language acquisition proposed by Nick Ellis (e.g., Ellis 2007b; Robinson & Ellis 2008), summarized briefly in section E3 of Chapter 3.

Here is a simple example, designed for use with elementary students, deployed recently to illustrate the procedure during an in-service training session for NS and NNS teachers from the community ESL program. (In a TBLT course, needless to say, the discourse samples chosen would be drawn from those collected during stage 2 of the needs analysis, making the plagiarized chunks more obviously relevant to the students concerned.) The topic was motivated by the 2012 election campaign underway in the USA at the time. The US media's relentless coverage of such spectacles meant that most students already possessed some background knowledge of the topic and, since the election was still a few weeks off, were unlikely to be able to avoid encountering much of the same language repeatedly outside the classroom in the coming weeks. While not good for their mental health, this could be useful for language learning.

Democrat or Republican?
Tuesday, November 6, 2014 is election day in the USA. US citizens can vote for the person they want as President. The two main candidates are Barak Obama (Democrat), the incumbent, and Mitt Romney (Republican), the challenger. Obama is younger than Romney. Romney is much wealthier. Obama has been President for four years. He would like a second term – four more years. The maximum term for US presidents is eight years. Polls show that the country is divided. Roughly 47% of the people support Obama, while roughly 46% prefer Romney. A minority – roughly 7% – in the middle are undecided. They are known as "swing voters." How they vote will determine who wins.

Memorizing this short passage took five minutes. Participants were then encouraged to use as much of the text as they liked to complete the following, with reference to a national or local election in the USA or their country of origin or any other country or jurisdiction. Note that the blanks are mostly for factual matters, such as names and dates. The shell provided, over which their eyes ran many times as they worked, contained the collocations of interest (election day, vote for, main candidates, maximum term, roughly X%, etc.).

Example from another country
_____ is election day in _____. _____ citizens can vote for the person they want as President. The _____ main candidates are _____ (_____), the incumbent, and _____ (_____) the challenger. _____ is _____er than _____, who is much _____er. _____ has been President for _____ years. He would like to be President for another _____ years. The maximum term for presidents in _____ is _____ years. Polls show that the country is divided. Roughly _____ % support _____, while roughly ____ % prefer _____. A minority – roughly ___% – are undecided. How they vote will determine the winner.

While I know of no empirical work directly evaluating "overt plagiarism" for language learning, its success would be predictable, based on the literature on so-called "transfer-appropriate training" (Morris, Bransford, & Franks 1977; Schmidt & Bjork 1992; Singley & Anderson 1989). Moreover, that repeated exposure to the same input has positive effects on acquisition, not just comprehension, should come as no surprise. Gass *et al.* (1999) showed that students who watched a video clip several times did not need to focus on meaning so much in the later viewings. That meant they had freed-up attentional resources they could devote to new forms in the input in the later viewings, with the result that they did better on measures of general proficiency, grammar, and vocabulary than those who saw the same video only once. Also of potential relevance, Dai and Ding (2010) report a study in which Chinese students who had memorized English texts over a school term, often through verbatim recitation, were found to use more varied and accurate formulaic sequences in their writing at the end of the term than a comparison group who had worked with the same texts in ways of their own choosing. Given the unquestioned importance of formulaic speech, including collocations, research directly addressing the effectiveness of "overt plagiarism" (for which a more positive term would be a good idea) and additional pedagogic procedures for teaching and learning collocations and other kinds of formulaic language are clearly a priority.

10.2.6. MP6: Focus on form

MP6: Focus on form, one of the three MPs original to TBLT (MP1 and MP3 are the other two), was first presented publicly as a free-standing item in a 1988 conference paper that was widely circulated before appearing in print (Long 1991). Since then, although not without its critics,[7] focus on form has taken on a life of its own (see, e.g., Doughty & Williams 1998a). This is because, like most of the other nine MPs (MPs 1 and 2 being the obvious exceptions), it is potentially relevant in language teaching more generally, especially for any communicative approach, task-based or otherwise. Many who have written about various aspects of the focus on form/focus on forms distinction seem unaware of its origins in TBLT.

While not the only one, focus on form is the principal mechanism in TBLT aimed at capturing the well-documented facilitative effects of instruction while respecting the

---

[7] For example, Batstone (2002) is undoubtedly correct when he notes that a teacher might intend a phase in a lesson as focus on form, but learners interpret it as focus on forms, and vice versa. Furthermore, I would add, different students' focus within a lesson will sometimes vary. Batstone's point was well illustrated in a lesson described by Samuda (2001). Also, R. Ellis (2012, pp. 274–275) argued that some activities, e.g., consciousness-raising (CR) tasks, can be hard to classify unambiguously as a means of delivering either focus on form or forms. My own view is that this is less of a problem. CR tasks' focus on particular target structures makes their typical use a focus on forms activity. However, as explained in Section 10.3, they can also serve as one of many pedagogic procedures teachers employ to provide corrective feedback during a communicative lesson, and *in that role, in that position in the discourse*, are equally clearly part of a focus on form. Even provision of an explicit grammar rule, after all, can constitute focus on form if it is provided *in response* to a problem that arises during a communicative exchange, then serving as the pedagogic procedure used to deliver focus on form. Such cases are further evidence of the importance of understanding that focus on form is by definition *reactive*, not proactive, and that the very same utterances or activities can constitute focus on form or focus on forms depending on when they occur. The timing is critical.

equally well-documented constraints on its effectiveness, not least the fact that learnability determines teachability (see Chapters 2 and 3). A rationale for focus on form was provided in Chapter 2, to which the reader is referred (see, also, Long 1988, 1991, 2000a; Long & Robinson 1998), and will not be repeated here. The following definition is from Chapter 2.5:

> *focus on form* involves *reactive* use of a wide variety of pedagogic procedures (PPs) to draw learners' attention to linguistic problems in context, as they arise during communication (in TBLT, typically as students work on problem-solving tasks), thereby increasing the likelihood that attention to code features will be synchronized with the learner's internal syllabus, developmental stage and processing ability. Focus on form capitalizes on a symbiotic relationship between explicit and implicit learning, instruction and knowledge.

The idea is simple, but not, I hope, simplistic. The key features are that focus on form involves learners' attention being briefly attracted to, or in some cases (see below) directed to, language form and form-meaning connections during a sequence (usually a whole lesson, in turn, part of a whole course) in which the primary focus is on meaning or communication. The brief switch in attention from meaning to form is usually (but by no means only) triggered by a communication problem, either receptive or productive, and thus is, by definition, *reactive*. It is a *response* to a difficulty – a missing vocabulary item, a problematic verb ending, and so on – due to a learner's current incomplete stage of L2 development.

The brief attentional switch, often lasting just a few seconds, typically originates with the learner, taking place without any external intervention, e.g., from the teacher or textbook. For example, a learner may attend to a reformulation by the teacher or a classmate of what he or she just said, or to a response to what another classmate has just said (the latter a process Slimani [1989] showed to be very effective), or, when the previous utterance contained errors, attend to a corrective recast. On other occasions, aware of a difficulty he or she is experiencing, a learner may pause briefly to try to recall a missing vocabulary item, the gender of a noun, a subjunctive verb form, and so on, or to re-read a sentence that is causing difficulty, or to ask a classmate or the teacher for help. The temporary new attentional focus may lead to effortful retrieval of the missing item from long-term memory, to the learning of a new item, or at least to noticing the item in the input. In all these cases, the attentional switch is initiated by the learner. The learner will then usually become aware of the form concerned, but without abstract knowledge of the form–meaning association, such as a rule. Intentional learning is brought to the aid of incidental learning, thereby improving the likelihood that a new form–meaning association will be perceived or perceived more quickly.

Communicative difficulties are not the only trigger for focus on form, however. A teacher or an interlocutor outside the classroom will sometimes repeat or reformulate something a learner has just said perfectly correctly. They may even explicitly draw a learner's attention to an alternative way of encoding what he or she just said, not because communication is threatened, but because a better option exists, e.g., a native-like collocation. Here, the attentional switch is other-initiated and recruits the learner's capacity for explicit learning. This is not the same as pre-teaching grammar points or vocabulary items *before* they are encountered in texts or tasks, which would be a case of focus on forms, not focus on form. With focus on form, even when a learner's attention is directed to linguistic form by an interlocutor, the direction is in *response* to what the learner has said or written (ideally, just said or just written) or has just failed to decode appropriately when listening or reading.

Numerous studies of the effectiveness of various types of L2 instruction have appeared in the SLA literature (for reviews, see, e.g., De Graaff & Housen 2009; R. Ellis 2012; and Chapter 11.5), including several of focus on form and/or comparative studies of focus on form and focus on forms, along with, in a number of additional studies, treatments which have been classified after the fact as exemplifying one or other approach. Two statistical meta-analyses of the available research have appeared, each of which draws conclusions about focus on form, as well as other dimensions of SLA, such as, more generally, explicit and implicit instruction. In the first, a landmark publication in its own right, as an accompanying editorial by Nick Ellis, then editor of *Language Learning* made clear, Norris and Ortega (2000) reviewed 49 experimental and quasi experimental studies conducted between 1980 and 1998. Their analysis showed (a) greater effects for explicit ($d = 1.13$) than implicit ($d = 0.54$) instructional treatments, and (b) that focus on form and focus on forms interventions resulted in equivalent and large effects. In fact, focus on form treatments ($d = 1.00$) produced slightly larger effect sizes than focus on forms treatments ($d = 0.93$). Not many studies provided data on pre-test to post-test gains within conditions, so results there must be considered cautiously, but among those that did, the average change across all instructional treatments was 1.66 standard deviations, with focus on form producing greater change than focus on forms. Based on average pre- to post-test improvements observed in control groups, however, as much as 18% of improvement in all conditions seems likely to have been due to practice effects and/or other naturally occurring changes. Of additional importance, (c) results on delayed post-tests in the small number of studies that included them showed the improvements to be durable, a finding since confirmed by analyses of more recent work. In related meta-analyses of the role of interaction and negative feedback in SLA (see, e.g., Goo & Mackey 2013; Li 2010; Mackey & Goo 2007), effects of implicit treatments have been found to be more durable than those of explicit treatments.

For several reasons, these results provide support for MP6, and for several reasons, even more support than might be obvious from a cursory inspection. First, by definition, focus on form achieved as much as focus on forms within communicative classrooms, not as a result of text-based lessons devoted chiefly to code-focused exercises and drills. Second, experimental (and most quasi-experimental) comparative studies of the relative effectiveness of focus on form and focus on forms instruction (and of explicit and implicit approaches) tend to be short-term – often lasting just a few hours, sometimes even just a few minutes – in the interest of maintaining control over the treatments and conditions and thereby avoiding threats to internal validity. Because demonstrating language learning within such short periods is a tall order, researchers tend to select simple target structures (learning hard grammar takes too long), which automatically favors focus on forms, since explicit instruction in any field generally works best, when it works at all, with simple learning tasks. Third, as Norris and Ortega pointed out, explicit treatments are typically more intense and varied than implicit treatments. Fourth, many researchers compound the inherent bias in short-term studies in favor of explicit treatments by employing outcome measures, e.g., discrete-point tests of various kinds (90% in Norris and Ortega's sample) that only require controlled L2 use and closely resemble the explicit treatments, and far fewer (10% in their sample) that consist of free productive L2 use. Doughty (2003) provides a detailed examination of these and other tricky methodological issues in effect-of-instruction research. Fifth, implicit learning takes time, so implicit treatments, Norris and Ortega observe, may require longer post-intervention observation periods for nonlinear learning curves to be detected.[8] Finally, whereas implicit treatments tend to have consisted of just one sort of implicit L2 exposure, explicit treatments often turn out to have comprised a medley of such pedagogic procedures as rule presentation, focused practice, negative feedback, and rule review. Some even included oral or written output, which can be an implicit learning activity.

While certainly encouraging, Norris and Ortega's results cannot be taken as a vindication of focus on form. First, many studies they considered required post hoc classification of instructional treatments as explicit/implicit and/or focus on form/ forms. Descriptions of treatments in the original reports were sometimes vague, and as noted above, supposedly explicit treatments, especially, often turned out to have included both explicit and implicit pedagogic procedures. Second, whereas average effect sizes for explicit and focus on forms treatments were large, that for implicit focus on form treatments was only medium ($0.50 < d < 0.80$). Third, standard deviations in many studies were high, indicating substantial variation in the effectiveness of all the treatments, possibly reflecting individual learner differences (aptitude–treatment interaction studies are clearly in order), and potentially, also, differences in the effectiveness of various sub-types of each treatment, as well as in learning context. Nevertheless, Norris and Ortega concluded as follows:

> These caveats notwithstanding, the current state of empirical findings indicates that explicit instruction is more effective than implicit instruction and that a focus on form and a focus on forms are equally effective. (Norris & Ortega 2000, p. 501)

This second conclusion is especially significant because it suggests that task-based, immersion and some content-based courses can potentially deal with at least some areas of students' language development without detracting from their intended primary focus on learning subject matter, accomplishing tasks, and developing communicative abilities in the L2.

The second statistical meta-analysis was a follow-up to Norris and Ortega's work, ten years on, by Goo *et al.* (2009). Goo *et al.* analyzed a total of 34 unique sample studies: 11 from Norris and Ortega's (2000) meta-analysis that met their stricter criteria for inclusion (see below), and 23 new studies published between 1999 and 2011. An important methodological improvement was their decision to consider only research treatments (e.g., Doughty 1991; Robinson 1996; Williams & Evans 1998) that had involved comparison of performance in *both* implicit and explicit conditions with that of a control or comparison group *within the same study*. This avoided the probability that the duration of implicit and explicit treatments would have been different, potentially affecting outcomes, in separate studies in which only one treatment (either implicit or explicit) had been compared with that of a control group (e.g., Lyster 1994; VanPatten & Sanz

---

[8] For insightful analyses of these and other issues in the identification and measurement of L2 development over time, especially when using time-series designs, see Mellow (1992) and Mellow, Reeder, and Forster (1996).

1995) or in which different implicit or different explicit treatments had been compared with one another or with a control or comparison condition (e.g., Fotos & Ellis 1991; Long, Inagaki, & Ortega 1998; VanPatten & Cadierno 1993). Inclusion of the latter two sorts of studies would have meant that effects in one would not be strictly comparable with those in another, whichever treatment type was involved. X amount of implicit instruction in one study would have been compared with Y amount of explicit instruction in another. Such studies had been included in the earlier meta-analysis.

The modified inclusion criteria notwithstanding, the findings of the new meta-analysis broadly confirmed those of the previous study. There was a large overall mean effect size for instruction ($g = 1.031$) across immediate and delayed post-tests, and a large mean pre-to-post effect size ($g = 1.515$), albeit a slightly lower one than that ($d = 1.66$) found by Norris and Ortega.[9] Explicit instruction was more effective than implicit instruction, regardless of the moderator variables examined: experimental or quasi-experimental studies, oral, written, or combined mode of instruction, provision or not of negative feedback, foreign or second language setting, type of target feature (grammar or pragmatics), and type of outcome measure. In performance across all post-tests, there was a large mean effect size for explicit instruction ($g = 1.290$) and an effect size for implicit instruction slightly short of what is considered large ($g = 0.774$). Explicit treatments led to greater gains than implicit treatments by 0.494 of a standard deviation unit. However, unlike Norris and Ortega, Goo *et al.* found that *both* implicit and explicit instruction yielded a large mean effect size on immediate post-tests ($gs = 1.361$ and 0.830 for explicit and implicit instruction, respectively). Their major conclusions echoed those of the earlier study:

> Our overall findings indicate, as in Norris and Ortega's meta-analysis, explicit instruction has been more effective at precipitating L2 development than implicit instruction, regardless of the moderator variables examined here. Nevertheless, implicit instruction still yielded a large effect size on immediate posttests in the present meta-analysis, unlike what Norris and Ortega found (a medium effect size). (Goo & Mackey 2013, p. 48)

The findings of the two statistical meta-analyses of the effects of instruction show that explicit treatments tend to produce larger learning gains than implicit treatments, especially when assessed by immediate post-tests, but that implicit treatments work well, too. It is important to bear in mind that most comparisons have involved short-term studies, easy learning targets, and outcome measures that favor explicit treatments. Implicit learning, in other words, is seldom allowed to show all it can do. Complex linguistic matters are very difficult to handle explicitly when they can be handled that way at all, and are very rarely the focus of these studies. Because of their primary focus on code features, moreover, explicit approaches preclude a primary focus on subject matter learning, immersion education, or TBLT; in other words, whatever they achieve comes at a major cost. In contrast, while preserving the benefits of such programs, MP6, Focus on form, presents an attractive alternative. It utilizes the learner's capacity for incidental learning, which will be necessary, due to both the size and complexity of the

---

[9] While demonstrating positive effects of formal instruction has become routine in recent years, there was a time when the value of instruction was seriously questioned, necessitating somewhat defensive reviews, such as my own (Long 1983a), of what was then admittedly a rather thin literature.

learning task, while improving on pure incidental learning through systematic recruit-ment of intentional learning, but doing so reactively, in harmony with the learner's developmental readiness.

10.2.7. MP7: Provide negative feedback

While negative feedback, usually in the form of traditional "error correction," is one of the most common features of language teaching (Krashen & Seliger 1975), dissenting opinions as to its value have appeared from time to time. More positive evidence, not negative evidence, has been proposed as the solution to error (e.g., Krashen & Terrell 1983). The "non-interface" position is that explicit and implicit knowledge are separate, non-interacting systems, such that neither explicit knowledge nor negative feedback can influence, much less morph into, implicit knowledge (see, e.g., Paradis 2004; Young-Scholten 1999, and for a nuanced supporting argument from a universal grammar [UG] perspective, Schwartz 1993). Those claims notwithstanding, MP7 is supported theoreti-cally and by a considerable body of empirical research. My own position is that negative evidence is (a) necessary in some cases and (b) facilitative in others. Since the topic was treated earlier, in Chapters 2 and 3, the present discussion will serve only as a brief reminder of the issues and relevant findings.

A compelling case for the *necessity* of negative evidence in L2A was made by White (1987, and elsewhere). When part of a L1 and L2 grammar are in a superset–subset relationship, i.e., when the L1 allows a wider range of grammatical options than the L2 with which to express the same or a similar meaning, L2 learners will need to "unlearn" one or more options that are perfectly acceptable in the L1, and some form of negative evidence will often be required for the purpose. For example, French and Spanish (among other languages) allow adverbials in initial and final position in simple S–V–DO sentences, and English does, too:

Toutes les jours, je bois du café. (Every day, I drink coffee.)
Je bois du café toutes les jours. (I drink coffee every day.)

However, French and Spanish (among other languages) also allow adverbials between verb and direct object, whereas English does not:

Je bois toujours du café. (*I drink every day coffee.)

Thus, a speaker of French or Spanish learning English will need to give up the third option. This can be tricky, White points out, because the meaning of 'I drink every day coffee' is clear, despite the error, so it will not cause a communication breakdown, and therefore, is unlikely to be "corrected" on the street. Classroom learners, however, may be made aware of the problem through provision of a simple grammar rule, overt "error correction," implicit negative feedback (clarification requests, recasts, etc.), or some combination thereof. Absent such negative evidence, they may remain unaware of the error and never learn the new rule, or constraint. An English speaker learning French, on the other hand, should have no problem with the same area of grammar, for then, the relationship is the reverse: a move from subset to superset. Learners will hear or read examples of the new permitted Subject–Verb–Adverbial–Direct Object option in the input (positive evidence) and simply add that to their repertoire. There are numerous such linguistic contrasts involving L1 superset–L2 subset relationships, some common to pairs of language families, and some, e.g., Spanish *por*/*para* for English *for*, and *rincón*/*esquina* for (indoor/outdoor) *corner*, unique to particular L1–L2 pairings. Such cases require negative evidence.[10]

White's argument is for the *necessity* of negative evidence in some (predictable) cases. Empirical evidence of its *facilitative* effects is plentiful. The reader is referred to the many sources on the effectiveness of both explicit negative feedback (e.g., DeKeyser 1993; Yilmaz 2012) and implicit negative feedback, especially recasts (Goo & Mackey 2013; Li 2010; Long 2007d; Mackey & Goo 2007; Russell & Spada 2006; Sagarra & Abbuhl 2013; Smith & Renaud 2013). (See also Chapter 11.5.3.) R. Ellis (2012, p. 262) summarizes an as yet unpublished classroom study by Mifka-Profozic (2011) of 50 high school students in New Zealand that compared the absolute effectiveness (using a control group) and relative effectiveness of two kinds of implicit negative feedback, one that does not require learner output, and one that does – recasts and clarification requests, respectively – for the teaching of two French verb tenses. Results showed that accuracy was statistically significantly higher on both the French preterite and imparfait on both immediate and delayed post-tests among students who had received recasts than among those in the control group. Accuracy was also higher, sometimes statistically significantly so, among students who had received recasts than among those who had received clarification requests for both structures on both immediate and delayed post-tests. These results are of special interest, given arguments between researchers (see, e.g., Goo & Mackey 2013; Long 2007b) who support the relative effectiveness of recasts, which contain contrastive positive evidence of the target structure, and those (see, e.g., Lyster & Saito 2010) who favor explicit negative feedback, especially prompts, that does not, but which has learners attempt to produce the target structure again.

Given that the major concern of language learners and teachers is efficiency, not necessity and sufficiency, overall justification for MP7 is strong. That is not to say that everything is known, that negative evidence is a cure-all, or that recasts, for example, are a panacea. Some errors, e.g., French gender marking for English speakers, and problems with article uses for speakers of Japanese and Russian, often prove resistant to treatment of any kind, as evidenced by lengthy stabilization of such errors in the interlanguages of Anglophone students in French immersion programs in Canada (Swain 1991) and in those of long-term residents in the target language environment (Master 1994, 1997). Despite the generally clear findings, much about negative evidence remains to be discovered. Where implicit negative feedback is concerned, for example, some studies of recasts (e.g., Doughty et al. 1999; Ono & Witzel 2002; Ortega & Long 1997) suggest the existence of an inverse relationship between the saliency of target linguistic features and the degree of explicitness required in negative evidence.

---

[10] It could also be the case that never encountering the ungrammatical options in the L2, e.g., the V–Adv–DO sequence, would cause the (L1) option simply to wither away over the years and eventually disappear for lack of support in the input – so-called "indirect negative evidence." But the process would take an unfortunately long time if it happened at all.

10.2.8. MP8: Respect learner syllabi and developmental processes

The psycholinguistic rationale for MP8 was prefigured in Chapters 2 and 3. To recapitulate, sudden categorical mastery of a full NS form or structure is rare, typically only witnessed with isolated lexical items, even if the full target version (e.g., the fully analyzed, stage 4 English negation system) is the only one that is taught and to which learners are exposed outside the classroom. The acquisition of target structures typically involves passage through each stage in a fixed developmental sequence manifested in target-like and/or non-target-like structures and independent of instructional sequences (for examples of common developmental ESL sequences for speakers of Polish and Vietnamese, see Johnston 1985, 1997, and for reviews, see Ortega 2009; Pienemann 2011). The transitional structures are often unattested in either the L1 or the L2. Learners cannot skip a stage.

Given these findings, it is unsurprising that research has shown that instruction needs to be pitched at a learner's current developmental stage or one step ahead to be effective (see, e.g., Ellis 1989; Lightbown 1983; Pienemann 1984, 1989), i.e., at the levels Krashen called "i" or "i + 1." The same is true of negative feedback (Mackey 1999). Both "i" and "i + 1" were unoperationalized, so untestable, constructs in Monitor Theory. Pienemann was able to operationalize them with reference to the developmental stages uncovered by the ZISA project (Clahsen, Meisel, & Pienemann 1983) and explained as reflections of universal cognitive underpinnings and constraints on production (Clahsen 1987). Specifically, progress to each new stage in a sequence was the result of a learner breaking through the constraints on what was processable at his or her current stage. For instance, at one stage, a learner could only move an element from a salient (e.g., final) position in a string to another salient one (e.g., initial position), as in English topicalization ('I love Barcelona' becoming 'Barcelona, I love!'). Later, the same learner could move items in less salient (string-internal) positions ('Which city did he love?' 'He asked which city he loved' not '*He asked which city did he love.'). In terms of Processability Theory (Pienemann 1998; Pienemann & Kessler 2011, 2012), what is teachable at any moment is constrained by what is processable at that moment, i.e., *learnability* determines *teachability*.

TBLT takes the findings on teachability into account first and foremost by not attempting to impose an unnatural instructional sequence on the learner. It does this by eschewing focus on forms and a linguistic syllabus of any kind – even a covert linguistic syllabus, as in task-*supported* language teaching (i.e., lower case tblt) – and replacing them with focus on form, which is by definition reactive, i.e., responsive to the learner's current stage of development. Second, TBLT recognizes the inevitability of errors and their positive role in language learning (Corder 1967; Dakin 1973; Nemser 1971; Selinker 1972). Third, learnability is respected by the *reactive* nature of focus on form and implicit negative feedback during communicative language use, especially recasts; a learner's attention is drawn or directed to linguistic code features in *response* to learner problems and/or because a preferable alternative form exists. Third, input that is provided is more likely to be at least roughly tuned to learners' current processing capacity by virtue of having been negotiated by them during collaborative work on PTs.

Teachers cannot teach whatever they choose, whenever they choose; nevertheless, the beneficial effects of instruction are well established. Instruction that is carefully timed, i.e., harmonized with internal learning processes and stages, helps accelerate passage through developmental sequences and extends the scope of application of grammatical rules (Pienemann 1989). It can deal with areas of the L2 grammar supposedly unlearnable from positive evidence alone (White 1991), and it improves accuracy, rate of learning, and level of ultimate attainment (Doughty 2003; Long 1988). TBLT seeks to deliver these benefits by respecting the learner's internal syllabus and "natural" developmental processes.

10.2.9. MP9: Promote cooperative collaborative learning

A philosophical argument in favor of cooperative collaborative learning was presented in Chapter 4 (see, especially, Section 4.9). As is frequently the case, progressive philosophical principles converge on psycholinguistically motivated learning and teaching practices, so it should come as no surprise that organizing plentiful opportunities for cooperative collaborative learning has important advantages for acquisition, too.

Studies of child L1A (e.g., Ochs & Schieffelin 1979; Scollon 1976) and child and adult L2A (for reviews, see Gass 1997, 2003; Hatch 1978; Long 1983b,c,d, 1996b; Pica 1994; Pica *et al.* 1996) reveal a facilitative role in language development for collaborative, "scaffolded" discourse across utterances and speakers. As usual, however, there are limits. In particular, while Sato's longitudinal study of early stages in two Vietnamese children (aged eight and ten) acquiring English showed the value of collaborative dialogue in the initial emergence of relative clauses and other complex English syntax (Sato 1988, 1990), her analyses of the same database also showed how participation in conversation with native speakers could hinder the acquisition of inflectional morphology (Sato 1986). Early-stage learners' reliance on their interlocutors' establishment of past time reference ('Did you go to the game yesterday?' 'Yes, I go.'), along with their own use of (mostly temporal) adverbials, could obviate the need for them to employ past time markings on verbs for the purpose ('I see game yesterday').

Research has documented the positive effects of cooperative, collaborative group work on attainment in subject-matter learning (e.g., Barnes 1976/1992; Barnes & Todd 1977, 1995; Hmelo-Silver & Chinn 2013; Holt 1993; Webb 1991). Strong support comes from meta-analyses of numerous studies in general education (Johnson, Johnson, & Stanne 2000; Slavin 1996). Johnson *et al.*'s analysis of 194 independent effect sizes from 164 studies, for example, showed consistently superior achievement among students learning through any of eight methods of cooperative learning over that of students learning competitively or individualistically. Research on cooperative learning and small group work in second language learning is far less extensive but has produced similar findings (Jacobs 1998; Liang, Mohan, & Early 1998; Long & Porter 1985; Nunan 1992; Oxford 1997; Pica *et al.* 1996). There is also the argument, again substantiated in both L1A and L2A (see Swain 1995) that, unlike comprehension, where listeners or readers can often decode meaning from context without understanding, or sometimes even noticing, small words that encode grammatical relationships, L2 production encourages, and sometimes obliges, learners to grammaticize meanings, a process often referred to as syntacticization.

All these lines of work converge on MP9. In addition, pair work and small group work offers learners relative privacy and anonymity. They can try out new language beyond the glare and scrutiny that typically comes with full class participation. As noted in Chapter 4, such "sheltered" communication has affective value, especially for shy students, and is one reason why in TBLT, individual, pair, and small group work often *precede* work in whole class formats, as distinct from their more traditional use as ways of organizing classroom participation to maximize listening and speaking opportunities after public lockstep work.. At the level of pedagogic procedure, for pros and cons of some of the many possible ways of organizing small group work, see, e.g., Jacobs (1998), Long (1977b), and McCafferty, Jacobs, and DaSilva Iddings (2006). The number of persons in a group, its internal communication structure, the way information is distributed when tasks are assigned, and other factors, can all affect the quantity and quality of such work. For findings and recommendations on related issues in collaborative work in network-based language teaching, see Fukuda *et al.* (2001) and Warschauer and Kern (2000).

10.2.10. MP10: Individualize instruction

As noted elsewhere, TBLT, unlike most other approaches, is radically learner-centered in at least two fundamental ways. First, course content is determined by student needs. Second, universal developmental processes and the learner's internal syllabus guide and mediate instruction. It would be wrong to stop there, however. To the extent allowed by logistical constraints – time, money, class size, student homogeneity, teacher expertise, etc. – there is no more reason to believe that one size fits all in language teaching than would be the case in other fields. Responsible care for sick people, for example, (usually) entails their receiving a treatment prescribed for what ails them, not someone else.

Individualizing learning and teaching is nothing new, of course. Research in general education and foreign language classrooms has long shown the benefits of tailoring instruction to cater to individual differences in goals, interests, motivation, cognitive style, and learning strategies (Altman & James 1980; Harlow 1987; Logan 1973; Sawyer & Ranta 2001; Wesche 1981). Improvements in the measurement of these and other individual difference variables, especially language learning aptitude and short-term memory (see, e.g., Doughty 2013; Ellis 2001; Granena 2013c; Grigorenko, Sternberg, & Ehrman 2000; Linck *et al.* 2013; Meara 2005; Miyake & Friedman 2001), now further justify the individualization of instruction in any language teaching program.

In TBLT, beyond the two above-mentioned basic adaptations to learners at the level of whole courses, individualization occurs ideally (i.e., when logistical constraints allow) in the form of modifications of the pace at which and manner in which instruction is delivered, as suggested by diagnostic information gathered on individual differences. For instance, modern aptitude measures, such as LLAMA (Granena 2013b,c; Meara 2005) and Hi-Lab (Doughty 2013; Doughty *et al.* 2010; Linck *et al.* 2013) are able to differentiate not only among levels of language aptitude within groups, but between relative strengths in capacity for implicit and explicit learning within individuals. So-called aptitude–treatment interaction (ATI) studies (Pashler *et al.* 2009; Perrachione *et al.* 2011) are currently starting to appear in the SLA literature (for reviews, see R. Ellis 2012, pp. 307–335; Vatz *et al.* 2013). They are beginning to show that modifying materials and/or instructional approaches (e.g., in the use of inductive and deductive presentations and provision of implicit and explicit feedback) to cater to students with relatively stronger implicit or explicit learning profiles can improve or hinder learning, depending on whether or not students and treatments are matched. Little of this work has affected classroom language teaching, including TBLT programs, as yet, but such individually tailored modifications, or modifications to learner groups formed by aptitude profile, are likely to become more common in the near future.

10.3. Pedagogic Procedures

Language teachers and learners feel, behave, and interact differently from day to day, and the language and tasks they work on vary, making every lesson unique. Global prescriptions and proscriptions, therefore, are unwarranted and doomed to failure. Teachers will have lesson plans, but they will need to react differently in real time to situations as they arise. They are in some ways like professional soccer coaches who have to make tactical alterations and substitutions during a match, except that the teacher's decisions are far more numerous and require judgments and responses in a matter of seconds as a lesson unfolds, whereas coaches can usually think for a few minutes and even consult with their assistants before making a change.

Responses to errors are a case in point. One error in a student's written work or overheard by the teacher as he or she moves around the classroom listening in on small groups as they work on a PT may merit quiet treatment at the individual level with the student who made it and no one else. Another error the teacher may have heard many times as he or she circulates: since it is currently pervasive, it may warrant a brief interruption of the group work to bring it to the attention of the whole class. A third error should simply be ignored (for now, at least) because it involves a linguistic issue that the teacher realizes is too advanced for students at their current level, and so is not teachable in Pienemann's sense. These and many more like them are all moment-by-moment decisions teachers make every day. The appropriate one will often vary from one error to another, from one student to another, from one linguistic item to another, and from one day to another. One error, for example, may involve a perceptually non-salient feature that the teacher knows to be especially problematic for speakers of the L1 concerned, and to require negative evidence of some kind (to speed up progress, at least), perhaps because it is the product of a superset–subset configuration. Another concerns a salient feature that will soon take care of itself through additional exposure to positive evidence.

In this light, it would be silly for anyone to prescribe "error correction" in all cases, much less the same form of "error correction." Good pedagogic decisions require local knowledge, and the person with the most knowledge and expertise concerning a particular group of students is the classroom teacher, not a textbook writer or methodologist or the author of a book like this who has never met his/her students (and in the case of all too many textbook writers and supposed experts on pedagogy, has not taught much at all). There is no single correct response to learner error, except to recognize the inevitable and constructive role errors play in language learning (Corder 1967; Dakin 1973). There is certainly no single correct method of responding to errors. Thus, although MP7: Provide negative feedback, is one of TBLT's ten MPs, the pedagogic procedures used to deliver negative feedback should vary. The teacher has several moment-by-moment decisions to make, some of which I attempted to model in an early paper on the topic (Long 1977c). Is the deviant utterance or sentence the result of a temporary slip of the kind even native speakers make from time to time, or the surface reflection of an underlying problem at the competence level, i.e., in Corder's terms (Corder 1967), is it just a mistake, not an error at all? If an error, is it one that is currently treatable? Does it need treating, or will it take care of itself? If treatment is called for, can it be provided in written form (are the students literate?) and/or involve metalinguistic information (are the students old enough and smart enough to benefit?), and will implicit negative feedback, such as a recast, suffice (is the target feature or construction salient?) or will more explicit, on-record "correction" be needed?

Just as many such decisions need to be made when a teacher chooses to withhold or provide negative feedback, so it is with many moment-by-moment decisions about pedagogic procedures during a lesson. And given that students are individuals, and differ, the same decision will not necessarily be appropriate for all students in a class at the same moment. Some may have relatively stronger or weaker implicit or explicit language aptitude, for example. In this respect, the teacher is rather like a chess master playing an exhibition game of simultaneous chess against (say) 20 opponents (which is not to suggest that students are opponents, of course). The decisions need to vary, but not randomly. Ideally, they will differ systematically, on the basis of a combination of research findings and teacher experience. An excellent example of a rational, research-based sequence of such decisions concerning when and how to deliver MP6, Focus on form, is provided by Doughty and Williams (1998b). More such treatments of pedagogic procedures are greatly needed in the literature. Regrettably, however, few options in pedagogic procedures have been the subject of systematic research, so teacher experience and familiarity with particular students is crucially important, and likely always to remain so, given the need to adjust delivery to fit what are at some level always unique local circumstances.

10.4. Summary

TBLT currently involves ten MPs, the product of theory and research in SLA, the philosophy of education, language teaching, and related fields. While putative universals, it is fully recognized that one or more will quite possibly turn out to be wrong in light of new findings. As in any field, the standard to which one tries to be accountable is best practice as judged by current understanding of theory, research, and practical experience. While the MPs are considered to be widely, potentially universally, applicable, the manner of their delivery is not, and should vary systematically to fit local circumstances. The classroom teacher is the expert on local needs and circumstances, so pedagogic procedures are the teacher's call. This does not mean that anything goes. Teachers should be aware of such research as exists on options at the level of PPs, melding findings with their classroom experience and knowledge of the student(s) concerned.

10.5. Suggested Readings

Barnes, D. (1992). *From communication to curriculum*. London: Heinemann.
Barnes, D., & Todd, F. (1995). *Communication and learning revisited: Making meaning through talk*. Portsmouth, NH: Boynton/Cook.

Boers, F., & Lindstromberg, S. (2012). Experimental and intervention studies on formulaic sequences in a second language. *Annual Review of Applied Linguistics* 32, 83–110.

Crookes, G., & Gass, S.M. (eds.) (1993a). *Tasks and language learning. Integrating theory and practice*. Clevedon, Avon: Multilingual Matters.

Crookes, G., & Gass, S.M. (eds.) (1993b). *Tasks in a pedagogical context. Integrating theory and practice*. Clevedon, Avon: Multilingual Matters.

Doughty, C.J. (2013). Optimizing post-critical-period language learning. In Granena, G., & Long, M.H. (eds.), *Sensitive periods, language aptitude, and ultimate L2 attainment* (pp. 153–175). Amsterdam and Philadelphia: John Benjamins.

Doughty, C.J., & Long, M.H. (2003). Optimal psycholinguistic environments for distance foreign language learning. *Language Learning and Technology* 7, 3, September, 50–80. Retrieved from http://llt.msu.edu

Doughty, C.J., & Williams, J. (1998). Pedagogical choices in focus on form. In Doughty, C.J., & Williams, J. (eds.), *Focus on form in classroom second language acquisition* (pp. 197–262). Cambridge, England: Cambridge University Press.

Garcia-Mayo, M.P. (ed.) (2007). *Investigating tasks in formal language learning*. Clevedon, Avon: Multilingual Matters.

Gass, S.M. (1997). *Input, interaction, and the development of second languages*. Mahwah, NJ: Erlbaum.

Goo, J., & Mackey, A. (2013). The case against the case against recasts. *Studies in Second Language Acquisition* 35, 1, 127–165.

Horst, M. (2005). Learning L2 vocabulary through extensive reading: A measurement study. *Canadian Modern Language Review* 61, 3, 355–382.

Long, M.H. (1991). Focus on form: A design feature in language teaching methodology. In de Bot, K., Ginsberg, R.B., & Kramsch, C. (eds.), *Foreign language research in crosscultural perspective* (pp. 39–52). Amsterdam: John Benjamins.

Long, M.H. (1998). Focus on form in Task-Based Language Teaching. *University of Hawai'i Working Papers in ESL* 16, 2, 35–49. Also in Lambert, R.L., & Shohamy, E. (eds.) (2000). *Language policy and pedagogy* (pp. 179–192). Amsterdam and Philadelphia: John Benjamins.

Long, M.H. (2009). Methodological principles in language teaching. In Long, M.H., & Doughty, C.J. (eds.), *Handbook of language teaching* (pp. 373–394). Oxford: Blackwell.

McCafferty, S.G., Jacobs, G.M., & DaSilvia Iddings, A.-M. (2006). *Cooperative learning and second language teaching*. Cambridge: Cambridge University Press.

Nation, P., & Chung, T. (2009). Teaching and testing vocabulary. In Long, M.H., & Doughty, C.J. (eds.), *Handbook of language teaching* (pp. 543–559). Oxford: Blackwell.

Sato, C.J. (1988). Origins of complex syntax in interlanguage development. *Studies in Second Language Acquisition* 10, 3, 371–395.

Vatz, K., Tare, M., Jackson, S.R., & Doughty, C.J. (2013). Aptitude-treatment interaction studies in second language acquisition: Findings and methodology. In Granena, G., & Long, M.H. (eds.), *Sensitive periods, language aptitude, and ultimate L2 attainment* (pp. 273–292). Amsterdam and Philadelphia: John Benjamins.

Chapter 11

Task-Based Assessment and Program Evaluation

11.1. Task-Based, Criterion-Referenced Performance Tests

Assessment, whether of language or other abilities, can take many forms and fulfill a variety of goals, so it is always important to specify a test's intended use before designing or evaluating a new one (Norris 2000). *Placement tests*, administered before a program begins, are designed to divide large numbers of students into groups of manageable size, preferably made up of those of similar L2 ability, language aptitude, and so on, for the purpose of instruction. They may be criterion-referenced or (because this is often more efficient with large numbers of students entering a program) norm-referenced, and linguistically and/or task focused. *Diagnostic tests* in traditional focus-on-forms L2 programs, typically employed during a course, will be linguistically focused, and usually discrete-point. In a task-based program, on the other hand, diagnostic tests will usually be task-based, although occasionally supplemented by a discrete-point section targeting specific linguistic phenomena known to be problematic for certain students in their performance of particular tasks. Task-based *achievement tests*, the main focus of this chapter, are used to determine whether students have learned what was

Second Language Acquisition and Task-Based Language Teaching, First Edition. Mike Long.
© 2015 John Wiley & Sons, Inc. Published 2015 by John Wiley & Sons, Inc.

intended in a TBLT program, so they can now do what they need to do in the L2. High-stakes L2 achievement tests can determine a person's educational life chances – whether he or she is admitted to a school or university, offered a job or a place on a vocational training program, or in some cases, even an immigrant visa or citizenship in a new country. Task-based achievement tests are also found outside language programs. They are often used for certification purposes in industry, the professions, and elsewhere, e.g., to assess an individual's ability to meet the standards required of a computer programmer, a nurse, an airline pilot, a marksman, and so on.

As described throughout this book, the goal of a TBLT program is to equip students with the abilities they need for successful completion of their target tasks. Those are identified by the needs analysis, after which they are classified into target task-types, from which pedagogic tasks are derived and sequenced to form the task syllabus. Now, the same target tasks constitute the focus of task-based performance tests – achievement tests that assess student abilities resulting from the course. These tests can take many forms, but they will have some features in common.

First, they will be *task-based performance tests*. That is, the focus will not be on language as object, but on a student's ability to *do* real tasks, or simulations thereof. Put another way, success or failure in the assessment will turn on whether or not the teacher or outside examiner observes specific behavior(s) on the part of the students called for by the needs analysis. To use an example with which we are already familiar, if the ability to follow street directions is a target task for a group of learners, the test will *not* consist of an assessment of their ability to do such things as provide missing words in a set of street directions (Go up Filbert Street and _____ left) or indicate whether directions like 'Go along two blocks and turning right' are grammatical or ungrammatical. Rather, they may be issued with a digital recording device containing real street directions and sent out to follow them from a given starting-point without being told the destination. The student will pass or fail, depending on whether he or she reaches the correct destination. If navigating real streets is logistically unfeasible or overly problematic, a simulation may be employed, with the student watching a video of a street scene on a computer while manipulating a cursor in response to directions received though headphones. (For a related example, see González-Lloret 2003.) A logistically still simpler, if less realistic, version may have students follow directions delivered through headphones, or lacking headphones, by the teacher, while they look at the street map of a real town. To assess success or failure, the series of directions might end with a question, such as 'What is the building on your left?' Alternatively, if the number of students to be tested is large, making objective and/or machine scoring necessary, the same question may be posed using a multiple-choice format, with (say) ten possible answers listed (library, church, mosque, supermarket, police station, etc.) or ten letters marked on the map to represent destinations, of which students must identify the one to which the directions have led them. This way, a teacher without access to high tech equipment could test a whole class of students simultaneously with the aid of nothing more sophisticated than photocopies of a section from a street map, accompanied by a set of multiple-choice items.

All these variants are task-based *achievement* tests. If *diagnosis* of remaining problems is desired, a version is possible in which students trace the route they take in response to the directions on a computer screen or (low tech version) in pencil on hard copy of the map. The resulting record will show any discrepancies between directions and behavior, allowing further work, if needed, to focus on the specific problems identified. As in this case, assessment in TBLT usually takes the form of the final, exit task in a module. Several more examples of such exit tasks were provided in the sample materials in Chapter 9.3.

Second, task-based performance tests in TBLT will be *criterion-referenced*. As with teaching, so with testing, the goal is not to compare one student's abilities against those of other students, as is the case with norm-referenced measures, but to determine whether each student can or cannot perform target tasks at a satisfactory level, i.e., to criterion. An everyday example of a task-based, criterion-referenced performance test with which most people are familiar is the one required to obtain a driver's license. Each candidate either passes or fails the test. The outcome does not depend on how other learner drivers do; it is simply a matter of whether the candidate meets the criteria. Did he or she pass the vision test by reading letters of a predetermined size projected on a screen, and then the written test satisfactorily by scoring at or above the predetermined threshold (35/40 points, or whatever)? Then, did he or she complete the practical part of the test to the satisfaction of the examiner (who rides along in the front passenger seat issuing instructions and taking notes and ticking boxes on a checklist) by navigating a fixed route on real streets safely and without violating any traffic laws? If so, a license is awarded. If not, the candidate failed the test and must try again after a set minimum period.

The criterion or criteria in criterion-referenced tests, it is important to note, will typically be determined by domain experts. In a test of students' ability to understand an undergraduate physics lecture, for example, the physics professor, not the language teacher or test designer, will be the judge of what is considered successful task completion. The goal is to ascertain whether students can extract the required information from the lecture, not their level of accuracy with (say) the third conditional. For example, the assessment may take the form of viewing a video of the lecture once, followed by a multiple-choice test focusing on (say) 50 important information bits (identified by the lecturer) that the lecture contained. The physics professor might decide that, in order to pass, candidates must show they understood (say) nine out of ten points that he or she identifies as critically important, and 36 out of the remaining 40 less important points, for a minimum total of 45/50. Whether students pass or fail will be determined by whether their score on the test meets or exceeds the minimum acceptable percentage of correct answers, or "cut score," as set by the domain expert. As with all criterion-referenced tests, it is unnecessary to compare a student's score against those of other students taking the test; the score itself will immediately indicate "pass" or "fail." (For detailed discussions of criterion-referenced testing, including the appropriate statistical procedures for evaluating test items and for assessing a test's reliability and validity, see Bachman 1989; Bachman & Palmer 1996; Brown 1990; Brown & Hudson 2002; Hudson & Lynch 1984; Lynch & Davidson 1994; Messick 1994; Popham 2000; and Popham & Husek 1969.)

Increasing numbers of task-based, criterion-referenced performance tests are being produced in areas not necessarily connected with TBLT programs, especially for certification purposes in the vocational and occupational sectors, and understandably often in high stakes situations, where predictive validity is at a premium. For examples and discussion, see, e.g., Brindley (2013); Coad (1984); Colpin & Gysen, 2006; McNamara (1996), Norris, Bygate, and Van den Branden (2009); Van den Branden, Depauw, and

Gysen (2002), and sample items from the test of English Language Proficiency for Aeronautical Communication (ELPAC) at http://www.elpac.info and the Lancaster Language Testing Research Group's ELPAC validation study, at http://elpac.info/index.php ?option=com_content&task=view&id=50&Itemid=42&Itemid=1.

In an important article, Fulcher (2008) has drawn attention to the need for empirical studies of learner and real-world task performance that would provide another way of assessing task-based test validity.

11.2. Task Completion and/or Language Abilities?

Following street directions and understanding a high school or university lecture are both tasks whose performance hinges on students' receptive abilities. This means that it is perfectly possible, and acceptable, for a student to pass a test despite missing some details due to gaps in his or her L2 abilities. For example, he or she might understand "Take the second turning on the right" without noticing 'the,' and without a clue as to the use of definite, indefinite, or zero articles in English. However, the test was not designed to assess command of articles, but the ability to follow street directions, and if what the student decoded was (in a worst-case scenario) no more than something like 'second turn right,' and that was sufficient for him or her to reach the correct destination, no matter, he or she passes. Things become a little more complicated when tasks require spoken or written production. Nevertheless, despite the option that production allows for an assessment to focus on linguistic accuracy, complexity or fluency, in *task-based* assessment, the focus remains on *task completion*, with a measurable behavioral outcome. Regardless of missing articles or a wrong preposition here and there, can the student perform the task or not?

For example, if the target task is buying train or plane tickets, or making a reservation for the theater, for a sports event, or for a dinner at a restaurant, learners might be issued with cue cards informing them of their destination, travel dates and budget, and/or the date, time, and number of people requiring seats. Their job will be to communicate their requirements to someone – in a genuine case, a real ticket clerk, airline reservations agent, or booking office agent (face to face, over the telephone, or online), or in a simulation, typically the teacher or a language tester – make the appropriate purchase for the specified time, date, and number of people, and do so within budget. In the case of a simulation, depending on the potential complexity of the target task, the examiner might also hold a cue card with information about train or flight (un)availability (direct or requiring stops/train changes, etc.), prices, seat (un)availability (economy, business, or first class, aisle, center or window seat, front row, gallery, etc.), restaurant table (un)availability (for the number of diners, corner or window table, for the game, on the day or at the time requested, etc.). In most such cases, successful task completion can be measured easily enough by observing the outcome. Did the student succeed in booking or buying what was needed within the price range allowed? But what about the language he or she used to do so? Should that be part of the assessment, too?

Views on this differ. It will ultimately depend on the uses that will be made of the assessment (for discussion, see Norris 2008) – who will use the results, for making what decisions or taking what actions? Some programs may choose to penalize students who completed the task, e.g., procured the tickets/seats/reservations they wanted, but employed some speech or writing that was ungrammatical (*I am needing two seats) and/or sociolinguistically inappropriate (e.g., familiar second person T form of verbs when the more formal V form was appropriate), and/or pragmatically or culturally inappropriate (e.g., the rude "I said *window* seats!" or in some cultures, not speaking first when one is the telephone *caller*) along the way. Others may opt to focus solely on task completion, regardless of linguistic, sociolinguistic, or pragmatic errors. While my own preference is for the latter (see, also, Long & Norris 2000; Mislevy, Steinberg, & Almond 2002; Robinson & Ross 1996), there is probably no uniformly correct answer. It is sometimes a judgment call, better made case by case. For example, grammatical and pragmatic errors may be unimportant in most service encounters involving buying and selling, but as shown by the Marriot and Yamada (1991) study of Australian duty-free shop service encounters (discussed in Chapter 7.4.2), they can sometimes be very important. Sociolinguistic and pragmatic errors might be overlooked in most cases, but could potentially be serious when committed by a hotel receptionist, a tour guide, or a diplomat.

The danger of opting for the addition of a linguistic "caboose" to a test of task-based abilities is that it can quickly lead to difficult questions regarding the frequency and/or degree of ungrammaticality or inappropriateness that will be tolerated. Questions will also arise as to how grammaticality, sociolinguistic appropriateness or pragmatic acceptability can be assessed and scored objectively, either in real time or on the basis of a recording. If students complete a task successfully, will they still pass if they made grammatical errors (if so, how many) or were impolite (if so, how impolite)? Worse, introduction of a linguistic caboose could eventually lead to a reorientation of a task-based course, as a result of washback, to one which devotes progressively larger segments of class time to work on language as object. TBLT's way of handling students' linguistic needs is through provision of appropriate input, task-based practice, focus on form (not forms), and negative feedback, all during work on pedagogic tasks, not by task-supported language teaching or by a return to some sort of bifurcated syllabus, part task, part structural, of the kind that has occasionally been proposed, e.g., by R. Ellis (1993, 2002, 2003, pp. 243–262). If pragmatic appropriateness, for example, is an important dimension of task completion, then students' attention can be drawn to pragmatic features as necessary, in context, in just the same way as it is drawn to grammatical, lexical, and collocational issues. The importance, if any, to be attached to linguistic accuracy and appropriateness will vary from one task to another, and should be decided during phase 2 of the needs analysis, when successful target task performance is first specified.

If a decision is made to add a language caboose, a holistic assessment of a student's linguistic performance will be more appropriate than measurement at the micro-level of accuracy with forms. The assessment can be made of the quality of the student's language overall while performing the task, or if more diagnostic information is desirable, at the level of sub-tasks. This was the approach taken by Nielson *et al.* (2009) for the evaluation of students' task-based abilities in an online course in Chinese as a foreign language (FL). The virtual role-play format they employed is reminiscent of the one described in Chapter 9.3.4.1 as PT6, the role-play exit task for assessing students' ability to negotiate a police traffic stop.

One example was the exit test in the course for the target task of *Buying a cell phone*. Nielsen *et al.* gave the students a list of features the cell phone was required to have, e.g., a camera, a qwerty keyboard, a wide screen, Internet-capability, and a maximum cost of $75. Students had to discuss phone options, with a conversation partner playing the role of the salesperson in the virtual language classroom. Both had pictures of four different possible cell phones in front of them. Nielsen *et al.* broke the transaction down into 11 sub-tasks: Uses appropriate greetings, Informs salesperson of item he/she wants to purchase, Informs salesperson of cell phone features, Discusses price, Negotiates price, Clarifies ambiguous information, Answers clarification questions about which features are most important, Maintains control of purchase, Determines final cost of cell phone, Successfully completes purchase of cell phone, and Closes conversation. Raters were provided with explicit criteria they were to consider when evaluating performance of each sub-task. For example, for 'Maintains control of purchase', the criterion was that the student redirect the salesperson when he attempts to sell the student a phone that is either beyond his or her budget or does not contain the necessary features. For 'Discusses price', the student had to inform the salesperson that the price was too high and request a discount. Raters had to place 11 check marks in the 'yes' or 'no' column of the rating sheet, depending on whether or not each sub-task was completed successfully.

Then came the linguistic caboose. For each sub-task, the evaluator had to provide a holistic rating of the student's general language skills, Chinese accuracy, and Chinese fluency. For general language skills, he or she had to indicate how well the criteria were met on a scale of 1, 'Student barely met success criteria' to 5, 'Student met success criteria perfectly.' The success criteria were that 'Student's questions, comments, and responses are appropriate to the situation.' For Chinese language accuracy, also rated on a scale of 1 to 5, the criteria for success were that 'Student's speech is clear and in Chinese (with the exception of proper names in English). Pauses and false starts do not detract from comprehensibility.' For Chinese language fluency, again using a five-point scale, the criteria were 'Conversation partner is able to understand student's pronunciation and responds to questions and comments appropriately.'

While one way of bringing language into an otherwise task-based assessment, there is obvious potential for the same degree of vagueness and impressionistic judgments that afflict global ratings based on oral proficiency interviews and similar "proficiency" tests. Similar problems arise with an approach that favors testing underlying constructs, discussed in the following section. Task completion can have tangible, observable, unambiguous, behavioral outcomes. Conversely, even when criteria are specified, holistic ratings of accuracy, fluency, general language skills, and proficiency, like underlying constructs, are inevitably impressionistic. Moreover, different tasks require different abilities. I can be good at reading novels, but lousy at reading legal documents, good (or if you prefer, a "2" or an "Intermediate High") at detailed, "closed" conversation over the telephone, e.g., canceling an airline reservation or obtaining information about the availability of a flight to Amsterdam, but poor at informal, open-ended, face-to-face conversation, e.g., chit-chat about family news or the evening news.

11.3. Target Tasks or Underlying Constructs and Abilities?

Assessment in TBLT consists of direct or indirect tests of students' ability to complete target tasks successfully. This sounds simple enough, but there are some hidden problems, chief among which is that there may simply be too many target tasks for all of them to be assessed in the time available. The potential solution is the same as that which was employed when dealing with the equivalent problem in syllabus design, i.e., teach for, and now test performance on, representative target tasks within sets grouped together as members of the same target task-type. While seemingly logical, the difficulty is the same in both cases: how does one know which target tasks share enough in common to be grouped together? More fundamentally, do task-based abilities transfer? Is it sufficient to test one or two tasks and assume that students who can complete those tasks successfully will be able to complete other tasks of the same type? If so, how can one be sure that two tasks are of the same type? Task classification and its reflex, transferability of task-based abilities, are long-standing questions (Norris *et al.* 1998) and one of the two major unresolved issues in TBLT. (The other, as noted in Chapter 8, is the identification of theoretically motivated and/or empirically attested criteria for sequencing pedagogic tasks by increasing task complexity.)

The transferability of classroom-produced abilities to the real world is a problem facing educators in all fields, and all approaches to language teaching and testing, of course, not just TBLT. It is a problem ignored altogether by most advocates of synthetic linguistic syllabi (as well as most critics of task-based assessments), where it takes the form of predicting (in reality, usually being unable to predict) communicative ability from performance on discrete-point grammar or vocabulary tests. Little is known, moreover, about how linguistic abilities relate to global proficiency levels (see Long, Gor, & Jackson 2012). The use of global "proficiency testing" is just to kick the can down the road. Despite all the work, rhetoric, and vast financial profits surrounding the creation and administration of tests tied to the ever-increasing plethora of so-called "proficiency scales" (Inter-Agency Language Roundtable [ILR], American Council on Teaching Foreign Languages [ACTFL], Common European Framework of Reference [CEFR], International English Language Testing System [IELTS], etc.), little is known about how global proficiency levels relate to task or job performance, and even less about how linguistic abilities relate to task or job performance. It is sometimes decreed by fiat that certain government employees, for example, must attain level X or Y on a particular proficiency scale, e.g., level 2 or 3 on the ILR scale in the USA, in order to perform their duties in a FL, but the assertion is rarely supported by any evidence.[1] TBLT at least has greater face validity where these issues are concerned, as it is the target tasks themselves for particular learners' jobs that are the focus of assessment. There is no need to find out how accurate someone is with the third conditional or whether they are a "2," "2+," or "3" on the ILR scale (whatever that may mean); assessment in TBLT shows whether they can or cannot perform the tasks they need to be able to do.

Some have argued against testing performance of discrete tasks, however (see, e.g., Bachman 2002, 2007). There is skepticism as to whether one really can predict performance on task C and D by assessing performance on tasks A and B, and even if that is possible, at least in some domains, about how time-consuming and costly it will be. Instead of assessing task performance itself, therefore, the suggestion is to test command of the constructs and abilities underlying task performance, with some attention to linguistic abilities, on the assumption that it will be less time-consuming, and with the expectation that predictions will then be possible about performance on other tasks

---

[1] In a recent development, ACTFL has mandated ACTFL oral proficiency interviews (OPIs) for FL teacher certification. For discussion, see Norris (2013).

sharing the same underlying constructs or requiring similar language. While logical enough, the problem lies in how to identify underlying constructs and abilities, which in most cases involves a high degree of inference. One could attempt to reduce the judgment factor by asking several experts to classify target tasks that way, and measuring inter-rater reliability. But in practice, that, too, could be time-consuming, and seems unlikely to work. What are the constructs and abilities underlying, say, understanding an undergraduate physics lecture, making an airline reservation or following a cooking recipe? Do following a cooking recipe and following street directions share the same or similar underlying constructs and abilities? The idea is not to dismiss this approach, but to point out the inevitable degree of subjectivity involved. To be sure, all assessment involves estimation, just with different kinds of inferences involved. The exception is a truly task-based test where an examinee is observed doing the task of interest in the real world or in a simulation. Even then, however, there is a hidden assumption/prediction that the given performance is representative of the likely quality of performance on other occasions.

In sum, discrete-point tests of linguistic knowledge reveal little or nothing about the ability to perform real-world tasks. Proficiency testing might be a solution if proficiency were not a vague, global construct, an epiphenomenon, whose measurement is, in any case, often disturbingly subjective, and if a common proficiency metric existed that was relevant for all tasks. In fact, different tasks require different abilities and proficiency of different kinds and in different domains. Testing underlying constructs and abilities would be fine if there were an algorithm for identifying the relevant underlying constructs and abilities in each case. None exists, so judgments will inevitably be impressionistic. Task-based, criterion-referenced performance testing, despite its logistical drawbacks, is feasible, viable, and provides hard, usable information. In addition, it offers the likelihood of more positive washback on teaching and learning than discrete-point, construct-based, skills or abilities testing.

11.4. The Transferability of Task-Based Abilities

To what extent do task-based abilities transfer? To what extent can performance on tasks 1 and 2 be used to predict performance on tasks 3, 4, and 5? For example, can someone who passed the test and obtained a driver's license in New York or Beijing subsequently drive safely in Tokyo or London, or in any of the 50+ countries that drive on the left, and where some laws, signs, and traffic conditions differ considerably? Very little has been published on these issues in the field of applied linguistics, but work has, at least, begun.

To determine if and when task-based abilities measured in the performance of one task can be used to predict performance on another entails knowing how to classify tasks into task-types reliably. In some of the only published empirical work of its kind, Norris *et al.* (2002) reported a study of the development of criterion-referenced, task-based performance tests. Part of their research involved an attempt to classify 13 tasks, based on work by Skehan (1996, 1998), according to "difficulty," and to predict the performance of 90 participants – three groups of non-native speakers (NNSs) divided by language proficiency, and a group of native speakers (NSs) – on tasks of certain types from their performance on tasks of the same types. Difficulty was decided according to whether a task involved one, two, or all three of three underlying 'cognitive factors': 'complexity of the language code to be processed,' 'complexity of the cognitive operations involved,' and 'processing demands associated with the required communicative activities.' The 13 tasks were selected from a larger set of integrated skills performance tasks in broad 'domains' (health, at the restaurant, etc.) developed in an earlier study (Norris *et al.* 1998). They varied from ordering a pizza with certain ingredients, size, and so on, to locating information in a library catalogue.

Norris *et al.* collected five kinds of data: (i) predictions of students' performance based on their English as a second language (ESL) proficiency level, (ii) estimates of task difficulty based on the one, two, or three cognitive processes each task was judged to involve, (iii) after they had completed seven of the tasks, student self-ratings of how familiar they were with each task, how well they thought they had performed it, and how easy or difficult they considered it, (iv) judgments by three external raters (experienced ESL teachers) of student performance on each task, using a five-point scale – from inadequate, through able/successful, to adept – specific to each task, and (v) rater judgments of each student's holistic ability for the three cognitive factors, based on the rating scales. The holistic ratings of perceived underlying abilities were to be used to see whether student performance could be predicted from one task to another with the same underlying cognitive abilities.

Interrater reliability in use of the rating scales was acceptably high. Implicational (Guttman) scaling showed a relationship between (higher) ESL proficiency and (more successful) task performance. Judges' assessments of a participant's success with each of whichever seven of the 13 tasks he or she performed broadly agreed with predictions from the participant's language proficiency. The assessments did not agree entirely with the a priori estimates of the difficulty of those seven tasks based on which of the three hypothesized cognitive factors each one involved; on the whole, however, the tasks predicted to be more complex were the ones students performed worst on, overall, and the ones that learners with higher proficiency levels did better on. There was a relatively high correlation between examinee familiarity and task performance ratings; essentially, if students knew the task, they did better. The level of agreement between participants' own ratings of their performance on the seven tasks and ratings by the three judges varied greatly from one task to the next (Pearson r from 0.27 to 0.76), and while there was some evidence of a broad overall relationship between "difficulty" as assessed according to the three cognitive criteria and the average level of participants' success in performing tasks, the relationship was inconsistent at the level of individual tasks. Of particular importance, the finding that the three judges' ratings of participants' holistic abilities (based on the three underlying cognitive abilities) correlated strongly ($r = 0.92$) with their task-specific ratings of the same participants suggested that ratings of holistic abilities might be usable to predict task performance. To assess this possibility, Norris *et al.* point out, would require that tasks and/or task-types be (a) reliably classifiable as related to one another at some level, and (b) systematically sampled from the discourse domains of interest. To test the prediction – essentially, the claim that task-based abilities are generalizable – it would be necessary to assess students' actual performance on a second representative sample of the tasks of interest. Norris (p.c., July 20, 2013) notes that the research team was dealing with an extremely variable collection of task-types, not even drawn from the same domain (e.g., English for Academic Purposes). Given a more specific domain, he thinks it might be possible to hone in relatively closely on elements that would enable transferability or predictability among tasks.

Clearly, much work remains to be done. Some guidance for testing may be found in the substantial psychology and education literature on "transfer-appropriate processing" (Morris, Bransford, & Franks 1977) in teaching and learning. The basic idea is that transfer of training is more likely to occur if the training (encoding) is conducted with tasks involving similar processing to the tasks to which transfer is sought (retrieval). On the other hand, while transfer is generally more likely the closer one task is to another in that and other respects, extensive practice with the same task(s) may result in narrower, task-specific abilities, and less ability to transfer what has been learned to new tasks, than variable practice involving a wider range of processing activities (Schmidt & Bjork 1992). There is also the possibility, noted by Gagne (1965), that transfer effects may occur not only laterally, to tasks and situations of similar complexity, but also vertically, to tasks involving more complex skills, part of which encompass the subset on the training task. Transfer predictions, whether in training or testing, might also take into account, on the one hand, task *content*, or *what* is transferred, including the skill that has been learned and the kinds of performance and memory demands involved, and on the other, the knowledge domain and modality, and physical, temporal, functional, and social *context*, i.e., *when* and *where* what has been learned is transferred (Barnett & Ceci 2002). As with 'underlying construct,' these are all abstract categories and characteristics that are difficult to operationalize, and all were originally proposed in an effort to understand transfer of learning. Nonetheless, they could motivate hypotheses in future work on the reliability of predictions concerning transfer of task-based abilities on one task to another for assessment purposes.

Hard evidence of transfer is sparse in psychology (Haskell 2001), where, as shown by a meta-analytic review of the literature (Blume *et al.* 2010), the problem has been compounded by the use of varied operationalizations of transfer. There has been some success, however. Gick and Holyoak (1980), for example, found evidence of so-called 'far transfer,' i.e., between distantly related tasks, in a prototypical analogical transfer experiment between a military context and medical context. Two L2 studies (Bygate 2001; Plough & Gass 1993), on the other hand, had potentially troubling findings, as noted in the section on familiar tasks in Chapter 8.4.5; it seemed that transfer might only occur with the same task, and not to tasks of the same type.

A small-scale study of the transfer issue was conducted by Benson (2013), whose goal was precisely to determine whether performance on one task can predict performance on a task of similar type and complexity, and secondarily, do so more accurately with a "near" than a "far" transfer task, i.e., with a second task in the same knowledge domain than with a task in a different knowledge domain. The study is presented in some detail here with the hope that others may be stimulated to take up the serious challenge the transferability issue presents.

Benson deployed two experimental versions of each of two receptive tasks identified by a task-based needs analysis as useful for students of low ESL proficiency in a community college ESL program in the southern USA: *Following directions to a destination* and *Evaluating product information in a store*. Proficiency was measured using the 20-item listening section of the standardized Levels of English Proficiency (LOEP) test. The cognitive complexity of the experimental versions of the tasks was a control variable, operationalized as the number of steps and elements in each task. Two knowledge

	Group 1a	Group1b	Group2a	Group2b	Group3a	Group3b
Treatment	Practice Following street directions	Practice Following street directions	Practice Buying the best television	Practice Buying the best television	Listen to stories unrelated to tasks	Listen to stories unrelated to tasks
Assessment 1	Following directions in a hospital	Buying the best refrigerator	Following directions in a hospital	Buying the best refrigerator	Following directions in a hospital	Buying the best refrigerator
Assessment 2	Buying the best refrigerator	Following directions in a hospital	Buying the best refrigerator	Following directions in a hospital	Buying the best refrigerator	Following directions in a hospital

Figure 11.1. Experimental groups and assessment item order (from Benson 2013, p. 17).

domains were selected for each, and two equivalent forms of each experimental task were prepared, use of which was counterbalanced. The difficulty and perceived similarity of the experimental tasks was established as comparable through a pilot study with 20 students from the same proficiency range as that of the participants in the main study. The language employed in all the training and assessment tasks was typical of that used for their performance by native speakers in the real world, as established by analysis of recordings of authentic target discourse made in preparation for the study. Two control groups listened to stories unrelated to the tasks, for a total of six conditions. Forty-eight students from a variety of L1 backgrounds with LOEP scores ranging from 44 to 98, and with ages ranging from 18 to 64, were randomly assigned to one of the six conditions (see Figure 11.1).

There were three questions. After training on one of the experimental tasks, either following street directions or buying a television, would performance on the hospital directions task predict performance on the refrigerator purchase task, and vice versa? Second, would performance on a task in one knowledge domain, e.g., street directions, predict performance on a task in a similar, i.e., 'near,' knowledge domain, e.g., hospital directions, more accurately than on a task in a dissimilar, i.e., 'far,' domain, e.g., the television purchase? Third, would the treatment groups outperform the control groups on the hospital directions or refrigerator purchase tasks, for which the control groups had received no training?

The training consisted of a 45-minute lesson for each task developed using ANGEL, an online learning management system (LMS) platform, which made it possible to control time on task and ensure identical exposure to treatment and assessment. Treatments consisted of listening to multiple spoken models while watching performance on a computer screen, e.g., hearing directions while watching an icon move on a real map, followed by practice hearing and following sets of progressively more complex directions. To counteract a potential Hawthorne effect, the unrelated stories were presented in a similar format within the LMS, so that the control groups would be unaware that they were not treatment groups. Participants could repeat videos and questions as often as they liked within the 45-minute period. The assessment tasks followed. Each comprised 15 short variations, one item per video, i.e., 15 sets of directions or 15 product information bits. Performance (scored out of 30) was assessed according to whether the correct destination was reached or the best product was chosen. To ensure that learning was not occurring during the assessments, item facility was plotted, and the mean score for items 2–8 was compared with the mean score for items 9–15 for both tasks. A brief exit survey showed that participants perceived the directions and purchase tasks as somewhat similar, possibly due to use of the same computer format, and (contrary to the eventual average scores on each) the purchase task as somewhat more difficult. Cronbach's alphas for the 15 items in the assessment measures were only moderate: 0.75 for the directions task and 0.74 for the shopping task.

Using a one-way MANCOVA, the effect of training (directions, shopping, or none) on directions and shopping assessment task scores was calculated, with English proficiency as a covariate. ESL proficiency was statistically significantly related to scores on the hospital directions and refrigerator purchase tasks. Contrary to the results for perceived difficulty, and regardless of training, both the experimental and control groups performed better on the hospital directions than on the refrigerator shopping task. Disappointingly, there was no main effect for training, i.e., no significant transfer between tasks of the same type and complexity. However, a post hoc analysis using an exploratory mixed effects logistic regression showed a treatment effect for the 12 learners with the lowest ESL proficiency scores (LOEP score < 55). In that group, those who learned to follow street directions during the treatment phase did follow hospital directions better than those who had learned how to shop for the best television, and better than those in the control group; those who had learned to shop for a television performed better on the refrigerator purchase task than those who had learned to follow street directions, and better than those in the control group. Both treatment groups outperformed the control group when assessed on similar ('near'), but not on dissimilar ('far'), tasks.

Thus, with the caveat that these latter findings were derived from a post hoc analysis of data from a small sub-sample of only 12 participants (360 total observations), Benson found some support for the idea that training on a task can transfer to performance on a second task involving a similar skill and situation, i.e., near transfer, as predicted by Haskell (2001), and content and context, as predicted by Barnett and Ceci (2002), and to a task of similar complexity with respect to its interactional and cognitive demands, i.e., lateral transfer (Gagne 1965), or horizontal transfer (Singley & Anderson 1989).

The heterogeneity of Benson's original sample of 48 in terms of L1, age, and ESL proficiency may have precluded the possibility of more supportive findings. It is possible that the tasks were simply too easy for many of the higher proficiency participants. Some participants showed no effect for training, and some may have had pre-existing ability with one or both tasks, as their performance was sometimes superior on the task for which transfer was not expected, further masking the effects of training. Future work could correct for this by using additional pretests to determine prior domain knowledge and an additional measure to document learning from the training. Lexical differences among the tasks, Benson suggests, may also have served to obscure the amount of observable transfer in this case. Were the results with the less proficient participants to be replicated with larger, more homogeneous samples and a wider array of task-types, however, the implications both for selection of tasks in syllabus design and sampling of tasks for assessment purposes would be profound. Further studies of these issues are clearly of the highest priority for TBLT, and for task-based assessment in general.

Full coverage of the many practical and psychometric issues in task-based language assessment would require a book-length treatment and lies well beyond the scope of this volume. Fortunately, others have been hard at work. For an example of so-called "integrated performance assessments" (which are task-based), see Adair-Hauck (2006). For examples of the development of task-specific rating criteria, see Deygers *et al.* (2013) and Norris (2001), and for steps in developing task-based assessments, see Long & Norris (2000) and Van Gorp & Deygers (2013). For the use of task-based assessment for washback purposes, see Byrnes (2002), and for task-based assessment at work in larger-scale policy-driven environments, see Fischer *et al.* (2011). For the implementation of task-based assessment in university courses, see Chouissa *et al.* (2012).

11.5. Program Evaluation

11.5.1. Some general requirements on TBLT evaluations

Evaluations of TBLT programs need to follow the procedures and meet the standards for evaluations in education and other fields, with use of multiple data sources and triangulation among them both important qualities. The typical approach is descriptive, the main purposes being to find out whether programs are achieving their goals, and to make data-based decisions as to whether they should continue as they are or should be modified. Are programs doing what they say they are doing? Are students learning what they need? Programs are unique, and are best considered holistically, *in situ*, recognizing that they are inevitably affected by the context in which they operate.

While they might be ideal, evaluations of whole programs using the pretest–posttest experimental designs favored in theory-driven research, with a TBLT group and one or more control or comparison groups, and random assignment of teachers and students to groups, are rarely feasible, especially in elementary and secondary school settings. Even at college level, where multiple sections of the same course (ESL 101, Persian 202, Spanish 301, etc.) are often available, teachers' and students' schedules usually make at least some of them unavailable to teach or take at a specific time, thereby precluding genuine random assignment. There are exceptions, though, as we shall see. True experiments and quasi-experimental designs using intact groups are occasionally possible when the focus is one or more particular dimensions of TBLT, such as methodological principles (MPs) or the very different kinds of teacher–student interaction found in TBLT and traditional focus-on-forms classrooms.

In either case – descriptive, with judgments based on whether or not program and learner goals are being achieved, or true experimental or quasi-experimental studies designed to compare the absolute or relative effectiveness of TBLT or parts thereof – it is important, but often difficult, to control for six classes of variables, any one of which can threaten the internal validity of either an evaluation or a research study.[2] They are usually referred to as history, maturation, testing, instrumentation, selection, and mortality. (For more detailed discussion of the threats within L2 studies, see Long 1984. For additional issues and alternative approaches when evaluating language programs, see Alderson & Beretta 1992; Beretta 1986; Lynch 1990, 1996).

---

[2] Such has been the case, for example, with quasi-experimental studies of content-and-language integrated learning (CLIL) using intact classes in Spanish secondary schools. For critical comments noting examples of failure to control for several of the six threats, see Bruton (2011a,b).

(i) History   The effects of something that occurs during the course of the program being evaluated, e.g., some students taking additional classes or gaining additional outside language exposure from L2-speaking friends, are not controlled for and could influence the results.

(ii) Maturation   Students may undergo changes during the course of a program independent of the instruction they receive, e.g., develop more positive attitudes toward the L2 and its speakers, resulting in increased motivation. Those changes may affect the results.

(iii) Testing   Although necessary in many cases, use of a pre-test can alert students to the subject matter being tested, e.g., particular L2 structures, or resuscitate latent knowledge of them, or even serve to help students learn the material for the first time and improve their performance on the post-test independent of the effects of instruction.

(iv) Instrumentation   Problems with the reliability or validity of tests used to measure learning will make interpretation of results impossible. So will inconsistencies in the way otherwise sound tests are administered, e.g., when students are allowed more or less time with one than the other. If pre- and post-tests are employed, they must be of equivalent difficulty, i.e., alternate forms of the same test.

(v) Selection   Students assigned to groups, or intact groups assigned to two or more conditions (e.g., four classes, two of which undergo a TBLT program, and two a traditional program), may already differ in ways which affect the outcome, because the assignment was not random. Some may be more proficient in the L2 before the courses begin, for instance, or have higher average language aptitude, or be more intelligent or more motivated. If measured, such pre-existing differences can sometimes be corrected for statistically (adjusting for their effects as covariates), but not always.

(vi) Mortality   Students occasionally drop out of programs altogether, miss important classes, or are absent on the days when one or more tests are taken. This can affect results in several ways. For instance, it may be that the weaker students are the ones who drop out or skip a test, with the result that the average score for their group increases simply because only the better students remain.

Given the difficulty of obtaining permission to conduct large-scale evaluations in educational settings, and where permission is granted, of dealing with all of these potential threats to the internal validity of a study, many researchers have chosen to conduct evaluations of various sub-components of task-based learning and teaching in small-scale laboratory studies, where control over extraneous variables is easier and identification of causal relationships more feasible. In such cases, the distinction between evaluations for decision-making and empirical research for testing theory becomes blurred, with results of each relevant to the other. While less than optimal from an evaluation perspective, far more empirical studies of this kind have already been completed on components of TBLT than on components of any other approach to language teaching, some of which have rarely been subjected to research or evaluations of any kind, despite having been utilized over a much longer period. Fortunately, as we shall see, most issues in TBLT have been addressed in classroom studies, as well. As a result, given its close connection with current research in instructed second language acquisition (SLA), where task has long been a moderator variable of interest in its own right, much of the work on TBLT has been conducted with both basic and applied interests in mind, often independently of the TBLT literature itself, but relevant, nonetheless, with reports often appearing in mainstream refereed SLA journals, such as *Language Learning* and *Studies in Second Language Acquisition*, as well as in periodicals with a more applied focus, such as *Language Teaching Research, Applied Linguistics, International Review of Applied Linguistics*, and *System*, and in several edited volumes. Despite its youth and whatever its limitations, TBLT is the closest thing to a researched language pedagogy that exists.

11.5.2. Laboratory and classroom studies

While limited from an evaluation perspective, laboratory studies have many positive features, the most important of which is their potential for establishing cause-and-effect relationships between instructional processes (e.g., focus on forms and focus on form), and learning processes (e.g., various dimensions of negotiation for meaning, including uptake from corrective feedback), on the one hand, and both performance outcomes (e.g., changes in output accuracy, complexity, and fluency) and learning outcomes (e.g., acquisition of new linguistic features), on the other. Whole program types are usually too complex to operationalize for long enough in the laboratory, and should be evaluated *in situ*, but particular MPs and pedagogic procedures (PPs) can be, and have been, isolated and their effectiveness evaluated there. Laboratory studies are also useful for developing and fine-tuning the instrumentation to be used in classroom studies – everything from observation checklists to outcome measures. They can sometimes be of limited ecological validity, it is true, but that is a problem which, for different reasons, afflicts many studies in natural settings as well. Generalization of findings from classroom studies can also be problematic, given how greatly classrooms and the kinds of instruction that occur in them differ among themselves. Compounding the problem, a number of studies, especially at the level of PPs, are hard to classify unambiguously as laboratory or classroom research. For example, in some cases (see, e.g., Long *et al.* 1976; Pica, Doughty, & Young 1986), data are collected from real students drawn from intact classes, but pulled out during lessons and recorded individually, in pairs or in small groups in a separate room, in order to cut down on background noise that would hinder the audibility if recordings were attempted in the main classroom with the teacher and many other students present and talking at the same time.

Can findings from experimental work be generalized to natural classroom settings? While much has been written about this issue (some of it by armchair pedagogues expressing skepticism about the value of empirical findings from any context compared with their own data-free prescriptions and proscriptions), little research has been conducted to compare findings on the same program elements in each setting, and there are grounds for concern. For example, as noted in Chapter 8.4.5, several laboratory studies (e.g., Long 1980a, 1983b; Pica & Doughty 1985a,b) have shown an advantage for two-way over one-way tasks in the amount of negotiation work, among other things, engendered by the two-way tasks. However, while some classroom studies (e.g., Newton 2013) have obtained the same result, some others (Eckerth 2008; Foster 1998; Foster &

Ohta 2005) of the relative effectiveness of two-way tasks, in which information exchange is required, and opinion-gap tasks, in which it is optional, have not found statistically significant advantages for either one (although Foster observed a trend in the data favoring two-way tasks). They have also unearthed troublesome differences in the amount of negotiation work completed by individual students, varying from a great deal to none at all. Another classroom study (Slimani-Rolls 2005) did find the same advantage for two-way tasks established in the laboratory work, but again noted considerable variation at the individual level.

It is also the case that laboratory studies have tended to produce stronger learning effects than classroom studies, at least on immediate post-tests, for such phenomena as recasts and negotiation work (Li 2010; Mackey & Goo 2007), perhaps because the intensity (frequency over time, and total input) is higher in the lab, and perhaps also because students there are aware that their performance is under a microscope, so they pay more attention and try harder. Of some encouragement, in a direct comparison of dyads completing two two-way tasks and one opinion-gap task in the laboratory and in their regular classroom settings, Gass, Mackey, and Ross-Feldman (2005) found statistically significantly higher frequencies of negotiation for meaning, recasts, and 'language-related episodes' (Swain 1998, p. 70), i.e., instances of student talk about, or "correction" of, their own or their partner's L2 use while working on the two-way tasks, but in each case, no statistically significant differences between the results in laboratory and classroom setting. Gass *et al.* (2005, p. 210) concluded that it is reasonable to support "cautious generalizations about laboratory based research findings to L2 classroom settings," while bearing in mind that "classrooms can vary tremendously, and not all laboratories are equivalent either."

My own view has always been, and remains, that research on, and evaluations of, language teaching (and other educational programs) does best, and the generalization issue can be finessed, by adopting a two-pronged approach. (For a more detailed rationale and some historical examples of the approach applied to a variety of topics in L2 classroom research, see Long in press.) The programmatic element(s) of interest (MPs, PPs, instructional materials, etc.), and where possible, the same whole program type (synthetic, analytic, traditional grammar-based curriculum, TBLT, notional-functional syllabus, lexical syllabus, etc.) should be evaluated under experimental conditions first. That usually means a laboratory study. While inevitably artificial in some respects, it is important to see whether it is possible to isolate a causal relationship (which true experiments permit) before attempting to assess the absolute or relative effectiveness of the same procedure(s) or program type(s) in natural classrooms, with the inevitable messiness they can create for a researcher. In intact classroom settings, as noted in Section 11.5.1, the effectiveness or ineffectiveness of a treatment may be masked by any number of confounding variables. Were the observed results really due to focus on form, not forms, or use of this or that PP or program type, or were they due, wholly or in part, to the fact that the teachers in the more successful group(s) were especially gifted, better trained, more enthusiastic, and so on, or their students more intelligent, more motivated, or of higher IQ or superior language aptitude?

If a clear relationship between the program, MP(s) or PP(s) of interest and learning outcomes cannot be established under laboratory conditions, where showing such relationships is easier, it is premature to attempt the classroom version of the study. However, if a causal relationship between the use of the program, principle(s), or procedure(s) –

TBLT, focus on form, input elaboration, referential questions, recasts, closed tasks, intentional plagiarism, input chunking, and so on – has been demonstrated in one or more laboratory studies under controlled conditions, the question then arises as to how results in one or more subsequent paired studies in natural classrooms should be interpreted. Clearly, if the same statistically significant advantages are obtained in real classrooms for the same program, principle(s), or procedure(s), or if, in the case of a program evaluation, as opposed to a research study, the same meaningful, large, beneficial, clear, valued effects are observed, the researcher/evaluator can begin to have confidence that he or she is on to something. If findings in the classroom study or evaluation are the reverse of those observed in the true experiment, conversely, it is "back to the drawing-board." The tricky case to interpret is when the trend in the classroom data on use of specific MPs or PPs is in the same direction as that in the experiment(s), but the effect does not reach statistical significance. In my view, case by case, it is a judgment call. Factors can sometimes be identified – inconsistent teacher delivery of an MP, mixed student L2 proficiency, low student language aptitude, or simply the small numbers involved making statistical significance hard to achieve in any case – that seem to have weakened the main effect of the independent variable of interest. If those factors are not inevitably problematic in natural classrooms, regardless of what an artificial and often misinterpreted p value might suggest, it is reasonable to present the findings of the paired studies or sets of studies to program designers, materials writers, teacher educators, and classroom practitioners with whatever implications for classroom practice they support, but being careful explicitly to note the failure of the classroom data to yield statistically significant findings. Others will assuredly disagree.[3]

11.5.3. Research findings on MPs

Numerous controlled studies have been carried out at the level of methodological principles (MPs). A full review is beyond the scope of this book. For readers interested in pursuing the topics further, the following are some of the findings (often citing just a few of the relevant studies) that have been reasonably consistent (not necessarily uniform) across laboratory and classroom settings. For more comprehensive and detailed treatments, see, e.g., R. Ellis (2003, 2012), Gass (1997), Mackey (2012), and Pica (1994, 2009). Seven MPs, in particular, have received some, and in five cases (MPs 1, 2, 3, 6, and 7) considerable, research attention.

[3] One or two prominent applied linguists have expressed skepticism over whether the results of laboratory and/or classroom studies can *ever* be used as a rationale for recommendations for practice. That view strikes me as self-defeating and inhibitory of progress in the field. First, some findings are surely better than none, and much language teaching practice is as yet based on no findings at all. Second, it is not as if one were in the position (as might be the case in medicine, engineering, etc.) of recommending a change from teaching practices whose effectiveness is well established to practices about which little is known. Some other writers on the topic have taken the position that research findings should not be valued above practicing teachers' classroom experience, above their "knowledge of what works." While teaching experience is, of course, a potentially valuable source of expertise, two problems with that view are that (i) "what works" is often unknown (or we wouldn't be having the discussion), and (ii) teaching experiences and teachers' opinions about "what works" differ, are usually largely impressionistic, and cannot possibly all be right. In any case, recommendations emanating from the two-pronged approach described above are in part based precisely on evaluation of the effectiveness of the practice of classroom teachers.

MP1: Use task, not text, as the unit of analysis and **MP2: Promote learning by doing**, are supported by the results of evaluation studies reported in Chapter 8.4.5. They are also consistent with studies showing that doing tasks produces negotiation for meaning, which, in turn, increases L2 comprehension. For laboratory studies, see, e.g., R. Ellis (1994), Long (1983b), and Varonis and Gass (1985). For a quasi-classroom study, see Pica, Young, and Doughty (1987). For a classroom study, see De Ridder, Vangehuchten, and Sesena Gomez (2007). Task-based negotiation for meaning has also been shown to increase L2 learning. For laboratory studies, see, e.g., Iwashita (2003) and Mackey (1999). For classroom studies, see, e.g., De la Fuente (2006) and Shintani (2011, 2013). For reviews, see, e.g., R. Ellis (2012), Gass (1997, 2003), and Mackey (2007, 2012). Statistical meta-analyses report significant positive effects of task-based conversation on the acquisition of targeted linguistic structures (Keck *et al.* 2006), on interaction in general (Mackey & Goo 2007), and on corrective feedback, in particular (Li 2010; Lyster & Saito 2010; Russell & Spada 2006).

MP3: Elaborate input has been the subject of approximately 20 laboratory studies in both spoken and written modalities. See, e.g., Kim (2003, 2006); Oh (2001); Urano (2000); Yano, Long, and Ross (1994); and additional studies and results summarized in Chapter 9.2.4. The general finding has been that elaborated input produces better comprehension than genuine input, probably in large part due to the redundancy it contains, rather than any lessening of grammatical complexity (Pica, Young, & Doughty 1987), and almost the same level (i.e., a non-statistically significantly different level) of improved comprehensibility as simplified input. When it is the result of adapting a genuine spoken or written text (as opposed to being written from scratch), elaborated input can retain all or close to 100% of the semantic content of the original version, whereas much of the meaning is lost when the same passage is simplified (Long & Ross 1993), a finding of obvious relevance for content-and-language-integrated learning (CLIL; Long *et al.* 2013).

MP5: Encourage inductive "chunk" learning is consistent with the findings of a number of studies (discussed in Chapter 10.2.5) of the importance of holistically acquired chunks for both learning and L2 proficiency ratings. It is also consistent with a still rather mixed set of findings on how best to facilitate the holistic learning of collocations and other formulaic sequences. Incidental learning of chunks is a capacity widely observed in language-learning children, but as recent work has shown, one that is still available to adults, albeit with lesser power. An immediate post-test can detect evidence of some learning from as little as a single exposure to a collocation, but multiple exposures are usually necessary for significant and sustained knowledge gains as a result of more typical PPs, such as student use of modified graded readers while simultaneously hearing the text read aloud. For laboratory studies, see, e.g., Durrant and Schmitt (2010) and Webb and Kagimoto (2011). For an experimental classroom study, see Webb, Newton, and Chang (2013). For reviews, see Boers and Lindstromberg (2012), Meara (2009), and Schmitt (2008); Wray (2002).

MP6: Focus on form has been shown to produce statistically significantly more learning than simple exposure, almost as much learning as focus on forms in some studies, and more learning than focus on forms in some others. These results were achieved despite the fact that most studies (a) were short-term, (b) targeted simple grammar, and (c) used "constrained response" tests that focused on controlled use of L2 knowledge, often in a similar format to the focus on forms treatments, all three factors favoring focus on forms and disfavoring focus on form. For a review of a number of laboratory studies, see Long and Robinson (1998). For classroom studies, see, e.g., Alcon (2007), De la Fuente (2006), Loewen (2005), Shintani (2011, 2013), and Williams (2001). For reviews of findings in both settings, see R. Ellis (2012), Long and Robinson (1998), Pica (2009), and Spada (1997). For statistical meta-analyses of findings, see Goo *et al.* (2009) and Norris and Ortega (2000). For a statistical meta-analysis of research on a related topic, the effects of comprehension-based and production-based grammar instruction, see Shintani, Li, and Ellis (2013).

MP7: Provide negative feedback has been supported by numerous studies showing short-term and long-term gains from both explicit and implicit negative feedback. For laboratory studies of explicit negative feedback, see, e.g., Varnosfadrani and Basturkmen (2009) and Yilmaz (2012). For classroom studies, see, e.g., Alcon (2007), Ammar and Spada (2006), DeKeyser (1993), Ellis, Loewen, and Erlam (2006), and Lightbown and Spada (1990). For laboratory studies of implicit negative feedback, especially recasts, see, e.g., Choi (2000), Mackey (2006), and Mackey and Philp (1998). For classroom studies, see, e.g., Braidi (2002), Doughty and Varela (1998), Ellis, Basturkmen, and Loewen (2001), Loewen and Philp (2005), Lyster (1998), Mifka-Profozic (2011), Oliver (1995), Sheen (2004), and Trofimovitch, Ammar, and Gatbonton (2007). For reviews, see Loewen (2012), Long (2007d), Mackey (2012), and Nicholas, Lightbown, and Spada (2001). For statistical meta-analyses of findings, see Goo and Mackey (2013), Li (2010), Lyster and Saito (2010), Mackey and Goo (2007), Russell and Spada (2006), and Spada and Tomita (2010). Important recent studies using eye-tracking methodology and heat maps by O'Rourke (2008), Smith (2010, 2012), Smith and Renaud (2013), and Godfroid (Godfroid, Boers, & Housen 2013; Godfroid, Housen, & Boers 2010) suggest that, at least in the written mode, learners' noticing of recasts, while already demonstrated to be good, may have been considerably underestimated by studies that relied on behavioral records (transcripts of conversation, think-aloud protocols, etc.). In Smith's 2011 study, for instance, heat maps, which record eye-fixation sites and gaze-duration in computer-mediated conversation, revealed a noticing rate for recasts of 71%, compared with a rate of 54% revealed by stimulated recalls, and a rate of only 25% by think-aloud protocols.

MP8: Respect learner syllabi and developmental processes has been supported by studies reporting non-effects of instruction (including negative feedback) that ignores learners' developmental readiness to acquire targeted L2 features, and by studies that show learning and/or faster rates of learning from developmentally well-timed instruction. For laboratory studies, see, e.g., Bonilla (2012), Mackey (1999), Pienemann (1984, 1989), and Trofimovitch, Ammar, and Gatbonton (2007). For some possible counterevidence (involving L1 transfer effects), see Spada and Lightbown (1999). For classroom studies, see, e.g., Ellis (1989), Hakansson and Norrby (2010), and Lightbown (1983). For a review, see Kessler, Liebner, and Mansouri (2011).

11.5.4. Evaluating task-based courses and programs

11.5.4.1. Establishing construct validity The so-called "comparative method" studies of the 1960s and 1970s frequently failed to ensure that the treatment, or even a whole "method," supposedly being evaluated had actually been delivered. Anyone now setting out to evaluate TBLT needs to be sure not to make the same mistake. How will the evaluator know that what he or she is observing is TBLT and not something else? This is an especially important issue given that (a) several other communicative approaches, especially analytic approaches, may feature some of the same MPs and PPs, and (b) many so-called "task-based" programs are really only cases of task-*supported* delivery of linguistic (usually grammatical, notional-functional, or lexical) syllabi of some kind. Before an evaluation of a TBLT course or program can be carried out, it is necessary to identify it as genuine TBLT, i.e., to establish construct validity.

To this end, it behooves the evaluator to confirm that the "treatments" being compared really are or were what they were supposed to be. As explained in detail elsewhere (Long 1980b), before examining the learning outcomes of various courses or whole programs, i.e., the *product*, it is essential to examine the *process* involved. The best way of doing this is to code systematically drawn samples of the classroom lessons, either in real time or using recordings, for a set of low inference, high frequency behaviors and parameters of language use known to reflect each of the programs concerned (see Long & Crookes 1987). For reliability and validity purposes, the behaviors selected should be *low inference*, i.e., behaviors or events about which two or more observers will readily agree because they do not require a significant degree of subjective interpretation or "judgment" on their part. Intra-rater and inter-rater reliability need to be acceptably high (for procedures, see Chaudron, Crookes, & Long 1988). For economy of time, effort, and money, they should also be *high frequency*, i.e., behaviors or events that occur early and often, so as to avoid the need for vast amounts of data, and so that the occurrence of copious instances will decrease the likelihood of error due to an insufficient number of cases.

Candidates for processes to be monitored and evaluated will vary somewhat according to the nature and purpose of the particular programs concerned. However, the theory and research findings underlying TBLT, coupled with my own and others' observations (see, e.g., Bennett & Dunne 1991; Chaudry 1991; Deen 1991; Shintani 2011, 2013) of communicative and genuine task-based programs and all too many traditional synthetic programs over the years, show that items in the following lists (see Table 11.1) are typical of what might be expected in skill-building approaches (whether in laboratory or classroom lessons), in which synthetic, focus-on-forms instruction is delivered, e.g., through a traditional present-practice-produce (sic) (PPP) approach, on the one hand, and on the other, in cognitive-interactionist approaches, lessons utilizing an analytic (TBLT) approach with a focus on form.

Absence or presence of the first group of items listed in Table 11.1 is usually easily ascertained simply by the evaluator requesting to see documentation (e.g., needs analysis findings, syllabus, pedagogic materials, tests, lesson plans) from the course or program coordinator and/or the teachers. The second group of items in each column contains several low inference, high frequency, easily quantified teacher and learner behaviors with which to distinguish the two broad instructional approaches. Data need not be gathered, or analyses conducted, on all of the items in this second group, needless to say. For instance, referential questions, student-initiated exchanges, implicit negative feedback, proportions of teacher and student topic-initiating moves, and ratio of topic-continuing to topic-initiating moves tend to co-occur. Differences in the use of some of the items in the two types of lessons will not be absolute, but a matter of degree, or rela-

Table 11.1. Distinguishing characteristics of PPP and TBLT

Synthetic/focus on forms/PPP	*Analytic/focus on form/TBLT*
Determined by inquiry and inspection	
Code-focused course objectives	Task-focused course objectives
No needs analysis	Needs analysis
Generic, commercially published textbook(s)	Local, program-specific materials[4]
Linguistic syllabus	Task syllabus
Code-focused tests	Task-focused tests
No TBLT-specific training of teachers or students	TBLT-specific training of teachers and students
Determined by observation of lessons (live or recorded)	
Focus on code feature(s)	Focus on pedagogic tasks
Early forced student output	Substantial, rich, task-related input
Language-like behavior (drills, etc.)	Communicative language use
Display questions	Referential questions
Mostly explicit "error correction"	Mostly implicit negative feedback (esp. recasts)
Meta-linguistic talk	Little or no meta-linguistic talk
Mostly teacher-initiated exchanges	At least some student-initiated exchanges
Low ratio of topic-continuing to topic-initiating moves	High ratio of topic-continuing to topic-initiating moves
Low proportion of student utterances/turns	High proportion of student utterances/turns

tive frequency of use. Research (e.g., Long & Sato 1983) shows that a PPP lesson may well include a handful of referential questions (usually for classroom management) and recasts, for example, but there should be statistically significantly more of both in a genuine TBLT lesson. In PPP lessons, most questions will be display questions, and much negative feedback will be explicit, not implicit.

Some additional behaviors, events, and activities can be expected to distinguish these two basic types of lessons, courses and programs over time, but they will not necessarily constitute reliable observational targets in single lessons. Teacher-fronted lessons with a large amount of, or sometimes exclusively, lockstep work, for example, will be more common in PPP classrooms, and pair-work and small group work more common in TBLT, over the duration of a course. Individual lessons may not differ in that way, however, making classroom organization an unreliable focus for the purpose

---

[4] Almost all PPP-type programs use commercially published "generic" textbooks. Most TBLT programs use locally produced materials designed specifically for their students. There are exceptions, however, and some TBLT programs use a combination of commercial and locally written materials, especially during the transition to complete TBLT.

of monitoring the fidelity of program delivery when observation is of only a small number of individual lessons.

11.5.4.2. Sample evaluations and findings   Full-fledged genuine TBLT programs are still few and far between, and satisfactory opportunities to investigate their effectiveness rare. Many of the published descriptions and evaluations (e.g., Carless 2002, 2003, 2004; Gatbonton & Gu 1994; Li 1998; McDonough & Chaitmongkol 2007; Sachs 2007; Zhang 2007) have been formative, only, far from comprehensive even then, and have not sought to capture any kind of program theory or logic underlying innovations or interventions. They have often focused on problems sometimes encountered when allegedly "western" task-based (or task-supported) LT is introduced to, or by, relatively inexperienced teachers in culturally different societies where teacher-fronted PPP-type language teaching has long been the norm – in the studies cited, Japan, Hong Kong, South Korea, Thailand, and the PRC. Similar problems, it is worth noting, have arisen when communicative language teaching of any variety, not just TBLT, has been introduced in some parts of the world (Butler 2011; Hu 2002).

Unfortunately, some of the early reports have provided insufficient information for readers to be clear about the true nature of the courses or programs concerned, which often seem to have been (at most) task-supported, not task-based. The most detailed formative evaluation of the implementation of a task-based program to date is Markee's account (Markee 2007, pp. 73–168) of the decade-long curricular and teacher innovation (CATI) project in a major public US university's ESL program for international students. Markee's report was intended as a case study in the diffusion of educational innovation (see, also, Markee 1993, 1994, 1997), to which we will return in Chapter 12. Meanwhile, the crucial link between curricular change and teacher development in such work is a major focus of Markee's book, as is the production of pedagogic materials by the generations of teaching assistants involved in the project he describes, improved through cycles of classroom trials and technology-supported teacher and ESL student feedback. It should come as no surprise, therefore (see, also, Lai, Zhao, & Wang 2011; McDonough & Chaitmongkol 2007), if things do not go smoothly when a TBLT program is suddenly introduced with insufficient (or no) preparation for teachers and students alike, especially if traditional approaches to teaching and learning in the existing program or broader educational context reflects dissimilar values and practices.

An example of an education authority taking the need for teacher preparation for task-based education seriously is provided by a nationwide in-service program in Belgium, where the Flemish government funded a large-scale initiative designed to raise the quality of second language education in Dutch for immigrants by introducing teachers to TBLT. Task-based programs have since been implemented to varying degrees in some 200 state primary and secondary schools, as well as in adult education, for about 20 years (see Van den Branden 2006a).

Aware of the need for teachers to be familiar not only with TBLT's theoretical rationale, but also to have a practical grounding in the new approach, the program consisted of explanations, demonstration lessons, and provision of a task-based syllabus and materials. Linsen (1994, reported in Van den Branden, 2006b) evaluated the in-service program from 1992 to 1994, using 114 teacher logs, 21 teacher interviews, and classroom observations in 20 schools. Aside from relinquishing the traditional focus-on-forms approach, the main difficulty teachers reported early on was their having to reduce the complexity of some of the task-based materials, which were occasionally too difficult for their students, or at least, were perceived by the teachers as too difficult. In a later classroom observational study of ten primary school teachers, Timmermans (2005) also found the need to simplify some tasks was the main problem the Flemish teachers encountered, as did Luyten and Houben (2002) in their study of the implementation of a task-based multi-media course in basic Dutch for adult migrants. Both studies are also reported in Van den Branden (2006b). In general, students reacted very enthusiastically to the multi-media course, but, reflecting the way they had been used to teaching, some teachers in that program and those in some task-based reading courses were skeptical about starting with tasks without first teaching the language that occurred in them (i.e., focus on forms). Some were also uncomfortable at the lesser degree of control they felt they had over what students were doing in parts of lessons, especially during group work. A few in Linsen's study were suspicious as to whether students could really be learning when they seemed to be enjoying themselves so much. In general, however, teacher reactions were positive, in part due to their students' enthusiasm for the materials:

> In addition, the majority of the teachers were charmed by the students' enthusiasm: their motivation to perform the language tasks contributed to the teachers being motivated themselves to use the syllabuses. (Van den Branden 2006b, p. 233)

Several other studies were conducted of the way TBLT was implemented in Belgian schools, and are summarized in Van den Branden (2006b). Of particular interest is a longitudinal (three-year) investigation by Devlieger *et al.* (2003) of implementation issues in a number of schools in Brussels. Teachers there could choose to participate (or not) in any or all of four kinds of in-service coaching: school-based, team-based, needs-based, and classroom practice-based. Devlieger *et al.* observed 170 coaching sessions and 21 classroom lessons, and conducted 277 interviews with teachers and head teachers. They found that each school was visited by coaches about 20 times a year. The researchers reported that teachers initially tended to adopt the task-based materials as supplements to their traditional code-focused materials, and often varied in the way they used them. Their questions to coaches ranged from aspects of the rationale to extremely detailed practical matters, such as how much time to devote to particular activities or how best to distribute pictures quickly. Overall, again, responses were positive, and an evaluation by Hillewaere (2000) involving 20 schools concluded that the Flemish government's program of teacher support for task-based education had been successful, especially in primary schools. In another study, this time comparing attitudes and practices before and after three years of implementing TBLT, Devlieger and Goosens (2004) found that teachers were still uncomfortable with the loss of control some felt when using group work, but had reoriented more toward functional language goals, provided more natural classroom input, and asked more of the kinds of questions that gave students room to express their own thoughts and opinions. Students were enjoying their classroom experiences much more, they found, and were more motivated.

Formative evaluations are important, but the long-term interest is in outcomes. Does TBLT work, and work better than alternative approaches? For those questions, summative, process-product evaluations are required. Closer to meeting the need was the post hoc study of the Bangalore Project (BP) (Prabhu 1987) conducted by Beretta and Davies (1985). As noted in Chapter 8.2.6, the BP involved use of a procedural syllabus delivered via an assortment of pedagogic tasks unmotivated by a needs analysis. It was not a TBLT program, but an important innovation, nevertheless. Contrary to the normal evaluation sequence, the first part of the study was an intact-groups *product* comparison (Beretta & Davies 1985) of the English abilities of four BP classes and four roughly comparable classes in the same schools that had been taught using a traditional grammar (TG) approach. A positive feature of the work (not always true of such studies) was that Beretta and Davies did not bias their findings by using a single type of outcome measure intended to favor one group over the other (see Beretta 1986, for a discussion of "program-fair" evaluations). Rather, they created a battery of tests – a task-based test reflecting the kind of reasoning-gap tasks used during the BP, a discrete-point grammar test, and other tests supposedly not biased in favor of either group: grammar in context, dictation, and listening and reading comprehension. The idea was to let both groups show what should have been their strongest suit, but also to see how well each program had equipped students to perform on a test favoring the other group's supposed strengths, as well as on neutral tests not favoring either. Beretta and Davies found that (i) all four BP groups did better than the TG groups on the task-based test, (ii) the TG groups did statistically significantly better than the BP groups on the discrete-point grammar test, (iii) three of the four BP groups outperformed the TG groups statistically significantly on the listening and reading comprehension tests, and (iv) the BP groups were better than the TG with grammatical structures they had not been explicitly taught.

At first sight, this might look like evidence that a rather idiosyncratic form of task-supported language teaching can achieve what it sets out to do, and without harming general L2 proficiency, provided proficiency is assessed meaningfully. However, as is often the case with educational evaluations in all subject areas, not just language teaching and learning, first appearances can be deceptive. To begin with, Beretta and Davies recognized that causal claims were unjustified because (i) there had been no random assignment of students or intact groups to each condition, and (ii) three of the four Project classes had been taught by "better qualified, more highly motivated teachers" (Beretta & Davies 1985, p. 123). Second, Beretta (1989, 1990) subsequently conducted a *process* evaluation (which normally *precedes* a product evaluation) in the form of a detailed analysis of the transcripts of videos of demonstration classes and other lessons provided by BP staff. Like so many such studies of classroom processes (see, e.g., Dinsmore 1985; Long & Sato 1983; Nunan 1987), it revealed a gap between what was supposed to have happened and what had actually happened. As noted in Section 8.2.6, unlike the supposedly purely communicative orientation in lessons that Prabhu had prescribed, teaching was in practice often linguistically quite tightly controlled, i.e., task-supported, not task-based, and featured some supposedly proscribed behaviors, such as traditional "error correction." In other words, (i) the seemingly positive results of a task-supported communicative program, as compared with those of a traditional synthetic approach, need to be treated with caution, and (ii) the findings of the process evaluation underscored the importance of first establishing construct validity in all such evaluations.

The finding that a communicative classroom, as in the BP project, can produce students able to function with acceptable levels of grammatical accuracy should come as no surprise. Few studies had been conducted until recently, but contrary to the alarmist pronouncements of some skeptics, communicative approaches have been found to fare well since as far back as the late 1960s (see Oller 1971; Oller & Obrecht 1968, 1969). For example, using intact groups, Hammond (1988) compared the grammatical accuracy of eight sections of Spanish 101 taught for one semester using the Natural Approach (Krashen & Terrell 1983), supplemented by traditional discrete-point written homework exercises, and that of 52 Spanish 101 sections taught using a modified grammar-translation methodology that included deductive grammar instruction. The same battery of discrete-point mid-term and final exams were administered to all 60 sections. The tests assessed students' mastery of verb forms, vocabulary items, possessive adjectives, relative pronouns, direct and indirect object pronouns, comparatives, and so on. The eight experimental sections consistently outperformed the traditional grammar-based sections on all tests, often statistically significantly so, despite their discrete-point format favoring students in the 52 traditionally taught sections. The fact that the study involved intact groups and the experimental curriculum included a supplementary focus-on-forms homework component makes it impossible to claim that a purely communicative approach with a focus-on-meaning led to the superior performance of students in the eight experimental sections. Nevertheless, use of the Natural Approach, with its reliance on comprehensible input and proscription of overt attention to grammar or corrective feedback, means the orientation of lessons in the eight experimental sections was radically communicative (assuming the treatment really was delivered as intended). The unusual size of the study in terms of numbers of teachers, sections, and students, lends its findings greater credibility, moreover, and should at least give pause to those who assert that communicatively oriented language teaching will inevitably result in poorer grammatical skills than traditional grammar-focused instruction. As summaries of the following studies will bear out, that is not at all what the research has shown.

Van den Branden (2006b) reports two outcomes studies of the Flemish programs. Based on classroom observations and test administrations in 20 primary schools, Jaspaert and Linsen (1997) found that students' Dutch language proficiency strongly correlated with the extent to which teachers appealed to learner initiation during language lessons. In a pre-test, post-test study, Devlieger and Goosens (2004) used standardized tests to compare students' Dutch proficiency before the teacher TBLT support program was implemented with their abilities three years later. They found significant gains in Dutch proficiency at kindergarten and primary levels, and more substantial gains than those observed among comparable students in schools whose teachers had been less intensively supported during the three-year period. There is insufficient information to judge the precise source of the gains, however. With a task-based approach seeming to have been only one component in language teaching in some of the Flemish schools, and the extent of the teacher support program another confounding variable, it is tempting, but unjustified, to attribute the gains to TBLT itself.

Still in Belgium, but this time in a study involving university studnts, De Ridder, Vangehuchten, and Sesena Gomez (2007) compared the results of a 'traditional communicative course' (sic), referred to as the control group, and a course for intermediate

(CEFR B2/C1) Dutch-speaking third-year students of business and economics at the University of Antwerp learning Spanish that, while not wholly task-based, featured a genuinely task-based component. Sixty-eight students aged 20–23 were randomly assigned to the two courses. Each group met for two 50-minute lessons a week for two 12-week terms separated by a seven-week gap. Both courses were communicative. Each included the same "strong systematic or focus-on-form (sic) component: presentation, explanation, exercises" (2007, p. 311). It was the fourth component, lasting an additional 10 hours (five 60-minute sessions per term), which differed. Students assigned to the 'traditional' course (traditional in Belgium, perhaps) applied what they had learned to a similar context, each compiling an individual dossier on the basis of reading 12 specialist business texts about 12 Spanish companies, additional information they gathered on the companies, and a brief oral presentation they made on each one. The fourth component for the experimental group was task-based, not text-based, and consisted of making an advertising spot for a new product, drawing on their specialist economic background, their knowledge of the world, and (meta)-linguistic knowledge of Spanish. Videos of each control group student's final oral presentation and each experimental group student's final oral advertisement were rated independently by two judges using a scale of 1 (insufficient) to 4 (outstanding) on six dimensions, for which inter-rater reliability ranged from 0.90 to 0.98.

De Ridder *et al.* found that the control group performed statistically significantly better than the experimental group on pronunciation and intonation. Contrary to expectations, given the control group's greater language practice opportunities in the additional 10-hour segment, there was no difference between the two groups on fluency, perhaps, the researchers suggest, because both groups had had the opportunity to prepare their final presentations. Of most interest, the experimental group, with the task-based component, outperformed the control group statistically significantly on grammar (present and past tense morphology and syntax, pronoun use, use of *ser/estar* and *por/para*, prepositions and concordance rules), lexis (core vocabulary, 'adjustment to the situation,' phraseology, richness), and sociolinguistic adequacy ('adjustment to the situation,' use of *tu/usted*).

The De Ridder *et al.* study is interesting on at least six counts. It involved (i) substantial (24-week) courses (ii) conducted in real classrooms, (iii) a homogeneous pool of students, (iv) crucially, random assignment of students to groups, and (v) assessments that covered a range of linguistic dimensions and features, (vi) based on a communicative sample of the learners' spoken Spanish. Students whose course had included a task-based component not only held their own in the areas of grammar, vocabulary, and sociolinguistic appropriateness, but outperformed students from the 'traditional' communicative course in those areas. Once again, however, caution is needed. First, ratings were provided by only two judges, who had also served as the course instructors (L. Vangehuchten, p.c., May 2, 2013). Second, while the post-test measures were the same, the content of the two groups' video presentations was different. Independent "blind" raters and a supplementary common task or set of tasks would have been preferable. Finally, De Ridder *et al.* did not measure student motivation and wondered (2007, p. 314) if the task-based students' superior performance might not partly have been because task-based programs are simply more motivating for students. If true – and as noted in earlier chapters, it is my own experience and that of others that students do indeed, and understandably, tend to prefer task-based courses – this would be an example of 'maturation' as a threat to internal validity, although simultaneously a very positive characteristic of task-based programs.[5]

More studies comparing TBLT and other approaches have begun to appear. As explained earlier, collecting data on such items as those in Table 11.1, i.e., the process components, addresses the need to establish that the programs in question (i) really differed from one another, and (ii) did so in appropriate ways – appropriate with reference to the characteristics of the approaches supposedly being evaluated. Some of the recent studies, like that of De Ridder *et al.*, have been conducted in naturally occurring classroom settings, with the researchers involved especially careful to establish construct validity as the first part of a full process-product evaluation.

In a short-term study, De la Fuente (2006) compared 30 adult English-speaking college students learning vocabulary in three intact first-semester Spanish-as-a-foreign-language classes in the USA under one of three conditions: PPP (FonFs), and two varieties of what were labeled 'TBLT,' one with a teacher-generated explicit focus on *forms* component (sic), and one without. Focus on forms has no place in TBLT, of course, but the study is included here because of what it showed about the relative effectiveness of PPP and a genuinely task-based (group 2) and task-*supported* (group 3) language teaching. There were ten students in each class, randomly assigned to one of the three conditions.

The study covered two sessions. On day 1, all three groups received the same 45-minute input-based lesson on the topic of food, using dialogues and activities designed to familiarize students with procedures, followed by a ten-minute pre-test of their vocabulary knowledge. The 15 target Spanish words for food items were deliberately not included in this first lesson. The second 50-minute session, on day 2, was used for the treatment sessions. The 50-minute experimental lesson for the PPP group consisted of three phases: explanation of the 15 new words (presentation), each of which occurred twice in a dialogue, linguistically controlled and focused oral and written production exercises (practice), and acting out a role-play restaurant situation ("free" production), performed by the students working in pairs. The task-based group began their second lesson with the same dialogue, but with the teacher only explaining the meaning of new words, with no focus on their formal aspects (pronunciation, agreement

---

[5] As described in Section 11.5.4.2, González-Lloret and Nielson (to appear) reported positive student attitudes to the TBLT program they examined. Linsen (1994) and Devlieger and Goosens (2004), as summarized in Van den Branden (2006b), reported that student motivation had been increased by TBLT, and that student enthusiasm for task-based lessons had motivated teachers in their use of the new program. The motivational aspect of task-based programs that De Ridder *et al.* noted came through clearly, as well, in an evaluation of a federally funded task-based Korean program at the University of Hawaii by Kim *et al.* (2000), also reported in Kong (2012), which likewise found very positive student and teacher reactions. All three Korean teachers in the Hawaii program were interviewed and reported that their students were "very excited with the materials because those were new and very authentic with the pictures and conversations extracted from real maps and pictures, and real everyday conversations. The general format was very new to the students, so their anxiety level went up in the beginning of each pedagogic task in each target task. However, as the pedagogic tasks progressed, they gradually adjusted to the format and showed much interest.... Some students, who showed high anxiety in a traditional language class, felt comfortable with these classes because they were not forced to produce as much as in traditional language classes.... The three teachers all agreed that it was a very interesting, fun, and challenging experience to implement the TBLT modules. They mentioned that this kind of TBLT could be an alternative to traditional grammar-based or drill-based language classes, which have been disappointing for years" (Kim *et al.* 2000, p. 6).

morphology, etc.). In pairs, they then performed two iterations of a one-way task in which one student, acting as the customer, had to order from a menu containing the new target words, enhanced by bolding, for the 15 food items. The other student, playing the part of the waiter, had the menu with those items, plus an image for each item. He or she had to explain (in Spanish) any of the words the student playing the role of customer did not understand. That is, they negotiated for meaning. They then repeated the role play, reversing parts. The pairs next had to agree on, write, and then read aloud to their classmates, a perfect menu. This activity was designed to induce *focus on form* and incidental learning of the target lexical items. Finally, they did more of the same restaurant-ordering free role-play in pairs. The third, task-supported, group did the same activities as group two, except that instead of repeating the final restaurant role-play, they received a teacher-generated *focus-on-forms* lesson component, targeting the 15 vocabulary items through the two explicit focus-on-forms activities done by the PPP group in its practice stage. The idea was that, already having acquired the meaning of the items, they could now focus advantageously on phonological, morphological, and spelling issues. All sessions were recorded, so that post hoc monitoring could be used to see that the three treatments had really been delivered as intended.

At the process level, De la Fuente found no negotiation of meaning of target lexical items in the PPP lesson, and little production of them during the "free" speech role-play. The fact that there was no fixed or correct outcome, i.e., the role-play was an open task, meant that the target words could simply be avoided much of the time. Conversely, in the TBLT lessons, there was more production of the target lexical items, more retrieval of them in real time, and considerable negotiation work for their meaning.

Where product was concerned, the only outcome measures employed, unfortunately, were two discrete-point tests. The first, used as an immediate post-test, had students produce the lexical items orally when shown slides depicting each of the 15 food items. They scored one point for each recognizably correct word, regardless of the way it was pronounced or its (masculine/feminine, singular/plural) morphological accuracy. A delayed post-test, administered one week later, used the same slides and picture-labeling oral production procedure to test word retrieval, but separately scored responses for the absence/presence of appropriate morphology (gender and plural marking). Despite the measures clearly favoring the PPP group, and not really allowing the task-based/supported groups to show their strengths, (i) there were no between-group differences on the immediate word retrieval post-test, (ii) both task-oriented groups outperformed the PPP group on the delayed post-test, (iii) there was no difference between the performance of the two task-oriented groups on word retrieval, and (iv) group 3, with the added focus on forms component, was more accurate with gender and number morphology than group 2. De la Fuente reported the study's results as providing support for a 'task-based' approach to teaching vocabulary (although group 3 was really task-supported, not task based), with deeper processing of the new lexical items during negotiation for meaning in the task-oriented lessons the likely source of the advantage. She quite reasonably attributed the morphological accuracy gains by group 3 to the focus-on-forms component they had received having allowed them to focus on the form of the new words, their meanings already having been established. It should be noted, however, that as seen, e.g., in the De Ridder *et al.* study, such improvements are typical of the short-term gains produced by explicit instruction when linguistic features are simple, as was the case here, and the study is short-term, as was also the case, and could equally well have been achieved through focus on form in a longer period of task-based instruction than a mere 50-minute lesson, with no need for an explicitly language-as-object instructional segment. Meanwhile, although the study was small-scale and of short duration, the results were again favorable for both task-based and task-supported instruction, compared with PPP. This was despite accuracy being assessed only via discrete-point tests. A more valid, "evaluation-fair" assessment would also have included finding out how accurate graduates of the PPP course were when having to use the L2 communicatively.

In another vocabulary study – this time more like a research study than a normal program evaluation, despite being conducted in real classrooms – Shintani (2011) used a quasi-experimental, pre-test, post-test, delayed post-test design to compare the learning of 24 concrete nouns by 36 Japanese children aged 6–8 during a 12-week course. The nouns included eight animals (ostrich, crocodile, etc.), eight household objects (cutting board, toothbrush, etc.), and eight fruits and vegetables (pear, radish, etc.). The children were all taught by the researcher in six intact classes. There were two groups in each of three conditions, one with four months of prior experience learning English, and the other 16 months. Two output-based groups (n = 11) received presentation-practice-production-based instruction in the form of five drill-like games suitable for young children. They were told at the beginning of the lessons that the purpose was for them to learn the new words (intentional learning, FonFs, PPP). Two input-based groups (n = 13) performed three simple, game-like "listen-and-do" pedagogic tasks involving manipulation of flash cards in response to their understanding of teacher utterances containing the target lexical items (incidental learning, FonF, TBLT). A control group (n = 12) received lessons featuring total physical response (TPR), English songs, and practice with writing the alphabet, but no exposure to the target vocabulary items. All lessons were audio- and video-recorded to enable *post hoc* monitoring of the intended treatments. After pre-testing in weeks 1 and 2, each group received two 30-minute lessons a week in weeks 3, 4, and 5. Post-testing took place in weeks 6 and 7, and delayed post-testing in weeks 11 and 12. Four vocabulary tests were administered – two production tests in the first week, and two comprehension tests in the second – during each of the three testing periods.

At the process level, Shintani found that discourse in the two PPP lessons analyzed featured a total of 200 of the well-known (teacher) initiation – (student) response – (teacher) feedback (IRF) sequences (Sinclair & Coulthard 1975), and no negotiation for meaning in either class, compared with a total of only 25 IRF sequences in two TBLT lessons and 25 negotiation sequences in one TBLT class (but none in the other, surprisingly). Based on an analysis of classroom discourse in the third lesson, total numbers of tokens to which students were exposed were roughly comparable in the four treatment group classes (two production-based and two input-based). Students' production of target word tokens (a combined total of 444 in the two lessons analyzed) was much higher than (the combined total of 144) in the two input-based lessons. Teacher-initiated tokens (e.g., where students repeat after the teacher) dominated in the production-based lessons and were non-existent in the input-based lessons. Student-initiated tokens (e.g., during negotiation for meaning) were few and far between in the production-based, and significantly more frequent in the input-based, lessons. Almost all tokens of the 24 target words were "isolated" in the production-based lessons analyzed (examples from Shintani 2011, p. 150):

> TEACHER: What is it?
> STUDENT: ...
> TEACHER: Hippopotamus. Hippopotamus.

but mostly "embedded" in the equivalent input-based lessons:

> TEACHER: Next one. Please take the <u>chopsticks</u> to the supermarket. Chopsticks.
> STUDENT: Chopsticks?
> TEACHER: Yes, you use <u>chopsticks</u> every day. You use <u>chopsticks</u> when you eat rice.

One production and one comprehension test in Shintani's study was discrete-point, and the second of each task-based, thereby potentially allowing students in each group to show both their strengths and potential weaknesses. For the discrete-point listening test, students heard recordings of 40 words read aloud (24 target items and 16 distractors) and had to choose the correct picture out of six choices provided. In the task-based listening test, students heard recordings of 24 sentences read aloud and had to decide in which setting it had been said: fruit and vegetable shop, kitchen, bathroom, or zoo. In the discrete-point production test, students had to name the objects depicted in 24 flash cards, with no points deducted for incorrect morphology. Task-based production was assessed using a two-way "Same or different?" test, which had each child, tested individually and separated from the researcher by a screen, name the 24 objects on their sheet. If the researcher indicated that she had the same item on her sheet, they wrote a check mark on the picture, and if not, a cross. The children received a point for each picture they named correctly, with or without the appropriate morphology.

In within-group comparisons, on both the discrete-point and task-based listening tests, both treatment groups improved statistically significantly from pre- to immediate and delayed post-test, whereas the control group's scores showed no change on either measure. On the discrete-point production test, both treatment groups improved statistically significantly from pre- to both immediate and delayed post-test, and the input-based (TBLT) group also from post-test to delayed post-test. The same pattern was observed on the task-based (Same or different?) production test. Both treatment groups again improved statistically significantly from pre- to both post- and delayed post-test, and the input-based (TBLT) group also from immediate to delayed post-test. The control group's scores on both production tests remained unchanged throughout.

Between-group comparisons showed that both treatment groups outperformed the control group on all four measures. On the discrete-point production test, there was no difference between the treatment groups on either post-test. On the task-based listening test, however, the input-based (TBLT) group outperformed the production-based (PPP) group statistically significantly on both post-tests. On the two production measures, there were no differences between the treatment groups on either post-test, despite the significantly fewer opportunities for student production in the input-based lessons. Shintani suggests that the degree of 'discourse control' (negotiation and initiation opportunities) enjoyed by students in the TBLT lessons was more important. In sum, the input-based/TBLT group performed as well as the production-based PPP group on both discrete-point measures (listening and speaking) and the task-based speaking measure, and better than the PPP group on the task-based listening measure. These results appear to provide more evidence for TBLT, for incidental L2 vocabulary learning (less surprising in young children), and for the development (seen in an earlier study by Ellis & He 1999) of both receptive and productive abilities from input-based instruction, just as the production-based instruction produced both productive and receptive gains. However, (i) it was a small study, (ii) with young children, and (iii) the scoring of both production measures ignored morphological accuracy, thereby potentially disfavoring the PPP group. On the other hand, the disappointing result for the task-based production test, where the TBLT group might have been expected to outperform the PPP group, may equally have been due to the fact that the task essentially boiled down to whether the children could remember and say the name of the objects pictured on their sheet, which seems little different from a second discrete-point measure.

In a similar, but extended, second study using new data, Shintani (2013) employed a pre-test and two post-tests to compare the absolute and relative effectiveness of focus on forms and focus on form for the learning of 24 nouns (zoo animals, etc.) and also, this time, 12 adjectives (denoting color, size, etc.) by 45 six-year-old Japanese children, all complete beginners studying English in a private school. The children were randomly assigned to form two treatment groups and a control group, with each group of 15 then divided into two classes of six to nine students for the purpose of instruction. Each group received nine 30-minute lessons, two lessons a week, over a five-week period. FonFs was operationalized as traditional PPP teaching, and FonF, which was delivered unobtrusively and reactively, as TBLT. Productive abilities were assessed using a discrete-point and a task-based test before the instruction began, one week after it finished, and again four weeks after it finished. Shintani acted as the teacher and tester for all three groups.

In the PPP classes, where the focus was on accuracy and intentional learning, the new words were first introduced explicitly and practiced via repetition of the individual words, then practiced chorally and individually in response to flash cards, and finally practiced further in "free production" activities, such as a modified version of solitaire, played with the flash cards, children winning a card if they could say the word referring to the card they chose from a set of 30. Students received corrective recasts from the teacher when they made errors, not explicit "on-record" negative feedback, as recasts have widely been found to be the most frequent form negative feedback takes in natural classrooms. In the TBLT lessons, which relied on incidental learning, students worked on pedagogic tasks designed to require their successful comprehension of input from the teacher containing the target items. With a focus on meaning throughout, their task was to respond to such commands as "Please take the crocodile to the zoo" by selecting the correct flashcard and placing it in the correct holder. The control group attended their regular lessons, which involved English songs, TPR activities, and copying the alphabet on work sheets, with no use of the target lexical items. The discrete-item oral production test involved showing a flash card accompanied by a verbal prompt, "What's this?" or "What color is this?" New objects were used when eliciting adjectives, e.g., "This box is ____?", said in Japanese, to avoid potential bias in favor of either group. The task-based assessment took the form of a communicative "Same-or-different?" task, conducted one-on-one. Teacher and student had a sheet containing 24 numbered pictures depicting the nouns and adjectives. The teacher asked such questions as "What color is it?" and "Is your soap pink?", and the student had to determine whether his or her picture matched that of the teacher. One point was awarded for each of the 24 nouns and 12 adjectives the student produced correctly. Intra-rater reliability was 100%.

Shintani first looked at processes in the two treatment classes. Input frequencies of the target nouns and adjectives were similar in both classes, but whereas the items often occurred as isolated words in PPP lessons, they were significantly more often embedded in complete teacher utterances in the TBLT classes. As was to be expected, output frequencies were much higher (a total of 3,846) in the production-oriented PPP classes, where the tokens were typically produced because they were requested by the teacher as part of IRF exchanges in lessons with an overall focus on intentional learning. The small total number (just 353) of output tokens in the TBLT lessons were always optional, i.e., "borrowed" (repeated or imitated) by pupils from a prior teacher utterance or self-initiated, never requested, and drew students' attention while they were focused on negotiating for meaning, learning incidentally while doing tasks. The option for self-initiation and negotiation for meaning, Shintani, notes, was especially important in this and the de la Fuente study. A post hoc regression analysis showed that learners who initiated the production of adjectives acquired more of them. The adjectives were always introduced preemptively in the FonFs/PPP lessons, but always reactively, contextually embedded, in the FonF/TBLT lessons, and with a communicative purpose, i.e., to help pupils identify correct noun referents in the teacher's commands. (Shintani notes that Jiang 2000, has claimed that learners must experience contextualized use of new L2 words if they are to develop a full representation.) In sum, the token frequencies and discourse-level differences were all entirely consistent with the supposed characteristics of both treatments. They demonstrated construct validity, or as Shintani puts it (2013, pp. 52–53), that "the *internal* characteristics of the two types of instruction (i.e., the activity that arises in the classroom) matched their *external* descriptions (i.e., the activity predicted by the design of instruction)."

Turning to learning outcomes, scores of both treatment groups on the 24 target nouns were significantly higher on each post-test than on the pre-test, but whereas the FonFs/PPP group did not improve from the first to the second post-test on either the discrete-point of task-based measure, the FonF/TBLT group improved statistically significantly on both measures. Within-group outcome measures favored the FonF/TBLT group. As expected, the control group's scores did not change across the pre-test and two post-tests. Scores on the 12 adjectives also favored the FonF/TBLT group. Once again, the control group showed no change across all three testing times. Both treatment groups' scores on the discrete-point test improved from pre-test to both post-tests, but not from the first to the second post-test. On the task-based test, however, the FonFs/PPP group improved from pre-test to post-test 1, but not from pre-test to post-test 2, or from one post-test to the next. The FonF/TBLT group, conversely, improved significantly from pre-test to both post-tests, i.e., the improvement was sustained, but like the PPP group, not from the first to the second post-test. Where between-group differences were concerned, the FonF/TBLT group did statistically significantly better than both the control group and the FonFs/PPP group on both the discrete-point and task-based measure on both post-tests. The FonFs group outperformed the control group on the discrete-point test on both post-tests, but failed to do so at either post-test on the communicative, task-based measure.

The two Shintani studies are valuable additions to the literature. The overt focus in both cases was the relative strengths of input-based and production-based instruction, but since the two treatments were operationalized as TBLT/focus on form and PPP/ focus on forms in each study, they are relevant to the present discussion. There are limitations, however. Shintani's studies both (i) concerned young children, who might be expected to benefit relatively more from incidental learning, and relatively less from explicit, intentional learning, opportunities than adults, (ii) were limited in scope to very early stages of language learning, and (iii) focused exclusively on vocabulary. (They do, incidentally, however, respond to skeptics who suggest that TBLT will not work with young, beginning learners, or in some cases, with beginners of any age, because communicative demands are too high, tasks too challenging, etc.)

With respect to (iii), similar findings for a grammatical morpheme were obtained in earlier work using the same data set as Shintani (2011). Shintani and Ellis (2010) found that the Japanese children had been able to acquire a grammatical target, plural -s, incidentally during the same lessons. There were three measures, used, again, three times, as pre-, post- and delayed post-tests. A comprehension test required the children to choose the correct picture, one showing one, the other two, of the same ten objects in response to hearing the singular or plural form. A modified Wug test (Berko 1958), using ten items, five of which were real and had appeared in the classes, and five of which were nonsense words, assessed the productivity of whatever had been acquired, i.e., the generalizability of the plural -s morpheme to new nouns. Third, also assessing productive use of the plural form, came the task-based "Same or different?" production test, administered individually following the same procedure as in the two Shintani studies described above. This time, the tester's and student's answer sheets contained 24 items, 12 singular and 12 plural, of which five had appeared in the lessons, and seven pertained to new items. The comprehension-based and production-based groups performed comparably, and with results similar to those in the two Shintani studies. Both treatment groups outperformed the control group on the comprehension and task-based production tests on both post-tests. Presumably because comprehension precedes production, the comprehension-based beginners group outperformed the production-based beginners group on the comprehension and task-based production task. However, very little learning was demonstrated by students from either treatment group on the Wug test, perhaps, Shintani and Ellis suggest (2010, p. 629), because the Wug test, unlike the other two measures, elicited a test-like, rather than a communicative, response. While constituting another positive result for comprehension-based instruction (CBI) and, indirectly, given the way CBI was operationalized, for TBLT, it needs to be remembered that this study, too, concerned young children, and in plural -s, a meaning-bearing item. In a classroom study, Loewen, Erlam, and Ellis (2009) found no evidence of incidental learning of functionally redundant, so less salient, third person -s by adults.

An evaluation of a full-fledged TBLT program for adults, also with Spanish as L2, was reported by Burwell, González-Lloret, and Nielsen (2009) and González-Lloret and Nielson (to appear). Starting with a thorough needs analysis, in which experienced field agents (domain experts) played critically important roles, and following the subsequent steps in designing a true TBLT program described in earlier chapters, the eight-week course, with eight hours of instruction per day, was developed specifically for US Border Patrol Academy (BPA) trainees, and launched in December, 2007. It replaced one considered unsatisfactory for (and by) the same population. The old course had used a traditional synthetic syllabus. With each lesson focusing on a grammatical topic, it had been delivered in English, and had used a written translation exercise for the final exam. Graduates had subsequently often been unable to perform their work in Spanish when needed, and had had to rely on native or heritage speakers among colleagues in the field.

Course modules in the new TBLT program, each of which lasts a week, are taught almost completely in Spanish. They begin with students watching and listening to genuine video- and audio-recordings of experienced agents performing the target tasks in one of seven scenarios in Spanish – conducting an emergency vehicle stop, offering and providing first aid, determining citizenship status, interviewing a detainee, and so on – that agents routinely encounter in the field. They continue with a series of peda-gogic tasks, gradually transitioning from simple ones that follow pre-determined story lines, focus mostly on comprehension, allow planning time, and require only limited production, to more complex ones with unpredictable scenarios and role-plays with native speakers in simulations of real-world conditions. There is no linguistic syllabus and no planned, explicit grammar instruction. Grammar is taught reactively through focus on form, and also learned incidentally as students work on pedagogic tasks, view thematically relevant movies (*El Norte*, etc.), play *La Chamba*, a video game created especially for the program, and take advantage of supplementary conversation oppor-tunities with native speakers. Exit tasks and the final criterion-referenced performance assessments occur in week eight, during which trainees are evaluated on their participa-tion with professional actors in life-like role-plays of each of the seven scenarios.

Trainees' performance is assessed by two instructors who score each learner's ability to perform the target tasks in a scenario to criterion. The seven critical target tasks are divided into two categories of sub-tasks: (i) compulsory, and (ii) expected but not required. That way, learners and teachers can be given more diagnostic information about any remaining weaknesses than would be available from a single dichotomous overall grade of pass or fail. The sub-tasks were identified by a team of experienced Border Patrol agents, using their knowledge of what really happens in the field, as well as videos of real agents performing the tasks. The assessments include no explicitly language-focused measures, but sub-tasks do have accompanying language-focused elements, e.g., 'Using appropriate Spanish, trainee ascertains subject's physical condi-tion.' By the time of the evaluation in 2009, several thousand students had completed the new program, all of whom were native speakers of English with no knowledge of Spanish when the course began. With close to a 100% pass rate, it had already demon-strated its effectiveness in meeting the main objective, i.e., graduation of agents capable of performing seven critical target tasks in Spanish (in simulations, at least; their per-formance in the field would require a separate study).

González-Lloret and Nielson's evaluation addressed three issues. First, in a small-scale study, they compared the oral proficiency of students in the prior grammar-based program with that of students in the TBLT program. This was possible because the need for a comparative evaluation had been anticipated while the TBLT program was being created. Permission was obtained to audio-record 19 students from the final group in the grammar-based course and 20 from the first cohort in the TBLT program during their fourth week of instruction completing the same picture-guided narrative about a boy on a bicycle who is forced off the road by an angry driver, only to pass him later when the driver's car breaks down. Identifying information about the participants was kept from the two raters, who were one of the authors and a NS teacher of Spanish. The recordings were judged for grammatical accuracy (target-like use of noun–modifier and noun–verb agreement), syntactic complexity (since these were low-proficiency speakers, mean length of utterance), lexical complexity, and fluency (following Gilabert 2004, operationalized as total number of syllables divided by the total number of seconds, multiplied by 60). Students from the TBLT course performed statistically significantly better than those from the grammar-based course on syntactic complexity and fluency. Grammatical accuracy was slightly better for the grammar-based group, but not statistically significantly so, and the groups performed comparably on the measures of lexical complexity and variety. These results are obviously positive for TBLT, especially since they were achieved with graduates from the very first cohort of the new TBLT program. However, Nielson and González-Lloret note that the samples were small, and the respectable grammatical accuracy scores of the TBLT students could have been due not only to the use of focus on form in their program, but to optional self-study use of computer-based exercises, some of which involved explicit grammar instruction.

The second part of the evaluation was an attempt to find out if completion of the program had simultaneously improved students' global proficiency scores, as measured by the 2008 version of the *Versant* test of oral Spanish abilities, assessed on the basis of a 15-minute telephone interview, and whether students' starting proficiency made a difference. Two hundred and fifty-four students were assessed using their *Versant* test scores when joining the BPA and again, with an alternate form of the test, on the very last day of the eight-week TBLT program. *Versant* scores could vary from a minimum of 20 to a maximum of 80. The mean "pre-test," i.e., BPA entry test, score was 30.21, and the mean post-test score was 37.68 (a roughly 12.5% improvement). Scores on all four dimensions of the test – fluency, pronunciation, sentence mastery, and vocabulary – had improved statistically significantly, with improvements greater on the last two. In other words, the TBLT program had achieved close to a 100% pass rate with respect to its intended focus, the ability to perform target tasks to criterion (a handful of the 3,000+ trainees at the time of the evaluation had had to take the final assessment for individual tasks again, and in two or three cases, to repeat the entire course), but simultaneously had improved their general Spanish proficiency. There was no statistically significant relationship between pre-test and post-test scores, indicating that the course had worked well for all students, regardless of the (relatively small) differences in their starting proficiency.

The third component was an online survey of 37 students, 21 of whom were enrolled in the TBLT program at the time, and 16 who had completed it and were now working as BP agents in the field. Both groups expressed broad satisfaction with the program, reporting that they appreciated its hands-on nature and obvious relevance to their work.

Overall, the results Burwell, González-Lloret, and Nielson report attest to the effectiveness of the BPA program in meeting trainee agents' job-related needs; this was clear from the task-based outcomes assessments and also from the students' recognition of its relevance. Moreover, the graduates were achieving the program's goals, regardless of some differences in starting proficiency, while simultaneously outperforming students from the previous grammar-based program in the complexity and fluency of their spoken Spanish and demonstrating a comparable level of grammatical accuracy. Nielson and González-Lloret note some limitations of their findings, mostly due to factors beyond their control. The main ones were the small n-sizes of the first and third parts of their study, and the unavailability of *Versant* test scores for graduates of the old grammar course. They suggest that follow-up data on agents' task performance and language use in the field would shed light on the transferability of abilities learned in the classroom to the real world outside. I would add that a comparison of their performance of tasks for which they were and were not specifically prepared would also be revealing.

An evaluation of an online course with a task-based component for the teaching of elementary Chinese to US high school students (Lai, Zhao, & Wang 2011) found positive attitudes toward the course on the part of the four instructors (three of them novices) and students (n = 38), and like other studies, superior performance on the outcome measure to that of students in a control group (n = 36) who devoted comparable time (roughly five hours per week) to a traditional grammar-focused course. Students, who ranged in age from 13 to 19 (average age was 16) completed 12 one-hour task-based modules, one each for 12 weeks of the 16-week course, written by the researchers to accompany use of the regular Chinese e-textbook. All lessons were recorded, and a randomly chosen lesson by each of the four teachers using the supplementary materials was examined to ensure that the instruction was indeed task-based. Data on teacher and student attitudes were derived from multiple sources: students' weekly blogs and course evaluations, notes on classroom observations, weekly debriefing sessions, and end-of-semester interviews with the teachers. Outcome data consisted of three measures applied to transcriptions of students' performance of an unplanned, untimed, monological picture-description task. The TBLT group scored slightly higher, but not statistically significantly so, than the control group on accuracy (error-free clauses) and syntactic complexity (mean length of T-units), and despite substantial variation in scores, statistically significantly higher on fluency (meaningful words per minute). The performance of students in the TBLT groups might have been even more impressive, Lai *et al.* suggest, but for the fact that most lacked prior experience with task-based language learning or with a course taught exclusively in the L2 and requiring more than the usual amount of independent and collaborative (small-group) work. Lai *et al.* recommend explaining the expectations and benefits afforded by task-based learning to both teachers and students, accompanied, if necessary, by training in appropriate teaching and learning strategies.

11.6. Summary

Assessment of L2 abilities might take any of four approaches, focusing on (i) measures of linguistic knowledge, (ii) global proficiency, (iii) the constructs underlying tasks, or (iv) tasks themselves – specifically, those shown by the needs analysis to be relevant for the students concerned. The approach taken in TBLT is the last of the four: using task-based, criterion-referenced performance tests. The addition of some kind of language measure to a task-based assessment is understandably attractive for those hitherto accustomed to language as the exclusive assessment focus. However, aside from the questionable advantage of attaching a linguistic caboose in the majority of cases, there is a danger that a backwash effect from such an approach can lead to a reorientation of task-based courses away from tasks and toward teaching and testing language abilities and skills, or whatever other dimensions of "proficiency" or "underlying constructs" take their place. While not without problems, in particular, the paucity of knowledge about the generalizability of task-based abilities, TBLT's approach, assessing students' ability to perform their target tasks, is tangible, usually logistically feasible, more direct, and more likely to yield reliable and valid results.

Evaluations of TBLT must meet the standard requirements for evaluating any educational program, e.g., recognizing and countering six common threats to internal validity, with formative and summative, process and product, dimensions all important. The need to establish cause-and-effect relationships to allow judgments of the absolute and relative effectiveness of program components and of entire programs requires a combination of laboratory and classroom studies, in that order. The suggestion is first to confirm construct validity (the process), focusing on low inference, high frequency behaviors, and then to compare the outcomes (the product) of programs that have employed TBLT and some alternative approach. The programs should involve comparable populations of teachers and students, randomly assigned to the groups being compared wherever possible.

Numerous studies of TBLT components – of relationships between pedagogic task-types and language use and language learning (reviewed briefly in Chapter 8.4.5), and of several of TBLT's MPs – have been reported in the SLA and applied linguistics literatures over the past 20 years. They amount to far more than for any alternative approach to language teaching, despite TBLT's appearance on the scene relatively recently compared with what are currently thought of as "traditional" PPP and other focus on forms approaches. Evaluations of full TBLT programs to date have been less numerous, and generally small-scale, although, again, more numerous than the vanishingly small number of evaluations of PPP-type programs conducted by their advocates. (Even if they do no research themselves, it would be nice if critics of TBLT and defenders of the status quo – often commercial textbook writers – could cite just one study to support their positions.) Results of both types of evaluations so far have been positive. Evidence is steadily accruing of TBLT's success in achieving its main objective, i.e., graduating students able to perform their target tasks, but also students as competent on linguistically focused measures as students whose only experience has been forms-focused instruction, with the latter less capable when it comes to communicative abilities, task-based or otherwise. Meanwhile, to repeat, program-level evaluations of TBLT are still insufficient in number and scale. Much more research and many more process-product evaluations are needed.

11.7. Suggested Readings

Bachman, L. (1989). The development and use of criterion-referenced tests of language proficiency in language program evaluation. In Johnson, R.K. (ed.), *The second language curriculum* (pp. 242–258). Cambridge: Cambridge University Press.

Bachman, L. (2002). Some reflections on task-based language performance assessment. *Language Testing* 19, 4, 453–476.

Bachman, L.F. (2007). What is the construct? The dialectic of abilities and contexts in defining constructs in language assessment. In Fox, J., Wesche, M., Bayliss, D., Cheng, L., Turner, C., & Doe, C. (eds.), *Language testing reconsidered* (pp. 41–71). Ottawa, Canada: University of Ottawa Press.

Brindley, G. (2013). Task-based assessment. In Chapelle, C. (ed.), *The encyclopedia of applied linguistics*. Oxford: Wiley-Blackwell.

Brown, J.D. (1990). Short-cut estimates of criterion-reference test consistency. *Language Testing* 7, 1, 77–97.

Brown, J.D., & Hudson, T. (2002). *Criterion-referenced language testing*. Cambridge: Cambridge University Press.

Buck, G., & Tatsuoka, K. (1998). Application of the rule-space procedure to language testing: Examining attributes of a free response listening test. *Language Testing* 15, 119–157.

East, M. (2012). *Task-based language teaching from the teachers' perspective: Insights from New Zealand*. Amsterdam: John Benjamins.

Gass, S., Mackey, A., & Ross-Feldman, L. (2005). Task-based interactions in classroom and laboratory settings. *Language Learning* 55, 575–611.

González-Lloret, M., & Nielson, K. (in Press). Does TBLT work? Evaluation of a task-based Spanish program. *Language Teaching Research*.

Gysen, S., & van Avermaet, P. (2005). Issues in functional language performance assessment: The case of the Certificate in Dutch as a Foreign Language. *Language Assessment Quarterly* 2, 1, 51–68.

Long, M.H. (1984). Process and product in ESL program evaluation. *TESOL Quarterly* 18, 3, 409–425.

Long, M.H. (in press). Experimental perspectives on classroom interaction. In Markee, N. (ed.), *Handbook of classroom discourse and interaction*. Oxford: Wiley-Blackwell.

Long, M.H., & Norris, J.M. (2000). Task-based teaching and assessment. In Byram, M. (ed.), *Encyclopedia of language teaching* (pp. 597–603). London: Routledge.

McNamara, T.F. (1996). Designing a performance test: The Occupational English Test. In McNamara, T. (ed.), *Measuring second language performance* (pp. 91–116). London: Longman.

Norris, J.M. (2001). Identifying rating criteria for task-based EAP assessment. In Hudson, T.D., & Brown, J.D. (eds.), *A focus on language test development: Expanding the language proficiency construct across a variety of tests* (pp. 163–204). Honolulu: University of Hawai'i Press.

Norris, J.M. (ed.) (2002). Special issue: "Interpretations, intended uses and designs in task-based language assessment." *Language Testing* 19, 4, 337–346.

Norris, J.M. (2009). Task-based teaching and testing. In Long, M.H., & Doughty, C.J. (eds.), *Handbook of language teaching* (pp. 578–594). Oxford: Blackwell.

Norris, J.M., Brown, J.D., Hudson, T.D., & Bonk, W. (2002). Examinee abilities and task difficulty in task-based second language performance assessment. *Language Testing* 19, 4, 395–418.

Robinson, P., & Ross, S. (1996). The development of task-based assessment in English for academic purposes programs. *Applied Linguistics* 17, 4, 455–476.

Shehadeh, A., & Coombe, C.A. (eds.) (2012). *Task-based language teaching in foreign language contexts: Research and implementation*. Amsterdam: John Benjamins.

Shintani, N., & Ellis, R. (2010). The incidental acquisition of English plural -*s* by Japanese children in comprehension-based and production-based lessons: A process-product study. *Studies in Second Language Acquisition* 32, 4, 607–637.

Van den Branden, K., Depauw, V., & Gysen, S. (2002). A computerized task-based test of second language Dutch for vocational training purposes. *Language Testing* 19, 4, 438–452.

Wigglesworth, G. (2008). Tasks and performance-based assessment. In Shohamy, E., & Hornberger, N. (eds.), *Encyclopedia of language and education: Language testing and assessment* (Vol. 7, 2nd edn, pp. 111–122). New York: Springer.

Part Three
The Road Ahead

Chapter 12

Does TBLT Have a Future?

12.1. Diffusion of Innovation

'Diffusion of innovation' is a term often used to refer to the study of when and how new ideas (or ideas perceived as new) catch on and spread, and when and why they often do not. While a long-standing research interest in other fields, including general education, the first serious treatments of the topic in applied linguistics, to the best of my knowledge, were those of Bailey (1992), Henrichsen (1989), Kennedy (1988), Maley (1984), Tickoo (1987), and most notably, Markee (1988) in his UCLA dissertation, followed by a series of publications (Markee 1993, 1994, 1997, 2007). Since Markee's pioneering work, much of it focusing on TBLT as described in this book (see Chapter 11.5.4.2), diffusion of innovation has become a topic of wider interest in language teaching (LT) and applied linguistics, with contributions by Alderson (2009), Carless (2007, 2012), Goto Butler (2011), Holliday (1994), Murray (2008), Van den Branden (2009), and Wedell (2009), among others.

The literature shows that numerous factors, both positive and negative, have been implicated in the diffusion of innovation in education, including LT and applied linguistics. While the labels vary, several conditions are considered likely to facilitate the adoption and spread of new ideas. They include the early involvement of teachers; practical demonstrations (not just chalk and talk) and successful working models (even if small-scale) that potential adopters can observe; a perception that the change involved is not too radically different from current practice, too complex to understand, or too hard to introduce, e.g., because it requires abilities or technology that teachers lack; a perception that the innovation has tangible advantages likely to accrue for adopters, including institutional support (e.g., the Flemish government's in-service training for

Second Language Acquisition and Task-Based Language Teaching, First Edition. Mike Long.
© 2015 John Wiley & Sons, Inc. Published 2015 by John Wiley & Sons, Inc.

TBLT, described in Chapter 11.5.4.2); a perception in the eyes of teachers, students, and institutions alike that the innovation is compatible with local systems and values; and (potentially as a result of several of the previous factors combined) teacher buy-in. Concluding his book, Prabhu (1987) writes of the need for a 'sense of plausibility' if teachers are to embrace curricular innovation. An external, top-down, mandated innovation, he believes, and I think rightly so, is less likely to be effective than new ideas that "invoke some corroborative experience in teachers" (p. 105).

Negative factors likely to impede change or block it altogether are essentially the opposites of the positive factors. In particular, innovative ideas or programs are likely to be ignored or rejected if they would entail an increased workload for teachers; they are difficult for them to understand; they require greater skills, abilities, technology, or training than they currently possess; they would cause disruptions to customary practices; and they come with no obvious benefits to potential adopters, including little or no institutional support. For example, as part of an interesting review of the history of English language teaching in India before and after the Bangalore Project, Tickoo (1987) identified the procedural syllabus' requirement of a command of spoken English far beyond that of most Indian secondary school teachers, and the relatively more important place in India of an ability to read English, as each having played a crucial role in the failure of Prabhu's ideas to influence Indian English as a foreign language (EFL) beyond the original locale.

A cultural clash, perceived or genuine, could also prove fatal. For example, the relative spontaneity and creative, communicative language use in typical TBLT lessons could initially sit uneasily with the heavy reliance on rote memorization in education in countries such as Saudi Arabia, where memorization goes back thousands of years. Long before the establishment of Islam, Arabs would memorize poems and folklore to pass them down to the next generation. When Islam was established, memorization continued because there were still few literate people able to write down the Quran (about 600 pages) and the *hadiths* (Al Thowaini 2011; Parker 1986).

The dictates of centralized state education systems can also be decisive. In many parts of the world, teachers find that helping their students to learn to speak a foreign language and to use it communicatively must take a back seat to getting them to complete a rigid "official" syllabus on schedule, and then to pass decidedly non-communicatively oriented final examinations, some more akin to IQ tests than measures of language abilities. (It is to be hoped that research findings like some of those reported in Chapter 11.5.4.2 will gradually allay fears in such settings.)

In my own view, perhaps most underestimated of all is teacher burnout, i.e., that state of cynicism, often combined with mental and/or physical exhaustion bordering on despair and depression, which is increasingly common in countries where those at the chalk-face are overworked, underpaid, and generally exploited. This is the situation, for reasons beyond their control, of all too many teachers and other education workers the world over, especially those in the many state systems in which public education is ever more obviously devalued by politicians and subjected to severe budget cuts, and where schools are increasingly regarded by social planners as useful primarily for warehousing children of the poor until they join their parents on the lower rungs of the labor force or among the ranks of the unemployed.

In light of the factors that have been identified as prone to favor or disfavor the diffusion of innovation, it is easy to see why TBLT is unlikely ever to displace traditional approaches to LT in some parts of the world, and in many schools and classrooms in all parts. As explained in Chapter 2 and detailed elsewhere in the book, TBLT differs radically from the dominant, traditional synthetic/focus-on-forms approaches to LT, but simultaneously may appear too planned and structured for supporters of purely analytic, non-interventionist, laissez-faire approaches. Although conceptually simple enough in my view, understanding TBLT implies a basic grasp of how people learn languages, an openness to genuinely student-centered learning, and a willingness to teach in harmony with learners' internal psycholinguistic processes, none of which are called for by traditional synthetic approaches, where such issues keep few textbook writers, teacher educators, or the teachers themselves awake at night. At a very basic level, but unfortunately, a relevant one, given the state of LT and the status of language teachers in all too many parts of the world, and in some classrooms and schools in all parts, the need for a decent command of the L2 and at least some specific training or re-training in TBLT will make adoption a daunting prospect for many teachers, especially as they are precisely the ones who most frequently work in resource-starved environments and lack institutional support. Finally, as Richards (1984) noted, no method or approach to LT can be expected to survive unless it comes with teaching materials, whereas those that are accompanied by well-marketed materials are likely to last and do well, whatever their merits.[1] Busy teachers rarely have the time or expertise to produce materials themselves, task-based or otherwise. In contrast, synthetic materials are only too readily available from commercial publishers, in whose interest it is to make sure they continue to sell as widely as possible.

Given the many potential obstacles, does TBLT have a future? Where, if anywhere, can it be expected to survive and thrive? The following speculations are impressionistic; they are based in part on individual cases with which I am familiar or about which I have read or heard, but whose representativeness is uncertain.

I think TBLT is more likely to be adopted, sustained, and successful in institutions, or with groups of teachers who pool their resources and work together, in situations exhibiting at least some of the following five positive characteristics:

1. Students are homogenous enough, their numbers large enough, throughput stable enough (i.e., successive generations are similar enough), and learning a functional command of the L2 recognized as important enough, to justify the initial societal or institutional investment of time and money in conducting (and periodically repeating) a properly conducted needs analysis.
2. Financial resources and institutional support are available.
3. Expertise already exists locally, or can be brought in, to produce (i) the initial sets of instructional materials (modules of pedagogic tasks) and (ii) criterion-referenced, task-based performance tests identified as required to meet student needs.
4. Teachers or faculty members, whether native or non-native speakers, have an adequate command of the L2 and sufficient expertise as language teachers, their preparation either having been originally included, or later been supplemented by, specific training in TBLT.

---

[1] Thirty years after it first appeared, Richards' (1984) article, 'The Secret Life of Methods,' is still worth reading for the insights it contains about some of the powerful commercial and quasi-governmental forces at work in LT, often in the shadows. It is a shame that sections of the even more revealing original version were deemed too sensitive for publication by *TESOL Quarterly* at the time.

5. At least some of those teachers or faculty members have long-term or permanent positions, preferably full-time. This will (a) guarantee some level of needed program stability, (b) make the effort required to create a new program, including retraining where necessary, both viable and visibly worthwhile to stakeholders, and (c) create the conditions essential for the development and maintenance of understanding, expertise, and institutional memory.

Those factors would be beneficial for any type of LT program, of course, but given the often higher than average standards and levels of expertise required are especially important for designing, implementing, and evaluating a TBLT program. I have worked as a language teacher, teacher educator, and materials writer in several programs that have had few or none of the optimal characteristics, most often for lack of genuine institutional interest in the students, high teacher turnover, and lack of resources. However, I have also seen first-hand how, given enlightened institutional support, genuine commitment to their students and solidarity among teachers, and with some outside help, a resource-starved community English as a second language (ESL) program can slowly transition to something approaching TBLT to the benefit of the many hard-working, low-income students who might otherwise not have acquired the kind of functional language proficiency they desperately needed.

How much easier sites for TBLT, then, are the circumstances of many government language programs (e.g., those for diplomatic, military, and intelligence agency person-nel), industry-sponsored programs (e.g., foreign language teaching in the travel industry and tourism), corporate-sponsored programs (e.g., in-house language courses designed specifically for employees of large companies with international interests), and more generally, foreign language programs in public and private universities or for large mis-sionary or volunteer organizations, such as the US Peace Corps, as well as some of the rapidly increasing numbers of private 'bilingual' or 'immersion' schools for young chil-dren in large parts of the world. Many such programs involve highly motivated learners, parents, and sponsors, are relatively well-funded, have a large, stable, homogeneous student throughput, a stable, well-qualified teaching cadre, and in some cases, more technology at their disposal than is good for language learning. In all those cases, moreover, the development of a high-level, functional command of the L2 concerned (most often English, but increasingly other languages, such as Chinese, Spanish, or Arabic) is widely understood by all but the youngest students, and by parents, institu-tions, and societies, alike, as critically important for educational and/or occupational purposes.

In contrast, and paradoxically, given that a large proportion of the research and writing on LT in general, and TBLT in particular, to date has come from within English-speaking societies, all too many ESL programs in those societies are underfunded or not funded at all and employ poorly paid teachers on a part-time, temporary basis, thus ensuring high teacher turnover and instability. The student populations, moreover, tend to vary greatly at any one time, and over time, e.g., as a direct result of geopolitical changes ranging from war to economic prosperity, either of which can result in sudden increases or decreases in the numbers and types of students in ESL classrooms from the countries affected. The combination of an ever-changing teaching staff and volatile student population makes high-quality LT programs of any kind, especially TBLT, less likely. Again, however, there are exceptions, with many admirable programs evident in the world of ESL, not just EFL, including, e.g., some cleverly designed English-for-academic-purposes programs at some colleges and universities.

It would be a shame if successful TBLT programs were gradually to become the preserve of well-resourced institutions catering to privileged social elites. It is to be hoped that grassroots TBLT programs, many of whose teachers and whose students, such as recently arrived refugees and migrant workers, come from the opposite end of the social spectrum, will receive the attention and support they deserve, too, on a voluntary basis if necessary. My own work as a volunteer with one such program has proved the most challenging of any I have experienced in many years as a language teacher and applied linguist, but also one of the most rewarding. One quickly learns the difference between what is helpful and makes LT run smoothly, and what is *necessary, sufficient, and available*, when working in such contexts. The highest level of general education achieved by many of the students may have been sixth grade, 15–20 years ago, in a tiny rural school in a war-torn country. They may arrive for their two-hour evening ESL class after a long day of poorly paid, hard physical work, often with few of the background learning skills and experiences (such as a reasonable level of literacy) one has unthinkingly taken for granted with different populations in the past. Many live and work in a L1 linguistic ghetto, so with very little contact with English or with English native speakers outside of those classes. Some have never used a computer or set foot in a library or a museum. Yet these students typically have urgent, clearly specifiable communicative needs, and are among those who can benefit most from TBLT.

12.2. A Research Program for TBLT

While I have attempted to bring theory and research findings to bear as part of the rationale for TBLT, there has, I hope, been no pretense that all is well and understood. There have been numerous ideas about how best to teach languages in the past, many of them innovative at the time. No one has got it all right before, or debates would have ceased long ago, and it would be irrational to assume that TBLT as described in this book will be any different. There may not be a single correct or a best way to teach languages, although there certainly are some wrong ways. As with the provision of any service, however, end users have a right to expect that providers will keep abreast of developments in the field and endeavor to follow what at any time is believed to be best practice, always open to change when new theory or research findings and/or practitioners' field experiences dictate.

Several obvious areas in need of a serious research effort – preferably coherent and coordinated research programs, not isolated one-off studies – were noted in previous chapters. The first is the identification of improved criteria for classifying and sequencing target and pedagogic tasks, knowledge of which would help improve the design of task syllabi. (See Chapter 8.4.4, and Chapter 8's fn. 8.) Second, and related to the first, (more standardized) work is needed on relationships between pedagogic task-types and various dimensions of linguistic performance (see Chapter 8.4.5). The third concerns the extent to which task-based abilities are task-specific or transferable, knowledge of which would be useful in making both syllabus design and task-based testing more efficient (see Chapter 11.4). Fourth, the whole field of task-based, criterion-referenced performance testing needs serious attention, with some of the outstanding issues also noted in Chapter 11. Fifth, detailed classroom studies of the ways teachers and students perform task-based classroom lessons are much needed, with work by Samuda (2001), Block (1994), and East (2012) suggesting some productive lines of inquiry. Among other matters, it will be important to identify if and when pedagogic tasks need to be "proofed" if they are to serve the designer's purpose, and how their roles can be modified by teachers and students, intentionally or unintentionally. For many additional proposals, see, also, the excellent discussion of research directions by Samuda and Bygate (2008, pp. 233–263). As described in earlier chapters, a considerable amount of research has been conducted on the first two issues, much less on the others. More work is needed on all aspects of TBLT, and more *in situ* evaluations of complete TBLT programs are another priority.

The research is labor-intensive, and only rarely is it adequately funded or funded at all. It would make obvious sense for the hundreds of individuals and numerous research centers around the world already engaged in the work to coordinate their efforts to a much greater extent than hitherto, e.g., with respect to (i) clarity as to precisely what they mean by 'task-based,' 'task-supported,' 'task-oriented,' and so on, and (ii) the operationalization and (some degree of, not complete, of course) standardization of the ways dependent variables are measured. This might perhaps be achieved under the auspices of the International Consortium on Task-Based Language Teaching (ICTBLT) and/or via the biannual international TBLT conferences the Consortium has organized since 2005.[2] The ICTBLT's founding members were John Norris, Martin Bygate, and Kris van den Branden, all of whom are still active in the organization. It includes a Scientific Committee and an International Advisory Board, and is best contacted via the TBLT website: http://www.tblt.org

12.3. Building the Road as We Travel

TBLT is a work in progress. It is not the only task-based approach, and it may turn out not to be the best one. It is certainly no panacea. There are problems – some we know of, and assuredly, others yet to be discovered. Many very talented researchers are hard at work on them in several countries, however, and I am guardedly optimistic that most can be solved.

During the early years of the Franco dictatorship that followed the Spanish Civil War, and inspired by the possibilities of the genuinely free society that the world had glimpsed in Barcelona and elsewhere in 1936–1937 (described vividly in George Orwell's firsthand account, *Homage to Catalonia*), what were initially no more than tiny isolated groups of Basque workers in Arrasate (Mondragon) set out to develop "a third way" between laissez-faire state capitalism and authoritarian state socialism (see Azurmendi 1984; Long 1996c; Morrison 1991; Whyte & Whyte 1991). Despite brutal repression by the fascists in the early years, the Basques persevered, and while very far from ideal, the vast, multi-billion-dollar Mondragon Cooperative Corporation of today provides a

---

[2] The five international TBLT conferences to date have been hosted by the Katolieke Universiteit Leuven (2005), the University of Hawaii (2007), Lancaster University (2009), the University of Auckland (2011), and the University of Alberta (2013). The conference will again be hosted by the Katolieke Universiteit Leuven in 2015.

vibrantly successful alternative economic model for societies of the future, owned and controlled by the people who work there.

In just the same way, developing an alternative to the two major traditional LT ortho-doxies – in my view, excessively interventionist, on the one hand, and irresponsibly non-interventionist, on the other – means a journey along a road as yet unbuilt. The rationale and the objectives are clear, but the route is uncertain. Jose-Maria Arizmen-diarrieta, spiritual father of the Mondragon co-ops wrote, "Se hace el camino al andar" – roughly, "We build the road as we travel" – and for those of us in the trenches today, that is what it is like with TBLT. Bidai ona izan! Buen viaje!

References

Abrahamsson, N., & Hyltenstam, K. (2008). The robustness of aptitude effects in near-native second language acquisition. *Studies in Second Language Acquisition* 30, 481–509.

Abrahamsson, N., & Hyltenstam, K. (2009). Age of onset and nativelikeness in a second language: Listener perception versus linguistic scrutiny. *Language Learning* 59, 249–306.

Adair-Hauck, B. (2006). The Integrated Performance Assessment (IPA): Connecting assessment to instruction and learning. *Foreign Language Annals* 39, 3, 359–382.

Adamson, D. (2009). *Interlanguage variation in theoretical and pedagogical perspective.* New York: Routledge.

Agar, M.H. (1986). *Speaking of ethnography* (Vol. 2), *Qualitative Research Methods Series.* Beverly Hills, CA: Sage.

Alcon, E. (2007). Incidental focus on form, noticing and vocabulary learning in the EFL classroom. *International Review of Applied Linguistics* 7, 1, 41–60.

Alderson, J.C. (ed.) (2009). *The politics of language education: Individuals and institutions.* Bristol: Multilingual Matters.

Alderson, J.C., & Beretta, A. (eds.) (1992). *Evaluating second language education.* Cambridge: Cambridge University Press.

Alexander, L. (1967). *First things first.* London: Longman.

Alexandrou, R., & Revard, D. (1990). *A task-based needs analysis for ELI listening courses.* Honolulu, HI: University of Hawai'i English Language Institute.

Allen, J.P.B., Frolich, M., & Spada, N. (1984). The communicative orientation of language teaching: An observation scheme. In Handscombe, J., Orem, R.A., & Taylor, B. (eds.), *On TESOL '83* (pp. 231–252). Washington, DC: TESOL.

Allen, W., & Spada, N. (1983). Designing a communicative syllabus in the People's Republic of China. In Jordan, R. (ed.), *Case studies in ELT* (pp. 132–145). London: Collins ELT.

Allwright, J., & Allwright, R. (1977). An approach to the teaching of medical English. In Holden, S. (ed.), *English for specific purposes* (pp. 58–62). Oxford: Modern English Publications.

Allwright, R. (1976). Language learning through communication practice. *ELT Documents* 76, 3, 2–14.

Second Language Acquisition and Task-Based Language Teaching, First Edition. Mike Long.
© 2015 John Wiley & Sons, Inc. Published 2015 by John Wiley & Sons, Inc.

Allwright, R. (1977). Language learning through communication practice. *ELT Documents* 76, 3, 2–14. Reprinted in Brumfit, C.J., & Johnson, K. (eds.) (1979). *The communicative approach to language teaching* (pp. 167–182). Oxford: Oxford University Press.

Allwright, R. (1982). Perceiving and pursuing learners' needs. In Geddes, M., & Sturtridge, G. (eds.), *Individualisation*. Oxford: Modern English Publications.

Al Thowaini, A. (2011). Implementing TBLT in Saudi Arabia: Context and constraints. Term paper, SLAA 754: TBLT. College Park, MD: University of Maryland.

Altman, H.B., & James, C.V. (eds.) (1980). *Foreign language teaching: Meeting individual needs*. Oxford: Pergamon.

Ammar, A., & Spada, N. (2006). One size fits all? Recasts, prompts, and L2 learning. *Studies in Second Language Acquisition* 28, 4, 543–574.

Amster, R., DeLeon, A., Fernandez, L.A., Nocella, A.J., & Shannon, D. (eds.) (2009). *Contemporary anarchist studies. An introductory anthology of anarchy in the academy*. London: Routledge.

Anderson, J.R. (1993). *Rules of the mind*. Hillsdale, NJ: Erlbaum.

Anderson, J.R., & Lebiere, C. (1998). *The atomic components of thought*. Hillsdale, NJ: Erlbaum.

Anderson-Hsieh, J., & Koehler, K. (1988). The effects of foreign accent and speaking rate on native speaker comprehension. *Language Learning* 38, 561–613.

Annett, J. (1969). *Feedback and human behaviour*. Baltimore, MD: Penguin Books.

Apple, M.W. (1996). *Cultural politics and education*. New York: Teachers College Press.

Arden-Close, C. (1993). Language problems in science lectures to non-native speakers. *English for Specific Purposes* 12, 3, 252–261.

Arnold, E. (1991). Authenticity revisited: How real is real? *English for Specific Purposes* 10, 237–244.

Asher, J.J. (1981). The total physical response: Theory and practice. *Annals of the New York Academy of Sciences* 379, 1, 324–331.

Aslin, R.N., & Newport, E.L. (2012). Statistical learning: From acquiring specific items to forming general rules. *Current Directions in Psychological Science* 21, 3, 170–176.

Au, K.H., & Jordan, C. (1981). Teaching reading to Hawaiian children: Finding a culturally appropriate solution. In Trueba, H., Guthrie, G.P., & Au, K.H. (eds.), *Culture in the bilingual classroom: Studies in classroom ethnography* (pp. 139–152). Rowley, MA: Newbury House.

Auerbach, E.R. (1992). *Making meaning, making change: Participatory curriculum development for adult ESL literacy*. Washington, DC: Center for Applied Linguistics and Delta.

Auerbach, E.R., & Burgess, D. (1985). The hidden curriculum of survival ESL. *TESOL Quarterly* 19, 3, 475–495.

Auerbach, E.R., & Wallerstein, N. (2005). *Problem-posing at work: English for action*. Edmonton, AB: Grass Roots Press.

Avrich, P. (1980). *The modern school movement. Anarchism and education in the United States*. Princeton, NJ: Princeton University Press.

Azurmendi, J. (1984). *El hombre cooperative. Pensamiento de Arizmendiarrieta*. Mondragon: Caja Laboral Popular.

Babbie, E.R. (1973). *Survey research methods*. Belmont, CA: Wadsworth.

Bachman, L.F. (1989). The development and use of criterion-referenced tests of language proficiency in language program evaluation. In Johnson, R.K. (ed.), *The second language curriculum* (pp. 242–258). Cambridge: Cambridge University Press.

Bachman, L.F. (2002). Some reflections on task-based language performance assessment. *Language Testing* 19, 4, 453–476.

Bachman, L.F. (2007). What is the construct? The dialectic of abilities and contexts in defining constructs in language assessment. In Fox, J., Wesche, M., Bayliss, D., Cheng, L., Turner, C., & Doe, C. (eds.), *Language testing reconsidered* (pp. 41–71). Ottawa, Canada: University of Ottawa Press.

Bachman, L.F., & Palmer, A.S. (1996). *Language testing in practice*. Oxford: Oxford University Press.

Baddeley, A.D. (1986). *Working memory*. Oxford: Clarendon Press.

Baddeley, A.D. (1996). Exploring the central executive. *Quarterly Journal of Experimental Psychology* 18, 1, 119–129.

Bahns, J., & Eldaw, M. (1993). Should we teach EFL students collocations? *System* 21, 1, 101–114.

Bailey, K.E. (1982). *Methods of social research*. New York: Free Press.

Bailey, K.M. (1990). The use of diary studies in teacher education programs. In Richards, J.C., & Nunan, D. (eds.), *Second language teacher education* (pp. 215–226). Cambridge: Cambridge University Press.

Bailey, K.M. (1992). The process of innovation in language teacher development: What, why and how teachers change. In Flowerdew, J., Brock, M., & Hsia, S. (eds.), *Perspectives on second language teacher development* (pp. 253–282). Hong Kong: City Polytechnic of Hong Kong.

Bailey, K.M., & Oschner, R. (1983). A methodological review of the diary studies: Windmill tilting or social science? In Bailey, K.M., Long, M.H., & Peck, B. (eds.), *Second language acquisition studies* (pp. 188–198). Rowley, MA: Newbury House.

Bardovi-Harlig, K. (1995). The interaction of pedagogy and natural sequences in the development of tense and aspect. In Eckman, F., Highland, D., Lee, P., Mileham, J., & Weber, R. (eds.), *Second language acquisition theory and pedagogy* (pp. 151–168). Mahwah, NJ: Lawrence Erlbaum.

Barnes, D. (1976/1992). *From communication to curriculum*. Harmondsworth: Penguin Books/London: Heinemann.

Barnes, D., & Todd, F. (1977). *Communication and learning in small groups*. London: Routledge.

Barnes, D., & Todd, F. (1995). *Communication and learning revisited: Making meaning through talk*. London: Boynton/Cook.

Barnett, S.M., & Ceci, S.J. (2002). When and where do we apply what we learn? A taxonomy for far transfer. *Psychological Bulletin* 128, 4, 612–637.

Barron, C. (1991). Material thoughts: ESP and culture. *English for Specific Purposes* 10, 173–187.

Bartlett, N.D. (2005). A double shot 2% mocha latte, please, with whip: Service encounters in two coffee shops and at a coffee cart. In Long, M.H. (ed.), *Second language needs analysis* (pp. 305–343). Cambridge: Cambridge University Press.

Bates, E., & MacWhinney, B. (1989). Functionalism and the competition model. In MacWhinney, B., & Bates, E. (eds.), *The cross-linguistic study of sentence processing* (pp. 3–73). Cambridge: Cambridge University Press.

Batstone, R. (2002). Contexts of engagement: A discourse perspective on "intake" and "pushed output." *System* 30, 1, 1–14.

Beatty, C.J., & Chan, M.J. (1984). Chinese scholars abroad: Changes in perceived academic needs. *English for Specific Purposes* 3, 1, 53–59.

Bell, R.T. (1981). Appendix A: Job analysis and ESP – Case study on the canteen assistant. In Bell, R.T. (ed.), *An introduction to applied linguistics. Approaches and methods in language teaching* (pp. 159–170). London: Batsford.

Bellack, A., Kliebard, M., Hyman, R.T., & Smith, F.L., Jr. (1966). *The language of the classroom*. New York: Teachers College Press.

Benesch, S. (1996). Needs analysis and curriculum development in EAP: An example of a critical approach. *TESOL Quarterly* 30, 4, 723–738.

Bennett, N., & Dunne, E. (1991). The nature and quality of talk in co-operative classroom groups. *Learning and Instruction* 1, 103–118.

Benson, M.J. (1989). The academic listening task: A case study. *TESOL Quarterly* 23, 3, 421–445.

Benson, S. (2013). TBLT: An empirical study of task transfer. Qualifying Paper. College Park, MD: University of Maryland, PhD in Second Language Acquisition Program.

Beretta, A. (1986). Towards a methodology for ESL program evaluation. *TESOL Quarterly* 20, 1, 144–155.

Beretta, A. (1989). Attention to form or meaning? Error treatment in the Bangalore Project. *TESOL Quarterly* 23, 2, 283–303.

Beretta, A. (1990). Implementation of the Bangalore Project. *Applied Linguistics* 11, 4, 321–337.

Beretta, A. (1991). Theory construction in SLA: Complementarity and opposition. *Studies in Second Language Acquisition* 13, 4, 493–511.

Beretta, A., & Davies, A. (1985). Evaluation of the Bangalore Project. *English Language Teaching Journal* 39, 121–127.

Berko, J. (1958). The child's learning of English morphology. *Word* 14, 150–177.

Bernard, H.R. (1994). *Research methods in anthropology. Qualitative and quantitative approaches* (2nd edn). Thousand Oaks, CA: Sage.

Berry, D., & Broadbent, D. (1984). On the relationship between task performance and associated verbalizable knowledge. *Quarterly Journal of Experimental Psychology* 36, 209–231.

Berwick, R. (1989). Needs assessment in language programming: From theory to practice. In Johnson, R.K. (ed.), *The second language curriculum* (pp. 48–62). Cambridge: Cambridge University Press.

Berwick, R. (1990). *Task variation and repair in English as a foreign language*. Kobe: Institute of Economic Research, Kobe University of Commerce.

Biber, D. (1988). *Variation across speech and writing*. Cambridge: Cambridge University Press.

Biber, D. (1993). Representativeness in corpus design. *Literary and Linguistic Computing* 8, 243–257.

Biber, D., Conrad, S., & Cortes, V. (2004). *If you look at* …: Lexical bundles in university teaching and textbooks. *Applied Linguistics* 25, 371–405.

Biber, D., Johansson, S., Leech, G., Conrad, S., & Finegan, E. (1999). *Longman grammar of spoken and written English*. London: Longman.

Blau, E.K. (1982). The effect of syntax on readability for ESL students in Puerto Rico. *TESOL Quarterly* 16, 4, 517–528.

Blau, E.K. (1990). The effect of syntax, speed, and pauses on listening comprehension. *TESOL Quarterly* 24, 4, 746–753.

Blau, E.K. (1991). More on comprehensible input: The effect of pauses and hesitation markers on listening comprehension. ERIC DOC NO. ED340 234.

Blessing, S., & Anderson, J.R. (1996). How people learn to skip steps. *Journal of Experimental Psychology: Learning, Memory, and Cognition* 22, 576–598.

Block, D. (1994). A day in the life of a class: Teacher/learner perceptions of task purpose in conflict. *System* 22, 4, 473–486.

Bloor, M., & Bloor, T. (1986). Languages for specific purposes: Practice and theory. Trinity College Dublin: Centre for Language and Communication Studies Occasional Paper No. 19.

Blume, B.D., Ford, K.J., Baldwin, T.T., & Huang, J.L. (2010). Transfer of training: A meta-analytic review. *Journal of Management* 36, 4, 1065–1105.

Boers, F., Demecheleer, M., Coxhead, A., & Webb, S. (2013). Gauging the effects of exercises on verb-noun collocations. *Language Teaching Research* 17. doi: 10.1177/ 1362168813505389

Boers, F., Eyckmans, J., Kappel, J., Stengers, H., & Demecheleer, M. (2006). Formulaic sequences and perceived oral proficiency: Putting a lexical approach to the test. *Language Teaching Research* 10, 245–261.

Boers, F., & Lindstromberg, S. (2012). Experimental and intervention studies on formulaic sequences in a second language. *Annual Review of Applied Linguistics* 32, 83–110.

Boggs, S.T., & Watson-Gegeo, K.A. (1985). Verbal play and talking story: The rhetoric of solidarity. In Boggs, S.T. (ed.), *Speaking, relating, and learning: A study of Hawaiian children at home and at school* (pp. 92–111). New York: Ablex.

Bonilla, C. (2012). Processability theory in L2 Spanish: A cross-sectional analysis of an oral corpus. Unpublished doctoral dissertation. Pittsburgh, PA: Department of Linguistics, University of Pittsburgh.

Bosher, S., & Smalkoski, K. (2002). From needs analysis to curriculum development: Designing a course in health-care communication for immigrant students in the USA. *English for Specific Purposes* 21, 1, 59–79.

Boswood, T. (1992). English for professional communication: Responding to Hong Kong employers' needs for English graduates. Research Report No. 20. Hong Kong: Department of English, City University of Hong Kong.

Boswood, T. (1994). Communication for specific purposes: Establishing the communicative event as the focus of attention in ESP. *Perspectives. Working Papers of the Department of English. City University of Hong Kong* 6, 1, 35–60.

Boswood, T., & Marriot, A. (1994). Ethnography for specific purposes: Teaching and training in parallel. *English for Specific Purposes* 13, 1, 3–21.

Boydell, T. (1970). *A guide to job analysis.* London: Bacie.

Braidi, S.M. (2002). Reexamining the role of recasts in native speaker/nonnative speaker interactions. *Language Learning* 52, 1, 1–41.

Braine, G. (1988). Academic writing task surveys: The need for a fresh approach. *Texas Papers in Foreign Language Education* 1, 101–118.

Brantmeier, C. (2005). Effects of reader's knowledge, text type, and test type on L1 and L2 reading comprehension in Spanish. *Modern Language Journal* 89, 1, 37–53.

Breen, M.P. (1984). Process syllabuses for the language classroom. In Brumfit, C.J. (ed.), *General English syllabus design. ELT Documents 118* (pp. 47–60). Oxford: Pergamon.

Breen, M.P. (1987a). Contemporary paradigms in syllabus design. Parts 1 and 2. *Language Teaching* 20, 2, 81–92, and 20, 3, 157–174.

Breen, M.P. (1987b). Learner contributions to task design. In Candlin, C.N., & Murphy, D.F. (eds.), *Language learning tasks* (pp.

23–46). Englewood Cliffs, NJ: Prentice-Hall.

Breen, M.P. (2001). *Learner contributions to language learning.* London: Pearson.

Breen, M.P., & Candlin, C. (1980). The essentials of a communicative curriculum in language teaching. *Applied Linguistics* 1, 2, 89–112.

Breen, M.P., Candlin, C.N., & Waters, A. (1979). Communicative materials design: Some basic principles. *RELC Journal* 10, 1–13.

Breen, M.P., & Littlejohn, A. (eds.) (2000). *Classroom decision-making: Negotiation and process syllabuses in practice.* Cambridge: Cambridge University Press.

Brett, D., & Gonzalez-Lloret, M. (2009). Technology enhanced materials. In Long, M.H., & Doughty, C.J. (eds.), *Handbook of language teaching* (pp. 351–369). Oxford: Blackwell.

Briggs, C. (1986). *Learning how to ask.* Cambridge: Cambridge University Press.

Brindley, G. (1984). *Needs analysis and objective setting in the Adult Migrant Education Service.* Sydney: Adult Migrant Education Service.

Brindley, G. (1989). *Assessing achievement in the learner-centred curriculum.* Sydney: Macquarie University, National Centre for English Language Teaching and Research.

Brindley, G. (2013). Task-based assessment. In Chapelle, C. (ed.), *The encyclopedia of applied linguistics.* Oxford: Wiley-Blackwell. doi: 10.1002/9781405198431. wbeal1141

Brindley, G., & Hood, S. (1990). Curriculum innovation in adult ESL. In Brindley, G. (ed.), *The second language curriculum in action* (pp. 232–248). Sydney: NCELTR, Macquarie University.

Brinton, D.M., Wesche, M., & Snow, M.A. (2003). *Content-based second language instruction.* Ann Arbor, MI: University of Michigan Press.

Broad, M. (1997). Overview of transfer of training: From learning to performance. *Performance Improvement Quarterly* 10, 2, 7–21.

Brooks, N. (1964). *Language and language learning*. New York: Harcourt.

Brown, C. (1985). Two windows on the classroom world: Diary studies and participant observation. In Larsen, P., Judd, E., & Messerschmitt, D. (eds.), *On TESOL '84* (pp. 121–134). Washington, DC: TESOL.

Brown, G., Anderson, A., Shilcock, R., & Yule, G. (1984). *Teaching talk strategies for production and assessment*. Cambridge: Cambridge University Press.

Brown, G., & Yule, G. (1983). *Teaching the spoken language*. Cambridge: Cambridge University Press.

Brown, J.D. (1990). Short-cut estimates of criterion-reference test consistency. *Language Testing* 7, 1, 77–97.

Brown, J.D. (1995). *Elements of language curriculum*. Boston, MA: Heinle & Heinle.

Brown, J.D. (2009). Foreign and second language needs analysis. In Long, M.H., & Doughty, C.J. (eds.), *Handbook of language teaching* (pp. 269–293). Oxford: Wiley-Blackwell.

Brown, J.D., & Hudson, T. (2002). *Criterion-referenced language testing*. Cambridge: Cambridge University Press.

Brown, J.D., Hudson, T., Norris, J., & Bonk, W.J. (2002). *An investigation of second language task-based performance assessments*. Honolulu, HI: Second Language Teaching and Curriculum Center.

Brown, R. (1987). A comparison of the comprehensibility of modified and unmodified reading materials for ESL. *University of Hawai'i Working Papers in ESL* 6, 1, 49–79.

Brown, R. (1991). Group work, task difference, and second language acquisition. *Applied Linguistics* 21, 1, 1–12.

Brumfit, C.J. (1979). Communicative language teaching: An educational perspective. In Brumfit, C.J., & Johnson, K. (eds.), *The communicative approach to language teaching*. Oxford: Oxford University Press.

Brumfit, C.J. (1981). Notional syllabuses revisited: A response. *Applied Linguistics* 2, 1, 90–92.

Brumfit, C.J. (ed.) (1984). *General English syllabus design. ELT Docs 118*. Oxford: Pergamon.

Brumfit, C.J., & Johnson, K. (eds.) (1979). *The communicative approach to language teaching*. Oxford: Oxford University Press.

Bruton, A. (2011a). Are the differences between CLIL and non-CLIL groups in Andalusia due to CLIL? A reply to Lorenzo, Casal and Moore (2010)? *Applied Linguistics 32*, 2, 236–241.

Bruton, A. (2011b). Is CLIL so beneficial, or just selective? Re-evaluating some of the research. *System 39*, 523–532.

Bruton, A. (2013). CLIL: Some of the reasons why … and why not. *System 41*, 3, 587–597.

Buck, G., & Tatsuoka, K. (1998). Application of the rule-space procedure to language testing: Examining attributes of a free response listening test. *Language Testing 15*, 119–157.

Burwell, G., Gonzalez-Lloret, M., & Nielsen, K. (2009). Evaluating a TBLT Spanish immersion program. Paper presented in the colloquium: Evaluating task-based language programs. 3rd Biannual Conference on TBLT. Lancaster, UK: University of Lancaster, September 13–16.

Butler, Y. (2011). The implementation of communicative and task-based language teaching in the Asia-Pacific region. *Annual Review of Applied Linguistics 31*, 36–57.

Bygate, M. (1987). *Speaking*. Oxford: Oxford University Press.

Bygate, M. (1988). Units of oral expression and language learning in small group interaction. *Applied Linguistics 9*, 1, 59–82.

Bygate, M. (2001). Effects of task repetition on the structure and control of language. In Bygate, M., Skehan, P., & Swain, M. (eds.), *Task-based learning: Language teaching, learning and assessment* (pp. 23–48). London: Longman.

Bygate, M., & Samuda, V. (2007). *Tasks in second language learning*. Basingstoke, HA: Palgrave Macmillan.

Bygate, M., Skehan, P., & Swain, M. (eds.) (2001). *Researching pedagogic tasks:*

Second language learning, teaching and testing. Harlow: Longman.

Byrnes, H. (2002). The role of task and task-based assessment in a content-oriented collegiate FL curriculum. *Language Testing* 19, 4, 425–443. Reprinted in Van den Branden, K., Bygate, M., & Norris, J.M. (eds.) (2009). *Task-based language teaching: A reader* (pp. 477–494). Philadelphia, PA/Amsterdam: John Benjamins.

Cadierno, T., & Robinson, P. (2009). Language typology, task complexity and the development of L2 lexicalization patterns for describing motion events. *Annual Review of Cognitive Linguistics* 7, 245–276.

Cain, P.S., & Green, B.F. (1983). Reliabilities of selected ratings available from the *Dictionary of Occupational Titles. Journal of Applied Psychology* 68, 1, 155–165.

Canagarajah, A.S. (1999). *Resisting linguistic imperialism in ELT.* New York: Oxford University Press.

Candlin, C.N. (1984). Syllabus design as a critical process. In Brumfit, C.J. (ed.), *General English syllabus design. ELT Documents 118* (pp. 29–46). Oxford: Pergamon.

Candlin, C.N. (1987). Towards task-based language learning. In Candlin, C.N., & Murphy, D.F. (eds.), *Language learning tasks* (pp. 5–22). London: Prentice Hall.

Candlin, C.N., Bruton, A., & Leather, J.M. (1976). Doctors in casualty: Specialist course design from a database. *International Review of Applied Linguistics* 14, 245–272.

Candlin, C.N., & Murphy, D.F. (eds.) (1987). *Language learning tasks.* Englewood Cliffs, NJ: Prentice-Hall.

Carless, D. (2002). Implementing task-based learning with young learners. *ELT Journal* 56, 389–396.

Carless, D. (2003). Factors in the implementation of task-based teaching in primary schools. *System* 31, 4, 485–500.

Carless, D. (2004). Issues in teachers' reinterpretation of a task-based innovation in primary schools. *TESOL Quarterly* 38, 4, 639–662.

Carless, D. (2007). The suitability of task-based approaches for secondary schools: Per-

spectives from Hong Kong. *System* 35, 4, 595–608.

Carless, D. (2012). Innovation in language teaching and learning. In Chapelle, C. (ed.), *The encyclopedia of applied linguistics.* Oxford: Wiley-Blackwell. doi: 10 .1002/9781405198431.wbeal0540

Carroll, J.B., & Sapon, S. (1959). *Modern language aptitude test: Form A.* New York: Psychological Corporation.

Castaños, F. (1976). The discourse of science and teaching ESP at the elementary level. *Languages for Specific Purposes 2.* Xochimilco, Mexico: Universidad Autónoma Metropolitana.

Castaños, F. (1977). Towards a coding system for the argumentative functions of language. *English for Specific Purposes, an International Seminar* (pp. 90–96). Bogotá: The British Council.

Cathcart, R. (1984). What really happened at the bank? A study of real language and textbook language. Paper presented at the 18th Annual TESOL Convention, Houston, TX.

Cathcart, R. (1989). Authentic discourse and the survival English curriculum. *TESOL Quarterly* 23, 1, 105–126.

Chalmers, D.J. (1999). *What is this thing called science?* Cambridge, MA: Hacket Publishing.

Chambers, F. (1980). A re-evaluation of needs analysis in ESP. *The ESP Journal* 1, 1, 25–33.

Chaudron, C. (1977). A descriptive model of discourse in the corrective treatment of learners' errors. *Language Learning* 27, 1, 29–46.

Chaudron, C. (1982). Vocabulary elaboration in teachers' speech to L2 learners. *Studies in Second Language Acquisition* 4, 2, 170–180.

Chaudron, C. (1985). On models and methods for discovering learners' processing of input. *Studies in Second Language Acquisition* 7, 1, 1–14.

Chaudron, C. (1988). *Second language classrooms: Research on teaching and learning.* Cambridge: Cambridge University Press.

Chaudron, C., Crookes, G., & Long, M.H. (1988). *Reliability and validity in second* language classroom research. Technical Report No. 8. Honolulu, HI: Center for Second Language Classroom Research, Social Science Research Institute, University of Hawai'i at Manoa.

Chaudron, C., Doughty, C.J., Kim, Y., Kong, D.-K., Lee, J., Lee, Y.-G., Long, M.H., Rivers, R., & Urano, K. (2005). A task-based needs analysis of a tertiary Korean as a foreign language program. In Long, M.H. (ed.), Second language needs analysis (pp. 225–261). Cambridge: Cambridge University Press.

Chaudron, C., Loschky, L., & Cook, J. (1995). Second language listening comprehension and lecture note-taking. In Flowerdew, J. (ed.), Academic listening (pp. 75–92). Cambridge: Cambridge University Press.

Chaudron, C., & Richards, J.C. (1986). The effects of discourse markers on the comprehension of lectures. Applied Linguistics 7, 2, 113–127.

Chaudry, L. (1991). TBLT vs. "regular" language teaching: A comparative analysis of classroom language. Term paper, ESL 730 (Task-based language teaching). Honolulu, HI: University of Hawai'i at Manoa, Department of ESL.

Chiang, C.S., & Dunkel, P. (1992). The effect of speech modification, prior knowledge, and listening proficiency on EFL lecture learning. TESOL Quarterly 26, 2, 345–374.

Choi, M.-Y. (2000). Effects of recasts on irregular past tense verb morphology in webchat. MA in ESL thesis. Honolulu, HI: University of Hawai'i, Department of Second Language Studies.

Chomsky, N. (1988). Language and problems of knowledge: The Managua Lectures. Cambridge, MA: MIT Press.

Chouissa, C., Dugovicova, S., Fischer, J., & Virkkunen-Fullenwider, A. (2012). Guidelines for task-based university language testing. Graz: Council of Europe, European Centre for Modern Languages.

Christison, M., & Krahnke, K. (1986). Student perceptions of academic language study. TESOL Quarterly 20, 1, 61–81.

Chung, H. (1995). Effects of elaborative modification on second language reading comprehension and incidental vocabulary learning. Unpublished MA in ESL thesis. Honolulu, HI: University of Hawai'i, Department of Second Language Studies.

Cicourel, A.V. (1974). Theory and methods in a study of Argentine fertility. New York: Wiley-Interscience.

Clahsen, H. (1987). Connecting theories of language processing and (second) language acquisition. In Pfaff, C. (ed.), First and second language acquisition processes (pp. 103–116). Cambridge, MA: Newbury House.

Clahsen, H., Meisel, J.M., & Pienemann, M. (1983). Deutsch als zweitsprache: Der spracherwerb auslandischer arbeiter. Tubingen: Gunter Narr.

Clapham, C. (2001). Discipline specificity and EAP. In Flowerdew, J., & Peacock, M. (eds.), Research perspectives on English for academic purposes (pp. 84–100). Cambridge: Cambridge University Press.

Clement, R. (1980). Ethnicity, contact and communicative competence in a second language. In Giles, H., Robinson, W.P., & Smith, P.M. (eds.), Language: Social psychological perspectives (pp. 147–154). Oxford: Pergamon.

Clement, R., & Kruidenier, B.G. (1985). Aptitude, attitude and motivation in second language proficiency: A test of Clement's model. Journal of Language and Social Psychology 4, 21–37.

Clifford, R.T., & Fischer, D.C. (1990). Foreign language needs in the US government. In Lambert, R.D., & Moore, S.J. (eds.), Foreign language in the workplace. Annals of the American Academy of Political and Social Science (pp. 109–121). Newbury Park, CA: Sage.

Cloud, N., Genesee, F., & Hamayan, E. (2000). Dual language instruction: A handbook for enriched education. London: Heinle.

Clyne, M. (1994). Inter-cultural communication at work: Discourse structures across cultures. Cambridge: Cambridge University Press.

Coad, C.P. (1984). Developing competency-based placement tests for machine shop training. *The ESP Journal* 3, 183–192.

Cobb, T. (2007). Computing the vocabulary demands of L2 reading. *Language Learning & Technology* 11, 38–63.

Coffey, B. (1984). State of the art: ESP – English for specific purposes. *Language Teaching* 17, 1, 2–16.

Cole, M. (1985). The zone of proximal development: Where culture and cognition create each other. In Wertsch, J.V. (ed.), *Culture, communication, and cognition: Vygotskian perspectives* (pp. 146–161). New York: Cambridge University Press.

Coleman, H. (1988). Analysing language needs in large organizations. *English for Specific Purposes* 7, 155–169.

Colpin, M., & Gysen, S. (2006). Developing and introducing task-based language tests. In Van den Branden, K. (ed.), *Task-based language education: From theory to practice* (pp. 151–174). Cambridge: Cambridge University Press.

Commonwealth Office of Education. (1967). *Situational English*. London: Longman.

Conrad, S. (1996). Investigating academic texts with corpus-based techniques: An example from biology. *Linguistics and Education* 8, 3, 299–314.

Cook, V.J. (1975). *English topics*. Oxford: Oxford University Press.

Cook, V.J. (1985). Chomsky's Universal Grammar and second language learning. *Applied Linguistics* 6, 1, 1–8.

Corder, S.P. (1967). The significance of learners' errors. *International Review of Applied Linguistics* 5, 161–170.

Coulthard, M., & Johnson, A. (2007). *An introduction to forensic linguistics. Language in evidence*. London: Routledge.

Courtney, M. (1988). Some initial considerations for course design. *English for Specific Purposes* 7, 195–203.

Cowling, J.D. (2007). Needs analysis: Planning a syllabus for a series of intensive workplace courses at a leading Japanese company. *English for Specific Purposes* 26, 426–442.

Cox, D. (2004). Can we predict language items from open tasks? In Edwards, C., & Willis, J. (eds.), *Teachers exploring tasks in English language teaching* (pp. 171–185). Basingstoke, Hampshire: Palgrave Macmillan.

Coxhead, A., & Nation, P. (2001). The specialised vocabulary of English for Academic Purposes. In Flowerdew, J., & Peacock, M. (eds.), *Research Perspectives on English for Academic Purposes* (pp. 252–267). Cambridge: Cambridge University Press.

Coxhead, A.J. (2000). *An academic word list*. Wellington: Victoria University of Wellington. English Language Institute Occasional Publication Number 18.

Crago, M. (1992). Communicative interaction and second language acquisition: An Inuit example. *TESOL Quarterly* 26, 3, 487–505.

Crandall, J. (1993). Content-centered learning in the United States. *Annual Review of Applied Linguistics* 13, 111–126.

Crandall, J., & Tucker, G.R. (1990). Content-based language instruction in second and foreign languages. In Anivan, S. (ed.), *Language teaching methodology for the nineties* (pp. 83–96). Singapore: SEAMEO Regional Language Center.

Crombie, W. (1985a). *Process and relation in discourse and language learning*. Oxford: Oxford University Press.

Crombie, W. (1985b). *Discourse and language learning: A relational approach to syllabus design*. Oxford: Oxford University Press.

Crookes, G. (1986a). *Task classification: A cross-disciplinary review*. Technical Report No. 4. Honolulu: Center for Second Language Classroom Research, Social Science Research Institute, University of Hawai'i at Manoa.

Crookes, G. (1986b). Towards a validated analysis of scientific text structure. *Applied Linguistics* 7, 57–70.

Crookes, G. (1989). Planning and interlanguage variation. *Studies in Second Language Acquisition* 11, 2, 367–383.

Crookes, G. (2009). Radical language teaching. In Long, M.H., & Doughty, C.J. (eds.), *Handbook of language teaching* (pp. 595–609). Malden, MA: Wiley-Blackwell.

Crookes, G., & Rulon, K. (1986). Topic and feedback in native speaker/non-native speaker conversation. *TESOL Quarterly* 22, 4, 675–681.

Crossley, S.A., McCarthy, P.M., Louwerse, M.M., & McNamara, D.S. (2007). A linguistic analysis of simplified and authentic texts. *Modern Language Journal* 91, 1, 15–30.

CREDIF. (1961). *Voix et Images de France.* Paris: Didier.

Culp, R.E., Watkins, R.V., Lawrence, H., Letts, D., Kelly, D.J., & Rice, M.L. (1991). Maltreated children's language and speech development: Abused, neglected, and abused and neglected. *First Language* 11, 377–389.

Cumaranatunge, L.K. (1988). An EOP case study: Domestic aids in West Asia. In Chamberlain, D., & Baumgardner, R.J. (eds.), *ESP in the classroom: Practice and evaluation. ELT Document 128* (pp. 127–133). London: Modern English Publications/The British Council.

Cummins, J. (1979). Cognitive/academic language proficiency, linguistic interdependence, the optimum age question, and some other matters. *Working Papers on Bilingualism* 19, 121–129.

Cummins, J. (1980a). The cross-lingual dimensions of language proficiency: Implications for bilingual education and the optimal age issue. *TESOL Quarterly* 14, 2, 175–187.

Cummins, J. (1980b). The construct of language proficiency in bilingual education. In Alatis, J.E. (ed.), *Georgetown University round table on languages and linguistics.* Washington, DC: Georgetown University Press.

Cummins, J. (2009). Bilingual and immersion programs. In Long, M.H., & Doughty, C.J. (eds.), *Handbook of language teaching* (pp. 161–181). Malden, MA: Wiley-Blackwell.

Curran, C.A. (1976). *Counseling-learning in second languages.* Apple River, IL: Apple River Press.

Curtiss, S. (1977). *Genie: A linguistic study of a modern day "wild child."* New York: Academic Press.

Curtiss, S. (1980). The critical period and feral children. *UCLA Working Papers in Cognitive Linguistics* 2, 21–36.

Curtiss, S. (1988). Abnormal language acquisition and the modularity of language. In Newmeyer, F.J. (ed.), *Linguistics: The Cambridge survey. Volume II. Linguistic theory: Extensions and implications* (pp. 96–116). Cambridge: Cambridge University Press.

Cutler, A. (2001). Listening to a second language through the ears of a first. *Interpreting* 5, 1, 1–18.

Cutler, A., & Otake, T. (1994). Mora or phoneme? Further evidence for language-specific listening. *Journal of Memory and Language* 33, 824–844.

Dai, Z., & Ding, Y. (2010). Effectiveness of text memorization in EFL learning of Chinese students. In Wood, D. (ed.), *Perspectives on formulaic language: Acquisition and communication* (pp. 71–87). New York: Continuum.

Dakin, J. (1973). *The language laboratory and language learning.* London: Longman.

Dalton-Puffer, C. (2011). Content-and-language integrated learning: From practice to principles? *Annual Review of Applied Linguistics* 31, 182–204.

Davies, A. (1981). Review of J. Munby, *Communicative syllabus design.* Cambridge: Cambridge University Press, 1981. *TESOL Quarterly* 15, 3, 332–344.

Day, E.M., & Shapson, S. (1994). *Studies in immersion education.* Philadelphia, PA: Multilingual Matters.

DeCarrico, J., & Nattinger, J.R. (1988). Lexical phrases for the comprehension of academic lectures. *English for Specific Purposes* 7, 91–102.

Deen, J.Y. (1991). Comparing interaction in a cooperative learning and teacher-centered foreign language classroom. *ITL Review of Applied Linguistics* 93–94, 153–181.

De Graaff, R. (1997). The eXperanto experiment: Effects of explicit instruction on second language acquisition. *Studies in Second Language Acquisition* 19, 249–276.

De Graaff, R., & Housen, A. (2009). Investigating the effects and effectiveness of instruction. In Long, M.H., & Doughty, C.J. (eds.), *Handbook of language teaching* (pp. 726–755). Oxford: Blackwell.

DeKeyser, R. (1993). The effect of error correction on L2 grammar knowledge and oral proficiency. *Modern Language Journal 77*, 4, 501–514.

DeKeyser, R. (2003). Implicit and explicit learning. In Doughty, C.J., & Long, M.H. (eds.), *Handbook of second language acquisition* (pp. 313–348). Oxford: Blackwell.

DeKeyser, R. (2005). What makes second-language grammar difficult? A review of issues. *Language Learning 55*, Suppl. 1, 1–25.

DeKeyser, R., & Larson-Hall, J. (2005). What does the critical period really mean? In Kroll, J.F., & De Groot, A.M.B. (eds.), *Handbook of bilingualism: Psycholinguistic approaches* (pp. 88–108). Oxford: Oxford University Press.

DeKeyser, R.M. (1994). Implicit and explicit learning of L2 grammar: A pilot study. *TESOL Quarterly 28*, 188–194.

DeKeyser, R.M. (1995). Learning second language grammar rules: An experiment with a miniature linguistic system. *Studies in Second Language Acquisition 17*, 379–410.

DeKeyser, R.M. (2000). The robustness of critical period effects in second language acquisition. *Studies in Second Language Acquisition 22*, 4, 499–533.

DeKeyser, R.M. (2001). Automaticity and automatization. In Robinson, P. (ed.), *Cognition and second language acquisition* (pp. 125–151). New York: Cambridge University Press.

DeKeyser, R.M. (2006). A critique of recent arguments against the critical period hypothesis. In Abello-Contesse, C., Chacón-Beltrán, R., López-Jiménez, M.D., & Torreblanca-López, M.M. (eds.), *Age in L2 acquisition and teaching* (pp. 49–58). Bern: Peter Lang.

DeKeyser, R.M. (2007a). Skill acquisition theory. In VanPatten, B., & Williams, J. (eds.), *Theories in second language acquisition* (pp. 97–113). Mahwah, NJ: Lawrence Erlbaum.

DeKeyser, R.M. (2007b). *Practice in a second language: Perspectives from applied linguistics and cognitive psychol-* ogy. Cambridge: Cambridge University Press.

DeKeyser, R.M. (2011). Differential age effects within and across linguistic domains. Paper presented at ISB 8 (International Symposium on Bilingualism), Oslo, Norway, June 18, 2011.

DeKeyser, R.M., Alfy-Shabtay, I., & Ravid, D. (2010). Cross-linguistic evidence for the nature of age effects in second language acquisition. *Applied Psycholinguistics 31*, 413–438.

De la Fuente, M.J. (2002). Negotiation and oral acquisition of L2 vocabulary: The roles of input and output in the receptive and productive acquisition of words. *Studies in Second Language Acquisition 24*, 1, 81–112.

De la Fuente, M.J. (2006). Classroom L2 vocabulary acquisition: Investigating the role of pedagogical tasks and form-focused instruction. *Language Teaching Research 10*, 263–295.

Denzin, N.K. (1970). *Sociological methods: A source book.* Chicago: Aldine.

De Ridder, I., Vangehuchten, L., & Sesena Gomez, M. (2007). Enhancing automaticity through task-based language learning. *Applied Linguistics 28*, 2, 309–315.

Derwing, T. (1996). Elaborative detail: Help or hindrance to the NNS listener? *Studies in Second Language Acquisition 18*, 283–297.

De Santillan, D.A. (1937/1996). *After the revolution. Economic reconstruction in Spain today.* New York: Greenberg/Sydney: Jura Media.

Devlieger, M., & Goosens, G. (2004). *Productinmeting taalvardigheid. Evaluatie Voorrangsbeleid Brussel.* Leuven: Steunpunt Nederlands als Tweede Taal.

Devlieger, M., Goosens, G., Labath, T., & Denolf, B. (2003). *Procesevaluatie Voorrangsbeleid Brussel eindverslag (2001–2003).* Leuven/Gent: Universiteit Gent, Steunpunt ICO & KU Leuven, Steunpunt NT2.

Dewey, J. (1933). *How we think: A restatement of the relation of reflective thinking to the educative process.* Boston, MA: Henry Holt.

Dewey, J. (1938). *Experience and education.* New York: Macmillan.

Dewey, J. (1939/1966). *Democracy and education: An introduction to the philosophy of education.* New York: The Free Press.

Deygers, B., Van Gorp, K., Luyten, L., & Joos, S. (2013). Rating scale design: A comparative study of two analytic rating scales in a task-based test. In Galaczi, E.D., & Weir, C.J. (eds.), *Exploring language frameworks: Proceedings of the ALTE Krakow Conference, July 2011* (pp. 271–287). Cambridge: Cambridge University Press.

Dictionary of Occupational Titles. (1991). Fourth edn, revised, Washington, DC: U.S. Employment Service, U.S. Department of Labor.

Dinsmore, D. (1985). Waiting for Godot in the EFL classroom. *ELT Journal* 39, 4, 225–234.

Donaldson, B. (2011). Left-dislocation in near-native French. *Studies in Second Language Acquisition* 33, 3, 399–432.

Dornyei, Z. (2005). *The psychology of the language learner: Individual differences in second language acquisition.* London: Routledge.

Dornyei, Z., & Skehan, P. (2003). Individual differences in second language learning. In Doughty, C.J., & Long, M.H. (eds.), *Handbook of second language acquisition* (pp. 589–630). New York: Basil Blackwell.

Doughty, C. (2001). Cognitive underpinnings of focus on form. In Robinson, P. (ed.), *Cognition and second language instruction* (pp. 206–257). Cambridge: Cambridge University Press.

Doughty, C. (2003). Instructed SLA: Constraints, compensation, and enhancement. In Doughty, C.J., & Long, M.H. (eds.), *Handbook of second language acquisition* (pp. 256–310). New York: Basil Blackwell.

Doughty, C., & Varela, E. (1998). Communicative focus on form. In Doughty, C.J., & Williams, J. (eds.), *Focus on form in classroom second language acquisition* (pp. 114–138). Cambridge: Cambridge University Press.

Doughty, C., & Williams, J. (1998a). *Focus on form in classroom second language acquisition.* Cambridge: Cambridge University Press.

Doughty, C.J., & Williams, J. (1998b). Pedagogical choices in focus on form. In Doughty, C.J., & Williams, J. (eds.), *Focus on form in classroom second language acquisition* (pp. 197–261). Cambridge: Cambridge University Press.

Doughty, C.J. (1991). Second language acquisition does make a difference: Evidence from an empirical study of SL relativization. *Studies in Second Language Acquisition* 13, 3, 431–469.

Doughty, C.J. (2013). Optimizing post-critical-period language learning. In Granena, G., & Long, M.H. (eds.), *Sensitive periods, language aptitude, and ultimate L2 attainment* (pp. 153–175). Amsterdam and Philadelphia, PA: John Benjamins.

Doughty, C.J., Campbell, S.G., Mislevy, M.A., Bunting, M.F., Bowles, A.R., & Koeth, J.T. (2010). Predicting near-native ability: The factor structure and reliability of Hi-LAB. In Prior, M.T., Watanabe, Y., & Lee, S. (eds.), *Selected proceedings of the 2008 Second Language Research Forum* (pp. 10–31). Somerville, MA: Cascadilla Proceedings Project.

Doughty, C.J., Izumi, S., Maciukaite, S., & Zapata, G. (1999). Recasts, focused recasts, and models: Effects on L2 Spanish word order. Paper presented at the Second Language Research Forum, University of Minnesota, September 1999.

Doughty, C.J., & Long, M.H. (2003). Optimal psycholinguistic environments for distance foreign language learning. *Language Learning & Technology* 7, 3, 50–80. Retrieved from http://llt.msu.edu

Duane, M. (1995). *The Terrace. An educational experiment in a state school.* London: Freedom Press.

Dubois, B.L. (1980). Genre and structure of biomedical speeches. *Forum Linguisticum* 5, 140–169.

Dudley-Evans, T. (1995). Variations in the discourse patterns favoured by different disciplines and their pedagogic implications. In Flowerdew, J. (ed.), *Academic listening* (pp. 146–158). Cambridge: Cambridge University Press.

Dudley-Evans, A., & Swales, J. (1980). Study modes and students from the Middle East. *ELT Documents* 109, 91–103.

Duff, P. (1986). Another look at interlanguage talk: Taking tasks to task. In Day, R. (ed.), *"Talking to learn": Conversation in second language acquisition* (pp. 147–181). Rowley, MA: Newbury House.

Dugatkin, L.A. (1997). *Cooperation among animals: An evolutionary perspective.* Oxford: Oxford University Press.

Dunkel, P., & Davis, J.N. (1994). The effects of rhetorical signalling cues on recall. In Flowerdew, J. (ed.), *Academic listening: Research perspectives* (pp. 55–74). Cambridge: Cambridge University Press.

Durrant, P., & Schmitt, N. (2010). Adult learners' retention of collocations from exposure. *Second Language Research* 26, 2, 163–188.

Eades, D. (1992). *Aboriginal English and the law: Communicating with Aboriginal English speaking clients: A handbook for legal practitioner.* Brisbane, CA: Queensland Law Society.

Eades, D. (1993). The case for Condren: Aboriginal English, pragmatics and the law. *Journal of Pragmatics* 20, 141–162.

Eades, D. (1994). Forensic linguistics in Australia: An overview. *Forensic Linguistics* 1, 2, 113–132.

Eades, D. (1995). Aboriginal English on trial: The case for Stuart and Condren. In Eades, D. (ed.), *Language in evidence: Issues confronting Aboriginal and multicultural Australia* (pp. 147–174). Sydney: University of New South Wales Press.

Eades, D. (1996). Legal recognition of cultural differences in communication: The case of Robyn Kina. *Language and Communication* 16, 215–227.

Eades, D. (2013). *Aboriginal ways of using English.* Canberra: Aboriginal Studies Press.

East, M. (2012). *Task-based language teaching from the teachers' perspective: Insights from New Zealand.* Amsterdam: John Benjamins.

Eckerth, J. (2008). Task-based language learning and teaching – Old wine in new bottles? In Eckerh, J., & Siekman, S. (eds.), *Task-based language learning and teaching: Theoretical, methodological, and pedagogical perspectives.* Frankfurt am Main: Peter Lang.

Eckman, F.R., Bell, L., & Nelson, D. (1988). On the generalization of relative clause instruction in the acquisition of English as a second language. *Applied Linguistics* 9, 1, 1–20.

Ellis, D. (2011). The role of task complexity in the linguistic complexity of native speaker output. Qualifying Paper, PhD in Second Language Acquisition Program. College Park, MD: University of Maryland.

Ellis, G., & Sinclair, B. (1989). *Learning how to learn.* Cambridge: Cambridge University Press.

Ellis, N.C. (1993). Rules and instances in foreign language learning: Interactions of explicit and implicit knowledge. *European Journal of Cognitive Psychology* 5, 289–318.

Ellis, N.C. (1994). Implicit and explicit processes in language acquisition: An introduction. In Ellis, N.C. (ed.), *Implicit and explicit learning of languages* (pp. 1–32). London: Academic Press.

Ellis, N.C. (2001). Memory for language. In Robinson, P. (ed.), *Cognition and second language instruction* (pp. 33–68). Cambridge: Cambridge University Press.

Ellis, N.C. (2002a). Frequency effects in language acquisition: A review with implications for theories of implicit and explicit language acquisition. *Studies in Second Language Acquisition* 24, 1, 143–188.

Ellis, N.C. (2002b). Reflections on frequency effects in language acquisition: A response to commentaries. *Studies in Second Language Acquisition* 24, 297–339.

Ellis, N.C. (2003). Constructions, chunking, and connectionism: The emergence of second language structure. In Doughty, C.J., & Long, M.H. (eds.), *Handbook of second language acquisition* (pp. 63–103). Oxford: Blackwell.

Ellis, N.C. (2005). At the interface: Dynamic interactions of explicit and implicit language knowledge. *Studies in Second Language Acquisition* 27, 305–352.

Ellis, N.C. (2006a). Selective attention and transfer phenomena in L2 acquisition: Contingency, cue competition, salience, interference, overshadowing, blocking, and perceptual learning. *Applied Linguistics* 27, 2, 164–194.

Ellis, N.C. (2006b). Language acquisition as rational contingency learning. *Applied Linguistics* 27, 1, 1–24.

Ellis, N.C. (2007a). The weak-interface, consciousness, and form-focussed instruction: Mind the doors. In Fotos, S., & Nassaji, H. (eds.), *Form-focused instruction and teacher education: Studies in honour of Rod Ellis* (pp. 17–33). Oxford: Oxford University Press.

Ellis, N.C. (2007b). The associative-cognitive CREED. In VanPatten, B., & Williams, J. (eds.), *Theories in second language acquisition. An introduction* (pp. 77–95). Mahwah, NJ: Lawrence Erlbaum.

Ellis, N.C. (2008a). Implicit and explicit knowledge about language. In Cenoz, J., & Hornberger, N.H. (eds.), *Encyclopedia of language and education: Knowledge about language* (2nd edn, Vol. 6, pp. 1–13). New York: Springer.

Ellis, N.C. (2008b). The psycholinguistics of the interaction hypothesis. In Mackey, A., & Polio, C. (eds.), *Multiple perspectives on interaction: Research in Honor of Susan M. Gass* (pp. 11–40). New York: Routledge.

Ellis, N.C. (2008c). Usage-based and form-focused language acquisition: The associative learning of constructions, learned attention, and the limited L2 end-state. In Robinson, P., & Ellis, N.C. (eds.), *Handbook of cognitive linguistics and second language acquisition* (pp. 372–405). New York: Routledge.

Ellis, N.C. (2009). Optimizing the input: Frequency and sampling in usage-based and form-focussed Learning. In Long, M.H., & Doughty, C.J. (eds.), *Handbook of language teaching* (pp. 139–158). Oxford: Blackwell.

Ellis, N.C. (2012). Frequency-based accounts of second language acquisition. In Gass, S.M., & Mackey, A. (eds.), *The Routledge handbook of second language acquisition* (pp. 193–210). New York: Routledge.

Ellis, N.C., & Laporte, L. (1997). Contexts of acquisition: Effects of formal instruction and naturalistic exposure on second language acquisition. In De Groot, A.M.B., & Kroll, J.F. (eds.), *Tutorials in bilingualism. Psycholinguistic perspectives* (pp. 53–83). Mahwah, NJ: Lawrence Erlbaum.

Ellis, R. (1985). *Understanding second language acquisition*. New York: Oxford University Press.

Ellis, R. (1987). Interlanguage variability in narrative discourse: Style-shifting in the use of the past tense. *Studies in Second Language Acquisition* 9, 1, 1–20.

Ellis, R. (1989). Are classroom and naturalistic acquisition the same? A study of the classroom acquisition of German word order rules. *Studies in Second Language Acquisition* 11, 3, 305–328.

Ellis, R. (1993). The structural syllabus and second language acquisition. *TESOL Quarterly* 27, 1, 91–113.

Ellis, R. (1994). A theory of instructed second language acquisition. In Ellis, N. (ed.), *Implicit and explicit learning of languages* (pp. 79–114). San Diego, CA: Academic Press.

Ellis, R. (1995). *Understanding second language acquisition*. Oxford: Oxford University Press.

Ellis, R. (1997). *SLA research and language teaching*. Oxford: Oxford University Press.

Ellis, R. (1999). Item versus system learning: Explaining free variation. *Applied Linguistics* 20, 4, 460–480.

Ellis, R., & He, X. (1999). The roles of modified input and output in the incidental acquisition of word meanings. *Studies in Second Language Acquisition* 21, 285–301.

Ellis, R. (2002). The place of grammar instruction in the second/foreign language curriculum. In Hinkel, E., & Fotos, S. (eds.), *New perspectives on grammar teaching in second language classrooms* (pp. 17–34). Mahwah, NJ: Lawrence Erlbaum.

Ellis, R. (2003). *Task-based language learning and teaching*. Oxford: Oxford University Press.

Ellis, R. (2005). Planning and task-based performance: Theory and research. In Ellis, R. (ed.), *Planning and task performance in a second language* (pp. 3–34). Amsterdam: John Benjamins.

Ellis, R. (2004). The effects of planning on fluency, accuracy, and complexity in second language narrative writing. *Studies in Second Language Acquisition 26*, 1, 59–84.

Ellis, R. (2012). *Language teaching research and language pedagogy*. Malden, MA: Wiley-Blackwell.

Ellis, R., & Barkhuizen, G. (2005). *Analyzing learner language*. Oxford: Oxford University Press.

Ellis, R., Basturkmen, H., & Loewen, S. (2001). Learner uptake in communicative classrooms. *Language Learning 51*, 2, 281–318.

Ellis, R., Loewen, S., & Erlam, R. (2006). Implicit and explicit corrective feedback and the acquisition of L2 grammar. *Studies in Second Language Acquisition 28*, 339–368.

Ellis, R., Tanaka, Y., & Yamazaki, A. (1994). Classroom interaction, comprehension, and the acquisition of L2 word meanings. *Language Learning 44*, 449–491.

Epling, S. (2011). Medicines make me sick: Synthesizing diversity of discourse and text structure into exemplar prescription labels for CASA de Maryland English language learners. Term paper, SLA 754: Task-Based Language Teaching. PhD in SLA Program: College Park, MD: University of Maryland.

Erlam, R. (2006). Elicited imitation as a measure of L2 implicit knowledge: An empirical validation study. *Applied Linguistics 27*, 3, 464–491.

Erlam, R. (2009). The elicited oral imitation test as a measure of implicit knowledge. In Ellis, R., Loewen, S., Elder, C., Erlam, R., Philp, J., & Reinders. H. (eds.), *Implicit and explicit knowledge in second language learning, testing and teaching* (pp. 65–93). Bristol: Multilingual Matters.

Erten, İ.H., & Tekin, M. (2008). Effects on vocabulary acquisition of presenting new words in semantic sets versus semantically unrelated sets. *System 36*, 407–422.

Eyckmans, J., Boers, F., & Stengers, H. (2007). Identifying chunks: Who can see the wood for the trees? *Language Forum 33*, 85–100.

Faerch, C., & Kasper, G. (1986). Strategic competence in foreign language teaching. In Kasper, G. (ed.), *Learning, teaching and communication in the foreign language classroom* (pp. 179–193). Aarhus, Denmark: Aarhus University Press.

Fanselow, J. (1977). Beyond "Rashomon" – Conceptualizing and describing the teaching act. *TESOL Quarterly 10*, 17–39.

Farrar, M.J. (1992). Negative evidence and grammatical morpheme acquisition. *Developmental Psychology 28*, 1, 90–98.

Felix, S. (1985). More evidence on competing cognitive systems. *Second Language Research 1*, 1, 47–72.

Ferreira, L. (1981). *Notion by notion*. Rowley, MA: Newbury House.

Ferrer y Guardia, F. (1909). *The rational education of children. The modern school*. New York: Mother Earth Publishing.

Ferrer y Guardia, F. (1913). *The origins and ideal of the modern school*. London: Watts.

Ferris, D., & Tagg, T. (1996). Academic oral communication needs of EAP learners: What subject-matter instructors really require. *TESOL Quarterly 30*, 1, 31–55.

Fidler, G.C. (1989). Anarchism and education: *Education integrale* and the imperative towards *fraternite*. *History of Education 18*, 1, 23–46.

Fischer, J., Chouissa, C., Dugovičová, S., & Virkkunen-Fullenwider, A. (2011). *Guidelines for task-based university language testing*. Graz: European Center for Modern Languages. Retrieved from http://gult.ecml.at/

Fishman, J. (1991). The cases of Basque and Frisian. In Fishman, J. (ed.), *Reversing language shift* (pp. 149–186). Clevedon, Avon: Multilingual Matters.

Fixman, C.S. (1990). The foreign language needs of U.S.-based corporations. In

Lambert, R., & Moore, S. (eds.), *Foreign language in the workplace: Special Issue of the Annals of the American Academy of Political and Social Science*. Newbury Park, CA: Sage Publications.

Fleishman, E.A., & Quaintance, M.K. (1984). *Taxonomies of human performance*. Orlando, FL: Academic Press.

Flowerdew, J. (1986). Cognitive style and specific purpose course design. *English for Specific Purposes* 5, 121–130.

Flowerdew, J. (1992). Student perceptions, problems and strategies in second language lecture comprehension. *RELC Journal* 23, 2, 60–80.

Flowerdew, J. (1993). Content-based language instruction in a tertiary setting. *English for Specific Purposes* 12, 2, 121–138.

Flowerdew, J. (1994). Specific language for specific purposes: Concordancing for the ESP syllabus. In Khoo, R. (ed.), *LSP: Problems and prospects* (pp. 97–113). Singapore: SEAMEO Regional Language Center.

Flowerdew, J. (ed.) (1995a). *Academic listening*. Cambridge: Cambridge University Press.

Flowerdew, J. (1995b). Research of relevance to second language lecture comprehension – An overview. In Flowerdew, J. (ed.), *Academic listening* (pp. 7–33). Cambridge: Cambridge University Press.

Flowerdew, J., & Peacock, M. (eds.) (2001). *Research perspectives on English for academic purposes*. Cambridge: Cambridge University Press.

Foster, P. (1996). Doing the task better: How planning time influences students' performance. In Willis, J., & Willis, D. (eds.), *Challenge and change in language teaching* (pp. 126–135). Oxford: Heinemann.

Foster, P. (1998). A classroom perspective on the negotiation of meaning. *Applied Linguistics* 19, 1, 1–23.

Foster, P., & Ohta, A. (2005). Negotiation for meaning and peer assistance in second language classrooms. *Applied Linguistics* 26, 402–430.

Foster, P., & Skehan, P. (1996). The influence of planning and task type on second language performance. *Studies in Second Language Acquisition* 18, 3, 299–323.

Foster, P., & Tavakoli, P. (2009). Lexical diversity and lexical selection: A comparison of native and non-native speaker peformance. *Language Learning* 59, 4, 866–896.

Foster, P., Tonkyn, A., & Wigglesworth, G. (2000). Measuring spoken language: A unit for all reasons. *Applied Linguistics* 21, 3, 354–375.

Fotos, S. (2005). Traditional and grammar translation methods for second language teaching. In Hinkel, E. (ed.), *Handbook of research in second language teaching and learning* (pp. 653–670). Mahwah, NJ: Erlbaum.

Fotos, S., & Ellis, R. (1991). Communicating about grammar: A task-based approach. *TESOL Quarterly* 25, 4, 605–628.

Franco, A.L. (1986). Beyond the classroom: Monitoring at industry. *The ESP Journal* 4, 153–160.

Frankel, R. (1984). From sentence to sequence: Understanding the medical encounter through microinteractional analysis. *Discourse Processes* 7, 135–170.

Freeman, D., & Cazden, C. (1991). Learning to talk like a professional: Some pragmatics of foreign language teacher training. In Kachru, Y., & Bouton, L. (eds.), *Pragmatics and language learning* (Vol. 2, pp. 225–245), *Monograph Series*. Urbana-Champaign: University of Illinois.

Freire, P. (1970). *Pedagogy of the oppressed*. New York: Herder and Herder.

Freire, P. (1972). *Cultural action for freedom*. Harmondsworth: Penguin.

Freire, P. (1981). *Education for critical consciousness*. New York: Continuum.

Fremeaux, I., & Jordan, J. (2012). Anarchist pedagogy in action: Paideai, Escuela libre. In Haworth, R.H. (ed.), *Anarchist pedagogies. Collective action, theories, and critical reflections on education* (pp. 107–123). Oakland, CA: PM Press.

Fries, C.C. (1945). *Teaching and learning English as a foreign language*. Ann Arbor, MI: University of Michigan Press.

Frigo, L., & McDonald, J.L. (1998). Properties of phonological markers that affect the acquisition of gender-like subclasses. *Journal of Memory and Language* 39, 2, 218–245.

Fujii, A., & Mackey, A. (2009). Interactional feedback in learner-learner interactions in a task-based EFL classroom. *International Review of Applied Linguistics* 47, 267–301.

Fukuda, C., Komatsu-Yonezawa, S., Komori, S., & Zimmerman, E. (2001). A meta-analysis of a CMC project for L2 Japanese learners. Paper presented at the Hawai'i Association of Language Teachers Conference, Honolulu.

Fulcher, G. (2008). Criteria for evaluating language quality. In Shohamy, E., & Hornberger, N. (eds.), *Encyclopedia of language and education: Language testing and assessment* (2nd edn, Vol. 7, pp. 157–176). New York: Springer.

Gagne, R.M. (1965). *The conditions of learning.* New York: Holt, Rinehart & Winston.

Garagorri, X., & Eguilior, E. (1983). Desarrollo y situacion actual de la ensenanza en las ikastolas. In Siguan, M. (ed.), *Lenguas y educacion en el ambito del estado espanol.* Barcelona: University of Barcelona Press.

Garcia-Mayo, M.P. (ed.) (2007). *Investigating tasks in formal language learning.* Clevedon, Avon: Multilingual Matters.

Gardner, R. (1988). The socio-educational model of second language learning: Assumptions, findings, and issues. *Language Learning* 38, 1, 101–126.

Gardner, R.C. (1985). *Social psychology and second language learning: The role of attitude and motivation.* London: Edward Arnold.

Gass, S.M. (1982). From theory to practice. In Hines, M., & Rutherford, W. (eds.), *On TESOL '81* (pp. 129–139). Washington, DC: TESOL.

Gass, S.M. (1988). Integrating research ideas: A framework for second language studies. *Applied Linguistics* 9, 198–217.

Gass, S.M. (1997). *Input, interaction, and the development of second languages.* Mahwah, NJ: Erlbaum.

Gass, S.M. (2003). Input and interaction. In Doughty, C.J., & Long, M.H. (eds.), *Handbook of second language acquisition* (pp. 224–255). Oxford: Blackwell.

Gass, S.M., & Mackey, A. (2007). Input, interaction, and output: An overview. *AILA Review* 19, 3–17.

Gass, S.M., Mackey, A., Alvarez-Torres, M., & Fernandez-Garcia, M. (1999). The effects of task repetition on linguistic output. *Language Learning* 49, 4, 549–581.

Gass, S.M., Mackey, A., & Pica, T. (1998). The role of input and interaction in second language acquisition: Introduction to the special issue. *Modern Language Journal* 82, 299–307.

Gass, S.M., Mackey, A., & Ross-Feldman, L. (2005). Task-based interactions in classroom and laboratory settings. *Language Learning* 55, 4, 575–611.

Gass, S.M., & Varonis, M. (1984). The effect of familiarity on the comprehensibility of non-native speech. *Language Learning* 34, 1, 65–89.

Gatbonton, E., & Gu, G. (1994). Preparing and implementing a task-based ESL curriculum in an EFL setting: Implications for theory and practice. *TESL Canada Journal* 11, 2, 9–29.

Gatbonton, E., & Segalowitz, N. (1988). Creative automatization: Principles for promoting fluency within a communicative framework. *TESOL Quarterly* 22, 3, 437–492.

Gattegno, C. (1972). *Teaching foreign languages in the schools the silent way.* New York: Educational Solutions.

Geertz, C. (1973). *The interpretation of cultures.* New York: Basic Books.

Genesee, F., Lindholm-Leary, K., Saunders, B., & Christian, D. (2006). *Educating English language learners: A synthesis of research evidence.* New York: Cambridge University Press.

Gholson, B., & Barker, P. (1985). Kuhn, Lakatos, and Laudan. Applications to the history of physics and psychology. *American Psychologist* 40, 7, 755–769.

Gick, M.L., & Holyoak, K.J. (1980). Analogical problem solving. *Cognitive Psychology* 12, 306–355.

Gijselaers, W.H. (1996). Connecting problem-based practices with educational theory. In Wilkerson, L., & Gijselaers, W.H. (eds.), *Bringing problem-based learning to higher education: Theory and practice* (pp. 13–21). San Francisco, CA: Jossey-Bass.

Gilabert, R. (2004). Task complexity and L2 narrative oral production. Unpublished PhD dissertation. Barcelona: Departament de Filologia Anglesa I Alemanya, Universitat de Barcelona.

Gilabert, R. (2005). Evaluating the use of multiple sources and multiple methods in needs analysis: A case study of journalists in the Autonomous Community of Catalonia (Spain). In Long, M.H. (ed.), *Second language needs analysis* (pp. 182–199). Cambridge: Cambridge University Press.

Gilabert, R. (2007a). Effects of manipulating task complexity on self repairs during L2 oral production. *International Review of Applied Linguistics* 45, 2, 215–240.

Gilabert, R. (2007b). The simultaneous manipulation of task complexity along planning time and [+/− here-and-now]: Effects on L2 oral production. In Garcia Mayo, M.P. (ed.), *Investigating tasks in formal language learning* (pp. 44–68). Clevedon, Avon: Multilingual Matters.

Gilabert, R., Baron, J., & Llanes, A. (2009). Manipulating cognitive complexity across task types and its impact on learners' interaction during oral performance. *International Review of Applied Linguistics* 47, 365–395.

Giles, H., & Byrne, J.L. (1982). An intergroup approach to second language acquisition. *Journal of Multilingual and Multicultural Development* 1, 17–40.

Givon, T. (1979). *On understanding grammar.* San Diego, CA: Academic Press.

Godfroid, A., Boers, F., & Housen, A. (2013). An eye for words: Gauging the role of attention in L2 vocabulary acquisition by means of eye-tracking. *Studies in Second Language Acquisition* 35, 3, 483–517.

Godfroid, A., Housen, A., & Boers, F. (2010). A procedure for testing the noticing hypothesis in the context of vocabulary acquisition. In Putz, M., & Sicola, L. (eds.), *Cognitive processing of second language acquisition inside the learner's mind* (pp. 169–197). Amsterdam: John Benjamins.

Godwin, W. (1793). *An enquiry concerning political justice and its influence upon modern morals and manners.* London: G. G. and J. Robinson.

Godwin, W. (1986). Education. In Marshall, P. (ed.), *The anarchist writings of William Godwin* (pp. 140–157). London: Freedom Press.

Goetz, J.P., & Le Compte, M.D. (1984). *Ethnography and qualitative design in educational research.* New York: Academic Press.

Goldberg, A., & Casenhiser, D. (2008). Construction learning and second language acquisition. In Robinson, P., & Ellis, N.C. (eds.), *Handbook of cognitive linguistics and second language acquisition* (pp. 197–215). New York: Routledge.

Goldman, E. (1917). Francisco Ferrer and the modern school. In Goldman, E. (ed.), *Anarchism and other essays* (pp. 151–172). New York: Mother Earth Publishing Association.

Goldman, E. (1931). *Living my life.* New York: Knopf.

Goldschneider, J.M., & DeKeyser, R.M. (2001). Explaining the "natural order of L2 morpheme acquisition" in English: A meta-analysis of multiple determinants. *Language Learning* 51, 1, 1–50.

González-Lloret, M. (2003). Designing task-based CALL to promote interaction: En Busca de Esmeraldas. *Language Learning & Technology* 7, 1, 86–104.

Gonzalez-Lloret, M., & Nielson, K. (to appear). Does TBLT work? Evaluation of a task-based Spanish program. *Language Teaching Research.*

Goo, J., Granena, G., Novella, M., & Yilmaz, Y. (2009). Implicit and explicit instruction in L2 learning: Norris and Ortega (2000) revisited and updated. Paper presented at the Second Language Research Forum, Michigan State University. In Rebuschat, P. (ed.), *Implicit and explicit learning of languages.* Amsterdam and Philadelphia: John Benjamins, to appear.

Goo, J., & Mackey, A. (2013). The case against the case against recasts. *Studies in Second Language Acquisition* 35, 1, 127–165.

Goodman, P. (1952). *Utopian essays and proposals.* New York: Random House.

Goodman, P. (1966). *Compulsory miseducation.* New York: Random House.

Gopnik, M. (1972). *Linguistic structures in scientific texts.* The Hague: Mouton.

Gor, K., & Long, M.H. (2009). Input and second language processing. In Ritchie, W.C., & Bhatia, T.K. (eds.), *The new handbook of second language acquisition* (pp. 445–472). Bingley: Emerald Group Publishing.

Goto Butler, Y. (2011). The implementation of communicative and task-based language teaching in the Asia-Pacific region. *Annual Review of Applied Linguistics 31,* 36–57.

Gould, S.J. (1997). Kropotkin was no crackpot. *Natural History* 106, June, 12–21.

Grabe, W. (1987). Contrastive rhetoric and text type research. In Connor, U., & Kaplan, R.B. (eds.), *Writing across cultures* (pp. 115–137). Reading, MA: Addison-Wesley.

Grabe, W. (ed.) (1994). *Language policy and planning. Annual Review of Applied Linguistics 14.* New York: Cambridge University Press.

Granena, G. (2008). Elaboration and simplification in scripted and genuine telephone service encounters. *International Review of Applied Linguistics 46,* 2, 137–166.

Granena, G. (2012). Age differences and cognitive aptitudes for implicit and explicit learning in ultimate L2 attainment. Unpublished PhD dissertation. College Park, MD: University of Maryland, Program in Second Language Acquisition.

Granena, G. (2013a). Language aptitude and degree of foreign accent in reading-aloud and oral production tasks. Ms. College Park, MD: University of Maryland, SLA Program.

Granena, G. (2013b). Individual differences in sequence learning ability and second language acquisition in early childhood and adulthood. *Language Learning* 63, 4, 665–703.

Granena, G. (2013c). Cognitive aptitudes for second language learning and the LLAMA Language Aptitude Test. In Granena, G., & Long, M.H. (eds.), *Sensitive periods, language aptitude, and ultimate L2 attainment* (pp. 105–129). Amsterdam: John Benjamins.

Granena, G., & Long, M.H. (2013a). Age of onset, length of residence, language aptitude, and ultimate L2 attainment in three linguistic domains. *Second Language Research* 29, 3, 311–343.

Granena, G., & Long, M.H. (eds.) (2013b). *Sensitive periods, language aptitudes, and ultimate L2 attainment.* Amsterdam: John Benjamins.

Grave, J. (1900). *Enseignement bourgeois et enseignement libertaire.* Paris: Les Temps Nouveaux.

Greenwood, D.J. (1991). Collective reflective practice through participatory action research: A case study from the Fagor cooperatives in Mondragon. In Schon, D.A. (ed.), *The reflective turn* (pp. 84–107). New York: Teachers College Press.

Greenwood, D.J., & Gonzales Santos, J.L. (1992). *Industrial democracy as process: Participatory action research in the Fagor Cooperative Group of Mondragon.* Stockholm: Arbeitslivscentrum.

Greenwood, J. (1985). Bangalore revisited: A reluctant complaint. *English Language Teaching Journal* 39, 4, 268–273.

Gregg, K.R. (1990). The variable competence model of second language acquisition, and why it isn't. *Applied Linguistics* 11, 4, 364–383.

Gregg, K.R. (1993). Taking explanation seriously; or, let a couple of flowers bloom. *Applied Linguistics* 14, 3, 278–294.

Gribble, D. (1998). *Real education. Varieties of freedom.* Bristol: Libertarian Education.

Griffiths, R. (1992). Speech rate and listening comprehension: Further evidence of the relationship. *TESOL Quarterly* 26, 2, 385–390.

Grigorenko, E.L., Sternberg, R.J., & Ehrman, M.E. (2000). A theory-based approach to the measurement of foreign language learning ability: The Canal-F theory and test. *Modern Language Journal* 84, 3, 390–405.

Grimshaw, G.M., Adelstein, A., Bryden, M.P., & MacKinnon, G.E. (1998). First-language acquisition in adolescence: Evidence for a critical period for verbal language development. *Brain and Language* 63, 237–255.

Gumperz, J. (1982). *Discourse strategies.* Cambridge: Cambridge University Press.

Gysen, S., & Van Avermaet, P. (2005). Issues in functional language performance assessment: The case of the Certificate Dutch as a Foreign Language. *Language Assessment Quarterly* 2, 1, 51–68.

Hagen, S. (ed.) (1988). *Languages in British business: An analysis of current needs.* Necastle upon Tyle: Newcastle upon Tyne Polytechnic Products, Ltd.

Hakansson, G., & Norrby, C. (2010). Environmental influence on language acquisition: Comparing second and foreign language acquisition of Swedish. *Language Learning* 60, 3, 628–650.

Halliday, M. (1975). *An introduction to functional grammar.* London: Edward Arnold.

Hama, M., & Leow, R.P. (2010). Learning without awareness revisited: Extending Williams (2005). *Studies in Second Language Acquisition* 32, 3, 465–491.

Hamann, K., Warneken, F., Greenberg, J.R., & Tomasello, M. (2011). Collaboration encourages equal sharing in children but not in chimpanzees. *Nature* 476, 7360, 328–331.

Hammersley, M., & Atkinson, P. (1983). *Ethnography: Principles and practice.* London: Tavistok.

Hammond, R. (1988). Accuracy versus communicative competency: The acquisition of grammar in the second language classroom. *Hispania (Madrid, Spain: 1940)* 71, 2, 408–417.

Hamrick, P. (2013). Recognition memory for novel syntactic structures. *Canadian Journal of Experimental Psychology/Revue Canadienne de Psychologie Expérimentale* 68, 1, 2–7. doi: 10.1037/cep0000002

Han, Z., & Odlin, T. (2005). *Studies of fossilization in second language acquisition.* Clevedon, Avon: Multilingual Matters.

Hanawalt, P.C. (1972). Repair of genetic material in living cells. *Endeavor* 31, 83–87.

Harley, B. (1989). Functional grammar in French immersion: A classroom experiment. *Applied Linguistics* 19, 331–359.

Harlow, L.L. (1987). Individualized instruction in foreign languages at the college level: A survey of programs in the United States. *Modern Language Journal* 7, 1, 389–394.

Harmer, J. (1998). *How to teach English.* Harlow: Longman.

Haskell, R.E. (2001). *Transfer of learning: Cognition, instruction, and reasoning.* San Diego, CA: Academic Press.

Hatch, E. (1992). *Discourse and language education.* Cambridge: Cambridge University Press.

Hatch, E.M. (1978). Discourse analysis and second language acquisition. In Hatch, E.M. (ed.), *Second language acquisition: A book of readings* (pp. 402–435). Rowley, MA: Newbury House.

Hatch, E.M., & Long, M.H. (1980). Discourse analysis, what's that? In Larsen-Freeman, D. (ed.), *Discourse analysis in second language research* (pp. 1–40). Rowley, MA: Newbury House.

Hawkey, R. (1980). Needs analysis and syllabus design for specific purposes. In Altman, H.B. (ed.), *Foreign language teaching: Meeting individual needs* (pp. 81–93). Oxford: Pergamon Press.

Hawkey, R. (1983). Programme development for learners of English. In Richterich, R. (ed.), *Case studies in identifying language needs* (pp. 79–87). Oxford: Pergamon Press.

Hawkins, B. (1985). Is an "appropriate response" always so appropriate? In Gass, S.M., & Madden, C.G. (eds.), *Input in second language acquisition* (pp. 162–178). Rowley, MA: Newbury House.

Haworth, R.H. (2012). *Anarchist pedagogies. Collective actions, theories, and critical reflections on education.* Oakland, CA: PM Press.

Henderson, M., Morris, L., & Fitz-Gibbon, C. (1987). *How to measure attitudes.* Newbury Park, CA: Sage.

Henrichsen, L. (1984). Sandhi-variation: A filter of input for learners of ESL. *Language Learning* 34, 3, 103–126.

Henrichsen, L.E. (1989). *Diffusion of innovations in English language teaching: The ELEC effort in Japan, 1956–1968*. New York: Greenwood.

Hern, M. (ed.) (2008). *Everywhere all the time: A new deschooling reader*. Oakland, CA: AK Press.

Hewetson, J. (1987). Mutual aid and the social significance of Darwinism. Introductory essay in Kropotkin, P. (1902/1987) (ed.). *Mutual aid. A factor of evolution* (pp. 1–11). London: Freedom Press.

Hillewaere, K. (2000). *Evaluatieonderzoek van het onderwijsbeleid ten aanzien van etnische minderheden in het lager onderwijs*. Gent: Universiteit Gent, Steunpunt ICO.

Hirshon, S. (1983). *And also teach them to read*. Westport, CT: Lawrence Hill.

Hmelo-Silver, C.E., & Chinn, C.A. (2013). *The international handbook of collaborative learning*. New York: Routledge.

Hoadley-Maidment, E. (1983). Methodology for the identification of language learning needs of immigrant learners of English through mother-tongue interviews. In Richterich, R., & Chancerel, J.-L. (eds.), *Identifying the needs of adults learning a foreign language* (pp. 39–51). Oxford: Pergamon.

Hodlin, S. (1970). Preliminary survey in a food factory: Introductory discussion, personnel records and participant observation. Southall, London: Pathway Industrial Unit.

Holliday, A. (1994). *Appropriate methodology and social context*. Cambridge, England: Cambridge University Press.

Holliday, A. (1995). Assessing language needs within an institutional context: An ethnographic approach. *English for Specific Purposes* 14, 2, 115–126.

Holliday, A., & Cooke, T. (1982). An ecological approach to ESP. In Waters, A. (ed.), *Issues in ESP*. Oxford: Pergamon.

Holmes, J. (2005). When small talk is a big deal: Sociolinguistic challenges in the workplace. In Long, M.H. (ed.), *Second language needs analysis* (pp. 344–372). Cambridge: Cambridge University Press.

Holt, J.C. (1964/1995). *How children fail*. Cambridge, MA: Da Capo Press.

Holt, J.C. (1967/1995). *How children learn*. Cambridge, MA: Da Capo Press.

Holt, J.C. (1972). *Freedom and beyond*. Harmondsworth: Penguin.

Holt, L.C. (1993). *Cooperative learning in action*. Westerville, OH: National Middle School Association.

Horowitz, D. (1986). What professors actually require: Academic tasks for the ESL classroom. *TESOL Quarterly* 20, 445–462.

Horst, M. (2005). Learning L2 vocabulary through extensive reading: A measurement study. *Canadian Modern Language Review* 61, 3, 355–382.

Horst, M. (2010). How well does teacher talk support incidental vocabulary acquisition? *Reading in a Foreign Language* 22, 1, 161–180.

Horst, M., Cobb, T., & Meara, P. (1998). Beyond a clockwork orange: Acquiring second language vocabulary through reading. *Reading in a Foreign Language* 11, 207–223.

Horst, M., Cobb, T., & Nicolae, I. (2005). Expanding academic vocabulary with an interactive on-line database. *Language Learning & Technology* 9, 90–110.

Housen, A., & Perriard, M. (2005). Investigating instructed second language acquisition. In Housen, A., & Perriard, M. (eds.), *Investigations in instructed second language acquisition* (pp. 1–30). Berlin: Mouton de Gruyter.

Howatt, A.P.R. (1984). *A history of English language teaching*. Oxford: Oxford University Press.

Howell-Richardson, C., & Parkinson, B. (1988). Learner diaries: Possibilities and pitfalls. In Grunwell, P. (ed.), *Applied linguistics in society*. Papers from the Annual Meeting of the British Association for Applied Linguistics (20th, Nottingham, England, United Kingdom, September 1987. British Studies in Applied Linguistics(Vol. 3, pp. 74–79).

Hoyer, W.J., & Lincourt, A.E. (1998). Ageing and the development of learning. In Stadler, M.A., & Frensch, P.A. (eds.),

Handbook of implicit learning (pp. 445–470). Thousand Oaks, CA: Sage.

Hu, G. (2002). Potential cultural resistance to pedagogical imports: The case of communicative language teaching in China. *Language, Culture and Curriculum* 15, 93–105.

Huckin, T.N., & Olson, L.A. (1984). On the use of informants in LSP discourse analysis. In Pugh, A.K., & Ulijn, J.M. (eds.), *Reading for professional purposes* (pp. 120–129). London: Heinemann.

Hudson, T., & Lynch, B. (1984). A criterion-referenced measurement approach to ESL achievement testing. *Language Testing* 1, 2, 171–201.

Huebner, T. (1983). Linguistic system and linguistic change in an interlanguage. *Studies in Second Language Acquisition* 6, 1, 33–53.

Hulstijn, J.H. (1989). Implicit and incidental second language learning: Experiments in the processing of natural and partly artificial input. In Dechert, H.W., & Raupach, M. (eds.), *Interlingual processing*. Tubingen: Gunter Narr.

Hulstijn, J.H. (1992). Retention of inferred and given word meanings: Experiments in incidental vocabulary learning. In Arnaud, P., & Bejoint, H. (eds.), *Vocabulary and applied linguistics* (pp. 113–125). London: Macmillan.

Hulstijn, J.H. (2003). Incidental and intentional learning. In Doughty, C.J., & Long, M.H. (eds.), *Handbook of second language acquisition* (pp. 349–381). Oxford: Blackwell.

Hutchinson, T., & Waters, A. (1987). *English for specific purposes: A learning-centred approach*. Cambridge: Cambridge University Press.

Hyland, K. (2009). Specific purpose programs. In Long, M.H., & Doughty, C.J. (eds.), *Handbook of language teaching* (pp. 201–217). Oxford: Wiley-Blackwell.

Hyland, K., & Hamp-Lyons, E. (2002). EAP: Issues and directions. *Journal of English for Academic Purposes* 1, 1–12.

Hyland, K., & Tse, P. (2007). Is there an academic vocabulary? *TESOL Quarterly* 41, 2, 235–254.

Hyltenstam, K. (1977). Implicational patterns in interlanguage syntax variation. *Language Learning* 27, 2, 383–411.

Hyltenstam, K. (1984). The use of typological markedness conditions as predictors in second language acquisition: The case of pronominal copies in relative clauses. In Andersen, R.W. (ed.), *Second language: A cross-linguistic perspective* (pp. 39–58). Rowley, MA: Newbury House.

Hyltenstam, K. (1992). Non-native features of non-native speakers: On the ultimate attainment of childhood L2 learners. In Harris, R.J. (ed.), *Cognitive processing in bilinguals* (pp. 351–368). New York: Elsevier.

Hyltenstam, K., & Abrahamsson, N. (2003). Maturational constraints in second language acquisition. In Doughty, C.J., & Long, M.H. (eds.), *Handbook of second language acquisition* (pp. 539–588). Oxford: Blackwell.

Hymes, D. (1962). The ethnography of speaking. In Gladwin, T., & Sturtevant, W. (eds.), *Anthropology and human behavior* (pp. 15–53), Washington, DC: Anthropological Society of Washington.

Hymes, D. (1971). *On communicative competence*. Philadelphia, PA: University of Pennsylvania Press.

Hymes, D. (1974). *Foundations in sociolinguistics: An ethnographic approach*. Philadelphia, PA: University of Pennsylvania Press.

Ikastola Irekia. (n.d.). Donostia, Pais Vasco: Almen Ikastola.

Illich, I. (1971). *Deschooling society*. Harmondsworth: Penguin.

Inman, M. (1979). Language and cross-cultural training in American multinational corporations. *Modern Language Journal* 69, 3, 247–255.

Ioup, G., Boustagui, E., El Tigi, M., & Moselle, M. (1994). Reexamining the critical period hypothesis. A case study of successful adult SLA in a naturalistic environment. *Studies in Second Language Acquisition* 16, 1, 73–98.

Ishikawa, T. (2006). The effects of task complexity and language proficiency on task-based language performance. *The Journal of Asia TEFL* 3, 4, 193–225.

Ishikawa, T. (2008a). Investigating the effects of intentional reasoning demands on L2 speech production. Unpublished PhD dissertation, Tokyo: Aoyama Gakuin Daigaku.

Ishikawa, T. (2008b). The effects of task demands of intentional reasoning on L2 speech performance. *The Journal of Asia TEFL* 5, 1, 29–63.

Iverson, P., Kuhl, P.K., Akahane-Yamada, R., Diesch, E., Tohkura, Y., & Ketterman, A. (2003). A perceptual interference account of acquisition difficulties for non-native phonemes. *Cognition* 87, B47–B57.

Iwai, T., Kondo, K., Lim, D.S.J., Ray, G.E., Shimizu, H., & Brown, J.D. (1999). *Japanese language needs analysis*. Ms. Honolulu, HI: National Foreign Language Research Center, University of Hawai'i at Manoa.

Iwashita, N. (2001). The effect of learner proficiency on interactional moves and modified output in nonnative-nonnative interaction in Japanese as a foreign language. *System* 29, 2, 267–287.

Iwashita, N. (2003). Negative feedback and positive evidence in task-based interaction: Differential effects on L2 development. *Studies in Second Language Acquisition* 25, 1, 1–36.

Izumi, S., & Bigelow, M. (2000). Does output promote noticing and second language acquisition? *TESOL Quarterly* 34, 2, 239–278.

Izumi, S., Bigelow, M., Fujiwara, M., & Fearnow, S. (1999). Testing the output hypothesis. *Studies in Second Language Acquisition* 21, 421–452.

Jackson, D.O., & Suethanapornkul, S. (2013). The cognition hypothesis: A synthesis and meta-analysis of research on second language task complexity. *Language Learning* 63, 2, 330–367.

Jackson, J., & Bilton, L. (1994). Lexis in science lectures. *English for Specific Purposes* 13, 1, 61–80.

Jacobs, B. (1988). Neurobiological differentiation of primary and secondary language acquisition. *Studies in Second Language Acquisition* 10, 3, 303–337.

Jacobs, G.M. (1998). Cooperative learning or just grouping students: The difference makes a difference. In Renandya, W.A., & Jacobs, G.M. (eds.), *Learners and language learning* (pp. 172–193). Singapore: SEAMEO Regional Language Centre.

Jacobson, W.H. (1986). An assessment of the communication needs of non-native speakers of English in an undergraduate physics lab. *English for Specific Purposes* 5, 2, 189–195.

Jacoby, S. (1999). Rethinking EST: What can "indigenous assessment" tell us about the communication culture of science? Ms. Department of Communication, University of New Hampshire.

Jacoby, S., & McNamara, T. (1999). Locating competence. *English for Specific Purposes* 18, 3, 213–241.

Janacsek, K., Fiser, J., & Nemeth, D. (2012). The best time to acquire new skills: Age-related differences in implicit sequence learning across the human lifespan. *Developmental Science* 15, 4, 496–505.

Jarvis, J. (1992). Using diaries for teaching reflection on in-service courses. *English Language Teaching Journal* 46, 2, 133–143.

Jaspaert, K., & Linsen, B. (1997). Succes verzekerd? Effecten van taakgericht onderwijs. *Moer* 6, 362–373.

Jasso-Aguilar, R. (1999/2005). Sources, methods and triangulation in needs analysis: A critical perspective in a case study of Waikiki hotel maids. *English for Specific Purposes* 18, 1, 1999, 27–46. Revised and expanded version in Long, M.H. (ed.) (2005). *Second language needs analysis* (pp. 127–58). Cambridge: Cambridge University Press.

Jiang, N. (2000). Lexical representation and development in a second language. *Applied Linguistics* 21, 1, 47–77.

Johns, A. (1981). Necessary English: A faculty survey. *TESOL Quarterly* 15, 1, 51–57.

Johns, A.M. (1988). The discourse communities dilemma: Identifying transferable skills for the academic milieu. *English for Specific Purposes* 7, 1, 55–60.

Johns, A.M. (1997). *Text, role and context*. Cambridge: Cambridge University Press.

Johnson, D.M. (1992). Survey research. In Johnson, D.M. (ed.), *Approaches to second language learning* (pp. 104–129). White Plains, NY: Longman.

Johnson, D.W., Johnson, R.T., & Stanne, M.B. (2000). *Cooperative learning methods: A meta-analysis*. Minneapolis, MN: University of Minnesota.

Johnson, K. (1996). *Language teaching and skill learning*. Oxford: Blackwell.

Johnson, K. (2003). *Designing language teaching tasks*. New York: Palgrave.

Johnson Nystrom, N. (1983). Teacher-student interaction in bilingual classrooms: Four approaches to error feedback. In Seliger, H.W., & Long, M.H. (eds.), *Classroom-oriented research in second language acquisition* (pp. 169–188). Rowley, MA: Newbury House.

Johnston, M. (1985). *Syntactic and morphological progressions in learner English*. Canberra: Commonwealth Department of Immigration and Ethnic Affairs.

Johnston, M. (1995). *Stages of acquisition of Spanish as a second language. Australian Studies in Language Acquisition*. NLLIA/LARC, University of Western Sydney, Macarthur.

Johnston, M. (1997). Development and variation in learner language. Unpublished doctoral dissertation, Australian National University, Canberra.

Johnston, M. (2000). *Stages of development for English as a second language. Australian Studies in Language Acquisition*. Language Acquisition Research Center, University of Western Sydney.

Jones, L. (1979). *Notions in English*. Cambridge: Cambridge University Press.

Jordan, R.R. (1978). Language practice materials for economists. In Mackay, R., & Mountford, A. (eds.), *English for specific purposes: A case study approach*. London: Longman.

Jordan, R.R. (1993). Study skills: Experience and expectations. In Blue, G. (ed.), *Language, learning and success: Studying through English*. London: Macmillan.

Jordan, R.R. (2002). The growth of EAP in Britain. *English for Academic Purposes* 1, 69–78.

Jordan, R.R., & Mackay, R. (1973). A survey of the spoken English problems of overseas postgraduate students at the universities of Manchester and Newcastle upon Tyne. *Journal of the Institutes of Education of the Universities of Newcastle upon Tyne and Durham* 25 (No. 125, November).

Julkunen, K. (1990). Open and closed vocabulary tasks in foreign language learning. In Tommola, J. (ed.), *Foreign language comprehension and production* (pp. 7–25). Turku, Finland: Finnish Association of Applied Linguistics.

Jupp, T.C. (1980). English language training for employment needs. *TEAL Occasional Papers* 4, 67–81.

Jupp, T.C., & Hodlin, S. (1975). *Industrial English*. London: Heinemann.

Keck, C.M., Iberri-Shea, G., Tracy-Ventura, N., & Wa-Mbaleka, S. (2006). Investigating the empirical link between interaction and acquisition: A quantitative meta-analysis. In Ortega, L., & Norris, J. (eds.), *Synthesizing research on language learning and teaching* (pp. 91–131). Amsterdam: John Benjamins.

Keenan, E.L., & Comrie, B. (1977). Noun phrase accessibility and universal grammar. *Linguistic Inquiry* 8, 1, 63–99.

Kelch, K. (1985). Modified input as an aid to comprehension. *Studies in Second Language Acquisition* 7, 1, 81–90.

Kelly, L.G. (1969). *Twenty-five centuries of language teaching*. Rowley, MA: Newbury House.

Kennedy, C. (1988). Evaluation of the management of change in ELT projects. *Applied Linguistics* 9, 4, 329–342.

Kennedy, G. (1990). Collocations: Where grammar and vocabulary meet. In Anivan, S. (ed.), *Language teaching methodology for the nineties* (pp. 215–229), *Anthology Series 24*. Singapore: SEAMEO Regional Language Centre.

Kessler, J.-U., Liebner, M., & Mansouri, F. (2011). Teaching. In Pienemann, M.P., &

Kessler, J.-U. (eds.), *Studying processability theory* (pp. 149–156). Amsterdam and Philadelphia, PA: John Benjamins.

Kim, Y. (2003). Effects of input elaboration and enhancement on vocabulary acquisition through reading by Korean EFL learners. Unpublished PhD dissertation. Honolulu, HI: University of Hawai'i, Department of Second Language Studies.

Kim, Y. (2006). Effects of input elaboration on vocabulary acquisition through reading by Korean learners of English as foreign language. *TESOL Quarterly* 40, 2, 341–373.

Kim, Y. (2009). The effects of task complexity on learner–learner interaction. *System* 37, 254–268.

Kim, Y., & McDonough, K. (2008). The effect of interlocutor proficiency on the collaborative dialogue between Korean as a second language learners. *Language Teaching Research* 12, 211–234.

Kim, Y., Kong, D.-K., Lee, J.-H., & Lee, Y.-G. (2000). Implementation and evaluation of an approach to task-based Korean language teaching. Honolulu, HI: National Foreign Language Resource Center, University of Hawai'i at Mānoa. [An abridged version of this paper appeared with the same title in Korean Language in America (Vol. 6, pp. 45–51, 2001), the Proceedings of the 6th Annual American Association of Teachers of Korean.].

Kirk, J., & Miller, M.L. (1986). *Reliability and validity in qualitative research*. Beverly Hills, CA: Sage.

Klein, W., & Dimroth, C. (2009). Untutored second language acquisition. In Ritchie, W.C., & Bhatia, T.K. (eds.), *The new handbook of second language acquisition* (pp. 503–521). Bingley: Emerald Group Publishing.

Klein, W., & Purdue, C. (1997). The basic variety (or: Couldn't natural languages be much simpler?) *Second Language Research* 13, 301–347.

Ko, J., Schallert, D., & Walters, K. (2003). Rethinking scaffolding: Examining negotiation of meaning in an ESL storytelling task. *TESOL Quarterly* 37, 303–324.

Kolb, D. (1984). *Experiential learning: Experience as the source of learning and development*. Englewood Cliffs, NJ: Prentice-Hall.

Kong, D.-K. (2002). Effects of task complexity on second-language production. Unpublished MA thesis. Honolulu, HI: University of Hawai'i, Department of Second Language Studies.

Kong, D.-K. (2012) Task-based language teaching in an advanced Korean language learning program. The Korean Language in America 17. American Association of Teachers of Korean.

Kouraogo, P. (1987). EFL curriculum renewal and INSET in difficult circumstances. *English Language Teaching Journal* 41, 3, 171–178.

Kramer, R. (1978). *Maria Montessori*. Oxford: Blackwell.

Krashen, S.D. (1985). *The input hypothesis. Issues and implications*. New York: Longman.

Krashen, S.D. (1991). Sheltered subject matter teaching. *Cross Currents* 18, 2, 183–189.

Krashen, S.D., & Scarcella, R. (1979). On routines and patterns in second language acquisition. *Language Learning* 28, 2, 283–300.

Krashen, S.D., & Seliger, H.W. (1975). The essential characteristics of formal instruction. *TESOL Quarterly* 9, 173–183.

Krashen, S.D., & Terrell, T. (1983). *The natural approach: Language acquisition in the classroom*. Oxford: Pergamon.

Kropotkin, P. (1890/1913). Brain work and manual work. The Nineteenth Century March, 456–75. In Ward, C. (ed.), *Peter Kropotkin's Fields, factories and workshops tomorrow* (pp. 161–187). London: Freedom Press. 1985.

Kropotkin, P. (1899/1985). *Fields, factories and workshops tomorrow*. Edited edition by Colin Ward. London: Freedom Press.

Kropotkin, P. (1902/1987). *Mutual aid. A factor of evolution*. London: Freedom Press.

Kropotkin, P. (1903). *Modern science and anarchism*. London: Mother Earth Publication Association. Retrieved from http://books .google.co.uk/books/about/Modern

_Science_and_Anarchism.html?id
=GVJqo2EFw_cC&redir_esc=y

Kuhl, P.K. (2007). Is speech learning gated by the "social brain"? *Developmental Science* 277, 684–686.

Kuhl, P.K., & Iverson, P. (1995). Linguistic experience and the "perceptual magnetic effect." In Strange, W. (ed.), *Speech perception and linguistic experience: Issues in cross-language research* (pp. 121–154). Timonium, MD: York Press.

Kuiken, F., Mos, M., & Vedder, I. (2005). Cognitive task complexity and second language writing performance. In Foster-Cohen, S., Garcia-Mayo, M., & Cenoz, J. (eds.), *EUROSLA yearbook 2005* (Vol. 5, pp. 195–222). Amsterdam: John Benjamins.

Kuiken, F., & Vedder, I. (2007). Task complexity and measures of linguistic performance in L2 writing. *International Review of Applied Linguistics* 45, 3, 261–284.

Kumaravadivelu, B. (1991). Language-learning tasks: Teacher intention and learner interpretation. *English Language Teaching Journal* 45, 2, 98–107.

Lackstrom, J., Selinker, L., & Trimble, L. (1973). Technical rhetorical principles and grammatical choice. *TESOL Quarterly* 7, 127–136.

Lado, R. (1957). *Linguistics across cultures.* Ann Arbor, MI: University of Michigan Press.

Lado, R. (1964). *Language teaching: A scientific approach.* New York: McGraw-Hill.

Lado, R., & Fries, C.G. (1958). *English pattern practices.* Ann Arbor, MI: University of Michigan Press.

Lai, C., Zhao, Y., & Wang, J. (2011). Task-based language teaching in online ab initio foreign language classrooms. *Modern Language Journal* 95, Suppl. Issue, 81–103.

Lambert, C. (2010). A task-based needs analysis: Putting principles into practice. *Language Teaching Research* 14, 99–112.

Lambert, R., & Moore, S. (1990). Foreign language in the workplace. *Annals of the American Academy of Political and Social Science* 511, 25–46.

Lamotte, J. (1981). Introspections and discourse in a physical therapy session.

Unpublished term paper. Philadelphia, PA: University of Pennsylvania, Graduate School of Education.

Lankshear, C., & Lawler, M. (1987). *Literacy, schooling and revolution.* Philadelphia, PA: Taylor and Francis.

Lantolf, J.P. (2012). Sociocultural theory: A dialectical approach to L2 research. In Gass, S.M., & Mackey, A. (eds.), *The Routledge handbook of second language acquisition* (pp. 57–72). New York: Routledge.

Lardiere, D. (1998a). Case and tense in the "fossilized" steady-state. *Second Language Research* 14, 1–26.

Lardiere, D. (1998b). Dissociating syntax from morphology in a divergent L2 end-state grammar. *Second Language Research* 14, 359–375.

Lardiere, D. (2006). *Ultimate attainment in second language acquisition: A case study.* Mahwah, NJ: Lawrence Erlbaum.

Lardiere, D. (2007). *Ultimate attainment in second language acquisition. A case study.* Mahwah, NJ: Lawrence Erlbaum.

Lardiere, D. (2012). Linguistic approaches to second language morphosyntax. In Gass, S.M., & Mackey, A. (eds.), *The Routledge handbook of second language acquisition* (pp. 106–126). New York: Routledge.

Larsen-Freeman, D. (1976). An explanation for the morpheme acquisition order of second language learners. *Language Learning* 26, 1, 125–134.

Larsen-Freeman, D., & Ellis, N. (2006). Language emergence: Implications for applied linguistics. *Applied Linguistics* 27, 4, 558–589.

LaRue, C. (2010). *LaRue Medical Literacy Exercises.* December 2. Retrieved from http://www.mcedservices.com/medex/medex.htm

Lasagabaster, D., & Ruiz de Zarobe, Y. (2010). *CLIL in Spain: Implementation, results, and teacher training.* Cambridge: Cambridge Scholars.

Lass, R. (1997). *Historical linguistics and language change.* Cambridge: Cambridge University Press.

Laudan, L. (1977). *Progress and its problems: Towards a theory of scientific growth.*

Berkeley and Los Angeles, CA: University of California Press.

Laudan, L. (1996). A problem-solving approach to scientific progress. In Laudan, L. (ed.), *Beyond positivism and relativism. Theory, method, and evidence* (pp. 77–87). Boulder, CO: Westview.

Laudan, L., & Laudan, R. (1989). Dominance and disunity of method: Solving the problems of innovation and consensus. *Philosophy of Science* 56, 221–237.

Laufer, B. (2005). Focus on form in second language vocabulary learning. *EUROSLA Yearbook* 5, 223–250.

Lave, J., & Wenger, E. (1991). *Situated learning: Legitimate peripheral participation*. Cambridge: Cambridge University Press.

Lebauer, R.S. (1984). Using lecture transcripts in EAP lecture comprehension courses. *TESOL Quarterly* 18, 1, 41–54.

Lee, Y.-G. (2002). Effects of task complexity on the complexity and accuracy of oral production in L2 Korean. Unpublished PhD dissertation. Honolulu, HI: University of Hawai'i, Department of East Asian Languages and Literatures.

Leech, G., Rayson, P., & Wilson, A. (2001). *Word frequencies in written and spoken English, based on the British national corpus*. London: Longman.

Leow, R.P. (2000). A study of the role of awareness in foreign language behavior: Aware vs. unaware learners. *Studies in Second Language Acquisition* 22, 3, 557–584.

Leow, R.P., & Hama, M. (2013). Implicit learning in SLA and the issue of internal validity: A response to Leung and Williams's (2011) "The implicit learning of mappings between forms and contextually derived meanings". *Studies in Second Language Acquisition* 35, 3, 545–557.

Lett, J.A. (2005). Foreign language needs assessment in the U.S. military. In Long, M.H. (ed.), *Second language needs analysis* (pp. 105–124). Cambridge: Cambridge University Press.

Leung, J., & Williams, J.N. (2006). Implicit learning of form-meaning connections. In Sun, R., & Miyake, N. (eds.), *Proceedings of the Annual Meeting of the Cognitive Science Society* (pp. 465–470). Mahwah, NJ: Erlbaum.

Leung, J.H.C., & Williams, J.N. (2011a). The implicit learning of mappings between forms and contextually derived meanings. *Studies in Second Language Acquisition* 33, 1, 33–55.

Leung, J.H.C., & Williams, J.N. (2011b). Constraints on implicit learning of grammatical form-meaning connections. *Language Learning* 62, 2, 634–662.

Leval, G. (1975). *Collectives in the Spanish Revolution*. London: Freedom Press.

Levin, L. (1972). *Comparative studies in foreign language teaching*. Godteborg Studies in Educational Sciences 9.

Li, D. (1998). It's always more difficult than you planned. Teachers' perceived difficulties in introducing the communicative approach in South Korea. *TESOL Quarterly* 32, 4, 677–703.

Li, S. (2010). The effectiveness of corrective feedback in SLA: A meta-analysis. *Language Learning* 60, 2, 309–365.

Liang, X., Mohan, B.A., & Early, M. (1998). Issues of cooperative learning in ESL classes: A literature review. *TESL Canada Journal* 1, 2, 13–23.

Lightbown, P.M. (1983). Exploring relationships between developmental and instructional sequences. In Seliger, H.W., & Long, M.H. (eds.), *Classroom-oriented research on second language acquisition* (pp. 217–243). Rowley, MA: Newbury House.

Lightbown, P.M., & Spada, N. (1990). Focus on form and corrective feedback in communicative language teaching: Effects on second language learning. *Studies in Second Language Acquisition* 12, 429–448.

Lin, Y.-H., & Hedgcock, J. (1996). Negative feedback incorporation among high-proficiency and low proficiency Chinese speaking learners of Spanish. *Language Learning* 46, 4, 567–611.

Linck, J.A., Hughes, M.M., Campbell, S.G., Silbert, N.H., Tare, M., Jackson, S.R., Smith, B.K., Bunting, M.F., & Doughty, C.J. (2013). Hi-LAB: A new measure of aptitude for high-level language proficiency. *Language Learning* 63, 3, 530–566.

Lincoln, Y.S., & Guba, E.G. (eds.) (1985). *Naturalistic inquiry.* Newbury Park, CA: Sage.

Linsen, B. (1994). Met vallen en opstaan: De introductie van taakgericht taalonderwijs. Een Praktijkbeschrijving uit het basisonderwijs in Vlaanderen. In Kroon, S., & Vallen, T. (eds.), *Nederalnds als tweede taal in het onderwijs. Parktijkbeschrijvingen uit Nederland en Vlaanderen* (pp. 131–159). 's-Gravenhage: Nederlandse Taalunie Voorzetten 46.

Liu, D. (2012). The most frequently-used multiword constructions in academic written English: A multi-corpus study. *English for Specific Purposes* 31, 25–35.

Lo Bianco, J. (1989). *National policy on languages.* Canberra: Australian Government Publishing Service.

Loewen, S. (2005). Incidental focus on form and second language learning. *Studies in Second Language Acquisition* 27, 361–386.

Loewen, S. (2012). The role of feedback. In Gass, S.M., & Mackey, A. (eds.), *The Routledge handbook of second language acquisition* (pp. 24–40). New York: Routledge.

Loewen, S., Erlam, R., & Ellis, R. (2009). *Implicit and explicit knowledge and second language learning: Testing and teaching.* Clevedon, Avon: Multilingual Matters.

Loewen, S., & Philp, J. (2005). Recasts in the adult English L2 classroom: Characteristics, explicitness, and effectiveness. *Modern Language Journal* 90, 536–556.

Logan, G.D. (1988). Toward an instance theory of automatization. *Psychological Review* 95, 492–527.

Logan, G.D. (1990). Repetitive priming and automaticity: Common underlying mechanisms? *Cognitive Psychology* 22, 1–35.

Logan, G.E. (1973). *Individualizing foreign language learning: An organic process.* Rowley, MA: Newbury House.

Long, M.H. (1977a). *Face to face.* London: Evans Bros.

Long, M.H. (1977b). Group work in the teaching and learning of English as a foreign language – Problems and potential. *English Language Teaching Journal* 31, 4, 285–292.

Long, M.H. (1977c). Teacher feedback on learner error: Mapping cognitions. In Brown, H.D., Yorio, C.A., & Crymes, R. (eds.), *On TESOL '77. Teaching and learning English as a second language: Trends in research and practice* (pp. 278–294). Washington, DC: TESOL. Reprinted in Robinett, B.W., & Schachter, J. (eds.) (1993). Second language learning: Contrastive analysis, error analysis, and related aspects (pp. 446–465). Ann Arbor, MI: University of Michigan Press.

Long, M.H. (1980a). Input, interaction, and second language acquisition. Unpublished PhD dissertation. Los Angeles, CA: University of California, Los Angeles.

Long, M.H. (1980b). Inside the "black box": Methodological issues in classroom research on language learning. *Language Learning* 30, 1, 1980, 1–42. Reprinted in Seliger, H.W., & Long, M.H. (eds.) (1983). *Classroom-oriented research on second language acquisition* (pp. 3–41). Rowley, MA: Newbury House.

Long, M.H. (1981). Input, interaction and second language acquisition. In Winitz, H. (ed.), Native language and foreign language acquisition. *Annals of the New York Academy of Sciences* 379, 259–278.

Long, M.H. (1982). Die Aushandlung verstehbarer Eingabe in Gesprachen zwishen muttersprachlichern Sprechern und Lernern. *Zeitschrift fur Literaturwissenschaft und Linguistik* 45, 12, 100–129.

Long, M.H. (1983a). Does second language instruction make a difference? A review of research. *TESOL Quarterly* 17, 3, 359–382.

Long, M.H. (1983b). Native speaker/non-native speaker conversation and the negotiation of comprehensible input. *Applied Linguistics* 4, 2, 126–141. Reprinted in Candlin, C.N., & Macnamara, T. (eds.) (2001). *A reader in applied linguistics.* London: Routledge.

Long, M.H. (1983c). Native speaker/non-native speaker conversation in the second language classroom. In Clark, M., &

Handscombe, J. (eds.), *On TESOL '82. Pacific perspectives on language learning* (pp. 207–225). Washington, DC: TESOL. Reprinted in Long, M.H., & Richards, J.C. (eds.) (1987). *Methodology in TESOL. A book of readings* (pp. 339–354). New York: Newbury House/Harper and Row.

Long, M.H. (1983d). Linguistic and conversational adjustments to non-native speakers. *Studies in Second Language Acquisition* 5, 2, 177–193.

Long, M.H. (1983e). Training the second language teacher as classroom researcher. In Alatis, J.E., Stern, H.H., & Strevens, P.D. (eds.), *GURT '83. Applied linguistics and the preparation of second language teachers: Towards a rationale* (pp. 281–297). Washington, DC: Georgetown University Press.

Long, M.H. (1984). Process and product in ESL program evaluation. *TESOL Quarterly* 18, 3, 409–425.

Long, M.H. (1985a). A role for instruction in second language acquisition: Task based language teaching. In Hyltenstam, K., & Pienemann, M. (eds.), *Modeling and assessing second language development* (pp. 77–99). Clevedon, Avon: Multilingual Matters.

Long, M.H. (1985b). Input and second language acquisition theory. In Gass, S.M., & Madden, C.G. (eds.), *Input in second language acquisition* (pp. 377–393). Rowley, MA: Newbury House.

Long, M.H. (1987). Task, group and task-group interactions. *University of Hawai'i Working Papers in ESL* 8, 2, 1–26. Also in Anivan, S. (ed.), *Language teaching methodology for the nineties* (pp. 31–50). Singapore: Regional English Language Centre/Singapore University Press.

Long, M.H. (1988). Instructed interlanguage development. In Beebe, L.M. (ed.), *Issues in second language acquisition: Multiple perspectives* (pp. 115–141). Cambridge, MA: Newbury House/Harper and Row.

Long, M.H. (1990a). The least a second language acquisition theory needs to explain. *TESOL Quarterly* 24, 4, 649–666. Reprinted in Brown, H.D., & Gonzo, S. (eds.) (1994). *Readings on second language acquisition* (pp. 470–490). Englewood Cliffs, NJ: Prentice Hall Regents.

Long, M.H. (1990b). Maturational constraints on language development. *Studies in Second Language Acquisition* 12, 3, 251–285.

Long, M.H. (1991). Focus on form: A design feature in language teaching methodology. In de Bot, K., Ginsberg, R.B., & Kramsch, C. (eds.), *Foreign language research in cross-cultural perspective* (pp. 39–52). Amsterdam: John Benjamins.

Long, M.H. (1992). Fragile features in language development, loss and impairment. Paper presented at the NIMH Colloquium on Second Language Acquisition and Philosophy of Science. Washington, DC.

Long, M.H. (1996a). Authenticity and learning potential in L2 classroom discourse. University of Hawai'i Working Papers in ESL 14, 2, 127–149. Also in Jacobs, G.M. (ed.), *Language classrooms of tomorrow: Issues and responses* (pp. 148–169). Singapore: SEAMEO Regional Language Centre.

Long, M.H. (1996b). The role of the linguistic environment in second language acquisition. In Ritchie, W.C., & Bahtia, T.K. (eds.), *Handbook of second language acquisition* (pp. 413–468). New York: Academic Press.

Long, M.H. (1996c). The Mondragon Co-operative Federation: A model for our times? *Libertarian Labor Review* 19, 19–36.

Long, M.H. (1998). Focus on form in task-based language teaching. University of Hawai'i Working Papers in ESL 16, 2, 35–49. Also in Lambert, R.L., & Shohamy, E. (eds.), *Language policy and pedagogy* (pp. 179–192). Amsterdam and Philadelphia, PA: John Benjamins. 2000.

Long, M.H. (2000a). Focus on form in task-based language teaching. In Lambert, R.L., & Shohamy, E. (eds.), *Language policy and pedagogy* (pp. 179–192). Philadelphia, PA: John Benjamins.

Long, M.H. (2000b). Acquisition and teaching. In Byram, M. (ed.), *Encyclopedia of language teaching* (pp. 4–5). London: Routledge.

Long, M.H. (2003a). Stabilization and fossilization in interlanguage development. In

Doughty, C.J., & Long, M.H. (eds.), *Handbook of second language acquisition* (pp. 487–535). Oxford: Blackwell.

Long, M.H. (2003b). Espanol para fines específicos: Textos o tareas? [Spanish for specific purposes: Texts or tasks?]. In Jauregui, K. (ed.), *Espanol para fines específicos. Actas del 11 CIEFE, Amsterdam, 2003* (pp. 15–39). Madrid: Ministerio de Educacion y Ciencia del Reino de Espana.

Long, M.H. (2005a). Problems with supposed counter-evidence to the critical period hypothesis. *International Review of Applied Linguistics* 43, 287–317.

Long, M.H. (2005b). A rationale for needs analysis and needs analysis research. In Long, M.H. (ed.), *Second language needs analysis* (pp. 1–16). Cambridge: Cambridge University Press.

Long, M.H. (2005c). Methodological issues in learner needs analysis. In Long, M.H. (ed.), *Second language needs analysis* (pp. 19–76). Cambridge: Cambridge University Press.

Long, M.H. (ed.) (2005d). *Second language needs analysis*. Cambridge: Cambridge University Press.

Long, M.H. (2007a). Second language acquisition theories. In Long, M.H. (ed.), *Problems in SLA* (pp. 3–20). Mahwah, NJ: Erlbaum.

Long, M.H. (2007b). Problem solving and theory change in SLA. In Long, M.H. (ed.), *Problems in SLA* (pp. 21–40). Mahwah, NJ: Erlbaum.

Long, M.H. (2007c). Age differences and the sensitive periods controversy in SLA. In Long, M.H. (ed.), *Problems in SLA* (pp. 43–74). Mahwah, NJ: Erlbaum.

Long, M.H. (2007d). Recasts in SLA: The story so far. In Long, M.H. (ed.), *Problems in SLA* (pp. 75–116). Mahwah, NJ: Erlbaum.

Long, M.H. (2007e). Texts, tasks, and the advanced learner. In Long, M.H. (ed.), *Problems in SLA* (pp. 119–138). Mahwah, NJ: Erlbaum.

Long, M.H. (2009). Methodological principles in language teaching. In Long, M.H., & Doughty, C.J. (eds.), *Handbook of language teaching* (pp. 373–394). Oxford: Blackwell.

Long, M.H. (2010). *The English language needs of international fellows and post-docs at NIH.* Technical Report. Silver Spring, MD.

Long, M.H. (2013a). Maturational constraints on child and adult SLA. In Granena, G., & Long, M.H. (eds.), *Sensitive periods, language aptitude, and ultimate L2 attainment* (pp. 3–41). Amsterdam and Philadelphia, PA: John Benjamins.

Long, M.H. (2013b). Needs analysis. In Chapelle, C. (ed.), *The encyclopedia of applied linguistics.* Oxford: Wiley-Blackwell.

Long, M.H. (2013c). Identifying and satisfying language needs in the tourist industry. Plenary address to the First Annual Conference on Language and Tourism. Mallorca: University of the Balearic Islands, April 14–15, 2011. In Bosch Roig, G.I. (ed.), *Teaching foreign languages for tourism: Research and practice* (pp. 21–44). Bern: Peter Lang.

Long, M.H. (in press). Experimental perspectives on classroom interaction. In Markee, N. (ed.), *Handbook of classroom discourse and interaction.* Oxford: Wiley-Blackwell.

Long, M.H., Adams, L., McLean, M., & Castanos, F. (1976). Doing things with words: Verbal interaction in lockstep and small group classroom situations. In Fanselow, J., & Crymes, R. (eds.), *On TESOL '76* (pp. 137–153). Washington, DC: TESOL. Reprinted in Allwright, D. (1988). *Observation in the language classroom* (pp. 153–171). Harlow, Essex: Longman.

Long, M.H., & Adamson, D. (2012). Valdez, G., & Faltis, C. (eds.), *SLA research and Arizona's Structured English Immersion policies, Implementing English language learning policy in Arizona: An examination of legal, historical and current practices of SEI* (pp. 39–55). Clevedon, Avon: Multilingual Matters.

Long, M.H., Allen, W., Cyr, A., Lemelin, C., Ricard, E., Spada, N., & Vogel, P. (1980). *Reading English for academic study.* Rowley, MA: Newbury House.

Long, M.H., Al-Thowaini, A., Al-Thowaini, B., Lee, J., & Vafaee, P. (2013). Input modification, language acquisition and subject matter learning in a laboratory study of a CLIL lesson. Paper presented at the Second Language Research Forum, Provo, UT, October 31–November 2.

Long, M.H., & Crookes, G. (1987). Intervention points in second language classrooms. In Das, B. (ed.), *Patterns of interaction in classrooms in Southeast Asia* (pp. 177–203). Singapore: Regional English Language Centre.

Long, M.H., & Crookes, G. (1992). Three approaches to task-based language teaching. *TESOL Quarterly* 26, 1, 27–56. Reprinted in Van den Branden, K., Bygate, M., & Norris, J.M. (eds.), *Task based language teaching: A reader* (pp. 57–81). Amsterdam: John Benjamins.

Long, M.H., & Crookes, G. (1993). Units of analysis in syllabus design: The case for task. In Crookes, G., & Gass, S.M. (eds.), *Tasks in pedagogical context. Integrating theory and practice* (pp. 9–54). Clevedon, Avon: Multilingual Matters.

Long, M.H., Gor, K., & Jackson, S. (2012). Linguistic correlates of proficiency. Proof of concept with ILR 2–3 in Russian. *Studies in Second Language Acquisition* 34, 1, 99–126.

Long, M.H., Inagaki, S., & Ortega, L. (1998). The role of implicit negative feedback in SLA: Models and recasts in Japanese and Spanish. *Modern Language Journal* 82, 3, 357–371.

Long, M.H., Kim, Y., Lee, Y.-G., & Doughty, C.J. (2003). *Task-based language teaching: A demonstration video* (NFLRC RN #37v). Honolulu, HI: University of Hawai'i, Second Language Teaching & Curriculum Center.

Long, M.H., & Norris, J.M. (2000). Task-based teaching and assessment. In Byram, M. (ed.), *Encyclopedia of language teaching* (pp. 597–603). London: Routledge.

Long, M.H., & Porter, P. (1985). Group work, interlanguage talk, and second language acquisition. *TESOL Quarterly* 19, 2, 207–227.

Long, M.H., & Robinson, P. (1998). Focus on form: Theory, research and practice. In Doughty, C.J., & Williams, J. (eds.), *Focus on form in second language acquisition* (pp. 15–41). Cambridge, England: Cambridge University Press.

Long, M.H., & Ross, S. (1993). Modifications that preserve language and content. In Tickoo, M. (ed.), *Simplification: Theory and application* (pp. 29–52). Singapore: SEAMEO Regional Language Centre.

Long, M.H., & Ross, S. (2009). Input elaboration: A viable alternative to "authentic" and simplified texts. In Namai, K., & Fukada, Y. (eds.), *Toward the fusion of language, culture and education: From the perspectives of international and interdisciplinary research. A feschrift for Yasukata Yano* (pp. 307–325). Tokyo: Kaitakusha.

Long, M.H., & Sato, C.J. (1983). Classroom foreigner talk discourse: Forms and functions of teachers' questions. In Seliger, H.W., & Long, M.H. (eds.), *Classroom-oriented research on second language acquisition* (pp. 268–285), Rowley, MA. Newbury House.

Long, M.H., & Sato, C.J. (1984). Methodological issues in interlanguage studies: An interactionist perspective. In Davies, A., Criper, C., & Howatt, A.P.R. (eds.), *Interlanguage* (pp. 253–280). Edinburgh: Edinburgh University Press.

Luke, A., McHoul, A.W., & Mey, J.L. (1990). On the limits of language planning: Class, state and power. In Baldouf, R., Jr., & Luke, A. (eds.), *Language planning and education in Australasia and the South Pacific* (pp. 25–44). Clevedon, Avon: Multilingual Matters.

Lukyanchenko, A., Idsardi, W.J., & Jiang, N. (2011). Opening your ears: The role of L1 in processing of nonnative prosodic contrasts. In Granena, G., Koeth, J., Lee-Ellis, S., Lukyanchenko, A., Prieto Botana, G., & Rhoades, E. (eds.), *Selected proceedings of the second language research forum 2010* (pp. 50–62). Somerville, MA: Cascadilla Press.

Lundstrom, P. (1994). Task-based language teaching in a learner-centered setting: A case study. Term paper, ESL 750 (Task-based language learning). Honolulu, HI: ESL Department, University of Hawai'i at Manoa.

Luyten, L., & Houben, L. (2002). *Bonte Was: Verslag pilootfase*. Leuven: Centrum voor Taal en Migratie. Internal report.

Lynch, B., & Davidson, F. (1994). Criterion-referenced language test development: Linking curricula, teachers, and tests. *TESOL Quarterly* 28, 4, 727–743.

Lynch, B.K. (1990). A context-adaptive model for program evaluation. *TESOL Quarterly* 24, 1, 23–42.

Lynch, B.K. (1995). Using triangulation in naturalistic research. Paper presented at the AAAL Conference, Long Beach, CA, March 27.

Lynch, B.K. (1996). *Language program evaluation: Theory and practice*. Cambridge: Cambridge University Press.

Lynch, T. (1987). Modifications to foreign listeners: The stories teachers tell. ERIC Document ED 274 255. Washington, DC: Center for Applied Linguistics.

Lynch, T., & Anderson, K. (1991). Do you mind if I come in here? – A comparison of EAP seminar/discussion materials and the characteristics of real academic interaction. In Adams, P., Heaton, B., & Howarth, P. (eds.), *Socio-cultural issues in English for specific purposes* (pp. 88–99). London: Modern English Publications.

Lynch, T., & Maclean, J. (2001). A case of exercising: Effects of immediate task repetition on learners' performance. In Bygate, M., Skehan, P., & Swain, M. (eds.), *Researching pedagogic tasks: Second language learning, teaching and testing* (pp. 141–162). Harlow: Longman.

Lyster, R. (1994). The effect of functional-analytic teaching on aspects of French immersion students' sociolinguistic competence. *Applied Linguistics* 15, 263–287.

Lyster, R. (1998). Recasts, repetition and ambiguity in L2 classroom discourse. *Studies in Second Language Acquisition* 20, 1, 51–81.

Lyster, R., & Ranta, L. (1997). Corrective feedback and learner uptake: Negotiation of form in communicative classrooms. *Studies in Second Language Acquisition* 19, 1, 37–66.

Lyster, R., & Saito, K. (2010). Oral feedback in classroom SLA: A meta-analysis. *Studies in Second Language Acquisition* 32, 265–302.

MacDonald, T. (1985). *Making a new people: Education in revolutionary Cuba*. Vancouver: North Star.

Mackay, R. (1978). Identifying the nature of the learner's needs. In Mackay, R., & Mountford, A. (eds.), *English for specific purposes* (pp. 21–42). London: Longman.

Mackay, R. (1993). Embarrassment and hygiene in the classroom. *ELT Journal* 47, 1, 32–39.

Mackay, R., & Bosquet, M. (1981). LSP curriculum development – From policy to practice. In Mackay, R., & Palmer, J.D. (eds.), *Languages for specific purposes* (pp. 1–28). Rowley, MA: Newbury.

Mackay, R., & Mountford, A. (eds.) (1978). *English for specific purposes*. London: Longman.

Mackey, A. (1999). Input, interaction and second language development. *Studies in Second Language Acquisition* 21, 4, 557–587.

Mackey, A. (2006). Feedback, noticing and instructed second language learning. *Applied Linguistics* 27, 405–430.

Mackey, A. (ed.) (2007). *Conversational interaction in second language acquisition*. Oxford: Oxford University Press.

Mackey, A. (2012). *Input, interaction, and corrective feedback in L2 learning*. Oxford: Oxford University Press.

Mackey, A., Abbuhl, R., & Gass, S.M. (2012). Interactionist approach. In Gass, S.M., & Mackey, A. (eds.), *The Routledge handbook of second language acquisition* (pp. 7–23). New York: Routledge.

Mackey, A., Fujii, A., Biesenbach-Lucas, S., Weger, H., Dolgova-Jacobson, N., Fogle, L., Lake, J., Sondermann, K., Kim, K., Tagarelli, M., Takada, A., Watanabe, A., & Abbuhl, R. (2012). Classrooms, FL and SL context, and task-based activities. In McDonough, K., & Mackey, A. (eds.), *New perspectives on classroom interaction in second language research*. Amsterdam: John Benjamins.

Mackey, A., & Goo, J. (2007). Interaction research in SLA: A meta-analysis and research synthesis. In Mackey, A. (ed.), *Conversational interaction in second language acquisition* (pp. 407–452). Oxford: Oxford University Press.

Mackey, A., Kanganas, P., & Oliver, R. (2007). Task familiarity and interactional feedback in child ESL classrooms. *TESOL Quarterly* 41, 2, 285–312.

Mackey, A., & Philp, J. (1998). Conversational interaction and second language development: Recasts, responses, and red herrings? *Modern Language Journal* 82, 3, 338–356.

Mackey, A., & Silver, R.E. (2005). Interactional tasks and English L2 learning by immigrant children in Singapore. *System* 33, 239–260.

Malcolm, L. (1987). What rules govern tense usage in scientific articles? *English for Specific Purposes* 6, 1, 31–43.

Maley, A. (1984). Constraints-based syllabuses. In Read, J.A.S. (ed.), *Trends in language syllabus design* (pp. 68–90). Singapore: SEAMEO Regional Language Centre.

Malvern, D., & Richards, B. (2002). Investigating accommodation in language proficiency interviews using a new measure of lexical diversity. *Language Testing* 19, 85–104.

Manheimer, R. (1993). Close the task, improve the discourse. *Estudios de Linguistica Aplicada* 17, 18–40.

Manicas, P.T. (1982). John Dewey: Anarchism and the political state. *Transactions of the Charles S. Peirce 539 Society* 18, 2, 133–157.

Mansbridge, J. (ed.) (1990). *Beyond self-interest*. Chicago: University of Chicago Press.

Marinova-Todd, S. (2003). Comprehensive analysis of ultimate attainment in adult second language acquisition. Unpublished doctoral dissertation. Boston, MA: Harvard University, Graduate School of Education.

Markee, N. (1986). The relevance of sociopolitical factors to communicative course design. *English for Specific Purposes* 5, 1, 3–16.

Markee, N. (1988). Toward an appropriate technology model of communicative course design. Unpublished PhD dissertation. UCLA.

Markee, N. (1993). The diffusion of innovation in language teaching. *Annual Review of Applied Linguistics* 13, 229–243.

Markee, N. (1994). Curricular innovation: Issues and problems. *Applied Language Learning* 5, 2, 1–30.

Markee, N. (1997). Second language acquisition research: A resource for changing teachers' professional cultures? *Modern Language Journal* 81, 1, 80–93.

Markee, N. (2007). *Managing curricular innovation*. Cambridge: Cambridge University Press.

Marriot, H.E. (1990). Intercultural business negotiations: The problem of norm discrepancy. *Australian Review of Applied Linguistics* 7, 33–65.

Marriot, H. (1991). Language planning and language management for tourism shopping situations. Australian Review of Applied Linguistics, Series S, No. 8. 191–222.

Marriot, H.E., & Yamada, N. (1991). Japanese discourse in tourism shopping situations. *Japan and the world*. (Vol. 3, pp. 155–168). Canberra: Australia-Japan Research Centre.

Martinez, R., & Schmitt, N. (2012). A phrasal expressions list. *Applied Linguistics* 33, 3, 299–320.

Marx, R.W., & Walsh, J. (1988). Learning from academic tasks. *The Elementary School Journal* 88, 3, 207–219.

Mason, D. (1989). An examination of authentic dialogues for use in the ESP classroom. *English for Specific Purposes* 8, 1, 85–92.

Master, P. (1994). The effect of systematic instruction on learning the English article system. In Odlin, T. (ed.), *Perspectives on pedagogical grammar* (pp. 229–252). Cambridge: Cambridge University Press.

Master, P. (1997). The English article system: Acquisition, function, and pedagogy. *System* 25, 215–232.

Mathews, R.C., Roussel, L.G., Cochran, B.P., Cook, A.E., & Dunaway, D.L. (2000). The role of implicit learning in the acquisition of generative knowledge. *Cognitive Systems Research* 1, 161–174.

Mawer, G. (1991). *Language audits and industry restructuring.* Sydney: Macquarie University, NCELTR.

Mayberry, R.I., & Eichen, E.B. (1991). The long-lasting advantage of learning sign language in childhood: Another look at the critical period for language acquisition. *Memory and Language* 30, 486–512.

Mayberry, R.I., & Lock, E. (2003). Age constraints on first versus second language acquisition: Evidence for linguistic plasticity and epigenesist. *Brain and Language* 87, 369–384.

McCafferty, S.G., Jacobs, G.M., & DaSilva Iddings, A.-M. (2006). *Cooperative learning and second language teaching.* Cambridge: Cambridge University Press.

McClelland, J.L., Fiez, J.A., & McCandliss, B.D. (2002). Teaching the /r/-/l/ discrimination to Japanese adults: Behavioral and neural aspects. *Physiology and Behavior* 77, 657–662.

McCormick, E.J. (1976). Job and task analysis. In Dunnette, M.D. (ed.), *Handbook of industrial and organizational psychology* (pp. 651–696). Chicago: Rand McNally.

McCormick, E.J., Jeanneret, R.R., & Meecham, R.C. (1972). A study of job characteristics and job dimensions based on the position analysis questionnaire. *Journal of Applied Psychology* 56, 4, 347–368.

McDonough, J. (1994). A teacher looks at teachers' diaries. *English Language Teaching Journal* 48, 1, 57–65.

McDonough, K. (2004). Learner-learner interaction during pair and small group activities in a Thai EFL context. *System* 32, 207–224.

McDonough, K., & Chaitmongkol, W. (2007). Teachers' and learners' reactions to a task-based EFL course in Thailand. *TESOL Quarterly* 41, 1, 107–132.

McIntosh, A. (1965). Saying. *Review of English literature* 6, 2, 9–20.

McKay, I. (2008). *Mutual aid: An introduction and evaluation.* Retrieved from http://anarchism.pageabode.com/anarcho/mutual-aid-an-introduction-and-evaluation (September 28, 2009).

McKay, S.L. (1980). On notional syllabuses. *Modern Language Journal* 64, 2, 179–186.

McKenna, E. (1987). Preparing foreign students to enter discourse communities in the US. *English for Specific Purposes* 6, 187–202.

McMahon, A. (1994). *Understanding language change.* Cambridge: Cambridge University Press.

McNamara, T. (1996). Designing a performance test: The occupational English test. In McNamara, T. (ed.), *Measuring second language performance* (pp. 91–116). London: Longman.

Mead, R. (1982). Review of Munby, J. Communicative syllabus design, 1978. *Applied Linguistics* 3, 1, 70–77.

Meara, P. (2005). *LLAMA language aptitude tests.* Swansea: Lognostics.

Meara, P. (2009). *Connected Words: Word associations and second language vocabulary acquisition.* Amsterdam: John Benjamins.

Medway, P. (1994). The language component of technological capability: Lessons from architecture. *International Journal of Technology and Design Education* 4, 85–107.

Medway, P., & Andrews, R. (1992). Building with words: Discourse in an architect's office. *Carleton Papers in Applied Language Studies* 9, 1–32.

Mehnert, U. (1998). The effects of different lengths of time for planning on second language performance. *Studies in Second Language Acquisition* 20, 1, 83–108.

Meisel, J.M. (1987). Reference to past events and actions in the development of natural second language acquisition. In Pfaff, C. (ed.), *First and second language acquisition processes* (pp. 206–224). Cambridge, MA: Newbury House.

Meisel, J.M. (2011). *First and second language acquisition.* Cambridge: Cambridge University Press.

Meisel, J.M. (2012). ZISA Project. In Robinson, P. (ed.), *The Routledge encyclopedia of second language acquisition* (pp. 708–709). London: Routledge.

Meisel, J.M., Clahsen, H., & Pienemann, M. (1981). On determining developmental stages in natural second language acquisition. *Studies in Second Language Acquisition* 3, 1, 109–135.

Mellow, D. (1992). Towards a theory of second language transition: Implications from constrained studies of instruction and attrition. Paper presented at SLRF, Michigan State University, April 3.

Mellow, D., Reeder, K., & Forster, E. (1996). Using time series research designs to investigate the effects of instruction on SLA. *Studies in Second Language Acquisition* 18, 3, 325–350.

Messick, S. (1994). The interplay of evidence and consequences in the validation of performance assessments. *Educational Researcher* 23, 13–23.

Met, M. (1991). Learning language through content: Learning content through language. *Foreign Language Annals* 24, 4, 281–295.

Michel, M., Kuiken, F., & Vedder, I. (2007). The influence of complexity in monologic versus dialogic tasks in Dutch L2. *International Review of Applied Linguistics* 45, 241–259.

Mifka-Profozic, N. (2011). Corrective feedback, individual differences, and the L2 acquisition of French preterite and imperfect tenses. Unpublished PhD thesis. Auckland: University of Auckland.

Millar, N. (2010). The processing of malformed formulaic language. *Applied Linguistics* 32, 129–148.

Miller, A.R., Trieman, D.J., Cain, P.S., & Roos, P.S. (eds.) (1980). *Work, jobs, and occupations: A critical review of the dictionary of occupational titles. Final report to the U.S. Dept. of Labor from the Committee on Occupational Classification and Analysis).* Washington, DC: National Academy Press.

Miller, M.A. (1976). *Kropotkin.* Chicago: University of Chicago Press.

Mintz, F. (2013). *Anarchism and workers' self-management in revolutionary Spain.* Oakland, CA: AK Press.

Mislevy, R.L., Steinberg, L.S., & Almond, R.G. (2002). Design and analysis in task-based language assessment. *Language Testing* 19, 4, 477–496.

Miyake, A., & Friedman, N.F. (2001). Individual differences in second language proficiency: Working memory as "language aptitude." In Healy, A.F., & Bourne, L.E. (eds.), *Foreign language learning: Psycholinguistic studies on training and retention* (pp. 339–364). Mahwah, NJ: Lawrence Erlbaum Associates.

Mochizuki, N., & Ortega, L. (2008). Balancing communication and grammar in the beginning-level foreign language classroom: A study of guided planning and relativization. *Language Teaching Research* 12, 1, 11–37.

Mohan, B. (1977). Towards a situational curriculum. In Brown, H.D., Yorio, C.A., & Crymes, R. (eds.), *On TESOL '77. Teaching and learning English as a second language: Trends in research and practice* (pp. 250–257). Washington, DC: TESOL.

Mohan, B., & Marshall Smith, S.M. (1992). Context and cooperation in academic tasks. In Nunan, D. (ed.), *Collaborative language learning and teaching* (pp. 81–89). Cambridge: Cambridge University Press.

Mohan, B.A., Leung, C., & Davison, C. (2001). *English as a second language in the mainstream.* London: Pearson.

Montrul, S., & Slabakova, R. (2003). Competence similarities between native and near-native speakers. An investigation of the preterite-imperfect contrast in Spanish. *Studies in Second Language Acquisition* 25, 351–398.

Morris, D.D., Bransford, J.D., & Franks, J.J. (1977). Levels of processing versus transfer-appropriate processing. *Journal of Verbal Learning and Verbal Behavior* 16, 519–533.

Morrison, J. (1978). Designing a course in advanced listening comprehension. In Mackay, R., & Mountford, A. (eds.), *English for specific purposes* (pp. 161–178). London: Longman.

Morrison, R. (1991). *We build the road as we travel: Mondragon, a co-operative system.* Philadelphia, PA: New Society Publishers.

Moskowitz, G. (1978, 1991). *Caring and sharing in the foreign language classroom*. Rowley, MA: Newbury House/Harper Collins.

Motta, S.C. (2012). The Nottingham free school: Notes towards a systematization of praxis. In Haworth, R.H. (ed.), *Anarchist pedagogies. Collective action, theories, and critical reflections on education* (pp. 145–161). Oakland, CA: PM Press.

Mountford, A. (1988). Factors influencing ESP materials production and use. In Chamberlain, D., & Baumgardner, R.J. (eds.), *ESP in the classroom: Practice and evaluation* (pp. 76–84). Oxford: Modern English Publications.

Munby, J. (1978). *Communicative syllabus design*. Cambridge: Cambridge University Press.

Munby, J. (1984). Communicative syllabus design: Principles and problems. In Read, J.A.S. (ed.), *Trends in language syllabus design*. Singapore: SEAMEO Regional Language Centre.

Munnich, E., & Landau, B. (2010). Developmental decline in the acquisition of spatial language. *Language Learning and Development* 6, 1, 32–59.

Muñoz, C. (2007). CLIL: Some thoughts on its psycholinguistics principles. *RESLA Models of Practice in CLIL*. Monographic Issue, 17–26.

Muranoi, H. (2000). Focus on form through interaction enhancement: Integrating formal instruction into a communicative task in EFL classrooms. *Language Learning* 50, 4, 617–673.

Murphy, D.F., & Candlin, C.N. (1979). Engineering lecture discourse and listening comprehension. *Practical Papers in Language Education* 2, 1–79. Lancaster: University of Lancaster.

Murray, D.E. (ed.) (2008). *Planning change, changing plans: Innovations in second language teaching*. Ann Arbor, MI: University of Michigan Press.

Musumeci, D. (1997). *An exploration of the historical relationship between theory and practice in second language teaching*. New York: McGraw-Hill.

Musumeci, D. (2009). History of language teaching. In Long, M.H., & Doughty, C.J. (eds.), *Handbook of language teaching* (pp. 42–62). Oxford: Blackwell.

Najar, R. (1992). Transfer of training and second language tasks. MA in ESL thesis. Honolulu, HI: University of Hawai'i at Manoa.

Nation, I.S.P. (2006). How large a vocabulary is needed for reading and listening? *Canadian Modern Language Review* 63, 59–82.

Nation, I.S.P., & Chung, M. (2009). Teaching and testing vocabulary. In Long, M., & Doughty, C. (eds.), *Handbook of language teaching* (pp. 543–559). Malden, MA: Wiley-Blackwell.

Nattinger, J.R., & DeCarrico, J.S. (1992). *Lexical phrases and language teaching*. Oxford: Oxford University Press.

Naves, T. (2009). Effective content and language integrated learning (CLIL) programmes. In Ruiz de Zarabe, Y., & Jimenez Catalan, R.M. (eds.), *Content and language integrated learning. Evidence from research in Europe* (pp. 22–40). Bristol: Multilingual Matters.

Navon, D. (1989). The locus of attentional selection: Is it early, late, or neither? *European Journal of Cognitive Psychology* 1, 47–68.

Nelson, K.E. (1987). Some observations from the perspective of the rare event cognitive comparison theory of language acquisition. In Nelson, K.E., & Van Kleek, A. (eds.), *Children's language* (Vol. 6, pp. 289–331). Hillsdale, NJ: Lawrence Erlbaum.

Nemeth, D., Janacsek, K., & Fiser, J. (2013). Age-dependent and coordinated shift in performance between implicit and explicit skill learning. *Frontiers in Computational Neuroscience* 7, 147, 1–13.

Nemser, W. (1971). Approximative systems in foreign language learners. *International Review of Applied Linguistics* 9, 115–123.

Neumann, O. (1996). Theories of attention. In Neumann, O., & Sanders, A.F. (eds.), *Handbook of perception and action: Attention* (Vol. 3, pp. 389–446). London: Academic Press.

Neustupny, J.V. (1988). Australia and Japan: Cross-cultural communication problems. *Vox* 1, 28–321.

Neustupny, J.V. (1995a). Problems in Australian-Japanese contact situations. In Pride, J.B. (ed.), *Cross-cultural encounters: Communication and Miscommunication* (pp. 44–64). Melbourne: River Seine.

Neustupny, J.V. (1995b). Language norms in Australian-Japanese contact situations. In Clyne, M.G. (ed.), *Australia, meeting-place of languages* (pp. 161–170). Canberra: Pacific Linguistics.

Newmark, L. (1966). How not to interfere with language learning. *International Journal of American Linguistics* 32, 1, 70–83. Reprinted in Lester, M. (ed.) (1970). *Readings in applied transformational grammar* (pp. 219–227). New York: Holt.

Newmark, L. (1971). A minimal language-teaching program. In Pimsleur, P., & Quinn, T. (eds.), *The psychology of second language learning* (pp. 11–18). Cambridge: Cambridge University Press.

Newmark, L., & Reibel, D. (1968). Necessity and sufficiency in language learning. *International Review of Applied Linguistics* 4, 2, 145–164.

Newport, E. (1990). Maturational constraints on language learning. *Cognitive Science* 14, 11–28.

Newport, E.L. (2002). Critical periods in language development. In Nadel, L. (ed.), *Encyclopedia of cognitive science* (pp. 737–739). London: Macmillan/Nature Publishing Group.

Newton, J. (1991). Negotiation: Negotiating what? Paper presented at the SEAMEO Conference on Second Language Acquisition and the Second/Foreign Language Classroom. Singapore: Regional English Language Center.

Newton, J. (2013). Incidental vocabulary learning in classroom communication tasks. *Language Teaching Research* 17, 2, 164–187.

Nicholas, H. (1993). *Languages at the crossroads: The report of the national enquiry into the employment and supply of teachers of languages other than English.* Canberra: Australian Government Publishing Service.

Nicholas, H., Lightbown, P.M., & Spada, N. (2001). Recasts as feedback to language learners. *Language Learning* 51, 4, 719–758.

Nielson, K. (2010). Results of the first stage of an initial needs analysis for CASA de Maryland. Unpublished manuscript. College Park, MD: University of Maryland, PhD Program in Second Language Acquisition.

Nielson, K.B., Masters, M.C., Rhoades, E., & Freynik, S. (2009). *Prototype implementation of an online Chinese course: An analysis of course implementation and learner performance. (TTO 82131).* College Park, MD: University of Maryland Center for Advanced Study of Language.

Nobblit, G.W., & Hare, R.D. (1988). *Meta-ethnography: Synthesizing qualitative studies.* Beverly Hills, CA: Sage.

Nore, G. (1990). Peer tutoring in vocational literacy skills. *TESL Canada Journal* 7, 2, 66–74.

Norris, J., Brown, J. D., Hudson, T., & Yoshioka, J. (1998). *Designing second language performance assessments.* Technical Report # 18. Honolulu, HI: University of Hawai'i, Second Language Teaching and Curriculum Center.

Norris, J.M. (2000). Purposeful language assessment. *English Teaching Forum* 38, 1, 18–23.

Norris, J.M. (2001). Identifying rating criteria for task-based EAP assessment. In Hudson, T.D., & Brown, J.D. (eds.), *A focus on language test development: Expanding the language proficiency construct across a variety of tests* (pp. 163–204). Honolulu, HI: University of Hawai'i Press.

Norris, J.M. (2002). Special issue: "Interpretations, intended uses and designs in task-based language assessment." *Language Testing* 19, 4, 337–346.

Norris, J.M. (2008). *Validity evaluation in language assessment.* New York: Peter Lang.

Norris, J.M. (2009). Task-based teaching and testing. In Long, M.H., & Doughty, C.J.

(eds.), *Handbook of language teaching* (pp. 578–594). Oxford: Blackwell.

Norris, J.M. (2013). Some challenges in assessment for teacher licensure, program accreditation, and educational reform. *Modern Language Journal* 97, 2, 554–560.

Norris, J.M., Brown, J.D., Hudson, T., & Yoshioka, J. (1998). *Designing second language performance assessments*. Technical Report #18. Honolulu, HI: Second Language Teaching and Curriculum Center, University of Hawai'i at Manoa.

Norris, J.M., Brown, J.D., Hudson, T.D., & Bonk, W. (2002). Examinee abilities and task difficulty in task-based second language performance assessment. *Language Testing* 19, 4, 395–418.

Norris, J.M., Bygate, M., & Van den Branden, K. (2009). Task-based language assessment. In Van den Branden, K., Bygate, M., & Norris, J.M. (eds.), *Task-based language teaching: A reader*. Amsterdam/Philadelphia, PA: John Benjamins.

Norris, J.M., & Ortega, L. (2000). Effectiveness of L2 instruction: A research synthesis and quantitative meta-analysis. *Language Learning* 50, 3, 417–528.

Norris, J.M., & Ortega, L. (2009). Towards an organic approach to investigating CAF in instructed SLA: The case of complexity. *Applied Linguistics* 30, 555–578.

Nuevo, A. (2006). Task complexity and interaction: L2 learning opportunities and development. Unpublished doctoral dissertation. Washington, DC: Georgetown University.

Nunan, D. (1987). Communicative language teaching: Making it work. *English Language Teaching Journal* 41, 2, 136–145.

Nunan, D. (1988). *The learner-centered curriculum*. Cambridge: Cambridge University Press.

Nunan, D. (1989). *Designing tasks for the communicative classroom*. Cambridge: Cambridge University Press.

Nunan, D. (1992). *Collaborative language learning and teaching*. Cambridge: Cambridge University Press.

Nunan, D. (1996). *Atlas*. Boston, MA: Heinle and Heinle.

Nunan, D. (2004). *Task-based language teaching*. Cambridge: Cambridge University Press.

Ochs, E.O., & Schieffelin, B.B. (eds.) (1979). *Developmental pragmatics*. New York: Academic Press.

O'Connell, S. (2012). A task-based language teaching approach to the police traffic stop. Term paper, SLA 754: Task-Based Language Teaching. PhD in SLA Program: College Park, MD: University of Maryland.

Ogata, M. (1992). Language needs of EFL students in Japanese high schools. Scholarly Paper. Honolulu, HI: Department of Second Language Studies, University of Hawai'i at Manoa.

Oh, S.-Y. (2001). Two types of input modification and EFL reading comprehension: Simplification versus elaboration. *TESOL Quarterly* 35, 1, 69–96.

Oliver, R. (1995). Negative feedback in child NS-NNS conversation. *Studies in Second Language Acquisition* 18, 4, 459–481.

Oliver, R., Grote, E., Rochecouste, J., & Exell, M. (2012). Addressing the language and literacy needs of aboriginal high school VET students who speak SAE as an additional language. *Australian Journal of Indigenous Education* 41, 2, 229–239.

Oller, J.W., & Obrecht, D.H. (1968). Pattern drill and communicative activity: A psycholinguistic experiment. *International Review of Applied Linguistics* 6, 165–174.

Oller, J.W., & Obrecht, D.H. (1969). The psycholinguistic principle of informational sequence: An experiment in second language learning. *International Review of Applied Linguistics* 7, 117–123.

Oller, J.W., Jr. (1971). Language communication and second language learning. In Pimsleur, P., & Quinn, T. (eds.), *The psychology of second language learning* (pp. 171–179). Cambridge: Cambridge University Press.

Olsen, L.A., & Huckin, T.N. (1990). Point-driven understanding in engineering lecture comprehension. *English for Specific Purposes* 9, 1, 33–47.

Ono, L., & Witzel, J. (2002) Recasts, salience, and morpheme acquisition. Scholarly Paper. Honolulu, HI: University of Hawai'i, Department of Second Language Studies. [Abbreviated version: Recasts, morpheme acquisition, and salience of form. *Proceedings of the Twentieth Annual Meeting of the Japanese Cognitive Science Society*, pp. 212–213.].

O'Neill, S., & Hatoss, A. (2003). Harnessing a nation's linguistic competence: Identifying and addressing needs for LOTE in the tourism and hospitality industry. *Australian Review of Applied Linguistics* 26, 2, 31–45.

Oppenheim, A.N. (1966). *Questionnaire design and attitude measurement*. New York: Basic Books.

Orikasa, K. (1989). A needs analysis for an EFL program in Japan: A systematic approach to program development. *University of Hawai'i Working Papers in ESL* 8, 1, 1–47.

Ortega, L. (1999). Planning and focus on form in oral L2 performance. *Studies in Second Language Acquisition* 21, 1, 109–148.

Ortega, L. (2009). Sequences and processes in language learning. In Long, M.H., & Doughty, C.J. (eds.), *Handbook of language teaching* (pp. 81–105). Oxford: Blackwell.

Ortega, L., & Long, M.H. (1997). The effects of models and recasts on object topicalization and adverb placement in L2 Spanish. *Spanish Applied Linguistics* 1, 1, 65–86.

Orwell, G. (1938/2000). *Homage to Catalonia*. New York: Martin Secker and Warberg/New York: Mariner Books.

O'Rourke, B. (2008). The other C in CMC: What alternative data sources can tell us about text-based synchronous computer-mediated communication and language learning. *Computer Assisted Language Learning* 21, 3, 227–251.

Oskarsson, M. (1972). Comparative method studies in foreign language teaching. *Moderna Sprak* 66, 350–366.

Oskarsson, M. (1973). Assesssing the relative effectiveness of two methods of teaching English to adults. *International Review of Applied Linguistics* 10, 3, 251–261.

Ostler, S. (1980). A survey of academic needs for advanced ESL. *TESOL Quarterly* 14, 4, 489–502.

Oxford, R.L. (1997). Cooperative learning; collaborative learning; and interaction: Three communicative strands in the language classroom. *The Modern Language Journal* 81, 4, 443–456.

Oyama, S. (1978). The sensitive period and comprehension of speech. *Working Papers on Bilingualism* 16, 1–17.

Pacton, S., & Perruchet, P. (2008). An attention-based associative account of adjacent and non-adjacent dependency learning. *Journal of Experimental Psychology. Learning, Memory, and Cognition* 34, 80–96.

Paradis, M. (2004). *A neurolinguistic theory of bilingualism*. Amsterdam: John Benjamins.

Paradis, M. (2009). *Declarative and procedural determinants of second languages*. Amsterdam: John Benjamins.

Paribakht, T.S., & Wesche, M. (1999). Reading and "incidental" L2 vocabulary acquisition: An introspective study of lexical inferencing. *Studies in Second Language Acquisition* 21, 195–224.

Parker, K., & Chaudron, C. (1987). The effects of linguistic simplification and elaborative modification on L2 comprehension. *University of Hawai'i Working Papers in ESL* 6, 2, 107–133.

Parker, O. (1986). Cultural clues to the Middle Eastern students. In Valdes, J. (ed.), *Culture bound: Bridging the cultural gap in language teaching* (pp. 94–101). Cambridge: Cambridge University Press.

Parkinson, B., & Howell-Richardson, C. (1990). Learner diaries. In Brumfit, C., & Mitchell, R. (eds.), *Research in the language classroom. ELT Documents 133* (pp. 128–140). Oxford: Pergamon.

Pashler, H., McDaniel, M., Rohrer, D., & Bjork, R. (2009). Learning styles: Concepts and evidence. *Psychological Science in the Public Interest* 9, 105–119.

Paul, M. (1991). Negotiating open and closed tasks. Term paper, ESL 650 (Second language acquisition). Honolulu, HI: University of Hawai'i at Manoa.

Paulston, C.B. (1970). Structural pattern drills: A classification. *Foreign Language Annals* 4, 2, 187–193.

Paulston, C.B. (1971). The sequencing of structural pattern drills. *TESOL Quarterly* 5, 3, 197–208.

Paulston, C.B. (1981). Notional syllabuses revisited: Some comments. *Applied Linguistics* 2, 1, 93–95.

Paulston, C.B., & Bruder, M.N. (1976). *Teaching English as a second language: Techniques and procedures.* Cambridge, MA: Winthrop.

Pavesi, M. (1986). Markedness, discoursal modes, and relative clause formation in a formal and an informal context. *Studies in Second Language Acquisition* 81, 1, 38–55.

Pellicer-Sanchez, A., & Schmitt, N. (2010). Incidental vocabulary acquisition from an authentic novel: Do *things fall apart? Reading in a Foreign Language* 22, 1, 31–55.

Perez, P., Jordana, M., Paz, A., & Ackelsberg, M. (n.d). *The modern school movement. Historical and personal notes on the Ferrer schools in Spain.* Croton-on-Hudson, NY: Friends of the Modern School.

Perrachione, T.K., Lee, J., Ha, L.Y.Y., & Wong, P.C.M. (2011). Learning a novel phonological contrast depends on interactions between individual differences and training paradigm design. *Journal of the Acoustical Society of America* 130, 461–472.

Peterson, N.G., & Bownas, D.A. (1982). Skill, task structure, and performance acquisition. In Dunnette, M.D., & Fleishman, E.A. (eds.), *Human performance and productivity* (pp. 49–106). Hillsdale, NJ: Lawrence Erlbaum.

Petitto, L.A., Berens, M.S., Kovelman, I., Dubins, M.H., Jasinska, K., & Shalinsky, M. (2012). The "perceptual wedge hypothesis" as the basis for bilingual babies' phonetic processing advantage: New insights from fNIRS brain imaging. *Brain and Language* 121, 130–143.

Peyton, J.K., & Reed, L. (1990). *Dialogue journal writing with nonnative English speakers: A handbook for teachers.* Alexandria, VA: TESOL.

Phillips, S.U. (1972). Participant structures and communicative competence: Warm Springs children in community and classroom. In Cazden, C.B., John, V.P., & Hymes, D. (eds.), *Functions of language in the classroom.* New York: Teachers College Press.

Phillipson, R. (1988). Linguicism: Structures and ideologies in linguistic imperialism. In Skutnabb-Kangas, T., & Cummins, J. (eds.), *Minority education: From shame to struggle* (pp. 339–358). Clevedon, Avon: Multilingual Matters.

Phillipson, R. (1992). *Linguistic imperialism.* Oxford: Oxford University Press.

Phillipson, R. (2009). *Linguistic imperialism continued.* Hyderabad: Orient Black Swan.

Phillipson, R., & Skutnabb-Kangas, T. (2009). The politics and policies of language and language teaching. In Long, M.H., & Doughty, C.J. (eds.), *Handbook of language teaching* (pp. 26–41). Malden, MA: Wiley-Blackwell.

Philp, J., Oliver, R., & Mackey, A. (2006). The impact of planning time on children's task-based interactions. *System* 34, 547–565.

Pica, T. (1983). Adult acquisition of English as a second language under different conditions of exposure. *Language Learning* 33, 4, 465–497.

Pica, T. (1987). Second language acquisition, social interaction, and the classroom. *Applied Linguistics* 8, 1, 1–25.

Pica, T. (1994). Research on negotiation: What does it reveal about second language learning conditions, processes, and outcomes? *Language Learning* 44, 4, 493–527.

Pica, T. (2002). Subject-matter content: How does it assist the interactional and linguistic needs of classroom language learners? *Modern Language Journal* 86, 1–19.

Pica, T. (2009). Second language acquisition in the instructional environment. In Ritchie, W.C., & Bhatia, T.K. (eds.), *The new handbook of second language acquisition* (pp. 473–501). Bingley: Emerald.

Pica, T., & Doughty, C.J. (1985a). Input and interaction in communicative language classrooms: A comparison of teacher-fronted and group activities. In Gass, S.M., & Madden, C. (eds.), *Input and second language acquisition* (pp. 115–132). Rowley, MA: Newbury House.

Pica, T., & Doughty, C.J. (1985b). The role of group work in classroom second language acquisition. *Studies in Second Language Acquisition* 7, 2, 233–248.

Pica, T., Doughty, C.J., & Young, R. (1986). Making input comprehensible: Do interactional modifications help? *ITL Review of Applied Linguistics* 72, 1–25.

Pica, T., Kanagy, R., & Falodun, J. (1993). Choosing and using communication tasks for second language research and instruction. In Crookes, G., & Gass, S.M. (eds.), *Tasks and language learning. Integrating theory and practice* (pp. 9–34). Clevedon, Avon: Multilingual Matters.

Pica, T., Lincoln-Porter, F., Paninos, D., & Linnell, J. (1996). Language learners' interaction: How does it address the input, output, and feedback needs of language learners? *TESOL Quarterly* 30, 1, 59–84.

Pica, T., Young, R., & Doughty, C. (1987). The impact of interaction on comprehension. *TESOL Quarterly* 21, 4, 737–758.

Pienemann, M. (1984). Psychological constraints on the teachability of languages. *Studies in Second Language Acquisition* 6, 2, 186–214.

Pienemann, M. (1985). Learnability and syllabus construction. In Hyltenastam, K., & Pienemann, M. (eds.), *Modelling and assessing second language acquisition* (pp. 23–75). Bristol: Multilingual Matters.

Pienemann, M. (1989). Is language teachable? Psycholinguistic experiments and hypotheses. *Applied Linguistics* 10, 1, 52–79.

Pienemann, M. (1998). *Language processing and second language development. Processability theory*. Amsterdam/Philadelphia, PA: John Benjamins.

Pienemann, M. (2011). Developmental schedules, and Explaining developmental schedules. In Pienemann, M., & Kessler, J.-U. (eds.), *Studying processability theory: An introductory textbook* (pp. 3–11, 50–63). Amsterdam: John Benjamins.

Pienemann, M., & Johnston, M. (1987). Factors influencing the development of language proficiency. In Nunan, D. (ed.), *Applying second language acquisition research* (pp. 45–141). Adelaide: National Curriculum Resource Centre, Adult Migrant Education Program.

Pienemann, M., & Kessler, J.-U. (2011). *Studying processability theory: An introductory textbook*. Amsterdam: John Benjamins.

Pienemann, M., & Kessler, J.-U. (2012). Processability Theory. In Gass, S.M., & Mackey, A. (eds.), *The Routledge handbook of second language acquisition* (pp. 228–246). New York: Routledge.

Pinter, A. (2007). Some benefits of peer-peer interaction: 10-year-old children practising with a communication task. *Language Teaching Research* 11, 187–207.

Pishwa, H. (1994). Abrupt restructuring versus gradual acquisition. In Blackshire-Belay, C.A. (ed.), *Current issues in second language acquisition and development* (pp. 143–166). Lanham, MD: University Press of America.

Plough, I., & Gass, S.M. (1993). Interlocutor and task familiarity effects on interactional structure. In Crookes, G., & Gass, S.M. (eds.), *Tasks and language learning. Integrating theory and practice* (pp. 35–56). Clevedon, Avon: Multilingual Matters.

Politzer, R. (1960). *Teaching French: An introduction to applied linguistics*. Boston, MA: Ginn.

Politzer, R.L. (1961). *Foreign language learning: A linguistic introduction*. Englewood Cliffs, NJ: Prentice-Hall.

Politzer, R.L. (1968). The role and place of the explanation in the pattern drill. *International Review of Applied Linguistics* 4, 4, 315–331.

Popham, W.J. (2000). *Modern educational measurement* (3rd edn). Englewood Cliffs, NJ: Prentice-Hall.

Popham, W.J., & Husek, T.R. (1969). Implications of criterion-referenced measurement. *Journal of Educational Measurement* 6, 1–9.

Poulisse, N. (1990). *The use of compensatory strategies by Dutch learners of English*. Eschede: Sneldruk.

Prabhu, N.S. (1980). Reactions and predictions [special issue]. *Bulletin* 4, 1. Bangalore Regional Institute of English, South India.

Prabhu, N.S. (1984). Procedural syllabuses. In Read, J.A.S. (ed.), *Trends in language syllabus design* (pp. 272–280). Singapore: SEAMEO Regional Language Centre.

Prabhu, N.S. (1987). *Second language pedagogy.* Oxford: Oxford University Press.

Prabhu, N.S. (1990a). Comments on Alan Beretta's "Attention to form or meaning? Error treatment in the Bangalore Project." *TESOL Quarterly* 24, 1, 112–115.

Prabhu, N.S. (1990b). Comments on Alan Beretta's paper: "Implementation of the Bangalore Project." *Applied Linguistics* 11, 4, 338–340.

Prator, C. (1979). The cornerstones of method. In Celce-Murcia, M., & McIntosh, L. (eds.), *Teaching English as a second or foreign language* (pp. 5–15). Rowley, MA: Newbury House.

Preston, D. (1989). *Sociolinguistics and second language acquisition.* Oxford: Basil Blackwell.

Purcell, E., & Suter, R. (1980). Predictors of pronunciation accuracy: A reexamination. *Language Learning* 30, 271–287.

Purchase, G. (1996). *Evolution and revolution. An introduction to the life and thought of Peter Kropotkin.* Sydney: Jura Media.

Quirk, R., Greenbaum, S., Leech, G., & Svartvik, J. (1972). *A grammar of contemporary English.* London: Longman.

Rahimpour, M. (1997). Task complexity, task condition, and variation in oral L2 discourse. Unpublished PhD dissertation. Brisbane: University of Queensland.

Rahimpour, M. (1999). Task complexity and variation in interlanguage. In Jungheim, N., & Robinson, P. (eds.), *Pragmatics and pedagogy: Proceedings of the 3rd Pacific Second Language Research Forum* (Vol. 2, pp. 115–134). Tokyo: PacSLRF.

Rahimpour, M., & Hosseini, P. (2010). The impact of task complexity on L2 learners' written narratives. *English Language Teaching* 3, 3, 198–205.

Ramani, E., Chacko, T., Singh, S.J., & Glendinning, E.H. (1988). An ethnographic approach to syllabus design: A case study of the Indian Institute of Science, Bangalore. *The ESP Journal* 7, 1, 81–90.

Rankin, J. (1990). A case for close-mindedness: Complexity, accuracy and attention in closed and open tasks. Term paper, ESL 730 (Task-based language teaching). Honolulu, HI: University of Hawai'i at Manoa.

Ravitch, D. (2010). *The death and life of the great American school system: How testing and choice are undermining education.* New York: Basic Books.

Reber, A. (1979). Implicit learning and tacit knowledge. *Journal of Experimental Psychology* 40, 2, 219–235.

Reber, A.S., & Allen, R. (2000). Individual differences in implicit learning: Implications for the evolution of consciousness. In Kunzendorf, R.G., & Wallace, B. (eds.), *Individual differences in conscious experience* (pp. 227–247). Amsterdam: John Benjamins.

Reber, A.S., Kassin, S.M., Lewsis, S., & Cantor, G.W. (1980). On the relationship between implicit and explicit modes in the learning of a complex rule structure. *Journal of Experimental Psychology: Human Learning and Memory* 6, 492–502.

Reber, A.S., Walkenfeld, F.F., & Hernstadt, R. (1991). Implicit and explicit learning: Individual differences and IQ. *Journal of Experimental Psychology: Learning, Memory, and Cognition* 17, 5, 888–896.

Rebuschat, P., & Williams, J.N. (2012). Implicit and explicit knowledge in second language acquisition. *Applied Psycholinguistics* 33, 4, 829–856.

Rebuschat, P.E. (2013). Measuring implicit and explicit knowledge in second language research. *Language Learning* 63, 3, 595–626.

Rebuschat, P.E. (ed.) (in press). *Implicit and explicit learning of languages.* Amsterdam and Philadelphia, PA: John Benjamins.

Rebuschat, P.E., & Williams, J.N. (2009). Implicit learning of word order. *Proceedings of the 31st Annual Conference of the*

Cognitive Science Society (pp. 425–430). Austin, TX: Cognitive Science Society.

Reeder, P.A., Newport, E.L., & Aslin, R.N. (2009). The role of distributional information in linguistic category formation. In Taatgen, N., & van Rijn, H. (eds.), *Proceedings of the 31st Annual Conference of the Cognitive Science Society* (pp. 2564–2569). Austin, TX: Cognitive Science Society.

Reeder, P.A., Newport, E.L., & Aslin, R.N. (2010). Novel words in novel contexts: The role of distributional information in form-class category learning. In Ohlsson, S., & Catrambone, R. (eds.), *Proceedings of the 32nd Annual Conference of the Cognitive Science Society* (pp. 2063–2068). Austin, TX: Cognitive Science Society.

Reibel, D. (1969). Language learning analysis. *International Review of Applied Linguistics* 7, 4, 283–294.

Reibel, D. (1971). Language learning strategies for the adult. In Pimsleur, P., & Quinn, T. (eds.), *The psychology of second language learning* (pp. 87–96). Cambridge: Cambridge University Press.

Reinharz, S. (1992). *Feminist methods in social research*. New York: Oxford University Press.

Reves, C. (1994). The use of journals in needs identification for academic reading. Term paper, ESL 750 (Task-based language learning). Honolulu, HI: Department of Second Language Studies, University of Hawai'i at Manoa.

Revesz, A. (2009). Task complexity, focus on form, and second language development. *Studies in Second Language Acquisition* 31, 3, 437–470.

Revesz, A. (2011). Task complexity, focus on L2 constructions, and individual differences: A classroom-based study. *Modern Language Journal* 95, Suppl. Issue, 162–181.

Richards, J., Gordon, D., & Harper, A. (1995). *Listen for it. A task-based listening course*. Oxford: Oxford University Press.

Richards, J.C. (1984). The secret life of methods. *TESOL Quarterly* 18, 1, 7–23.

Richardson, M.A. (1995). The use of negative evidence in the second language acquisition of grammatical morphemes. Unpub-

lished MEd thesis. Perth: Graduate School of Education, University of Western Australia.

Richterich, R. (1972). *A model for the definition of language needs of adults learning a modern language*. Strasbourg: Council of Europe.

Richterich, R. (1979). Identifying language needs as a means of determining educational objectives with the learners. *A European unit/credit system for modern language learning by adults* (pp. 71–75). Strasbourg: Council of Europe. Report of the Ludwigshafen Symposium, 1979.

Richterich, R. (ed.) (1983). *Case studies in identifying language needs*. Oxford: Pergamon.

Richterich, R., & Chancerel, J.-L. (1977/1980). *Identifying the needs of adults learning a foreign language*. Strasbourg, France: Council of Europe/Oxford, England: Pergamon.

Richterich, R., & Chancerel, J.-L. (1978). *Identifying the needs of adults learning a foreign language*. Strasbourg: Council for Cultural Cooperation of the Council of Europe.

Riggs, P.J. (1992). Laudan's theory of evolving research traditions. In Riggs, P.D. (ed.), *Whys and ways of science. Introducing philosophical and sociological theories of science* (pp. 95–123). Carlton, Victoria: Melbourne University Press.

Rivers, W. (1964). *The psychologist and the foreign language teacher*. Chicago: University of Chicago Press.

Roberts, C. (1981). Needs analysis for ESP programmes. *Language Learning and Communication* 1, 1, 105–120.

Roberts, C., Davis, E., & Jupp, T. (1992). *Language and discrimination. A study of communication in multi-ethnic workplaces*. London: Longman.

Roberts, J.L. (1982). Recent developments in ELT. In Kinsella, V. (ed.), *Surveys 1 and 2*. Cambridge: Cambridge University Press.

Robinson, P. (1981). *ESP (English for specific purposes: The present position)*. Oxford: Pergamon.

Robinson, P. (1994). Comments on Rod Ellis' "The structural syllabus and second language acquisition." Implicit knowledge, second language learning and syllabus construction. *TESOL Quarterly* 28, 1, 161–166.

Robinson, P. (1995a). Aptitude, awareness, and the fundamental similarity of implicit and explicit second language learning. In Schmidt, R.W. (ed.), *Attention and awareness in foreign language learning* (pp. 303–358). Honolulu, HI: Second Language Teaching and Curriculum Center.

Robinson, P. (1995b). Task complexity and second language narrative discourse. *Language Learning* 45, 2, 283–331.

Robinson, P. (1996). Learning simple and complex second language rules under implicit, incidental, rule-search, and instructed conditions. *Studies in Second Language Acquisition* 18, 1, 27–67.

Robinson, P. (1998). State of the art: SLA theory and second language syllabus design. *The Language Teacher* 22, 4, 7–14.

Robinson, P. (2001a). Task complexity, cognitive resources, and syllabus design. In Robinson, P. (ed.), *Cognition and second language instruction* (pp. 287–318). Cambridge: Cambridge University Press.

Robinson, P. (2001b). Task complexity, task difficulty and task production: Exploring interactions in a componential framework. *Applied Linguistics* 22, 1, 27–57.

Robinson, P. (ed.) (2002a). *Individual differences and instructed language learning.* Amsterdam and Philadelphia, PA: John Benjamins.

Robinson, P. (2002b). Learning conditions, aptitude complexes and SLA: A framework for research and pedagogy. In Robinson, P. (ed.), *Individual differences and instructed language learning* (pp. 113–133). Amsterdam: John Benjamins.

Robinson, P. (2003a). Attention and memory during SLA. In Doughty, C.J., & Long, M.H. (eds.), *Handbook of second language acquisition* (pp. 630–678). Oxford: Blackwell.

Robinson, P. (2003b). Cognitive complexity and task sequencing: A review of studies in a componential framework for second language task design. *International Review of Applied Linguistics* 43, 1, 1–33.

Robinson, P. (2005). Cognitive complexity and task sequencing: Studies in a componential framework for second language task design. *International Review of Applied Linguistics* 43, 1, 1–32.

Robinson, P. (2007a). Criteria for classifying and sequencing pedagogic tasks. In Garcia-Mayo, M.P. (ed.), *Investigating tasks in formal language learning* (pp. 7–26). Clevedon, UK: Multilingual Matters.

Robinson, P. (2007b). Task complexity, theory of mind, and intentional reasoning: Effects on L2 speech production, interaction, uptake and perceptions of task difficulty. *International Review of Applied Linguistics* 45, 193–213.

Robinson, P. (2009). Syllabus design. In Long, M.H., & Doughty, C.J. (eds.), *Handbook of language teaching* (pp. 294–310). Oxford: Blackwell.

Robinson, P. (2010). Situating and distributing cognition across task demands: The SSARC model of pedagogic task sequencing. In Putz, M., & Sicola, L. (eds.), *Cognitive processing in second language acquisition: Inside the learner's mind* (pp. 243–268). Amsterdam: John Benjamins.

Robinson, P. (2011a). Task-based language learning: A review of issues. *Language Learning* 61, Suppl. 1, 1–36.

Robinson, P. (2011b). Second language task complexity, the cognition hypothesis, language learning, and performance. In Robinson, P. (ed.), *Second language task complexity. Researching the cognition hypothesis of language learning and performance* (pp. 3–37). Amsterdam: John Benjamins.

Robinson, P., Cadierno, T., & Shirai, Y. (2009). Time and motion: Measuring the effects of the conceptual demands of tasks on second language speech production. *Applied Linguistics* 30, 4, 533–554.

Robinson, P., & Ellis, N.C. (2008). Conclusion: Cognitive linguistics, second language acquisition and L2 instruction – Issues for research. In Robinson, P., & Ellis, N.C. (eds.), *Handbook of cognitive linguistics and second language acquisition* (pp. 489–545). New York: Routledge.

Robinson, P., & Gilabert, R. (2007). Task complexity, the cognition hypothesis, and second language instruction [special issue]. *International Review of Applied Linguistics* 45, 3, 161–284.

Robinson, P., & Ha, M. (1993). Instance theory and second language rule learning under explicit conditions. *Studies in Second Language Acquisition* 15, 4, 413–438.

Robinson, P., Mackey, A., Gass, S.M., & Schmidt, R.W. (2012). Attention and awareness in second language acquisition. In Gass, S.M., & Mackey, A. (eds.), *The Routledge handbook of second language acquisition* (pp. 247–267). Abingdon, Oxford: Routledge.

Robinson, P., & Ross, S. (1996). The development of task-based assessment in English for academic purposes programs. *Applied Linguistics* 17, 4, 455–476.

Robinson, P., Ting, S.C.-C., & Erwin, J.J. (1995). Investigating second language task complexity. *RELC Journal* 26, 2, 62–79.

Rosenshine, B.V. (1986). Synthesis of research on explicit teaching. *Educational Leadership* 43, 7, 60–69.

Rost, M., & Stratton, R. (1978). *Listening in the real world*. Tucson, AZ: Lingual House.

Russell, J., & Spada, N. (2006). The effectiveness of corrective feedback for the acquisition of L2 grammar. In Norris, J.D., & Ortega, L. (eds.), *Synthesizing research on language learning and teaching* (pp. 133–164). Philadelphia, PA: John Benjamins.

Sachs, G.T. (2007). The challenges of adopting and adapting task-based cooperative teaching and learning in an EFL context. In Van den Branden, K., Van Gorp, K., & Verhelst, M. (eds.), *Tasks in action: Education from a classroom-based perspective*. Newcastle: Cambridge University Press.

Saffran, J.R., Newport, E.L., & Aslin, R.N. (1996). Word segmentation: The role of distributional cues. *Journal of Memory and Language* 35, 606–621.

Sagarra, N., & Abbuhl, R. (2013). Optimizing the noticing of recasts via computer-delivered feedback: Evidence that oral input enhancement and working memory help second language learning. *Modern Language Journal* 97, 1, 196–216.

Samuda, V. (2001). Guiding relationships between form and meaning during task performance: The role of the teacher. In Bygate, M., Skehan, P., & Swain, M. (eds.), *Researching pedagogic tasks: Second language learning, teaching and testing*. Harlow: Pearson Education.

Samuda, V., & Bygate, M. (2008). *Tasks in second language learning*. New York: Palgrave Macmillan.

Sanchez Carrion, J.M. ("Txepetx") (1991). *Un futuro para nuestro pasado. Claves para la recuperacion del euskera y teoria social de las lenguas*. Donostia-San Sebastian: Jose Maria Sanchez Carrion.

Sato, C.J. (1984). Phonological processes in second language acquisition: Another look at interlanguage syllable structure. *Language Learning* 34, 1, 43–57.

Sato, C.J. (1985). Task variation in interlanguage phonology. In Gass, S.M., & Madden, C. (eds.), *Input and second language acquisition* (pp. 181–196). Rowley, MA: Newbury House.

Sato, C.J. (1986). Conversation and interlanguage development: Rethinking the connection. In Day, R.R. (ed.), *"Talking to learn": Conversation in second language acquisition* (pp. 23–45). Rowley, MA: Newbury House.

Sato, C.J. (1988). Origins of complex syntax in interlanguage development. *Studies in Second Language Acquisition* 10, 3, 371–395.

Sato, C.J. (1989). A nonstandard approach to Standard English. *TESOL Quarterly* 23, 2, 259–282.

Sato, C.J. (1990). *The syntax of conversation in interlanguage development*. Tubingen: Gunter Narr.

Savage, W., & Storer, G. (1992). An emergent language program framework: Actively involving learners in needs analysis. *System* 20, 2, 187–198.

Savage, W., & Whisenand, R. (1993). Logbooks and language learning objectives in an intensive ESP workshop. *TESOL Quarterly* 27, 4, 741–746.

Sawyer, M., & Ranta, L. (2001). Aptitude, individual differences, and instructional design. In Robinson, P. (ed.), *Cognition and second language instruction* (pp. 310–353). Cambridge: Cambridge University Press.

Saxton, M. (1997). The contrast theory of negative input. *Journal of Child Language* 24, 139–161.

Schank, R.C., & Abelson, R. (1977). *Scripts, plans, goals and understanding.* Hillsdale, NJ: Lawrence Erlbaum.

Scherer, A.C., & Wertheimer, M. (1964). *A psycholinguistic experiment in foreign language teaching.* New York: McGraw-Hill.

Schieffelin, B., & Ochs, E. (1986). Language socialization. *Annual Review of Anthropology* 15, 163–191.

Schieffelin, B. & Ochs, E. (1996). The microgenesis of competence: Methodology in language socialization. In Slobin, D., Gerhardt, J., Kyratzis, A., & Guo, J. (eds.), *Social interaction, social context and language: Essays in honor of Susan Ervin-Tripp* (pp. 251–264). Mahwah, NJ: Lawrence Erlbaum Associates.

Schmidt, M. (1981). Needs assessment for English for specific purposes: The case study. In Selinker, L., Tarone, E., & Hanzeli, V. (eds.), *English for academic and technical purposes: Studies in honor of Louis Trimble* (pp. 199–209). Rowley, MA: Newbury House.

Schmidt, R.A., & Bjork, R.A. (1992). New conceptualizations of practice: Common principles in three paradigms suggest new concepts for training. *Psychological Science* 3, 4, 207–217.

Schmidt, R.W. (1983). Interaction, acculturation, and the acquisition of communicative competence: A case study of an adult. In Wolfson, N., & Judd, E. (eds.), *Sociolinguistics and second language acquisition* (pp. 137–174). Rowley, MA: Newbury House.

Schmidt, R.W. (1990). The role of consciousness in second language learning. *Applied Linguistics* 11, 2, 129–158.

Schmidt, R.W. (1994). Deconstructing consciousness in search of useful definitions for applied linguistics. *AILA Review* 11, 11–26.

Schmidt, R.W. (1995). Consciousness and foreign language learning: A tutorial on the role of attention and awareness in learning. In Schmidt, R.W. (ed.), *Attention and awareness in foreign language learning* (pp. 1–63). Honolulu, HI: National Foreign Language Resource Center.

Schmidt, R.W. (2001). Attention. In Robinson, P. (ed.), *Cognition and second language instruction* (pp. 3–32). Cambridge: Cambridge University Press.

Schmidt, R.W. (2010). Attention, awareness, and individual differences in language learning. In Chan, W.M., Chi, S., Cin, K.N., Istanto, J., Nagami, M., Sew, J.W., Suthiwan, T., & Walker, I. (eds.), *Proceedings of CLaSIC 2010, Singapore, December 2–4* (pp. 721–737). Singapore: National University of Singapore, Centre for Language Studies.

Schmidt, R.W., & Frota, S. (1986). Developing basic conversational ability in a second language: A case study of an adult learner of Portuguese. In Day, R. (ed.), *"Talking to learn": Conversation in second language acquisition* (pp. 237–326). Rowley, MA: Newbury House.

Schmitt, N. (2008). Instructed second language vocabulary learning. *Language Teaching Research* 12, 329–363.

Schumann, J.H. (1978). The acculturation model for second language acquisition. In Gingras, R. (ed.), *Second language acquisition and foreign language teaching* (pp. 27–50). Arlington, VA: Center for Applied Linguistics.

Schumann, J.H. (1986). Research on the acculturation model for second language acquisition. *Journal of Multilingual and Multicultural Development* 7, 379–392.

Schwartz, B.D. (1993). On explicit and negative data effecting and affecting competence and linguistic behavior. *Studies in Second Language Acquisition* 15, 147–163.

Scollon, R. (1976). *Conversations with a one-year-old. A case study of the developmental foundation of syntax.* Honolulu, HI: University of Hawai'i Press.

Scotton, C., & Bernstein, J. (1988). Natural conversations as a model for textbook dialogue. *Applied Linguistics* 9, 372–384.

Scovel, T. (1978). The effect of affect on foreign language learning: A review of the anxiety research. *Language Learning* 28, 1, 129–142.

Scrivener, M.H. (1982). *Radical Shelley: The philosophical anarchism and utopian thought of Percy Bysshe Shelley*. Princeton, NJ: Princeton University Press.

Segalowitz, N. (2003). Automaticity and second languages. In Doughty, C.J., & Long, M.H. (eds.), *Handbook of second language acquisition* (pp. 382–408). New York: Blackwell.

Segalowitz, N. (2010). *Cognitive bases of second language fluency*. New York: Routledge.

Seig, M.T., & Winn, M. (2003). Guardians of America's gate: Discourse-based training lessons from INS interviews. Paper presented at the panel on high-stakes gatekeeping encounters, American Association for Applied Linguistics Conference, Arlington, VA, March 22–25.

Seliger, H.W. (1978). Implications of a multiple critical periods hypothesis for second language learning. In Ritchie, W.C. (ed.), *Second language acquisition research: Issues and implications* (pp. 11–19). New York: Academic Press.

Selinker, L. (1972). Interlanguage. *International Review of Applied Linguistics* 10, 3, 209–231.

Selinker, L. (1979). On the use of informants in discourse analysis and "language for specialized purposes." *International Review of Applied Linguistics* 17, 3, 189–215.

Selinker, L. (1988). Using research methods in LSP: Two approaches to applied discourse analysis. In Tickoo, M. L. (ed.), *ESP: State of the art* (pp. 33–52). Anthology Series 21. Singapore: SEAMEO Regional Language Centre.

Selinker, L., & Douglas, D. (1985). Wrestling with "context" in interlanguage theory. *Applied Linguistics* 6, 190–204.

Selinker, L., & Douglas, D. (1989). Research methodology in contextually based second language research. *Second Language Research* 5, 1, 1–34.

Selinker, L., & Lakshmanan, U. (1992). Language transfer and fossilization: The multiple effects principle. In Gass, S.M., &

Selinker, L. (eds.), *Language transfer in language learning* (pp. 176–217). Amsterdam: John Benjamins.

Selinker, L., Tarone, E., & Hanzelli, V. (eds.) (1981). *English for academic and technical purposes: Studies in honor of Louis Trimble*. Rowley, MA: Newbury House.

Serafini, E.J., Lake, J., & Long, M.H. (2013). Is your needs analysis valid and reliable? Methodological improvements for assessing specialized learner needs. Paper presented at the 5th Biannual International Conference on Task-Based Language Teaching, Banff, Alberta, Canada, October 3–5.

Shanks, D.R. (2005). Implicit learning. In Lamberts, K., & Goldstone, R. (eds.), *Handbook of cognition* (pp. 202–220). London: Sage.

Shantz, J. (2012). Spaces of learning: The anarchist free school. In Haworth, R.H. (ed.), *Anarchist pedagogies. Collective action, theories, and critical reflections on education* (pp. 124–144). Oakland, CA: PM Press.

Shavelson, R.L., & Stern, P. (1981). Research on teachers' pedagogical thoughts, judgments and behavior. *Review of Educational Research* 51, 4, 455–498.

Sheen, Y. (2004). Corrective feedback and learner uptake in communicative classrooms across instructional settings. *Language Teaching Research* 8, 3, 263–300.

Shehadeh, A. (2001). Self- and other-initiated modified output during task-based interaction. *TESOL Quarterly* 35, 433–457.

Shehadeh, A. (2005). Task-based learning and teaching: Theories and applications. In Edwards, C., & Willis, J. (eds.), *Teachers exploring tasks* (pp. 13–30). Basingstoke: Palgrave Macmillan.

Shehadeh, A., & Coombe, C.A. (eds.) (2012). *Task-based language teaching in foreign language contexts: Research and implementation*. Amsterdam: John Benjamins.

Shintani, N. (2011). A comparative study of the effects of input-based and production-based instruction on vocabulary acquisition by young EFL learners. *Language Teaching Research* 15, 137–158.

Shintani, N. (2012). Repeating input-based tasks with young beginner learners. *RELC Journal* 43, 1, 39–51.

Shintani, N. (2013). The effect of focus on form and focus on forms instruction on the acquisition of productive knowledge of L2 vocabulary by young beginner learners. *TESOL Quarterly* 47, 1, 36–62.

Shintani, N., & Ellis, R. (2010). The incidental acquisition of English plural -*s* by Japanese children in comprehension-based and production-based lessons: A process-product study. *Studies in Second Language Acquisition* 32, 4, 607–637.

Shintani, N., Li, S., & Ellis, R. (2013). Comprehension-based versus production-based grammar instruction: A meta-analysis of comparative studies. *Language Learning* 63, 2, 296–329.

Shortreed, I. (1993). Variation in foreigner talk input: The effects of task and proficiency. In Crookes, G., & Gass, S.M. (eds.), *Tasks and language learning. Integrating theory and practice* (pp. 96–122). Clevedon, Avon: Multilingual Matters.

Shotton, J. (1992). Libertarian education and state schooling in England, 1918–90. *Educational Review* 44, 1, 81–91.

Shotton, J. (1993). A century of libertarian education. A theory, a practice, a future. In Shotton, J. (ed.), *No master high or low. Libertarian education and schooling in Britain 1890–1990* (pp. 259–273). Bristol: Libertarian Education.

Silva, A.D. (2000). Text elaboration and vocabulary learning. Unpublished MA in ESL thesis. Honolulu, HI: University of Hawai'i, Department of Second Language Studies.

Simpson, R.C., Briggs, S.L., Ovens, J., & Swales, J.M. (2002). *The Michigan corpus of academic spoken English.* Ann Arbor, MI: The Regents of the University of Michigan.

Simpson-Vlach, R.C., & Ellis, N.C. (2010). An academic formulas list (AFL): New methods in phraseology research. *Applied Linguistics* 31, 4, 487–512.

Sinclair, J.H. (1987). Collocation: A progress report. In Steele, R., & Threadgold, T. (eds.), *Language topics: Essays in honor of Michael Halliday* (pp. 319–331). Amsterdam: John Benjamins.

Sinclair, J.H., & Coulthard, M. (1975). *The English used by teachers and pupils.* Oxford: Oxford University Press.

Sinclair, J.H., & Renouf, A. (1988). A lexical syllabus for language learning. In Carter, R., & McCarthy, M. (eds.), *Vocabulary and language teaching* (pp. 140–158). New York: Longman.

Singley, M.K., & Anderson, J.R. (1989). *The transfer of cognitive skill.* Cambridge, MA: Harvard University Press.

Skehan, P. (1996). A framework for the implementation of task-based instruction. *Applied Linguistics* 17, 1, 38–62.

Skehan, P. (1998). *A cognitive approach to language learning.* Oxford, England: Oxford University Press.

Skehan, P. (2001). Tasks and language performance assessment. In Bygate, M., Skehan, P., & Swain, M. (eds.), *Researching pedagogic tasks: Second language learning, teaching, and testing.* Harlow: Pearson Education.

Skehan, P. (2003). Task-based instruction. *Language Teaching* 36, 1–14.

Skehan, P. (2012). Language aptitude. In Gass, S.M., & Mackey, A. (eds.), *The Routledge handbook of second language acquisition* (pp. 381–395). New York: Routledge.

Skehan, P., & Foster, P. (1997). Task type and task processing conditions as influences on foreign language performance. *Language Teaching Research* 1, 3, 185–211.

Skehan, P., & Foster, P. (1999). The influence of task structure and processing conditions on narrative retellings. *Language Learning* 49, 1, 93–120.

Skehan, P., & Foster, P. (2001). Cognition and tasks. In Robinson, P. (ed.), *Cognition and second language instruction* (pp. 183–205). Cambridge: Cambridge University Press.

Skehan, P., & Foster, P. (2005). Strategic and on-line planning: The influence of surprise information and task time on second language performance. In Ellis, R. (ed.),

Planning and task performance in a second language (pp. 193–216). Amsterdam: John Benjamins.

Skehan, P., & Foster, P. (2007). Complexity, accuracy, fluency, and lexis in task-based performance: A meta-analysis of the Ealing research. In Van Daele, S., Housen, A., Kuiken, F., Pierrard, M., & Vedder, I. (eds.), *Complexity, accuracy, and fluency in second language use, learning, and teaching* (pp. 207–226). Brussels: KVAB.

Skutnabb-Kangas, T. (2000). *Linguistic genocide in education – Or world diversity and human rights?* Mahwah, NJ: Lawrence Erlbaum.

Skutnabb-Kangas, T., & Cummins, J. (eds.) (1988). *Minority education: From shame to struggle.* Clevedon, Avon: Multilingual Matters.

Skutnabb-Kangas, T., & Phillipson, R. (eds.) (1994). *Linguistic human rights: Overcoming linguistic discrimination.* Berlin & New York: Mouton de Gruyter.

Slavin, R.E. (1996). Research on cooperative learning and achievement: What we know, what we need to know. *Contemporary Educational Psychology* 21, 43–69.

Slimani, E. (1989). The role of topicalization in classroom language learning. *System* 17, 223–234.

Slimani-Rolls, A. (2005). Rethinking task-based language learning: What we can learn from the learners. *Language Teaching Research* 9, 2, 195–218.

Slobin, D.I. (1985). Introduction: Why study acquisition cross-linguistically? In Slobin, D.I. (ed.), *The cross-linguistic study of language acquisition: The data* (Vol. 1, pp. 3–24). Hillsdale, NJ: Erlbaum.

Smith, B. (2010). Employing eye-tracking technology in researching the effectiveness of recasts in CMC. In Hult, F.M. (ed.), *Directions and prospects for educational linguistics* (pp. 79–97). New York: Springer.

Smith, B., & Renaud, C. (2013). Using eye tracking as a measure of foreign language learners' noticing of recasts during computer-mediated writing conferences. In McDonough, K., & Mackey, A. (eds.), *New perspectives on classroom interaction in second language research* (147–156) Amsterdam: John Benjamins.

Smith, M.P. (1983). *The libertarians and education.* London: George Allen & Unwin.

Smith, M.P. (1989). Kropotkin and technical education: An anarchist voice. In Goodway, D. (ed.), *For anarchism: History, theory, and practice* (pp. 217–234). London: Routledge. Also in The Raven 10, Vol. 3, 2, 1990, 122–138.

Smith, P.D. (1970). *A comparison of the cognitive and audiolingual approaches to foreign language instruction: The Pennsylvania foreign language project.* Philadelphia, PA: Center for Curriculum Development.

Sorace, A. (2003). Near-nativeness. In Doughty, C.J., & Long, M.H. (eds.), *Handbook of second language acquisition* (pp. 130–152). Oxford: Blackwell.

Spack, R., & Sadow, C. (1983). Student-teacher working journals in ESL composition. *TESOL Quarterly* 17, 4, 575–591.

Spada, N. (1997). Form-focussed instruction and second language acquisition: A review of classroom and laboratory research. *Language Teaching* 30, 2, 73–87.

Spada, N., & Lightbown, P.M. (1999). Instruction, first language influence, and developmental readiness in second language acquisition. *Modern Language Journal* 83, 1, 1–22.

Spada, N., & Tomita, Y. (2010). Interactions between type of instruction and type of language feature: A meta-analysis. *Language Learning* 60, 2, 263–308.

Spadaro, K. (1996). Maturational constraints on lexical acquisition in a second language. Unpublished doctoral dissertation, University of Western Australia, Perth.

Spadaro, K. (2013). Maturational constraints on lexical acquisition in a second language. In Granena, G., & Long, M.H. (eds.), *Sensitive periods, language aptitudes, and ultimate L2 attainment* (pp. 43–68). Amsterdam: John Benjamins.

Spence, P., & Liu, G.-Z. (2013). Engineering English and the high-tech industry: A case study of an English needs analysis of process integration engineers at a semiconductor manufacturing company in Taiwan. *English for Specific Purposes* 32, 97–109.

Spinner, P. (2013). Language production and reception: A processability theory study. *Language Learning* 63, 4, 704–739.

Spradley, J.P. (1979). *The ethnographic interview.* New York: Holt, Rinehart and Winston.

Spradley, J.P. (1980). *Participant observation.* New York: Holt, Rinehart and Winston.

Spradley, J.P., & McCurdy, D.V. (1972). *The cultural experience. Ethnography in a complex society.* Chicago: Science Research Associates, Inc.

Spring, J. (1975). *A primer of libertarian education.* Montreal: Black Rose.

Spring, J. (1994a). Free schools, and free space and no schools. In Spring, J. (ed.), *Wheels in the head: Educational philosophies of authority, freedom, and culture from Socrates to Paulo Freire* (pp. 51–78). New York: McGraw-Hill.

Spring, J. (1994b). *Wheels in the head: Educational philosophies of authority, freedom, and culture from Socrates to Paulo Freire.* New York: McGraw-Hill.

Stadler, M., & Frensch, P. (eds.) (1998). *Handbook of implicit learning.* Thousand Oaks, CA: Sage.

Stanley, J., Ingram, D.E., & Chittick, G. (1990). *The relationship between international trade and linguistic competence.* Canberra: Australian Government Publishing Service.

Stanley, W., Mathews, R., Buss, R., & Kotler-Cope, S. (1989). Insight without awareness: On the interaction of verbalization, instruction, and practice in a process control task. *Quarterly Journal of Experimental Psychology* 41, 553–577.

Stauble, A.-M. (1984). A comparison of the Spanish-English and Japanese-English interlanguage continuum. In Andersen, R.W. (ed.), *Second language: A cross-linguistic perspective* (pp. 323–353). Rowley, MA: Newbury House.

Stengers, H., Boers, F., Housen, A., & Eyckmans, J. (2010). Does chunking foster chunk-uptake? In De Knop, S., Boers, F.,

& De Rycker, A. (eds.), *Fostering language teaching efficiency through cognitive linguistics* (pp. 99–117). Berlin: Mouton de Gruyter.

Stenhouse, M. (1975). *An introduction to curriculum research and development.* London: Heinemenan.

Stern, D. (1983). *Fundamental concepts of language teaching.* Oxford: Oxford University Press.

Stockwell, R.P., Bowen, J.D., & Martin, J.W. (1965). *The grammatical structures of English and Spanish.* Chicago, IL: University of Chicago Press.

Strauss, A., & Corbin, J. (1990). *Basics of qualitative research: Grounded theory, procedures and techniques.* Beverly Hills, CA: Sage.

Stufflebeam, D.L., McCormick, C.H., Brinkerhoff, R.O., & Nelson, C.O. (1985). *Conducting educational needs assessments.* Boston, MA: Kluwer-Nijhoff.

Sugito, S., & Sawaki, M. (1979). Gengo koudo no kijutsu [Description of language behaviour in shopping situations]. In Minami, F. (ed.), *Gengo to Koudo [Language and behaviour]* (pp. 271–319). Japan: Taishukan Shoten.

Suissa, J. (2006). *Anarchism and education: A philosophical perspective.* London: Routledge.

Sullivan, P., & Girginer, H. (2002). The use of discourse analysis to enhance ESP teacher knowledge: An example using aviation English. *English for Specific Purposes* 21, 397–404.

Svendsen, C., & Krebs, K. (1984). Identifying English for the job: Examples from healthcare occupations. *The ESP Journal* 3, 153–164.

Swaffer, J.K., Arens, K., & Morgan, M. (1982). Teacher classroom practices: Redefining method as task hierarchy. *Modern Language Journal* 66, 1, 24–33.

Swain, M. (1991). French immersion and its off-shoots: Getting two for one. In Freed, B.F. (ed.), *Foreign language acquisition research and the classroom* (pp. 91–103). Lexington, MA: D. C. Heath.

Swain, M. (1995). Three functions of output in second language learning. In Cook, G., &

Seidlhofer, B. (eds.), *Principles and practice in applied linguistics* (pp. 125–144). Oxford: Oxford University Press.

Swain, M. (1998). Focus on form through conscious reflection. In Doughty, C.J., & Williams, J. (eds.), *Focus-on-form in classroom second language acquisition* (pp. 64–81). Cambridge: Cambridge University Press.

Swales, J. (1981). Definitions in science and law – Evidence for subject-specific course components? *Fachsprache* 3, 106–112.

Swales, J.M. (1984). A review of ESP in the Arab world 1977–1983 – Trends, developments and retrenchments. In Swales, J.M., & Mustafa, H. (eds.), *English for specific purposes in the Arab world* (pp. 9–20). Birmingham: The University of Aston.

Swales, J.M. (1985a). ESP: The heart of the matter or the end of the affair? In Quirk, R., & Widdowson, H.G. (eds.), *English in the world: Teaching and learning the language and literatures* (pp. 212–223). Cambridge: Cambridge University Press.

Swales, J.M. (1985b). *Episodes in ESP*. Hemel-Hemstead: Prentice-Hall.

Swales, J.M. (1986). ESP in the big world of reprint requests. *English for Specific Purposes* 5, 1, 81–85.

Swales, J.M. (1990a). *Genre analysis*. Cambridge: Cambridge University Press.

Swales, J.M. (1990b). The concept of task. In Swales, J.M. (ed.), *Genre analysis* (pp. 68–82). Cambridge: Cambridge University Press.

Swales, J.M. (2001). EAP-related linguistic research: An intellectual history. In Flowerdew, J., & Peacock, P. (eds.), *Research perspectives on English for academic purposes* (pp. 42–54). Cambridge: Cambridge University Press.

Swales, J.M., & Mustafa, H. (1984). *English for specific purposes in the Arab world*. Birmingham: The University of Aston.

Swan, M. (2005). Legislation by hypothesis: The case of task-based instruction. *Applied Linguistics* 26, 3, 376–410.

Swan, M. (2006). Teaching grammar – Does teaching grammar work? *Modern English Teacher* 15, 2, 5–13.

Taatgen, N.A., & Wallach, D. (2002). Whether skill acquisition is rule or instance based is determined by the structure of the task. *Cognitive Science Quarterly* 2, 1–42.

Tarantino, M. (1988). Italian in-field EST users self-assess their macro- and micro-level needs: A case study. *English for Specific Purposes* 7, 1, 33–52.

Tarone, E., & Yule, G. (1989). *Focus on the language learner*. New York: Oxford University Press.

Tarone, E., Dwyer, S., Gillette, S., & Icke, V. (1981). On the use of the passive in two astrophysics journals. *The ESP Journal* 1, 2, 123–140.

Tarone, E.E. (1983). On the variability of interlanguage systems. *Applied Linguistics* 4, 2, 142–164.

Tavakoli, P., & Foster, P. (2008). Task design and second language performance: The effect of narrative type on learner output. *Language Learning* 58, 2, 439–473.

Taylor, A. (1993). Cultural differences and teaching EST writing in Micronesia. ESL 610 term paper. Honolulu, HI: University of Hawai'i at Manoa, ESL Department.

Teasdale, A. (1994). Authenticity, validity and task design for tests of well defined LSP domains. In Khoo, R. (ed.), *The practice of LSP: Perspectives, programmes and projects* (pp. 230–42). Anthology Series 34. Singapore: SEAMEO Regional Language Centre.

Thomas, M., & Reinders, H. (2010). *Task-based language learning and teaching with technology*. London: Continuum.

Thompson, S. (1994). Frameworks and contexts: A genre-based approach to analyzing lecture introductions. *English for Specific Purposes* 13, 2, 171–186.

Thornbury, S. (1999). *How to teach grammar*. Harlow: Longman.

Tickoo, M.L. (1987). Ideas and practice in state-level syllabuses: An Indian perspective. In Tickoo, M.L. (ed.), *Language syllabuses: State of the art* (pp. 110–146). Singapore: SEAMEO Regional Language Centre.

Timmermans, S. (2005). *Zin in lezen. Ondrzoek naar krachtige leeromgevingen voor begrijpend lezen in het eerste leerjaar*. Leuven: Steunpunt Nederlands als Tweede Taal/

Centrum voor Taal en Migratie (intern rapport).

Titone, R. (1968). *Teaching foreign languages: A historical sketch.* Washington, DC: Georgetown University Press.

Todd, A.D. (1984). The prescription of contraception: Negotiating between doctors and patients. *Discourse Processes* 7, 171–200.

Tollefson, J.W. (1989). *Alien winds: The reeducation of America's Indo-Chinese refugees.* New York: Praeger.

Tollefson, J.W. (1991). *Planning language, planning inequality.* New York: Longman.

Tollefson, J.W. (ed.) (1995). *Power and inequality in language education.* Cambridge: Cambridge University Press.

Tolstoy, L.N. (1862, 1863/1967). *Tolstoy on education.* Chicago: University of Chicago Press.

Tomasello, M. (2003). *Constructing a language.* Boston, MA: Harvard University Press.

Tomlin, R., & Villa, V. (1994). Attention in cognitive science and SLA. *Studies in Second Language Acquisition* 16, 183–204.

Tong-Fredericks, C. (1984). Types of oral communication activities and the language they generate: A comparison. *System* 12, 133–134.

Topping, D. (1992). Oracy, literacy and education in Micronesia. Technical Report. Honolulu, HI: University of Hawai'i, Social Science Research Institute.

Toya, M. (1992). Form of explanation in modification of listening input in L2 vocabulary learning. Unpublished MA in ESL thesis. Honolulu, HI: University of Hawai'i, Department of Second Language Studies.

Trim, J.L.M., Richterich, R., van Ek, J., & Wilkins, D. (1973). *Systems development in adult language learning.* Strasborg: Council of Europe.

Trimble, L. (1985). *English for science and technology: A discourse approach.* Cambridge: Cambridge University Press.

Trofimovitch, P., Ammar, A., & Gatbonton, E. (2007). How effective are recasts? The role of attention, memory, and analytic ability. In Mackey, A. (ed.), *Conversational interaction in second language acquisition* (pp.

171–195). Oxford: Oxford University Press.

Tsang, W.K. (1987). Text modification in ESL reading comprehension. Unpublished Scholarly Paper. Honolulu, HI: University of Hawai'i, Department of Second Language Studies.

Tsuda, A. (1984). *Sales talk in Japan and the United States: An ethnographic analysis of contrastive speech events.* Washington, DC: Georgetown University Press.

Tucker, G.R. (1994). TESOL and NAFTA: Challenges for the 21st century. *TESOL Matters* 4, 1, 4–5.

Tway, P. (1975). Workplace isoglosses: Lexical variation and change in a factory setting. *Language in Society* 4, 2, 171–183.

Ulijn, J.M., & Strother, J.B. (1990). The effect of syntactic simplification on reading EST texts as L1 and L2. *Journal of Research in Reading* 13, 1, 38–54.

Ullman, R. (1982). A broadened curriculum framework for second languages. *ELT Journal* 36, 4, 255–262.

Urano, K. (2000). Lexical simplification and elaboration: Sentence comprehension and incidental vocabulary acquisition. Unpublished MA in ESL thesis. Honolulu, HI: University of Hawai'i, Department of Second Language Studies.

U.S. Department of Labor. (1991). *Dictionary of occupational titles.* Washington, DC: Department of Labor.

U.S. Department of the Army. (1994). Soldier's manual of common tasks. Washington, DC.

U.S. Food and Drug Administration. (2009). The FDA announces new prescription drug information format. Retrieved from http://www.fda.gov/Drugs/GuidanceComplianceRegulatoryInformation/LawsActsandRules/ucm188665.htm

U.S. Food and Drug Administration. (2010). The new over-the-counter medicine label: Take a look. Retrieved from http://www.fda.gov/Drugs/EmergencyPreparedness/BioterrorismandDrugPreparedness/ucm133411.htm

Utley, D. (1992). The language audit. In Embleton, D., & Hagen, S. (eds.), *Languages in international business: A practical guide* (pp. 33–46). London: Hodder and Stoughton.

Van Avermaet, P., & Gysen, S. (2006). From needs to tasks: Language learning needs in a task-based approach. In Van den Branden, K. (ed.), *Task-based language education: From theory to Practice* (pp. 17–46). Cambridge: Cambridge University Press.

Van Boxtel, S. (2005). *Can the late bird catch the worm? Ultimate attainment in L2 syntax.* Utrecht: LOT (Landelijke Onderzoekschool Taalwetenschap).

Van Boxtel, S., Bongaerts, T., & Coppen, P.-A. (2005). Native-like attainment of dummy subjects in Dutch and the role of the L1. *IRAL* 43, 355–380.

Van den Branden, K. (1997). Effects of negotiation on language learners' output. *Language Learning* 47, 4, 589–636.

Van den Branden, K. (2000). Does negotiation of meaning promote reading comprehension? A study of multilingual primary school classes. *Reading Research Quarterly* 35, 426–443.

Van den Branden, K. (ed.) (2006a). *Task-based language education: From theory to practice.* Cambridge: Cambridge University Press.

Van den Branden, K. (2006b). Training teachers: Task-based as well? In Van den Branden, K. (ed.), *Task-based language education: From theory to practice* (pp. 217–248). Cambridge: Cambridge University Press.

Van den Branden, K. (2009). Diffusion of innovations. In Long, M.H., & Doughty, C.J. (eds.), *Handbook of language teaching* (pp. 659–672). Oxford: Blackwell.

Van den Branden, K., Depauw, V., & Gysen, S. (2002). A computerized task-based test of second language Dutch for vocational training purposes. *Language Testing* 19, 4, 438–452.

Van den Branden, K., Bygate, M., & Norris, J.M. (eds.) (2009). *Task-based language teaching. A reader.* Amsterdam: John Benjamins.

Vandermeeren, S. (2005). Foreign language needs of business firms. In Long, M.H.

(ed.), *Second language needs analysis* (pp. 160–181). Cambridge: Cambridge University Press.

Van Ek, J.A. (1976). *The threshold levels for modern language learning in schools.* London: Longman.

Van Els, T., & Oud-de-Glas, M. (eds.) (1983). *Research into foreign language needs.* Augsberg: University of Augsberg.

Van Gorp, K., & Deygers, B. (2013). Task-based language assessment. In Kunan, A. (ed.), *The companion to language assessment: Approaches and development* (Vol. 2, pp. 578–593). Oxford: Wiley-Blackwell.

Van Hest, E., & Oud-de-Glas, M. (1990). *A survey of techniques used in the diagnosis and analysis of foreign language needs in industry.* Brussels: Lingua.

Van Lier, L. (1988). *The classroom and the language learner.* New York: Longman.

VanPatten, B. (1996). *Input processing and grammar instruction in second language acquisition.* Westport, CT: Ablex.

VanPatten, B., & Cadierno, T. (1993). Explicit instruction and input processing. *Studies in Second Language Acquisition* 12, 225–243.

VanPatten, B., & Sanz, C. (1995). From input to output: Processing Instruction and, communicative tasks. In Eckman, F., Highland, D., Lee, P.W., Mileham, J., & Weber, R.R. (eds.), *Second language acquisition theory and pedagogy* (pp. 169–185). Mahwah, NJ: Erlbaum.

Varnosfadrani, A.D., & Basturkmen, H. (2009). The effectiveness of implicit and explicit error correction on learners' performance. *System* 37, 82–98.

Varonis, E.M., & Gass, S.M. (1985). Non-native/non-native conversations: A model for negotiation for meaning. *Applied Linguistics* 6, 1, 71–90.

Vatz, K., Tare, M., Jackson, S.R., & Doughty, C.J. (2013). Aptitude-treatment interaction studies in second language acquisition: Findings and methodology. In Granena, G., & Long, M.H. (eds.), *Sensitive periods, language aptitude, and ultimate L2 attainment* (pp. 272–292). Amsterdam and Philadelphia, PA: John Benjamins.

Ventola, E. (1983). Contrasting schematic structures in service encounters. *Applied Linguistics* 4, 3, 242–258.

Ventola, E. (1984). Orientation to social semiotics in foreign language teaching. *Applied Linguistics* 4, 242–258.

Ventola, E. (1987). Textbook dialogues and discourse realities. In Lorscher, W., & Schulze, R. (eds.), *Perspectives on language in performance* (pp. 399–411). Tubingen: Gunter Narr.

Vignola, M.-J., & Wesche, M. (1991). Le savoir ecrire en langue maternelle et en langue seconde chez les diplomes d'immersion francaise. *Etudes de linguistique appliequee* 82, 94–115.

Vilas, C.M. (1986). *The Sandinista Revolution: National liberation and social transformation in Central America*. New York: Monthly Review Press.

Virjo, I., Holmberg-Mattila, D., & Mattila, K. (2001). Task-based learning (TBL) in undergraduate medical education. *Medical Teacher* 23, 1, 55–58.

Von Elek, T., & Oskarsson, M. (1972). *Teaching foreign language grammar to adults. Research Bulletin No. 10.* Gothenburg: Gothenburg School of Education.

Wallerstein, N. (1983). *Language and culture in conflict: Problem-posing in the ESL classroom*. Reading, MA: Addison-Wesley.

Ward, C. (1996). *Talking schools*. London: Freedom Press.

Waring, R. (1997). The negative effects of learning words in semantic sets: A replication. *System* 25, 261–274.

Waring, R., & Takaki, M. (2003). At what rate do learners learn and retain new vocabulary from reading a graded reader? *Reading in a Foreign Language* 15, 130–163.

Warneken, F. (2013). Young children proactively remedy unnoticed accidents. *Cognition* 126, 1, 101–108.

Warneken, F., Hare, B., Melis, A.P., Hanus, D., & Tomasello, M. (2007). Spontaneous altruism by chimpanzees and young children. *PLoS Biology* 5, 7, 1414–1420.

Warneken, F., & Tomasello, M. (2008). Extrinsic rewards undermine altruistic tenden-

cies in 20-month-olds. *Developmental Psychology* 44, 6, 1785–1788.

Warneken, F., & Tomasello, M. (2009a). The roots of human altruism. *British Journal of Psychology* 100, 3, 455–471.

Warneken, F., & Tomasello, M. (2009b). Varieties of altruism in children and chimpanzees. *Trends in Cognitive Sciences* 13, 9, 397–402.

Warner, S.N. (1999). Hawaiian language regenesis: Planning for intergenerational use of Hawaiian beyond the school. In Huebner, T., & Davis, K.A. (eds.), *Sociopolitical perspectives on language policy and planning in the USA* (pp. 313–332). Philadelphia, PA: John Benjamins.

Warschauer, M., & Kern, R. (2000). *Network-based language teaching*. Cambridge: Cambridge University Press.

Watanabe, Y. (1999). Input, intake, and retention: Effects of increased processing on incidental learning of foreign language vocabulary. *Studies in Second Language Acquisition* 19, 3, 287–307.

Watanabe, Y., & Swain, M. (2007). Effects of proficiency differences and patterns of pair interaction on second language learning: Collaborative dialogue between adult ESL learners. *Language Teaching Research* 11, 121–142.

Watson-Gegeo, K.A. (1975). Transferable communicative routines: Strategies and group identity in two speech events. *Language in Society* 4, 1, 53–70.

Watson-Gegeo, K.A. (1988). Ethnography in ESL: Defining the essentials. *TESOL Quarterly* 22, 4, 575–592.

Watson-Gegeo, K.A. (1992). Thick explanation in the ethnographic study of child socialization: A longitudinal study of the problem of schooling for Kwawa'ae (Solomons Islands) children. In Corsaro, W.A., & Miller, P.J. (eds.), *Interpretive approaches to children's socialization. Special issue of New Directions for Child Development 58* (pp. 51–66).

Watson-Gegeo, K.A., & Gegeo, D.W. (1995). Understanding language and power in the Solomons Islands: Methodological lessons for educational intervention. In Tollefson, J.W. (ed.), *Power and inequality in language education* (pp. 59–72). New York: Cambridge University Press.

Watson-Gegeo, K.A., & Nielsen, S. (2003). Language socialization in SLA. In Doughty, C.J., & Long, M.H. (eds.), *Handbook of second language acquisition* (pp. 155–177). Oxford: Blackwell.

Watts, N. (1994). The use of foreign languages in tourism: Research needs. *Australian Review of Applied Linguistics* 17, 1, 73–84.

Webb, N.M. (1991). Task-related verbal interaction and mathematics learning in small groups. *Journal for Research in Mathematics Education* 22, 5, 366–389.

Webb, S. (2007). The effects of repetition on vocabulary knowledge. *Applied Linguistics* 28, 46–65.

Webb, S., & Kagimoto, E. (2011). Learning collocations: Do the number of collocates, position of the node word, and synonymy affect learning? *Applied Linguistics* 32, 259–276.

Webb, S., Newton, J., & Chang, A.C.-S. (2013). Incidental learning of collocation. *Language Learning* 63, 1, 91–120.

Wedell, M. (2009). *Planning for educational change: Putting people and their contexts first.* London: Continuum.

Wells, G. (1993). Reevaluating the IRF sequence: A proposal for the articulation of theories of activity and discourse for the analysis of teaching and learning in the classroom. *Linguistics and Education* 5, 1–37.

Werker, J. (1995). Exploring developmental changes in cross-language speech perception. In Gleitman, L., & Liberman, M. (eds.), *An invitation to cognitive science: Language* (Vol. 1, pp. 87–106). Cambridge, MA: MIT Press.

Werker, J.E., & Lalonde, C.E. (1988). Cross-language speech perception: Initial capabilities and developmental change. *Developmental Psychology* 24, 672–683.

Werker, J.E., & Tees, R.C. (1984). Cross-language speech perception: Evidence for perceptual reorganization during the first year of life. *Infant Behavior and Development* 7, 49–63.

Wesche, M. (1981). Language aptitude measures in streaming, matching students with methods, and diagnosis of learning problems. In Diller, K.C. (ed.), *Individual differences and universals in language learning aptitude* (pp. 119–154). Rowley, MA: Newbury House.

West, M. (1953). *A general service list of English words.* London: Longman.

West, R. (1994). Needs analysis in language teaching. *Language Teaching* 27, 1, 1–19.

White, L. (1987). Against comprehensible input: The input hypothesis and the development of L2 competence. *Applied Linguistics* 8, 1, 95–110.

White, L. (1991). Adverb-placement in second language acquisition: Some effects of positive and negative evidence in the classroom. *Second Language Research* 7, 133–161.

White, L. (2003a). Fossilization in steady state L2 grammars: Persistent problems with inflectional morphology. *Bilingualism: Language and Cognition* 6, 2, 129–141.

White, L. (2003b). On the nature of interlanguage representation: Universal grammar in the second language. In Doughty, C.J., & Long, M.H. (eds.), *Handbook of second language acquisition* (pp. 19–42). Oxford: Blackwell.

White, L. (2007). Linguistic theory, universal grammar, and second language acquisition. In VanPatten, B., & Williams, J. (eds.), *Theories in second language acquisition: An introduction* (pp. 37–55). Mahwah, NJ: Lawrence Erlbaum.

White, R. (1988). *The ELT curriculum: Design, management, innovation.* Oxford: Blackwell.

Whyte, W.F., & Whyte, K.K. (1991). *Making Modragon: The growth and dynamics of the worker co-operative complex* (2nd edn). Ithaca, NY: ILR Press.

Widdowson, H.G. (1971). The teaching of rhetoric to students of science and technology. Science and Technology as a Second Language 7. Reprinted in Widdowson, H.G. (ed.), *Explorations in applied linguistics* (pp. 7–17). Oxford: Oxford University Press.

Widdowson, H.G. (1972). The teaching of English as communication. *English Language Teaching* 27, 1, 15–19.

Widdowson, H.G. (1976). The authenticity of language data. In Fanselow, J.F., & Crymes,

R. (eds.), *On TESOL '76* (pp. 261–270). Washington, DC: TESOL.

Widdowson, H.G. (1978). *Teaching language as communication*. Oxford: Oxford University Press.

Widdowson, H.G. (1981). English for specific purposes: Criteria for course design. In Selinker, L., Tarone, E., & Hanzeli, V. (eds.), *English for academic purposes: Studies in honor of Louis Trimble* (pp. 1–11). Rowley, MA: Newbury House.

Widdowson, H.G. (1983). *Learning purpose and language use*. Oxford: Oxford University Press.

Widdowson, H.G. (1987). Aspects of syllabus design. In Tickoo, M.L. (ed.), *Language syllabuses: State of the art* (pp. 65–89). Singapore: SEAMEO Regional Language Centre.

Widdowson, H.G. (1996). Authenticity and autonomy in ELT. *English Language Teaching Journal* 50, 1, 67–68.

Wigglesworth, G. (2008). Tasks and performance-based assessment. In Shohamy, E., & Hornberger, N. (eds.), *Encyclopedia of language and education: Language testing and assessment* (2nd edn, Vol. 7, pp. 111–122). New York, NY: Springer.

Wilkins, D. (1974). Notional syllabuses and the concept of a minimum adequate grammar. In Corder, S.P., & Roulet, E. (eds.), *Linguistic insights in applied linguistics*. Brussels: AIMAV/Paris: Didier.

Wilkins, D. (1976). *Notional syllabuses*. Oxford: Oxford University Press.

Wilkins, D.A. (1981). Notional syllabuses revisited. *Applied Linguistics* 2, 1, 83–89.

Williams, J. (2001). The effect of spontaneous attention to form. *System* 29, 325–340.

Williams, J., & Evans, J. (1998). What kind of focus and on which forms? In Doughty, C.J., & Williams, J. (eds.), *Focus on form in classroom second language acquisition* (pp. 139–155). Cambridge: Cambridge University Press.

Williams, J.N. (1999). Memory, attention, and inductive learning. *Studies in Second Language Acquisition* 21, 1–48.

Williams, J.N. (2004). Implicit learning of form-meaning connections. In Van Patten, B., Williams, J., Rott, S., & Over-

street, M. (eds.), *Form-meaning connections in SLA* (pp. 203–218). Mahwah, NJ: Erlbaum.

Williams, J.N. (2005). Learning without awareness. *Studies in Second Language Acquisition* 27, 2, 269–304.

Williams, J.N. (2009). Implicit learning. In Ritchie, W.C., & Bhatia, T.K. (eds.), *The new handbook of second language acquisition* (pp. 319–353). Bingley: Emerald Group Publishing.

Williams, J.N., & Kuribara, C. (2008). Comparing a nativist and emergentist approach to the initial stage of SLA: An investigation of Japanese scrambling. *Lingua* 118, 522–553.

Williams, M. (1988). Language taught for meetings and language used in meetings: Is there anything in common? *Applied Linguistics* 1, 45–58.

Willis, D. (1990). *The lexical syllabus: A new approach to language teaching*. London: Collins.

Willis, D. (1993). Comments on Michael H. Long and Graham Crookes's (sic) "three approaches to task-based syllabus design." *TESOL Quarterly* 27, 4, 726–729.

Willis, D., & Willis, J. (1988). *Collins COBUILD English course*. London: Collins.

Willis, D., & Willis, J. (2001). Task-based language learning. In Carter, R., & Nunan, D. (eds.), *The Cambridge guide to teaching English to speakers of other languages* (pp. 173–179). Cambridge: Cambridge University Press.

Willis, D., & Willis, J. (2007). *Doing task-based teaching*. Oxford: Oxford University Press.

Winn, M. (2005). Collecting target discourse: The case of the US naturalization interview. In Long, M.H. (ed.), *Second language needs analysis* (pp. 265–304). Cambridge: Cambridge University Press.

Wode, H. (1981). Language-acquisitional universals: A unified view of language acquisition. In Winitz, H. (ed.), *Native language and foreign language acquisition* (pp. 218–234), *Annals of the New York Academy of Sciences 379*.

Wolfson, N. (1976). Speech acts and natural speech: Some implications for sociolinguistic methodology. *Language in Society* 5, 2, 189–209.

Wong, J. (2002). "Applying" conversation analysis in applied linguistics: Evaluating English as a second language textbook dialogue. *International Review of Applied Linguistics* 40, 1, 37–60.

Wood, A.S. (2001). International scientific English: The language of research scientists around the world. In Flowerdew, J., & Peacock, P. (eds.), *Research perspectives on English for academic purposes* (pp. 71–83). Cambridge: Cambridge University Press.

Wozniak, S. (2010). Language needs analysis from a perspective of international professional mobility: The case of French mountain guides. *English for Specific Purposes* 29, 243–252.

Wray, A. (2000). Formulaic sequences in second language teaching: Principle and practice. *Applied Linguistics* 21, 4, 463–489.

Wray, A. (2002). *Formulaic language and the lexicon*. Cambridge: Cambridge University Press.

Wright, N. (1989a). *Free School: The White Lion experience*. Leire, Leicestershire: Libertarian Education.

Wright, N. (1989b). Chapter 8: Radical perspectives on learning; and Chapter 9: Learning in society. In Wright, N. (ed.), *Assessing radical education* (pp. 115–146). Milton Keynes: Open University Press.

Yalden, J. (1987). Three case studies. In Yalden, J. (ed.), *Principles of course design for language teaching* (pp. 102–168). Cambridge: Cambridge University Press.

Yamaguchi, Y. (1994). *Negative evidence and Japanese as a foreign language acquisition*. Ms. Perth: Graduate School of Education, University of Western Australia.

Yamashita, J., & Jiang, N. (2010). L1 influence on the acquisition of L2 collocations: Japanese ESL users and EFL learners acquiring English collocations. *TESOL Quarterly* 44, 647–668.

Yano, Y., Long, M.H., & Ross, S. (1994). The effects of simplified and elaborated texts on foreign language reading comprehension. *Language Learning* 44, 2, 189–219.

Yilmaz, Y. (2012). The relative effects of explicit correction and recasts on two target structures via two communication modes. *Language Learning* 62, 4, 1134–1169.

Younes, M. (2006). *Living Arabic: A comprehensive introductory course*. Ithaca, NY: Cornell University Language Resource Center.

Young, L. (1995). University lectures – Macrostructure and micro-features. In Flowerdew, J. (ed.), *Academic listening* (pp. 159–176). Cambridge: Cambridge University Press.

Young-Scholten, M. (1999). Focus on form and linguistic competence: Why Krashen is still right about acquisition. Paper presented at the Annual Meeting of the American Association for Applied Linguistics, Stamford, CT.

Yule, G., & MacDonald, D. (1990). Resolving referential conflicts in L2 interaction: The effect of proficiency and interactive role. *Language Learning* 40, 4, 539–556.

Zemelman, S. (1978). Writing in other disciplines: A questionnaire for teachers. Conference on Language Attitudes and Composition Newsletter (Portland State University) 5, 12–16.

Zhang, E.Y. (2007). TBLT-innovation in primary school English language teaching in mainland China. In Van den Branden, K., Van Gorp, K., & Verhelst, M. (eds.), *Tasks in action: Task-based language education from a classroom-based perspective* (pp. 68–91). Cambridge: Cambridge Scholars Publishing.

Zobl, H. (1980). The formal and developmental selectivity of L1 influence on L2 acquisition. *Language Learning* 30, 1, 102–119.

Zobl, H. (1982). A direction for contrastive analysis: The comparative study of developmental sequences. *TESOL Quarterly* 16, 2, 169–183.

Zuck, L.V., & Zuck, J.G. (1984). The main idea: Specialist and non-specialist judgments. In Pugh, A.K., & Ulijn, J.M. (eds.), *Reading for professional purposes* (pp. 130–195). London: Heinemann.

Zughoul, M.R., & Hussein, R.F. (1985). English for higher education in the Arab world: A case study of needs analysis at Yarmouk University. *The ESP Journal* 4, 133–152.

Appendix

List of Abbreviations

ACTFL	American Council on Teaching Foreign Languages
AD	analysis of discourse
ALM	audiolingual method
AO	age of onset, the age at which sustained meaningful L2 exposure began
BALEAP	British Association of Lecturers in English for Academic Purposes
BICS	basic interactional communication skills
BP	Bangalore Project
BPA	Border Patrol Academy
CALP	cognitive academic language proficiency
CASL	Center for the Advanced Study of Language, University of Maryland
CEFR	Common European Framework of Reference
CH	cognition hypothesis
CLIL	content-and-language integrated learning
CLT	communicative language teaching
CNP	communication needs processor
CP	critical period
D1	first dialect
DA	discourse analysis
DOT	*Dictionary of Occupational Titles*
EAP	English for academic purposes
EC	evaluation criteria
EFL	English as a foreign language
EOP	English for occupational purposes
ESL	English as a second language
ESP	English for specific purposes
EST	English for science and technology
FA	flight attendant

Second Language Acquisition and Task-Based Language Teaching, First Edition. Mike Long.
© 2015 John Wiley & Sons, Inc. Published 2015 by John Wiley & Sons, Inc.

FDA	Food and Drug Administration
FL	foreign language
FonF	focus on form
FonFs	focus on forms
GJT	grammaticality judgment test
GT	grammar translation
ID	individual difference
IELTS	International English Language Testing System
IL	interlanguage
ILR	Interagency Language Roundtable
INS	Immigration and Naturalization Service
IQ	intelligence (quotient)
IRB	Institutional Review Board
IRF	initiation–response–feedback
ISLA	instructed second language acquisition
L1	first language
L1A	first language acquisition
L2	second language
L2A	second language acquisition
LACM	limited attention capacity model
LAD	language acquisition device
LMS	learning management system
LOR	length of residence
LSP	language for specific purposes
LT	language teaching
MEP	multiple effects principle
MLAT	Modern Language Aptitude Test
MLU	mean length of utterance
MP	methodological principle
MSA	Modern Standard Arabic
NA	needs analysis
NEH	neurological enrichment hypothesis
NIH	National Institutes of Health
NS	native speaker
NNS	non-native speaker
OTC	over the counter (drugs)
OVS	object–verb–subject
PBL	problem-based learning
PI	principal investigator
PP	pedagogic procedure
PPP	present–practice–produce
PT	pedagogic task
PT	processability theory
PTT	pedagogic task-type
SCMC	synchronous computer-mediated communication
SELMOUS	special English language materials for overseas university students
SLA	second language acquisition

SOC	supplied in obligatory contexts
SP	sensitive period
STM	short-term memory
SUV	sports utility vehicle
SVO	subject–verb–object
tblt	task-supported language teaching
TBLT	task-based language teaching as described in this book
TCF	triadic componential framework
TDS	target discourse sample
TL	target language
TLU	target-like use
TPR	total physical response
TSA	target situation analysis
TT	target task
TTT	target task-type
UG	Universal Grammar
UH	University of Hawai'i
V1	verb-first
V2	verb-second
VESL	vocational English as a second language
VET	vocational education training
VF	verb-final

Index

Note:
Figures indicated by *italics*
Table indicated by **bold**
Footnote indicated by 'fn'